IPHONE® FOR PROGRAMMERS: AN APP-DRIVEN APPROACH

DEITEL® DEVELOPER SERIES

Deitel® Ser

Deitel® Developer Series

AJAX, Rich Internet Applications and Web Development
   for Programmers

C++ for Programmers

C# 2008 for Programmers, 3/E

iPhone for Programmers: An App-Driven Approach

Java for Programmers

JavaScript for Programmers

Visual Basic® 2005 for Programmers, 2/E

How to Program Series

C How to Program, 6/E

C++ How to Program, 7/E

Internet & World Wide Web How to Program, 4/E

Java How to Program, Early Objects Version, 8/E

Java How to Program, Late Objects Version, 8/E

Visual Basic® 2008 How to Program

Visual C#® 2008 How to Program, 3/E

Visual C++® 2008 How to Program, 2/E

Simply Series

Simply Visual Basic® 2008, 3/E: An
   Application-Driven Tutorial
   Approach

Simply C++: An Application-Driven
   Tutorial Approach

Simply Java™ Programming: An
   Application-Driven Tutorial
   Approach

Simply C#: An Application-Driven
   Tutorial Approach

ies Page

CourseSmart Web Books

www.deitel.com/books/CourseSmart.html

C++ How to Program, 5/E, 6/E & 7/E

Java How to Program, 6/E, 7/E & 8/E

Simply C++: An Application-Driven
Tutorial Approach

Simply Visual Basic® 2008: An
Application-Driven Tutorial
Approach, 3/E

Small C++ How to Program, 5/E

Small Java How to Program, 6/E

Visual Basic® 2008 How to Program

Visual C#® 2008 How to Program, 3/E

LiveLessons Video Learning Products

www.deitel.com/books/LiveLessons/

Java Fundamentals Parts 1 and 2

C# Fundamentals Parts 1 and 2

C++ Fundamentals Parts 1 and 2

JavaScript Fundamentals Parts 1 and 2

To receive updates on Deitel publications, Resource Centers, training courses, partner offers and more, please register for the free *Deitel® Buzz Online* e-mail newsletter at:

www.deitel.com/newsletter/subscribe.html

follow us on Twitter®

@deitel

and Facebook®

www.deitel.com/deitelfan/

To communicate with the authors, send e-mail to:

deitel@deitel.com

For information on government and corporate *Dive-Into® Series* on-site seminars offered by Deitel & Associates, Inc. worldwide, visit:

www.deitel.com/training/

or write to

deitel@deitel.com

For continuing updates on Prentice Hall/Deitel publications visit:

www.deitel.com
www.pearsonhighered.com/deitel

Check out our Resource Centers for valuable web resources that will help you master various programming languages, software and Internet- and web-related topics:

www.deitel.com/ResourceCenters.html

iPhone for Programmers is not endorsed by nor is affiliated with Apple, Inc.

Library of Congress Cataloging-in-Publication Data

On file

ISBN-10: 0-13-705842-X
ISBN-13: 978-0-13-705842-6

Text printed in the United States on recycled paper at R.R . Donnelley in Crawfordsville, Indiana.
5th Printing   September 2010

IPHONE® FOR PROGRAMMERS: AN APP-DRIVEN APPROACH

DEITEL® DEVELOPER SERIES

Paul Deitel • Harvey Deitel
Abbey Deitel • Eric Kern • Michael Morgano
All of Deitel & Associates, Inc.

PRENTICE
HALL

Upper Saddle River, NJ • Boston • Indianapolis • San Francisco
New York • Toronto • Montreal • London • Munich • Paris • Madrid
Capetown • Sydney • Tokyo • Singapore • Mexico City

Trademarks

DEITEL, the double-thumbs-up bug and Dive Into are registered trademarks of Deitel & Associates, Inc.

Apple, iPhone, iPod, iPod Touch, Xcode, Objective-C and Cocoa are registered trademarks of Apple, Inc.

Google is a trademark of Google, Inc.

Twitter is a registered trademark of Twitter, Inc.

Dedicated to the wonderful folks at Apple
For making such great products.

Paul, Harvey, Abbey, Eric and Michael

Deitel Resource Centers

Our Resource Centers focus on the vast amounts of free content available online. Find resources, downloads, tutorials, documentation, books, e-books, journals, articles, blogs, RSS feeds and more on many of today's hottest programming and technology topics. For the most up-to-date list of our Resource Centers, visit:

www.deitel.com/ResourceCenters.html

Let us know what other Resource Centers you'd like to see! Also, please register for the free *Deitel®* *Buzz Online* e-mail newsletter at:

www.deitel.com/newsletter/subscribe.html

Computer Science
Functional Programming
Regular Expressions

Programming
ASP.NET 3.5
Adobe Flex
Ajax
Apex
ASP.NET Ajax
ASP.NET
C
C++
C++ Boost Libraries
C++ Game Programming
C#
Code Search Engines and Code Sites
Computer Game Programming
CSS 2.1
Dojo
Facebook Developer Platform
Flash 9
Functional Programming
Java
Java Certification and Assessment Testing
Java Design Patterns
Java EE 5
Java SE 6
Java SE 7 (Dolphin) Resource Center
JavaFX
JavaScript
JSON
Microsoft LINQ
Microsoft Popfly
.NET
.NET 3.0
.NET 3.5
OpenGL
Perl
PHP
Programming Projects
Python
Regular Expressions
Ruby
Ruby on Rails
Silverlight

UML
Visual Basic
Visual C++
Visual Studio Team System
Web 3D Technologies
Web Services
Windows Presentation Foundation
XHTML
XML

Apple
iPhone
Objective-C
Cocoa

Games and Game Programming
Computer Game Programming
Computer Games
Mobile Gaming
Sudoku

Internet Business
Affiliate Programs
Competitive Analysis
Facebook Social Ads
Google AdSense
Google Analytics
Google Services
Internet Advertising
Internet Business Initiative
Internet Public Relations
Link Building
Location-Based Services
Online Lead Generation
Podcasting
Search Engine Optimization
Selling Digital Content
Sitemaps
Web Analytics
Website Monetization
YouTube and AdSense

Java
Java
Java Certification and Assessment Testing

Java Design Patterns
Java EE 5
Java SE 6
Java SE 7 (Dolphin) Resource Center
JavaFX

Microsoft
ASP.NET
ASP.NET 3.5
ASP.NET Ajax
C#
DotNetNuke (DNN)
Internet Explorer 7 (IE7)
Microsoft LINQ
.NET
.NET 3.0
.NET 3.5
SharePoint
Silverlight
Visual Basic
Visual C++
Visual Studio Team System
Windows Presentation Foundation
Windows Vista
Microsoft Popfly

Open Source & LAMP Stack
Apache
DotNetNuke (DNN)
Eclipse
Firefox
Linux
MySQL
Open Source
Perl
PHP
Python
Ruby

Software
Apache
DotNetNuke (DNN)
Eclipse
Firefox
Internet Explorer 7 (IE7)
Linux
MySQL

Open Source
Search Engines
SharePoint
Skype
Web Servers
Wikis
Windows Vista

Web 2.0
Alert Services
Attention Economy
Blogging
Building Web Communities
Community Generated Content
Facebook Developer Platform
Facebook Social Ads
Google Base
Google Video
Google Web Toolkit (GWT)
Internet Video
Joost
Location-Based Services
Mashups
Microformats
Recommender Systems
RSS
Social Graph
Social Media
Social Networking
Software as a Service (SaaS)
Virtual Worlds
Web 2.0
Web 3.0
Widgets

***Dive Into*® Web 2.0 eBook**
Web 2 eBook

Other Topics
Computer Games
Computing Jobs
Gadgets and Gizmos
Ring Tones
Sudoku

Contents

Illustrations   **xvii**

Preface   **xxvii**

Before You Begin   **xxxiii**

1 Introduction to iPhone App Development   **1**

1.1   Introduction to *iPhone for Programmers*   2
1.2   iPhone Overview   3
1.3   Key New iPhone 3GS and OS 3.x Features and Enhancements   6
1.4   Downloading Apps from the App Store   7
1.5   iPhone OS 3.x   8
1.6   Objective-C Programming Language   9
1.7   Design Patterns   10
1.8   Cocoa Frameworks   11
1.9   New iPhone SDK 3 Features   13
1.10   Xcode Toolset   14
1.11   Basics of Object Technology   15
1.12   Web 2.0   17
1.13   Test-Driving the **Painter** App in the iPhone Simulator   17
1.14   Wrap-Up   22
1.15   Deitel Resource Centers   22

2 iPhone App Store and App Business Issues   **23**

2.1   Introduction   24
2.2   iPhone Developer Program: Setting Up Your Profile for Testing and Submitting Apps   25
    2.2.1   Setting Up Your iPhone Development Team   25
    2.2.2   Getting an iPhone Development Certificate   26
    2.2.3   Registering Devices for Testing   27
    2.2.4   Creating App IDs   27
    2.2.5   Creating a Provisioning Profile   27
    2.2.6   Using the Provisioning Profile to Install an App on an iPhone or iPod Touch   28
    2.2.7   Submitting Your App for Distribution   29

2.3   iPhone Human Interface Guidelines   30
2.4   Testing Your App   32
2.5   Preparing Your App for Submission through iTunes Connect   32
2.6   Characteristics of Great iPhone Apps   34
2.7   Avoiding Rejection of Your App   35
2.8   Pricing Your App: Free or Fee   36
2.9   Adding an App to iTunes Connect   38
2.10   Monetizing Paid Apps: Using In App Purchase to Sell Virtual Goods   41
2.11   Using iTunes Connect to Manage Your Apps   42
2.12   Marketing Your App   43
2.13   iPhone Anecdotes and Humor   48
2.14   Other Platforms   49
2.15   iPhone Developer Documentation   50
2.16   Wrap-Up   50

3   Welcome App   51
Dive-Into® Xcode, Cocoa and Interface Builder

3.1   Introduction   52
3.2   Overview of the Technologies   52
3.3   Xcode 3.x IDE and Cocoa   53
3.4   Building the Application   56
3.5   Building the GUI with Interface Builder   57
3.6   Running the **Welcome** App   61
3.7   Wrap-Up   63

4   Tip Calculator App   64
Introducing Objective-C Programming

4.1   Introduction   65
4.2   Test-Driving the **Tip Calculator** App   66
4.3   Overview of the Technologies   66
4.4   Building the App   66
4.5   Adding Functionality to Your App   71
4.6   Connecting Objects in Interface Builder   73
4.7   Implementing the Class's Methods   76
4.8   Wrap-Up   81

5   Favorite Twitter® Searches App   83
Collections and Cocoa GUI Programming

5.1   Introduction   84
5.2   Test-Driving the **Favorite Twitter Searches** App   85
5.3   Technologies Overview   86
5.4   Building the App   86
5.5   Wrap-Up   101

6   Flag Quiz Game App   **102**
Controllers and the Utility Application Template
6.1   Introduction   103
6.2   Test-Driving the **Flag Quiz Game** App   106
6.3   Technologies Overview   106
6.4   Building the App   107
    6.4.1   The **MainView** and Class `MainViewController`   107
    6.4.2   The **FlipsideView** and Class `FlipsideViewController` 122
6.5   Wrap-Up   127

7   Spot-On Game App   **129**
Using `UIView` and Detecting Touches
7.1   Introduction   130
7.2   Test-Driving the **Spot-On Game** App   132
7.3   Overview of the Technologies   132
7.4   Building the App   132
7.5   Wrap-Up   147

8   Cannon Game App   **154**
Animation with `NSTimer` and Handling Drag Events
8.1   Introduction   155
8.2   Test-Driving the **Cannon Game** app   156
8.3   Overview of the Technologies   156
8.4   Building the App   157
8.5   Wrap-Up   171

9   Painter App   **173**
Using Controls with a `UIView`
9.1   Introduction   174
9.2   Overview of the Technologies   174
9.3   Building the App   175
9.4   Wrap-Up   191

10 Address Book App   **193**
Tables and `UINavigationController`
10.1   Introduction   194
10.2   Test-Driving the **Address Book** App   196
10.3   Technologies Overview   196
10.4   Building the App   197
    10.4.1   Class `RootViewController`   197

	10.4.2 Class `AddViewController`	205
	10.4.3 Class `ContactViewController`	212
	10.4.4 Class `EditableCell`	215
10.5	Wrap-Up	219

11 Route Tracker App 220

Map Kit and Core Location (GPS and Compass)

11.1	Introduction	221
11.2	Test-Driving the **Route Tracker** App	224
11.3	Technologies Overview	224
11.4	Building the App	225
	11.4.1 Class `TrackingMapView`	225
	11.4.2 Class `Controller`	231
11.5	Wrap-Up	238

12 Slideshow App 240

Photos and iPod Library Access

12.1	Introduction	241
12.2	Test-Driving the **Slideshow** App	244
12.3	Technologies Overview	245
12.4	Building the App	245
	12.4.1 Class `RootViewController`	246
	12.4.2 Class `SlideshowViewController`	256
	12.4.3 Class `NameViewController`	264
	12.4.4 Class `SlideshowDataViewController`	266
12.5	Wrap-Up	276

13 Enhanced Slideshow App 278

Serialization Data with NSCoder and Playing Video

13.1	Introduction	279
13.2	Test-Driving the **Enhanced Slideshow** App	281
13.3	Overview of the Technologies	282
13.4	Building the App	282
	13.4.1 Class `MediaItem`	282
	13.4.2 Class `Slideshow`	286
	13.4.3 Class `RootViewController`	291
	13.4.4 Class `SlideshowDataViewController`	294
	13.4.5 Class `EnhancedSlideshowAppDelegate`	302
	13.4.6 Class `SlideshowViewController`	303
13.5	Suggested Enhancements	309
13.6	Wrap-Up	309

14 Voice Recorder App 310
Audio Recording and Playback

14.1 Introduction 311
14.2 Test-Driving the **Voice Recorder** App 314
14.3 Overview of the Technologies 314
14.4 Building the App 315
    14.4.1 Class `VoiceRecorderViewController` 315
    14.4.2 Class `NameRecordingViewController` 322
    14.4.3 Class `Visualizer` 325
    14.4.4 Class `PlaybackViewController` 328
14.5 Speech Synthesis and Recognition 341
14.6 Wrap-Up 341

15 Enhanced Address Book App 342
Managing and Transferring Persistent Data

15.1 Introduction 343
15.2 Test-Driving the **Enhanced Address Book** App 345
15.3 Technologies Overview 345
15.4 Building the App 346
    15.4.1 Building the Core Data Model 346
    15.4.2 Class `ContactViewController` 346
    15.4.3 Class `RootViewController` 351
15.5 Wrap-Up 362

16 Twitter® Discount Airfares App 364
Internet Enabled Applications

16.1 Introduction 365
16.2 Test-Driving the **Twitter Discount Airfares** App 366
16.3 Technologies Overview 366
16.4 Building the App 366
16.5 Wrap-Up 386

Index 387

Illustrations

Preface

1   *iPhone for Programmers* apps and the technologies they introduce.   xxx

1 Introduction to iPhone App Development

1.1   Key online documentation for iPhone developers.   3
1.2   iPhone gestures.   4
1.3   iPhone hardware.   5
1.4   iPhone 3.x default apps.   5
1.5   New landscape keyboard.   6
1.6   Popular iPhone apps in the App Store.   7
1.7   New iPhone 3.x software features
        (www.apple.com/iphone/softwareupdate/).   8
1.8   Design patterns used in *iPhone for Programmers*.   10
1.9   Cocoa frameworks (developer.apple.com/iPhone/library/
        navigation/Frameworks/index.html).   11
1.10   iPhone gestures on the simulator (developer.apple.com/IPhone/
        library/documentation/Xcode/Conceptual/iphone_development/
        125-Using_iPhone_Simulator/iphone_simulator_application.html).   15
1.11   Clicking the **Build and Go** button to run the **Painter** app.   18
1.12   **Painter** app with a blank canvas.   19
1.13   **Painter** app settings.   19
1.14   Drawing with a new brush color.   20
1.15   Changing the line color and line size to draw the stem and grass.   21
1.16   Changing the line color and line size to draw the rain.   21

2 iPhone App Store and App Business Issues

2.1   iPhone Development Team responsibilities. (*iTunes Connect Developer
        Guide version 4.7*, July 10, 2009.)   25
2.2   Points and suggestions from the *iPhone Human Interface Guidelines*.   31
2.3   iPhone functionality that is not available on the simulator.   32
2.4   Custom app icon design firms.   33
2.5   Languages available for localizing your iPhone apps.   34
2.6   Characteristics of great apps.   35
2.7   Reasons apps are rejected by Apple.   36
2.8   Ways to monetize your app.   36
2.9   Free iPhone apps that are building brand awareness.   37

2.10   iTunes Connect **Overview** page for adding an app.   38
2.11   App ratings.   39
2.12   App Stores worldwide.   40
2.13   Virtual goods.   41
2.14   Categorizing your products for sale using In App Purchase.   42
2.15   iTunes Connect modules.   43
2.16   Marketing Resources for iPhone app developers
       (developer.apple.com/iphone/).   43
2.17   Popular social media sites.   44
2.18   iPhone app review sites.   45
2.19   Internet public relations resources.   46
2.20   Mobile advertising networks.   47
2.21   iPhone development anecdotes, tips and humor.   48
2.22   Other popular platforms.   49
2.23   iPhone Reference Library documentation.   50

3   Welcome App

3.1   **Welcome** app.   52
3.2   Instruments capabilities.   53
3.3   **Welcome to Xcode** window.   54
3.4   Xcode templates.   54
3.5   Xcode toolbar.   55
3.6   Xcode toolbar elements.   55
3.7   Common Xcode keyboard shortcuts.   55
3.8   **New Project** window.   56
3.9   Naming your project.   57
3.10   **WelcomeTest** project window.   57
3.11   Adding a file to the **Welcome** project.   58
3.12   **MainMenu.xib** window.   58
3.13   Interface Builder's app window.   59
3.14   Interface Builder's **Library** window.   59
3.15   Adding an **Image View** via the **Library Window**.   60
3.16   Sizing handles on an **Image View**.   60
3.17   **Image View Attributes** tab in the **Inspector** window.   61
3.18   Adding a **Label** to a window.   62
3.19   **Label Attributes** tab of the **Inspector** window.   62
3.20   Completed **Welcome** app.   63
3.21   Xcode toolbar while an app is running.   63

4   Tip Calculator App

4.1   Entering the bill total and calculating the tip.   65
4.2   Adding a **Text Field** to the app window.   67
4.3   Adding a **Label** to the app window.   67
4.4   Placing a **Label** in the app window.   68
4.5   Adding a **Slider** to the app window.   69

4.6	App window after adding and sizing the **Slider**.	69
4.7	Positioning the "**Tip**" and "**Total**" **Text Field**s.	70
4.8	Completed **Tip Calculator** user interface.	70
4.9	Adding a new **Objective-C** class file to your Xcode project.	71
4.10	Controller class for the **Tip Calculator** app.	72
4.11	Adding a **Custom Object** to a nib file.	74
4.12	Changing the class of a custom object via the **Identity** tab.	74
4.13	**Controller's Connections** tab of the **Inspector** window.	74
4.14	Connecting an outlet to a **Text Field**.	75
4.15	Connecting an action to a **Controller** object.	76
4.16	`Controller` class for the **Tip Calculator** app.	76
4.17	Relational operators in Objective-C.	80
4.18	Arithmetic operators in Objective-C.	81

5 Favorite Twitter® Searches App

5.1	**Favorite Twitter Searches** app.	84
5.2	Running the **Favorite Twitter Searches** app.	85
5.3	Interface Builder **Button** styles.	86
5.4	App window with a **Label** and two **Text Field**s.	87
5.5	Adding the "**Save**" **Button** to the app window.	88
5.6	**View** with a colored background and a white **Label** at the top.	88
5.7	App window with a **Round Rect Button** at the bottom.	89
5.8	Adding a `UIScrollView` to the app window.	89
5.9	Controller class for the **Favorite Twitter Searches** app.	90
5.10	Adding a **Custom Object** to a nib file.	92
5.11	Controller class for the **Favorite Twitter Searches** app.	93
5.12	Method `awakeFromNib` of class `Controller`.	95
5.13	Method `refreshList` of class `Controller`.	95
5.14	Method `infoButtonTouched:` of class `Controller`.	97
5.15	Methods `addTag:` and `clearTags:` of class `Controller`.	97
5.16	Method `addNewButtonWithTitle:` of class `Controller`.	99
5.17	Method `buttonTouched:` of class `Controller`.	100
5.18	`UIButton`'s sorting category.	101

6 Flag Quiz Game App

6.1	**Flag Quiz Game** app.	103
6.2	Correct answer in the **Flag Quiz Game** app.	104
6.3	Disabled incorrect answer in the **Flag Quiz Game** app.	104
6.4	Options screen of the **Flag Quiz Game** app.	105
6.5	**Results** alert after quiz completion.	105
6.6	Completed **MainView** GUI design.	107
6.7	`MainViewController` interface declaration.	108
6.8	Initializing the `MainViewController` class.	110
6.9	`MainViewController`'s `viewDidLoad` method.	111
6.10	`MainViewController`'s `loadNextFlag` method.	113

6.11   `MainViewController`'s `submitGuess:` method.   116
6.12   Resetting the quiz.   118
6.13   `showInfo` and `flipsideViewControllerDidFinish:` methods.   119
6.14   `NSString`'s `displayName` category.   121
6.15   **Segmented Control** in the **FlipsideView**.   122
6.16   **Switches** in the **FlipsideView**.   123
6.17   `FlipsideViewController` interface declaration.   123
6.18   `FlipsideViewController` class implementation.   125

7   Spot-On Game App

7.1   **Spot-On Game** app.   130
7.2   **Spot-On Game** with a touched spot.   131
7.3   **Game Over** alert.   131
7.4   `SpotOnViewController` interface declaration.   132
7.5   `SpotOnViewController`'s user interface.   134
7.6   `SpotOnViewController`'s `viewDidLoad` method.   135
7.7   `SpotOnViewController`'s `resetGame` method.   136
7.8   `SpotOnViewController`'s `addNewSpot` method.   137
7.9   `SpotOnViewController`'s `beginSpotAnimation:` method.   139
7.10   `SpotOnViewController`'s `touchesBegan:withEvent:` method.   140
7.11   `SpotOnViewController`'s `touchedSpot:` method.   142
7.12   `SpotOnViewController`'s `beginSpotEndAnimation` method.   143
7.13   `SpotOnViewController`'s `finishedAnimation:finished:Context:`
        method.   144
7.14   `SpotOnViewController`'s methods `alertView:clickedButtonAtIndex:`,
        `shouldAutoRotateToInterfaceOrientation:` and `dealloc`.   146

8   Cannon Game App

8.1   Completed **Cannon Game** app.   155
8.2   **Cannon Game** app with cannonball in flight.   156
8.3   `CannonView`'s interface declaration.   157
8.4   Global variable declarations in `CannonView.m`.   159
8.5   `CannonView`'s `initWithCoder:` and `awakeFromNib` methods.   160
8.6   `CannonView`'s `newGame` method.   161
8.7   `CannonView`'s `timerFired:` method.   162
8.8   `CannonView`'s `showAlertwithTitle:message:` and
        `alertView:clickedButtonAtIndex:` methods.   165
8.9   `CannonView`'s `drawRect:` method.   166
8.10   `CannonView`'s `touchesBegan:withEvent:`, `touchesMoved:withEvent:`
        and `processTouch:` methods.   170

9   Painter App

9.1   **Painter** app and its control panel.   174
9.2   Class `Squiggle` represents the points, color and width of one line.   175

9.3   Squiggle class implementation.   176
9.4   View for the frontside of the **Painter** app.   177
9.5   Method initWithCoder: of class MainView.   178
9.6   Methods resetView and drawRect: of class MainView.   178
9.7   Method drawSquiggle: of class MainView.   179
9.8   Touch-handling methods of class MainView.   180
9.9   Methods motionEnded:withEvent:, alertView:clickedButtonAtIndex:,
        canBecomeFirstResponder and dealloc of class MainView.   183
9.10   MainViewController interface.   184
9.11   Controller for the front side of the **Painter** app.   185
9.12   FlipsideViewController interface.   187
9.13   FlipsideViewController class.   188
9.14   The finished flipside interface.   191

10   Address Book App

10.1   List of contacts.   194
10.2   Viewing a single contact's details.   195
10.3   **Add Contact** screen.   195
10.4   Deleting a contact.   196
10.5   Controller for the main table of the **Address Book** app.   197
10.6   Method viewDidLoad of class RootViewController.   199
10.7   Method addContact of class RootViewController.   200
10.8   Method addViewControllerDidFinishAdding: of class
        RootViewController.   200
10.9   Methods and tableView:NumberOfRowsInSection: and
        tableView:cellForRowAtIndexPath: of class RootViewController.   201
10.10   Method tableView:didSelectRowAtIndexPath: of class
        RootViewController.   202
10.11   Methods tableView:commitEditingStyle:forRowAtIndexPath:,
        shouldAutorotateToInterfaceOrientation: and dealloc of class
        RootViewController.   203
10.12   NSDictionary's sorting category.   204
10.13   AddViewController.xib in Interface Builder after placing the
        default **TableView**.   205
10.14   AddViewController's interface declaration.   205
10.15   Methods initWithNibName:bundle: and viewDidLoad of class
        AddViewController.   207
10.16   Methods doneAdding: and values of class AddViewController.   208
10.17   Methods editableCellDidBeginEditing:, editableCellDidEndEditing:
        and editableCellDidEndOnExit: of class AddViewController.   209
10.18   Methods numberOfSectionsInTableView:,
        tableView:numberOfRowsInSection: and
        tableView:titleForHeaderInSection: of class AddViewController.   210
10.19   Method tableView:cellForRowAtIndexPath: of
        class AddViewController.   211

10.20 `ContactViewController`'s interface declaration. 212
10.21 `ContactViewController` class displays information for a contact. 213
10.22 Interface for a `UITableViewCell` that contains a **Label** and a **Text Field**. 215
10.23 `EditableCell`'s class definition. 216

11   Route Tracker App

11.1 Approximate user location on world map. 221
11.2 Map just after the user presses **Start Tracking**. 222
11.3 User's route displayed on the map with arrows showing the
     user's direction. 222
11.4 Satellite and hybrid map views. 223
11.5 Statistics for a completed route. 223
11.6 **MainWindow.xib** in Interface Builder. 225
11.7 `TrackingMapView` interface declaration. 226
11.8 Method `initWithFrame:` of class `TrackingMapView`. 226
11.9 Method `drawRect:` of class `TrackingMapView`. 227
11.10 Methods `addPoint:` and `reset` of class `TrackingMapView`. 230
11.11 Methods `mapView:regionWillChangeAnimated:` and
      `mapView:regionDidChangeAnimated:` of class `TrackingMapView`. 231
11.12 `Controller` class for the **Route Tracker** app interface declaration. 232
11.13 Method `viewDidLoad` of class `Controller`. 233
11.14 Method `toggleTracking` of class `Controller`. 234
11.15 Methods `resetMap`, `selectMapMode:` and `mapView:viewForAnnotation:`
      of class `Controller`. 236
11.16 Method `locationManager:didUpdateToLocation:fromLocation:` of
      class `Controller`. 237
11.17 Methods `locationManager:didUpdateHeading:` and
      `locationManager:didFailWithError:` of class `Controller`. 238

12   Slideshow App

12.1 List of saved slideshows. 241
12.2 Slideshow playing in portrait and landcape orientations. 242
12.3 Editing the list of slideshows. 242
12.4 Creating a new slideshow. 243
12.5 Photo library. 243
12.6 Picking a photo. 244
12.7 `RootViewController` class controls the main list of slideshows. 246
12.8 Methods `viewDidLoad` of class `RootViewController`. 246
12.9 Method `viewWillAppear:` and `addSlideshow` of class
     `RootViewController`. 247
12.10 `RootViewController` methods `nameViewController:didGetName:`,
      and `tableView:numberOfRowsInSection:`. 248
12.11 Method `tableView:cellForRowAtIndexPath:` of class
      `RootViewController`. 249

12.12 Methods `slideshowCellDidSelectEditButton:` and
`slideshowCellDidSelectPlayButton:` of class `RootViewController`.   250

12.13 Method `tableView:commitEditingStyle:forRowAtIndexPath:`
of class `RootViewController`.   251

12.14 Methods `tableView:moveRowAtIndexPath:toIndexPath:` and
`tableView:canMoveRowAtIndexPath:` of class `RootViewController`.   252

12.15 `UITableViewCell` for previewing a slideshow.   253

12.16 `SlideshowCell` method `initWithFrame:reuseIdentifier:`.   254

12.17 Methods `editSlideshow` and `playSlideShow` of class `SlideshowCell`.   255

12.18 Controller for a **View** that shows a slideshow.   256

12.19 Methods `loadView` and `nextImageView` of class
`SlideshowViewController`.   257

12.20 Methods `exitShow` and `timerFired` of class `SlideshowViewController`.   259

12.21 Methods `transitionFinished:finished:context:`, `viewWillAppear`
and `viewDidDisappear` of class `SlideshowViewController`.   261

12.22 Methods `shouldAutorotateToInterfaceOrientation:` and
`willRotateToInterfaceOrientation:` of class
`SlideshowViewController`.   263

12.23 Scaling category of `UIImageView`.   263

12.24 Controls a **View** for naming a slideshow.   265

12.25 Implementation of `NameViewController`.   265

12.26 Manages the pictures, sounds and effects of a slideshow.   266

12.27 Method `viewDidLoad` of class `SlideshowDataViewController`.   268

12.28 Method `viewDidAppear:` and `viewDidDisappear:` of class
`SlideshowDataViewController`.   269

12.29 Methods `addPhoto` and
`imagePickerController:didFinishPickingImage:` of class
`SlideshowDataViewController`.   271

12.30 Methods `addMusic` and `mediaPicker:didPickMediaItems:` of class
`SlideshowDataViewController`.   272

12.31 Methods `addEffect` and `startSlideshow` of class
`SlideshowDataViewController`.   273

12.32 Method `tableView:cellForRowAtIndexPath:` of class
`SlideshowDataViewController`.   274

12.33 Methods `tableView:commitEditingStyle:forRowAtIndexPath:`,
`tableView:moveRowAtIndexPath:toIndexPath:` and
`tableView:canMoveRowAtIndexPath:` of class
`SlideshowDataViewController`.   275

13 Enhanced Slideshow App

13.1 iPhone photo library.   279

13.2 Viewing a video.   280

13.3 Setting the image transition effect.   280

13.4 **Flip** effect—rotates slide horizontally revealing the next slide underneath.   281

13.5 `MediaItem` class represents an image or a video.   283

13.6   `MediaItem` class implementation.   283
13.7   Presents the user with an interface for creating a `MediaItem`.   285
13.8   `MediaItemCreator` class implementation.   286
13.9   Interface for class `Slideshow` which represents a slideshow.   287
13.10   Methods `init` and `initWithCoder:` of class `Slideshow`.   288
13.11   Methods `encodeWithCoder:` and `firstImage` of class `Slideshow`.   289
13.12   NSCoding category For UIImage.   290
13.13   Method `viewDidLoad` of class `RootViewController`.   291
13.14   Method `nameViewController:didGetName:` of class
        `RootViewController`.   292
13.15   Method `slideshowCellDidSelectEditButton:` of class
        `RootViewController`.   293
13.16   Method `tableView:cellForRowAtIndexPath:` of class
        `RootViewController`.   294
13.17   Method `initWithSlideshow:` of class `SlideshowDataViewController`.   295
13.18   Method `addPhoto` of class `SlideshowDataViewController`.   295
13.19   Method `imagePickerController:didFinishPickingMediaWithInfo:`
        of class `SlideshowDataViewController`.   296
13.20   Method `mediaItemCreator:didCreateMediaItem:` of class
        `SlideshowDataViewController`.   298
13.21   Methods `mediaPicker:didPickMediaItems:` and `addEffect` of class
        `SlideshowDataViewController`.   299
13.22   Methods `startSlideshow` and `actionSheet:clickedButtonAtIndex:`
        of class `SlideshowDataViewController`.   299
13.23   Method `tableView:cellForRowAtIndexPath:` of class
        `SlideshowDataViewController`.   300
13.24   Method `tableView:moveRowAtIndexPath:toIndexPath:` of class
        `SlideshowDataViewController`.   302
13.25   Method `applicationWillTerminate:` of class
        `EnhancedSlideshowAppDelegate`.   303
13.26   Controller for a view that shows a slideshow.   303
13.27   Method `nextImageViewWithMedia:` of class `SlideshowViewController`.   305
13.28   Method `changeSlide` of class `SlideshowViewController`.   306
13.29   Method `displayNewImage:` of class `SlideshowViewController`.   306
13.30   Method `displayNewVideo:` of class `SlideshowViewController`.   308

14   Voice Recorder App

14.1   **Voice Recorder** app ready to record.   311
14.2   Visualizer during a recording.   312
14.3   Naming a recording.   312
14.4   Playing a saved recording.   313
14.5   E-mailing a recording.   313
14.6   `VoiceRecorderViewController` interface declaration.   315
14.7   `VoiceRecorderViewController`'s finished view.   316
14.9   Method `record:` of class `VoiceRecorderViewController`.   317

14.8 Methods `initWithNibName:bundle:` and `viewDidLoad` of class `VoiceRecorderViewController`. 317

14.10 Method `nameRecordingViewController:didGetName:` of class `VoiceRecorderViewController`. 320

14.11 Method `flip:` of class `VoiceRecorderViewController`. 321

14.12 Methods `playbackViewControllerDidFinish:` and `timerFired:` of class `VoiceRecorderViewController`. 322

14.13 Controls a **View** for naming a recording. 322

14.14 Finished layout of `NameRecordingViewController`'s view. 323

14.15 Implementation of `NameRecordingViewController`. 324

14.16 **View** that displays a visualization of a recording in progress. 326

14.17 Method `initWithCoder:` of class `Visualizer`. 326

14.18 Methods `setPower:` and `clear` of class `Visualizer`. 327

14.19 Method `drawRect:` of class `Visualizer`. 327

14.20 Controls the **View** where the user plays existing sound files. 329

14.21 Completed `PlaybackViewController` GUI. 330

14.22 Implementation for `PlaybackViewController`. 331

14.23 Methods `sliderMoved:`, `togglePlay` and `updateVolume:` of class `PlaybackViewController`. 332

14.24 `PlaybackViewController` methods `timerFired:` and `record:`. 333

14.25 Method `playSound` of class `PlaybackViewController`. 334

14.26 Methods `stopSound`, `numberOfSectionsInTableView:` and `tableView:numberOfRowsInSection:` of class `PlaybackViewController`. 335

14.27 Method `tableView:cellForRowAtIndexPath:` of class `PlaybackViewController`. 336

14.28 Method `tableView:commitEditingStyle:forRowAtIndexPath:` of class `PlaybackViewController`. 337

14.29 Method `tableView:didSelectRowAtIndexPath:` of class `PlaybackViewController`. 338

14.30 Methods `tableView:accessoryButtonTappedForRowWithIndexPath:` and `mailComposeController:didFinishWithResult:error:` of class `PlaybackViewController`. 339

15 Enhanced Address Book App

15.1 Viewing a contact. 343

15.2 Requesting a connection. 344

15.3 Getting a Bluetooth **Connection Request**. 344

15.4 Data model editor. 346

15.5 Controller that displays the contact information for a created contact. 347

15.6 Methods `viewDidLoad` and `send` of class `ContactViewController`. 347

15.7 Method `peerPickerController:didConnectPeer:toSession:` of class `ContactViewController`. 348

15.8 Methods `peerPickerControllerDidCancel:`, `updateTitle` and `tableView:numberOfRowsInSection:` of class `ContactViewController`. 349

15.9 Method `tableView:cellForRowAtIndexPath:` of class `ContactViewController`. 350

15.10   Controls the main view of the **Enhanced Address Book** app.   351
15.11   Method `viewDidLoad` of class `RootViewController`.   352
15.12   Method `session:didReceiveConnectionRequestFromPeer:` of class
        `RootViewController`.   353
15.13   Methods `alertView:clickedButtonAtIndex:` and `alertViewCancel:`
        of class `RootViewController`.   354
15.14   Method `receiveData:fromPeer:inSession:context:` of class
        `RootViewController`.   355
15.15   Methods `insertNewObject` and `addViewControllerDidFinishAdding:`
        of class `RootViewController`.   356
15.16   Methods `numberOfSectionsInTableView:` and
        `tableView:numberOfRowsInSection:` of class `RootViewController`.   358
15.17   Methods `tableView:cellForRowAtIndexPath:` and
        `tableView:didSelectRowAtIndexPath:` of class `RootViewController`.   359
15.18   Methods `tableView:commitEditingStyle:forRowAtIndexPath:` and
        `tableView:canMoveRowAtIndexPath:` of class `RootViewController`.   360
15.19   Method `fetchedResultsController` of class `RootViewController`.   361

16 Twitter® Discount Airfares App

16.1   **Twitter Discount Airfares** app showing several discount airfares.   365
16.2   Class that represents an airfare.   366
16.3   Implementation of class `Airfare`.   367
16.4   Controller for the root **View** of the **Twitter Discount Airfares** app.   367
16.5   `RootViewController` class implementation.   368
16.6   `UITableView` delegate and data source methods of class
        `RootViewController`.   370
16.7   **View** that displays the website for purchasing flight tickets.   371
16.8   **View** that displays a website for purchasing flight tickets.   372
16.9   Class that connects with Twitter web services and returns data.   373
16.10   Implementation of `TwitterConnection`.   374
16.11   Class that gets tweets and parses them for information.   376
16.12   `AirfareFinder` class implementation.   377
16.13   XML containing information about a single tweet.   378
16.14   `NSXMLParser` delegate methods.   379
16.15   Method `parseCost` of category parsing of class `NSString`.   381
16.16   Method `parseLocation` of category parsing of class `NSString`.   382
16.17   Method `removeLink` of category parsing of class `NSString`.   383
16.18   `UITableViewCell` that displays information about an airfare.   383
16.19   `AirfareCell` class implementation.   384

Preface

Welcome to the world of iPhone app development with the iPhone Software Development Kit (SDK) 3.x, the Objective-C® programming language, the Cocoa® frameworks and the Xcode® development tools.

This book presents leading-edge computing technologies for professional software developers. At the heart of the book is our "app-driven approach"—we present concepts in the context of 14 completely coded iPhone apps, rather than using code snippets. The introduction and app test drives at the beginning of each chapter show one or more sample executions. The book's source code is available at www.deitel.com/books/iPhoneFP/.

Sales of the iPhone and app downloads have been growing explosively. The first-generation iPhone sold 6.1 million units in its initial five quarters of availability.[1] The second-generation iPhone 3G sold 6.9 million units in its first quarter alone. The iPhone 3GS, launched in June 2009, sold 5.2 million units in its first month! At the time of this writing, there were approximately 75,000 apps in the App Store, and in just one year, over 1.5 billion apps were downloaded.[2] The potential for iPhone apps is enormous.

iPhone for Programmers was fun to write! We got to know (and love) the iPhone and many of its most popular apps. Then we let our imaginations run wild as we started developing our own iPhone apps. Some of the apps appear in this book, and some we'll sell through the iTunes App Store. The book's apps were carefully designed to introduce you to key iPhone features and frameworks (e.g., audio, video, animation, the compass, peer-to-peer connectivity, GPS and much more). You'll quickly learn everything you'll need to start building iPhone apps—starting with a test-drive of the **Painter** app in Chapter 1, then building your first app in Chapter 3. Chapter 2, iPhone App Store and App Business Issues walks you through what makes a great app, the submission process including uploading your apps for consideration by Apple, criteria for approval, what to expect in the process, why Apple rejects apps, deciding whether to sell your apps or offer them for free, and marketing them using the Internet, word-of-mouth, and so on.

Copyright Notice and Code License

This book is copyrighted by Pearson. All of the code and iPhone apps in this book are copyrighted by Deitel & Associates, Inc. *As a user of the book, we grant you the nonexclusive right to copy, distribute, display the code, and create derivative apps based on the code **for non-commercial purposes only**—so long as you attribute the code to Deitel & Associates, Inc. and reference **www.deitel.com/books/iPhoneFP/**. If you have any questions, or specifically would like to use our code for commercial purposes, contact **deitel@deitel.com**.*

---

1. www.apple.com/pr/library/2009/07/21results.html.
2. www.apple.com/pr/library/2009/07/14apps.html.

Intended Audience

We assume that you're comfortable with Mac OS X, as you'll need to work on a Mac to develop iPhone apps. We also assume that you're a programmer with significant experience working in a C-based object-oriented language such as Objective-C, C++, Java or C#. If you have not worked in any of these languages, you should still be able to master iPhone app development and object-oriented programming by reading the code and our code walkthroughs, running the apps and observing the results. You'll quickly learn a great deal about object-oriented iPhone app development in Objective-C and Cocoa. We overview the basics of object-oriented programming in Chapter 1.

Key Features

Here are some of the book's key features:

App-Driven Approach. You'll learn the programming technologies in the context of 14 complete working iPhone apps. Each chapter presents one app—we discuss what the app does, show screen shots, test-drive it and overview the technologies and the architecture you'll use to build it. Then we build the app, present the complete code and do a detailed code walkthrough. As part of the code walkthrough, we discuss the programming concepts and demonstrate the functionality of the iPhone APIs (application programming interfaces). Figure 1 lists the 14 apps in the book and the key technologies we introduce as we present each.

iPhone for Programmers apps and the technologies they introduce	
Chapter 3, **Welcome** App *Introducing Xcode, Cocoa and Interface Builder*	Chapter 10, **Address Book** App *Tables and UINavigationController*
Chapter 4, **Tip Calculator** App *Introducing Objective-C Programming*	Chapter 11, **Route Tracker** App *Map Kit and Core Location (GPS and Compass)*
Chapter 5, **Favorite Twitter® Searches** App *Collections and Cocoa GUI Programming*	Chapter 12, **Slideshow** App *Photos and iPod Library Access*
Chapter 6, **Flag Quiz Game** App *Controllers and the Utility Application Template*	Chapter 13, **Enhanced Slideshow** App *Saving Data and Playing Video*
Chapter 7, **Spot-On Game** App *Using UIView and Detecting Touches*	Chapter 14, **Voice Recorder** App *Audio Recording and Playback*
Chapter 8, **Cannon Game** App *Animation with NSTimer and Handling Drag Events*	Chapter 15, **Enhanced Address Book** App *Managing and Transferring Persistent Data*
Chapter 9, **Painter** App *Using Controls with a UIView*	Chapter 16, **Twitter® Discount Airfares** App *Internet Enabled Applications*

Fig. 1 | *iPhone for Programmers* apps and the technologies they introduce.

Objective-C. This book is not an Objective-C tutorial, but it teaches a good portion of this object-oriented programming language in the context of iPhone app development.

Cocoa Frameworks. Cocoa is the set of frameworks and the runtime environment for the iPhone. Throughout the book, we use many of the Cocoa features and frameworks. (Figure 1.9 in Chapter 1 shows the Cocoa frameworks.)

iPhone SDK 3.x. We cover many of the new features included in iPhone Software Development Kid (SDK) 3.x—the Game Kit framework for Bluetooth peer-to-peer connectivity, the Map Kit framework for embedding Google Maps[3], the Media Player framework for accessing the iPod music library, the Core Location framework for accessing the compass and the Core Data framework for managing app data.

Xcode. Apple's Xcode integrated development environment (IDE) and its associated tools for Mac OS, combined with the iPhone SDK, provide everything you need to develop and test iPhone apps.

Instruments. The Instruments tool, which is packaged with the SDK, is used to inspect apps while they're running to check for memory leaks, monitor CPU usage and network activity, and review the objects allocated in memory. We discuss how we used the Instruments tool to fix memory leaks and performance problems in Chapter 6's **Flag Quiz Game** App and Chapter 8's **Cannon Game** App, respectively.

Multimedia. The apps use a broad range of iPhone multimedia capabilities, including graphics, images, audio, video, speech synthesis and speech recognition.

iPhone App Design Patterns. This book adheres to Apple's app coding standards, including the Model-View-Controller (MVC) design pattern. (Figure 1.8 in Chapter 1 shows many of the design patterns we use directly or indirectly in the book.)

Web Services. Web services enable information sharing, e-commerce and other interactions using standard Internet protocols and technologies. Web services allow you to use the web as a library of reusable software components. Chapter 11's **Route Tracker** app uses built-in Apple APIs to interact with the Google Maps web services. In Chapter 16's **Twitter® Discount Airfares** app, you'll work directly with Twitter's REST-based web services.

Uploading Apps to the App Store. In Chapter 2, iPhone App Store and App Business Issues, we walk you through the process of obtaining development certificates, creating provisioning profiles, submitting your apps to the App Store for approval, deciding whether your app should be free or fee based, marketing it and much more.

Features

Syntax Shading. For readability, we syntax shade the code, similar to Xcode's use of syntax coloring. Our syntax-shading conventions are as follows:

```
comments appear in gray
keywords appear in bold black
constants and literal values appear in bold gray
all other code appears in black
```

---

3. *Note:* The **Route Tracker** App uses the Map Kit framework which allows you to incorporate Google™ Maps in your app. Before developing any app using the Map Kit, you must agree to the Google Maps Terms of Service for the iPhone (including the related Legal Notices and Privacy Policy) at: code.google.com/apis/maps/iphone/terms.html.

Code Highlighting. We use gray rectangles to emphasize the key code segments in each program that exercise the new technologies the program presents.

Using Fonts for Emphasis. We place the defining occurrences of key terms in ***bold italic*** text for easier reference. We emphasize on-screen components in the **bold Helvetica** font (e.g., the **Project** menu) and emphasize Objective-C and Cocoa program text in the `Lucida` font (e.g., `int x = 5;`).

In this book you'll create GUIs using a combination of visual programming (drag and drop) and writing code. We'll constantly be referring to GUI elements on the screen. We use different fonts when we refer to GUI components. For example, if a button is part of the IDE, we write the word "button" in lowercase and plain text, as in "**Build and Go** button." If on the other hand, it's a button that we create as part of an app, we use the name **Button** as it appears in the library of controls you can use in an app. When we refer to a **Button**'s class, we use the class name `UIButton`.

Source Code. All of the source-code examples are available for download from:

> `www.deitel.com/books/iPhoneFP/`

Documentation. All of the manuals that you'll need to develop iPhone apps are available free at `developer.apple.com/iphone/`.

Chapter Objectives. Each chapter begins with a list of objectives.

Figures. Abundant charts, tables, app source code listings and iPhone screen shots are included.

Index. We include an extensive index, which is especially useful when you use the book as a reference. Defining occurrences of key terms are highlighted with a **bold** page number.

The Deitel Online Resource Centers

Our website `www.deitel.com` provides more than 100 Resource Centers on various topics including programming languages, software development, Web 2.0, Internet business and open-source projects—see the list of Resource Centers in the first few pages of this book and visit `www.deitel.com/ResourceCenters.html`. Each week we announce our latest Resource Centers in our newsletter, the *Deitel*® *Buzz Online* (`www.deitel.com/newsletter/subscribe.html`). The Resource Centers evolve out of the research we do to support our publications and business operations. We've found many exceptional iPhone and iPhone programming resources online, including tutorials, documentation, software downloads, articles, blogs, podcasts, videos, code samples, books, e-books and more—most of them are free. Check out the growing list of iPhone-related Resource Centers, including:

- iPhone (`www.deitel.com/iPhone/`)
- Objective-C (`www.deitel.com/ObjectiveC/`)
- Cocoa (`www.deitel.com/Cocoa/`)
- iPhone App Development (`www.deitel.com/iPhoneAppDev/`)

Deitel® *Buzz Online* Free E-mail Newsletter

The *Deitel® Buzz Online* e-mail newsletter will keep you posted on issues related to this book. It also includes commentary on industry trends and developments, links to free articles and resources from our published books and upcoming publications, product-release schedules, errata, challenges, anecdotes, information on our corporate instructor-led training courses delivered at client locations worldwide and more. To subscribe, visit

    www.deitel.com/newsletter/subscribe.html

Follow Deitel on Twitter® and Facebook®

To receive updates on Deitel publications, Resource Centers, training courses, partner offers and more, follow us on Twitter®

    @deitel

and join the Deitel & Associates group on Facebook®

    www.deitel.com/deitelfan/

Acknowledgments

We're fortunate to have worked on this project with the talented and dedicated team of publishing professionals at Prentice Hall/Pearson. We appreciate the extraordinary efforts and mentorship of Mark L. Taub, Editor-in-Chief of Pearson Technology Group. Sandra Schroeder designed the book's cover. John Fuller managed the book's production.

Reviewers

We wish to acknowledge the efforts of our reviewers. Adhering to a tight time schedule, they scrutinized the manuscript and the programs and provided constructive suggestions for improving the accuracy and completeness of the presentation:

- Marcantonio Magnarapa, Research & Development on Mobile Platforms, Ogilvy Interactive
- Zach Saul, Founder, Retronyms
- Rik Watson, Senior Software Engineer, Lockheed Martin

Well, there you have it! This book will quickly get you comfortable developing iPhone apps. As you read the book, we'd sincerely appreciate your comments, criticisms, corrections and suggestions for improvement. Please address all correspondence to:

    deitel@deitel.com

We'll respond promptly, and post corrections and clarifications on:

    www.deitel.com/books/iPhoneFP/

We hope you enjoy reading *iPhone for Programmers: An App-Driven Approach* as much as we enjoyed writing it!

Paul Deitel
Harvey Deitel
Abbey Deitel
Eric Kern
Michael Morgano
October 2009

About Deitel & Associates, Inc.

Deitel & Associates, Inc., founded by Paul Deitel and Harvey Deitel, is an internationally recognized authoring, corporate training and software development organization specializing in computer programming languages, object technology, Internet and web software technology, iPhone app development and training, and Internet business development. The company offers instructor-led courses delivered at client sites worldwide on major programming languages and platforms, such as Objective-C and iPhone app development, C, C++, Visual C++®, Java™, Visual C#®, Visual Basic®, XML®, Python®, object technology, Internet and web programming, and a growing list of additional programming and software-development-related courses. The company's clients include many of the world's largest companies, government agencies, branches of the military, and academic institutions. Through its 33-year publishing partnership with Prentice Hall/Pearson, Deitel & Associates, Inc., publishes leading-edge programming professional books, textbooks, *LiveLessons* DVD- and web-based video courses, and e-content for popular course-management systems. Deitel & Associates, Inc., and the authors can be reached via e-mail at:

    deitel@deitel.com

To learn more about Deitel's *Dive Into*® *Series* Corporate Training curriculum, visit:

    www.deitel.com/training/

To request a proposal for on-site, instructor-led training at your company or organization, e-mail:

    deitel@deitel.com

To learn more about the company and its publications, subscribe to the free *Deitel*® *Buzz Online* e-mail newsletter at:

    www.deitel.com/newsletter/subscribe.html

Individuals wishing to purchase Deitel books and *LiveLessons* DVD- and web-based training courses can do so through www.deitel.com. Bulk orders by corporations, the government, the military and academic institutions should be placed directly with Pearson. For more information, visit www.prenhall.com/mischtm/support.html#order.

Before You Begin

This section contains information and instructions you should review to ensure that your Mac is set up properly for use with this book. We'll post updates (if any) to this Before You Begin section on the book's website:

www.deitel.com/books/iPhoneFP/

Font and Naming Conventions

We use fonts to distinguish between on-screen components (such as menu names and menu items) and Objective-C code or commands. Our convention is to show on-screen components in a sans-serif bold **Helvetica** font (for example, **Project** menu) and to show file names, Objective-C code, label text and commands in a sans-serif Lucida font (for example, @interface).

Software and Hardware System Requirements

To develop apps for the iPhone you need an Intel-based Mac running Mac OS X Leopard or later. There are no versions of the Software Development Kit (SDK) or the Xcode toolset for non-Intel-based Macs or for Windows®. To view the latest operating-system requirements visit:

www.apple.com/downloads/macosx/development_tools/iphonesdk.html

Installing the Software

To download the iPhone SDK you must first register for a free Apple developer account at:

developer.apple.com/iphone/program/start/register/

This account allows you access to the latest released version of the SDK, documentation and code examples. There is also a paid developer program that lets you download the latest SDK betas, upload finished apps to the App Store and load your apps directly onto an iPhone for testing. After registering for a developer account (free or paid), you can download the SDK from

developer.apple.com/iphone/index.action#downloads

Click the link for your version of Mac OS X to download the SDK.

We demonstrate most of the apps in this book using the iPhone SDK's iPhone Simulator; however, some of the apps use features that are available only on an actual iPhone, not the iPhone simulator. In addition, some features are available only on the iPhone 3GS. Testing apps on your iPhone requires a paid Apple developer account.

Installation Instructions and Installers

When the iPhone SDK finishes downloading, double click its disk-image (.dmg) file to mount it. Open the mounted image in the Finder and double click iPhoneSDK.mpkg installer package. This executes the installer, which walks you through the rest of the installation process. When you arrive at the **Installation Type** step, the default items checked will be adequate for this book.

Once the installation finishes, you can begin programming with the iPhone SDK. The default install location for the SDK is /Developer/. The development tools you use in this book are located in /Developer/Applications/.

Obtaining the Code Examples

The examples for *iPhone for Programmers* are available for download at

> www.deitel.com/books/iPhoneFP/

If you are not already registered at our website, go to www.deitel.com and click the **Register** link below our logo in the upper-left corner of the page. Fill in your information. There is no charge to register, and we do not share your information with anyone. We send you only account-management e-mails unless you register separately for our free, double-opt-in *Deitel® Buzz Online* e-mail newsletter at

> www.deitel.com/newsletter/subscribe.html

After registering for our website, you'll receive a confirmation e-mail with your verification code. *You'll need this code to sign in at www.deitel.com for the first time.* Configure your e-mail client to allow e-mails from deitel.com to ensure that the confirmation e-mail is not filtered as junk mail.

Next, visit www.deitel.com and sign in using the **Login** link below our logo in the upper-left corner of the page. Go to www.deitel.com/books/iPhoneFP/. Click the **Examples** link to download the Examples.zip file to your computer. Double click Examples.zip to unzip the archive. We assume that you extract the example code to your Documents folder.

You are now ready to begin developing iPhone apps with *iPhone for Programmers*. We hope you enjoy the book!

Introduction to iPhone App Development

OBJECTIVES

In this chapter you'll be introduced to:

- The history of the iPhone.
- The history of Objective C® and the iPhone SDK.
- Some basics of object technology.
- Key software for iPhone app development, including the Xcode® integrated development environment and Interface Builder.
- The Objective-C programming language and the Cocoa® frameworks.
- Important Apple iPhone publications.
- The iPhone Developer Program.
- The iPhone Developer University Program.
- Test-driving an iPhone app that enables you to draw on the screen.
- The Deitel online iPhone Resource Centers.

Outline

1.1 Introduction to *iPhone for Programmers*
1.2 iPhone Overview
1.3 Key New iPhone 3GS and OS 3.x Features and Enhancements
1.4 Downloading Apps from the App Store
1.5 iPhone OS 3.x
1.6 Objective-C Programming Language
1.7 Design Patterns
1.8 Cocoa Frameworks
1.9 New iPhone SDK 3 Features
1.10 Xcode Toolset
1.11 Basics of Object Technology
1.12 Web 2.0
1.13 Test-Driving the **Painter** App in the iPhone Simulator
1.14 Wrap-Up
1.15 Deitel Resource Centers

1.1 Introduction to *iPhone for Programmers*

Welcome to iPhone app development! We hope that working with *iPhone for Programmers* will be an informative, challenging, entertaining and rewarding experience for you. This book is geared toward experienced programmers who have worked in a C-based object-oriented language like C++, Java™, C# or Objective-C®. If you don't specifically know object-oriented programming using the Objective-C programming language and the Cocoa® frameworks, you should be able to absorb it by running the book's iPhone apps and carefully studying the detailed code walkthroughs and feature presentations.

The book uses an *app-driven approach*—each new technology is discussed in the context of a complete working iPhone app, with one app per chapter. Most of our apps will also work on the iPod Touch®.[1] We start by describing the app, then test-driving it. Next, we briefly overview the key *Xcode®* (integrated development environment), Objective-C and Cocoa technologies we'll use to implement the app. For apps that require it, we walk through designing the GUI visually using Interface Builder. Then we provide the complete source-code listing using line numbers, syntax shading (to mimic the syntax coloring used in the Xcode IDE) and code highlighting to emphasize the key portions of the code. We also show one or more screen shots of the running app. Then we do a code walkthrough, explaining any new programming concepts we introduced in the app. The source code for all of the book's apps may be downloaded from www.deitel.com/books/iPhoneFP/. We encourage you to read Apple's online documentation (Fig. 1.1) to learn more about the technologies discussed throughout the book, design guidelines, and so on.

To download the software for building iPhone apps, you'll need to become a Registered iPhone Developer at developer.apple.com/iphone/. This account allows you to access free downloads plus documentation, how-to videos, coding guidelines and more. As a Registered iPhone Developer, you'll be able to build and test iPhone apps on your Mac computer. To load apps onto your iPhone for testing, and to submit your apps to Apple's App Store, you'll need to join Apple's fee-based iPhone Developer Program, also at developer.apple.com/iphone/. This program allows you to access the latest iPhone SDK betas and features such as Store Kit and Push Notification, and it includes technical support.

---

1. Chapter 11's **Route Tracker** app works with limited functionality because the iPod Touch does not have a compass.

Title	URL

iPhone Human Interface Guidelines	`developer.apple.com/iphone/library/`
	`documentation/userexperience/conceptual/`
	`mobilehig/Introduction/Introduction.html`

The Objective-C 2.0 Programming Language	`developer.apple.com/documentation/Cocoa/` `Conceptual/ObjectiveC/ObjC.pdf`

Objective-C 2.0 Runtime Programming Guide	`developer.apple.com/documentation/Cocoa/`
	`Conceptual/ObjCRuntimeGuide/`
	`ObjCRuntimeGuide.pdf`

Xcode Overview	`developer.apple.com/documentation/`
	`DeveloperTools/Conceptual/Xcode_Overview/`
	`Contents/Resources/en.lproj/Xcode_Overview.pdf`

Xcode Debugging Guide	`developer.apple.com/documentation/`
	`DeveloperTools/Conceptual/XcodeDebugging/`
	`Xcode_Debugging.pdf`

Understanding XCode Projects	`developer.apple.com/tools/xcode/` `xcodeprojects.html`

Cocoa Fundamentals Guide	`developer.apple.com/documentation/Cocoa/`
	`Conceptual/CocoaFundamentals/`
	`CocoaFundamentals.pdf`

Coding Guidelines for Cocoa	`developer.apple.com/documentation/Cocoa/`
	`Conceptual/CodingGuidelines/`
	`CodingGuidelines.pdf`

Fig. 1.1 | Key online documentation for iPhone developers.

Colleges and universities interested in offering iPhone programming courses can apply to the ***iPhone Developer University Program*** for free (`developer.apple.com/iphone/program/university.html`). Qualifying schools receive free access to all the developer tools and resources. Students can share their apps with each other, and the schools can apply to include their apps in the App Store.

1.2 iPhone Overview

The first-generation iPhone was released in June 2007 and was an instant blockbuster success. Sales have grown significantly with each new version. According to Apple, 6.1 million first-generation iPhones were sold in the initial five quarters of availability.[2] The second-generation iPhone 3G included GPS and was released in July 2008; it sold 6.9 million units in the first quarter alone. The faster iPhone 3GS includes a compass; it was launched in June 2009 and sold 5.2 million in its first month of availability.

Gestures
The iPhone wraps the functionality of a mobile phone, Internet client, iPod, gaming console, digital camera and more into a handheld smartphone with a full-color, 480-by-320-

---

2.   `www.apple.com/pr/library/2009/07/21results.html`.

pixel resolution *Multi-Touch® screen*. Apple's patented Multi-Touch screen allows you to control the device with *gestures* involving one touch or multiple simultaneous touches (Fig. 1.2).

Gesture	Action	Used to
Tap	Tap the screen once.	Open an app, select a button.
Double Tap	Tap the screen twice.	Select text to cut, copy and paste.
Touch and Hold	Touch the screen and hold finger in position.	Move the cursor in e-mail and SMS messages, move app icons, and so on.
Drag	Touch and drag your finger across the screen.	Move a slider left and right.
Swipe	Touch the screen, then move your finger in the swipe direction and release.	Flip through photos or music album covers.
Flick	Touch and quickly flick your finger across the screen in the direction you'd like to move.	Scroll through a **Table View** (e.g., Contacts) or a **Picker View** (e.g. dates and times in the Calendar)
Pinch	Using two fingers, touch and pinch your fingers together, or spread them apart.	Zoom in and out on the screen (for example, enlarging text and pictures).

Fig. 1.2 | iPhone gestures.

iPhone Buttons and Features
The device itself is uncomplicated and easy to use (Fig. 1.3). The top of the phone has a headset jack, SIM card tray and a Sleep/Awake button—used to lock and unlock the iPhone, and to power it on and off. On the left side of the iPhone are the Ring/Silent switch and the Volume buttons. On the bottom of the iPhone are the speaker, the microphone and the Dock Connector (to plug-in a USB cable to charge or sync the device). On the front of the phone at the bottom is the Home button—used to exit apps and return to the home screen. On the back of the iPhone is the camera.

Multi-Touch Screen
Using the Multi-Touch screen, you can easily navigate between your phone, apps, your iTunes® music, web browsing, and so on. The screen can display a keyboard for typing e-mails and text messages and entering data in apps. Using two fingers, you can zoom in (moving your fingers apart) and out (pinching your fingers together) on photos, videos and web pages. You can scroll up-and-down or side-to-side by just swiping your finger across the screen.

Default Apps
The iPhone comes with several default apps, including **Phone, Contacts, Mail, iPod, Safari** and more (Fig. 1.4). To access any app, simply touch its icon.

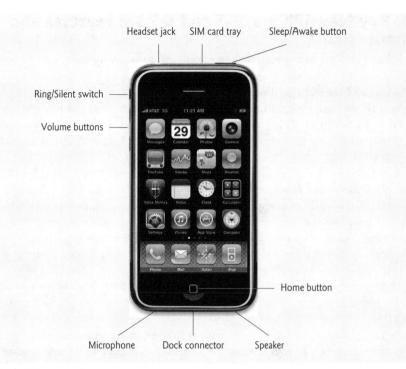

Fig. 1.3 | iPhone hardware.

Icon	App	Icon	App	Icon	App
	Phone		Photos		Voice Memos
	Contacts		Camera		Notes
	Mail		Settings		Calculator
	iPod		YouTube		Settings
	Safari		Stocks		iTunes
	Calendar		Maps		App Store
	Messages (SMS/MMS)		Weather		Compass (iPhone 3GS only)

Fig. 1.4 | iPhone 3.x default apps.

1.3 Key New iPhone 3GS and OS 3.x Features and Enhancements

The iPhone 3GS features several new hardware and software updates.

3-Megapixel Camera and Video

The new iPhone includes a 3-megapixel autofocus camera. You can touch the screen to focus on a particular subject. You can capture and edit videos. You can share photos and videos via e-mail, your MobileMe^{SM} gallery (where your friends can view and download your photos or add their own) or YouTube®.

Find My iPhone and Remote Wipe

If you misplace your iPhone, log in to Apple's *MobileMe* (a fee-based subscription service) from any computer and use the *Find My iPhone* feature to view a map with the iPhone's approximate location. You can then have the iPhone play a sound to help you locate the device, or display a message to help the person who finds your iPhone return it to you. If you're unable to find your iPhone, the *Remote Wipe* feature restores the device to the factory settings (removing all personal data), thus protecting the privacy of your information.

Compass

The digital compass can be used on its own or to orient maps in your apps—e.g., to point in the direction you're facing. We use the compass in Chapter 11's **Route Tracker** app.

Accelerometer

The accelerometer, included in all iPhones, allows the device to respond to motion. For example, you can rotate the phone from portrait to landscape (vertical to horizontal) to change the orientation of pictures, e-mails, web pages and more. You can also use the accelerometer to control games by shaking or tilting the iPhone. With the updated iPhone OS 3.x accelerometer-based apps, you can shake the iPhone to "shuffle" randomly to a different song in your music library, or turn the iPhone sideways to display a *landscape keyboard* for easier typing (Fig. 1.5). We use the accelerometer in Chapter 12's **Slideshow** app.

Fig. 1.5 | New landscape keyboard.

Bluetooth
You can connect compatible Bluetooth stereo headphones and other accessories to your iPhone. OS 3.x provides for peer-to-peer connectivity via Bluetooth. Also, *Internet tethering* enables users in some countries to connect to a Wi-Fi or 3G network on their laptop by using their iPhone as a modem (connected to their laptop via Bluetooth or USB cable).

Accessibility
The iPhone 3GS includes several *accessibility* features to help vision- and hearing-impaired users. *VoiceOver* is a gesture-based screen reader program. It allows vision-impaired users to interact with objects on the screen and understand their context. For example, users can touch the screen to hear a description of the item they touch, then drag their finger to hear descriptions of the surrounding content. It's also used with the keyboard to speak each character touched, or each complete word. The iPhone 3GS voice-recognition capabilities allow you to use voice commands to access features on the phone, such as making phone calls and playing music.

For hearing-impaired users, the iPhone 3GS has closed-captioning capabilities, MMS texting (not available in the U.S. at the time of this writing), visible and vibrating alerts and more. To learn about these and other accessibility features, visit `www.apple.com/iphone/iphone-3gs/accessibility.html`.

1.4 Downloading Apps from the App Store

Figure 1.6 lists some popular iPhone apps. You can download additional apps directly onto your iPhone through Apple's *App Store*, or download apps through iTunes, then *sync* your iPhone to install them. To sync the iPhone, use the USB cable to connect the device to a computer with iTunes. Syncing allows you to back up your information (contacts, apps and their data, music, photos, videos, and so on) and download new information onto the device. The App Store notifies you when updates to your downloaded apps are available.

Category	Sample apps
Books	B&N Bookstore, Kindle for iPhone, Classics
Business	QuickOffice® Mobile Office Suite, PDF Reader, Job Search
Education	Wheels on the Bus, 24/7 Tutor Spanish, USA Presidents
Entertainment	Backgrounds, Fandango®, i.TV
Finance	Bank of America Mobile Banking, PayPal™, Mint.com Personal Finance
Games	Hero of Sparta, Flight Control, Paper Toss, Monkey Sling
Healthcare and Fitness	iFitness, Lose It!, Restaurant Nutrition, Pedometer, BMI Calculator
Lifestyle	AroundMe, Shopper, GroceryIQ, eBay Mobile, OpenTable
Medical	Epocrates, EyeChart, Cardio Calc, BLACKBAG™, Dog First Aid
Music	Shazam, Pandora Radio, SIRIUS XM Premium Online, MiniPiano
Navigation	MapQuest® 4 Mobile, Free Wi-Fi, MotionX™ GPS

Fig. 1.6 | Popular iPhone apps in the App Store. (Part 1 of 2.)

Category	Sample apps
News	CNNMoney, NYTimes, USA Today, WSJ, Pro RSS Reader, Yahoo!®
Photography	Crop for Free, Camera Zoom, ColorSplash, Vint B&W
Productivity	iTranslate, Todo, Documents To Go®, Excuse Generator
Reference	Google® Mobile App, Dictionary.com, Wiki Mobile
Social Networking	Facebook®, MySpace™ Mobile, Skype™, Tweetie, LinkedIn®
Sports	ESPN® Score Center, Sportacular, Golfshot: Golf GPS
Travel	Google Earth, Urbanspoon, Yelp®, Cheap Gas!, Currency
Utilities	iHandyLevel Free, textPlus, Bug Spray—Ultrasonic, myLite Flashlight
Weather	The Weather Channel®, WeatherBug®, Surf Report

Fig. 1.6 | Popular iPhone apps in the App Store. (Part 2 of 2.)

The number of apps available is growing rapidly. At the time of this writing, there were approximately 75,000 apps in the App Store. In just one year, over 1.5 billion apps were downloaded.[3] Visit `www.apple.com/iphone/apps-for-iphone/` to check out Apple's featured apps. Some are free and some are fee based. Developers set the prices for their apps sold through the App Store and receive 70% of the revenue. Many app developers offer basic versions of their apps for free as a marketing strategy, so users can download apps and see whether they like them, then purchase more feature-rich versions. We discuss this so-called "lite" strategy in more detail in Section 2.8.

1.5 iPhone OS 3.x

The iPhone operating system is derived from Apple's Mac OS X and is used in the iPhone and iPod Touch devices. iPhone OS 3.0 was released in June 2009 and includes several new features and enhancements (Fig. 1.7). For example, you can cut, copy and paste text—even between apps. The new landscape keyboard—which appears when you turn the iPhone sideways in Mail, Safari, Notes and Messages—provides more room to type messages (and makes it easier to type with your thumbs). And you can record voice memos using the built-in microphone.

Feature	Description
Landscape Keyboard	Larger keyboard—for use with Mail, Messages, Safari and Notes—makes typing easier.
Cut, Copy and Paste	Cut, copy and paste text and images between apps.

Fig. 1.7 | New iPhone 3.x software features (`www.apple.com/iphone/softwareupdate/`). (Part I of 2.)

---

3.   `www.apple.com/pr/library/2009/07/14apps.html`.

Feature	Description
MMS	Multimedia Messaging Service (not available in the U.S. at the time of this writing)—send photos, audio and videos with messages.
Voice Controls	Access Contacts and your iPod music library via voice controls.
Voice Memos	Record audio messages with the new Voice Memos.
Spotlight	Search e-mail, contacts, calendars, notes and your iPod library.
Parental Controls	Restrict children's access to videos, music and apps.
Safari	Improvements to the Safari browser help you surf the web faster.
Notes	Sync your Notes to your computer.
Calendar	Improved functionality allows you to create meetings using Microsoft Exchange ActiveSync, and subscribe to calendars that use CalDAV—the standardized protocol to access information on a server and schedule meetings with other users (`caldav.calconnect.org`).
Wi-Fi	Automatically log in to Wi-Fi hotspots you've accessed previously.
iTunes	Create and access iTunes Store accounts directly from your iPhone, and purchase movies, TV shows and audiobooks directly from iTunes on the iPhone.
Shake to Shuffle	Shake the iPhone to skip to a different song in your iTunes library.
Shake to Undo	Shake the iPhone to undo an operation, such as a text edit.
Language Support	The iPhone supports 30 languages and over 40 keyboard layouts.
Peer-to-Peer Bluetooth Connectivity	Transfer data among nearby iPhones using Bluetooth. We use peer-to-peer functionality in Chapter 15's **Enhanced Address Book** app.
YouTube	Log in to your YouTube account to sync bookmarks, rate your favorite videos and more.

Fig. 1.7 | New iPhone 3.x software features (`www.apple.com/iphone/softwareupdate/`). (Part 2 of 2.)

1.6 Objective-C Programming Language

Apple was founded in 1976 by Steve Jobs and Steve Wozniak, and quickly became a leader in personal computing. In 1979, Jobs and several Apple employees visited Xerox PARC (Palo Alto Research Center) to learn about Xerox's desktop computer that featured a graphical user interface. That GUI served as the inspiration for the Apple Lisa personal computer (designed for business customers) and, more notably, the Apple Macintosh, which was launched with much fanfare in a memorable Super Bowl ad in 1984. Steve Jobs left Apple in 1985 and founded NeXT Inc.

The *Objective-C* programming language, created by Brad Cox and Tom Love at Stepstone in the early 1980s, added capabilities for object-oriented programming *(OOP)* to the C programming language. In 1988, NeXT licensed Objective-C from StepStone and developed an Objective-C compiler and libraries which were used as the platform for the NeXTSTEP operating system's user interface and Interface Builder—used to construct graphical user interfaces (we discuss Interface Builder in more detail in Section 1.10). Apple's Mac OS X is a descendant of NeXTSTEP.

Objective-C is object oriented and has access to the ***Cocoa frameworks*** (powerful class libraries of prebuilt components), enabling you to develop apps quickly. The Cocoa frameworks are discussed in Section 1.8. Cocoa Touch is the version of Cocoa for the iPhone and iPod Touch. We'll simply refer to it as Cocoa from now on.

Cocoa programming in Objective-C is event driven—in this book, you'll write apps that respond to timer firings and user-initiated events such as touches and keystrokes. In addition to directly programming portions of your Objective-C apps, you'll also use Interface Builder to conveniently drag and drop predefined objects like buttons and textboxes into place on your screen, and label and resize them. With Xcode, you can create, run, test and debug iPhone apps quickly and conveniently.

1.7 Design Patterns

Besides using predefined objects in your code, you'll also use several predefined ***design patterns***[4] to help you design and implement your apps according to Apple's guidelines (Fig. 1.8). Like a pattern a dressmaker uses to create clothing, a design pattern provides programmers with an architectural template for designing and implementing apps.

Design Pattern	Where it's used	How it's used
Abstract Factory	Introduced in Chapter 4's **Tip Calculator** app; used in every later app.	Many Foundation framework classes (Fig. 1.9) allow programmers to use one familiar interface to interact with different data structures.
Chain of Responsibility	Introduced in Chapter 7's **Spot-On** app; seen in several later apps.	Built into Cocoa as the mechanism for dealing with events.
Command	Introduced in Chapter 5's **Favorite Twitter Searches** app; used in most later apps.	To bind GUI components to actions (i.e., event handlers) that are triggered in response to events.
Composite	Introduced in Chapter 5's **Favorite Twitter Searches** app; used in most later apps.	To create a hierarchy of objects that can all be manipulated through the root object.
Decorator	Introduced in Chapter 6's **Flag Quiz** app; used in most later apps.	To add new functionality to an existing class without subclassing.
Facade	Introduced in Chapter 6's **Flag Quiz** app.	To provide a simple interface for the behaviors of a complex subsystem.
Model View Controller	Introduced in Chapter 4's **Tip Calculator** app; used in every later app.	To separate app data (contained in the model) from graphical presentation (the view) and input-processing logic (the controller).

Fig. 1.8 | Design patterns used in *iPhone for Programmers*. (Part 1 of 2.)

4. Some books you'll want to consult on design patterns are the seminal "gang of four" book, *Design Patterns: Elements of Reusable Object-Oriented Software*, by Gamma, Helm, Johnson and Vlissides, ©1994, Addison Wesley, and *Cocoa Design Patterns*, by Buck and Yacktman, ©2010, Addison Wesley.

Design Pattern	Where it's used	How it's used
Memento	Introduced in Chapter 5's **Favorite Twitter Searches** app; used in every later app that needs to save data.	To represent an object as a bit stream so it can be saved to a file or transferred over a network (also called "serialization").
Singleton	Introduced in Chapter 5's **Favorite Twitter Searches** app.	To ensure that only one object of a class is created. Other objects in the app can share the singleton object.
Template Methods	Introduced in Chapter 4's **Tip Calculator** app; used in every later app.	To define an algorithm in a superclass, parts of which a subclass can override.

Fig. 1.8 | Design patterns used in *iPhone for Programmers*. (Part 2 of 2.)

1.8 Cocoa Frameworks

Cocoa, a collection of frameworks, also evolved from projects at NeXT. OpenStep was developed at NeXT as an object-oriented programming API to be used in developing an operating system. After Apple acquired NeXT, the OpenStep operating system evolved into Rhapsody, and many of the base libraries became the Yellow Box API. Rhapsody and Yellow Box eventually evolved into OS X and Cocoa, respectively.

Cocoa consists of many frameworks (Fig. 1.9) that allow you to conveniently access iPhone OS features and incorporate them into your apps. Many of these frameworks are discussed in this book. They're written mainly in Objective-C and are accessible to Objective-C programs. The Cocoa frameworks help you create apps which adhere to the Mac's unique look and feel (see `developer.apple.com/cocoa/`).

Framework	Description
Cocoa Touch Layer—Frameworks for building graphical, event-driven apps.	
Address Book UI	GUI for accessing the user's Address Book contacts. Used in Chapter 15's **Enhanced Address Book** app.
Game Kit	Voice and Bluetooth networking capabilities for games and other apps. Used in Chapter 15's **Enhanced Address Book** app.
Map Kit	Add maps and satellite images to location-based apps. Used in Chapter 11's **Route Tracker** app.
Message UI	Create e-mail messages from within an app.
UIKit	Classes for creating and managing a user interface, including event handling, drawing, windows, views and Multi-Touch interface controls. Introduced in Chapter 3's **Welcome** app, and used throughout the book.

Fig. 1.9 | Cocoa frameworks (`developer.apple.com/iPhone/library/navigation/Frameworks/index.html`). (Part 1 of 3.)

Framework	Description
Media Layer—Frameworks for adding audio, video, graphics and animations to your apps.	
Audio Toolbox	Interface for audio recording and playback of streamed audio and alerts.
Audio Unit	Interface for opening, connecting and using the iPhone OS audio processing plug-ins.
AV Foundation	Interface for audio recording and playback (similar to the Audio Toolbox). Used in Chapter 7's **Spot-On Game** app and Chapter 8's **Cannon Game** app.
Core Audio	Framework for declaring data types and constants used by other Core Audio interfaces. Used in Chapter 7's **Spot-On Game** app and Chapter 8's **Cannon Game** app.
Core Graphics	API for drawing, rendering images, color management, gradients, coordinate-space transformations and handling PDF documents. Used in Chapter 7's **Spot-On Game** app and Chapter 8's **Cannon Game** app.
Media Player	Finds and plays audio and video files within an app. Used in Chapter 12's **Slideshow** app.
OpenGL ES	Supports integration with the Core Animation layer and UIKit views. Subset of the OpenGL API for 2D and 3D drawing on embedded systems.
Quartz Core	Framework for image and video processing, and animation using the Core Animation technology. Used in Chapter 7's **Spot-On Game** app.
Core Services Layer—Frameworks for accessing core iPhone OS 3.x services.	
Address Book	Used to access the user's Address Book contacts. Used in Chapter 15's **Enhanced Address Book** app.
Core Data	Framework for performing tasks related to object life-cycle and object graph management. Used in Chapter 15's **Enhanced Address Book** app.
Core Foundation	Library of programming interfaces that allow frameworks and libraries to share code and data. Also supports internationalization. Introduced in Chapter 5's **Favorite Twitter Searches** app and used throughout the book.
Core Location	Used to determine the location and orientation of an iPhone, then configure and schedule the delivery of location-based events. Used in Chapter 11's **Route Tracker** app.
Foundation	Includes NSObject (used to define object behavior), plus tools for creating graphical, event-driven apps. Also includes design patterns and features for making your apps more efficient. Introduced in Chapter 5's **Favorite Twitter Searches** app and used throughout the book.
Mobile Core Services	Includes standard types and constants.

Fig. 1.9 | Cocoa frameworks (developer.apple.com/iPhone/library/navigation/Frameworks/index.html). (Part 2 of 3.)

Framework	Description
Store Kit	In-app purchase support for processing transactions.
System Configuration	Determines network availability and state on an iPhone.
Core OS Layer—Frameworks for accessing the core iPhone OS 3.x kernel.	
CFNetwork	Framework using network protocols in apps to perform tasks including working with HTTP and authenticating HTTP and HTTPS servers, working with FTP servers, creating encrypted connections and more. Used in Chapter 16's **Twitter Discount Airfares** app.
External Accessory	Allows the iPhone to interact with third party authorized accessories connected via Bluetooth or the Dock Connector.
Security	Framework for securing data used in an app.
System	BSD operating system and POSIX API functions.

Fig. 1.9 | Cocoa frameworks (`developer.apple.com/iPhone/library/navigation/Frameworks/index.html`). (Part 3 of 3.)

1.9 New iPhone SDK 3 Features

iPhone SDK 3 includes several new frameworks for building powerful functionality into your iPhone apps. We use most of these new frameworks in this book. We also use *web services*. With web services, you can create *mashups*, which enable you to rapidly develop apps by combining the complementary web services of several organizations and possibly other forms of information feeds. A popular mashup is `www.housingmaps.com`, which uses web services to combine `www.craigslist.org` real estate listings with the mapping capabilities of Google Maps to offer maps that show the locations of apartments for rent in a given area. We use Twitter web services in Chapter 16's **Twitter Discount Airfares** app.

In App Purchase

In App Purchase allows you to build purchasing capabilities into your apps using the *Store Kit framework*, which processes payments through the iTunes Store. From a paid app, you can solicit the user to pay for additional content or functionality for that app. When the user chooses to make a purchase through your paid app, the app sends a payment request to the iTunes Store, which verifies and approves the payment and alerts the app to unlock new features or download new content. You'll receive 70% of the purchase price (Apple retains 30%), paid to you monthly. In App Purchase is discussed in more detail in Chapter 2, iPhone App Store and App Business Issues.

Apple Push Notification

The new *Apple Push Notification* service allows apps to receive notifications, even when the apps aren't running. The service can be used to notify the user when a new version of your app is available for download, to send news and messages to users, and so on. The Apple Push Notification service operates mostly on the server side, thus limiting the impact on the app user's iPhone performance and battery life.

Accessories

Accessory manufacturers can create protocols that allow the iPhone to interact with their accessories connected via Bluetooth or the Dock Connector. For example, you can create an app that interacts with a heart-rate monitor, pedometer or Nike + iPod Sensor to keep track of fitness goals, calories burned, and so on.

Peer-to-Peer Connectivity

The *Game Kit framework* includes *peer-to-peer connectivity* and in-game voice communication features, so you can add multiplayer and chat functionality to your games and apps. Multiple iPhones in close proximity can connect wirelessly via Bluetooth. Players can compete with one another. The Game Kit can also be used to exchange data, photos, and the like. This framework is used in Chapter 15's **Enhanced Address Book** app.

Maps

The *Map Kit framework* (which uses the Google Mobile Maps Service) creates location-based apps—for example, an app that displays a map of the nearest gas stations or public parking garages. The Map Kit framework is used in Chapter 11's **Route Tracker** app.

iPod Library Access

The *Media Player framework* allows apps to access music, podcasts and audio books in the user's iPod library. For example, in Chapter 12's **Slideshow** app, you'll use the Media Player framework in a **Slideshow** app that allows the user to create a slideshow of pictures set to a song from the music library.

1.10 Xcode Toolset

The Xcode 3 toolset, bundled with all Mac OS X versions since v10.5, is available for free through the Apple Developer Connection at developer.apple.com/. The toolset includes the Xcode IDE, Interface Builder, support for the Objective-C 2.0 language, the Instruments tool (used to improve performance) and more.

Xcode Integrated Development Environment (IDE)

Xcode is Apple's standard integrated development environment for Mac OS X. Xcode supports many programming languages including Java, C++, C, Python and Objective-C, but only Objective-C can be used for iPhone development. It includes a code editor with support for syntax coloring, autoindenting and autocomplete. It also includes a debugger and a version control system. You'll start using Xcode in Chapter 3, **Welcome** App.

Interface Builder

Interface Builder is a visual GUI design tool. GUI components can be dragged and dropped into place to form simple GUIs without any coding. Interface Builder files use the .xib extension, but earlier versions used .nib—short for NeXT Interface Builder. For this reason, Interface Builder .xib files are commonly referred to as "nib files." You'll learn more about Interface Builder in Chapter 3, **Welcome** App.

The iPhone Simulator

The iPhone simulator, included in the iPhone SDK, allows you to run iPhone apps in a simulated environment within OS X. The simulator displays a realistic iPhone user-interface window. We used this (not an actual iPhone) to take most of the iPhone screen shots for this book. You can reproduce on the simulator many of the iPhone gestures using your Mac's keyboard and mouse (Fig. 1.10). The gestures on the simulator are a bit limited, since your computer cannot simulate all the iPhone hardware features. For example, when running GPS apps, the simulator always indicates that you're at Apple's headquarters in Cupertino, California. Also, although you can simulate orientation changes (to portrait or landscape mode) and the shake gesture, there is no way to simulate particular accelerometer readings. You can, however, upload your app to an iPhone to test these features. You'll see how to do this in Chapter 11, **Route Tracker** app. You'll start using the simulator to develop iPhone apps in Chapter 3's **Welcome** app.

Gesture	Simulator action	App in which gesture is introduced
Tap	Click the mouse once.	Chapter 4's **Tip Calculator** app
Double Tap	Double click the mouse.	Chapter 8's **Cannon Game** app
Touch and Hold	Click and hold the mouse.	
Drag	Click, hold and drag the mouse.	Chapter 8's **Cannon Game** app
Swipe	Click and hold the mouse, move the pointer in the swipe direction and release the mouse.	Chapter 10's **Address Book** app
Flick	Click and hold the mouse, move the pointer in the flick direction and quickly release the mouse.	Chapter 10's **Address Book** app
Pinch	Press and hold the *Option* key. Two circles that simulate the two touches will appear. Move the circles to the start position, click and hold the mouse and drag the circles to the end position.	Chapter 11's **Route Tracker** app

Fig. 1.10 | iPhone gestures on the simulator (`developer.apple.com/IPhone/library/documentation/Xcode/Conceptual/iphone_development/125-Using_iPhone_Simulator/iphone_simulator_application.html`).

1.11 Basics of Object Technology

Objects are reusable software components that model items in the real world. A modular, object-oriented approach to design and implementation can make software-development groups much more productive than is possible using earlier programming techniques. Object-oriented programs are often easier to understand, correct and modify.

What are objects, and why are they special? *Object technology* is a packaging scheme for creating meaningful software units. There are date objects, time objects, invoice objects, automobile objects, people objects, audio objects, video objects, file objects and so on. There are graphics objects such as circles and squares, and GUI objects such as buttons, text boxes and sliders. In fact, almost any noun can be reasonably represented as a software object. Objects have *properties* (also called *attributes*), such as color, size and weight; and perform *methods* (also called *behaviors*), such as moving, sleeping or drawing.

Classes are types of related objects. For example, all cars belong to the "car" class, even though individual cars vary in make, model, color and options packages. A class specifies the general format of its objects, and the properties and actions available to an object depend on its class.

Different objects can have similar attributes and can exhibit similar behaviors. Comparisons can be made, for example, between babies and adults, and between humans and chimpanzees.

With object technology, properly designed classes can be *reused* on future projects. Using class libraries greatly reduces the effort required to implement new systems.

Object-oriented design (OOD) models software in terms similar to those that people use to describe real-world objects. It takes advantage of class relationships, where objects of a certain class, such as a class of vehicles, have the same characteristics—cars, trucks, little red wagons and roller skates have much in common. OOD takes advantage of *inheritance* relationships, where new classes of objects are derived quickly by absorbing characteristics of existing classes and adding unique characteristics of their own. For example, an object of class "convertible" certainly has the characteristics of the more general class "automobile," but more specifically, the roof goes up and down.

Object-oriented design provides a natural and intuitive way to view the software design process—namely, modeling objects by their attributes, behaviors and interrelationships, just as we describe real-world objects. OOD also models communication between objects. For example, a bank account object may receive a message to decrease its balance by a certain amount because the customer is withdrawing that amount of money.

OOD *encapsulates* (i.e., wraps) attributes and behaviors into objects—an object's attributes and behaviors are intimately tied together. Objects have the property of *information hiding*. This means that objects may know how to communicate with one another across well-defined interfaces, but normally they're not allowed to know how other objects are implemented—the implementation details are hidden within the objects themselves. We can drive a car effectively, for instance, without knowing the details of how engines, transmissions, brakes and exhaust systems work internally—as long as we know how to use the accelerator pedal, the brake pedal, the steering wheel and so on. Information hiding is crucial to good software engineering.

Languages like Objective-C are object oriented. Programming in such a language is called *object-oriented programming (OOP),* and it allows you to implement object-oriented designs as working software systems. In Objective-C, the unit of programming is the *class* from which objects are eventually *instantiated* (an OOP term for "created"). An object is said to be an *instance* of its class. Objective-C classes contain methods that implement behaviors and data that implements attributes.

Classes, Instance Variables and Methods

Objective-C programmers concentrate on creating their own classes and reusing existing classes, most notably those of the Cocoa frameworks. Each class contains data and the methods that manipulate that data and provide services to *clients* (i.e., other classes or functions that use the class). The data components of a class are implemented as *instance variables* and properties. For example, a bank account class might include an account number and a balance. The class might include member functions to make a deposit (increasing the balance), make a withdrawal (decreasing the balance) and inquire what the current balance is. The *nouns* in a system specification help the Objective-C programmer determine the set of classes from which objects will be created to work together to implement the system.

Classes are to objects as blueprints are to houses—a class is a "plan" for building an object of the class. Just as we can build many houses from one blueprint, we can instantiate (create) many objects from one class. You cannot cook meals in the kitchen of a blueprint; you *can* cook meals in the kitchen of a house. You cannot sleep in the bedroom of a blueprint; you *can* sleep in the bedroom of a house.

Classes can have relationships—called *associations*—with other classes. For example, in an object-oriented design of a bank, the "bank teller" class needs to relate to other classes, such as the "customer" class, the "cash drawer" class, the "safe" class, and so on.

Packaging software as classes makes it convenient to reuse the software. Reuse of existing classes when building programs saves time and money. Reuse also helps you build more reliable and effective systems, because existing classes and components often have gone through extensive testing, debugging and performance tuning. Indeed, with object technology, you can build much of the new software you'll need by combining existing classes, exactly as we do throughout this book.

1.12 Web 2.0

The web literally exploded in the mid-to-late 1990s, but the "dot com" economic bust brought hard times in the early 2000s. The resurgence that began in 2004 or so has been named *Web 2.0*. Google is widely regarded as the signature company of Web 2.0. Some others are FaceBook and MySpace (social networking), Twitter (social messaging), Flickr (photo sharing), Craigslist (free classified listings), delicious (social bookmarking), YouTube (video sharing), Salesforce (business software offered as online services), Second Life (a virtual world), Skype (Internet telephony) and Wikipedia (a free online encyclopedia).

At Deitel & Associates, we launched our Web 2.0-based Internet business initiative in 2005. We share our research in the form of Resource Centers at `www.deitel.com/resourcecenters.html`. Each lists many links to mostly free content and software on the Internet. We announce our latest Resource Centers in our weekly newsletter, the *Deitel*® *Buzz Online* (`www.deitel.com/newsletter/subscribe.html`).

To follow the latest developments in Web 2.0, read `www.techcrunch.com` and `www.slashdot.org` and check out the growing list of Internet- and web-related Resource Centers at `www.deitel.com/resourcecenters.html`.

1.13 Test-Driving the Painter App in the iPhone Simulator

In this section, you'll run and interact with your first iPhone app. The **Painter** app allows the user to "paint" on the screen using different brush sizes and colors. You'll build this app in Chapter 9.

We use fonts to distinguish between IDE features (such as menu names and menu items) and other elements that appear in the IDE. The following steps show you how to test-drive the app.

1. *Checking your setup.* Confirm that you've set up your computer properly by reading the Before You Begin section located after the Preface.

2. *Locating the app folder.* Open a **Finder** window and navigate to the Documents/ Examples/Painter folder or the folder where you saved the chapter's examples.

3. *Opening the Painter project.* Double click the file name Painter.xcodeproj to open the project in Xcode.

4. *Launching the Painter app.* In Xcode, select **Project > Set Active SDK** from the menu bar. Make sure **iPhone Simulator 3.0** (or **3.1**) is selected. Once this is done, click the **Build and Go** button (Fig. 1.11) to run the app in the simulator. [*Note:* Apple continuously updates Xcode. Depending on your version and how you last executed an app, this button may be called **Build and Run** or **Build and Debug**.]

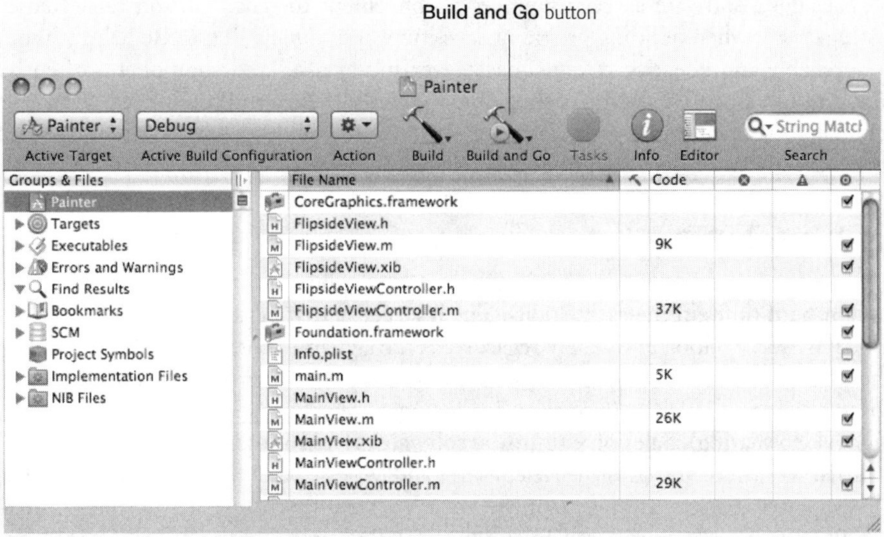

Fig. 1.11 | Clicking the **Build and Go** button to run the **Painter** app.

5. *Exploring the app.* The only items on the screen are the drawing canvas and the info (🛈) button (Fig. 1.12). When the app is installed on an iPhone, you can create a new painting by dragging your finger anywhere on the canvas. In the simulator, you "touch" the screen by using the mouse.

   To change the brush size or color, touch the info (🛈) button. The view changes to display the app settings. In Fig. 1.13 several graphical elements— called components—are labeled. The components include **Sliders**, **Labels**, **Buttons** and a **View** (these controls are discussed in depth later in the book). The app allows you to set the color and thickness of the brush. You'll explore these options momentarily. You can also clear the entire drawing to start from scratch.

   Using preexisting GUI components, you can create powerful apps in Cocoa much faster than if you had to write all the code yourself. In this book, you'll use many preexisting Cocoa components and write your own Objective-C code to customize your apps.

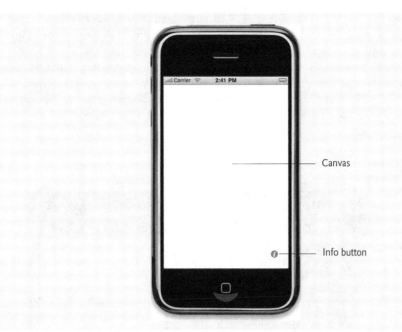

Fig. 1.12 | **Painter** app with a blank canvas.

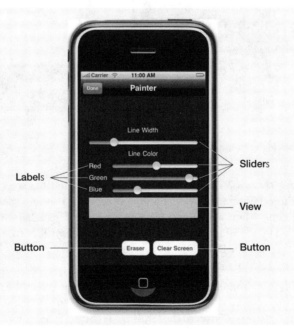

Fig. 1.13 | **Painter** app settings.

6. *Changing the brush color.* To change the brush color, drag any of the three sliders under the "**Line Color**" **Label**. As you drag a slider, the **View** below the **Sliders** dis-

plays the new color. Moving these **Red**, **Green** and **Blue** sliders enables the user to control the amounts of red, green and blue used to form the new color. iPhones also support alpha transparency (partial transparency), which you'll use in Chapter 7's **Spot-On Game** app. Once you've selected a color, touch the **Done** button to return to the canvas. Select a red color now by dragging the "**Red**" Slider to the right and the "**Blue**" **Slider** and "**Green**" **Slider** to the left Fig. 1.14(a). Touch the **Done** button to return to the canvas. Drag your finger on the screen to draw flower petals (Fig. 1.14(b)).

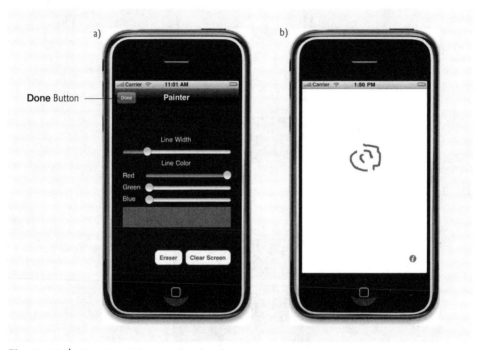

Fig. 1.14 | Drawing with a new brush color.

7. *Changing the brush color and size.* Change to the settings screen again by touching the info (ⓘ) button. Select a green color by dragging the "**Green**" **Slider** to the right and "**Red**" and "**Blue**" **Sliders** to the left (Fig. 1.15(a)). The line width is controlled by the slider labeled **Line Width**. Drag this slider to the right to thicken the line. Touch the **Done** button to return to the canvas. Draw grass and a flower stem (Fig. 1.15(b)).

8. *Finishing the drawing.* Switch back to the settings screen by touching the info (ⓘ) button. Select a blue color by dragging the "**Blue**" **Slider** to the right and the "**Red**" and "**Green**" **Sliders** to the left (Fig. 1.16(a)). Switch back to the canvas and draw the raindrops (Fig. 1.16(b)).

9. *Closing the app.* Close your running app by clicking the Home button on the bottom of the iPhone Simulator, or by selecting **iPhone Simulator > Quit iPhone Simulator** from the menu bar.

Fig. 1.15 | Changing the line color and line size to draw the stem and grass.

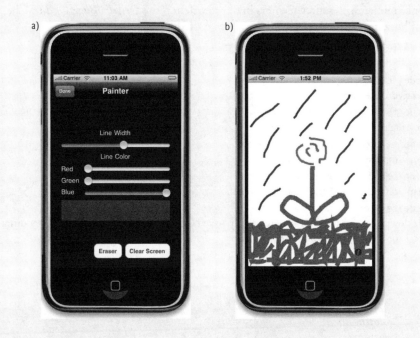

Fig. 1.16 | Changing the line color and line size to draw the rain.

1.14 Wrap-Up

This chapter presented a brief history of the iPhone and discussed its functionality. You learned about the new and updated hardware and software features of the iPhone 3GS and the iPhone 3.x operating system. You learned the iPhone gestures, and how to perform each on the iPhone and using the iPhone simulator. We introduced the Cocoa frameworks that enable you to use the iPhone hardware and software functionality to build your iPhone apps. You'll use many of these frameworks in this book. You also learned about the history of Objective-C programming and Apple's iPhone SDK 3. We listed the design patterns that we use in the book's apps. We discussed basic object-technology concepts, including classes, objects, attributes and behaviors. We discussed Web 2.0. Finally, you test-drove the **Painter** app.

In Chapter 2, we discuss the business side of iPhone app development. You'll see how to prepare your app for submission to the app store, including making icons and launch images. We provide tips for pricing and marketing your app. We also show how to use iTunes Connect to track app sales, payments and more.

1.15 Deitel Resource Centers

Our website (www.deitel.com) provides more than 100 Resource Centers on various topics including programming languages, software development, Web 2.0, Internet business and open-source projects. The Resource Centers evolve out of the research we do to support our publications and business endeavors. We've found many exceptional resources online, including tutorials, documentation, software downloads, articles, blogs, podcasts, videos, code samples, books, e-books and more—most of them are free. Each week we announce our latest Resource Centers in our newsletter, the *Deitel® Buzz Online*. Check out the iPhone-related Resource Centers to get started:

www.deitel.com/iPhone/
Apple iPhone Resource Center.

www.deitel.com/ObjectiveC/
Objective-C Resource Center.

www.deitel.com/Cocoa/
Cocoa Frameworks Resource Center.

www.deitel.com/iPhoneAppDevelopment/
iPhone App Development Resource Center.

www.deitel.com/ResourceCenters.html
The master list of all Deitel Resource Centers.

www.deitel.com/books/iPhoneFP/
Code downloads, updates, errata, Frequently Asked Questions (FAQs), hot links and additional resources for *iPhone for Programmers*.

iPhone App Store and App Business Issues

OBJECTIVES

In this chapter you'll be introduced to:

- iPhone Human Interface Guidelines for designing your app.
- Characteristics of great apps.
- Setting up an iPhone Developer Program profile so you can test your apps on devices and submit your apps to the App Store.
- Submitting your app to the App Store through iTunes Connect.
- Common reasons an app might be rejected by Apple.
- Pricing your app and the benefits of free vs. paid apps.
- Marketing and monetizing your app.
- Using iTunes Connect to track sales and trends.
- iPhone anecdotes and humor.
- Other popular platforms to which you can port your app.

Outline

2.1   Introduction

2.2   iPhone Developer Program:

    2.2.1   Setting Up Your iPhone Development Team

    2.2.2   Getting an iPhone Development Certificate

    2.2.3   Registering Devices for Testing

    2.2.4   Creating App IDs

    2.2.5   Creating a Provisioning Profile

    2.2.6   Using the Provisioning Profile to Install an App on an iPhone or iPod Touch

    2.2.7   Submitting Your App for Distribution

2.3   iPhone Human Interface Guidelines

2.4   Testing Your App

2.5   Preparing Your App for Submission through iTunes Connect

2.6   Characteristics of Great iPhone Apps

2.7   Avoiding Rejection of Your App

2.8   Pricing Your App: Free or Fee

2.9   Adding an App to iTunes Connect

2.10 Monetizing Paid Apps: Using In App Purchase to Sell Virtual Goods

2.11 Using iTunes Connect to Manage Your Apps

2.12 Marketing Your App

2.13 iPhone Anecdotes and Humor

2.14 Other Platforms

2.15 iPhone Developer Documentation

2.16 Wrap-Up

2.1 Introduction

In Chapters 3–16, you'll learn how to develop a wide variety of iPhone apps. Once you've developed and tested your own app—both in the simulator and on iPhones—the next step is to submit it to Apple's App Store for approval for distribution. At the time of this writing, Apple indicated that "94% of apps are being approved within 14 days."[1] In this chapter, you'll learn how to set up your iPhone Developer Program profile so you can test your app on iPhones and submit it to the App Store for approval. We'll discuss the *iPhone Human Interface Guidelines* to follow when you design your app's user interface, and general characteristics of great apps. We'll list some common reasons why Apple rejects apps. You'll learn how to submit your app through iTunes Connect (part of the iPhone Developer Program). We'll discuss some considerations for making your app free or selling it for a fee, and refer you to resources for monetizing apps. We'll provide resources for marketing your app. We'll introduce you to iTunes Connect where you can track your app sales, payments and more. And, we'll point you to lots of online resources, mostly free, where you can find additional information.

There's a lot of useful information in this chapter that you should keep in mind as you develop your iPhone apps and that we kept in mind as we developed the 14 apps in Chapters 3–16. If you're eager to plunge into iPhone app development, you can skip right to Chapter 3. At a minimum, you should glance through this chapter to see what's covered. You can then return to this chapter as you like while reading the rest of the book.

---

1. "Announcements and News for iPhone Developers," developer.apple.com/iphone.

2.2 iPhone Developer Program: Setting Up Your Profile for Testing and Submitting Apps

To test your apps on actual iPhones and to submit your apps to the App Store for approval, you must join the fee-based iPhone Developer Program at `developer.apple.com/iphone/`. As a member, you'll have access to numerous resources, including:

- Getting started guides
- Tips on submitting your apps to the App Store
- Programming guides
- Sample code
- Downloads
- Preview/beta releases of the iPhone OS and iPhone SDK
- Developer forums, and more.

As we completed this book for publication, Apple released the "App Store Resource Center" (`developer.apple.com/iphone/appstore/`), which provides additional information about the issues we discuss in Sections 2.2.1–2.2.7.

2.2.1 Setting Up Your iPhone Development Team

Log into the iPhone Developer Program site and click **iPhone Developer Program Portal** (the link for this appears after you've bought and activated the developer program membership). Here you'll find the resources for testing your apps and submitting them for approval. You'll need to set up your *iPhone Development Team* (Fig. 2.1)—you and/or the people in your organization who'll be able to log into the iPhone Developer Program Portal, test apps on iPhones, add iPhones to the account for testing, and so on. To set up your team, click the **Team** link on the iPhone Developer Program Portal page. The person who registers is designated as the *Team Agent*. If you register as a company, you can assign Team Members. The Team Agent has all primary responsibilities for the account.

---

iPhone Development Team

Team Agent
- Primary responsibilities for the account—assigned to the person who enrolls in the iPhone Developer program.
- Accepts all legal program agreements through iTunes Connect.
- Assigns Team Admins and Team Members.
- Creates Provisioning Profiles, which include your development certificates, devices and App IDs (an alphanumeric identifier of your choice).
- Obtains the iPhone Distribution Certificate for App Store and Ad Hoc distribution.
- Designated as a Team Admin if the team consists of two or more people.
- Tests apps on designated iPhones.

Fig. 2.1 | iPhone Development Team responsibilities. (*iTunes Connect Developer Guide version 4.7*, July 10, 2009.) (Part 1 of 2.)

---

iPhone Development Team

Team Admin
- Assigns Team Admins and Team Members who'll be eligible to test your apps on iPhones.
- Approves Development Certificate requests.
- Assigns iPhones to your account for testing.
- Creates Provisioning Profiles.
- Tests apps on designated iPhones.

Team Member
- Makes (but does not approve) Development Certificate requests.
- Downloads Provisioning Profiles.
- Tests apps on designated iPhones.

Fig. 2.1 | iPhone Development Team responsibilities. (*iTunes Connect Developer Guide version 4.7*, July 10, 2009.) (Part 2 of 2.)

2.2.2 Getting an iPhone Development Certificate

You'll also need to get an *iPhone Development Certificate*—an encrypted certificate that serves as your digital identification. You must sign your app using the certificate before you can run and test the app on an iPhone.

To get a development certificate, you must first generate a *Certificate Signing Request (CSR)* using the pre-installed Mac OS X Keychain Access application (**Applications > Utilities > Keychain Access**).

1. Go to the **Keychain Access** menu and select **Preferences**.

2. Click the **Certificates** tab and set the **Online Certificate Status Protocol** and **Certificate Revocation List** to **Off**. Close this dialog.

3. Next, in the **Keychain Access** menu, select **Certificate Assistant > Request a Certificate from a Certificate Authority** to display the **Certificate Assistant**. Enter the same e-mail address and name you used to enroll in the iPhone Developer Program. Select the **Saved to Disk** radio button and check the **Let me specify key pair information** checkbox. Click **Continue** then **Save** to save the request to disk.

4. In the **Key Pair Information** screen, set the **Key Size** to **2048 bits** and the **Algorithm** to **RSA**, then click **Continue**. The CSR is now saved on your computer.

Go back to the **iPhone Developer Program Portal** and click the **Certificates** link to add the certificate.

1. Ensure that the **Development** tab is selected.

2. Click the **Request Certificate** button to display the **Create iPhone Development Certificate** instructions page.

3. Click the **Browse...** (for Team Admins) or **Choose File** (for Team Members) button near the bottom of the page to find the CSR you saved on your computer. Select the file then click **Open**.

4. On the **Create iPhone Development Certificate** instructions page, click **Submit**.

A request for approval will be sent to the Team Admin(s). An admin (or the Team Agent) must go to the **Certificates** page and click **Approve** (for a certificate requested by an admin) or **Approve Selected** (for a request from a Team Member) to approve the request. Upon approval, the developer who submitted the CSR will be able to download the certificate. The developer may need to refresh the browser window to see the **Download** button.

Next, go to the **iPhone Developer Program Portal** and click the **Certificates** link, where you'll see your development certificate listed. Before downloading the development certificate, you must install the *WWDR intermediate certificate* on your computer. Just below your certificate you'll see "**If you do not have the WWDR intermediate certificate installed, click here to download now.**"

1. Click the link and save the WWDR intermediate certificate to your computer.

2. In **Finder**, double-click the WWDR intermediate certificate file to open it in Keychain Access and install it. Click **OK** to complete the installation.

3. Return to the **Certificates** page in the **iPhone Developer Program Portal**. Click the **Download** button next to your certificate and save it to your computer. In **Finder**, double-click the development certificate file to open it in Keychain Access and install it on your computer. Click **OK** to complete the installation.

It's possible to use the same developer certificate on multiple computers, which can be handy and really cut down on all of the certificate requesting overhead.

2.2.3 Registering Devices for Testing

Next, click **Devices** to register up to 100 iPhone and iPod Touch devices on which to test your apps. For each, provide a *device name* of your choosing and a *Unique Device Identifier (UDID)*—a 40-character identification code that is associated with a particular device. To find the UDID for a device, connect it to your Mac. Open Xcode and go to **Window > Organizer**. Select the connected device. The UDID appears in the **Identifier** field. To add a device, click the Add Devices button, enter the device's name and ID, then click **Submit**.

2.2.4 Creating App IDs

Return to the iPhone Developer Program Portal and click the **App IDs** link. The *App ID* (part of the Provisioning Profile, which we'll discuss shortly) identifies an app or a suite of related apps. It's used when communicating with hardware accessories and the Apple Push Notification service, and when sharing data in a suite of apps. Click the **New App ID** button. Enter an alphanumeric description of your app (e.g., the app's name). Next, add the *Bundle Seed ID*—the App ID prefix—by going to **Bundle Seed App ID** and selecting **Generate New** from the drop-down menu. Finally, in the **Bundle Identifier** textbox, enter a unique *Bundle Indentifier*—the App ID suffix. Apple recommends using the reverse-domain-name style (e.g., com.*DomainName*.*AppName*). Click **Submit** to add the new App ID.

2.2.5 Creating a Provisioning Profile

Now, click the **Provisioning** link on the iPhone Developer Program Portal page. A *Development Provisioning Profile* assigns your authorized iPhone Development Team members to your approved devices, allowing the Team Members to test an app on the devices. It's installed on each device and contains the iPhone Development Certificates for each Team Member, the UDID and the App ID. To create a **Provisioning Profile**:

1. Click the **New Profile** button.

2. In the **Profile Name** textbox, enter the name you wish to use for this profile.

3. In the **Certificates** section, check the boxes for each approved Team Member.

4. Go to the **App ID** drop-down menu and select the name of the app associated with the profile.

5. Under **Devices**, check the boxes for the devices on which the profile will be used.

6. Click the **Submit** button to create the profile.

Next, the development Team Members must download the profile and add it in Xcode. Each approved Team Member should perform the following steps:

1. Go to the **iPhone Developer Program Portal** and click the **Provisioning** link.

2. Click the **Download** button next to the appropriate provisioning profile and save it to your computer.

3. In **Finder**, double-click the provisioning profile that you saved to your computer (ending with .mobileprovision) to install the provisioning profile in Xcode.

4. To confirm that the profile was installed in Xcode, select **Window > Organizer**, then clicking **Provisioning Profiles** under the **IPHONE DEVELOPMENT** category.

2.2.6 Using the Provisioning Profile to Install an App on an iPhone or iPod Touch

The steps in this section should be performed once you've created an app and would like to install it on an actual device for testing.

1. In Xcode, open the project for the app that you'd like to install on a device.

2. In the Project's **Resources** group, double click the info.plist file (now called *AppName*-info.plist in newer Xcode versions).

3. Change the **Bundle identifier** to the bundle identifier you specified when you created your App ID, then save the file.

4. In Xcode, select **Project > Edit Project Settings** to display the **Project Info** dialog.

5. **Under Code Signing > Code Signing Identity**, select **iPhone Developer** under **Automatic Profile Selector**. [*Note:* In Xcode 3.2, click the **Build** tab to see this option.] This will choose the appropriate developer certificate for the app and will allow other developers on the team to build the app if you pass your project to them. You can also select your specific developer certificate if you like, but this will allow the app to be built only on your computer.

6. To get the app onto your device, ensure that your device is connected to your computer. Then, in Xcode, select **Project > Set Active SDK > iPhone Device 3.x** (where **x** is the most recent SDK version) and click **Build and Go**. In the latest version of Xcode, **Build and Go** is **Build and Run** or **Build and Debug**, depending on how you last ran an app.

The project will be compiled (if it is not up to date), then the app will be installed on the device and executed. [*Note:* If you have trouble getting the app to run on your device, it is sometimes helpful to reboot your iPhone or to select **Build > Clean All Targets** in Xcode.]

2.2.7 Submitting Your App for Distribution

The steps so far enable you to build and test apps on iPhones and iPod Touches. If you'd like to distribute your apps, you'll also need to perform the steps described in this subsection. In the **iPhone Developer Program Portal**, click the **Distribution** link to learn how to prepare and submit your app for App Store or *Ad Hoc distribution*, which allows you to distribute your app to up to 100 users via e-mail, a website or a server. Only the Team Agent can create an *iPhone Distribution Certificate* and submit an app for distribution. Assuming you are the Team Agent, generate a CSR in Keychain Access as follows:

1. In the **Keychain Access** menu, select **Preferences**.

2. Click the **Certificates** tab and set the **Online Certificate Status Protocol** and **Certificate Revocation List** to **Off**.

3. In the **Keychain Access** menu, select **Certificate Assistant > Request a Certificate from a Certificate Authority** to display the **Certificate Assistant**. Enter the same e-mail address and name you used to enroll in the iPhone Developer Program. Select the **Saved to Disk** radio button and check the **Let me specify key pair information** checkbox. In the **Key Pair Information** screen, set the **Key Size** to **2048 bits** and the **Algorithm** to **RSA**. Click **Continue** then **Save** to save the request to disk.

4. Click **Done**.

Next, return to the **iPhone Developer Program Portal** to upload the certificate request.

1. Click the **Certificates** link, then click the **Distribution** tab.

2. Upload and submit the CSR, then approve your distribution certificate using the same steps we described earlier in Section 2.2.2.

3. If you do not already have the WWDR intermediate certificate on your computer, follow the steps in Section 2.2.2 to download it.

4. Next, download the distribution certificate. Return to the **Certificates** link (and the **Distribution** tab) on the **iPhone Developer Program Portal**. Click the **Download** button next to distribution certificate and save it to your computer.

5. In **Finder**, double-click the distribution certificate file to open it in Keychain Access and install it on your computer.

To distribute your app through the App Store, you'll need to create a *Distribution Provisioning Profile*. [*Note:* Before performing these steps, some developers prefer to make copies of the projects they intend to distribute, rather than modifying the settings on their development projects.] On the **Create iPhone Distribution Provisioning Profile** page, you'll be able to create a profile for either App Store distribution of Ad Hoc distribution.

1. In the **iPhone Developer Program Portal**, click the **Provisioning** link.

2. Click the **Distribution** tab, then click the **New Profile** button.

3. Select the **App Store** radio button. In the **Profile Name** textbox, enter the name you wish to use for your Distribution Provisioning Profile. The **Distribution Cer-**

tificates section should show your distribution certificate. In the **App ID** drop-down menu, select the name of the app (or suite of apps) associated with the pro-file.

4. For Ad Hoc distribution, under **Devices**, check the boxes for the devices on which the app will be run. This section is disabled for App Store distribution profiles.

5. Click the **Submit** button. Once the Distribution Provisioning Profile is created, click the name of the file to download it to your computer, then double click it to install it in Xcode.

6. To use this profile, you'll need to select it in your project's settings. In Xcode, se-lect **Project > Edit Project Settings** to display the **Project Info** dialog. Then **Under Code Signing > Code Signing Identity**, select **iPhone Distribution** under **Automatic Profile Selector**. [*Note:* In Xcode 3.2, click the **Build** tab to see this option.]

To use Ad Hoc distribution, build your app, then provide each approved device's owner with both the application file and the Ad Hoc Distribution Provisioning Profile. The de-vice owner must drag *both* of these into iTunes, then sync the device. For App Store dis-tribution, see Section 2.5.

After building your appl, locate and compress your app for distribution as follows:

1. In Xcode, open the **Products** group under **Groups & Files** for your project.

2. Right click the app name under **Products** and select **Reveal in Finder** to locate the app bundle in Finder.

3. In Finder, right click the app bundle (which looks like a file with the .app exten-sion) and select compress.

You now have a zipped app bundle—required since app bundles are actually folders—that you can distribute. For more detail on building and verifying your app for distribu-tion, visit developer.apple.com/iphone/manage/distribution/index.action in the iPhone Developer Program Portal.

2.3 iPhone Human Interface Guidelines

It's important when creating iPhone apps to follow the *iPhone Human Interface Guide-lines*:

> developer.apple.com/iphone/library/documentation/userexperience/
> conceptual/mobilehig/Introduction/Introduction.html

Part One, "Planning Your iPhone Software Product," provides guidelines for developing apps that run efficiently and effectively on the iPhone platform. For example, you'll need to consider the screen size, memory limitations and the ease of use of your apps, particu-larly because your app cannot include extensive help documentation. The guide also in-cludes principles for creating good user interfaces, such as designing easy-to-use controls, providing status updates and other feedback, and more.

Part Two, "Designing the User Interface of Your iPhone Application," walks through the proper use and appearance of views and controls including:

• Navigation bars and toolbars,

• Alerts,

- Table views,

- App controls (e.g., date and time pickers, labels, etc.),

- Buttons and icons (e.g., the **Done** button, the info (ⓘ) button, etc.) ,

- Creating custom icons and images,

- and more.

Figure 2.2 lists some of the many suggestions that appear in the 130-page document *IPhone Human Interface Guidelines.*

Points and Suggestions from the *iPhone Human Interface Guidelines*

- Most important, read the document *IPhone Human Interface Guidelines.*
- If you're going to create web applications, also read the document *iPhone Human Interface Guidelines for Web Applications.*
- Make your apps aesthetically pleasing.
- Keep your apps simple and easy to use.
- Keep in mind that iPhone apps are designed differently from desktop apps because of the small screen.
- Avoid cluttering the screen.
- Design your app to work well given that the iPhone displays *only* a single screen at a time.
- Keep in mind that the iPhone runs *only* one app at a time. Leaving an app quits the app, so be sure to save anything you need immediately after it's created.
- Carefully manage memory as a limited resource.
- Keep in mind *why* the user is using your app.
- Keep your app's *goals* in mind as you design it.
- Your app should be modeled after the way things work in the real world.
- People feel closer to your app's interface because they touch it directly (rather than indirectly through a mouse).
- Give people lists and let them touch the choice they want rather than requiring key stroking, if possible.
- Provide feedback to user actions—for example, use an activity indicator to show that an app is working on a task of unpredictable duration.
- Be consistent—for example, always prefer standard buttons and icons provided by the iPhone OS to creating your own customized buttons and icons.
- If you do provide custom icons, make sure that they're easily distinguishable from system icons.
- Although you can have as many buttons as you like on alerts, you should provide two. Avoid the complexity of alerts with more than two buttons.
- Your apps should be intuitive—the user should be able to figure out what to do at any given time, with minimal help.
- Support the standard iPhone gestures in the standard way.
- Make your apps accessible for people with disabilities.
- If a button does something destructive, make it red.

Fig. 2.2 | Points and suggestions from the *iPhone Human Interface Guidelines.* (Part 1 of 2.)

Points and Suggestions from the *iPhone Human Interface Guidelines*
• Make your application icons 57 x 57 pixels with square corners. • The user's finger is generally much larger than a mouse pointer (used in desktop applications), so make the "hit region" of each user interface element 44 x 44 pixels.

Fig. 2.2 | Points and suggestions from the *iPhone Human Interface Guidelines*. (Part 2 of 2.)

2.4 Testing Your App

Before submitting your app for approval for App Store or Ad Hoc distribution, test your app thoroughly to make sure it works properly on iPhone OS 3.x. Although the app might work perfectly using the simulator on your Mac, problems could arise when running the app on an iPhone. Figure 2.3 lists iPhone functionality that isn't available on the simulator. To learn more about the simulator and the frameworks it uses, read the *iPhone Development Guide*.

iPhone functionality that is not available on the simulator	
Compass	Camera
Bluetooth data transfer	3D graphics (works differently)
iPod music library access	Accelerometer (allows only orientation changes)
GPS	

Fig. 2.3 | iPhone functionality that is not available on the simulator.

Check out the **iPhone OS 3.0 Readiness Checklist** on the password-protected Developer Connection website. Here you'll find:

- Getting Started guides for the latest iPhone OS 3.x features including Apple Push Notification, In App Purchase and Parental Controls.

- Programming guides for additional iPhone OS 3.x features including Accessibility, Game Kit, iPod Library Access, Open GL ES 2.0 and Store Kit.

- The *iTunes Connect Developer Guide*, which provides guidelines for adding an app to the App Store; testing, creating and managing In-App Purchases; updating your app on the App Store; and more.

2.5 Preparing Your App for Submission through iTunes Connect

When submitting your app for approval through iTunes Connect, you'll be asked to provide keywords, icons, a launch image, screenshots and translated app data if you intend to offer localized versions of your app for international App Stores. In this section, we'll tell you what to prepare. In Section 2.9, Adding an App to iTunes Connect, we'll walk you through the steps of uploading everything for approval.

Keywords

When submitting your app, you'll provide a comma-separated list of descriptive keywords that will help users find your app on the App Store. Your keyword list is limited to 100 characters. This is similar to the tagging schemes used by websites such as Flickr and You-Tube, except that only you can provide keywords for your own apps. Although Apple doesn't provide guidelines or suggested keywords, they do state that *you cannot use the names of other people's apps.*

Icons

Design an icon for your app that will appear in the App Store and on the user's iPhone. You can use your company logo, an image from the app or a custom image. Create the icon in two different sizes:[2]

- 57 x 57 pixels
- 512 x 512 pixels

Both icons should have square corners and no shine effects. The iPhone OS will automatically apply three visual effects to give your icon a similar appearance to the built-in iPhone app icons:

- Rounded corners
- Drop shadow to give the icons a 3-D appearance
- Glass-like reflective shine

In addition, every app should provide a 29 x 29 icon that will appear next to the app's name in Spotlight searches and possibly the iPhone's Settings app. For further specifications and best practices, see the *iPhone Human Interface Guidelines* (under **Creating Custom Icons and Images**) and the *iTunes Connect Developer Guide*. You might also consider hiring an experienced graphic designer to help you create a compelling, professional icon (Fig. 2.4).

Company	URL	Services
icondesign	www.icondesign.dk/	In addition to paid services, they offer a "free for free" deal—free icon design for your free app.
The Iconfactory	iconfactory.com/home	Custom and stock icons. Also offers IconBuilder software (for use with Adobe® Photoshop®) for creating your own icons.
IconDrawer	www.icondrawer.com/main.php/	Custom icon design and some free downloadable icons.
Razorianfly Graphic Design	www.rflygd.com/services/	Custom icons and launch images.

Fig. 2.4 | Custom app icon design firms.

---

2. *iTunes Connect Developer Guide* (version 4.7, July 10, 2009).

Launch Images

Next, create a *launch image*, which will be displayed when the icon is tapped on the screen so that the user sees an immediate response while waiting for the app to load. For example, tap any of the default icons on the iPhone (e.g., **Stocks**, **Camera**, **Contacts**) and you'll notice that they immediately display a launch image that resembles the app's user interface— often just an image of the background elements of the GUI. To add a launch image to your app, open the project in Xcode. Go to the **Project** menu and select **Add to Project**. Locate the file and click **Add**. Name the launch image `Default.png`. For additional information, see the *iPhone Human Interface Guidelines*, the *iPhone Application Programming Guide* and the *Bundle Programming Guide*.

Primary Screenshot(s)

Take between one and four screenshots of your app that will be included with your app description in the App Store. These provide a preview of your app since users can't test the app before downloading it. See the *iTunes Connect Developer Guide* for screenshot size and resolution specifications.

Contract Information

To sell your app through the App Store, the Team Admin must agree to the terms of the *Paid Applications contract*—this may take some time while Apple verifies your financial information. If you intend to offer your app for free, the Team Admin must agree to the *Free Applications contract*.

Additional Languages (Optional)

You may offer your app in foreign languages (Fig. 2.5) through international iTunes App Stores. You'll be asked to enter your translated data into iTunes Connect as part of the submission process (see Section 2.9). You can offer your app in the international stores without translating your metadata—if you do so, the international users see English. You can actually localize the app to many more languages, but you can only localize the store description and other metadata to the the languages in Fig. 2.5.

Languages for localizing apps		
Dutch	UK English	Italian
English	French	Japanese
Australian English	Canadian French	Spanish
Canadian English	German	Mexican Spanish

Fig. 2.5 | Languages available for localizing your iPhone apps.

2.6 Characteristics of Great iPhone Apps

With over 75,000 apps in the App Store, how do you create an iPhone app that people will find, download, use and recommend to others? Consider what makes an app fun, useful, interesting, appealing and enduring. A clever app name, an attractive icon and an engaging description might lure people to your app on the App Store. But once users download the app, what will make them use it and recommend it to others? Figure 2.6

shows some characteristics of great apps. You can find additional tips in the **News and Announcements** section of the **iPhone Dev Center** (accessible by logging into the iPhone Developer Program).

Characteristics of great apps

General Characteristics
- Compatible with the latest iPhone OS 3.x.
- Updated frequently with new features.
- Features work properly (and bugs are fixed promptly).
- Follow standard iPhone app GUI conventions.
- Responsive and don't require too much memory, bandwidth or battery power.
- Novel and creative—possess a "wow" factor.
- Enduring—something that you'll use regularly.
- Use quality graphics.
- Intuitive and easy-to-use (don't require extensive help documentation).
- Accessible to people with disabilities (see the *Accessibility Programming Guide for iPhone OS*).
- Give users reasons and a means to tell others about your app.
- Provide additional content (for content-driven apps).

Great Games
- Entertaining.
- Challenging (progressive levels of difficulty).
- Show your scores and record high scores.
- Provide audio and visual feedback.
- Offer single player, multi-player and networked games.

Useful Utilities
- Provide useful functionality and accurate information.
- Make tasks more convenient.
- Make the user better informed.
- Topical—provide information on current subjects of interest (e.g., Swine Flu, stock prices).
- Provide access on-the-go to your favorite websites (e.g., stores, banks, etc.).
- Increase your personal and business productivity.

Fig. 2.6 | Characteristics of great apps.

2.7 Avoiding Rejection of Your App

Apple doesn't list all of the reasons why an app might be rejected, so we researched the web for insights from developers who have gone through the approval process. Figure 2.7 includes some of the common reasons iPhone apps have been rejected by Apple.[3,4,5]

---

3. www.mobileorchard.com/avoiding-iphone-app-rejection-from-apple/.
4. stackoverflow.com/questions/308479/reasons-for-rejecting-iphone-application-by-apple-store.
5. appreview.tumblr.com/.

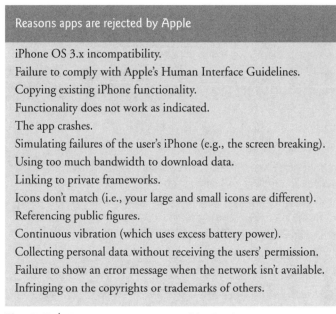

Reasons apps are rejected by Apple
iPhone OS 3.x incompatibility.
Failure to comply with Apple's Human Interface Guidelines.
Copying existing iPhone functionality.
Functionality does not work as indicated.
The app crashes.
Simulating failures of the user's iPhone (e.g., the screen breaking).
Using too much bandwidth to download data.
Linking to private frameworks.
Icons don't match (i.e., your large and small icons are different).
Referencing public figures.
Continuous vibration (which uses excess battery power).
Collecting personal data without receiving the users' permission.
Failure to show an error message when the network isn't available.
Infringing on the copyrights or trademarks of others.

Fig. 2.7 | Reasons apps are rejected by Apple.

2.8 Pricing Your App: Free or Fee

You set the price for your app that is distributed through the App Store. An increasing number of developers offer their apps for free as a marketing and publicity tool, earning revenue through increased sales of products and services, sales of more feature-rich versions of the same app, or in-app advertising. Figure 2.8 lists ways to monetize your app.

Paid apps	Free apps
Sell the app on the App Store.	Use mobile advertising services for in-app ads (see Section 2.12, Marketing Your App).
Sell paid upgrades to the app.	Sell in-app advertising space directly to your customers.
Sell virtual goods (see Section 2.10).	Use it to drive sales of a more feature-rich version of the app.

Fig. 2.8 | Ways to monetize your app.

Paid Apps

According to a study by O'Reilly® Radar, the average price of paid apps is around $2.65 (the median is $1.99).[6] When setting a price for your app, you should start by researching your competition. How much do their apps cost? Do theirs have the similar functionality?

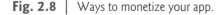

6. radar.oreilly.com/2009/04/itunes-app-store-billionth-download.html.

Is yours more feature-rich? Will offering your app at a lower price than the competition attract users? Is your goal is to recoup development costs and generate additional revenue?

All of the financial transactions for paid apps are handled by the App Store. Apple retains 30% of the purchase price and distributes 70% to you. Earnings are paid to you on a monthly basis, though Apple will withhold payment until you reach the minimum payment amount.

Free Apps

Approximately 22% of apps on the App Store are free, but they comprise the vast majority of downloads.[7] Given that users are more likely to download an app if it's free, consider offering a free "lite" version of your app to encourage users to download and try it. For example, if your app is a game, you might offer a free version with the first few levels. Once users complete these, the app would provide a message encouraging users to buy your more robust app with numerous game levels through the App Store. According to a recent study by AdMob, *upgrading from the "lite" version was the number one reason why users purchased a paid app.*[8]

Many companies use free apps to build brand awareness and drive sales of other products and services (Fig. 2.9).

Free app	Functionality
Amazon® Mobile	Browse and purchase items on Amazon.
Bank of America	Locate ATMs and bank branches in your area, check balances and pay bills.
ESPN® ScoreCenter	Set up personalized scoreboards to track your favorite college and professional teams in football, basketball, baseball, hockey, soccer and more.
Comcast® Mobile	Check your Comcast home phone voice mail and e-mail, forward calls to your iPhone, check television listings, watch trailers for Comcast On Demand movies and more.
Nationwide® Mobile	If you're in a car accident, use the accident toolkit to record the other driver's information, start an accident claim report, find a Nationwide agent and find a nearby repair shop.

Fig. 2.9 | Free iPhone apps that are building brand awareness.

Some developers offer free apps that are monetized with *in-app advertising*—often banner ads similar to those you find on websites. Mobile advertising networks such as AdMob (www.admob.com/) and Tapjoy (www.tapjoy.com/) aggregate advertisers for you and serve the ads to your app (see Section 2.12, Marketing Your App). You earn advertising revenue based on the number of views. According to a report by Adwhirl, a mobile

---

7. radar.oreilly.com/2009/07/news-providers-are-embracing-t.html.
8. metrics.admob.com/wp-content/uploads/2009/08/AdMob-Mobile-Metrics-July-09.pdf.

advertising network, the top 100 free apps earn about $400–5000 per day from in-app advertising.[9] They estimate that it takes about 2500 daily downloads for an app to make it into the top 100 of a given category.[10] In-app advertising does not generate significant revenue for most apps, so if your goal is to recoup development costs and generate profits, you may be better off selling your app. According to a study by Pinch Media, 20% of people who download a free app will use it within the first day after they download it, but only 5% will continue to use it after 30 days.[11] *Unless your app is widely downloaded and used, it will generate minimal advertising revenue.*

2.9 Adding an App to iTunes Connect

Once you've prepared all of your files and you're ready to submit your app to the App Store for approval, log into iTunes Connect at itunesconnect.apple.com. Click the **Manage Your Applications** link, then click the **Add New Application** button. The following is a walkthrough of the steps to add a new app. The *iTunes Connect Developer Guide* provides detailed descriptions of, and technical specifications for, each of the items you'll need to provide. [*Note:* You can also use the Application Loader to upload your apps. To get it, click the **Get Application Loader** link on the **Manage Your Applications** page.]

Add New Application

Chose the primary language for your app on the App Store (Fig. 2.5) and enter your company name, as it will appear on the App Store. Click the **Continue** button to proceed to the **Export Compliance** page.

Export Compliance

If your app includes encryption, you'll be asked a series of questions and you may need to provide Apple with copies of proper United States government authorization forms for exporting your app. To learn more about the U.S. Commerce Department export controls, go to (www.bis.doc.gov/licensing/exportingbasics.htm). Once you've provided the appropriate information, click the **Continue** button to proceed to the **Overview** page.

Overview

Enter the information in Fig. 2.10 (most of which will appear in the App Store), then click the **Continue** button to proceed to the **Ratings** page.

iTunes Connect **Overview** page for adding an app
App name.
App description (4000 characters or less).

Fig. 2.10 | iTunes Connect **Overview** page for adding an app. (Part 1 of 2.)

---

9. www.techcrunch.com/2009/05/06/just-how-much-money-can-free-iphone-apps-make-quite-a-bit/.
10. Adwhirl, "Over 50,000 Apps in the App Store—How do Apps Get Discovered?" (June 2009).
11. www.techcrunch.com/2009/02/19/pinch-media-data-shows-the-average-shelf-life-of-an-iphone-app-is-less-than-30-days/.

iTunes Connect Overview page for adding an app

Device requirements—choose from the drop-down menu (e.g, iPhone only, iPhone and iPod Touch).

Primary category—choose from the drop-down menu (see Fig. 1.6 for a list of categories on the App Store).

Subcategory—choose up to two subcategories from the drop-down menus (for games only—subcategories include action, adventure, kids, trivia, etc.).

Secondary category—choose from the drop-down menu (again, see Figure 1.6 for a list of categories on the App Store).

Copyright holder and year of copyright.

App version number (e.g., 1.0).

SKU (your own unique alphanumeric stock keeping unit number).

Keywords (see Section 2.5, Preparing Your App for Submission through iTunes Connect).

App URL (not required—website with additional information about your app.).

Support URL (where users can submit feedback forms, find bug reports, etc.).

Support e-mail (where users can send bug reports, feedback, etc.).

Demo account—full access (not required—usernames and passwords for any test accounts that Apple may use to test your app).

End User License Agreement (not required).

Fig. 2.10 | iTunes Connect **Overview** page for adding an app. (Part 2 of 2.)

Ratings

iTunes requires ratings for apps sold through the App Store. The ratings—used for the new iPhone parental controls—are displayed in the App Store below the price of the app so that parents can determine if the app contains material that is not suitable for children of a certain age. Parental controls enable users to restrict access to an app based on the rating. On the ratings page, you'll be asked if your app contains violence, sexual content, profanity, mature themes, gambling or horror themes. Next to each, select the radio button corresponding to the frequency of such content in your app—**None, Infrequent/Mild** or **Frequent/Intense**. Based on your responses, Apple will assign one of the ratings in Fig. 2.11. As you respond to each category, you're app rating will be displayed on the screen. Click the **Continue** button to proceed to the **Upload** page.

Age rating	Description
4+	No objectionable material.
9+	Suitable for children 9 years and older.
12+	Suitable for children 12 years and older.
17+	Frequent or intense objectionable material, suitable only for people 17 years and older.

Fig. 2.11 | App ratings.

Upload

On this page, you'll upload the files for your app, including:

- 2GB or smaller zipped app binary (which includes your app code, launch image and 57 x 57 icon)
- Large icon (512 x 512)
- Primary screenshot
- Additional screenshots

Once you've uploaded all of the files, click the **Continue** button to proceed to the **Pricing and Availability** page.

Pricing and Availability

On this page you'll select the price for your app.

- Select the date that you wish to make your app available through the App Store. The App Store will display the app release date as either the date you enter here or the date your app is approved, whichever is earlier.
- Next, select a *price tier* for your app. Click **See Pricing Matrix** to view a list of the numbered price tiers and the corresponding app price for each. Select a tier to view a table displaying the customer price for your app in the local currency for each App Store worldwide, and the proceeds you'll receive in each currency based on that price.
- Finally, select the App Stores (Fig. 2.12) in which you'll sell your app by clicking the checkbox next to each country name. Click the **Continue** button to proceed to the **Localization** page.

App Stores		
Australia	Greece	Norway
Austria	Ireland	Portugal
Belgium	Italy	Spain
Canada	Japan	Sweden
Denmark	Luxembourg	Switzerland
Finland	Mexico	United Kingdom
France	Netherlands	United States
Germany	New Zealand	Rest of World

Fig. 2.12 | App Stores worldwide.

Localization

You may enter your app information (which you supplied on the **Overview** page) in other languages to be used in international App Stores. For example, enter the information in Spanish for use in App Stores in Spanish-speaking countries. See Fig. 2.5 for a list of available languages. Click the **Continue** button to proceed to the **Review** page. To learn more about designing your app for international markets, search "Internationalization Programming Topics" in the iPhone Developer Program.

Review

The **Review** page provides a summary of all of the information you entered. If everything is correct, click the **Submit Application** button to send the information to the App Store for approval. Once you've submitted your app for approval, you can check the status of the app by going to the **Manage Your Applications** link in iTunes Connect. If you make changes to your app (e.g., upgrades, bug fixes, etc.) after it's approved and need to upload a new version, you must re-submit it to the App Store for approval. Your existing users will be notified that an update to the app is available when they access the App Store from their iPhone and tap the **Updates** icon.

2.10 Monetizing Paid Apps: Using In App Purchase to Sell Virtual Goods

As we discussed in Chapter 1, In App Purchase—a new feature in iPhone OS 3.x and part of the Store Kit framework—allows you to sell *virtual goods* (e.g., digital content) through a paid app (Fig. 2.13). *In App Purchase is not available in free apps.* In App Purchase items have a separate approval process, e.g., if you offer books for sale through a bookstore app, each book has to be approved as it is added to the catalog. According to Viximo, a virtual goods company, sales of virtual goods will reach $400 million in the United States and $5.5 billion globally in 2009.[12] In App Purchase opens this lucrative market to iPhone app developers. Selling virtual goods can generate higher revenue per user than advertising.[13]

Virtual goods		
Magazine subscriptions	Localized guides	Avatars
Virtual apparel	Game levels	Game scenery
Add-on features	Ringtones	Icons
E-cards	E-gifts	Virtual currency
Wallpaper	Images	Virtual pets
Audio	Video	And more.

Fig. 2.13 | Virtual goods.

Using In App Purchase

There are two ways to use In App Purchase:

- You can build the additional functionality into your app. When the user opts to make a purchase, the app notifies the App Store which handles the financial

---

12. viximo.com/publishers/about/why.
13. www.virtualgoodsnews.com/2009/04/super-rewards-brings-virtual-currency-platform-to-social-web.html.

transaction and returns a message to the app verifying payment. The app then unlocks the additional functionality.

• Your app can download the additional content on demand. When the user makes a purchase, the app notifies the App Store which handles the financial transaction. The app then notifies your server to send the new content. Before doing so, your server can verify that the app has a valid receipt.[14]

Your app provides the purchasing interface, allowing you to control the user experience. The Store Kit framework processes the payment request through the iTunes store, then sends your app confirmation of the purchase. To learn more about the In App Purchase using the Store Kit framework, read the *Store Kit Programming Guide* and the *Store Kit Framework Reference* (available at the iPhone Developer Program website).

If your app uses In App Purchase functionality, it's important that you select the correct category for the item you're selling (Fig. 2.14) as *you cannot modify the settings later*. For step-by-step instructions on setting up in app purchases, read the In App Purchases section of the *iTunes Connect Developer Guide* (available in the iPhone Developer Program website).

Category	Description
Consumables	Users pay for the item each time it is downloaded and it cannot be downloaded on multiple devices.
Non-consumables	Users pay for the content once. Subsequent downloads are free and can be used across multiple devices (e.g., your new iPhone or iPod).
Subscription	Users pay for content that is delivered for a set period of time (e.g., a six-month subscription). Content cannot be downloaded on multiple devices.

Fig. 2.14 | Categorizing your products for sale using In App Purchase.

2.11 Using iTunes Connect to Manage Your Apps

iTunes Connect (itunesconnect.apple.com/), which is part of the iPhone Developer Program, allows you to manage your account and your apps, track sales, request promotional codes for your products and more (Fig. 2.15). Promotional codes allow you to distribute up to 50 complimentary copies of your for-sale app per update of your app. In addition, iTunes reports app crashes from the devices on which your app is installed back to iTunes Connect. When managing an app in iTunes Connect, you can view crash information in the app's **App Details** page by clicking the **View Crash Reports** button. This information can help you fix bugs in your app.

14. For more information see "Verifying Store Receipts" in the *In App Purchase Programming Guide* (developer.apple.com/iphone/library/documentation/NetworkingInternet/Conceptual/ StoreKitGuide/StoreKitGuide.pdf).

iTunes Connect module	Description
Sales/Trend Reports	View daily, weekly and monthly sales reports.
Contracts, Tax & Banking Information	Sign paid applications agreements to sell your apps through the App Store. Set up banking information and tax withholdings. Manage your iTunes contracts.
Financial Reports	Access your monthly financial reports.
Manage Users	Add or remove authorized users for your iTunes Connect account and designate the modules each is able to access.
Manage Your Applications	Add new apps to be approved for the App Store.
Request Promotional Codes	Get promotional codes that allow selected users to download your app for free (see Section 2.12, Marketing Your App).
Contact Us	Find answers to frequently asked questions or fill out forms to contact an Apple representative.

Fig. 2.15 | iTunes Connect modules.

2.12 Marketing Your App

Once your app has been approved by Apple, you need to market it to your audience. Start by going to the **Marketing Resources for iPhone Developers** page on the iPhone Developer Center website at `developer.apple.com/iphone/`—log into the site and you'll see the **Marketing Resources for iPhone Developers** link under **iPhone Developer Program** (Fig. 2.16).

Resource	Description
App Store Logo License Program	Promote awareness by including the "Available on the App Store" logo in marketing materials. You must sign the *App Marketing License Agreement* and comply with the *App Marketing and Identity Guidelines for Developers* to use the artwork in your marketing materials.
iTunes Affiliate Program	If you're promoting apps on your website and in e-mail newsletters, sign up for the iTunes Affiliate Program (offered through LinkShare™) to earn a 5% commission on sales generated from your links to the App Store. Visit `www.apple.com/itunes/affiliates/`.
Sales and Trend Reporting	Available through iTunes Connect.
Keywords for App Store Search	Choose keywords that you believe will help users find your app when searching the App Store (see Section 2.5).

Fig. 2.16 | Marketing Resources for iPhone app developers (`developer.apple.com/iphone/`). (Part 1 of 2.)

Resource	Description
iTunes Deep Links	Use deep links to take users directly to your app on the App Store. Deep links are simply of the form `itunes.com/apps/`*appName*. For example, `itunes.com/apps/facebook`.
App Store Promo Codes (US-based developers only)	Use your promotional codes to increase awareness of your app. Give them to reviewers, bloggers or others who might spread the word (see Fig. 2.18 for a list of popular app review sites).

Fig. 2.16 | Marketing Resources for iPhone app developers (`developer.apple.com/iphone/`). (Part 2 of 2.)

Viral marketing and word-of-mouth marketing through social media sites such as Facebook and Twitter, and video sites such as YouTube, can help you get your message out. Figure 2.17 lists some of the most popular social media sites. Also, e-mail and electronic newsletters are still effective and often inexpensive marketing tools.

Social media sites	URL	Description
Facebook	`www.facebook.com`	Social networking.
Twitter	`www.twitter.com`	Micro blogging, social networking.
MySpace	`www.myspace.com`	Social networking.
Orkut	`www.orkut.com`	Google's social networking site.
YouTube	`www.youtube.com`	Video sharing.
LinkedIn	`www.linkedin.com`	Social networking for business.
Flickr	`www.flickr.com`	Photo sharing.
Digg	`www.digg.com`	Content "sharing and discovery."
StumbleUpon	`www.stumbleupon.com`	Social bookmarking.
Delicious	`www.delicious.com`	Social bookmarking.
Tip'd	`www.tipd.com/`	Social news for finance and business.
Blogger	`www.blogger.com`	Blogging sites.
Wordpress	`www.wordpress.com`	Blogging sites.
Squidoo	`www.squidoo.com`	Publishing platform and community.

Fig. 2.17 | Popular social media sites.

Facebook

Facebook, the premier social networking site, has over 250 million active users, each with an average of 120 friends.[15] It's an excellent resource for viral (word-of-mouth) marketing. Start by setting up a fan page for your app. Use the fan page to post:

- App information
- News

---

15. `www.facebook.com/press/info.php?statistics`.

- Updates
- Reviews
- Tips
- Videos
- Screenshots
- High scores for games
- User feedback
- Links to the App Store where users can download your app

Next, you need to spread the word. Encourage your co-workers and friends to become fans and to tell their friends to become fans as well. As people interact with your fan page, stories will appear in their friends' news feeds, building awareness to a growing audience.

Twitter
Twitter is a micro blogging, social networking site. You post *tweets*—messages of 140 characters or less. Twitter then distributes your tweets to all your followers (several Twitter users already have more than a million followers). Many people use Twitter to track news and trends. Tweet about your app—include announcements about new releases, tips, facts, comments from users, etc. Also encourage your colleagues and friends to tweet about your app. Use a *hashtag* (#) to reference your app. For example, when tweeting about this book on our Twitter page, @deitel, we use the hashtag #iPhoneFP. This enables you to easily search our tweets for messages related to *iPhone for Programmers*.

YouTube
Viral video is another great way to spread the word about your app. If you create a compelling video, which is often something humorous or even outrageous, it may quickly rise in popularity and the video may be tagged by users across multiple social networks.

E-Mail Newsletters
If you have an e-mail newsletter, use it to promote your app. Include links to the App Store where users can download it. Also include links to your Facebook fan page and Twitter page where users can stay up-to-date with the latest news about your app.

App Reviews
Contact influential bloggers and app review sites (Fig. 2.18) and tell them about your app. Provide them with a promotional code to download your app for free (see Section 2.11). Influential bloggers and reviewers receive numerous requests, so keep yours concise and informative without too much marketing hype. Many app reviewers post video app reviews on YouTube.

iPhone app review sites	URL
What's on iPhone	www.whatsoniphone.com/
iPhone App Reviews	www.iphoneappreviews.net/

Fig. 2.18 | iPhone app review sites. (Part 1 of 2.)

iPhone app review sites	URL
iusethis	iphone.iusethis.com/
Apple iPhone School	www.appleiphoneschool.com/
AppVee	www.appvee.com/
AppCraver	www.appcraver.com/
The App Podcast	theapppodcast.com/
Gizmodo	gizmodo.com/tag/iphone-apps-directory/
iPhone Toolbox	iphonetoolbox.com/category/application/
Fresh Apps	www.freshapps.com/
Apptism	www.apptism.com/
148Apps	www.148apps.com/
Macworld	www.macworld.com/appguide/index.html
Ars Technica	arstechnica.com/apple/iphone/apps/
Appletell	www.appletell.com/apple/tag/iphone+app+reviews/

Fig. 2.18 | iPhone app review sites. (Part 2 of 2.)

Internet Public Relations

The public relations industry uses traditional media outlets to help companies get their message out to consumers. With the phenomenon known as Web 2.0, public relations practitioners are incorporating blogs, podcasts, RSS feeds and social media into their PR campaigns. Figure 2.19 lists some of the free and fee-based Internet public relations resources, including press release distribution sites, press release writing services and more. For additional resources, check out our Internet Public Relations Resource Center at www.deitel.com/InternetPR/.

Site	URL	Description
PRWeb®	www.prweb.com	Online press release distribution service offering free and fee-based services.
ClickPress™	www.clickpress.com	Submit your news stories for approval (free of charge). If approved, they'll be available on the ClickPress site and to news search engines.
PR Leap	www.prleap.com	Fee-based online press release distribution service.
Marketwire	www.marketwire.com	Fee-based press release distribution service allows you to target your audience by geography, industry, etc.

Fig. 2.19 | Internet public relations resources. (Part 1 of 2.)

Site	URL	Description
PRLog	www.prlog.org/pub/	Free press release submission and distribution.
i-Newswire	www.i-newswire.com	Free press release submission and distribution.
InternetNews-Bureau.com®	www.internetnewsbureau.com	Online press release services for businesses and journalists.
openPR®	www.openpr.com	Free press release publication.
PRX Builder	www.prxbuilder.com/x2/	Tool for creating social media press releases.
Press Release Writing	www.press-release-writing.com	Press release distribution and services including press release writing, proofreading and editing. Check out the tips for writing effective press releases.

Fig. 2.19 | Internet public relations resources. (Part 2 of 2.)

Mobile Advertising Networks

Purchasing advertising space—in other apps, online, in newspapers and magazines or on television—is one means of marketing your app. Mobile advertising networks (Fig. 2.20) specialize in advertising iPhone (and other) mobile apps on mobile platforms. You can pay these networks to market your iPhone apps, or monetize your free apps by including their banner ads within the apps. Many of these mobile advertising networks are able to target audiences by location, carrier, device (e.g., iPhone, BlackBerry, etc.) and more.

Mobile ad networks	URL	Description
AdWhirl	www.adwhirl.com/	Free service that aggregates multiple mobile ad networks, allowing you to increase your advertising fill rate. Also use it to sell virtual goods in your apps.
AdMob	www.admob.com/	Advertise your app online and in other apps, or incorporate ads in your app for monetization.
Medialets	www.medialets.com/	Mobile Advertising SDK allows you to incorporate ads into your app. The analytics SDK enables you to track usage of the app and ad clickthroughs.
Quattro Wireless	www.quattrowireless.com/	Advertise your app online and in other apps, or incorporate targeted, location-based ads in your app for monetization.

Fig. 2.20 | Mobile advertising networks. (Part 1 of 2.)

Mobile ad networks	URL	Description
Decktrade	www.decktrade.com/	Advertise your app on mobile sites, or incorporate ads in your app for monetization.
Pinch Media	www.pinchmedia.com/ #pinchanalytics	Analytics tools for tracking downloads, usage and revenue for your iPhone app.
Tapjoy	www.tapjoy.com	Aggregates seven mobile ad networks, allowing you to increase your advertising fill rate. Also use it to sell virtual goods in your apps.

Fig. 2.20 | Mobile advertising networks. (Part 2 of 2.)

Advertising Costs
According to AdWhirl, the eCPM (effective cost per 1000 impressions) for ads in iPhone apps ranges from $0.50 to $4.00, depending on the ad network and the ad. Most ads on the iPhone pay based on click-through rate (CTR) of the ads rather than the number of impressions generated. If the CTRs of the ads in your app are high, your ad network may serve you higher paying ads, thus increasing your eCPM (earnings per thousand impressions). CTRs are generally 1 to 2% on iPhone apps (though this varies based on the app).

2.13 iPhone Anecdotes and Humor
Figure 2.21 lists sites where you'll find iPhone-related anecdotes and humor.

URL	Description
Anecdotes	
blog.wundrbar.com/	True story about the process of submitting an app to the App Store for approval.
www.touchtip.com/iphone-and-ipod-touch/worlds-youngest-iphone-developer/	The article, "Worlds Youngest iPhone Developer."
www.techcrunch.com/2009/02/15/experiences-of-a-newbie-iphone-developer/	The TechCrunch article, "Experiences of a Newbie iPhone Developer."
www.wired.com/gadgets/wireless/magazine/16-02/ff_iphone?currentPage=all	The Wired Magazine article, "The Untold Story: How the iPhone Blew Up the Wireless Industry."
stackoverflow.com/questions/740127/how-was-your-iphone-developer-experience	Feedback from developers who have submitted apps to the App Store for approval.

Fig. 2.21 | iPhone development anecdotes, tips and humor. (Part I of 2.)

URL	Description
Humor	
www.iphonebuzz.com/category/ apple-iphone-humor	Humorous iPhone blog posts from iPhone Buzz.
twitter.com/Humorforiphone	Send your favorite iPhone jokes to iPhone Humor on Twitter.
dailymobile.se/2009/02/11/ iphone-humor-cell-phone- reunion/	The video, "Cell Phone Reunion," by CollegeHumor, features iPhone apps such as Google Maps.
gizmodo.com/5300060/find-my- iphone-saved-my-phone-from-a- thief	The story, "*Find My iPhone* Saved my Phone from a Thief," that tells you how an iPhone owner used MobileMe to get his iPhone back.

Fig. 2.21 | iPhone development anecdotes, tips and humor. (Part 2 of 2.)

2.14 Other Platforms

iPhone for Programmers is the first of our platform development titles in our Deitel Developer Series published by Pearson Technology Group. There are numerous other platforms that you may want to consider when creating applications (Fig. 2.22). You could reach an even larger audience by porting your iPhone apps to other platforms.

Platforms	URL	Description
Mobile Platforms		
BlackBerry (RIM)	na.blackberry.com/eng/ services/appworld/?	BlackBerry development platform.
Android (Google)	www.google.com/mobile/ #p=android	Google apps for Android, Blackberry, iPhone, Windows Mobile, Nokia S60 and other devices.
webOS (Palm)	developer.palm.com/	Palm's webOS developer program.
Windows Mobile	msdn.microsoft.com/en-us/ windowsmobile/default.aspx	Windows Mobile Developer Center.
Symbian	developer.symbian.org/	Symbian developer program.
Internet Platforms		
Facebook	developers.facebook.com/	Facebook Platform.
Twitter	apiwiki.twitter.com/	Twitter API.
Google	code.google.com	Google APIs.
Yahoo!	developer.yahoo.com	Yahoo! Developer Network APIs.
Bing	www.bing.com/developers	Bing API.
Chrome	code.google.com/chromium/	Google's open-source Internet browser.

Fig. 2.22 | Other popular platforms. (Part 1 of 2.)

Platforms	URL	Description
LinkedIn	www.linkedin.com/static?key=developers_widgets&trk=hb_ft_widgets	LinkedIn Applications Platform.
MySpace	developer.myspace.com/community/	MySpace Open Platform.

Fig. 2.22 | Other popular platforms. (Part 2 of 2.)

2.15 iPhone Developer Documentation

Figure 2.23 is a list of freely available iPhone Reference Library documentation mentioned in this chapter. For additional documentation, go to developer.apple.com/iphone/library/navigation/index.html.

Document	URL
iPhone Development Guide	developer.apple.com/iphone/library/documentation/Xcode/Conceptual/iphone_development/000-Introduction/introduction.html
iPhone Human Interface Guidelines	developer.apple.com/iphone/library/documentation/UserExperience/Conceptual/MobileHIG/Introduction/Introduction.html
iPhone Application Programming Guide	developer.apple.com/iphone/library/documentation/iPhone/Conceptual/iPhoneOSProgrammingGuide/Introduction/Introduction.html
Bundle Programming Guide	developer.apple.com/iphone/library/documentation/CoreFoundation/Conceptual/CFBundles/Introduction/Introduction.html

Fig. 2.23 | iPhone Reference Library documentation.

2.16 Wrap-Up

In Chapter 2, you learned how to prepare your apps for submission to the App Store, including testing them on the simulator and on iPhones, creating icons and launch images and following the *iPhone Human Interface Guidelines*. We walked through the steps for submitting your apps through iTunes Connect. We provided tips for pricing your apps, and resources for monetizing free apps. You learned how to use iTunes Connect to manage your apps and track sales. And we included resources for marketing your apps once they're available through the App Store.

Chapters 3–16 present 14 complete working iPhone apps exercising a broad range of functionality, including the latest iPhone 3GS features. In Chapter 3, you'll use the Xcode IDE to create your first iPhone app, using visual programming, without writing any code! And you'll become familiar with Xcode's extensive help features.

3

Welcome App
Dive-Into® Xcode, Cocoa and Interface Builder

OBJECTIVES

In this chapter you'll learn:

- The basics of the Xcode integrated development environment (IDE) for writing, running and debugging your iPhone apps.

- How to create an Xcode project to develop a new app.

- The purpose of the various Xcode and Interface Builder windows.

- To design a Cocoa GUI visually using Interface Builder.

- To edit the properties of Cocoa GUI components.

- To build and launch a simple iPhone app.

Outline

3.1 Introduction

3.2 Overview of the Technologies

3.3 Xcode 3.x IDE and Cocoa

3.4 Building the Application

3.5 Building the GUI with Interface Builder

3.6 Running the **Welcome** App

3.7 Wrap-Up

3.1 Introduction

In this chapter, you'll build the **Welcome** app—a simple iPhone app that displays a welcome message and an image of the Deitel bug—without writing any code. The Xcode 3.x toolset is Apple's suite of development tools for creating and testing Mac OS X and iPhone applications. The toolset includes an Integrated Development Environment (IDE), also referred to as Xcode—and Interface Builder, which is used to construct graphical user interfaces quickly and conveniently. We'll overview Xcode and show you how to create a simple iPhone app (Fig. 3.1) by dragging and dropping predefined building blocks onto your app using Interface Builder. Finally, you'll compile your app and execute it in the iPhone simulator.

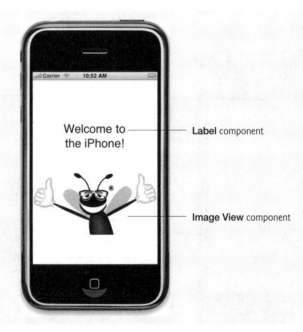

Welcome to the iPhone! ——— Label component

——— Image View component

Fig. 3.1 | **Welcome** app.

3.2 Overview of the Technologies

This chapter introduces the Xcode IDE and Interface Builder. You'll learn how to navigate Xcode and create a new project. With Interface Builder, you'll display a picture using an

Image View (an object of class *UIImageView*) and display text using a *Label* (an object of class *UILabel*). You'll see how to edit the properties of GUI components (e.g., the **Text** property of a **Label** and the **Image** property of an **Image View**) to customize them for your app and you'll run your app in the iPhone simulator.

3.3 Xcode 3.x IDE and Cocoa

The book's examples are based on Xcode 3.x, which is bundled with all Mac OS X versions since v10.5. Apple offers it free through the Apple Developer Connection at

```
developer.apple.com/
```

We assume you're familiar with Mac OS X.

Introduction to Xcode 3.x

To start Xcode 3.x, double click the **Xcode** icon in the /Developer/Applications folder. This folder also contains Interface Builder—a tool for designing graphical interfaces that you'll use throughout the book, and Instruments—a tool for inspecting your running app that can monitor memory usage, CPU load and more (Fig. 3.2). If this is your first time running Xcode 3.x, the *Welcome to Xcode* window will open (Fig. 3.3). This contains a list of links to local and online Xcode 3.x resources. Close this window for now—you can access it any time by selecting **Help > Xcode News**. From this point forward, we'll refer to the Xcode 3.x IDE simply as "Xcode" or "the IDE." We use the > character to indicate selecting a menu item from a menu. For example, we use the notation **File > Open...** to indicate that you should select the **Open...** menu item from the **File** menu.

Instruments Capabilities
Automate testing of your app.
Monitor file usage in your app—record what files are opened, closed, read from and written to.
Detect memory leaks and monitor object allocation.
Stress test your app.
Record a set of user interactions and play them back to automate human interaction with your app.

Fig. 3.2 | Instruments capabilities.

Customizing the IDE and Creating a New Project

To begin programming in Xcode, select either **File > New Project...** to create a new project or **File > Open...** to open an existing project. A *project* is a group of related files, such as the Objective-C code files and any images that make up an app.

When you select **File > New Project...**, the *New Project dialog* appears. Dialogs are windows that facilitate user-computer communication. You'll see how to create new projects in Section 3.4.

Fig. 3.3 | **Welcome to Xcode** window.

Xcode provides several *Templates* (Fig. 3.4) that represent the different project types you can create in Xcode, such as navigation-based applications, tab bar applications, utility applications and more. For iPhone development you'll use the templates listed under **iPhone OS > Application.**

Template	Template Description
Navigation-based Application	An application that involves traversing a hierarchy of views, such as the **Address Book** app you'll build in Chapter 10.
OpenGL ES Application	An application with a view configured to render complex 3D graphics using the OpenGL ES graphics API (www.khronos.org/opengles).
Tab Bar Application	An application with a tab bar at the bottom configured for switching between multiple views.
Utility Application	An application that has a frontside and a flipside. The flipside is generally used to configure the app. Examples of this template are the iPhone's **Stocks** and **Weather** apps.
View-based Application	An application containing a single view in which you can draw custom graphics or add subviews.
Window-based Application	An application containing only the basic elements required to run an iPhone app.

Fig. 3.4 | Xcode templates.

Toolbar
The Xcode toolbar (Fig. 3.5) contains menus and buttons that cause Xcode to perform specific actions. Figure 3.6 overviews each of these elements.

Fig. 3.5 | Xcode toolbar.

Control	Description
Overview	Drop-down menu for changing the project's build settings, such as the active SDK, target and executable.
Action	Drop-down menu containing actions specific to the currently selected item. Many of these are also available when you right click an item in your app.
Build and Go	Compiles then runs the project. [*Note:* In the latest version of Xcode, this is **Build and Run** or **Build and Debug**, depending on how you last ran an app. We'll refer to it as **Build and Go** from this point forward.]
Tasks	Terminates a task, such as a build or the running app.
Info	Opens an **Info** window with information on the currently selected item.
Search	Searches filenames in the project.

Fig. 3.6 | Xcode toolbar elements.

Groups and Files

The **Groups and Files** list in the project window provides access to all of a project's components. It consists of a series of groups containing error messages, bookmarks, breakpoints and more. The most used group is the ***project structure group***—the topmost group whose title is the same as that of the project. This group contains all the files currently in your project, including source files, preference files and frameworks. Frameworks are Cocoa libraries that you use to develop your app. The hierarchy in the project structure group does not affect the program, but there are some general guidelines for organizing your files:

- **Classes** group—source files.
- **Resources** group—Interface Builder files, preference files and images.
- **Frameworks** group—frameworks used in the app.

Keyboard Shortcuts

Xcode provides many keyboard shortcuts for useful commands. Figure 3.7 shows some of the most useful shortcuts.

Shortcut	Function	Shortcut	Function
shift + ⌘ + *N*	Creates a new project.	⌘ + *B*	Builds the project.
⌘ + *N*	Creates a new file.	⌘ + *R*	Builds and runs the project.
⌘ + *S*	Saves the current file.	⌘ + *I*	Displays additional information about the selected file.

Fig. 3.7 | Common Xcode keyboard shortcuts.

Interface Builder

Interface Builder is a tool for visually laying out your GUI. You can use it to drag and drop **Button**s, **Text Field**s, **Slider**s and other GUI components onto an app. Interface Builder files now use the .xib extension, but earlier versions used .nib, short for NeXT Interface Builder. For this reason, Interface Builder files are commonly referred to as "nib files." Interface Builder opens when you double click a nib file in your project.

Cocoa

Cocoa is a collection of APIs, frameworks and runtimes used in Mac OS X development (developer.apple.com/cocoa/). A successor of the NeXTSTEP programming environment developed by NeXT, Cocoa provides the easiest way to develop iPhone apps that match the Mac look and feel. In this chapter, we use the UIKit framework, which contains the **Text Field**, **Image View** and many other GUI components. Other frameworks provide libraries for networking, 3D graphics and more.

3.4 Building the Application

Creating a New Project

Open Xcode and select **File > New Project...** to create a new project. The **New Project** window (Fig. 3.8) appears, prompting you to choose a template for your new project.

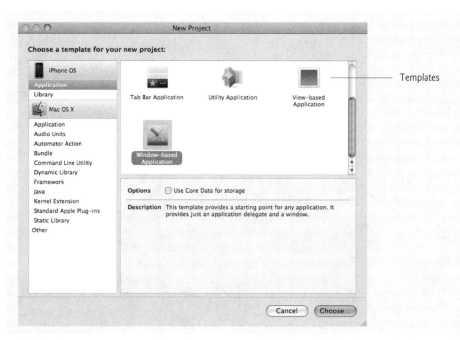

Fig. 3.8 | **New Project** window.

Select ***Window-based Application***—the simplest template provided by Xcode. All other iPhone app templates are enhanced versions of this template. When you click the **Choose...** button, a dialog box appears attached to the top of the **New Project** window. This is known as a *sheet*. In this case, it prompts you to choose a project name and to specify where to save the project (Fig. 3.9). Name the project Welcome, choose where you'd like to save it and click **Save**.

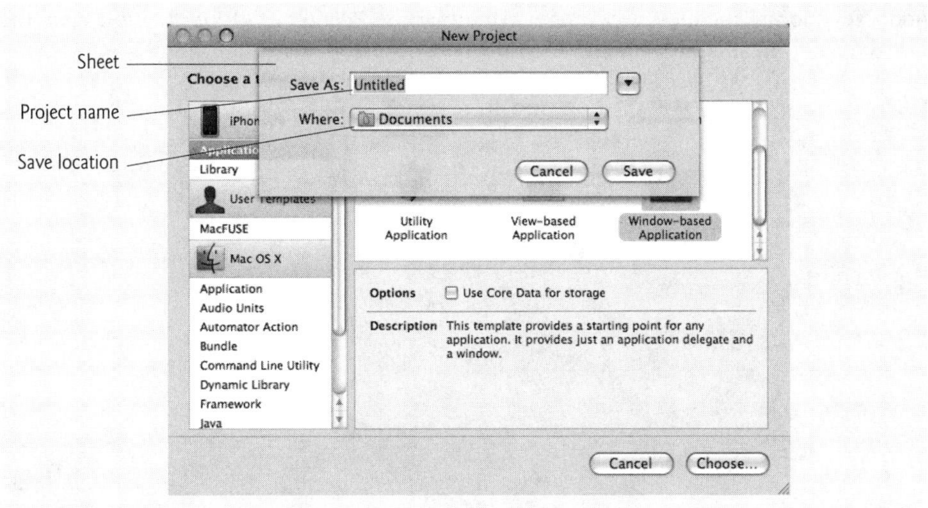

Fig. 3.9 | Naming your project.

3.5 Building the GUI with Interface Builder

Next, you'll create the GUI for the **Welcome** app. After you've created a new project, the project window appears (Fig. 3.10). The column on the left shows all of the files in your project.

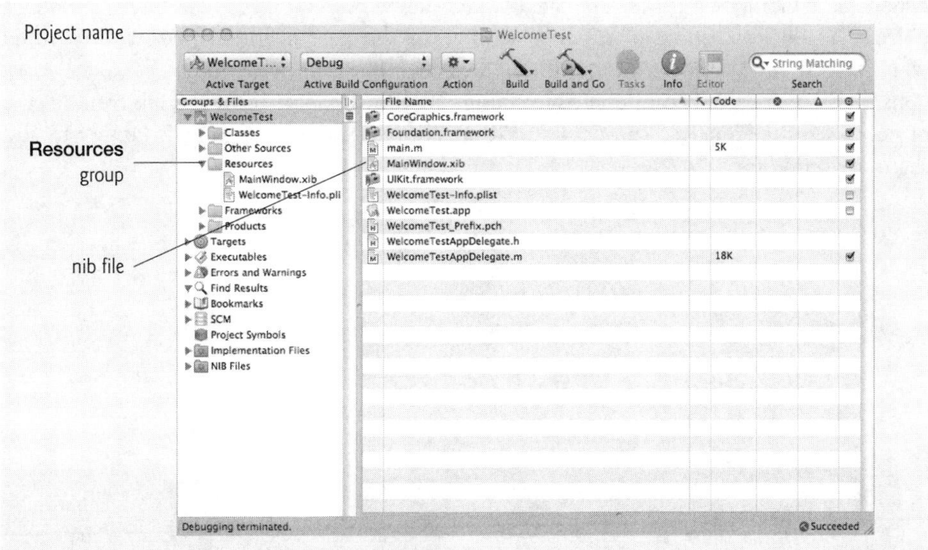

Fig. 3.10 | **WelcomeTest** project window.

To create the **Welcome app**, you need to add the Deitel bug image file from the Finder to the project. The image (bug.png) is located in this chapter's examples folder. Drag the file to the **Resources** group. A sheet appears (Fig. 3.11). Check **Copy items into destination group's folder (if needed)** to make sure all files are stored in the project's folder and click **Add**. Next, locate the file MainWindow.xib under the **Resources** group. Double click the file to open it in Interface Builder.

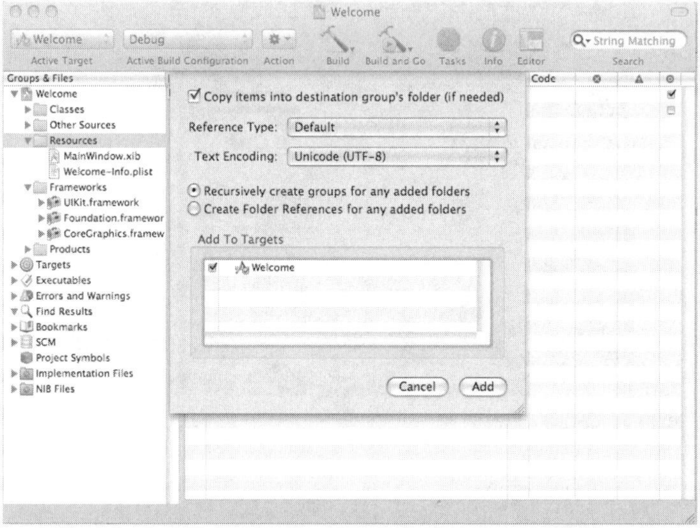

Fig. 3.11 | Adding a file to the **Welcome** project.

Once MainWindow.xib opens in Interface Builder, you'll see the **MainWindow.xib, Window** and **Library** windows. The **MainWindow.xib** window (Fig. 3.12) is used to manage objects. You'll learn more about this window in the next chapter. The window titled **Window** (Fig. 3.13) represents the iPhone's screen. The **Library** window (Fig. 3.14) contains the standard GUI components for designing iPhone apps. Its **Media** tab contains the project's resource images. You drag and drop GUI components from the **Library** to add them to your app.

Fig. 3.12 | **MainMenu.xib** window.

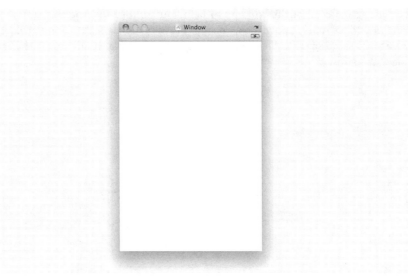

Fig. 3.13 | Interface Builder's app window.

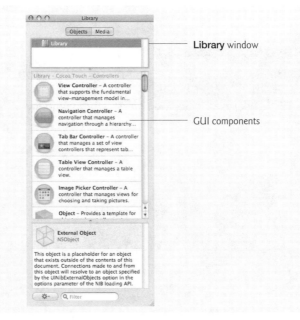

Fig. 3.14 | Interface Builder's **Library** window.

To create the **Welcome** app, you need to add the **Image View** that will display the bug.png image. In Cocoa, images are usually displayed using the UIImageView class. In the **Library** window, locate **Image View** by scrolling or by typing Image View into the **Filter** field at the bottom of the window (Fig. 3.15). Drag and drop an **Image View** from the **Library** onto the window (Fig. 3.15). Resize the view using the sizing handles that appear along the edges (Fig. 3.16) until it fills the bottom half of the window. Notice the blue lines that appear along the edge of the window to help you conform to Apple's Human Interface Guidelines (developer.apple.com/iphone/library/documentation/userexperience/ conceptual/mobilehig/). The blue lines suggest spacing and alignment that adhere to Apple's standards.

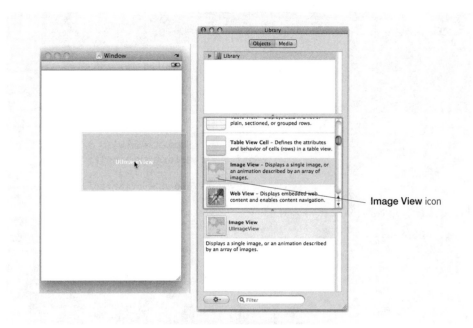

Fig. 3.15 | Adding an **Image View** via the **Library Window**.

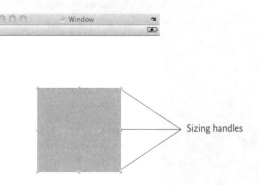

Fig. 3.16 | Sizing handles on an **Image View**.

Next, select the **Image View** you just created then open the **Inspector** window by selecting **Tools > Inspector**. The ***Inspector window*** allows you to customize the GUI components. In most cases it's helpful to leave the **Inspector** open while designing your interface. In the **Inspector** window, locate the **Image View** section, select the **Image** field, then enter bug.png for the image name (Fig. 3.17). This tells the **Image View** to display this picture. Then set the **Mode** field to Aspect Fit to force your image to fit in the **Image View**. When you press *Enter*, the image should appear in the **Image View**. Interface Builder can also create the **Image View** for you and configure it to display the proper image—simply drag the image from the **Library** window's **Media** tab to the app window.

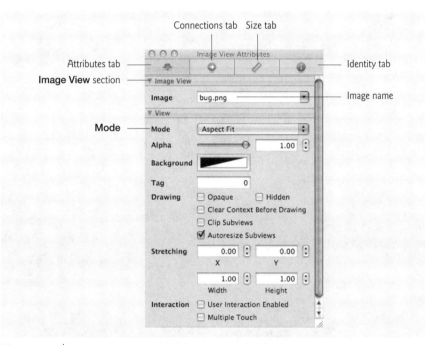

Fig. 3.17 | **Image View Attributes** tab in the **Inspector** window.

Next, you'll add the text. Drag and drop a **Label** from the **Library** window onto the app window above the image (Fig. 3.18). When you select the **Label**, the **Inspector** window will change to display the **Label** properties. Under the **Label** header set the **Text** property to Welcome to the iPhone! (you can also set the text by double clicking the **Label**), set **Layout** to the middle option for centered alignment, set **# Lines** to 2 and set the minimum font size to 30 (Fig. 3.19). Once the properties are set, change the size of the **Label** to fit the larger text, then recenter the **Label** (Fig. 3.20).

3.6 Running the Welcome App

Save the nib file and return to Xcode. To run the project, select either **Build > Build and Run** or click the **Build and Go** button in the **Project** window (Fig. 3.21). The **Build and Go** button repeats the last build action, such as build and run, build and debug or build and launch in the Instruments tool. Because this is the first time we've run this project, the

Build and Go button builds the project and runs the app in the iPhone Simulator. While your app is running, the **Tasks** button becomes enabled. Clicking the **Tasks** button terminates the app. You can also close your app by quitting the iPhone Simulator or by pressing the home button on the simulator.

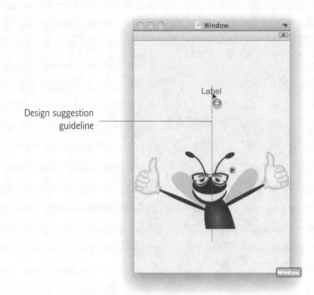

Fig. 3.18 | Adding a **Label** to a window.

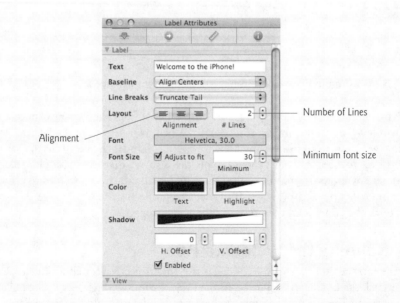

Fig. 3.19 | **Label Attributes** tab of the **Inspector** window.

Fig. 3.20 | Completed **Welcome** app.

Fig. 3.21 | Xcode toolbar while an app is running.

3.7 Wrap-Up

This chapter introduced key features of Xcode and Interface Builder. You used Interface Builder to create a working iPhone app without writing any code! You used the **Image View** and **Label** GUI components to display an image and accompanying text. You edited the properties of GUI components to customize them for your app. You then compiled your app and tested it in the iPhone simulator.

In the next chapter we introduce Objective-C programming. iPhone development is a combination of GUI design and Objective-C coding:

- Interface Builder allows you to develop GUIs visually, avoiding tedious GUI programming.
- Objective-C programming allows you to specify the behavior of your apps.

You'll develop the **Tip Calculator** app, which calculates a range of tip possibilities when given a restaurant bill amount. You'll design the GUI using Interface Builder as you did in this chapter, but you'll also add Objective-C code to specify how the app should process user input and display the results of its calculations.

4

Tip Calculator App

Introducing Objective-C Programming

OBJECTIVES

In this chapter you'll learn:

- Basic Objective-C syntax and keywords.

- To use object-oriented features of Objective-C, including objects, classes, interfaces and inheritance.

- Arithmetic and relational operators.

- **Text Field** and **Slider** GUI components.

- To design an app following the Model-View-Controller (MVC) design pattern.

- To programmatically interact with GUI components.

- To invoke methods of objects via object messaging.

- To build and run an interactive iPhone app.

Outline

4.1 Introduction

4.2 Test-Driving the **Tip Calculator** App

4.3 Overview of the Technologies

4.4 Building the App

4.5 Adding Functionality to Your App

4.6 Connecting Objects in Interface Builder

4.7 Implementing the Class's Methods

4.8 Wrap-Up

4.1 Introduction

The **Tip Calculator** app (Fig. 4.1) calculates and displays tips for a restaurant bill. As the user enters a bill total, the app calculates and displays the tip amount and total bill for three standard tipping percentages—10%, 15% and 20%. The user can also specify a custom tip percentage by moving the thumb of a **Slider**. The tip and the total are updated in response to each user interaction.

This app uses various object-oriented Objective-C features including class declarations (known as interfaces in Objective-C), class implementations and inheritance. You'll also learn basic Objective-C keywords and syntax as you write the code that responds to user interactions and programmatically updates the GUI.

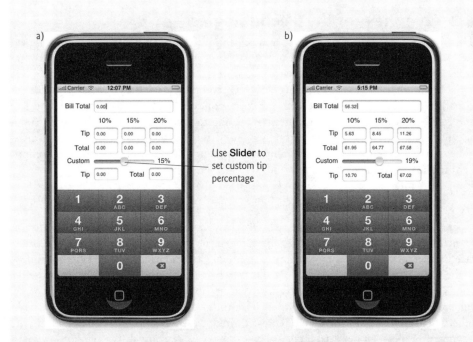

Fig. 4.1 | Entering the bill total and calculating the tip.

4.2 Test-Driving the Tip Calculator App

Opening the Completed Application
Open the folder on your local computer containing the **Tip Calculator** app project. Double click TipCalculator.xcodeproj to open the project in Xcode.

Running the App
Click the **Build and Go** button to run the app in the iPhone Simulator. The user enters a restaurant bill amount in the "**Bill Total**" **Text Field**. The **Text Field**s under **10%**, **15%** and **20%** display the tip and the total bill for the corresponding tip percentage. The **Slider** allows the user to enter a custom percentage, and the **Text Field**s below the **Slider** display the corresponding tip and the total bill. The numeric keypad in the bottom half of the app is always present and is used to enter the bill amount.

Entering a Bill Total
Enter **56.32** into the "**Bill Total**" **Text Field** by touching the numeric keypad. If you make a mistake, press the delete button (⌫) in the bottom right corner of the keypad to erase the last digit you entered. Notice that the "**Tip**" and "**Total**" **Text Field**s update as you enter or delete digits.

Selecting a Custom Tipping Percentage
Drag the **Slider**'s thumb to the right until the custom percentage reads **19%**. The totals for this custom tip percentage now appear below the **Slider**.

4.3 Overview of the Technologies

This chapter introduces Objective-C and several of its object-oriented programming capabilities, including objects, classes, interfaces and inheritance. The app's code requires various Objective-C data types, operators, control statements and keywords. You'll declare variables to programmatically interact with GUI components and use Interface Builder to visually "connect" each variable with the corresponding GUI component. You'll declare and implement methods, and use message passing to invoke an object's methods. You'll also use event handling to process the user's GUI interactions. To set up the event handling, you'll use drag-and-drop capabilities of Interface Builder to link each GUI component to the method that should respond to their events.

4.4 Building the App

Open Xcode and create a new project. Select the **Window-based Application** template and name the project TipCalculator. Double click MainWindow.xib to open the file in Interface Builder so you can design the app's GUI. Drag a **Text Field** from the **Library** window to the top of the app window (Fig. 4.2). This is where the bill total will be displayed. Select your **Text Field** from the **Inspector** window. Set the **Text** property's value to 0.00. The new value will appear in the app window. Uncheck the checkbox **Clear When Editing Begins**—otherwise, the **Text Field** will be cleared each time the user enters a digit. Next, locate the **Keyboard** property under **Text Input Traits**—this property controls the type of keyboard that is displayed when the user touches the **Text Field**. Since we need only digits, change the value to **Number Pad**.

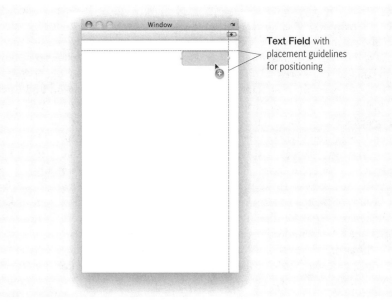

Fig. 4.2 | Adding a **Text Field** to the app window.

Next, to identify the **Text Field** in the GUI, drag a **Label** from the **Library** onto the app window (Fig. 4.3). Double click the **Label** and change its **Text** property to Bill Total. Select the previously created **Text Field** and use the resizing handles to stretch it to the left. When the **Text Field** reaches the recommended minimum distance from the **Label**, a blue guideline appears to indicate that you should stop resizing the **Text Field**.

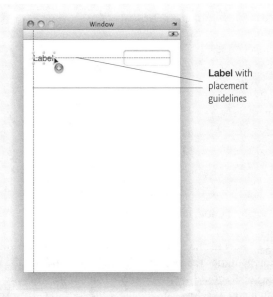

Fig. 4.3 | Adding a **Label** to the app window.

Next, drag three more **Labels** onto the app window and name them **10%**, **15%** and **20%**—these will label tip calculation results. Arrange the **Labels** side by side in the window as shown in Fig. 4.1. Select the **Text Field** and duplicate it by pressing ⌘D or by holding the *option* key and dragging the **Text Field**. Resize the new **Text Field** to be approximately one quarter of its original size and position it under the "**10%**" **Label**. Select the new **Text Field** and open the **Inspector**. Scroll down to the **Control** section and uncheck **Enabled**. This prevents the user from manually editing the **Text Field**. You can also use the **Inspector**'s **Size** (🖉) tab to view a component's size and position, and you can see a component's position by holding the *option* key and moving the cursor over the component.

Make two copies of this **Text Field** and position them under the "**15%**" and "**20%**" **Labels**. These three **Text Fields** will display the standard tip amounts. You may need to adjust their sizes to make them fit. When the **Text Fields** are aligned, select all three by holding the ⌘ key and clicking each, then make a duplicate by typing ⌘D. Position the three new **Text Fields** directly under the originals, using the blue guidelines to adjust the spacing. These will display the totals for standard tip amounts.

Drag and drop two more **Labels** and set their **Text** attributes to Tip and Total, respectively. These will label the standard tip and total **Text Fields**. Position **Tip** next to the first row of fields and **Total** next to the second row (Fig. 4.4). In the **Layout** section of the **Inspector** for each of these **Labels**, set the **Alignment** to be right aligned. This ensures that the text of each **Label** is the same distance from the **Text Fields**.

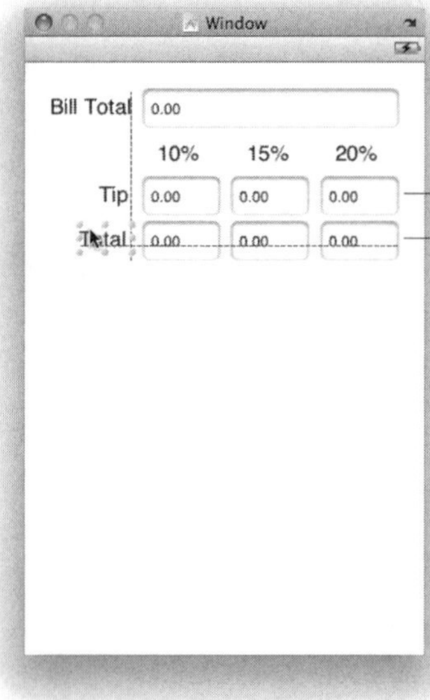

Fig. 4.4 | Placing a **Label** in the app window.

Add a new **Label** to the app window and set its **Text** attribute to 15%. Move it to the right side, directly under the last row of **Text Fields**, and use the blue guidelines to align it properly. The **Label** should snap into place when it gets close to the lines.

Next, you'll add a **Slider** that will allow the user to customize the tip percentage from 0% to 30%. Drag a **Slider** from the **Library** window onto the app and left-align it below the "**Total**" **Text Field**s (Fig. 4.5). Resize the **Slider** until a guideline appears at its side to specify the correct distance from the "**15%**" **Label** (Fig. 4.6).

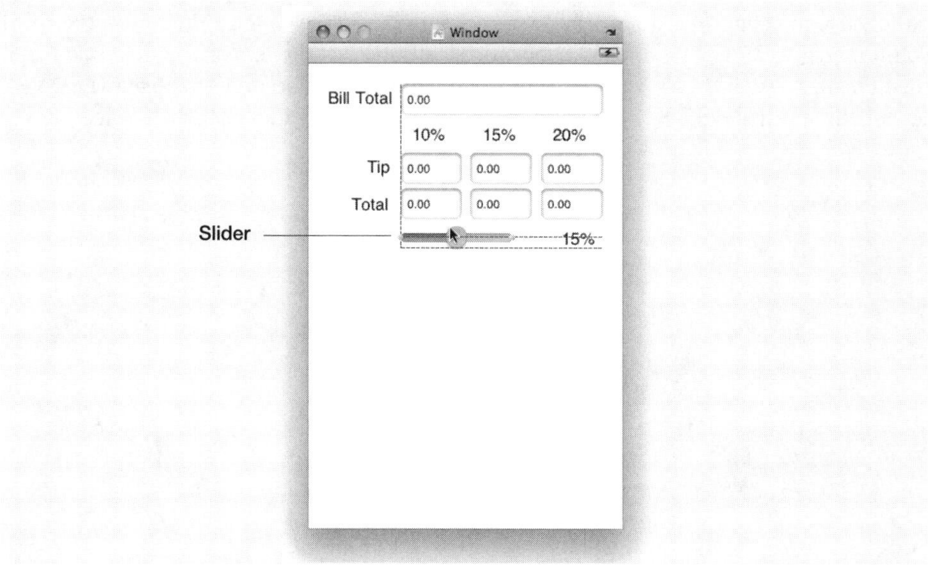

Fig. 4.5 │ Adding a **Slider** to the app window.

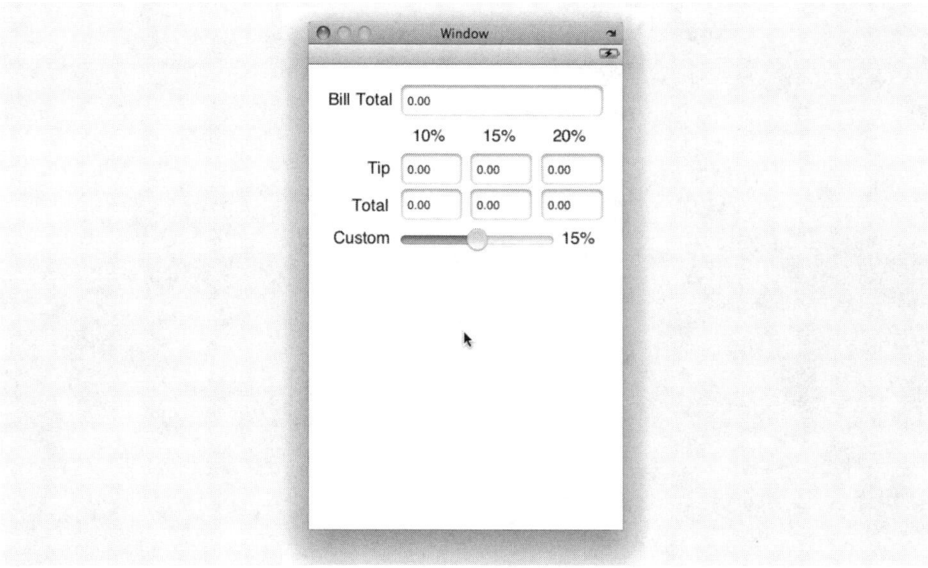

Fig. 4.6 │ App window after adding and sizing the **Slider**.

Select the **Slider**, then locate the **Values** field in the **Inspector** and set **Minimum** to 0.00, **Maximum** to 0.30 and **Initial** to 0.15. This tells the **Slider** that its value is 0.00 when the thumb is fully to the left, 0.30 when the thumb is fully to the right and 0.15 in its initial state when the app is launched.

Now that the **Slider** is configured, add another **Label** to the **Slider**'s left and set its text to Custom (Fig. 4.6). To complete the user interface, you need to add **Labels** and **Text Fields** for the custom percentage tip and total. Copy one of the existing small **Text Fields** and paste it twice. Align one under the first column of **Text Fields** and one under the third column (Fig. 4.7). Create a "**Tip**" **Label** and position it to the left of the first **Text Field**, then create a "**Total**" **Label** and position it to the left of the second **Text Field** (Fig. 4.8). Each **Label**'s text should be right aligned. Save the file and switch back to Xcode.

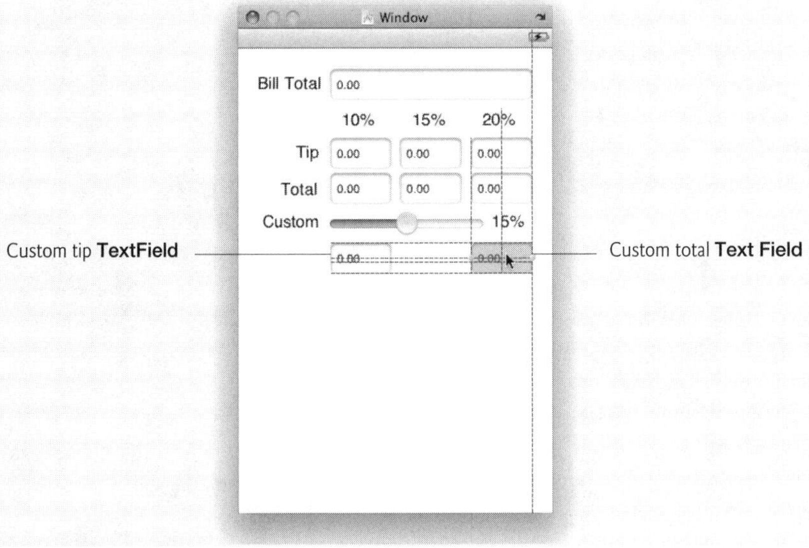

Fig. 4.7 | Positioning the "**Tip**" and "**Total**" **Text Field**s.

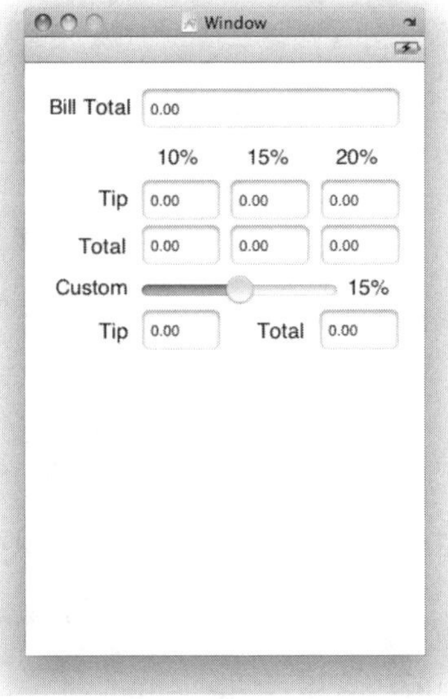

Fig. 4.8 | Completed **Tip Calculator** user interface.

4.5 Adding Functionality to Your App

In Xcode, click the **Build and Go** button to run the app in the iPhone simulator. You can touch the "**Bill Total**" **Text Field** to display the numerical keyboard and you can move the **Slider** left and right, but the app's functionality is still missing. In this section, you'll write the code to calculate the tips and totals, and display them in the GUI.

This app adheres to the ***Model-View-Controller (MVC)*** design pattern, which separates app data (contained in the model) from graphical presentation (the view) and input-processing logic (the controller). Most iPhone apps use this design pattern. You created **Tip Calculator**'s view using Interface Builder; you'll construct the controller in Objective-C. This app's data is trivial, so we implement the model in the same file as the controller. As your apps get more complex, you'll find it beneficial to separate the two, which we'll do in later examples. A key benefit of the MVC design pattern is that you can modify the model, view and controller individually without modifying the others.

Creating the App's `Controller` *Class*

Close the simulator. In Xcode's **Groups and Files** list, select the **Classes** group and select **File > New File...** to add a new file to the project. A window will appear, prompting you to choose a template (Fig. 4.9). In the left column, ensure that **Cocoa Touch Class** is selected, then select **Objective-C class** in the right column. Make sure the **Subclass of** list is set to **NSObject**[1] and click the **Next** button. Name the file `Controller.m`, then click **Finish**.

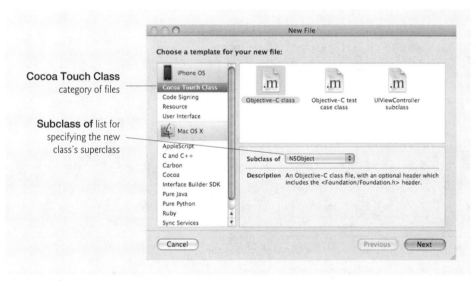

Cocoa Touch Class
category of files

Subclass of list for
specifying the new
class's superclass

Fig. 4.9 | Adding a new **Objective-C** class file to your Xcode project.

This creates two files in the **Classes** folder—`Controller.h` and `Controller.m`. Controller.h (Fig. 4.10) is a ***header file***, in which you'll declare the instance variables and methods of the new class. `Controller.m` is a source file in which you'll implement those methods. The separation between the declaration (header file) and implementation

---

1. Normally, controllers are defined as `UIViewController` subclasses—introduced in Chapter 6.

(source file) is an important aspect of Objective-C and object-oriented programming. Splitting a class into separate files is not required, but it's considered to be good practice.

Examining the Completed Controller.h File

Figure 4.10 begins with three lines of comments (lines 1–3) that indicate the name and purpose of the file. The symbol // indicates that the remainder of each line is a comment. Line 4 is a directive to the *preprocessor*. Lines beginning with # are processed by the preprocessor before the program is compiled. The *#import* directive tells the preprocessor to include the contents of the *UIKit header file (<UIKit/UIKit.h>)* in the program. The #import directive ensures that a header file is included only once in the compilation unit—an improvement over C and C++ #includes, for which you must guard against this. UIKit.h represents a system library containing the declarations for the common user-interface components, such as **Slider**s (UISlider) and **Text Field**s (UITextField).

```
 1   // Fig. 4.10: Controller.h
 2   // Controller class for the Tip Calculator app.
 3   // Methods defined in Controller.m.
 4   #import <UIKit/UIKit.h>
 5
 6   @interface Controller : NSObject
 7   {
 8       // outlets
 9       IBOutlet UITextField *billField;
10       IBOutlet UITextField *tipFieldTen;
11       IBOutlet UITextField *tipFieldFifteen;
12       IBOutlet UITextField *tipFieldTwenty;
13       IBOutlet UITextField *tipFieldCustom;
14       IBOutlet UITextField *totalFieldTen;
15       IBOutlet UITextField *totalFieldFifteen;
16       IBOutlet UITextField *totalFieldTwenty;
17       IBOutlet UITextField *totalFieldCustom;
18       IBOutlet UILabel *customPercentLabel;
19       IBOutlet UISlider *customPercentSlider;
20
21       NSString *billTotal; // string for the "Bill Total" field
22   } //end instance variable declarations
23
24   - (IBAction)calculateTip:(id)sender; // calculates the tips
25   @end
```

Fig. 4.10 | Controller class for the **Tip Calculator** app.

The declaration of class Controller's interface (line 6) states that this class *inherits* from NSObject. Inheritance is a form of software reuse in which a new class is created by absorbing an existing class's members and enhancing them with new or modified capabilities. All Cocoa classes in the UIKit framework inherit from NSObject. The class on the left of the : is the subclass and the class on the right is the superclass.

We must declare instance variables for each GUI component that the Controller will interact with programmatically (lines 9–19). *IBOutlet* is a macro that evaluates to nothing. Its purpose is to let Interface Builder know that the variable being declared is an *outlet*—meaning that it will be connected to a GUI component through Interface Builder.

Outlets allow you to programmatically interact with the GUI via Objective-C variables.[2] IBOutlet is followed by a type name and a variable name. The asterisk (*) before each variable name indicates that the variable is a pointer—it contains an object's location in memory. All objects in Objective-C are manipulated via pointers.

The nine UITextField pointers (lines 9–17) represent the nine **Text Field**s you put in your nib file. The UISlider (line 19) represents the **Slider**. We declare only one UILabel (line 18), even though we created 10 **Label**s in the nib file. This is because only the **Label** next to the **Slider** will change in response to user interactions. The rest of the **Label**s will not change, so Controller doesn't need to interact with them. The last instance variable (line 21) is an *NSString*, a class that represents a sequence of characters. This variable does not point to a GUI component, so it's not preceded by IBOutlet. It will store a string used during the tip calculation.

Finally, line 24 declares the calculateTip: method. The - symbol indicates that this is an *instance method*, meaning it's associated with an instance of the class (an object) as opposed to the class itself. This allows the method access to instance variables and other instance methods. *Static methods* are preceded by a + and are associated with a class. They cannot access instance variables or instance methods directly. The method's return type is placed in parentheses to the right of the + or - symbol. The return type IBAction is a macro that evaluates to void, similar to IBOutlet. It indicates to Interface Builder that the method can be used as an event handler that responds to user interactions with GUI components. Such a method is known as an *action*. After the return type is the method name. The colon is a part of the name and signifies that the method takes an argument. A method takes the same number of arguments as the number of colons in its name. Before each argument is text that describes the argument (which you'll see in later examples). The next item in parentheses is the type of the argument. This is followed by the argument's name. The type *id* represents a pointer to any type of object. Since this type does not provide any information about the object, the object's type must be determined at runtime. This *dynamic typing* is used for event handlers, because many different types of objects can generate events. Objective-C also has *static typing* in which an object's type is known at compile time. Line 24 can be read as "instance method calculateTip takes a pointer to an object as an argument and returns nothing." The *@end keyword* (line 25) terminates the class declaration.

4.6 Connecting Objects in Interface Builder

Now that you've declared your class, let's connect the IBOutlet instance variables to the GUI components you placed on your app with Interface Builder. If you've closed Interface Builder, reopen it by double clicking MainWindow.xib. In the Interface Builder **Library** window, locate **Object**. This isn't a GUI component, so you aren't going to drag it onto the app window. Instead, drag it onto the **MainWindow.xib** window (Fig. 4.11). This **Object** will be used to create an instance of the Controller class so that we can connect each IBOutlet instance variable to the appropriate GUI component.

With the new object selected, open the **Inspector** window. In the **Identity** tab change **Class** from **NSObject** to **Controller** (Fig. 4.12). Then change to the **Connections** tab

---

2. In Chapter 6, we introduce memory management and a feature called "properties." From that point forward, we'll declare all outlets as properties, as recommended by Apple.

(Fig. 4.13). Here you'll see all the outlets (IBOutlets) and actions (IBActions) you defined in the header file. Click the small dot next to the billField outlet and drag to the topmost **Text Field** in the app window (Fig. 4.14). This connects the billField variable to the specified **Text Field**—when you modify billField's text property programmatically, the text in the **Text Field** will change accordingly.

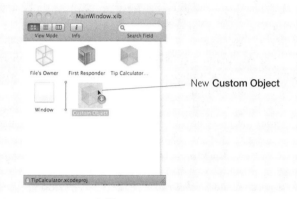

Fig. 4.11 | Adding a **Custom Object** to a nib file.

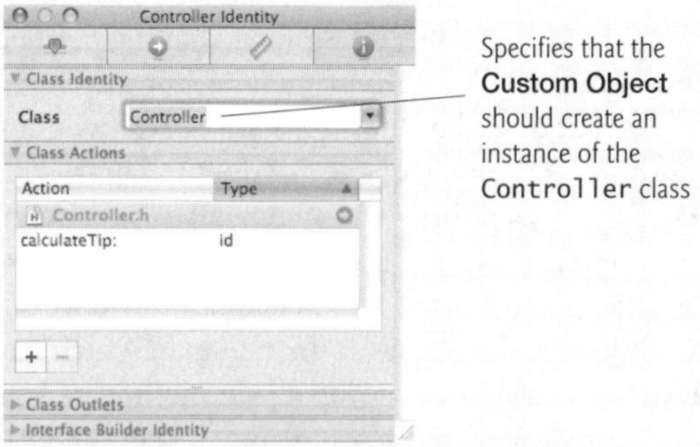

Fig. 4.12 | Changing the class of a custom object via the **Identity** tab.

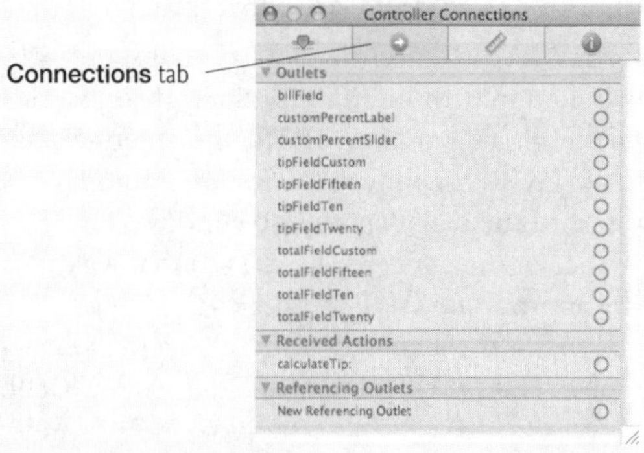

Fig. 4.13 | **Controller's Connections** tab of the **Inspector** window.

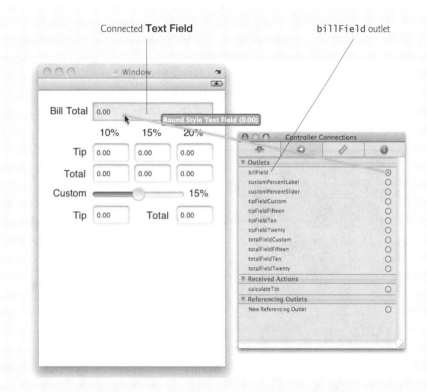

Fig. 4.14 | Connecting an outlet to a **Text Field**.

Next you need to connect the rest of the outlets to their corresponding GUI components. Once all the outlets are connected, you need to connect the events sent by the GUI components to their respective actions. We want to call the `calculateTip:` method every time the user enters or removes a digit to change the bill total and when the user moves the **Slider**'s thumb. To do this, first select the top **Text Field**, then click the **Connections** tab in the **Inspector** window. In the **Events** section, you can see all the possible events for the **Text Field**. An *event*, such as user interaction with the GUI, triggers a message to be sent to an object. This could be pushing a button, typing text or shaking the iPhone. You want the **Text Field** to send the `Controller` a message every time the user presses a key—the corresponding event for this is **Editing Changed**. A *message* tells an object to execute a method. In this case, the event is triggered when the user edits the **Text Field**. When that occurs, a message is sent to the `Controller` object to execute the `calculateTip:` method. Click the circle next to the **Editing Changed** event and drag it to the **Controller** object in the **MainWindow.xib** window (Fig. 4.15). A small gray overlay will appear to let you choose which method you want to connect to the event. Choose the `calculateTip:` method.

You also want the **Slider** to call the `calculateTip:` method when the user moves the thumb, so select the **Slider** and open the **Connections** tab in the **Inspector** window. **Editing Changed** events are primarily used for **Text Fields**. For **Sliders** you typically handle the **Value Changed** event. Drag a connection from the circle next to **Value Changed** to your `Controller` object and select the `calculateTip:` method.

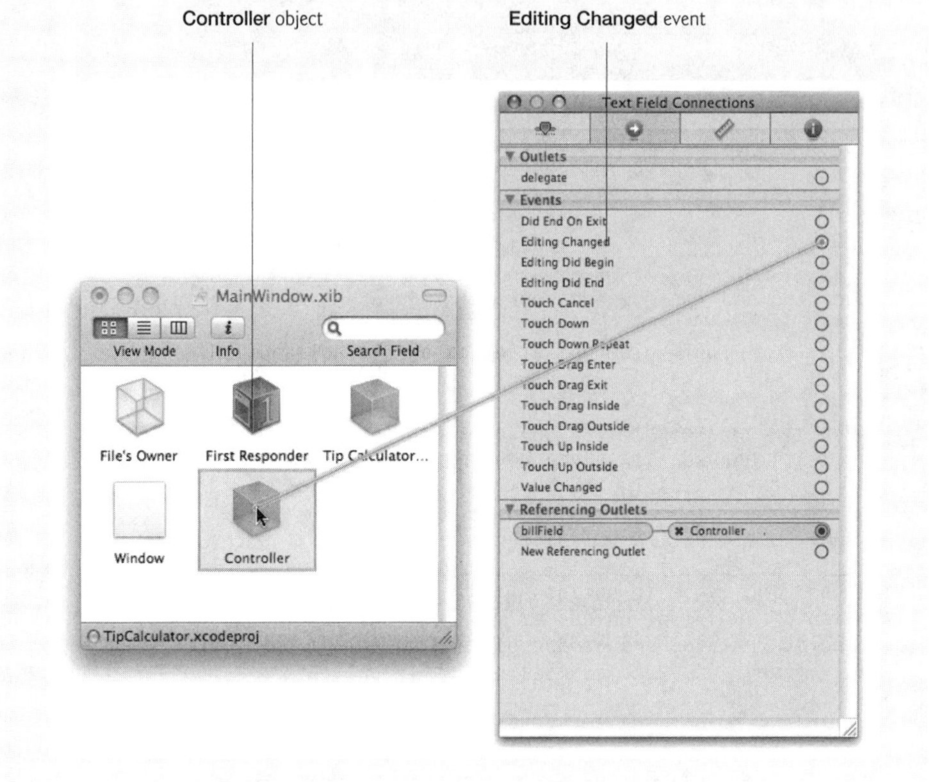

Fig. 4.15 | Connecting an action to a **Controller** object.

4.7 Implementing the Class's Methods

Now that you've connected the outlets and actions, you'll implement the Controller's logic for handling the user-interface events. Figure 4.16 shows the completed code for the file Controller.m. As you type the code, Xcode suggests completions for the class and method names. You can also press the *esc* key to show a list of all the possible completions.

```
 1   // Fig. 4.16: Controller.m
 2   // Controller class for the tip calculator app.
 3   #import "Controller.h"
 4
 5   @implementation Controller // begin implementation of Controller
 6
 7   // called after all the GUI elements have been loaded
 8   - (void)awakeFromNib
 9   {
10       [billField becomeFirstResponder]; // display keyboard for billField
11   } // end method awakeFromNib
12
```

Fig. 4.16 | Controller class for the **Tip Calculator** app. (Part 1 of 3.)

```objc
13   // called when the user touches a key or button
14   - (IBAction)calculateTip:(id)sender
15   {
16       static BOOL toggle = YES; // was this method trigger by the user?
17
18       // the user touched the keypad or moved the Slider
19       if (toggle)
20       {
21           toggle = NO; // this method will next be called programmatically
22           // retrieve the string in billField
23           NSString *billFieldText = billField.text;
24
25           // convert billFieldText to a float
26           float newTotal = [billFieldText floatValue];
27
28           // retrieve the slider value (between 0 and 0.3)
29           float customTipPercent = customPercentSlider.value;
30
31           // determine if billField generated the event
32           if (sender == billField)
33           {
34               // delete key pressed
35               if (billFieldText.length < billTotal.length)
36                   billTotal = [NSString stringWithFormat:@"%.02f",
37                       newTotal / 10];
38               else // new digit entered
39                   billTotal = [NSString stringWithFormat:@"%.02f",
40                       newTotal * 10];
41
42               // update billField with the properly formatted number
43               billField.text = billTotal;
44
45               // update newTotal with the new value
46               newTotal = [billTotal floatValue];
47
48               // calculate the tips for 10, 15 and 20%
49               float tenTip = newTotal * 0.10;
50               float fifteenTip = newTotal * 0.15;
51               float twentyTip = newTotal * 0.20;
52
53               // set the values for the "Tip" fields
54               tipFieldTen.text = [NSString stringWithFormat:@"%.02f", tenTip];
55               tipFieldFifteen.text =
56                   [NSString stringWithFormat:@"%.02f", fifteenTip];
57               tipFieldTwenty.text =
58                   [NSString stringWithFormat:@"%.02f", twentyTip];
59
60               // set the values for the "Total" fields
61               totalFieldTen.text =
62                   [NSString stringWithFormat:@"%.02f", newTotal + tenTip];
63               totalFieldFifteen.text =
64                   [NSString stringWithFormat:@"%.02f", newTotal + fifteenTip];
```

Fig. 4.16 | Controller class for the **Tip Calculator** app. (Part 2 of 3.)

```
65              totalFieldTwenty.text =
66                [NSString stringWithFormat:@"%.02f", newTotal + twentyTip];
67          } // end if
68          // determine if customPercentSlider generated the event
69          else if (sender == customPercentSlider)
70          {
71              // the "Custom" slider was moved
72              // round the value to a whole number
73              int percentage = (int)(customTipPercent * 100);
74
75              // update the label with the new percentage followed by %
76              customPercentLabel.text =
77                [NSString stringWithFormat:@"%i%%", percentage];
78
79              // convert percentage back to float and assign to Slider's value
80              float newSliderValue = ((float) percentage) / 100;
81              customPercentSlider.value = newSliderValue;
82
83              // slider Thumb moved; update customTipPercent
84              customTipPercent = newSliderValue;
85          } // end else
86
87          // calculate customTip
88          float customTip = customTipPercent * newTotal;
89
90          // update tipFieldCustom with the new custom tip value
91          tipFieldCustom.text = [NSString stringWithFormat:@"%.02f",
92              customTip];
93
94          // update totalFieldCustom
95          totalFieldCustom.text =
96              [NSString stringWithFormat:@"%.02f", customTip + newTotal];
97      } // end if
98      else // the method was called programmatically
99      {
100         toggle = YES; // the method will next be called by user interaction
101     }
102 } // end method calculateTip:
103 @end // Controller's implementation
```

Fig. 4.16 | Controller class for the **Tip Calculator** app. (Part 3 of 3.)

Controller.m contains the implementation of the class's methods. This *implementation file* begins by importing the Controller's interface header file (line 3). This is required so that you can implement methods declared in class Controller's interface and methods declared in class Controller's direct and indirect superclasses. You may notice that the header file name is enclosed in quotes on line 3, but line 4 of Controller.h (Fig. 4.10) enclosed a header file name in angle brackets. To help the compiler locate the files, quotes are used for files you create in your project, and angle brackets are used for files in system libraries. The Controller class's implementation starts at line 5 with the @implementation keyword and ends at line 103 with the @end keyword. This implementation contains two methods—awakeFromNib and calculateTip:.

Launching and Initializing the App

When a user launches the app, the app's main function is called to begin the app's execution. This function is defined by each application template in the file main.m. When an app executes, its main nib file loads to create the application's GUI. After all the objects in the nib file are created, the runtime sends an ***awakeFromNib** message* to each object in the nib file to perform app-specific initialization. Recall that an object of class Controller was added to the nib file in Fig. 4.11.

Implementing awakeFromNib is an example of using the *template method design pattern* in which an algorithm pre-exists, but one of its steps is defined elsewhere. In this app, the algorithm for loading objects from a nib file is built into the process of starting up the app. However, what to do when the algorithm calls method awakeFromNib on a particular object is left to that object's class.

In this app, we want billField to be the selected object and we want to display the numeric keyboard immediately. To do this, we send a message to the billField object in the Controller's awakeFromNib method (lines 8–11). The syntax for sending a message is

[*receiver message*] ;

where *receiver* is an object and *message* is the name of one of the object's methods. In line 10, billField is the *receiver* and becomeFirstResponder is the *message*. The billField's ***becomeFirstResponder** method* programmatically makes billField the active component on the screen—as if the user touched it. Recall that we previously configured billField such that when it's selected, the numeric keypad is displayed in the lower half of the screen, so line 10 also causes this keypad to be displayed when the app loads. Method becomeFirstResponder does not receive any arguments—you'll see how to pass arguments to methods momentarily.

calculateTip: Method

The calculateTip: method (lines 14–102) gets the current values of billField and customPercentSlider and uses them to calculate the new tip and total values. Line 16 declares a static BOOL and initializes it to YES. Local variables that are declared static are initialized the first time the method is called and retain their values between calls—so toggle is set to YES only the first time this method is called. Method calculateTip: was designed to be called in response to user interactions with the GUI, but setting billField's value programmatically also generates an event that results in a call to this method. We want to update billField's text when calculateTip: was called as a result of a user interaction, not by changing the **Text Field**'s value programmatically. If toggle is YES (line 19), we update billField, otherwise we do nothing. This prevents infinite recursion.

Line 23 accesses billField's text property using dot (.) notation to obtain the **Text Field**'s string content. This notation can be used only to access instance variables declared as properties.[3] In Objective-C, unlike many other object-oriented languages, dot notation *cannot* be used to invoke methods. For methods, you must use the syntax for sending messages shown in our discussion of method awakeFromNib. Line 26 invokes billField's floatValue method to convert that string to a floating-point number. Line 29 gets customPercentSlider's value by accessing its value property, which returns a float.

---

3. We discuss properties in Chapter 6.

As you know, method `calculateTip:` is invoked in response to a user interaction with `billField` or `customPercentSlider`. When an object receives a message from a GUI component, it also receives a pointer to that component (known as the *sender*) as an argument. Parameter `sender`'s type—*id*—represents a *generic pointer* that can point to any object. Line 32 determines whether `sender` and `billField` point to the same object. When comparing pointers, the equality operator compares the addresses stored in its operands—if these addresses are equal, the pointers point to the same object. In this case, that means the user interacted with the `billField`. We perform a similar test at line 69 to determine whether the user interacted with the `customPercentSlider`. This nested `if...else` statement enables us to perform different tasks based on the component that caused the event.

Lines 35–40 calculate a new bill total based on whether the user added a digit to the total or removed a digit from the total, then display the updated total in `billField`. We do this by comparing the current length of `billField`'s string to the previous string's length (stored in `billTotal`); if the current string is shorter (line 35), the user deleted a digit, so we divide `newTotal` by 10 to reposition the decimal point; otherwise, the user entered a digit, so we multiply `newTotal` by 10 to reposition the decimal point.[4] Lines 36 and 39 use `NSString` literals of the form *@"string"*. A string literal that begins with @ represents an `NSString` object, whereas *"string"* (without the @ symbol) represents a C-style string in Objective-C.

Lines 35–40 create a formatted string with two digits to the right of the decimal point by calling `NSString`'s `static` class method `stringWithFormat:`, which performs *string formatting*. The `%.02f` *format specifier* is a placeholder for the value `newTotal / 10`. The `.02` forces the string to include two places to the right of the decimal point (with trailing 0's if necessary) and the letter `f` indicates that the value is a floating-point number. Complete documentation for formatting strings can be found at

> developer.apple.com/iphone/library/documentation/Cocoa/Conceptual/
> Strings/introStrings.html

under **Formatting String Objects**. After the string `billTotal` is updated, line 43 programmatically changes `billField`'s text to the new value.

The length comparison in line 35 uses the less-than (<) relational operator. The relational operators are shown in Figure 4.17.

Standard algebraic relational operators	Objective-C relational operator	Sample Objective-C condition	Meaning of Objective-C condition
=	==	x == y	x is equal to y
≠	!=	x != y	x is not equal to y

Fig. 4.17 | Relational operators in Objective-C. (Part 1 of 2.)

---

4. This app assumes that "." is the decimal separator. Many countries use "," instead. To obtain the locale-specific decimal separator, use the expression:

   `[[NSLocale currentLocale] objectForKey:NSLocaleDecimalSeparator]`

   You can use this and the `NSNumberFormatter` class for localized currency formatting.

Standard algebraic relational operators	Objective-C relational operator	Sample Objective-C condition	Meaning of Objective-C condition
<	<	x < y	x is less than y
>	>	x > y	x is greater than y
≥	>=	x >= y	x is greater than or equal to y
≤	<=	x <= y	x is less than or equal to y

Fig. 4.17 | Relational operators in Objective-C. (Part 2 of 2.)

Lines 46–51 update newTotal with the floating-point value of the string billTotal, then calculate the tips for 10%, 15% and 20% using the multiplication operator (*). The arithmetic operators are shown in (Fig. 4.18). Lines 54–66 create formatted strings to display the updated tip and total amounts in the 10%, 15% and 20% tip and total **Text Field**s.

Objective-C operation	Arithmetic operator	Algebraic expression	Objective-C expression
Addition	+	$f + 7$	f + 7
Subtraction	–	$p - c$	p - c
Multiplication	*	$b \cdot m$	b * m
Division	/	x / y or $\frac{x}{y}$ or $x \div y$	x / y
Remainder	%	$r \bmod s$	r % s

Fig. 4.18 | Arithmetic operators in Objective-C.

Lines 69–85 change the value of customPercentLabel and customPercentSlider when the user moves the **Slider**. Line 73 obtains the **Slider**'s percentage value, then rounds down to the nearest integer. Lines 76–77 update customPercentLabel with the new value—formatted with the %i format specifier for integers. The %% format specifier inserts a single % in the formatted string. Lines 80–81 compute and set a new **Slider** value using the rounded number. This prevents the **Slider** from stopping between whole numbers. Lines 88–96 update the custom tip and total **Text Field**s outside the inner if statement, since those need to be updated regardless of which GUI component generated the event.

If this method was called programmatically (line 98), we set toggle to YES. This indicates that this method will next be called in response to an event generated by a user interaction and prevents infinite recursion when the events are generated programmatically.

4.8 Wrap-Up

In this chapter, you created your first interactive iPhone app using object-oriented programming in Objective-C. You learned how to control GUI components, receive messages from the GUI and respond by updating the display. The user interacted with the app via two new GUI components—**Text Field**s and **Slider**s. You learned how to create a class's interface and implementation. You used various Objective-C data types, keywords, operators and control statements while building your app.

In the next chapter, we introduce data structures while building the **Favorite Twitter Searches** app. More advanced object-oriented techniques will be used, including inheritance and the `self` and `super` keywords. You'll also use C-style structures, and you'll lay out a GUI programmatically—allowing you to add and remove components in response to user interactions.

5

Favorite Twitter® Searches App

Collections and Cocoa GUI Programming

OBJECTIVES

In this chapter you'll learn:

- To use **View** objects in Interface Builder to add color to an app.

- To enable users to interact with an app via **Button**s.

- To use a **Scroll View** to display objects that do not fit on the screen.

- To write a custom `init` method to initialize an object's data when the object is created.

- To use the classes NSMutableArray and NSMutableDictionary to store mutable app data.

- To create GUI components programmatically to add components to the user interface in response to user interactions.

- To write the contents of an NSMutableDictionary to a file and read the contents from a file.

- To programmatically open a website in the Safari browser.

Outline

5.1 Introduction

5.2 Test-Driving the **Favorite Twitter Searches** App

5.3 Technologies Overview

5.4 Building the App

5.5 Wrap-Up

5.1 Introduction

The **Favorite Twitter Searches** app allows users to save their favorite (possibly lengthy) Twitter search strings with user-chosen, short tag names that are easy to remember. It enables users to quickly and easily follow the tweets on their favorite topics. Twitter search queries can be finely tuned using Twitter's search operators—often resulting in lengthy queries that are time consuming to type on an iPhone. (A complete list of Twitter search operators can be found at `search.twitter.com/operators`.) The user's favorite searches are saved on the iPhone, so they're available each time the app launches. Figure 5.1(a) shows the app with four saved searches—the user can save many searches and scroll through them. The tags are maintained in alphabetical order. Search queries and their corresponding tags are entered in the top **Text Field**s, and the "**Save**" **Button** adds the search to the favorites list. Tapping a search button opens the Twitter search results in the Safari web browser. Figure 5.1(b) shows the result of touching the "**Deitel**" **Button** button, which we specified should search for `c OR java from:deitel`. You can edit the search using the ⊚ **Button**s to the right of each favorite search **Button**. This enables you to tweak your searches for better results after you save them as favorites. The "**Clear All Tags**" **Button** at the bottom of the screen removes all the searches from the favorites list.

Fig. 5.1 | **Favorite Twitter Searches** app.

5.2 Test-Driving the Favorite Twitter Searches App

Opening the Completed Application

Open the directory on your computer containing the **Favorite Twitter Searches** app project. Double click FavoriteTwitterSearches.xcodeproj to open the project in Xcode.

Running the App

Click the **Build and Go** button to run the app in the iPhone Simulator (Fig. 5.2). The top two **Text Field**s allow you to enter new searches, and the bottom section will display previously saved searches (in this case none).

Fig. 5.2 | Running the **Favorite Twitter Searches** app.

Adding a New Favorite Search

Enter **Apple OR iPhone** into the top **Text Field** specifying your search subject. Enter iPhone into the bottom **Text Field**. This will be the short name displayed in the **Tagged Searches** section. Press the "**Save**" **Button** to save the search—a new search **Button** appears in the **Tagged Searches** section.

Editing a Search

To the right of each search **Button** is a **Detail Disclosure Button** ( ). Touch this **Button** to reload your query and tag into the **Text Field**s at the top of the app for editing. Let's restrict our search to within five miles of Apple's headquarters by adding near:Cupertino within:5 mi to the end of the query. Touching **Save** updates the saved search.

Viewing Twitter Search Results

To see the search results touch the "**iPhone**" **Button**. This opens the Safari web browser and accesses the Twitter website to obtain and display the results.

5.3 Technologies Overview

This app uses three new GUI components—View, Scroll View and Button. A *View* provides the fundamental capabilities of many other GUI components. Labels and Image Views are types of Views. Buttons and Sliders are types of Controls. A Control is a type of View, so Buttons and Sliders are also Views. Such components respond to touches, display complicated graphics and perform 3D animations. In this app, we'll use a View simply to place a background color in the area of the app where saved searches are displayed.

A *Scroll View* is a View that lets you scroll to access content that's too large to display on the screen. We use a Scroll View to display an arbitrarily large list of saved searches, because the user may have more favorite searches than can fit on the screen.

A *Button* sends actions when tapped. Five Button styles are available in Interface Builder (Fig. 5.3). Additional button styles are available for Toolbars (Bar Button Items; discussed in Chapter 10) and Tab Bars (Tab Bar Items; not discussed in this book). In this app, we use Rounded Rect and Detail Disclosure Buttons. The *Detail Disclosure Button* (⊙) allows the user to edit an existing search. The large Buttons that open each search in Safari are *Rounded Rect Buttons*.

Button Style	Sample	Description
Rounded Rect		Multipurpose Button used to perform an action.
Detail Disclosure	⊙	Used to display additional information about an element.
Add Contact	⊕	Used to display a "people picker" for choosing an existing contact from the address book.
Info Dark	ⓘ	Info Button with dark background. Often used to access an app's settings.
Info Light	ⓘ	Info Button with light background. Often used to access an app's settings.

Fig. 5.3 | Interface Builder **Button** styles.

We store the search query/tag pairs in an NSDictionary. We maintain the set of Rounded Rect Buttons in an NSArray. This app uses the mutable (or editable) counterparts of these collections—NSMutableArray and NSMutableDictionary, respectively—since the immutable versions cannot be changed after they are created and initialized.

We also show how to create GUI components programmatically to modify the GUI in response to user interactions. We use this technique to create a Round Rect Button for each new search the user adds. We programmatically set the Button's sizes and positions on the screen. We also programmatically specify their target objects and actions.

5.4 Building the App

Open Xcode and create a new **Window-based Application** project named FavoriteTwitterSearches. Double click MainWindow.xib to open Interface Builder.

Laying Out the GUI

Drag a **Label** from the **Library** and name it Favorite Twitter Searches. In the **Inspector**, increase **Font Size** to 18. Center the **Label** in the top of the window by using **Layout > Alignment > Align Horizontal Center in Container**. Next, drag two **Text Fields** to the app window. Select the first **Text Field**. In the **Inspector**'s **Attributes** tab, add the text Enter query expression here in the **Placeholder** field. Select the second **Text Field** and set its **Placeholder** text to Tag your search. Resize the **Text Field** objects and arrange them so that your app window looks like Fig. 5.4.

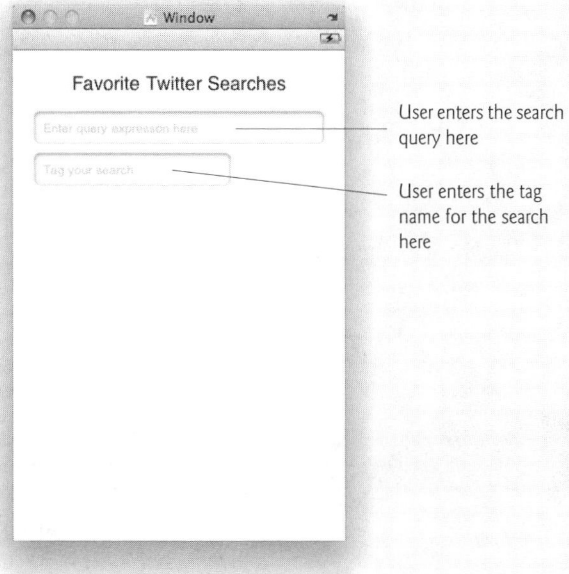

Fig. 5.4 | App window with a **Label** and two **Text Fields**.

Next, drag a **Round Rect Button** from the **Library** window onto the app window. In the **Inspector**'s **Attributes** tab, set the **Title** to Save.

Next, drag a **View** from the **Library** onto the app window. Expand the **View** to cover the app window below the **Text Fields**. Select this **View** and open the **Inspector**. Under the **Attributes** tab click the color swatch next to **Background**. This opens the **Colors** window. Click the second tab (⊞), and select **RGB Sliders** from the list. Every color can be created from a combination of red, green and blue components called *RGB values*, each in the range 0–255. The first value defines the amount of red in the color, the second the amount of green and the third the amount of blue. The larger a particular value, the greater the amount of that color. Enter the value 129 for **Red**, 160 for **Green** and 168 for **Blue** (or use your own preferred color values). Close the **Color** window and switch back to the app window. The color of the **View** changes to reflect the new color.

Drag a **Label** onto the **View** and set its text to Tagged Searches. In the **Inspector**, click the color swatch next to the **Color** label. Change the color to white, then center the **Label** at the top of the **View** (Fig. 5.6).

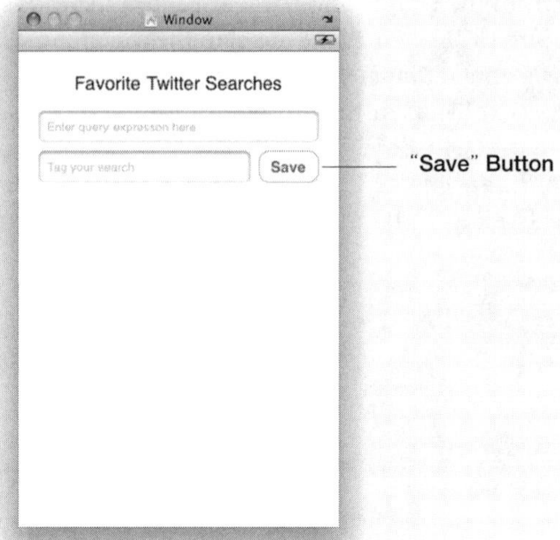

Fig. 5.5 | Adding the "**Save**" **Button** to the app window.

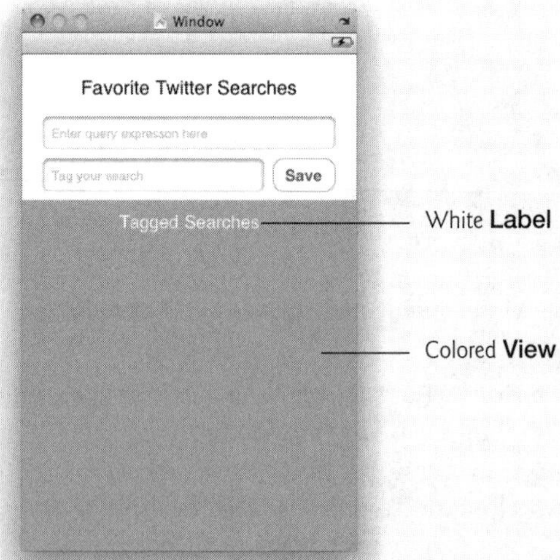

Fig. 5.6 | **View** with a colored background and a white **Label** at the top.

Next, drag a **Round Rect Button** from the **Library** and position it at the bottom of the **View**. Double click the **Button** and set its title to Clear All Tags (Fig. 5.7).

Next, you'll add a **Scroll View** (an instance of the UIScrollView class), which enables the user to scroll through content that's too large to display on the screen. Position a **Scroll View** in the colored **View** between the **Button** and the **Label** (Fig. 5.8). You've now completed the GUI design. Save the nib file and switch back to Xcode.

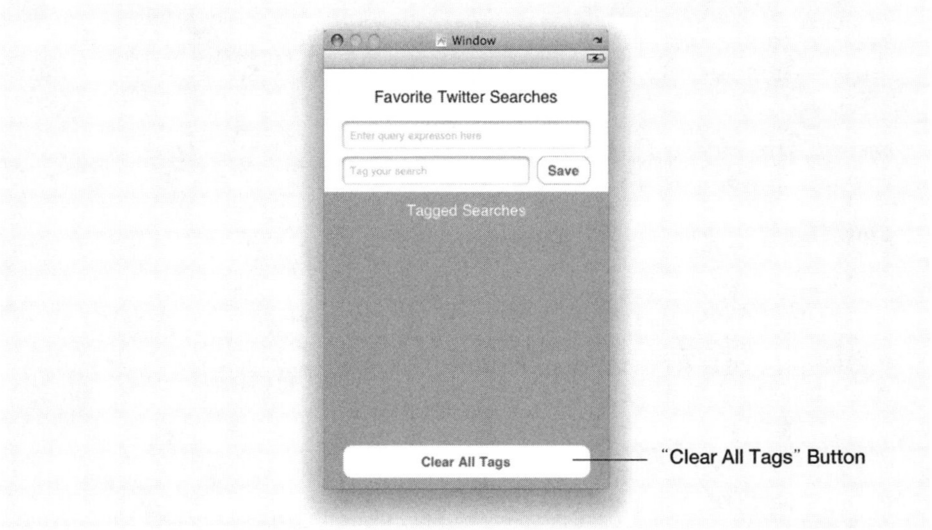

Fig. 5.7 | App window with a **Round Rect Button** at the bottom.

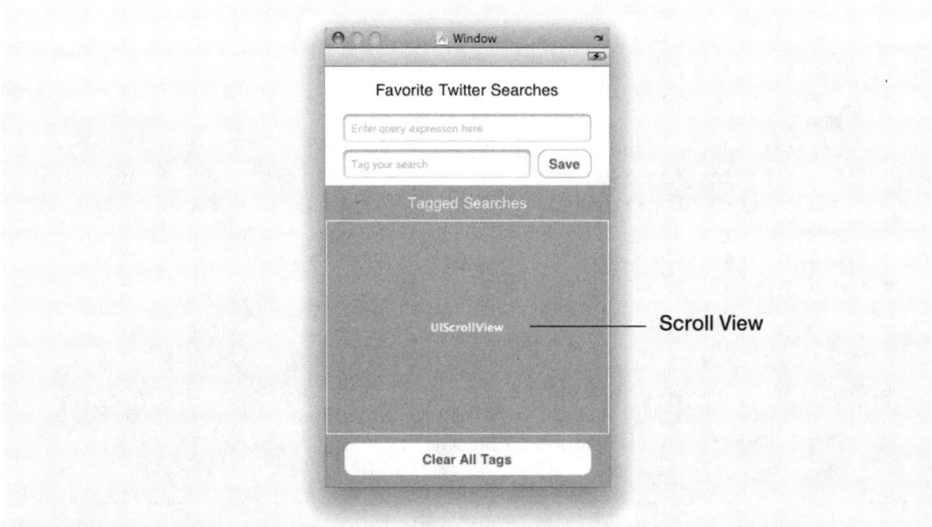

Fig. 5.8 | Adding a UIScrollView to the app window.

Defining the Controller Class

In Xcode, select the **Classes** group and create a new class (as discussed in Section 4.5). Make sure **NSObject** is selected in the **Subclass of** list. Click **Finish** and open the newly created file Controller.h. Figure 5.9 shows the completed class declaration.

Lines 6–7 define two *constants*. In Chapter 6, we'll introduce the preferred way to create constants with static const. BUTTON_SPACING defines the spacing between **Button**s in the **Scroll View**, and BUTTON_HEIGHT represents the height of each **Button**. If you want to change how each **Button** is displayed, you can simply alter these values.

```
 1   // Controller.h
 2   // Controller class for the Favorite Twitter Searches app.
 3   #import <UIKit/UIKit.h> // this line is auto-generated
 4
 5   // constants that control the height of the buttons and the spacing
 6   #define BUTTON_SPACING 10
 7   #define BUTTON_HEIGHT 40
 8
 9   @interface Controller : NSObject // this line is auto-generated
10   {
11      // Interface Builder outlets
12      IBOutlet UIScrollView *scrollView; // for scrollable favorites
13      IBOutlet UITextField *tagField; // text field for entering tag
14      IBOutlet UITextField *queryField; // text field for entering query
15
16      // stores the tag names and searches
17      NSMutableDictionary *tags;
18
19      // stores the Buttons representing the searches
20      NSMutableArray *buttons;
21
22      // stores the info buttons for editing existing searches
23      NSMutableArray *infoButtons;
24
25      // location of the file in which favorites are stored
26      NSString *filePath;
27   } // end instance variable declarations
28
29   - (IBAction)addTag:sender; // adds a new tag
30   - (IBAction)clearTags:sender; // clears all of the tags
31   - (void)addNewButtonWithTitle:(NSString *)title; // creates a new button
32   - (void)refreshList; // refreshes the list of buttons
33   - (void)buttonTouched:sender; // handles favorite button event
34   - (void)infoButtonTouched:sender; // handles info button event
35   @end // end Controller interface
36
37   // begin UIButton's sorting category
38   @interface UIButton (sorting)
39      // compares this UIButton's title to the given UIButton's title
40      - (NSComparisonResult)compareButtonTitles:(UIButton *)button;
41   @end // end category sorting of interface UIButton
```

Fig. 5.9 | Controller class for the **Favorite Twitter Searches** app.

Lines 12–14 define a UIScrollView and two UITextField pointers. These IBOutlets correspond to the **Scroll View** and **Text Fields** we created with Interface Builder.

Line 17 declares an NSMutableDictionary pointer named tags which will point to an object that stores Twitter search queries and their corresponding tags. **NSMutableDictionary** is a subclass of **NSDictionary**, a collection of key–value pairs in which each key has a corresponding value. The word "mutable" in the name indicates that an object of this class can be modified after it's created—by contrast, the entries in an NSDictionary object *cannot* be modified after the collection is initialized. The keys are the tags you entered, and the corresponding value for each key is the search query. The collection must be mutable, because we insert a new key–value pair every time the user adds a new search.

We also use collections to store the **Button**s created for each search and their corresponding **Button**s for editing favorites. Lines 20 and 23 declare ***NSMutableArray*** pointers, named buttons and infoButtons. NSMutableArray (a subclass of ***NSArray***) represents a mutable array of objects. Similarly to NSMutableDictionary, NSMutableArray allows you to alter the elements of the array without creating a new array object.

Lines 29–34 declare the methods of our class. The first two are IBActions that will appear in Interface Builder as actions that components can invoke to handle events. Method addTag: adds a new search favorite. Method clearTags: clears all previously saved favorites. Method addNewButtonWithTitle: adds a new **Button** to the GUI when the user adds a new search favorite. Method refreshList updates the **Button**s on the screen when the user adds a new favorite. Method buttonTouched: loads a selected search into the web browser. Method infoButtonTouched: loads an existing search into the **Text Field**s for editing.

Lines 38–41 add the sorting category to UIButton. A *category* is a group of related method implementations that enhance an existing class. Category methods are added to a class at runtime, so we can add methods to UIButton even though we cannot edit the original class declaration and implementation. The sorting category has only one method— compareButtonTitles: (defined in Fig. 5.18), which compares two UIButtons' titles alphabetically. We use this method to sort an NSMutableArray of UIButtons.

The Abstract Factory Design Pattern

NSArray and NSDictionary are examples of the ***abstract factory design pattern.*** In this pattern the abstract factory hides from the client code the details of creating objects of classes that are typically in a class hierarchy. The client code does not know the actual type of the object that is returned by the factory, only that the object has the capabilities that the client needs. Typically, an abstract factory provides methods that the client calls to obtain appropriate objects. When you create an NSArray, the object you receive is actually an object of a private NSArray subclass. The client code interacts with the object via the abstract NSArray superclass's public interface. NSArray and its private subclasses are collectively known as a ***class cluster***.

Connecting Objects in Interface Builder

Once you've finished editing Controller.h, save it and open MainWindow.xib in Interface Builder. Drag an **Object** from the **Library** window onto the window labeled **MainWindow.xib** (Fig. 5.10). Select your new object and open the **Inspector**. In the **Identity** tab change the value in the **Class** list to **Controller**. The actions and outlets we've defined should appear under the **Class Outlets** and **Class Actions** headers.

Switch to the **Connections** tab in the **Inspector**. There are three outlets to connect to GUI components. Connect the queryField outlet to the top **Text Field** by dragging from the circle to the right of the outlet name to the corresponding component. Similarly, connect scrollView to the **Scroll View** in the middle of the screen and tagField to the second **Text Field**. Make these connections now. You can also access the connections by right clicking the **Controller** in the **MainWindow.xib** window.

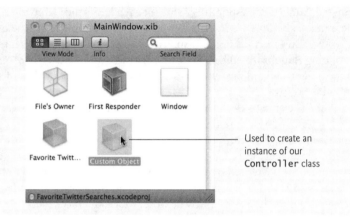

Fig. 5.10 | Adding a **Custom Object** to a nib file.

Next you'll connect the events generated by GUI components to their corresponding actions. The events generated in this app are sent by the two **Button** objects. Select the "Save" **Button** and open the **Connections** tab of the **Inspector**. In this case, we use the **Button**'s *Touch Up Inside event*, which is triggered when the user touches and releases a **Button** while staying inside its bound. This means the event is not triggered if the user drags outside the **Button** while maintaining contact with the screen. Connect the **Touch Up Inside** event to your **Controller** object. When the dialog box appears prompting you to pick a method, choose addTag: from the list. Next, select the "**Clear All Tags**" **Button**. Connect its **Touch Up Inside** event to the **Controller** object and select the clearTags: method. Save the file and close Interface Builder.

Defining Class Controller's *Implementation*
Now that we've declared class Controller and connected our actions and outlets, we need to provide the class's implementation. For this app, we must implement the six methods we declared in Controller.h. We also override two others inherited from class NSObject—the init method (used to initialize the object) and the dealloc method (used to release the object from memory). Finally, we define the awakeFromNib method because we added an instance of the class to the nib file in Interface Builder. This method will be invoked after the nib file loads and the GUI is created. In Xcode, open the file Controller.m.

init *Method of Class* Controller
The method *init* (Fig. 5.11, lines 8–44), which we inherit from NSObject and override here, initializes our Controller class's instance variables. In this example, method init is called automatically when the nib file is loaded, which creates the GUI components and the Controller object. When you override this method, you must call the superclass's version to ensure that inherited instance variables are properly initialized (line 10). Every object can access a pointer to itself with the keyword *self*. The keyword *super* references the same object as self, but super is used to access members inherited from the superclass. Line 10 sends the init message to super, which calls the init method of superclass NSObject. It's important to initialize the inherited superclass instance variables before performing custom initialization.

```
 1   // Fig. 5.11: Controller.m
 2   // Controller class for the Favorite Twitter Searches app.
 3   #import "Controller.h" // this line is auto-generated
 4
 5   @implementation Controller // this line is auto-generated
 6
 7   // called when object is initialized
 8   - (id)init
 9   {
10      self = [super init]; // initialize the superclass members
11
12      if (self != nil) // if the superclass initialized properly
13      {
14         // creates list of valid directories for saving a file
15         NSArray *paths = NSSearchPathForDirectoriesInDomains(
16            NSDocumentDirectory, NSUserDomainMask, YES);
17
18         // get the first directory
19         NSString *dir = [paths objectAtIndex:0];
20
21         // concatenate the file name "tagsIndex.plist" to the path
22         filePath = [[NSString alloc] initWithString:
23            [dir stringByAppendingPathComponent:@"tagsIndex.plist"]];
24
25         NSFileManager *fileManager = [NSFileManager defaultManager];
26
27         // if the file does not exist, create an empty NSMutableDictionary;
28         // otherwise, initialize an NSDictionary with the file's contents
29         if ([fileManager fileExistsAtPath:filePath] == NO)
30         {
31            tags = [[NSMutableDictionary alloc] init];
32         } // end if
33         else
34         {
35            tags = [[NSMutableDictionary alloc]
36               initWithContentsOfFile:filePath];
37         } // end else
38
39         buttons = [[NSMutableArray alloc] init]; // create array
40         infoButtons = [[NSMutableArray alloc] init]; // create array
41      } // end if
42
43      return self; // if self == nil, object not initialized properly
44   } // end method init
45
```

Fig. 5.11 | Controller class for the **Favorite Twitter Searches** app.

If the superclass doesn't instantiate properly, init returns a "pointer to nothing," which is represented by the keyword *nil*. Line 12 ensures that the superclass was properly initialized by comparing self to nil. Line 43 returns self. If self is not nil, initialization was successful; otherwise, initialization failed.

If initialization of the superclass's members succeeds, lines 15–40 initialize class Controller's instance variables. To initialize filePath, we need to ask the operating system where we're allowed to save files for the app. According to the iPhone developer documentation, it's poor practice to specify hard coded paths in iPhone apps, because the underlying directory structure could change in future iPhone OS releases. Calling NSSearchPathForDirectoriesInDomains (lines 15–16) returns an NSArray containing possible locations. The method takes three arguments and returns an NSArray containing a list of paths matching our search. The first argument indicates that we're looking for a directory that can store documents. The second says that we're looking for the directory relative to the current user. The iPhone SDK does not give you access to shared system folders; you can use only folders that are specific to your app. The last argument tells the function to return complete path strings by expanding any tildes (~), which are used in UNIX systems to represent the user's home directory. To see what the iPhone's file system looks like, navigate to the folder ~/Library/Application Support/iPhone Simulator/User/Applications. Because each iPhone app has one documents directory, the function NSSearchPathForDirectoriesInDomains returns an NSArray containing only one object. Line 19 obtains the path to that directory from the array with method *objectAtIndex*, which returns the object at the specified index.

Lines 22–23 create a new string and initialize it with a string containing the name of the file in which we'll save the favorites (tagsIndex) appended to the string dir. NSString method *initWithString:* initializes a string with another string's contents. NSString method *stringByAppendingPathComponent:* returns a new string with its argument appended to the string on which the method is called. The method ensures that the path components are separated by the path-separator character (/). Variable filePath now contains the path where we'll save and load the app's data.

Line 25 retrieves the default *NSFileManager*—used to perform common file-system operations such as adding, copying and removing files. This is another example of the singleton design pattern. Lines 29–32 check if the file already exists using NSFileManager method *fileExistsAtPath:*, which receives the file's name and path as an argument and returns YES or NO. The file will already exist if it was created during a previous execution of the app. If it does not exist, we initialize tags as an empty NSMutableDictionary. To create the object, we call NSMutableDictionary's *alloc method*. We then initialize the object by calling NSMutableDictionary's *init method*. If the file exists, we initialize tags with the contents of that file (lines 35–36). NSMutableDictionary method *initWithContentsOfFile:* receives the file's name and path as an argument and initializes the NSMutableDictionary with the file's contents. Lines 39–40 initialize buttons and infoButtons as empty NSMutableArrays. Note that, unlike many other object-oriented programming languages, Objective-C does not have constructors that are guaranteed to get called when an object is created. It's the responsibility of the object's creator to invoke an appropriate initialization method on the object.

awakeFromNib *Method of Class* Controller

The awakeFromNib method (Fig. 5.12, lines 47–51) creates **Buttons** for each search saved by the user. We do this here rather than in method init to ensure that the GUI has loaded before trying to programmatically attach new **Buttons** to it. Recall that awakeFromNib is called once your GUI objects have finished loading. Method init is called *before* the GUI is created. Method `awakeFromNib` iterates over the entries in `tags` and creates a new `UIButton` for each one. We use a `for...in` loop, which iterates through the items in a collection. For an `NSDictionary`, a `for...in` loop iterates through the collection's keys by default. For each key, we call the `addNewButtonWithTitle:` method (lines 151–197), passing the user-specified tag as the text to display on the **Button**.

```
46   // called when the GUI components finish loading
47   - (void)awakeFromNib
48   {
49      for (NSString *title in tags)
50         [self addNewButtonWithTitle:title];
51   } // end method awakeFromNib
52
```

Fig. 5.12 | Method `awakeFromNib` of class `Controller`.

refreshList *Method of Class* Controller

Method `refreshList` (Fig. 5.13, lines 54–99) updates the list of searches on the screen to reflect changes to the number of **Button**s in the **Scroll View**. First, lines 57–58 remove all the **UIButton**s.[1] The ***subviews property*** of `scrollView` returns all the **View**s currently managed by `scrollView`, or in our case all the `UIButton` objects previously added. A *subview* is a **View** contained in a larger **View**. In this case, each **Button** is an individual **View** in `scrollView`. The containing **View** is called the *superview*. For each `UIButton`, we call the ***removeFromSuperview method***, which tells the `UIButton` to remove itself from `scrollView`. We also clear the `NSMutableArray` `infoButtons` (line 60) by calling its ***removeAllObjects method***. We'll be adding new objects to it later.

```
53   // remove all buttons and populate View with favorites
54   - (void)refreshList
55   {
56      // remove all the buttons from the GUI
57      for (UIButton *button in scrollView.subviews)
58         [button removeFromSuperview];
59
60      [infoButtons removeAllObjects];
61
62      float buttonOffset = BUTTON_SPACING; // reset the spacing
63
64      // repopulate the scroll view with buttons
65      for (UIButton *button in buttons)
66      {
67         CGRect buttonFrame = button.frame; // fetch the frame of button
68         buttonFrame.origin.x = BUTTON_SPACING; // set the x-coordinate
69         buttonFrame.origin.y = buttonOffset; // set the y-coordinate
```

Fig. 5.13 | Method `refreshList` of class `Controller`. (Part 1 of 2.)

---

1. This method of removing all the `UIButton`s and re-adding them will become slow if the number of `UIButton`s is large. To better manage large lists of items, you can use the `UITableView` class, which we present in Chapter 10.

```
70
71          // button width is the size of the view minus padding on each side
72          buttonFrame.size.width =
73              scrollView.frame.size.width - 5 * BUTTON_SPACING;
74          buttonFrame.size.height = BUTTON_HEIGHT; // set the height of button
75          button.frame = buttonFrame; // assign the new frame to button
76          [scrollView addSubview:button]; // add button as a subview
77
78          // create detail button
79          UIButton *infoButton =
80              [UIButton buttonWithType: UIButtonTypeDetailDisclosure];
81          [infoButtons addObject:infoButton]; // add infoButton to infoButtons
82
83          // position button to the right of the button we just added
84          buttonFrame = infoButton.frame; // fetch the frame of infoButton
85          buttonFrame.origin.x = scrollView.frame.size.width - 35;
86
87          // this button is a bit shorter than normal buttons, so we adjust
88          buttonFrame.origin.y = buttonOffset + 3;
89          infoButton.frame = buttonFrame; // assign the new frame
90
91          // make the button call infoButtonTouched: when it is touched
92          [infoButton addTarget:self action:@selector(infoButtonTouched:)
93              forControlEvents:UIControlEventTouchUpInside];
94          [scrollView addSubview:infoButton]; // add infoButton as a subview
95
96          // increase the offset so the next button is added further down
97          buttonOffset += BUTTON_HEIGHT + BUTTON_SPACING;
98      } // end for
99  } // end refreshList
100
```

Fig. 5.13 | Method refreshList of class Controller. (Part 2 of 2.)

Lines 65–98 iterate through the buttons array and set each UIButton's width, height and location in scrollView. Line 67 gets the current **Button**'s *frame property*. This property (of type *CGRect*) is a structure containing a CGSize named size and a *CGPoint* named origin. A *structure* is an aggregate type capable of storing related data items of different types under one name. The size property controls the width and height of the UIButton, and origin controls its placement in the superview. In this case, the superview is scrollView. Line 68 sets the distance of the UIButton from the left side of the **Scroll View**, and line 69 sets the distance from the top. Lines 72–73 set the width of the UIButton, which is the entire width of the scrollView object minus the padding on either side, minus the size of the UIButton we'll be placing next to it. We then set the height (line 74), assign the new frame to the UIButton (line 75) and add the UIButton to scrollView (line 76).

Next we create a **Detail Disclosure Button** (⊙) that will be displayed to the right of the UIButton we just added. We create the UIButton (lines 79–80), add it to infoButtons (line 81), then set its frame property. This is similar to how we set the frame of the previous UIButton. We don't set width and height, because we want to keep the default values. Lines 92–93 specify that the action infoButtonTouched: should be called in response to infoButton's UIControlEventTouchUpInside event.

infoButtonTouched: *Method of Class* Controller

The infoButtonTouched: method (Fig. 5.14, lines 102–114) allows the user to edit an existing search. This method is called when the user touches a **Detail Disclosure Button** in the scrollView. When this happens, we update tagField and queryField with the appropriate values. First, line 105 gets the index in infoButtons of the UIButton that was touched. The sender argument (which implicitly has the type id if no type is specified) is passed into the event handler automatically and represents the component with which the user interacted. The UIButton next to the touched **Detail Disclosure Button** is at the same index in buttons, so we get that UIButton and retrieve its title (line 108). We then set tagField's text property to the title (line 109), look up the title in tags (line 112) by calling NSMutableDictionary's *valueForKey* method and update queryField's text property with the returned value (line 113).

```
101    // called when the user touches an info button
102    - (void)infoButtonTouched:sender
103    {
104       // get the index of the button that was touched
105       int index = [infoButtons indexOfObject:sender];
106
107       // get the title of the button
108       NSString *key = [[buttons objectAtIndex:index] titleLabel].text;
109       tagField.text = key; // update tagField with the button title
110
111       // get the search query using the button title
112       NSString *value = [tags valueForKey:key];
113       queryField.text = value; // update queryField with the value
114    } // end method infoButtonTouched:
115
```

Fig. 5.14 | Method infoButtonTouched: of class Controller.

addTag: *and* clearTags: *Methods of Class* Controller

The addTag: method (Fig. 5.15, lines 117–139) adds a new **Button** to the app when the user touches the "**Save**" **Button**. Lines 120–121 hide the keyboard by deselecting tagField and queryField. Lines 123–124 obtain the values in tagField and queryField. If either field is empty, we exit the method (line 128). Line 130 checks whether an entry for this tag already exists. If not, we add a new UIButton (line 131). Otherwise, we simply alter the existing tag's value using NSMutableDictionary's *setValue:forKey:* method (line 133). This method takes an NSString as the key and an object as the value.

```
116    // add a favorite search
117    - (IBAction)addTag:sender
118    {
119       // make the keyboard disappear
120       [tagField resignFirstResponder];
121       [queryField resignFirstResponder];
122
```

Fig. 5.15 | Methods addTag: and clearTags: of class Controller. (Part 1 of 2.)

```
123     NSString *key = tagField.text; // get the text in tagField
124     NSString *value = queryField.text; // get the text in queryField
125
126     // test if either field is empty
127     if (value.length == nil || key.length == nil)
128        return; // exit from the method
129
130     if ([tags valueForKey:key] == nil) // test if the tag already exists
131        [self addNewButtonWithTitle:key]; // if not, add a new button
132
133     [tags setValue:value forKey:key]; // add a new entry in tags
134
135     tagField.text = nil; // clear tagField of text
136     queryField.text = nil; // clear queryField of text
137
138     [tags writeToFile:filePath atomically:NO]; // save the data
139  } // end method addTag:
140
141  // remove all the tags
142  - (IBAction)clearTags:sender
143  {
144     [tags removeAllObjects]; // clear tags
145     [tags writeToFile:filePath atomically:NO]; // update favorite file
146     [buttons removeAllObjects]; // clear buttons
147     [self refreshList]; // update the display
148  } // end clearTags:
149
```

Fig. 5.15 | Methods addTag: and clearTags: of class Controller. (Part 2 of 2.)

We next clear the text in queryField and tagField (lines 135–136). Because a new entry has been added, we need to update the file containing the saved favorites (line 138). The *writeToFile:atomically:* method of NSDictionary writes the entire contents of the NSDictionary to a file.[2] Providing NO as the second argument tells the NSDictionary to write directly to the file rather than using a temporary file. This will perform the write operation faster but could corrupt the file if a write got interrupted.

The clearTags: method (lines 142–148) empties the tags collection, then writes its contents to the file (thus clearing the file's contents). We then remove all the **Button**s from the buttons collection and call refreshList to update the app's user interface.

addNewButtonWithTitle: *Method of Class* Controller

The addNewButtonWithTitle: method (Fig. 5.16, lines 151–197) adds a new UIButton in alphabetical order to NSArray buttons. Line 154 creates the UIButton as a **Round Rect Button**. Line 157 sets the title of the UIButton. Lines 160–161 connect the UIButton's *UIControlTouchUpInside* event to our Controller's buttonTouched: action. Method *addTarget:action:forControlEvents:* receives three arguments. The first is a pointer to the object that defines the action, the second is the action to invoke and the third is a constant representing the event that invokes the action. In the second argument, *@selector*

---

2. The file uses Apple's property list (also called plist) format, which is an XML document with the .plist extension by convention.

is a compiler directive that enables you to pass a method name as data in a method call. This is similar to a function pointer in C and C++.

```
150    // add a new button with the given title to the bottom of the list
151    - (void)addNewButtonWithTitle:(NSString *)title
152    {
153        // create a new button
154        UIButton *button = [UIButton buttonWithType:UIButtonTypeRoundedRect];
155
156        // give the button the title of the tag
157        [button setTitle:title forState:UIControlStateNormal];
158
159        // tell the button to call buttonTouched: when it is touched
160        [button addTarget:self action:@selector(buttonTouched:)
161            forControlEvents:UIControlEventTouchUpInside];
162
163        [buttons addObject:button]; // add the UIButton to the end of the array
164
165        // sort the NSMutableArray by the UIButton's titles
166        [buttons sortUsingSelector:@selector(compareButtonTitles:)];
167        [self refreshList]; // refresh the list of favorite search Buttons
168
169        // Adjust the content size of the view to include the new button. The
170        // view scrolls only when the content size is greater than its frame.
171        CGSize contentSize = CGSizeMake(scrollView.frame.size.width,
172            buttons.count * (BUTTON_HEIGHT + BUTTON_SPACING) + BUTTON_SPACING);
173        [scrollView setContentSize:contentSize];
174    } // end addNewButtonWithTitle:
175
```

Fig. 5.16 | Method `addNewButtonWithTitle:` of class `Controller`.

Line 163 inserts the UIButton at the end of the array using NSMutableArray's addObject: method. Next, we sort the UIButtons in alphabetical order by their titles using ***NSMutableArray's sortUsingSelector: method***. We pass the UIButton category method compareButtonTitles:, which we define in Figure 5.18. This method compares the NSStrings that represent the titles of two UIButtons.

So far, we haven't changed the GUI—we've modified only a list of UIButton objects. To update the GUI with the updated list of **Button**s, we call our refreshList method (line 167). We'll review this method shortly.

The last step in adding a new UIButton is adjusting the contentSize property of scrollView, which sets the size of scrollView's contents so it knows how much to let the user scroll in any given direction. Lines 171–172 pass dimensions to the ***CGSizeMake*** function, creating a new ***CGSize*** (a data structure containing width and height) representing those dimensions. The first argument is the width, which we don't want to change since this app does not require horizontal scrolling. The second argument is the height. This is the sum of the heights of a UIButton and the spacing below it, multiplied by the number of UIButtons. We also add space before the first UIButton. Line 173 readjusts the size of the **Scroll View** to accommodate the new **Button** by calling the UIScrollView's ***setContentSize:*** method.

The Command Design Pattern

The method ***addTarget:action:forControlEvents:*** that we use to register an event handler programmatically is an example of the ***command design pattern*** in which an object contains the information necessary to call a method at a later time—typical of event handlers. This information includes the method name and the object on which that method should be called. In this case, a UIButton object is storing information necessary to call the buttonTouched: event-handling method on the Controller object when a user touches the button.

buttonTouched: Method of Class Controller

The buttonTouched: method (Fig. 5.17, lines 177–190) tells the Safari browser to open the search query related to the touched **Button**. First we get the touched UIButton's text (line 179). Notice that to access sender's titleLabel property we use object messaging and not dot notation. Since sender is of the generic type id, which defines no properties, trying to access titleLabel via dot notation would result in a compilation error.[3] In object messaging the receiving object and calling method are dynamically bound at runtime. The compiler does not check whether you call a method that is not applicable for the receiving object—such an error would cause your app to fail at runtime. In this case, we know that sender is a UIButton which defines a titleLabel property. We look up this title in tags (lines 182–183) to retrieve the search string, then URL encode it.

```
176   // load selected search in web browser
177   - (void)buttonTouched:sender
178   {
179      NSString *key = [sender titleLabel].text; // get Button's text
180
181      // get the search and URL encode any special characters
182      NSMutableString *search = [[tags valueForKey:key]
183         stringByAddingPercentEscapesUsingEncoding:NSUTF8StringEncoding];
184
185      // format the URL
186      NSString *urlString = [NSString stringWithFormat:
187         @"http://search.twitter.com/search?q=%@", search];
188      NSURL *url = [NSURL URLWithString:urlString];
189      [[UIApplication sharedApplication] openURL:url];
190   } // end buttonTouched
191   @end // end implementation controller
192
```

Fig. 5.17 | Method buttonTouched: of class Controller.

Method stringByAddingPercentEscapesUsingEncoding: encodes the special characters in the string so that it's a properly formatted URL that can be passed to the web browser. We append this formatted search string to the Twitter search URL (lines 186–187) and create an ***NSURL*** object (line 188). The %@ format specifier is a placeholder for an object that should be converted to a string. Line 189 tells the operating system to open the URL. Each application running on the iPhone OS has one instance of ***UIApplication***—

---

3. If you cast sender to a UIButton*, you can use dot notation to access its properties.

used to manage the app (e.g., managing windows and opening outside resources). This is an example of the *singleton design pattern*, which guarantees that a system instantiates a maximum of one object of a given class. For class UIApplication, we retrieve this object by invoking *sharedApplication* and call *openURL* to open the web page in Safari. Any NSURL beginning with http:// is opened by Safari by default. This causes your app to quit. The page is then loaded and displayed by Safari.

UIButton's sorting Category
Lines 194–201 implement method compareButtonTitles: of UIButton's sorting category (Fig. 5.18). Lines 198–199 use NSString's caseInsensitiveCompare: method to compare the text property of the UIButton argument to that of the UIButton receiving the compareButtonTitles: message, then return the result. This method is used to determine the sorting order of the UIButtons.

```
193  // define UIButton's sorting category method
194  @implementation UIButton (sorting)
195  - (NSComparisonResult)compareButtonTitles:(UIButton *)button
196  {
197      // compare this UIButton's title to that of the given UIButton
198      return [self.titleLabel.text
199          caseInsensitiveCompare:button.titleLabel.text];
200  } // end method compareButtonTitles
201  @end // end UIButtons's sorting category
```

Fig. 5.18 | UIButton's sorting category.

5.5 Wrap-Up

In this chapter, we created the **Favorite Twitter Searches** app. First we designed the GUI, introducing the **Button** and **View** components. We then wrote Objective-C code, using the classes NSMutableDictionary and NSMutableArray. We introduced the init method along with the self and super keywords for getting pointers to the current object and accessing its superclass's members. Later, you saw how to create GUI components programmatically. This allowed you to modify the GUI dynamically in response to user interactions. We showed how to programmatically add a target object and an action to a control. You then saw how to format a URL and use the iPhone OS to open it in the Safari web browser. We also showed how to sort elements in an NSMutableArray using its sortUsingSelector method. In Chapter 16, we'll revisit Twitter—creating an app which calls Twitter web services.

In Chapter 6, you'll build the **Flag Quiz** app, which uses the **Utility Application** template to create an app with two **View**s. We show a more complex **View** while managing frontside and flipside **View**s. We'll also introduce basic memory management and UIViewController.

6

Flag Quiz Game App
Controllers and the Utility Application Template

OBJECTIVES

In this chapter you'll learn:

- To create an app with a frontside and a flipside (commonly used for app settings), using the **Utility Application** template.

- To extend the UIViewController class to manage multiple views.

- To use the **Segmented Control** GUI component to create multiple selectable items.

- To vary the quiz answers each time the app runs using random number generation.

- To avoid memory leaks using basic memory management.

- To load resource files from your iPhone to display the flag images.

Outline

6.1 Introduction

6.2 Test-Driving the **Flag Quiz Game** App

6.3 Technologies Overview

6.4 Building the App

    6.4.1 The **MainView** and Class `MainViewController`

    6.4.2 The **FlipsideView** and Class `FlipsideViewController`

6.5 Wrap-Up

6.1 Introduction

The **Flag Quiz Game** app tests the user's ability to correctly identify flags from around the world (Fig. 6.1). The user is presented with a flag image and three, six or nine country names—one matches the flag and the others are randomly selected. The user chooses the country by touching its name on the screen. If the choice is correct, the app displays "**Correct!**" in green (Fig. 6.2) and loads the next flag after a three-second delay. An incorrect choice disables the chosen country and displays "**Incorrect**" in red (Fig. 6.3)—the user must keep choosing until the correct country is picked. The app displays in the lower-left corner the user's progress throughout the quiz. The user can customize the quiz using an options screen which is hidden behind the game (Fig. 6.4)—and accessed by touching the **Info Button** (ⓘ). The user can increase the number of country choices from the default of 3 to 6 or 9 to make the quiz more difficult. **Switch**es are used to restrict the quiz to certain regions of the world—five of the major continents and Oceania, which consists of Australia, New Zealand and various South Pacific Islands. Touching a **Switch** to turn it to the

Fig. 6.1 | Flag Quiz Game app.

OFF position removes the corresponding region's countries from the quiz. The "**Done**" **Button** applies the configuration changes and begins a new quiz. After 10 flags are matched, a popup alert displays the user's total number of guesses and the percentage of correct answers (Fig. 6.5). The "**Reset Quiz**" **Button** starts a new quiz.

Fig. 6.2 │ Correct answer in the **Flag Quiz Game** app.

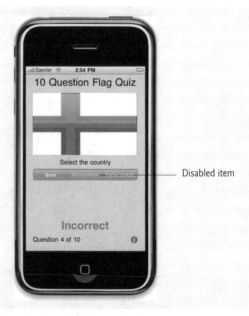

Fig. 6.3 │ Disabled incorrect answer in the **Flag Quiz Game** app.

Fig. 6.4 | Options screen of the **Flag Quiz Game** app.

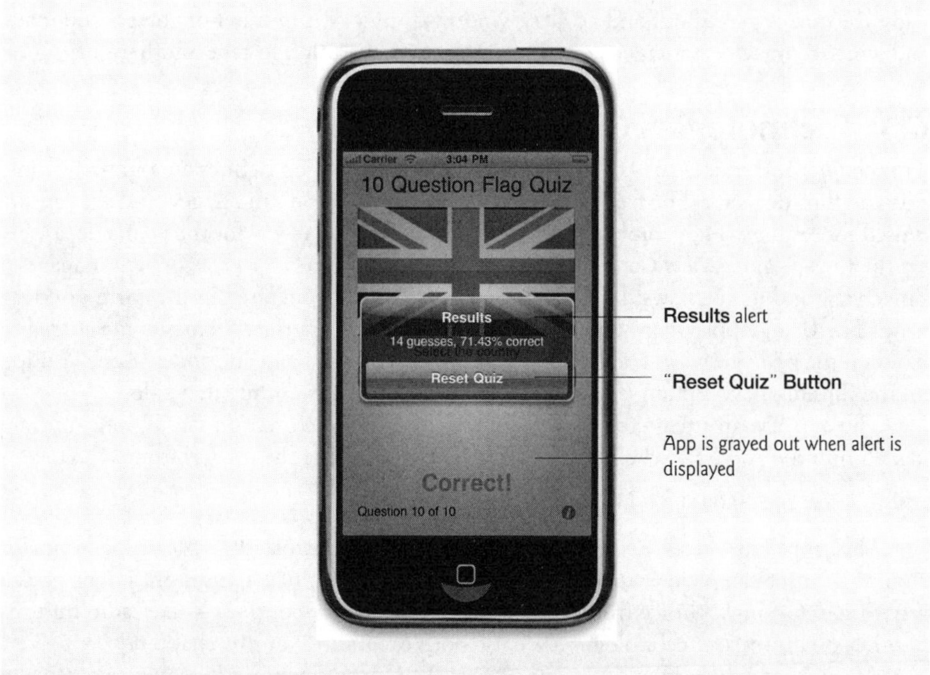

Fig. 6.5 | **Results** alert after quiz completion.

6.2 Test-Driving the Flag Quiz Game App

Opening the Completed Application
Open the directory on your computer containing the **Flag Quiz Game** app project. Double click FlagQuizGame.xcodeproj to open the project in Xcode.

Running the App
Click **Build and Go** to run the app in the iPhone Simulator. A new quiz begins automatically. The flag at the top of the app matches one of the three countries below the image. The flag and the answer choices are selected randomly, varying each time you run the app.

Configuring the Quiz
Touch the **Info Button** (●) to view the options screen. The three topmost items specify the number of answers that should be displayed with each flag. The item reading **3** is initially selected. Touch the middle item to double the answer pool to **6**. Each of the six **Switch**es in the lower part of the options screen represents a region of the world. They all currently read **ON**—meaning that any of the world's flags can be selected randomly for the quiz. Touch the **Switch**es next to **Africa** and **Oceania** to set them to the **OFF** position and exclude the corresponding countries from the quiz. Press the "**Done**" **Button** at the top of the options screen to start a new game with your specified options.

Completing the Quiz
A new quiz starts with six answer choices and no flags from either Africa or Oceania. Work through the quiz by touching the country you think matches each flag. If you guess incorrectly, keep guessing until you get the right answer. After you've successfully matched 10 flags, the quiz is grayed out and an alert window displays the number of guesses you made and your accuracy percentage. Touch the "**Reset Quiz**" **Button** to take another quiz.

6.3 Technologies Overview

This chapter introduces the **Utility Application** template, which defines an app with frontside and flipside views. The frontside typically displays the app's main view and the flipside is used for settings. The template generates several classes—a view for the frontside, a view for the flipside and a **View Controller** for each. A **View Controller** is a class which manages a single view and its subviews. It usually responds to events generated in the corresponding view. The **Utility Application** template also autogenerates interface elements for changing between the two views. An **Info Button** (●) is placed on the frontside and a "**Done**" **Button** on the flipside. Each **Button** is preconfigured to flip the app to the other side.

The app has an image for each flag. The images are stored on the iPhone and are loaded into the app only when they're needed. We obtained the images from

            www.free-country-flags.com

This app introduces **Segmented Control**s—GUI controls that present a series of choices the user can pick. **Segmented Control**s can act either like a series of **Button**s or as a way to select a single choice from a set of mutually exclusive options—like radio buttons in other user interface technologies. We use both capabilities in this chapter.

We also introduce memory management. In Cocoa, memory is managed manually using a system called retain counting. Every descendent of NSObject has an integer *retain count.* When this reaches zero, the object's memory is deallocated. If a part of your program relies on an object, it sends the object a ***retain*** message, which adds one to the object's retain count. When that part of the program is finished using the object, it sends the object a ***release*** message, which subtracts one from the retain count. As a rule, you're responsible for releasing any object you retain or create with `alloc` or `copy`.

You do not have to release any object returned from methods or created using a convenience constructor, such as `stringWithFormat:`. Such an object is autoreleased—the object will be sent a `release` message at some point in the future. For more information on memory management, visit `developer.apple.com/iPhone/library/documentation/Cocoa/Conceptual/MemoryMgmt/MemoryMgmt.html`.

6.4 Building the App

Section 6.4.1 presents the **MainView** and class `MainViewController`. Section 6.4.2 presents the **FlipsideView** and class `FlipsideViewController`.

6.4.1 The MainView and Class `MainViewController`

Open Xcode and create a new **Utility Application**. Remember to drag the folders containing this example's images from the Finder into the project's **Resources** group. Open **MainView.xib** in Interface Builder. Center a **Label** at the top of the screen and set its text to 10 Question Flag Quiz. Set the **Label**'s **Minimum Font Size** to 27 in the Inspector window. Drag an **Image View** to the top of the app window. This **Image View** displays the flag images. Next, center a **Label** underneath the **Image View**, then change its text to Select the country. Drag two more **Labels** onto the app window. Center the first **Label** near the bottom of the app and set its **Minimum Font Size** property to **30**—this **Label** is used to display whether each answer is correct or incorrect. Set this **Label**'s text to Answer. You'll soon see how to hide the **Label** until the user selects an answer. The **Label** in the bottom-left corner will display the user's progress—showing the number of flags seen so far in the quiz. Set this **Label**'s text to Question 0 of 10. Figure 6.6 shows the completed layout for **MainView**.

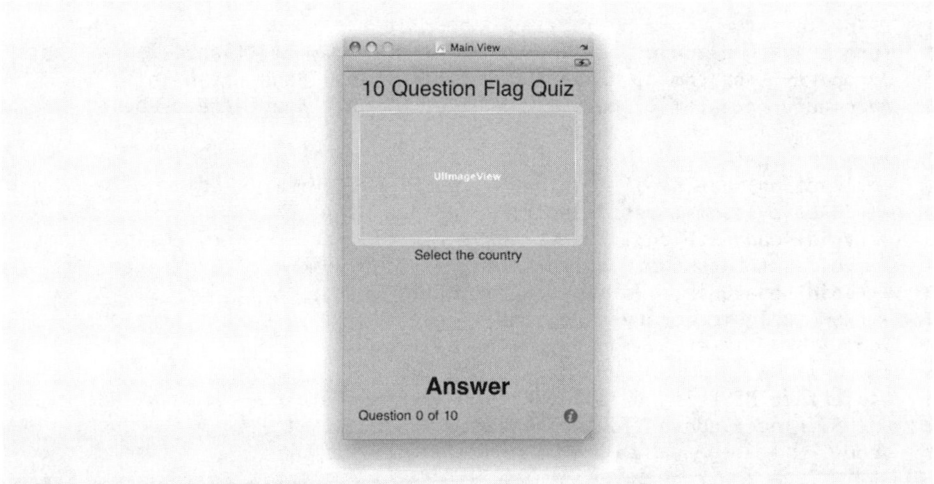

Fig. 6.6 | Completed **MainView** GUI design.

The ***Info Button*** () at the bottom-right corner of the app window was automatically generated by the **Utility Application** template. Touching this **Button** displays the **FlipsideView**, which contains this app's options screen. This **Button**'s functionality is provided by the template. You can move the **Info Button**, but Apple's *iPhone Human Interface Guidelines* recommend leaving it in the lower-right corner when appropriate.

The MainView *interface*
Under the **Main View** folder of Xcode's **Groups and Files** window, select MainViewController.h. This is the automatically generated header file for class MainViewController. Initially, the class includes method showInfo, which is called to display the **FlipsideView**. Figure 6.7 contains the completed interface declaration.

```
 1  // MainViewController.h
 2  // Controller for the front side of the Flag Quiz app.
 3  // Implementation in MainViewController.m
 4  #import "FlipsideViewController.h"
 5
 6  @interface MainViewController : UIViewController
 7     <FlipsideViewControllerDelegate>
 8  {
 9     IBOutlet UIImageView *flagView; // displays the flag image
10     IBOutlet UILabel *answerLabel; // displays if guess is correct
11     IBOutlet UILabel *numCorrectLabel; // displays quiz's progress
12     NSMutableArray *bars; // stores Segmented Controls
13     NSMutableArray *filenames; // list of flag image file names
14     NSMutableArray *quizCountries; // names of 10 countries in the quiz
15     NSMutableDictionary *regions; // stores whether each region is enabled
16     NSString *correctAnswer; // the correct country for the current flag
17     int totalGuesses; // number of guesses made
18     int numCorrect; // number of correct guesses
19     int guessRows; // number of Segmented Controls displaying choices
20  } // end instance variable declarations
21
22  // declare the three outlets as properties
23  @property (nonatomic, retain) IBOutlet UIImageView *flagView;
24  @property (nonatomic, retain) IBOutlet UILabel *answerLabel;
25  @property (nonatomic, retain) IBOutlet UILabel *numCorrectLabel;
26
27  // method declarations
28  - (IBAction)showInfo; // displays the FlipsideView
29  - (IBAction)submitGuess:sender; // processes a guess
30  - (void)loadNextFlag; // displays a new flag and country choices
31  - (void)setGuessRows:(int)rows; // sets the number of Segmented Controls
32  - (void)resetQuiz; // starts a new quiz
33  - (NSMutableDictionary *)regions; // returns the regions dictionary
34  @end // end interface MainViewController;
35
36  @interface NSString (displayName) // begin NSString's displayName category
37  - (NSString *)convertToDisplayName; // converts file name to country name
38  @end // end category displayName of interface NSString
```

Fig. 6.7 | MainViewController interface declaration.

MainViewController is a subclass of UIViewController (line 6) that implements the *FlipSideViewContollerDelegate protocol* (line 7). A *protocol* describes a set of methods that can be called on an object—this is similar to the concept of an "interface" in other programming languages. The FlipSideViewControllerDelegate protocol was automatically defined in the FlipSideViewController class by the **Utility Application** template. This protocol declares the flipsideViewControllerDidFinish method, which returns the app to the **MainView** when the user touches the "**Done**" **Button** on the options screen.

There are three outlets (lines 9–11) representing the three dynamic GUI components on the **MainView** that we'll interact with programmatically—flagView, answerLabel and numCorrectLabel. Lines 12–14 declare NSMutableArrays to store the quiz's **Segmented Controls**, flag file names and country names, respectively. NSMutableDictionary regions stores whether each region's countries are included in the quiz (line 15). Lines 16–19 declare other variables used to maintain the game's state.

Lines 23–25 declare each of our outlets as properties. A *property* is a member variable that defines a *get* and a *set* method. As you'll soon see, these methods can be automatically generated. The *nonatomic* keyword affects the performance and threading of a property. More information can be found in the Performance and Threading section of Apple's Objective-C documentation, located at

```
developer.apple.com/documentation/Cocoa/Conceptual/ObjectiveC/
Articles/ocProperties.html#//apple_ref/doc/uid/TP30001163-CH17-SW12
```

The *retain* keyword specifies that the *set* method will release the old object, assign a new one and invoke the new one's retain method. This is typical with outlets. Other keywords can be used to specify that the generated set method simply assigns a new value to the pointer without releasing the old object or retaining the new one, or make a copy of the object being used to set the property.

MainViewController contains six methods (lines 28–33):

- showInfo:—displays the **FlipsideView** (options) when the "**Info**" **Button** is touched.

- submitGuess—processes the answer when the user touches a country name on a **Segmented Control**.

- loadNextFlag—loads a new flag and set of answers.

- setGuessRows:—sets the number of country choices. Each row is a **Segmented Control** that contains three countries.

- resetQuiz:—resets the game after the user completes the quiz.

- regions—returns an NSMutableDictionary indicating which regions were chosen to be included in the quiz. By default, all regions are chosen.

Lines 36–38 add the displayName category to NSString. The displayName category has only one method—convertToDisplayName (defined in Fig. 6.14). This converts the flag-image file names to readable country names for display in the app.

Implementing the *MainViewController* Class
Under the **Main View** folder of Xcode's **Groups and Files** window, double click MainViewController.m. The completed initialization methods appear in Fig. 6.8. The class begins by declaring the BAR_OFFSET *global variable* (line 8). Because the variables are declared

outside any interface definition, they're accessible to any class. BAR_OFFSET represents the space between the top of the **MainView** and the top-most **Segmented Control** (247 pixels). The *const qualifier* informs the compiler that the variable's value cannot be modified. If an attempt is made to modify a const variable, the compiler catches it and issues an error. The *static* keyword indicates that the variable is known only in this compilation unit.

```
1   // MainViewController.m
2   // Controller for the front side of the Flag Quiz app.
3   #import <AVFoundation/AVFoundation.h>
4   #import <MediaPlayer/MediaPlayer.h>
5   #import "MainViewController.h"
6   #import "MainView.h"
7
8   static const int BAR_OFFSET = 247; // top Segmented Control's y-coordinate
9
10  @implementation MainViewController
11
12  // generate get and set methods for outlet properties
13  @synthesize flagView;
14  @synthesize answerLabel;
15  @synthesize numCorrectLabel;
16
17  // initialize the controller
18  - (id)initWithNibName:(NSString *)nibNameOrNil
19      bundle:(NSBundle *)nibBundleOrNil
20  {
21      // initialize the superclass
22      if (self = [super initWithNibName:nibNameOrNil bundle:nibBundleOrNil])
23      {
24          guessRows = 1; // default to one row of choices
25          bars = [[NSMutableArray alloc] init]; // initialize the list of bars
26          filenames = [[NSMutableArray alloc] init];
27
28          // initialize the list of flags to be displayed
29          quizCountries = [[NSMutableArray alloc] initWithCapacity:10];
30
31          // create the dictionary of regions
32          regions = [[NSMutableDictionary alloc] init];
33
34          // default all the regions to on
35          NSNumber *yesBool = [NSNumber numberWithBool:YES];
36          [regions setValue:yesBool forKey:@"Africa"];
37          [regions setValue:yesBool forKey:@"Asia"];
38          [regions setValue:yesBool forKey:@"Europe"];
39          [regions setValue:yesBool forKey:@"North_America"];
40          [regions setValue:yesBool forKey:@"Oceania"];
41          [regions setValue:yesBool forKey:@"South_America"];
42      } // end if
43
44      return self; // return this MainViewController
45  } // end method initWithNibName:bundle:
46
```

Fig. 6.8 | Initializing the MainViewController class.

Lines 13–15 use *@synthesize* to "synthesize each outlet's property." This automatically generates *get* and *set* methods (also known as *get* and *set* accessors) for the properties, based on the options specified in the @property declarations. In this case, property flagView can be modified using setFlagView: and accessed using flagView. These follow the default naming scheme for a property's methods. It's also possible to define your own custom *get* and *set* methods for a property as we show for a *get* method in Fig. 10.14.

The initWithNibName:bundle: method (lines 18–45) initializes class MainViewController's instance variables. The guessRows instance variable is initialized to 1 row, so that three answer choices are displayed for each flag (line 24). Lines 25–26 initialize two NSMutableArrays—one to store the **Segmented Controls** displaying country names and one to store the flag image file names. NSMutableArray quizCountries (line 29) will contain the names of the 10 flag images used in the quiz. Since we know exactly how many flag path names we need to store for each quiz (10), we can use NSMutableArray's *init-WithCapacity method* to allocate exactly 10 elements. This prevents the array from having to resize itself when we add new objects to it, thus increasing the app's performance. Line 35 calls NSNumber's *numberWithBool: method* to create the yesBool NSNumber. The *NSNumber class* represents a numeric value as an object. We perform this operation because only objects that derive from NSObject can be stored in an NSArray, and a BOOL is not an object. Supplying YES as an argument to numberWithBool: returns an NSNumber representing YES's numerical equivalent, which is 1. Lines 36–41 initialize the NSDictionary containing the world's six regions—using yesBool to enable each region by default. All the world's regions are included in the quiz unless the user disables any in the **FlipsideView**.

Method viewDidLoad of Class MainViewController
Method viewDidLoad (Fig. 6.9) is inherited from UIViewController (MainViewController's superclass) and overridden. This method initializes instance variables that can be created only after the view has been initialized (i.e., loaded). Line 50 calls the superclass's viewDidLoad method. Line 51 seeds the random number generator. The *srandom library method* uses an integer seed to produce a different sequence of random numbers for each execution of the app. We use the current time as the seed by calling the *time library function*. Lines 53–54 set the **Text** property of answerLabel and numCorrectLabel to their initial states.

```
47   // called when the view finishes loading
48   - (void)viewDidLoad
49   {
50       [super viewDidLoad]; // call superclass's viewDidLoad method
51       srandom(time(0)); // seed random number generator
52
53       [answerLabel setText:nil]; // clear answerLabel
54       [numCorrectLabel setText:@"Question 1 of 10"]; // initialize label
55
56       // get a list of all the png files in the app
57       NSMutableArray *paths = [[[NSBundle mainBundle]
58           pathsForResourcesOfType:@"png" inDirectory:nil] mutableCopy];
59
```

Fig. 6.9 | MainViewController's viewDidLoad method. (Part 1 of 2.)

```
60      // loop through each png file
61      for (NSString *filename in paths)
62      {
63          // separate the file name from the rest of the path
64          filename = [filename lastPathComponent];
65          [filenames addObject:filename]; // add the display name
66      } // end for
67
68      [paths release]; // release the paths NSMutableArray
69      [self resetQuiz]; // start a new quiz
70  } // end viewDidLoad
71
```

Fig. 6.9 | MainViewController's viewDidLoad method. (Part 2 of 2.)

Lines 57–58 obtain an array containing all of the flag images' (.png) path names. NSBundle's static *mainBundle method* returns the NSBundle for the **Flag Quiz Game** app's directory. An *NSBundle* represents a special directory in the file system that groups an app's executables and corresponding resources. The NSBundle method *pathsForResources-OfType:* returns an NSArray of NSStrings representing the paths of all files that have the specified type (.png). Calling *mutableCopy* on the NSArray returns an NSMutableArray so we can shuffle the elements later. NSArray inherits this method from NSObject. Lines 61–66 extract the file names from the paths and add them to NSArray filenames. NSString method *lastPathComponent* returns the part of the path after the last path separator (/)—this represents the file name. The method returns the entire string if there are no path separators.

Line 68 decrements paths' retain count using NSObject's *release method*. When an object's *retain count* reaches zero, its internal pointer is deleted and its dealloc method is called. All objects are created with a retain count of 1. NSObject's retain and release methods increment and decrement the retain count, respectively. In this case, paths had a retain count of 1—unchanged since the array was created (line 58). Line 68 lowers its retain count to zero, thus deallocating its memory. It's important to release objects when they're no longer needed. If another object still relied on paths (e.g., a view or a collection class) the retain count would be higher than 1 and invoking release would not destroy the paths object, thus ensuring that the object remained in memory if other parts of the app were referencing it. Calling resetQuiz (line 69) begins the game.

Method *loadNextFlag* of Class *MainViewController*
The loadNextFlag method (lines 73–206) displays a new flag and answer choices on the **MainView** (Fig. 6.10). Line 76 gets the file name of the next flag image from the end of array quizCountries. NSObject's *retain method* ensures that the NSString representing the file name is not released from memory when we remove it from the array in line 77. The correctAnswer NSString stores the flag's image name (which is its country's name). Line 81 creates a new UIImage using the flag's file name.

We now need to display the next flag's image. Lines 84–85 create a new UIImage using the next flag's file name. Because **Image Views** are immutable, it's not possible to change the image displayed by the **Image View**—a new **Image View** must be created. UIView's *removeFromSuperview method* (line 89) removes the flagView from the **MainView**, then line 85 releases it from memory. Lines 91–92 set flagView equal to a new **Image View**, then attach it to the **MainView** to display the new flag.

```
72   // called 3 seconds after the user guesses a correct flag
73   - (void)loadNextFlag
74   {
75      // get file name of the next flag
76      NSString *nextImageName = [[quizCountries lastObject] retain];
77      [quizCountries removeLastObject]; // remove that flag from list
78      correctAnswer = nextImageName; // update the correct answer
79
80      // create a new flag image using the given file name
81      UIImage *nextImage = [UIImage imageNamed:nextImageName];
82
83      // create a UIImageView for the next flag
84      UIImageView *nextImageView =
85         [[UIImageView alloc] initWithImage:nextImage];
86
87      // delete the current flagView and put nextImageView in its place
88      [nextImageView setFrame:[flagView frame]]; // copy the frame over
89      [flagView removeFromSuperview]; // remove flagView from view
90      [flagView release]; // release the flagView's memory
91      flagView = nextImageView; // reassign flagView to the new view
92      [self.view addSubview:flagView]; // add the new view to view
93
94      int offset = BAR_OFFSET + 40 * bars.count; // set offset for next bar
95
96      // add new UISegmentedControls if necessary
97      for (int i = bars.count; i < guessRows; i++)
98      {
99         // create a new bar with three empty items
100        UISegmentedControl *bar = [[UISegmentedControl alloc] initWithItems:
101           [NSArray arrayWithObjects:@"", @"", @"", nil]];
102        bar.segmentedControlStyle = UISegmentedControlStyleBar;
103
104        // make the segments stay selected only momentarily
105        bar.momentary = YES;
106
107        // tell the bar to call the given method whenever it's touched
108        [bar addTarget:self action:@selector(submitGuess:)
109           forControlEvents: UIControlEventValueChanged];
110        CGRect frame = bar.frame; // get the current frame for the bar
111        frame.origin.y = offset; // position it below the last bar
112        frame.origin.x = 20; // give it some padding on the left
113
114        // expand the bar to fill the screen with some padding on the right
115        frame.size.width = self.view.frame.size.width - 40;
116        bar.frame = frame; // assign the new frame
117        [self.view addSubview:bar]; // add the bar to the main view
118        [bars addObject:bar]; // add the bar to the list of bars
119        [bar release]; // release the bar Segmented Control
```

Fig. 6.10 | MainViewController's loadNextFlag method. (Part 1 of 3.)

```
120        offset += 40; // increase the offset so the next bar is farther down
121     } // end for
122
123     // delete bars if there are too many on the screen
124     for (int i = bars.count; i > guessRows; i--)
125     {
126        UISegmentedControl *bar = [bars lastObject]; // get the last bar
127        [bar removeFromSuperview]; // remove the bar from the main view
128        [bars removeLastObject]; // remove the bar from the list of bars
129     } // end for
130
131     // enable all the bars
132     for (UISegmentedControl *bar in bars)
133     {
134        bar.enabled = YES; // enable the Segmented Control
135
136        // enable each segment of the bar
137        for (int i = 0; i < 3; i++)
138           [bar setEnabled:YES forSegmentAtIndex:i];
139     } // end for
140
141     // shuffle filenames
142     for (int i = 0; i < filenames.count; i++)
143     {
144        // pick a random int between the current index and the end
145        int n = (random() % (filenames.count - i)) + i;
146
147        // swap the object at index i with the index randomly picked
148        [filenames exchangeObjectAtIndex:i withObjectAtIndex:n];
149     } // end for
150
151     // get the index of the string with the correct answer
152     int correct = [filenames indexOfObject:correctAnswer];
153
154     // put the correct answer at the end
155     [filenames exchangeObjectAtIndex:filenames.count - 1
156        withObjectAtIndex:correct];
157
158     int flagIndex = 0; // start adding flags from the beginning
159
160     // loop through each bar and choose incorrect answers to display
161     for (int i = 0; i < guessRows; i++)
162     {
163        // get the bar at the current index
164        UISegmentedControl *bar =
165           (UISegmentedControl *)[bars objectAtIndex:i];
166        int segmentIndex = 0;
167
168        // loop through each segment of the bar
169        while (segmentIndex < 3)
170        {
171           NSString *name; // store country name
172
```

Fig. 6.10 | MainViewController's loadNextFlag method. (Part 2 of 3.)

```
173              // if there is another file name
174              if (flagIndex < filenames.count)
175                 name = [filenames objectAtIndex:flagIndex]; // get filename
176              else // there aren't enough names to display
177                 name = nil; // set name to nil
178
179              // get the region from the file name
180              NSString *region =
181                 [[name componentsSeparatedByString:@"-"] objectAtIndex:0];
182
183              // if the region of the selected country is enabled
184              if ([[regions valueForKey:region] boolValue])
185              {
186                 [bar setTitle:[name convertToDisplayName]
187                    forSegmentAtIndex:segmentIndex];
188                 ++segmentIndex;
189              } // end if
190
191              ++flagIndex; // move to the next entry in the array
192           } // end while
193        } // end for
194
195        int z = random() % guessRows; // pick a random bar
196        UISegmentedControl *bar = [bars objectAtIndex:z];
197
198        // put the correct answer on a randomly chosen segment
199        [bar setTitle:[correctAnswer convertToDisplayName]
200           forSegmentAtIndex:random() % 3];
201
202        // update the label to display the current question number
203        [numCorrectLabel setText:[NSString stringWithFormat:
204           @"Question %i of 10", numCorrect + 1]];
205        [answerLabel setText:nil]; // clear the answer label
206     } // end method loadNextFlag
207
```

Fig. 6.10 | `MainViewController`'s `loadNextFlag` method. (Part 3 of 3.)

Lines 97–121 dynamically create **Segmented Controls** for displaying the answer countries. We initialize the loop's control variable to the current number of **Segmented Controls** (guessRows). If guessRows equals the current number of **Segmented Controls**, the loop does nothing. Otherwise, each iteration of the loop creates a **Segmented Control**. Lines 100–101 create a new **Segmented Control** containing three empty items. Line 102 specifies the **Segmented Control**'s appearance by setting its segmentedControlStyle property. Line 105 sets bar's momentary property to YES—specifying that the **Segmented Control**'s items do not remain selected once touched. Lines 108–109 specify the submitGuess: method as the action that responds to a touch of the **Segmented Control**. Lines 110–112 position the **Segmented Control** in the **MainView**. Line 115 sets frame's width to fill most of the screen and line 116 sets bar's frame property to frame. Lines 117–118 add the bar object to the **MainView** and the bars NSMutableArray. After releasing bar (line 119), we increase offset to ensure that the next **Segmented Control** is placed below this one (line 120).

If guessRows is less than the current number of **Segmented Controls**, the excess components must be deleted from the quiz. Lines 124–129 remove each extra **Segmented Control** from the superview (line 127) and the bars array (line 128). Lines 132–139 enable the items in all the **Segmented Controls**.

When the flag is updated, new answers need to be generated. To do this we shuffle the array of possible answers, then move the correct answer to the end of the array. We then choose the displayed answers from the front of the shuffled array (the correct answer will not get chosen). We overwrite a random incorrect answer with the correct one.

Lines 142–149 shuffle the answers. Line 145 chooses a random index in the array. To produce a value inside the array's bounds, the random number is scaled using the modulus operator (%) and the size of the array. The randomly chosen array element is swapped with the element at index i (line 148). This is repeated for each item in the array. Once the array is shuffled, the correct answer is located and moved to the end of the array so that it's out of the way (lines 155–156). Next, we set the title of each item in the **Segmented Controls** by picking names from the filenames array. Lines 161–193 loop through each **Segmented Control**. For each item in a **Segmented Control**, we extract the country name and region from the next element in filenames (lines 171–181). Finally, a random segment is picked to display the correct answer, which is currently at the end of the array (lines 199–200). Lines 203–205 update the quiz's **Labels** to reflect the user's progress.

Method submitGuess: of Class MainViewController
The submitGuess: method (Fig. 6.11) is called when the user submits an answer by touching a **Segmented Control** item. The selected country is determined by getting the touched segment's index (line 212). Lines 215 retrieves the title of that segment using UISegmentedControl's titleForSegmentAtIndex: method. If the chosen country matches the current flag (line 219), the answerLabel's Text property is set to "**Correct!**" (lines 222–224). All of the other segments are then disabled (lines 220–244). If the game is finished (line 249), lines 252–254 create an NSString to display the total number of guesses and the percentage accuracy. If the game isn't over, the ***performSelector:withObject:AfterDelay:*** method (inherited from class NSObject) invokes the loadNextFlag method after a three-second delay (lines 266–267). Method performSelector:withObject:AfterDelay: receives as arguments a method to call, an object to pass to the method and a time in seconds to wait before invoking the method. If the user did not choose correctly, lines 272–273 display "**Incorrect**" in red text in answerLabel. Line 276 then disables the incorrect segment so the answer cannot be selected again.

```
208  // called when the user touches one of the Segmented Control items
209  - (IBAction)submitGuess:sender
210  {
211      // get the index of the selected item
212      int index = [sender selectedSegmentIndex];
213
214      // get the title of the bar at that segment, which is the guess
215      NSString *guess = [sender titleForSegmentAtIndex:index];
216      ++totalGuesses; // increment the number of times the user has guessed
217
```

Fig. 6.11 | MainViewController's submitGuess: method. (Part 1 of 3.)

```objc
218     // if the guess is correct
219     if ([guess isEqualToString:[correctAnswer convertToDisplayName]])
220     {
221        // make the text color a medium green
222        answerLabel.textColor =
223           [UIColor colorWithRed:0.0 green:0.7 blue:0.0 alpha:1.0];
224        answerLabel.text = @"Correct!"; // set the text in the label
225
226        // get the correct answer from the correct file name
227        NSString *correct = [correctAnswer convertToDisplayName];
228
229        // loop through each bar
230        for (UISegmentedControl *bar in bars)
231        {
232           bar.enabled = NO; // don't let the user choose another answer
233
234           // loop through the bar segments
235           for (int i = 0; i < 3; i++)
236           {
237              // get the segment's title
238              NSString *title = [bar titleForSegmentAtIndex:i];
239
240              // if this segment does not have the correct choice
241              if (![title isEqualToString:correct])
242                 [bar setEnabled:NO forSegmentAtIndex:i]; // disable segment
243           } // end for
244        } // end for
245
246        ++numCorrect; // increment the number of correct answers
247
248        // is the game finished?
249        if (numCorrect == 10)
250        {
251           // create the message which includes guess number and percentage
252           NSString *message = [NSString stringWithFormat:
253              @"%i guesses, %.02f%% correct", totalGuesses,
254              1000 / (float)totalGuesses];
255
256           // create an alert to display the message
257           UIAlertView *alert = [[UIAlertView alloc] initWithTitle:
258              @"Results" message:message delegate:self cancelButtonTitle:
259              @"Reset Quiz" otherButtonTitles:nil];
260           [alert show]; // show the alert
261           [alert release]; // release the alert UIAlertView
262        } // end if
263        else // the game is not finished so load another flag
264        {
265           // load a new flag after 3 seconds
266           [self performSelector:@selector(loadNextFlag) withObject:nil
267              afterDelay:3];
268        } // end else
269     } // end if
```

Fig. 6.11 | MainViewController's submitGuess: method. (Part 2 of 3.)

```
270        else // the user has guessed incorrectly
271        {
272            answerLabel.textColor = [UIColor redColor]; // set text color to red
273            answerLabel.text = @"Incorrect"; // set the text of the label
274
275            // disable the incorrect choice
276            [sender setEnabled:NO forSegmentAtIndex:index];
277        } // end else
278    } // end method submitGuess:
279
```

Fig. 6.11 | MainViewController's submitGuess: method. (Part 3 of 3.)

Resetting the Quiz

Recall that at the end of each quiz, the submitGuess: method creates a UIAlertView displaying the user's total guesses and percentage (lines 257–260). The UIAlertView contains a **Button** titled "**Reset Quiz**." Touching this **Button** calls the alertView:clickedButtonAtIndex method (Fig. 6.12, lines 281–285), which invokes the resetQuiz method.

Note that line 261 releases the UIAlertView because it's retained automatically when it's displayed. When we built this app, we initially forgot to call release on this object. By running the app in the Instruments tool (as we did with every app), we were able to see a memory leak each time the "**Reset Quiz**" **Button** was touched to start a new quiz. We examined the leaked object in the Instruments tool, determined where the leak occurred and added the appropriate release call to eliminate the leak.

After the user completes a quiz and chooses to start a new one, the resetQuiz method (lines 294–325) returns the game to its initial state. Lines 296–297 reset numGuesses and totalGuesses to zero. Ten flags must be randomly chosen for the new quiz. We begin by picking a random file name from the filenames array (lines 303–306). Each file name begins with its region, followed by a hyphen. Line 310 extracts the region. If the region is enabled and has not already been chosen (lines 316–317), the flag's file name is added to the quizCountries array (line 319). Method setGuessRows: (lines 288–291) takes an int argument and sets it as the value of guessRows (line 290). This sets the number of rows of answers—which is used by loadNextFlag method when creating the **Segmented Controls**.

```
280    // called when the user touches the "Reset Quiz" button in the alert
281    - (void)alertView:(UIAlertView *)alertView clickedButtonAtIndex:
282        (NSInteger)buttonIndex
283    {
284        [self resetQuiz]; // reset the quiz
285    } // end method alertView:clickedButtonAtIndex:
286
287    // set the number of bars for displaying choices
288    - (void)setGuessRows:(int)rows
289    {
290        guessRows = rows;
291    } // end method setGuessRows:
292
```

Fig. 6.12 | Resetting the quiz. (Part 1 of 2.)

```
293  // reset the quiz
294  - (void)resetQuiz
295  {
296     numCorrect = 0; // reset the number of correct answers the user made
297     totalGuesses = 0; // reset the total number of guesses the user made
298     int i = 0; // initialize i to 0
299
300     // add 10 random file names to quizCountries
301     while (i < 10)
302     {
303        int n = random() % filenames.count; // choose a random index
304
305        // get the filename from the end of the path
306        NSString *filename = [filenames objectAtIndex:n];
307        NSArray *components = [filename componentsSeparatedByString:@"-"];
308
309        // get the region from the beginning of the filename
310        NSString *region = [components objectAtIndex:0];
311
312        // check if the region is enabled
313        NSNumber *regionEnabled = [regions valueForKey:region];
314
315        // if the region is enabled and it hasn't already been chosen
316        if ([regionEnabled boolValue] &&
317           ![quizCountries containsObject:filename])
318        {
319           [quizCountries addObject:filename]; // add the file to the list
320           ++i; // increment i
321        } // end if
322     } // end for
323
324     [self loadNextFlag]; // load the first flag
325  } // end method resetQuiz:
326
```

Fig. 6.12 | Resetting the quiz. (Part 2 of 2.)

Methods regions, flipsideViewControllerDidFinish: and showInfo of Class MainViewController

The regions method (Fig. 6.13, lines 328–331) is a *get* method for the regions NSMutableDictionary. Calling this method allows other classes to access the regions variable. In Objective-C, *get* methods are typically named the same as the variable they return, and *set* methods begin with the word set followed by the variable name, as in set *Variable*:.

```
327  // returns the NSMutableDictionary regions
328  - (NSMutableDictionary *)regions
329  {
330     return regions; // return the regions NSMutableDictionary
331  } // end method regions
332
```

Fig. 6.13 | showInfo and flipsideViewControllerDidFinish: methods. (Part 1 of 2.)

```
333  // called by a FlipsideViewController when the user touches "Done"
334  - (void)flipsideViewControllerDidFinish:
335     (FlipsideViewController *)controller
336  {
337     // flip the app back to the front side
338     [self dismissModalViewControllerAnimated:YES];
339  } // end method flipsideViewControllerDidFinish:
340
341  // called when the user touches the info button
342  - (IBAction)showInfo
343  {
344     // create a new FlipsideViewController
345     FlipsideViewController *controller = [[FlipsideViewController alloc]
346        initWithNibName:@"FlipsideView" bundle:nil];
347     controller.delegate = self; // set the delegate
348
349     // set the animation style to a horizontal flip
350     controller.modalTransitionStyle = UIModalTransitionStyleFlipHorizontal;
351
352     // show the flipside of the app
353     [self presentModalViewController:controller animated:YES];
354
355     // set the controls on the flipside
356     [controller setSwitches:regions]; // set each region's switch
357     [controller setSelectedIndex:guessRows - 1]; // set number of choices
358
359     [controller release]; // release the controller FlipsideViewController
360  } // end method showInfo
361
362  - (void)dealloc
363  {
364     [filenames release]; // release the filenames NSMutableArray
365     [bars release]; // release the bars NSMutableArray
366     [quizCountries release]; // release quizCountries NSMutableDictionary
367     [flagView release]; // release the flagView UIImageView
368     [answerLabel release]; // release the answerLabel UILabel
369     [numCorrectLabel release]; // release the numCorrectLabel UILabel
370     [super dealloc]; // release the superclass
371  } // end method dealloc
372  @end // end implementation of MainViewController
373
```

Fig. 6.13 | showInfo and flipsideViewControllerDidFinish: methods. (Part 2 of 2.)

The flipsideViewControllerDidFinish method (lines 334–339) is called when the user touches the **"Done" Button** on the option screen. This method (automatically generated by the **Utility Application** template) returns the user to the **MainView** by invoking its *dismissModalViewControllerAnimated: method* (line 338).

Method showInfo (Fig. 6.13, lines 342–360) creates and shows the game's options screen. Lines 345–346 create a new FlipsideViewController. Line 347 sets its delegate property to self so that the FlipSideViewController can call this class's flipside-ViewControllerDidFinish: method. It also gives controller access to NSMutableDictionary regions and the setGuessRows: method—allowing it to apply user settings from

FlipsideView. The FlipsideViewController class, which was autogenerated by the **Utility Application** template, controls the **FlipsideView.** Line 350 sets controller's *modalTransitionStyle property* to UIModalTransitionStyleFlipHorizontal—telling the transition style to flip the screen horizontally. Normally, the new view slides in from the bottom of the screen. We then tell the MainViewController to display the options screen by passing our FlipsideViewController object to presentModalViewController:animated: (line 353). Lines 356–357 set the GUI components on the **FlipsideView** to match the current quiz settings. FlipsideViewController controller can now be released, since it's no longer needed by this class (line 359). The FlipsideViewController is retained when its view appears on the screen, so the controller will not be deallocated right away. When the FlipsideViewController's view disappears from the screen, the controller will be released. If it hasn't been retained elsewhere, it will also be deallocated.

Delegation and the Decorator Design Pattern

Delegates are used frequently in iPhone app development to handle events. A delegate implements the functionality specified in a delegate protocol. When an event occurs, the component calls the delegate's appropriate method to handle the event. Delegation implements a form of the *decorator design pattern*, which allows new functionality to be added to an existing class without creating a subclass. This is particularly important in event handling, since the designers of the GUI components cannot know in advance what each app should do in response to a particular user interaction. For this reason, the GUI components use delegate protocols to specify the methods that can be called in response to events. Classes that implement these protocols enhance the functionality of existing GUI component classes by specifying what should happen when events occur.

displayName Category

Lines 374–394 implement method convertToDisplayName of NSString's displayName category (Fig. 6.14). (Categories are another example of the decorator design pattern—they're used to add functionality to a class without subclassing.)

```
374  @implementation NSString (displayName)
375  - (NSString *)convertToDisplayName
376  {
377     // get the name from the end of the string after the hyphen
378     NSString *name = [[self componentsSeparatedByString:@"-"]
379        objectAtIndex:1];
380
381     // get a mutable copy of the name for editing
382     NSMutableString *displayName = [[name mutableCopy] autorelease];
383
384     // remove the .png from the end of the name
385     [displayName replaceOccurrencesOfString:@".png" withString:@""
386        options:NSLiteralSearch range:NSMakeRange(0, displayName.length)];
387
388     // replace all underscores with spaces
389     [displayName replaceOccurrencesOfString:@"_" withString:@" "
390        options:NSLiteralSearch range:NSMakeRange(0, displayName.length)];
```

Fig. 6.14 | NSString's displayName category. (Part 1 of 2.)

```
391
392      return displayName;
393  } // end method convertToDisplayName
394  @end // end implementation of NSString
```

Fig. 6.14 | NSString's displayName category. (Part 2 of 2.)

We use NSString's componentsSeparatedByString: method and NSArray's object-AtIndex: method to remove the part of the file name before the hyphen (lines 379–380). After retrieving a mutable copy of the file name (line 382), we remove the .png file extension using NSString's replaceOccurrencesOfString:withString:options:range: method (lines 385–386). Lines 389–390 remove the underscores and line 392 returns the formatted country name. We send the ***autorelease*** message to displayName (line 382) to add displayName to the current ***autorelease pool*** (an instance of class NSAutoreleasePool). Autorelease pools contain objects that have received the autorelease message. When a pool is destroyed, it sends a release message to all the objects it contains. Typically, objects that are returned from methods are autoreleased, so that the caller is not responsible for releasing objects it did not create. Every app has an event-handling loop, generally known as the ***run loop***. Each iteration of this loop creates an autorelease pool that can be used during that iteration, and releases the pool at the end of the iteration. This ensures that autoreleased objects are released when the event handler finishes executing.

6.4.2 The FlipsideView and Class FlipsideViewController

Open **FlipsideView.xib** from the **Groups and Files** list. Double click title and change the text to Flag Quiz. Center a **Label** at the top of the app window and change its **Text** property to Number of Choices. Drag a **Segmented Control** from the **Library** to the app window below the **Label** (Fig. 6.15). Select the **Segmented Control**. In the **Inspector** window's **Attributes**

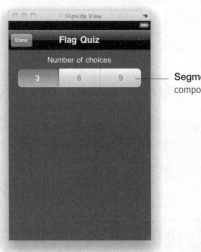

Fig. 6.15 | Segmented Control in the **FlipsideView**.

tab set the **Segments** property to 3. Each segment represents the number of country choices for each flag, where only one choice can be selected at a time. The advantage of using a **Segmented Control**, as opposed to manually adding three **Buttons**, is that a **Segmented Control** ensures that each item has the same width. Use the drop-down menu in the **Inspector Window** to set the text in each segment to read 3, 6 and 9, respectively, from left to right. Alternatively, you can edit this text by double clicking the center of each segment.

Switch components are used in this app to allow the user to exclude certain regions from the quiz. ***Switch***es correspond to boolean values and are tapped to change between the **ON** and **OFF** positions—corresponding to the values YES and NO, respectively. Drag six **Switch**es from the **Library** to the right side of the app window (Fig. 6.16). Six **Label**s are added, representing the six regions of the world. You can use Interface Builder's align tool, located in the **Inspector**'s ruler tab, to align the components. Select all the components to align, then click the appropriate button under the **Alignment** header. The "**Done**" **Button** in the top-left corner of the app was placed there by the **Utility Application** template. Its default functionality is to return to the **MainView**.

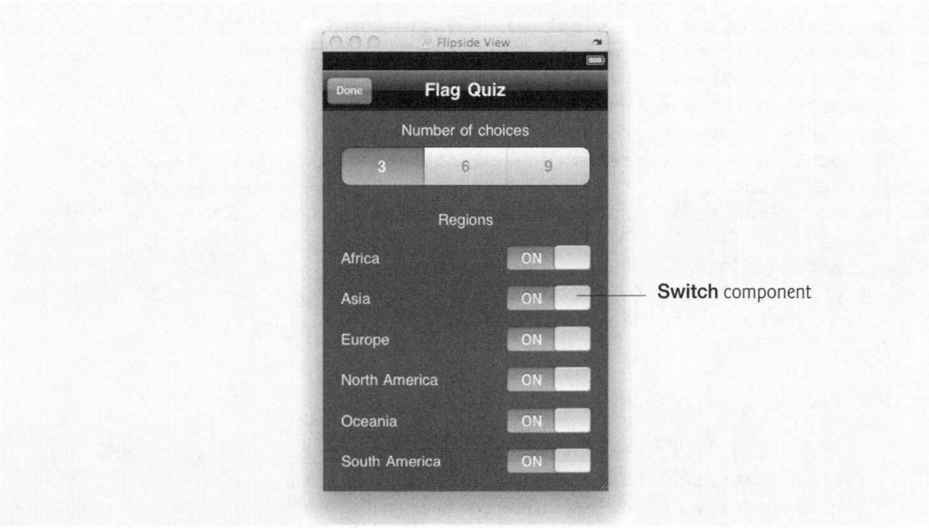

Fig. 6.16 | Switches in the **FlipsideView**.

Declaring the FlipsideViewController Class's Interface
The FlipsideViewController class controls the options screen used to customize the **Flag Quiz Game** app (Fig. 6.17). In addition to declaring the FlipsideViewController interface, FlipsideViewController.h declares the FlipsideViewControllerDelegate protocol—which is implemented by MainViewController.

```
1   // FlipsideViewController.h
2   // Controller for the flipside of the Flag Quiz app
3   // Implementation in FlipsideViewController.m
4   @protocol FlipsideViewControllerDelegate;
```

Fig. 6.17 | FlipsideViewController interface declaration. (Part 1 of 2.)

```
5
6   @interface FlipsideViewController : UIViewController
7   {
8       // stores an object that will receive the delegate messages
9       id <FlipsideViewControllerDelegate> delegate;
10
11      // control for selecting the number of choices in the quiz
12      IBOutlet UISegmentedControl *choicesControl;
13
14      // switches to include/exclude each region in the quiz
15      IBOutlet UISwitch *africaSwitch;
16      IBOutlet UISwitch *asiaSwitch;
17      IBOutlet UISwitch *europeSwitch;
18      IBOutlet UISwitch *northAmericaSwitch;
19      IBOutlet UISwitch *oceaniaSwitch;
20      IBOutlet UISwitch *southAmericaSwitch;
21  } // end instance variable declarations
22
23  // declare delegate and outlets as properties
24  @property(nonatomic, assign) id <FlipsideViewControllerDelegate> delegate;
25  @property(nonatomic, retain) IBOutlet UISegmentedControl *choicesControl;
26  @property(nonatomic, retain) IBOutlet UISwitch *africaSwitch;
27  @property(nonatomic, retain) IBOutlet UISwitch *asiaSwitch;
28  @property(nonatomic, retain) IBOutlet UISwitch *europeSwitch;
29  @property(nonatomic, retain) IBOutlet UISwitch *northAmericaSwitch;
30  @property(nonatomic, retain) IBOutlet UISwitch *oceaniaSwitch;
31  @property(nonatomic, retain) IBOutlet UISwitch *southAmericaSwitch;
32
33  - (IBAction)done; // return to the MainView
34  - (void)setSwitches:(NSDictionary *)dictionary; // set the Switch's states
35  - (void)setSelectedIndex:(int)index; // set selected segment
36  @end // end interface FlipsideViewController
37
38  @protocol FlipsideViewControllerDelegate  // begin delegate protocol
39
40  // notifies MainViewController that the "Done" button was touched
41  - (void)flipsideViewControllerDidFinish:
42      (FlipsideViewController *)controller;
43  @end // end protocol FlipsideViewControllerDelegate
```

Fig. 6.17 | FlipsideViewController interface declaration. (Part 2 of 2.)

Line 9 declares a variable of type id that implements the FlipsideViewControllerDelegate protocol. This will be used to call the flipsideViewControllerDidFinish method on the object that implements this method. Outlets are declared for the **Segmented Control** (line 12) and all of the **Switch**es used in the options screen (lines 15–20). Line 24 declares the variable delegate (of type id) as a property. The **assign** keyword specifies that the generated *set* method simply assigns a new value to the pointer without releasing the old object or retaining the new one. This is typical with delegates. Lines 25–31 declare each of FlipsideViewController's outlets as properties.

Class FlipsideViewController contains three methods—done, setSwitches and setSelectedIndex (lines 33–35). The done method applies all of the option settings and returns the user to the **MainView**. Methods setSwitches and setSelectedIndex update the GUI components on the **FlipsideView** to reflect the current quiz settings.

Lines 38–42 declare the FlipsideViewDelegate protocol. Classes implementing this protocol define the flipsideViewControllerDidFinish: method. MainViewController implements this protocol—using the flipsideViewControllerDidFinish method to hide the **FlipsideView** when the "**Done**" **Button** is touched.

Implementing the FlipsideViewController class

The FlipsideViewController class defines all of the methods that coordinate data between the **MainView** and the **FlipsideView** (Fig. 6.18). This includes applying option settings to the quiz and initializing the **FlipsideView** to reflect the current settings. The **FlipsideView** is recreated each time the user touches the **Info Button**.

```
1   //  FlipsideViewController.m
2   //  Controller for the flipside of the Flag Quiz app
3   #import "FlipsideViewController.h"
4   #import "MainViewController.h"
5
6   @implementation FlipsideViewController
7
8   // generate get and set methods for our properties
9   @synthesize delegate;
10  @synthesize choicesControl;
11  @synthesize africaSwitch;
12  @synthesize asiaSwitch;
13  @synthesize europeSwitch;
14  @synthesize northAmericaSwitch;
15  @synthesize oceaniaSwitch;
16  @synthesize southAmericaSwitch;
17
18  // called when the main view finishes initializing
19  - (void)viewDidLoad
20  {
21     // set the background color to the standard background color
22     self.view.backgroundColor = [UIColor viewFlipsideBackgroundColor];
23  } // end method viewDidLoad
24
25  // called when the user touches the "Done" button
26  - (IBAction)done
27  {
28     // if none of the switches are selected
29     if (!africaSwitch.on && !asiaSwitch.on && !europeSwitch.on &&
30        !oceaniaSwitch.on && ! northAmericaSwitch.on &&
31        !southAmericaSwitch.on)
32     {
33        // show an alert prompting the user to select at least one region
34        UIAlertView *alert = [[UIAlertView alloc] initWithTitle:@"Error"
35           message:@"Please select at least one region" delegate:self
36           cancelButtonTitle:@"Ok" otherButtonTitles:nil];
37        [alert show]; // show the alert
```

Fig. 6.18 │ FlipsideViewController class implementation. (Part 1 of 3.)

```
38          [alert release]; // release the alert UIAlertView
39       } // end if
40       else
41       {
42          // get the selected index of choicesControl
43          int index = [choicesControl selectedSegmentIndex];
44
45          // update the number of guess rows on the frontside
46          [(MainViewController *)self.delegate setGuessRows:index + 1];
47
48          // update the enabled regions on the fronside with the switch values
49          NSMutableDictionary *regions =
50             [(MainViewController *)self.delegate regions];
51          [regions setValue:[NSNumber numberWithBool:africaSwitch.on]
52             forKey: @"Africa"];
53          [regions setValue:[NSNumber numberWithBool:asiaSwitch.on]
54              forKey: @"Asia"];
55          [regions setValue:[NSNumber numberWithBool:europeSwitch.on]
56              forKey: @"Europe"];
57          [regions setValue:[NSNumber numberWithBool:
58             northAmericaSwitch.on] forKey:@"North_America"];
59          [regions setValue:[NSNumber numberWithBool:oceaniaSwitch.on]
60             forKey: @"Oceania"];
61          [regions setValue:[NSNumber numberWithBool:
62             southAmericaSwitch.on] forKey:@"South_America"];
63
64          // create a new quiz on the frontside
65          [(MainViewController *)self.delegate resetQuiz];
66
67          // flip back to the frontside
68          [self.delegate flipsideViewControllerDidFinish:self];
69       } // end else
70    } // end method done
71
72    // update the switches with values from the frontside
73    - (void)setSwitches:(NSDictionary *)dictionary
74    {
75       // update each switch with its corresponding entry in the dictionary
76       [africaSwitch setOn:[[dictionary valueForKey:@"Africa"] boolValue]];
77       [asiaSwitch setOn:[[dictionary valueForKey:@"Asia"] boolValue]];
78       [europeSwitch setOn:[[dictionary valueForKey:@"Europe"] boolValue]];
79       [northAmericaSwitch setOn:
80          [[dictionary valueForKey:@"North_America"] boolValue]];
81       [oceaniaSwitch setOn:[[dictionary valueForKey:@"Oceania"] boolValue]];
82       [southAmericaSwitch setOn:
83          [[dictionary valueForKey:@"South_America"] boolValue]];
84    } // end method setSwitches:
85
86    // update choicesControl with the value from the frontside
87    - (void)setSelectedIndex:(int)index
88    {
89       choicesControl.selectedSegmentIndex = index;
90    } // end method setSelectedIndex:
```

Fig. 6.18 | FlipsideViewController class implementation. (Part 2 of 3.)

```
 91
 92    // free FlipsideViewController's memory
 93    - (void)dealloc
 94    {
 95        [choicesControl release]; // release choicesControl UISegmentedControl
 96        [africaSwitch release]; // release africaSwitch UISwitch
 97        [asiaSwitch release]; // release asiaSwitch UISwitch
 98        [europeSwitch release]; // release europeSwitch UISwitch
 99        [northAmericaSwitch release]; // release northAmericaSwitch UISwitch
100        [oceaniaSwitch release]; // release oceaniaSwitch UISwitch
101        [southAmericaSwitch release]; // release southAmericaSwitch UISwitch
102        [super dealloc]; // call the superclass's dealloc method
103    } // end dealloc method
104    @end // end FlipsideViewController class
```

Fig. 6.18 | `FlipsideViewController` class implementation. (Part 3 of 3.)

Initialization

The `viewDidLoad` method (lines 19–23) sets **FlipsideView**'s background color when the view is created. The `setSwitches:` and `setSelectedIndex:` methods are called by the `MainViewController` class immediately after creating the **FlipsideView** to set the GUI components to reflect the current quiz configuration.

done and setSwitches Methods of Class `MainViewController`

The done method (lines 26–70) returns to the **MainView** when the user touches the "**Done**" **Button**. We want to switch **View**s only if there's at least one region included in the quiz. If none of the **Switch**es are in the **ON** position (lines 29–31), a **UIAlert** (lines 34–36) tells the user to select a region, and the method exits without returning to the **MainView**. Otherwise, we retrieve the selected index from our **Segmented Control** (line 43) and update the number of answer choices in the quiz by invoking `setGuessRows:` on `delegate` (line 46).

Lines 49–62 update `delegate`'s regions dictionary by invoking NSMutableDictionary's `setValue:forKey:` method—matching each key with the state of its respective **Switch**. Line 65 starts a new quiz and line 68 informs the delegate that the user touched the **Button**. We assume that `delegate` implements the `flipsideViewControllerDidFinish:` method—this might not be the case, since classes that implement a protocol don't have to implement every method. We know it is implemented here, however, because we defined the method in `MainViewController.m`.

The `setSwitches:` method (lines 73–84) sets each **Switch** to display whether that region's flags are included in the quiz. The method updates the **Switch**es to match an NSMutableDictionary it receives from `MainViewController`. This dictionary stores boolean values for each region—specifying whether or not that region is included in the quiz. The `setSelectedIndex` method (lines 87–90) selects an item in the `choicesControl` **Segmented Control**. The selected item's text matches the number of possible answers displayed for each flag.

6.5 Wrap-Up

In this chapter we created the **Flag Quiz Game** app, testing the user's knowledge of the world's flags. We used the **Utility Application** template and UIViewController so that our app could have a quiz game on the front side and game options on the flipside. On the **FlipsideView**, the user could select the regions included in the quiz and the number of answers to display. The quiz selected random flags and answers, and used a **Segmented Control** to display the answers. We began to consider memory management—retaining objects when they might be needed beyond the current scope and releasing them when they were no longer needed to avoid memory leaks.

In Chapter 7, you'll create a game called **Spot-On** using Cocoa's Core Animation libraries. This app will test the user's reflexes by animating multiple custom **Views** (spots) that the user must touch before they disappear. You'll manually process touch gestures for the first time. The spots will be animated using Core Animation, and the AVFoundation framework will be used to add sound effects to the game.

7

Spot-On Game App
Using UIView and Detecting Touches

OBJECTIVES

In this chapter you'll learn:

- To create a simple game app that's easy to code and fun to play.

- To animate **View**s using Core Animation.

- To use **UIImageView**s to display custom images.

- To add sound to your app using the AVFoundation framework.

- To process multitouch gestures when several fingers simultaneously touch the iPhone.

- To create an app containing a single **UIView**, using the **View-based Application** template.

Outline

7.1 Introduction

7.2 Test-Driving the **Spot-On Game** App

7.3 Overview of the Technologies

7.4 Building the App

7.5 Wrap-Up

7.1 Introduction

The **Spot-On Game** tests your reflexes by requiring you to touch moving spots before they disappear (Fig. 7.1). The spots shrink as they move—the longer a spot is on the screen the harder it is to touch. The game begins on level one and each higher level is reached by touching 10 spots. The spots move faster at higher levels—making the game increasingly challenging. When you touch a spot, the app makes a popping sound and the spot turns green then fades away (Fig. 7.2). The player receives points (10 times the current level) for each touched spot. Accuracy is important—any touch that isn't on a spot decreases the score by 20 times the current level. The score is tallied in the top-left corner of the screen. The player begins the game with *three* lives, which are displayed in the bottom-left corner of the app. If a spot disappears before it's touched, the player hears a flushing sound and loses a life. The player gains a life for each new level reached, up to a maximum of *seven* lives. When all the lives are lost, the game ends (Fig. 7.3).

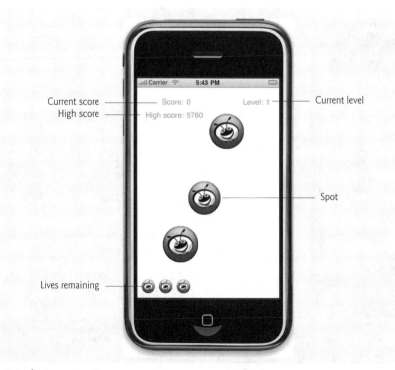

Fig. 7.1 | Spot-On Game app.

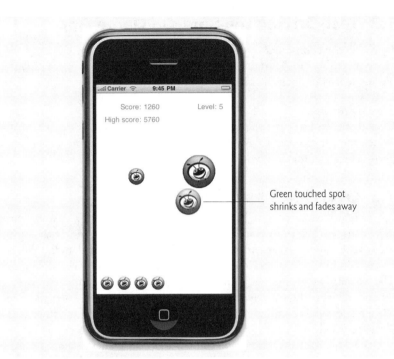

Fig. 7.2 | **Spot-On Game** with a touched spot.

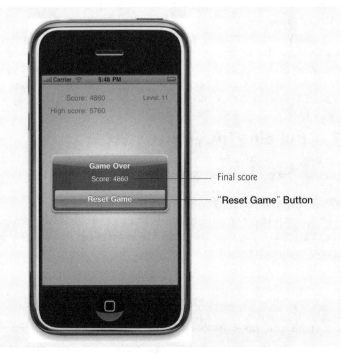

Fig. 7.3 | **Game Over** alert.

7.2 Test-Driving the Spot-On Game App

Opening the completed application
Open the directory containing the **Spot On Game** app project. Double click Spot-On.xcodeproj to open the project in Xcode.

Playing the app
Click **Build and Go** to run the app in the iPhone Simulator. The game begins immediately. Touch the red spots as fast as you can! Don't delay in touching a spot—if the spot disappears before you touch it, you'll lose a life!

7.3 Overview of the Technologies

For each animated spot, we'll use a UIImageView to display a custom image. We change this image when a spot is touched by setting the UIImageView's image property to a new UIImage. In SpotOnViewController, we'll implement touch handling for our game. We'll process multi-touch events—allowing the player to touch several spots simultaneously. The touchesBegan method inherited from UIView gets touch information from the iPhone. This method receives pointers to UITouch objects when the screen is touched. We'll retrieve the coordinates of each touch, and use that information to determine if the player touched a spot.

We'll use the Core Animation framework to animate the spots—making them move, get smaller and disappear. As you'll see, UIImageView has built-in animation methods, which provide easy access to basic animations. We'll also access the underlying CALayer (Core Animation Layer) to perform more complex functions that are not provided by class UIImageView.

Sounds are added to the app using the AVFoundation framework. AVAudioPlayers are used to play back .wav files stored on the iPhone. Each file will have an associated AVAudioPlayer object to control playback of that file. The NSObject method performSelector:withObject:afterDelay: allows us to call functions after a specified delay (in seconds). We use this to add the first three spots to a new game at one-second intervals.

7.4 Building the App

To begin, open XCode and create a new project. Select the **View-based Application** template and name the project SpotOn.

Declaring the SpotOnViewController Interface
The SpotOnViewController (Fig. 7.4) manages the game, keeping track of the current score, high score, current level and lives remaining. It's also responsible for animating the spots, and touch handling.

```
1   // Fig. 7.4: SpotOnViewController.h
2   // SpotOnViewController interface declaration.
3   // Implementation in SpotOnViewController.m
4   #import <UIKit/UIKit.h>
```

Fig. 7.4 | SpotOnViewController interface declaration. (Part 1 of 2.)

```
5   #import <CoreGraphics/CGBase.h>
6   #import <QuartzCore/CoreAnimation.h>
7   #import <AVFoundation/AVFoundation.h>
8
9   @interface SpotOnViewController : UIViewController <UIAlertViewDelegate>
10  {
11     IBOutlet UILabel *scoreLabel; // label for displaying the score
12     IBOutlet UILabel *levelLabel; // label for displaying the level
13     IBOutlet UILabel *highScoreLabel; // label for displaying high score
14     NSMutableArray *spots; // stores the spot images
15     NSMutableArray *lives; // stores the Views representing remaining lives
16     AVAudioPlayer *hitPlayer; // plays a sound when a spot is touched
17     AVAudioPlayer *missPlayer; // plays a sound when a spot is missed
18     AVAudioPlayer *disappearPlayer; // plays a sound when a spot disappears
19     int spotsTouched; // number of spots touched
20     int score; // current score
21     int level; // current level
22     float drawTime; // duration that each spot remains on the screen
23     BOOL gameOver; // has the game ended?
24     UIImage *touchedImage; // touched spot image
25     UIImage *untouchedImage; // untouched spot image
26  } // end instance variable declaration
27
28  // declare our outlets as properties
29  @property(nonatomic, retain) IBOutlet UILabel *scoreLabel;
30  @property(nonatomic, retain) IBOutlet UILabel *levelLabel;
31  @property(nonatomic, retain) IBOutlet UILabel *highScoreLabel;
32
33  - (void)resetGame; // starts a new game
34  - (void)addNewSpot; // adds a new spot to the game
35
36  // called when spots disappear
37  - (void)finishedAnimation:(NSString *)animationId finished:(BOOL)finished
38     context:(void *)context;
39  - (void)touchedSpot:(UIImageView *)spot; // called when a spot is touched
40  @end // end interface SpotOnViewController
```

Fig. 7.4 | SpotOnViewController interface declaration. (Part 2 of 2.)

SpotOnViewContoller's instance variables are declared at lines 11–25. Labels score-Label and levelLabel display the current score and level (lines 11–12). NSMutableArrays spots and lives store the UIImageViews representing the current spots and the player's remaining lives (lines 14–15). *AVAudioPlayer* objects are used to play sound files included in the app (lines 16–18). Each AVAudioPlayer is initialized with a single sound file, which the AVAudioPlayer can play. The number of spots already touched is stored in spots-Touched, which is used to calculate the score (line 19). The level variable stores the current level (line 21). The time it takes spots to disappear is stored in drawTime (line 22). This decreases by five percent each time a new level is reached. The SpotOnViewController class contains four methods (lines 33–39):

- resetGame—resets the score and begins a new game.
- addNewSpot—adds a new spot to the display.

- finishedAnimation:finished:context:—called when a spot disappears from the screen. This method creates a new spot, determines if the finished spot was ever touched, and decreases the remaining lives if it wasn't.

- touchedSpot—increases the score when a spot is touched. It will increase the level if the touched spot was the tenth of the current level.

Building the Interface

Double-click the file SpotOnViewController.xib to open it in Interface Builder. When it opens, double-click **View** in the window labeled **SpotOnViewController.xib** to edit the contents of the view. Drag three **Labels** onto the view and arrange them as you see in Fig. 7.5. Change the opacity of each **Label** to 50% by editing the **Color** property in the **Inspector**.

Fig. 7.5 | SpotOnViewController's user interface.

Next, connect the outlets from SpotOnViewController to their corresponding **Labels**. In the window labeled **MainViewController.xib**, the MainViewController object is represented by the object named **File's Owner**. If you select this object, you'll see the outlets you defined in MainViewController.h appear in the **Inspector**. Connect each of these outlets to the appropriate **Label**.

Implementing the SpotOnViewController Class

Exit Interface Builder and open the file SpotOnViewController.m in XCode. The SpotOnViewContoller class controls the game's animation. It creates, destroys and displays spots and processes the player's touch gestures.

Figure 7.6 shows the viewDidLoad method (lines 14–65), which initializes the game when the main view loads. After initializing the superclass view members (line 16), we seed a random number generator and initialize the NSMutableArrays spots and lives (lines 17–19). Lines 22–23 load the spot UIImages. NSBundle's pathForResource:ofType: method is used to retrieve the full file path for hit.wav (lines 26–27). We create an NSURL to store the path of the hit sound (line 30) and use the path to initialize the hitPlayer AVAudioPlayer (lines 33–34). Line 35 sets hitPlayer's volume to 0.3 (on a scale of 0 to 1). Lines 38–62 perform similiar operations to initialize the other sound effects. Line 64 starts the new game by calling the resetGame method.

```
1   //  Fig. 7.6: SpotOnViewController.m
2   //  Controller for the Spot On Game app
3   #import "SpotOnViewController.h"
4   static const int BALL_RADIUS = 40;
5
6   @implementation SpotOnViewController
7
8   // generate get and set methods for our properties
9   @synthesize scoreLabel;
10  @synthesize levelLabel;
11  @synthesize highScoreLabel;
12
13  // called when the view finishes loading
14  - (void)viewDidLoad
15  {
16      [super viewDidLoad]; // pass the message to the superclass
17      srandom(time(0)); // seed random number generation
18      spots = [[NSMutableArray alloc] init]; // initialize spots
19      lives = [[NSMutableArray alloc] init]; // initialize lives
20
21      // initialize the two spot images
22      touchedImage = [UIImage imageNamed:@"touched.png"];
23      untouchedImage = [UIImage imageNamed:@"untouched.png"];
24
25      // get the path of the sound file
26      NSString *soundPath = [[NSBundle mainBundle] pathForResource:@"hit"
27          ofType:@"wav"];
28
29      // create a URL with the given path
30      NSURL *fileURL = [[NSURL alloc] initFileURLWithPath:soundPath];
31
32      // initialize the AVAudioPlayer with the sound file
33      hitPlayer = [[AVAudioPlayer alloc] initWithContentsOfURL:fileURL
34          error:nil];
35      hitPlayer.volume = 0.3; // set hitPlayer's volume
36
37      // get the path of the sound file
38      soundPath = [[NSBundle mainBundle] pathForResource:@"miss"
39          ofType:@"wav"];
40
41      // create a URL with the given path
42      [fileURL release];
43      fileURL = [[NSURL alloc] initFileURLWithPath:soundPath];
44
45      // initialize the AVAudioPlayer with the sound file
46      missPlayer = [[AVAudioPlayer alloc] initWithContentsOfURL:fileURL
47          error:nil];
```

Fig. 7.6 | SpotOnViewController's viewDidLoad method. (Part 1 of 2.)

```
48      missPlayer.volume = 0.7; // set missPlayer's volume
49
50      // get the path of the sound file
51      soundPath =
52         [[NSBundle mainBundle] pathForResource:@"disappear" ofType:@"wav"];
53
54      // create a URL with the given path
55      [fileURL release];
56      fileURL = [[NSURL alloc] initFileURLWithPath:soundPath];
57
58      // initialize the AVAudioPlayer with the sound file
59      disappearPlayer =
60         [[AVAudioPlayer alloc] initWithContentsOfURL:fileURL error:nil];
61      disappearPlayer.volume = 0.3; // set disappearPlayer's volume
62      [fileURL release]; // release the fileURL NSURL
63
64      [self resetGame]; // begin a new game
65   } // end method viewDidLoad
66
```

Fig. 7.6 | SpotOnViewController's viewDidLoad method. (Part 2 of 2.)

Method resetGame of class SpotOnViewController

The resetGame method (Fig. 7.7) removes any spots from previous games and sets the game's instance variables to their initial states. The method adds the new game's first three spots at one-second intervals.

```
67   // removes old objects and begins a new game
68   - (void)resetGame
69   {
70      [spots removeAllObjects]; // empty the array of spots
71      drawTime = 3.0; // reset the draw time
72      spotsTouched = 0; // reset the number of spots touched
73      score = 0; // reset the score
74      level = 1; // reset the level
75      [scoreLabel setText:@"Score: 0"]; // reset the score label
76      [levelLabel setText:@"Level: 1"]; // reset the level label
77
78      // get the high score from the preferences file
79      NSNumber *highScore =
80         [[NSUserDefaults standardUserDefaults] valueForKey:@"highScore"];
81
82      // if there isn't a current high score
83      if (highScore == nil)
84         highScore = [NSNumber numberWithInt:0]; // set the high score to 0
85
86      // update the high score label with the high score
87      [highScoreLabel setText:
88         [NSString stringWithFormat:@"High Score: %@", highScore]];
89      gameOver = NO; // reset the gameOver boolean
```

Fig. 7.7 | SpotOnViewController's resetGame method. (Part 1 of 2.)

```
90
91      // add three lives
92      for (int i = 0; i < 3; i++)
93      {
94          UIImageView *life = [[UIImageView alloc]
95              initWithImage:touchedImage];
96
97          // position the views next to each other at the bottom left
98          CGRect frame = CGRectMake(10 + 40 * i, 420, 30, 30);
99          life.frame = frame; // assign the new frame
100         [lives addObject:life]; // add the view to the list of lives
101         [self.view addSubview:life]; // add the image to the view
102         [life release];
103     } // end for
104
105     // add three new spots, each spaced by a one-second delay
106     [self addNewSpot];
107     [self performSelector:@selector(addNewSpot) withObject:nil
108         afterDelay:1.0]; // call addNewSpot after 1 second
109     [self performSelector:@selector(addNewSpot) withObject:nil
110         afterDelay:2.0]; // call addNewSpot after 2 seconds
111 } // end method resetGame
112
```

Fig. 7.7 | SpotOnViewController's resetGame method. (Part 2 of 2.)

Lines 70–76 reset SpotOnViewController's instance variables to their states for the start of a new game. Lines 79–80 get an NSNumber representing the current high score. *NSUserDefault's standardUserDefaults method* returns the *NSUserDefault* representing this app's preferences. This information is stored in the app's .plist file. *NSUserDefault's valueForKey: method* returns the value for highScore saved in this file. If there is no current high score (line 83), we set highScore to 0. Lines 87–88 update the high-score label.

Lines 92–103 add three small versions of the green spot image to the lower-left corner of the app. These images represent the player's remaining lives.

To begin the game, we must add the initial spots to the screen. Lines 106–110 create three new spots, invoking addNewSpot three times. The second and third calls to addNewSpot are performed by NSObject's performSelector:withObject:afterDelay: method to add these spots at one-second intervals.

Method addNewSpot of class SpotOnViewController
The addNewSpot method (Fig. 7.8) creates new UIImageViews and adds them to the display. Once a new spot is added, its beginSpotAnimation method is called to start its animation.

```
113 // adds a new spot at a random location
114 - (void)addNewSpot
115 {
```

Fig. 7.8 | SpotOnViewController's addNewSpot method. (Part 1 of 2.)

```
116    // get the view width and height
117    float viewWidth = self.view.bounds.size.width;
118    float viewHeight = self.view.bounds.size.height;
119
120    // pick random coordinates inside the view
121    float x = random() % (int)(viewWidth - 2 * BALL_RADIUS);
122    float y = random() % (int)(viewHeight - 2 * BALL_RADIUS);
123
124    // create a new spot
125    UIImageView *spot = [[UIImageView alloc] initWithImage:untouchedImage];
126    [spots addObject:spot]; // add the spot to the spots NSMutableArray
127    [self.view addSubview:spot]; // add the spot to the main view
128
129    // set the frame of variable spot with the random coordinates
130    [spot setFrame:CGRectMake(x, y, BALL_RADIUS * 2, BALL_RADIUS * 2)];
131
132    // delay beginning animation to give the spot time to redraw
133    [self performSelector:@selector(beginSpotAnimation:) withObject:spot
134       afterDelay:0.01];
135
136    [spot release]; // release the spot UIImageView
137 } // end method addNewSpot
138
```

Fig. 7.8 | SpotOnViewController's addNewSpot method. (Part 2 of 2.)

Lines 117–118 retrieve the screen size. We access the SpotOnViewController's UIView, which has a bounds property that, in turn, contains a size property from which we obtain the view's width and height. We then compute random *x*- and *y*-coordinates in that area (lines 121–122). Line 127 invokes UIView's addSubview method to attach the UIImageView representing a spot to the main view. The UIImageView's frame is created at the random coordinates (line 130) and the method beginSpotAnimation is invoked, starting the UIImageView's movement (lines 133–134). A small (.01 second) delay is used to allow the spot to render before the animation begins. Line 136 releases the UIImageView because it's no longer needed by this method; howerver, the UIImageView isn't deallocated, because it was added to the spots NSMutableArray and as a subview of the main view—both of which automatically send a retain messages to the object being added.

Method beginSpotAnimation of class SpotOnViewController

The beginSpotAnimation method (Fig. 7.9) selects random coordinates inside the main view and animates the UIImageView to that point. This method and method beginSpot-EndAnimation (Fig. 7.12) are not declared in SpotOnViewController.h—this is required in Objective-C only for methods that will be called from outside the class.

First, we pick the coordinates to which the UIImageView will move (lines 143–148). We then move the UIImageView to that point by using a *Core Animation block*—a section of code in which changes to the UIView are animated rather than performed immediately. A Core Animation block always begins with UIView's **beginAnimations:context: *method*** (line 150) and ends with its **commitAnimations *method*** (line 163).

The first parameter to beginAnimations:withContext: is the animation identifier. This doesn't affect the animation—it's used only to identify the animation in the delegate

```
139  // start the animation of the given spot
140  - (void)beginSpotAnimation:(UIImageView *)spot
141  {
142      // get the width and height of view
143      float viewWidth = [self.view bounds].size.width;
144      float viewHeight = [self.view bounds].size.height;
145
146      // pick random coordinates inside the view
147      float x = random() % (int)(viewWidth - 2 * BALL_RADIUS);
148      float y = random() % (int)(viewHeight - 2 * BALL_RADIUS);
149
150      [UIView beginAnimations:nil context:spot]; // begin the animation block
151      [UIView setAnimationDelegate:self]; // set the delegate as this object
152
153      // call the given method of the delegate when the animation ends
154      [UIView setAnimationDidStopSelector:
155          @selector(finishedAnimation:finished:context:)];
156      [UIView setAnimationDuration:drawTime]; // set the animation length
157
158      // make the animation start slow and speed up
159      [UIView setAnimationCurve:UIViewAnimationCurveEaseIn];
160
161      // set the ending location of the spot
162      [spot setFrame:CGRectMake(x + BALL_RADIUS, y + BALL_RADIUS, 0, 0)];
163      [UIView commitAnimations]; // end the animation block
164  } // end method beginSpotAnimation:
165
```

Fig. 7.9 | SpotOnViewController's beginSpotAnimation: method.

methods so that separate animations can be treated differently by the delagate. We pass nil because we won't need the identifier in this app. The second argument represents the view that the delegate will manipulate. We pass the animating view (spot) because we'll need to interact with it in the delegate methods. Line 151 sets the SpotOnViewController as the animation's delegate. This means that the SpotOnViewController will be notified when this animation starts and stops. Next, we specify the message sent (i.e., the method that is called on the delegate) when the animation stops by calling UIView's ***setAnimationDidStopSelector: method*** (lines 154–155).

UIView's setAnimationDuration: method (line 156) sets drawTime as the time it takes the animation to complete. This means that the life of a spot—from when it first appears on the screen until it disappears—takes place in this time frame. Line 159 uses UIView's ***setAnimationCurve: method*** to specify that the UIImageView will begin moving slowly, then accelerate over the course of the animation. After setting the ending location of the animation using the setFrame: method (line 162), line 163 calls UIView's commit-Animations method to end the Core Animation block. The animation begins as soon as beginSpotAnimation: finishes executing.

Method touchesBegan:withEvent: of class SpotOnViewController

Touch handling is performed in the touchesBegan:withEvent: method (Fig. 7.10, lines 167–218), which is called every time the player touches the screen. We override it to make spots disappear when the player touches them. The method's first argument is an NSSet containing all the new touches. An *NSSet* is a collection of unique objects. In this case, it contains one *UITouch* object for each new touch on the screen. A UITouch represents a single touch on the screen. It contains information such as where and when the touch occurred and the type of touch.

```
166  // method is called when the player touches the screen
167  - (void)touchesBegan:(NSSet *)touches withEvent:(UIEvent *)event
168  {
169     BOOL hitSpot = NO; // initialize hitSpot
170
171     for (UITouch *touch in touches) // loop through all the new touches
172     {
173        // get the location of the touch in the main view
174        CGPoint point = [touch locationInView:self.view];
175
176        // loop through all the spots to check if the player hit any;
177        // iterate backwards so foreground spots get checked first
178        for (int i = spots.count - 1; i >= 0 && !hitSpot; i--)
179        {
180           UIImageView *spot = [spots objectAtIndex:i];
181
182           // We need to get the current location of spot, but the frame
183           // of spot is already set to its ending location. To get the
184           // displayed frame, we need to access the Core Animation layer.
185           CGRect frame = [[spot.layer presentationLayer] frame];
186
187           // compute the point at the center of the spot
188           CGPoint origin =  CGPointMake(frame.origin.x + frame.size.width /
189              2, frame.origin.y + frame.size.height / 2);
190
191           // compute the distance between the spot's center and the touch
192           float distance =
193              pow(origin.x - point.x, 2) + pow(origin.y - point.y, 2);
194           distance = sqrt(distance); // square root to complete formula
195
196           // check if the touch is within the spot
197           if (distance <= frame.size.width / 2)
198           {
199              spot.image = touchedImage; // change to touched spot image
200              [self touchedSpot:spot]; // call the touchedSpot: method
201              hitSpot = YES; // a spot has been touched
202           } // end if
203        } // end for
204     } // end for
205
206     if (!hitSpot) // if the player missed
207     {
208        [missPlayer play]; // play the miss sound
209        score -= 20 * level; // remove some points
210
211        if (score < 0)
212           score = 0;
```

Fig. 7.10 | SpotOnViewController's touchesBegan:withEvent: method. (Part 1 of 2.)

```
213
214        // update the score label
215        [scoreLabel setText:
216            [NSString stringWithFormat:@"Score: %i", score]];
217    } // end if
218 } // end method touchesBegan:withEvent:
219
```

Fig. 7.10 | SpotOnViewController's touchesBegan:withEvent: method. (Part 2 of 2.)

Lines 171–204 loop through each UITouch object. To get the location of a touch, we call UITouch's *locationInView: method*, which returns a CGPoint containing the location of the touch in the specified UIView (line 174). Lines 178–203 loop through each spot UIImageView, determining if the UITouch is in the UIImageView's bounds. If the player touches two spots that overlap, we want only the top one to be destroyed. To accomplish this, we loop through the array of spots backwards, so the top UIImageView is checked first.

Next, we determine the UIImageView's location. The UIImageView is currently being animated, so its frame corresponds to where the animation eventually finishes. To find the location when the player touches the screen, we need to access its Core Animation layer. UIImageView's *layer property* provides access to UIImageView's Core Animation layer (an object of class CALayer). CALayer's *presentationLayer method* returns a copy of the layer in the position currently shown on the screen. The frame of this layer is the one we want.

Lines 188–189 determine the UIImageView's center, then lines 192–194 get the distance between the player's touch and the UIImageView's center (lines 192–194). If the player touched inside the UIImageView (line 197), we change the spot's image property to display the green spot image and invoke SpotOnViewController's touchedSpot method. Otherwise, we play a sound effect indicating a miss (line 208), decrease the score by the product of 20 and the current level (line 209). If the score is below 0 (line 211), we set it to 0 to avoid negative scores (line 212). Lines 215–216 update scoreLabel appropriately.

The Chain of Responsibility Design Pattern

The touchesBegan:withEvent: method responds to events in a manner that is consistent with the *chain-of-responsibility design pattern*. In this pattern, a series of processing objects is given the opportunity to respond to a so-called command object—typically, an event. If the first object in the chain cannot handle the event (i.e., no event handler was registered for that event), the event is passed to the next object in the chain. If the event gets handled, processing stops.

In Cocoa, the *responder chain* is a series of linked objects that respond to events. First the view that the user interacts with receives the event. If that object does not have an event handler, then the event is passed to the next object in the chain (i.e., the containing view), and so on. When an event such as a touch occurs, the event is sent down the responder chain until an object is encountered that has an appropriate event handler to process the event. If none of the objects can handle the event, it's ignored.

Method touchedSpot: of class SpotOnViewController

SpotOnViewController's touchedSpot: method (Fig. 7.11) is called when the player successfully touches a spot UIImageView. This method updates the score, level and lives remaining, then starts the animation that causes the touched UIImageView to fade away.

First, we increment `spotsTouched` and add 10 times the current level to the score (lines 222–223). Then, we play a sound indicating that a spot was touched. First, we reset `hitPlayer` to the beginning (line 224), so that if it's already playing (most likely because the player touched multiple spots quickly) it will play again.

```
220   - (void)touchedSpot:(UIImageView *)spot
221   {
222       ++spotsTouched; // increment the number of spots touched
223       score += 10 * level; // increment the score
224       hitPlayer.currentTime = 0; // reset the playback to the beginning
225       [hitPlayer play]; // play the sound for when the player hits a spot
226
227       // update the score label
228       [scoreLabel setText:[NSString stringWithFormat:@"Score: %i", score]];
229
230       // increment level if the player touched 10 spots in the current level
231       if (spotsTouched % 10 == 0)
232       {
233           ++level; // increment the level
234           drawTime *= 0.95; // speed up the game
235
236           // update the level label
237           [levelLabel setText:
238             [NSString stringWithFormat:@"Level: %i", level]];
239
240           // add a new life if it fits on the screen
241           if (lives.count < 7)
242           {
243               // load the life image
244               UIImageView *life = [[UIImageView alloc]
245                   initWithImage:touchedImage];
246
247               // position the View to the right of the previous life View
248               CGRect frame = CGRectMake(10 + 40 * lives.count, 420, 30, 30);
249               life.frame = frame; // set life's frame
250               [self.view addSubview:life]; // add life to View
251               [lives addObject:life]; // add life to lives array
252               [life release]; // release the life UIImageView
253           } // end if
254       } // end if
255
256       // stop the current animation and start a new one at the same place
257       CGRect frame = [[spot.layer presentationLayer] frame]; // get the frame
258       [spot.layer removeAllAnimations]; // stop the animation
259       spot.frame = frame; // move the spot to where the old animation ended
260       [spot setNeedsDisplay]; // redraw the spot
261
262       // give the spot time to redraw by delaying the end animation
263       [self performSelector:@selector(beginSpotEndAnimation:) withObject:spot
264           afterDelay:0.01];
265   } // end method touchedSpot:
266
```

Fig. 7.11 | SpotOnViewController's touchedSpot: method.

Line 231 determines if the level needs to be increased by checking if this spot was the tenth one touched in the current level. If so, we increment the level then decrease draw-Time, which controls how long the spot animations last. Because the animations have less time to complete, the spots move faster to reach their end locations. We update the level-Label (lines 237–238), then add a new life to reward the player for completing the previous level (lines 241–252)—if the player has fewer than seven lives.

Next, we end spot's current animation and start its fade away animation. If we just end the animation, the spot UIImageView will jump to the end location. To keep the UIImageView where it was touched, we use its CALayer to get its current position, stop the animation, then update the UIImageView's frame (lines 257–259).

We want the spot to turn green when it is touched, so we flag it for redrawing using the setNeedsDisplay method (line 260). This tells the app that the view needs to be redrawn. It will be redrawn once this method exits. Lines 263–264 call the perform-Selector:withObject:afterDelay method to begin the touched spot UIImageView's fade away animation.

Method beginSpotEndAnimation: of class SpotOnViewController

The beginSpotEndAnimation: method (Fig. 7.12) causes the passed UIImageView to shrink, fade away and disappear. This method is called by the touchedSpot: method once the spot's first animation has been stopped.

```
267  // starts the fade-away animation for a spot that's been touched
268  - (void)beginSpotEndAnimation:(UIImageView *)spot
269  {
270      [UIView beginAnimations:@"end" context:spot]; // begin animation block
271      [UIView setAnimationDuration:0.8]; // set the time for the animation
272      [UIView setAnimationDelegate:self]; // set the animation delegate
273
274      // set the method to call when the animation ends
275      [UIView setAnimationDidStopSelector:
276          @selector(finishedAnimation:finished:context:)];
277
278      // make the spot stay in the same place and disappear
279      CGRect frame = spot.frame; // get the current frame
280      frame.origin.x += frame.size.width / 2; // set x to the center
281      frame.origin.y += frame.size.height / 2; // set y to the center
282      frame.size.width = 0; // set the width to 0
283      frame.size.height = 0; // set the height to 0
284      [spot setFrame:frame]; // assign the new frame
285      [spot setAlpha:0.0]; // set the spot to be fully transparent
286      [UIView commitAnimations]; // end the animation block
287  } // end method beginSpotEndAnimation:
288
```

Fig. 7.12 | SpotOnViewController's beginSpotEndAnimation method.

Line 270 begins a new Core Animation block, passing end as the identifier and spot as the context. We specify an identifier in this animation block because we need to differentiate between this animation and other animations in the delegate methods. UIView's setAnimationDuration method specifies that the animation will last 0.8 seconds, allowing it to be visible but ensuring that the spot disappears quickly. Line 272 sets the animation's delegate to self, which allows the SpotOnViewController to receive messages when the animation starts and ends. UIView's ***setAnimationDidStopSelector method*** is used to specify that SpotOnViewController's finishedAnimation:finished:Context method is called when the animation ends. Lines 279–283 create a new CGRect at the center of spot's current location. The CGRect's width and height are set to 0 so the spot UIImageView will vanish from the screen. This CGRect is set as spot's final frame (line 284), which will cause the UIImageView to fade and shrink once the animation begins. The animation block ends with UIView's commitAnimations method. The animation will begin once beginSpotAnimation: finishes executing.

Method finishedAnimation:finished:context: of class SpotOnViewController

The finishedAnimation method (Fig. 7.13) is called when a spot UIImageView animation ends. This occurs when both touched and untouched spots disappear from the screen.

```
289  // method is automatically called when an animation ends
290  - (void)finishedAnimation:(NSString *)animationId finished:(BOOL)finished
291     context:(void *)context
292  {
293     // if the game has already been lost, exit
294     if (gameOver)
295        return;
296
297     UIImageView *spot = (UIImageView *)context; // get the finished spot
298
299     // if it was an ending animation that finished, add a new spot
300     if (animationId == @"end")
301     {
302        // remove spot from the spots NSMutableArray
303        [spots removeObject:spot];
304        [spot removeFromSuperview]; // remove the old spot
305        [self addNewSpot]; // add a new spot
306     } // end if
307     else if ([spot.image isEqual:untouchedImage]) // a spot was missed
308     {
309        [disappearPlayer play]; // play disappearing spot sound effect
310
311        // the game has been lost
312        if (lives.count == 0)
313        {
314           for (UIImageView *spot in spots) // delete all old spots
315           {
316              [spot removeFromSuperview]; // remove the spot from the View
317              [spot.layer removeAllAnimations]; // stop existing animations
318           } // end for
319
320           gameOver = YES; // the game is over
```

Fig. 7.13 | SpotOnViewController's finishedAnimation:finished:Context: method. (Part I of 2.)

```
321
322          // display the game-over alert
323          NSString *message =
324              [NSString stringWithFormat:@"Score: %i", score];
325
326          // get the standard user defaults
327          NSUserDefaults *defaults = [NSUserDefaults standardUserDefaults];
328
329          // get the current high score
330          int highScore = [[defaults valueForKey:@"highScore"] intValue];
331
332          // if the score of the last game is greater than the high score
333          if (score > highScore)
334
335              // update the file with the new high score
336              [defaults setValue:[NSNumber numberWithInt:score]
337                  forKey:@"highScore"];
338
339          UIAlertView *alert = [[UIAlertView alloc]
340              initWithTitle:@"Game Over" message:message delegate:self
341              cancelButtonTitle:@"Reset Game" otherButtonTitles:nil];
342          [alert show]; // show the alert
343          [alert release]; // release the alert UIAlertView
344      } // end else
345      else // remove one life
346      {
347          UIImageView *life = [lives lastObject]; // get the last life
348          [lives removeLastObject]; // remove the life from the array
349          [life removeFromSuperview]; // remove the life from the screen
350
351          // remove the old spot and create a new one
352          [spot removeFromSuperview]; // remove old spot
353          [self addNewSpot]; // add a new spot
354      } // end else
355  } // end else
356 } // end method finishedAnimation:finished:context:
357
```

Fig. 7.13 | SpotOnViewController's finishedAnimation:finished:Context: method.
(Part 2 of 2.)

If the game is over, the method exits (lines 294–295). Otherwise, we cast context to a UIImageView (line 297)—remember that we attached animations only to UIImageViews. If the animation that just finished is an ending animation (line 300), we remove the UIImageView from the spots NSMutableArray (line 301). We then remove the old UIImageView and add a new one (line 304–305). If it's a spot that's never been touched (line 307), we play the sound effect for a missed spot (line 309). We determine whether the game is over by checking if the player has any lives remaining (line 312). If it's over, lines 314–318 loop through the spots NSMutableArray and remove any UIImageViews from the previous game. UIView's removeFromSuperView method erases each UIImageView from the screen. Line 317 ends each UIImageView's animation. We use UIImageView's layer property to access the UIImageView's Core Animation layer (an object of class CALayer), which provides the view with animation support. CALayer's ***removeAllAnimations*** *method* removes any animations attached to the layer. If we don't remove the animations, Core Animation will continue animating a view that no longer exists, causing the app to crash.

We get the high score using NSUserDefault's valueForKey: method. If the player's score is greater than the old high score (line 333), we write the new high score to the app's preferences file using ***NSUserDefault's setValue:forKey: method*** (lines 336–337). We then display a UIAlertView with the final score. Otherwise, we remove one life and update the display.

Methods altertView:clickedButtonAtIndex:, shouldAutorotateTo-InterfaceOrientation: *and* dealloc *of class* SpotOnViewController

The alertView:clickedButtonAtIndex: method (Fig. 7.14) is called when the player touches the "**Reset Game**" **Button** on UIAlertView displayed at the end of the game. Line 362 starts a new game, by invoking the resetGame method.

Method shouldAutoRotateToInterfaceOrientation: (lines 366–371) is inherited from UIViewController. It's called by the iPhone OS to determine whether this view should rotate when the iPhone's orientation changes. Method dealloc (lines 374–385) releases SpotOnViewController's remaining objects and calls the superclass's dealloc method.

```
358  // called when the player touches the "Reset Game" Button
359  - (void)alertView:(UIAlertView *)alertView
360      clickedButtonAtIndex:(NSInteger)buttonIndex
361  {
362     [self resetGame]; // create a new game
363  } // end method alertView:clickedButtonAtIndex:
364
365  // called to determine what orientations our View allows
366  - (BOOL)shouldAutorotateToInterfaceOrientation:
367      (UIInterfaceOrientation)interfaceOrientation
368  {
369     // allow only the portrait orientation
370     return (interfaceOrientation == UIInterfaceOrientationPortrait);
371  } // end method shouldAutorotateToInterfaceOrientation:
372
373  // free SpotOnViewController's memory
374  - (void)dealloc
375  {
376     [spots release]; // release the spots NSMutableArray
377     [lives release]; // release the lives NSMutableArray
378     [hitPlayer release]; // release the hitPlayer AVAudioPlayer
379     [missPlayer release]; // release the missPlayer AVAudioPlayer
380     [disappearPlayer release]; // release the disappearPlayer AVAudioPlayer
381     [scoreLabel release]; // release the scoreLabel UILabel
382     [levelLabel release]; // release the levelLabe UILabel
383     [highScoreLabel release]; // release the highScoreLabel UILabel
```

Fig. 7.14 | SpotOnViewController's methods alertView:clickedButtonAtIndex:, shouldAutoRotateToInterfaceOrientation: and dealloc. (Part 1 of 2.)

```
384     [super dealloc]; // invokes the superclass's dealloc method
385   } // end method dealloc
386   @end
```

Fig. 7.14 | SpotOnViewController's methods alertView:clickedButtonAtIndex:, shouldAutoRotateToInterfaceOrientation: and dealloc. (Part 2 of 2.)

7.5 Wrap-Up

In this chapter, we created the **Spot-On Game** app, using Core Animation to animate multiple views. We used Core Animation blocks to animate UIImageViews. We provided an ending location and size for each spot UIImageView and the length of the animation. Core Animation then moved the UIImageViews and shrunk them, in accordance with the parameters we set. We used AVAudioPlayers to play sound effects in the game. Each AVAudioPlayer was tied to an individual sound file and gave us the ability to play the file programmatically.

In Chapter 8, the **Cannon Game** app makes further use of many of the technologies used in this chapter. We handle multitaps and swipe gestures. Rather than animating the game with the Core Animation framework, we introduce an NSTimer to generate events and update the display in response to those events. We also show how to group related objects in structures, and how to perform simple collision detection.

This page intentionally left blank.

This page intentionally left blank.

This page intentionally left blank.

This page intentionally left blank.

This page intentionally left blank.

This page intentionally left blank.

8

Cannon Game App

Animation with NSTimer and Handling Drag Events

OBJECTIVES

In this chapter you'll learn:

- To use an NSTimer to generate events at fixed time intervals.

- To group common variables under one name using a struct type.

- To perform simple collision detection.

- To use the touchesMoved:withEvent: method to aim the cannon as the player drags a finger on the screen.

- To process double-tap events to fire the cannon.

- To use the typedef keyword to declare easier-to-understand aliases for previously defined data types.

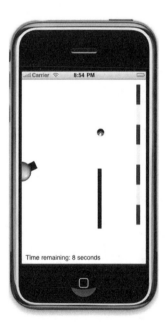

Outline

8.1 Introduction

8.2 Test-Driving the **Cannon Game** app

8.3 Overview of the Technologies

8.4 Building the App

8.5 Wrap-Up

8.1 Introduction

The **Cannon Game** app challenges the player to destroy a seven-piece target before a ten-second time limit runs out (Fig. 8.1). The game consists of three visual components—a cannon that the player controls, the target and a blocker that defends the target. The player aims the cannon by touching the screen—the cannon then aims at the touched point. The cannon fires a cannonball when the player double-taps the screen (Fig. 8.2).

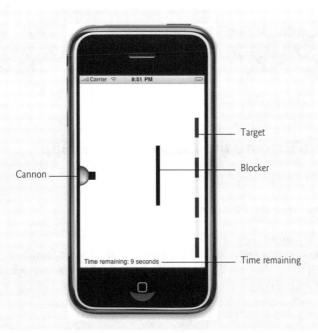

Fig. 8.1 | Completed **Cannon Game** app.

The target consists of seven pieces, each of which the player must hit to win the game. When a cannonball hits the target, a glass-breaking sound plays and that piece of the target disappears from the screen. When the cannonball hits the blocker, a "hit" sound plays and the cannonball bounces back. The blocker cannot be destroyed. The target and blocker move vertically, changing direction when they hit the top or bottom of the screen.

The game begins with a 10-second time limit. Each time a cannonball hits the target, three seconds are added to the time limit, and each time a cannonball hits the blocker, two seconds are subtracted. The player wins by destroying all seven target sections before time runs out. If the timer reaches zero, the player loses.

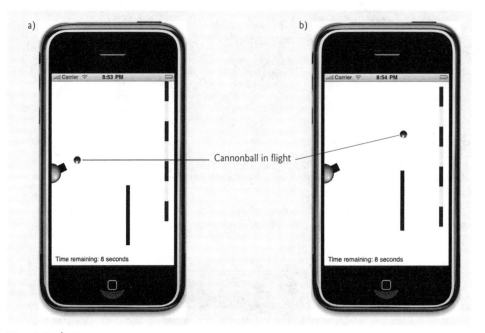

a)   b)

Cannonball in flight

Fig. 8.2 | **Cannon Game** app with cannonball in flight.

8.2 Test-Driving the Cannon Game App

Opening the Completed Application
Open the directory containing the **Cannon Game** app project. Double click Cannon-Game.xcodeproj to open the project in Xcode.

Running the Game
Click the **Build and Go** button to run the app in the iPhone Simulator. Drag your finger on the screen or tap it to aim the cannon, and double tap the screen (i.e., tap it twice quickly in the same place) to fire a shot. Try to destroy the target as fast as you can—if the timer in the lower-left corner of the app runs out, the game is over.

8.3 Overview of the Technologies

In the previous chapter, we used the Core Animation framework to animate several views in our app. In this chapter, we manually perform the animations by responding to NSTimer events that occur at fixed time intervals. This gives us more control over the animations but sacrifices some of the simplicity of using Core Animation.

An *NSTimer* object is initialized with a time interval and a method to call when that interval expires. In this app, the NSTimer generates an event every 0.025 second, and the method that is called in response to the event redraws the entire display. This will cause the app to refresh the display 40 times per second.

To refresh the display, we must compute new coordinates for each item on the screen, checking for collisions and adjusting velocities accordingly. This is straightforward in our app, because only four pieces move (the cannon, cannonball, blocker and target) and only the cannonball can collide with the other elements.

We introduce structures and use a structure in this app to group two points that represent the endpoints of a line. Variables of this new type are used to represent the endpoints of both the blocker and the target.

This chapter also introduces Core Graphics framework functionality. We show how to draw lines, draw text, change line thicknesses, change colors, and save and restore graphics contexts.

8.4 Building the App

Declaring the CannonView Interface

The CannonView class controls the game—storing the locations of the cannon, cannonball, target and blocker. An NSTimer refreshes the game every .025 second to update the position of each item on the screen. Figure 8.3 shows CannonView's interface declaration.

```
1   // CannonView.h
2   // CannonView's interface declaration
3   // Implementation in CannonView.m
4   #import <UIKit/UIKit.h>
5   #import <AVFoundation/AVFoundation.h>
6   #define TARGET_PIECES 7 // number of sections in the target
7
8   typedef struct line // groups two points that represent a line
9   {
10     CGPoint start; // the line's start point
11     CGPoint end; // the line's endpoint
12  } Line; // end typedef struct line
13
14  @interface CannonView : UIView
15  {
16     AVAudioPlayer *cannonFireSound; // plays the cannon firing sound
17     AVAudioPlayer *targetHitSound; // plays the target hit sound
18     AVAudioPlayer *blockerHitSound; // plays the blocker hit sound
19
20     Line blocker; // stores the points representing the blocker
21     Line target; // stores the points representing the target
22     BOOL targetPieceHit[TARGET_PIECES]; // is each target piece hit?
23     int targetPiecesHit; // number of target pieces hit
24     float blockerVelocity; // blocker's velocity
25     float targetVelocity; // target's velocity
26
27     CGPoint cannonball; // cannonball image's upper-left corner
28     CGPoint cannonballVelocity; // cannonball's velocity
29     CGPoint barrelEnd; // the endpoint of the cannon's barrel
30     NSTimer *timer; // the main timer
31     BOOL cannonballOnScreen; // is the cannonball on the screen?
32
33     int timerCount; // times the timer fired since the last second
```

Fig. 8.3 | CannonView's interface declaration. (Part 1 of 2.)

```
34        int timeLeft; // the amount of time left in seconds
35        int shotsFired; // the number of shots the user has made
36        int timeElapsed; // the number of seconds elapsed
37   } // end instance variable declaration
38
39   - (void)timerFired:(NSTimer *)theTimer; // updates the entire display
40
41   // shows an alert with the given title and message
42   - (void)showAlertWithTitle:(NSString *)title message:(NSString *)message;
43   - (void)newGame; // starts a new game
44   - (void)processTouch:(UITouch *)touch; // process a player's touch
45   @end // end interface CannonView
```

Fig. 8.3 | CannonView's interface declaration. (Part 2 of 2.)

The constant TARGET_PIECES specifies the number of sections in the target (line 6). Lines 8–12 define a *structure*—a collection of related variables under one name. Unlike an array, a structure can contain variables of different data types. The *struct keyword* begins the structure declaration. The identifier line is the *structure tag*, which names the declaration. Variables declared within the braces of the structure declaration are the structure's *members*. Members of the same structure type must have unique names, but two different structure types may contain members of the same name without conflict. The struct keyword is normally used to declare variables of a structure *type*. In this example, the structure type is struct line. The *typedef specifier* (line 8) declares synonyms (aliases) for previously defined data types. We use typedef to create shorter, more readable type names. Here, we create the alias Line (line 12) for the struct line structure type. When a struct declaration begins with typedef struct, we place the alias name between the struct's closing brace and semicolon. In this example, we can declare variables of our structure type by using the alias Line.

The declaration for the CannonView interface states that it's a subclass of UIView. Lines 16–18 declare three AVAudioPlayer pointers—which are used to play sound effects when the cannon is fired, when the cannonball hits the blocker and when the cannonball hits the target.

Line 30 declares an NSTimer pointer. The timer will call the setNeedsDisplay method every .025 seconds, which will indirectly cause CannonView's drawRect: method to be called to update the view. Class CannonView defines four methods (lines 39–44):

- timerFired:—updates the status of the game each time the timer fires.

- showAlertWithTitle:message:—displays results at the end of the game.

- newGame—resets all of the game components restoring all of the target's pieces, removing the ball from sight and aiming the cannon horizontally, then starts a new game.

- processTouch—processes taps, double taps and drag touches.

CannonView Class Implementation

The CannonView (Fig. 8.4) will display all of the game's visual elements and perform the animation. A CannonView is later added to the main view through Interface Builder, but none of the visual design takes place outside the CannonView class.

```
 I   // CannonView.m
 2   // Main view for the Cannon Game.
 3   #import <AVFoundation/AVFoundation.h>
 4   #import "CannonView.h"
 5
 6   static const int CANNON_BASE_RADIUS = 25; // radius of the cannon base
 7   static const int CANNON_LENGTH = 40; // length of the cannon barrel
 8
 9   static const int CANNONBALL_RADIUS = 10; // radius of the cannonball
10   static const int CANNONBALL_VELOCITY = 600; // cannonball's velocity
11
12   static const int LINE_WIDTH = 10; // width of the target and blocker
13   static const int BLOCKER_DISTANCE = 200; // blocker distance from left
14   static const int BLOCKER_BEGINNING = 50; // blocker distance from top
15   static const int BLOCKER_END = 200; // blocker bottom's distance from top
16   static const int BLOCKER_VELOCITY = 300; // blocker's velocity
17
18   static const int TARGET_VELOCITY = -100; // target's velocity
19   static const int TARGET_DISTANCE = 300; // target's distance from left
20   static const int TARGET_BEGINNING = 50; // target's distance from top
21   static const int TARGET_END = 400; // target bottom's distance from top
22
23   static const int MISS_PENALTY = 2; // seconds subtracted for a miss
24   static const int HIT_REWARD = 3; // seconds added for a hit
25
26   static const float TIME_INTERVAL = 0.025; // interval for timer events
27
```

Fig. 8.4 | Global variable declarations in CannonView.m.

Lines 6–26 declare static const global variables used throughout class CannonView. CANNON_BASE_RADIUS and CANNON_LENGTH are used to set the cannon's size (line 6–7). CANNONBALL_RADIUS declares the size of the cannonball and CANNONBALL_VELOCITY controls how fast the cannonball moves across the screen (lines 9–10). LINE_WIDTH (line 12) defines the width of the blocker and target. BLOCKER_DISTANCE sets the blocker's x-coordinate, BLOCKER_BEGINNING sets the blocker's top y-coordinate and BLOCKER_END sets the blocker's bottom y-coordinate (lines 13–15). The blocker's speed is defined by BLOCKER_VELOCITY (line 16). The target's velocity is set by TARGET_VELOCITY and its x-coordinate is TARGET_DISTANCE (lines 18–19). The target's top y-coordinate is set by TARGET_BEGINNING; TARGET_END sets its bottom y-coordinate (lines 20–21). MISS_PENALTY is the number of seconds subtracted from the remaining time when the player fires a missed shot and HIT_REWARD is the number of seconds added back when the target is hit (lines 23–24). TIME_INTERVAL is used to set how often the timer generates events to update the display (line 26).

Methods initWithCoder: and awakeFromNib of Class CannonView

The *initWithCoder: method* is called by the iPhone OS when loading nib files. Since we add CannonView to a nib file in Interface Builder, we use the initWithCoder: method (Fig. 8.5) to initialize the CannonView. If the superview's initialization is successful (line 34), the cannon's position is initialized to be parallel to the bottom of the screen. This is set using the barrelEnd CGPoint, which represents the point at the tip of the cannon. Changing this point changes the cannon's angle. We initialize the point halfway down the screen at the end of the cannon (line 37). CannonView's frame's size property returns a CGSize object representing the size of the entire view. Lines 40–41 invoke NSBundle's pathForResource:ofType: method to get the file path of cannon_fire.wav. Line 44 converts this path to an NSURL. This NSURL is used to initialize the cannonFireSound AVAudio-Player (lines 47–48). Lines 52–73 initialize the remaining AVAudioPlayers.

The awakeFromNib method (lines 80–83) is called after the nib file has finished loading. At this point, we start a new game by calling the newGame method.

```
28  @implementation CannonView
29
30  // initialize the view
31  - (id)initWithCoder:(NSCoder *)aDecoder
32  {
33      // if the superclass initialized properly
34      if (self = [super initWithCoder:aDecoder])
35      {
36          // make the cannon initially point horizontally
37          barrelEnd = CGPointMake(CANNON_LENGTH, self.frame.size.height / 2);
38
39          // get the path for the cannon firing sound
40          NSString *soundPath = [[NSBundle mainBundle]
41              pathForResource:@"cannon_fire" ofType:@"wav"];
42
43          // create a URL from the path
44          NSURL *soundURL = [[NSURL alloc] initFileURLWithPath:soundPath];
45
46          // initialize cannonFireSound with the URL
47          cannonFireSound =
48              [[AVAudioPlayer alloc] initWithContentsOfURL:soundURL error:nil];
49          [soundURL release]; // release the soundURL NSURL
50
51          // get the path for the target hit sound
52          soundPath = [[NSBundle mainBundle] pathForResource:@"target_hit"
53              ofType:@"wav"];
54
55          // create a URL from the path
56          soundURL = [[NSURL alloc] initFileURLWithPath:soundPath];
57
58          // initialize targetHitSound with the URL
59          targetHitSound =
60              [[AVAudioPlayer alloc] initWithContentsOfURL:soundURL error:nil];
61          [soundURL release]; // release the soundURL NSURL
62
63          // get the path for the blocker hit sound
64          soundPath = [[NSBundle mainBundle] pathForResource:@"blocker_hit"
65              ofType:@"wav"];
66
67          // create a URL from the path
68          soundURL = [[NSURL alloc] initFileURLWithPath:soundPath];
```

Fig. 8.5 | CannonView's initWithCoder: and awakeFromNib methods. (Part 1 of 2.)

```
69
70        // initialize blockerHitSound with the URL
71        blockerHitSound =
72           [[AVAudioPlayer alloc] initWithContentsOfURL:soundURL error:nil];
73        [soundURL release]; // release the soundURL NSURL
74     } // end if
75
76     return self;
77  } // end method initWithCoder:
78
79  // called when the nib file finishes loading
80  - (void)awakeFromNib
81  {
82     [self newGame]; // view is loaded, so start a new game
83  } // end method awakeFromNib
84
```

Fig. 8.5 | CannonView's initWithCoder: and awakeFromNib methods. (Part 2 of 2.)

newGame *method of Class* CannonView

The newGame method (Fig. 8.5) resets the display and begins a new game. The newGame method begins by declaring the endpoints for the blocker and target Lines (lines 89–94). We then loop through the targetPieceHit array, declaring that each segment of the target has not yet been hit (lines 97–98). The targetPiecesHit instance variable begins at 0 and cannonballVelocity and targetVelocity are initialized to their respective constants' values (lines 102–103). The game begins with timeLeft set to 10. Lines 100–113 initialize CannonView's remaining instance variables to their initial game states. Lines 112–113 create a new NSTimer by invoking its static method ***scheduledTimerWithTimeInterval***—which automatically allocates memory for the new NSTimer. It also adds the timer to the current run loop, which retains the timer. TIME_INTERVAL specifies how often the timer will generate events and the next two arguments state that the timer will invoke the timerFired method of self. The userInfo parameter can be used to store any object you want to use in the specified method, but we pass nil in this app since we have no need. The last argument specifies that we wish the timer to keep generating events throughout the game as opposed to generating a single event.

```
85  // reset all the screen elements and start a new game
86  - (void)newGame
87  {
88     // set the initial blocker position based on the defined constants
89     blocker.start = CGPointMake(BLOCKER_DISTANCE, BLOCKER_BEGINNING);
90     blocker.end = CGPointMake(BLOCKER_DISTANCE, BLOCKER_END);
91
92     // set the initial target position based on the defined constants
93     target.start = CGPointMake(TARGET_DISTANCE, TARGET_BEGINNING);
94     target.end = CGPointMake(TARGET_DISTANCE, TARGET_END);
95
```

Fig. 8.6 | CannonView's newGame method. (Part 1 of 2.)

```
96      // set every element of targetPieceHit to NO
97      for (int i = 0; i < TARGET_PIECES; i++)
98         targetPieceHit[i] = NO; // this piece hasn't been hit
99
100     targetPiecesHit = 0; // no target pieces have been hit
101
102     blockerVelocity = BLOCKER_VELOCITY; // set the initial blocker velocity
103     targetVelocity = TARGET_VELOCITY; // set the initial target velocity
104
105     timeLeft = 10; // start the countdown at 10 seconds
106     timerCount = 0; // the timer has fired 0 times so far
107     cannonballOnScreen = NO; // the cannonball is not on the screen
108     shotsFired = 0; // set initial number of shots fired
109     timeElapsed = 0; // set the time elapsed to zero
110
111     // start the timer with the defined time interval
112     timer = [NSTimer scheduledTimerWithTimeInterval:TIME_INTERVAL target:
113        self selector:@selector(timerFired:) userInfo:nil repeats:YES];
114  } // end method newGame
115
```

Fig. 8.6 | CannonView's newGame method. (Part 2 of 2.)

Method timerFired: of Class CannonView

Method timerFired: (Fig. 8.7) updates the game each time the timer generates an event. Global constant TIME_INTERVAL global variable indicates that the timer generates events every .025 second; however, these events may not be processed at .025 second intervals. For example, if another event is still being handled, the new timer event will be queued for processing as soon as possible. Therefore, timerFired: might not be called precisely when each timer event occurs. Method timerFired: is called approximately 40 times per second for smooth animation. Fewer refreshes start to make the animation choppy.

```
116  // refreshes all the elements on the screen
117  - (void)timerFired:(NSTimer *)theTimer
118  {
119     // if the cannonball is on the screen
120     if (cannonballOnScreen)
121     {
122        // update cannonball position
123        cannonball.x += TIME_INTERVAL * cannonballVelocity.x;
124        cannonball.y += TIME_INTERVAL * cannonballVelocity.y;
125
126        // check for collision with blocker
127        if (cannonball.x > BLOCKER_DISTANCE - CANNONBALL_RADIUS * 2 &&
128           cannonball.x < BLOCKER_DISTANCE + LINE_WIDTH / 2 &&
129           cannonball.y + CANNONBALL_RADIUS * 2 > blocker.start.y &&
130           cannonball.y < blocker.end.y)
131        {
```

Fig. 8.7 | CannonView's timerFired: method. (Part 1 of 3.)

```
132              cannonballVelocity.x *= -1;
133              [blockerHitSound play]; // play the blocker hit sound
134              timeLeft -= MISS_PENALTY;
135           } // end if
136
137           // check for collisions with the left and right walls
138           else if (cannonball.x > self.frame.size.width || cannonball.x +
139              CANNONBALL_RADIUS * 2 < 0 && cannonballVelocity.x < 0)
140              cannonballOnScreen = NO; // make the cannonball disappear
141
142           // check for collisions with top and bottom walls
143           else if (cannonball.y + CANNONBALL_RADIUS * 2 < 0 ||
144              cannonball.y > self.frame.size.height + CANNONBALL_RADIUS * 2)
145              cannonballOnScreen = NO; // make the cannonball disappear
146
147           // check for a hit on the target
148           else if (cannonball.x > TARGET_DISTANCE - CANNONBALL_RADIUS * 2 &&
149              cannonball.x < TARGET_DISTANCE + LINE_WIDTH / 2 &&
150              cannonball.y + CANNONBALL_RADIUS * 2 > target.start.y &&
151              cannonball.y < target.end.y)
152           {
153              // calculate the length of each piece of the target
154              float pieceLength =
155                 (TARGET_END - TARGET_BEGINNING) / TARGET_PIECES;
156
157              // determine which section number was hit (0 is the top)
158              int section =
159                 (int)((cannonball.y - target.start.y) / pieceLength);
160
161              // check if the piece hasn't been hit yet
162              if (!targetPieceHit[section])
163              {
164                 targetPieceHit[section] = YES; // the piece was hit
165                 cannonballOnScreen = NO; // make the cannonball disappear
166                 timeLeft += HIT_REWARD; // add reward to remaining
167                 [targetHitSound play]; // play the target hit sound
168
169                 // if all the target's pieces have been hit
170                 if (++targetPiecesHit == TARGET_PIECES)
171                 {
172                    NSString *message = [NSString stringWithFormat:
173                       @"Shots fired: %i\nTime elapsed: %i seconds",
174                       shotsFired, timeElapsed];
175
176                    // display the game won alert
177                    [self showAlertWithTitle:@"You Win!" message:message];
178                 } // end if
179              } // end if
180           } // end else
181        } // end if
182
```

Fig. 8.7 | CannonView's timerFired: method. (Part 2 of 3.)

```
183    // update the blocker's position
184    blocker.start.y += TIME_INTERVAL * blockerVelocity;
185    blocker.end.y += TIME_INTERVAL * blockerVelocity;
186
187    // update the target's position
188    target.start.y += TIME_INTERVAL * targetVelocity;
189    target.end.y += TIME_INTERVAL * targetVelocity;
190
191    // check if the blocker has hit the top or bottom walls
192    if (blocker.start.y < 0 || blocker.end.y > self.bounds.size.height)
193       blockerVelocity *= -1; // reverse the blocker's direction
194
195    // check if the target has hit the top or bottom walls
196    if (target.start.y < 0 || target.end.y > self.bounds.size.height)
197       targetVelocity *= -1; // reverse the target's direction
198
199    ++timerCount; // increment the timer event counter
200
201    // if one second has passed
202    if (TIME_INTERVAL * timerCount >= 1)
203    {
204       --timeLeft; // subtract one from the timer
205       ++timeElapsed; // increment the time elapsed
206       timerCount = 0; // reset the count
207    } // end if
208
209    // if the timer reached zero
210    if (timeLeft <= 0 && timerCount > 0)
211
212       // display game over alert
213       [self showAlertWithTitle:@"Game Over" message:nil];
214
215    [self setNeedsDisplay]; // redraw the entire display
216 } // end method timerFired:
217
```

Fig. 8.7 | CannonView's timerFired: method. (Part 3 of 3.)

Line 120 checks whether the cannonball is currently on the screen. If it is, we update its position by adding the distance it should have traveled since the last timer event. This is calculated by multiplying its velocity by the amount of time that passed (lines 123–124). Lines 127–130 check whether the cannonball has collided with the blocker. We perform simple collision detection in this app based on the rectangular boundaries of the cannon-ball image. There are four conditions that must be met if the cannonball is in contact with the blocker. The left edge of the cannonball must be greater than the blocker's *x*-coordinate (BLOCKER_DISTANCE) minus the diameter of the cannonball (line 127). This means that the cannonball has reached the blocker. The cannonball's *x*-coordinate must also be less than the blocker's position plus the width of the line (line 128). This ensures that the cannonball has not yet passed the blocker. Part of the cannonball must also be lower than the top of the blocker (line 129) and higher than the bottom of the blocker (line 130). If all these conditions are met, we remove the cannonball from the screen by setting cannon-ballOnScreen to NO, then play the blockerHitSound AVAudioPlayer.

We remove the cannonball if it reaches any of the screen's edges. Lines 143–145 remove the cannonball if any part of it has reached the right or left edge. Lines 148–151 remove the cannonball if it reaches the top or bottom of the screen. We then check whether the cannonball has hit the `target`. Four conditions must be met if the cannonball has made contact with the `target` (142–145). These are exactly the same as the conditions used to determine collision with the `blocker`, but using `target`'s coordinates.

If the cannonball hit the `target`, we determine which section of the `target` was hit. Lines 154–155 calculate the length of each `target` section by dividing the total length of the `target` by the number of sections. Lines 158–159 determine which section has been hit—dividing the distance between the cannonball and the bottom of the `target` by the size of a piece. This returns 0 for the top-most section and 6 for the bottom-most. We check whether that section was previously hit, using the `targetPieceHit` array (line 162). If it wasn't, line 164 sets the appropriate element of `targetPieceHit` to `YES` and the cannonball is removed from the screen. We then add `HIT_REWARD` to `timeLeft`, increasing the game's time remaining, and play the `targetHitSound`. We increment `targetPiecesHit`—if it's equal to `TARGET_PIECES` (line 170), the game is over. The `showAlertwith-Title:message:` method is called to display a `UIAlertView` containing a string detailing the number of shots fired and time elapsed during the game (lines 172–177).

Now that all possible cannonball collisions have been checked, the `blocker` and `target` positions must be updated. Lines 184–185 change the `blocker`'s position by multiplying `blockerVelocity` by the amount of time that has passed since the last update and adding that value to the current *x*- and *y*-coordinates. Lines 188–189 do the same for `target`. If the `blocker` has collided with the top or bottom wall, its direction is reversed by multiplying its velocity by -1 (lines 192–193). Lines 196–197 perform the same check and adjustment for `target`.

We increment the `timerCount`, keeping track of the number of times the timer has generated an event. If the product of `TIME_INTERVAL` (`.025`) and `timerCount` is one, `timerCount` must equal 40 and one second has passed since `timeLeft` was last updated. If so, we decrement `timeLeft`, increment `timeElapsed` and reset `timerCount` (205–207). If the timer has reached zero, the `showAlertwithTitle:message:` method is called to display a `UIAlertView` reading "**Game Over**" (line 213). Line 215 invokes `UIView`'s `setNeedsDisplay` method, causing the `CannonView` to redraw.

Methods *showAlertwithTitle:message:* and *alertView:clickedButtonAtIndex:* of class *CannonView*

The `showAlertwithTitle:message:` method (Fig. 8.8, lines 219–229) displays a `UIAlertView` at the end of the game.

```
218  // show an alert with the given title and message
219  - (void)showAlertWithTitle:(NSString *)title message:(NSString *)message
220  {
221     [timer invalidate]; // stop and release the timer
222     timer = nil; // set timer to nil
223
```

Fig. 8.8 | CannonView's showAlertwithTitle:message: and alertView:clickedButtonAtIndex: methods. (Part 1 of 2.)

```
224     // create the game over alert
225     UIAlertView *alert = [[UIAlertView alloc] initWithTitle:title
226        message:message delegate:self cancelButtonTitle:@"New Game"
227        otherButtonTitles:nil];
228     [alert show]; // show the alert
229     [alert release]; // release the alert UIAlertView
230  } // end method displayAlertWithTitle:
231
232  // called when the player touches the new game button in an alert
233  - (void)alertView:(UIAlertView *)alertView clickedButtonAtIndex:
234     (NSInteger)buttonIndex
235  {
236     [self newGame]; // start a new game
237  } // end method alertView:clickedButtonAtIndex:
238
```

Fig. 8.8 | CannonView's showAlertwithTitle:message: and alertView:clickedButtonAtIndex: methods. (Part 2 of 2.)

Line 221 invokes NSTimer's *invalidate method* to prevent the timer from generating events and line 222 sets the timer to nil. Lines 225–228 create and display a UIAlertView displaying the title taken in as an argument. The cancelButtonTitle: argument is set to read "New Game" and will call CannonView's alertView:clickedButtonAtIndex: method, which starts a new game by calling the newGame method (lines 233–237).

drawRect method of class CannonView

The drawRect: method (Fig. 8.9) redraws the CannonView after the timerFired: method updates each screen item's position in the view.

```
239  // draw the display in the given rectangle
240  - (void)drawRect:(CGRect)rect
241  {
242     // get the current graphics context
243     CGContextRef context = UIGraphicsGetCurrentContext();
244
245     // save the context because we need to flip it upside down
246     CGContextSaveGState(context);
247
248     // translate the context down
249     CGContextTranslateCTM(context, 0, self.bounds.size.height);
250     CGContextScaleCTM(context, 1.0, -1.0); // flip context up over itself
251
252     // create a string with the time remaining
253     NSString *str =
254        [NSString stringWithFormat:@"Time remaining: %i seconds", timeLeft];
255
256     // make the font 16pt Helvetica
257     CGContextSelectFont(context, "Helvetica", 16, kCGEncodingMacRoman);
258     CGContextSetTextDrawingMode(context, kCGTextFill); // set drawing mode
```

Fig. 8.9 | CannonView's drawRect: method. (Part 1 of 3.)

```
259
260    // set the text color to black
261    CGContextSetRGBFillColor(context, 0.0, 0.0, 0.0, 1.0);
262
263    // // convert str to a C string and display it
264    CGContextShowTextAtPoint(context, 10.0, 10.0,
265       [str cStringUsingEncoding:[NSString defaultCStringEncoding]],
266       str.length);
267    CGContextRestoreGState(context); // restore the context
268
269    // if the cannonball is on the screen
270    if (cannonballOnScreen)
271    {
272       // create the rectangle to draw the cannonball in
273       CGRect cannonballRect = CGRectMake(cannonball.x, cannonball.y,
274          CANNONBALL_RADIUS * 2, CANNONBALL_RADIUS * 2);
275
276       // load the cannonball image
277       UIImage *image = [UIImage imageNamed:@"cannonball80.png"];
278
279       // draw the image into the rectangle
280       CGContextDrawImage(context, cannonballRect, image.CGImage);
281    } // end if
282
283    // draw the cannon barrel
284    // move to the middle of the cannon base
285    CGContextMoveToPoint(context, 0, self.frame.size.height / 2);
286
287    // add a line to the endpoint of the cannon barrel
288    CGContextAddLineToPoint(context, barrelEnd.x, barrelEnd.y);
289    CGContextSetLineWidth(context, 20); // set line thickness
290    CGContextSetRGBStrokeColor(context, 0.0, 0.0, 0.0, 1.0); // black color
291    CGContextStrokePath(context); // draw the line
292
293    // create the rectangle for the cannon base
294    CGRect cannonBase = CGRectMake(0, self.frame.size.height / 2 -
295       CANNON_BASE_RADIUS, CANNON_BASE_RADIUS, CANNON_BASE_RADIUS * 2);
296
297    // load the image for the cannon base
298    UIImage *baseImage = [UIImage imageNamed:@"cannon_base.png"];
299
300    // draw the cannon base image into the rectangle
301    CGContextDrawImage(context, cannonBase, baseImage.CGImage);
302
303    // add a line between the two points of the blocker
304    CGContextMoveToPoint(context, blocker.start.x, blocker.start.y);
305    CGContextAddLineToPoint(context, blocker.end.x, blocker.end.y);
306    CGContextSetLineWidth(context, LINE_WIDTH); // set the line width
307
308    CGContextStrokePath(context); // draw the line
309
```

Fig. 8.9 | CannonView's drawRect: method. (Part 2 of 3.)

```
310    // calculate the length of each piece in the target
311    float pieceLength = (TARGET_END - TARGET_BEGINNING) / TARGET_PIECES;
312
313    // move to the start point of the target
314    CGContextMoveToPoint(context, target.start.x, target.start.y);
315
316    // draw each target piece
317    for (int i = 1; i <= TARGET_PIECES; i++)
318    {
319       // make the pieces different colors between yellow and blue
320       if (i % 2 == 0)
321          CGContextSetRGBStrokeColor(context, 1, 1, 0, 1);
322       else
323          CGContextSetRGBStrokeColor(context, 0, 0, 0.5, 1);
324
325       // move to the ending point of the next segment
326       CGContextMoveToPoint(context, target.end.x,
327          target.start.y + pieceLength * (i - 1));
328
329       // if the piece hasn't been hit yet
330       if (!targetPieceHit[i - 1])
331       {
332          // add a line for the piece
333          CGContextAddLineToPoint(context, target.end.x,
334             target.start.y + pieceLength * i);
335          CGContextStrokePath(context); // draw the piece
336       } // end if
337    } // end for
338 } // end method drawRect:
339
```

Fig. 8.9 | CannonView's drawRect: method. (Part 3 of 3.)

To perform a custom drawing in a view, we must first get the current graphics context. A *graphics context* (of type struct CGContext) represents a drawing canvas. It stores drawing information such as the color, line width and font. Before calling drawRect:, a UIView configures the current graphics context for itself. The *UIGraphicsGetCurrentContext function* of the UIKit framework returns the current graphics context that has been configured for the current UIView (line 243).

Line 246 saves the state of context, because we'll be altering its coordinates to display the time remaining but will want to restore the original coordinate system afterward. We must change the context's coordinate system to draw text properly. By default, the origin for drawing graphics is the upper-left (0,0) coordinate of the view. The x-coordinates increase toward the right and the y-coordinates increase toward the bottom. For drawing directly to a graphics context, however, the origin is in the lower-left corner, and the y-coordinates increase toward the top. For the text to draw properly, we must change the context to the correct coordinate system. First we move the origin to the lower-left corner by calling the *CGContextTranslateCTM function* of CGContextRef (line 249), which takes two parameters—the amount to shift the origin horizontally and the amount to shift it vertically. We then use the *CGContextScaleCTM function* of CGContextRef to invert the y-axis (line 250). The function takes two parameters—the amount to scale the x-axis and the amount to scale the *y*-axis. We pass 1 for the first parameter to keep the *x*-axis as it is, and pass -1 for the second parameter to invert the *y*-axis.

Line 253–254 creates an NSString which will be used to display the remaining time. The %i format specifier (line 254) indicates that timeLeft contains an integer value that will be converted to string format. The **CGContextSelectFont** *function* sets the graphics context's font to 16 point Helvetica (line 257). Line 258 sets context's text drawing mode to CGTextFill, telling the graphics context to display text using a fill operation. The **CGContextSetRGBFillColor** *function* sets the text color to black. Lines 264–266 call the CGContextShowTextAtPoint function to display the text at point (10.0, 10.0). This function requires a C-style string as an argument, so line 265 calls NSString's **cStringUsing-Encoding** method to obtain the C-string version of str. Next, line 267 restores the original coordinate system.

We next draw the cannonball if it's on the screen (lines 270–281). The CGMakeRect function creates the cannonballRect CGRect, providing cannonball's coordinates and circumference. Line 277 loads the cannonball image, creating a new UIImage using cannonball80.png. The CGContextDrawImage function draws the cannonball to context (line 280). UIView's CGImage property returns a pointer to a CGImage copy of cannonball-Image, which can be written to a graphics context (unlike UIImages). The image is drawn inside the cannonballRect CGRect.

We next draw the cannon's barrel. The CGContextMoveToPoint function selects the point halfway down the left side of the screen (line 285). When we draw to context, this will be the starting point. Lines 288–291 add a black line 20 pixels wide from the point we just selected to barrelEnd (which stores the point at the end of the barrel). The CGContextStrokePath function draws that line.

Lines 294–295 create a CGRect for the cannon's base using the CGRectMake function. The cannon's base is a half circle attached to the left side of the screen. We use CANNON_BASE_RADIUS as the width and double that (the circumference) as the height. The baseImage UIImage is created using cannon_base.png then the CGContextDrawImage function draws the cannon's base to context (lines 298 and 301).

The blocker is drawn using a single line in a manner similar to the drawing of the cannon's barrel. Line 304 selects the blocker's starting location in context, and lines 305–306 draw a 10-pixel-wide line from that point to the blocker's end location.

Line 311 calculates the length of each section of the target by dividing the height of the target by the number of sections. Line 314 uses the CGContextMoveToPoint function to select the target's starting point. Lines 317–337 loop through each of the target's sections, drawing each section if it hasn't been hit. Lines 320–323 alternate the colors of each target section between yellow and dark blue. We then select the point starting the section to be drawn. Multiplying pieceLength by the index of the current section calculates each section's distance from the start of the target. Lines 330–336 draw the section if it has not yet been hit.

Using the Instruments Tool to Detect Performance Problems

When we first created this app, we used circles with gradients rather than images to draw the cannon's base and cannonball. When we ran the app, the animation was choppy and unpredictable. So, we ran the app in the Instruments tool using the Activity Monitor template. According to the tool, our app was using little memory and few threads; however, the CPU load was nearly 100%. With that knowledge, we modified the processor-intensive sections of our code. After removing the gradients and replacing them with images, the animation sped up considerably.

Methods *touchesBegan:withEvent* and *touchesMove:withEvent:* and *processTouch:withEvent:* of Class *CannonView*

The touchesBegan:withEvent: (Fig. 8.10, lines 341–344) and touchesMovedwithEvent: (lines 347–350) methods both perform the same touch handling. The touchesBegan:withEvent: method is called when the player first makes contact with the screen and touchesMoved:withEvent: is called when the user drags a finger across the screen. Each of these methods uses NSSet's anyObject method to pass as an argument one of its touch objects to the processTouch: method (chosen at the collection's convenience) (lines 353–391).

```
340  // handle new touches
341  - (void)touchesBegan:(NSSet *)touches withEvent:(UIEvent *)event
342  {
343     [self processTouch:[touches anyObject]];
344  } // end method touchesBegan:withEvent:
345
346  // exactly the same as touchesBegan:withEvent: minus double-tapping
347  - (void)touchesMoved:(NSSet *)touches withEvent:(UIEvent *)event
348  {
349     [self processTouch:[touches anyObject]];
350  } // end method touchesMoved:withEvent:
351
352  // aims the cannon and fires the cannonball if appropriate
353  - (void)processTouch:(UITouch *)touch
354  {
355     // get the location of the touch in this view
356     CGPoint touchPoint = [touch locationInView:self];
357
358     // calculate the angle the barrel makes with the horizontal
359     float angle =
360        atan(touchPoint.x / (self.frame.size.height / 2 - touchPoint.y));
361
362     // if the touch is on the lower half of the screen
363     if (touchPoint.y > self.frame.size.height / 2)
364        angle += M_PI; // adjust the angle
365
366     // calculate the endpoint of the cannon barrel
367     barrelEnd.x = CANNON_LENGTH * sin(angle);
368     barrelEnd.y = -CANNON_LENGTH * cos(angle) + self.frame.size.height / 2;
369
370     // update the display only in the area of the cannon
371     [self setNeedsDisplayInRect:CGRectMake(0, self.frame.size.height / 2 -
372        CANNON_BASE_RADIUS - CANNON_LENGTH, CANNON_BASE_RADIUS +
373        CANNON_LENGTH, (CANNON_BASE_RADIUS + CANNON_LENGTH) * 2)];
374
```

Fig. 8.10 | CannonView's touchesBegan:withEvent:, touchesMoved:withEvent: and processTouch: methods. (Part 1 of 2.)

```
375     // fire a cannonball on a double-tap
376     if (touch.tapCount >= 2 && !cannonballOnScreen)
377     {
378        // move the cannonball to be inside the cannon
379        cannonball.x = -CANNONBALL_RADIUS; // align x-coordinate with cannon
380        cannonball.y = self.frame.size.height / 2 - CANNONBALL_RADIUS;
381
382        // get the x component of the total velocity
383        cannonballVelocity.x = CANNONBALL_VELOCITY * sin(angle);
384
385        // get the y component of the total velocity
386        cannonballVelocity.y = -CANNONBALL_VELOCITY * cos(angle);
387        cannonballOnScreen = YES; // the cannonball is now visible
388        ++shotsFired; // increment number of shots fired
389        [cannonFireSound play]; // play the firing sound
390     } // end if
391  } // end method processTouch:
392
393  // releases CannonView's memory
394  - (void)dealloc
395  {
396     [cannonFireSound release]; // release the cannonFireSound AVAudioPlayer
397     [targetHitSound release]; // release the targetHitSound AVAudioPlayer
398     [blockerHitSound release]; // release the blockerHitSound AVAudioPlayer
399     [super dealloc]; // invokes the superclass's dealloc method
400  } // end method dealloc
401  @end // end implementation of CannonView
```

Fig. 8.10 | CannonView's touchesBegan:withEvent:, touchesMoved:withEvent: and processTouch: methods. (Part 2 of 2.)

Invoking UITouch's locationInView method (line 356) returns a CGPoint representing the point where the touch was made. Lines 359–360 determine the angle that aims the cannon at the point where the player touches. We then redraw the cannon at the new angle (lines 371–373). Each UITouch object contains a ***tapCount*** *property* storing how many rapid touches occur in a short period of time. If there are at least two taps (line 376) the cannonball is fired. Lines 386–389 initialize the cannonball at the end of the cannon and set cannonballOnScreen to YES.

8.5 Wrap-Up

In this chapter we created the **Cannon Game** app by drawing graphics on a single UIView. To make this possible we introduced several new technologies. We demonstrated how to group variables using structures and used the typedef keyword to declare an alias for the structure type. We used an NSTimer to generate events that continually updated the game. Finally, you saw how to use the Core Graphics framework to draw the images, lines and text that make up the game. We handled player touches using the touchesBegan:withEvent and touchesDragged:withEvent: methods. We accessed each touch's tapCount property, firing the cannon only if the user double tapped the screen.

In Chapter 9, we create the **Painter** app—tranforming the iPhone's screen to a virtual canvas. This app will be designed using the Utility Application template—creating a **Main-View** and **FlipsideView**. We'll define a class representing painted lines and add new points to these lines as the user moves fingers across the screen. The iPhone's accelerometer generates an event which allows the user to erase the painting by shaking the phone.

9

Painter App
Using Controls with a UIView

OBJECTIVES

In this chapter you'll learn:

- How to combine custom views with Cocoa GUI components to create a richer app.

- How to process multiple screen touches.

- How to detect when touches move and leave the screen.

- How to detect motion events to clear the screen when the user shakes the iPhone.

- How to add variables of primitive and **struct** types to collections.

Outline

9.1 Introduction
9.2 Overview of the Technologies
9.3 Building the App
9.4 Wrap-Up

9.1 Introduction

The **Painter** app turns the iPhone screen into a virtual canvas (Fig. 9.1). The user paints by dragging one or more fingers across the screen. The line color and thickness can be set by touching the info button in the lower-right corner of the screen. The control panel (Fig. 9.2) includes a slider for line width and red, green and blue sliders for line color. As the **Line Width** slider is moved from left to right, the width of the line increases. At the bottom of the screen, two buttons allow the user to turn a finger into an eraser or clear the screen entirely. At any point while painting, the user can shake the iPhone to clear the entire drawing from the screen.

Fig. 9.1 | **Painter** app and its control panel.

9.2 Overview of the Technologies

The **Painter** app stores painted lines using the custom Squiggle class. Each Squiggle contains an array of points, a UIColor object and a numeric line-width value. When the user touches the screen, a new Squiggle is created, given a unique key and placed in an NSMutableDictionary. New points are added to the Squiggle as the user drags a finger along the screen. When the touch ends, the Squiggle is transferred from the dictionary to an array of finished Squiggles.

The app uses the **Utility Application** template. The MainView displays the user's painting—showing all the finished Squiggles and any Squiggles currently in progress. The user sets the line characteristics in the FlipsideView. The color is set using three **Sliders**, representing the RGB values of the painted line. We display the currently selected color using a UIView's backgroundColor property that is updated dynamically as the user moves any of the **Sliders**. When the user flips from the FlipsideView to the MainView, the values for the color and line width are loaded from the **Sliders** and passed to the MainView.

9.3 Building the App

To begin, open Xcode and create a new project. Choose the **Utility Application** template and name the project Painter.

Declaring the Squiggle Interface
Create a new file and name it Squiggle. Squiggle.h declares a class named Squiggle, which represents a single stroke of a finger on the iPhone screen. A Squiggle saves each point touched by the user's finger between where the first touch occurred and where the finger was finally lifted from the screen. It also saves the color and line width at the time of the stroke—representing all of the information needed to draw the stroke to the screen. Let's take a look at the interface (Fig. 9.2).

```
 1   // Squiggle.h
 2   // Class Squiggle represents the points, color and width of one line.
 3   // Implementation in Squiggle.m
 4   #import <UIKit/UIKit.h>
 5
 6   @interface Squiggle : NSObject
 7   {
 8      NSMutableArray *points; // the points that make up the Squiggle
 9      UIColor *strokeColor; // the color of this Squiggle
10      float lineWidth; // the line width for this Squiggle
11   } // end instance variable declaration
12
13   // declare strokeColor, lineWidth and points as properties
14   @property (retain) UIColor* strokeColor;
15   @property (assign) float lineWidth;
16   @property (nonatomic, readonly) NSMutableArray *points;
17
18   - (void)addPoint:(CGPoint)point; // adds a new point to the Squiggle
19   @end // end interface Squiggle
```

Fig. 9.2 | Class Squiggle represents the points, color and width of one line.

The points are stored in an NSMutableArray (line 8), and the color, line width and points are stored as properties (lines 14–16). The addPoint: method adds a new point to a Squiggle. We declared the points property as readonly so that other classes can modify the points array only by calling the addPoint: method.

Implementing the Squiggle *Class*

Class Squiggle (Fig. 9.3) contains the information required to display a Squiggle but it does not define how to draw one. Drawing is handled by the view containing a Squiggle.

```
1   // Squiggle.m
2   // Squiggle class implementation.
3   #import "Squiggle.h"
4
5   @implementation Squiggle
6
7   @synthesize strokeColor; // generate set and get methods for strokeColor
8   @synthesize lineWidth; // generate set and get methods for lineWidth
9   @synthesize points; // generate set and get methods for points
10
11  // initialize the Squiggle object
12  - (id)init
13  {
14      // if the superclass properly initializes
15      if (self = [super init])
16      {
17          points = [[NSMutableArray alloc] init]; // initialize points
18          strokeColor = [[UIColor blackColor] retain]; // set default color
19      } // end if
20
21      return self; // return this object
22  } // end method init
23
24  // add a new point to the Squiggle
25  - (void)addPoint:(CGPoint)point
26  {
27      // encode the point in an NSValue so we can put it in an NSArray
28      NSValue *value =
29          [NSValue valueWithBytes:&point objCType:@encode(CGPoint)];
30      [points addObject:value]; // add the encoded point to the NSArray
31  } // end method addPoint:
32
33  // release Squiggle's memory
34  - (void)dealloc
35  {
36      [strokeColor release]; // release the strokeColor UIColor
37      [points release]; // release the points NSMutableArray
38      [super dealloc];
39  } // end method dealloc
40  @end
```

Fig. 9.3 | Squiggle class implementation.

Lines 7–9 synthesize *get* and *set* methods for the strokeColor, lineWidth and points properties. The compiler generates only a *get* method for points because it's readonly. The init method (lines 12–22) initializes a Squiggle by allocating the points array and setting the strokeColor to black (line 18), which is the default color for a Squiggle.

The addPoint: method adds a new point to the Squiggle (lines 25–31). This method takes a CGPoint as an argument. You cannot add a CGPoint directly to an NSArray because

CGPoint is a struct not a class. For this reason, we convert the CGPoint to an *NSValue* object, which is used as a container to store nonobject types, such as ints, floats, structs and pointers. We perform the conversion using NSValue's *valueWithBytes:objCType:* method (lines 28–29), which takes two arguments—a pointer to the value being encoded and its type. We obtain a pointer to the CGPoint using the *& (address of) operator*, which returns a pointer to the variable (i.e., its location in memory). The *@encode compiler directive* converts a type's name to the C string representing the type. This technique can be used when you need to store a nonobject type (such as a primitive value or a struct) in a collection. Line 30 adds the NSValue object to the array. When a Squiggle is removed from memory, the dealloc method releases all of the objects initialized in the init method (lines 34–39).

Declaring the MainView Interface
MainView.h (Fig. 9.4) declares class MainView—a UIView subclass that represents the app's canvas. MainView handles touches, draws the Squiggles and stores the painting.

```
 1   // MainView.h
 2   // View for the frontside of the Painter app.
 3   // Implementation in MainView.m
 4   #import <UIKit/UIKit.h>
 5   #import "Squiggle.h"
 6
 7   @interface MainView : UIView
 8   {
 9      NSMutableDictionary *squiggles; // squiggles in progress
10      NSMutableArray *finishedSquiggles; // finished squiggles
11      UIColor *color; // the current drawing color
12      float lineWidth; // the current drawing line width
13   } // end instance variable declaration
14
15   // declare color and lineWidth as properties
16   @property(nonatomic, retain) UIColor *color;
17   @property float lineWidth;
18
19   // draw the given Squiggle into the given graphics context
20   - (void)drawSquiggle:(Squiggle *)squiggle inContext:(CGContextRef)context;
21   - (void)resetView; // clear all squiggles from the view
22   @end // end interface MainView
```

Fig. 9.4 | View for the frontside of the **Painter** app.

To display the painting, the MainView stores all the Squiggles on the screen in two data structures—one for Squiggles in progress and one for finished Squiggles (lines 9–10). MainView also stores the current drawing color and line width (lines 11–12). The drawSquiggle:inContext: method displays one Squiggle in the given graphics context, and resetView clears the entire painting.

Implementing the MainView Class
MainView.m (Fig. 9.5) contains class MainView's implementation. Lines 7–8 synthesize properties color and lineWidth (lines 7–8). The initWithCoder: method is called when

the **MainView** is created in a nib file. If the superclass is initialized properly (line 14), we initialize the `squiggles` NSMutableDictionary and the `finishedSquiggles` NSMutable-Array (lines 17–18). The drawing color is initially set to black (line 21) and the line width is initially set to 5 pixels (line 22).

```
1   // MainView.m
2   // View for the frontside of the Painter app.
3   #import "MainView.h"
4
5   @implementation MainView
6
7   @synthesize color; // generate getters and setters for color
8   @synthesize lineWidth; // generate getters and setters for lineWidth
9
10  // method is called when the view is created in a nib file
11  - (id)initWithCoder:(NSCoder*)decoder
12  {
13      // if the superclass initializes properly
14      if (self = [super initWithCoder:decoder])
15      {
16          // initialize squiggles and finishedSquiggles
17          squiggles = [[NSMutableDictionary alloc] init];
18          finishedSquiggles = [[NSMutableArray alloc] init];
19
20          // the starting color is black
21          color = [[UIColor alloc] initWithRed:0 green:0 blue:0 alpha:1];
22          lineWidth = 5; // default line width
23      } // end if
24
25      return self; // return this object
26  } // end method initWithCoder:
27
```

Fig. 9.5 | Method `initWithCoder:` of class `MainView`.

Methods *resetView* and *drawRect:* of Class *MainView*

The `resetView` method (Fig. 9.6, lines 29–34) clears the painting from the screen by calling the `removeAllObjects` method on both the `squiggles` dictionary and finished-Squiggles array. Calling UIView's `setNeedsDisplay` method (line 33) forces the **MainView** to redraw, thus clearing the screen. The `drawRect:` method draws the entire painting using the stored squiggles. Line 40 retrieves the current graphics context to use for drawing. Then we loop through `finishedSquiggles`, passing each `Squiggle` and the graphics context to the `drawSquiggle:inContext:` method (lines 43–44). Finally, we loop through the `squiggles` NSMutableDictionary to draw any `Squiggles` still in progress (lines 47–51).

```
28  // clears all the drawings
29  - (void)resetView
30  {
31      [squiggles removeAllObjects]; // clear the dictionary of squiggles
```

Fig. 9.6 | Methods `resetView` and `drawRect:` of class `MainView`. (Part 1 of 2.)

```
32      [finishedSquiggles removeAllObjects]; // clear the array of squiggles
33      [self setNeedsDisplay]; // refresh the display
34    } // end method resetView
35
36    // draw the view
37    - (void)drawRect:(CGRect)rect
38    {
39       // get the current graphics context
40       CGContextRef context = UIGraphicsGetCurrentContext();
41
42       // draw all the finished squiggles
43       for (Squiggle *squiggle in finishedSquiggles)
44          [self drawSquiggle:squiggle inContext:context];
45
46       // draw all the squiggles currently in progress
47       for (NSString *key in squiggles)
48       {
49          Squiggle *squiggle = [squiggles valueForKey:key]; // get squiggle
50          [self drawSquiggle:squiggle inContext:context]; // draw squiggle
51       } // end for
52    } // end method drawRect:
53
```

Fig. 9.6 | Methods `resetView` and `drawRect:` of class `MainView`. (Part 2 of 2.)

Method `drawSquiggle:inContext:` of Class `MainView`

The `drawSquiggle:inContext:` method receives a `Squiggle` and a graphics context, then draws the `Squiggle` into the graphics context using the `Squiggle`'s color and line width.

```
54    // draws the given squiggle into the given context
55    - (void)drawSquiggle:(Squiggle*)squiggle inContext:(CGContextRef)context
56    {
57       // set the drawing color to the squiggle's color
58       UIColor *squiggleColor = squiggle.strokeColor; // get squiggle's color
59       CGColorRef colorRef = [squiggleColor CGColor]; // get the CGColor
60       CGContextSetStrokeColorWithColor(context, colorRef);
61
62       // set the line width to the squiggle's line width
63       CGContextSetLineWidth(context, squiggle.lineWidth);
64
65       NSMutableArray *points = [squiggle points]; // get points from squiggle
66
67       // retrieve the NSValue object and store the value in firstPoint
68       CGPoint firstPoint; // declare a CGPoint
69       [[points objectAtIndex:0] getValue:&firstPoint];
70
71       // move to the point
72       CGContextMoveToPoint(context, firstPoint.x, firstPoint.y);
73
```

Fig. 9.7 | Method `drawSquiggle:` of class `MainView`. (Part 1 of 2.)

```
74      // draw a line from each point to the next in order
75      for (int i = 1; i < [points count]; i++)
76      {
77        NSValue *value = [points objectAtIndex:i]; // get the next value
78        CGPoint point; // declare a new point
79        [value getValue:&point]; // store the value in point
80
81        // draw a line to the new point
82        CGContextAddLineToPoint(context, point.x, point.y);
83      } // end for
84
85      CGContextStrokePath(context);
86    } // end method drawSquiggle:inContext:
87
```

Fig. 9.7 | Method drawSquiggle: of class MainView. (Part 2 of 2.)

First, the color of the Squiggle is retrieved and set as the current stroke color (lines 58–60). Line 63 then gets the Squiggle's line width and updates the graphics context with it. Next, we draw the Squiggle. Lines 68–69 get the first point in the Squiggle and move to it. Recall that we added each CGPoint to the points array by storing it in an NSValue object. To retrieve the CGPoint from the NSValue, we use the ***getValue: method***, which receives a pointer to where the value will be stored.

Once we move to the first point, we add lines to each of the Squiggle's remaining points in sequence (lines 72–83). We get the next NSValue (line 77), get the CGPoint contained in the NSValue (lines 78–79) and add a line to the CGPoint (line 82). We then call the CGContextStrokePath function (line 85) to draw the Squiggle we just defined.

Touch-Handling Methods of Class MainView
The next three methods defined in MainView.m perform touch handling (Fig. 9.8). The method touchesBegan:withEvent: is called when the user touches the screen, touches-Moved:withEvent: is called when the user drags a finger and touchesEnded:withEvent: is called when the user lifts a finger.

```
88   // called whenever the user places a finger on the screen
89   - (void)touchesBegan:(NSSet *)touches withEvent:(UIEvent *)event
90   {
91      NSArray *array = [touches allObjects]; // get all the new touches
92
93      // loop through each new touch
94      for (UITouch *touch in array)
95      {
96        // create and configure a new squiggle
97        Squiggle *squiggle = [[Squiggle alloc] init];
98        [squiggle setStrokeColor:color]; // set squiggle's stroke color
99        [squiggle setLineWidth:lineWidth]; // set squiggle's line width
100
```

Fig. 9.8 | Touch-handling methods of class MainView. (Part 1 of 3.)

```
101        // add the location of the first touch to the squiggle
102        [squiggle addPoint:[touch locationInView:self]];
103
104        // the key for each touch is the value of the pointer
105        NSValue *touchValue = [NSValue valueWithPointer:touch];
106        NSString *key = [NSString stringWithFormat:@"%@", touchValue];
107
108        // add the new touch to the dictionary under a unique key
109        [squiggles setValue:squiggle forKey:key];
110        [squiggle release]; // we are done with squiggle so release it
111     } // end for
112 } // end method touchesBegan:withEvent:
113
114 // called whenever the user drags a finger on the screen
115 - (void)touchesMoved:(NSSet *)touches withEvent:(UIEvent *)event
116 {
117    NSArray *array = [touches allObjects]; // get all the moved touches
118
119    // loop through all the touches
120    for (UITouch *touch in array)
121    {
122        // get the unique key for this touch
123        NSValue *touchValue = [NSValue valueWithPointer:touch];
124
125        // fetch the squiggle this touch should be added to using the key
126        Squiggle *squiggle = [squiggles valueForKey:
127           [NSString stringWithFormat:@"%@", touchValue]];
128
129        // get the current and previous touch locations
130        CGPoint current = [touch locationInView:self];
131        CGPoint previous = [touch previousLocationInView:self];
132        [squiggle addPoint:current]; // add the new point to the squiggle
133
134        // Create two points: one with the smaller x and y values and one
135        // with the larger. This is used to determine exactly where on the
136        // screen needs to be redrawn.
137        CGPoint lower, higher;
138        lower.x = (previous.x > current.x ? current.x : previous.x);
139        lower.y = (previous.y > current.y ? current.y : previous.y);
140        higher.x = (previous.x < current.x ? current.x : previous.x);
141        higher.y = (previous.y < current.y ? current.y : previous.y);
142
143        // redraw the screen in the required region
144        [self setNeedsDisplayInRect:CGRectMake(lower.x - lineWidth,
145           lower.y - lineWidth, higher.x - lower.x + lineWidth * 2,
146           higher.y - lower.y + lineWidth * 2)];
147    } // end for
148 } // end method touchesMoved:withEvent:
149
150 // called when the user lifts a finger from the screen
151 - (void)touchesEnded:(NSSet *)touches withEvent:(UIEvent *)event
152 {
```

Fig. 9.8 | Touch-handling methods of class `MainView`. (Part 2 of 3.)

```
153    // loop through the touches
154    for (UITouch *touch in touches)
155    {
156        // get the unique key for the touch
157        NSValue *touchValue = [NSValue valueWithPointer:touch];
158        NSString *key = [NSString stringWithFormat:@"%@", touchValue];
159
160        // retrieve the squiggle for this touch using the key
161        Squiggle *squiggle = [squiggles valueForKey:key];
162
163        // remove the squiggle from the dictionary and place it in an array
164        // of finished squiggles
165        [finishedSquiggles addObject:squiggle]; // add to finishedSquiggles
166        [squiggles removeObjectForKey:key]; // remove from squiggles
167    } // end for
168 } // end method touchesEnded:withEvent:
169
```

Fig. 9.8 | Touch-handling methods of class `MainView`. (Part 3 of 3.)

In `touchesBegan:withEvent:`, we first get all the new touches by using the `allObjects` method of `NSSet` (line 91). This method returns an `NSArray` containing all the `UITouch` objects in the `NSSet`. We then loop through all the new touches (lines 94–111). For each touch, we create a new `Squiggle` and add it to the dictionary under a unique key. For the entire duration of a touch (from when it begins to when it ends), we are always guaranteed to be passed the same `UITouch` object in our touch-handling methods. So, we can use the memory address of the `UITouch` object as the key for the new `Squiggle`. We create the new `Squiggle` (line 97), customize it (lines 98–99) and add its first point (line 100). We then create the key (105–106). We use the *valueWithPointer:* method of `NSValue` to convert the memory address of the `UITouch` into an object (line 105). We then convert the `NSValue` to an `NSString` (line 106) and store the `Squiggle` in the dictionary using the `NSString` as the key (line 109).

In the `touchedMoved:withEvent:` method (lines 115–148), we add new points to the `Squiggles` in the `squiggles` dictionary for each touch that moved. For each moved touch, we get the unique key for that touch (line 123), then get the `Squiggle` using that key (lines 126–127). We then get the point the touch was moved to (line 130) and add it to the `Squiggle` (line 132).

Now that the `Squiggle` is updated, we need to update the view to draw the new line (lines 137–146). We could use the `setNeedsDisplay` method to redraw the entire view, but this is inefficient because only a portion of the view is changing. Instead, we use the `setNeedsDisplayInRect:` method (lines 144–146) to tell the view to update the display only in the area defined by the `CGRect` argument. To determine the `CGRect` that encloses the line segment, we first calculate the upper-left and bottom-right corners of the `CGRect` (lines 137–141) using the *?: (conditional) operator*, which takes three arguments. The first is a condition. The second is the value for the entire expression if the condition is true, and the third is the value for the entire expression if the condition is false. Once we calculate the points, we use them, along with some padding on either side to account for the line's thickness, to create the `CGRect` (lines 144–146).

In the touchesEnded:withEvent: method (lines 151–168), we transfer the Squiggles that correspond to the finished touches from the NSMutableDictionary of Squiggles in progress to the NSMutableArray of finished Squiggles. We loop through each finished touch (lines 154–167), and for each touch we get its corresponding Squiggle, using the touch's memory address as the key (157–161). We then add this Squiggle to the finishedSquiggles NSMutableArray (line 165) and remove it from the squiggles NSMutableDictionary (line 166).

Methods motionEnded:withEvent:, alertView:clickedButtonAtIndex:, canBecome-FirstResponder *and* dealloc *of Class* MainView

The next three methods in MainView (Fig. 9.9) clear the painting when the user shakes the iPhone. The method *motionEnded:withEvent:* is called when the user finishes a motion event, such as a shake. If the ended event was a shake (line 174), we display an alert asking whether the user really wanted to erase the painting (lines 177–182). The alertView:clickedButtonAtIndex: method is called when the user touches one of the buttons in the alert. If the user touched the button labeled Clear (line 194), we clear the entire painting (line 195). The *canBecomeFirstResponder* method is called to determine whether an object of this class can become the first responder. Only the first responder receives notifications about motion events, so we need MainView to be the first responder. We return YES (line 201) to enable this.

```
170  // called when a motion event, such as a shake, ends
171  - (void)motionEnded:(UIEventSubtype)motion withEvent:(UIEvent *)event
172  {
173     // if a shake event ended
174     if (event.subtype == UIEventSubtypeMotionShake)
175     {
176        // create an alert prompting the user about clearing the painting
177        NSString *message = @"Are you sure you want to clear the painting?";
178        UIAlertView *alert = [[UIAlertView alloc] initWithTitle:
179           @"Clear painting" message:message delegate:self
180           cancelButtonTitle:@"Cancel" otherButtonTitles:@"Clear", nil];
181        [alert show]; // show the alert
182        [alert release]; // release the alert UIAlertView
183     } // end if
184
185     // call the superclass's moetionEnded:withEvent: method
186     [super motionEnded:motion withEvent:event];
187  } // end method motionEnded:withEvent:
188
189  // clear the painting if the user touched the "Clear" button
190  - (void)alertView:(UIAlertView *)alertView clickedButtonAtIndex:
191     (NSInteger)buttonIndex
192  {
193     // if the user touched the Clear button
194     if (buttonIndex == 1)
195        [self resetView]; // clear the screen
196  } // end method alertView:clickedButtonAtIndex:
```

Fig. 9.9 | Methods motionEnded:withEvent:, alertView:clickedButtonAtIndex:, canBecomeFirstResponder and dealloc of class MainView. (Part 1 of 2.)

```
197
198    // determines if this view can become the first responder
199    - (BOOL)canBecomeFirstResponder
200    {
201        return YES; // this view can be the first responder
202    } // end method canBecomeFirstResponder
203
204    // free MainView's memory
205    - (void)dealloc
206    {
207        [squiggles release]; // release the squiggles NSMutableDictionary
208        [finishedSquiggles release]; // release finishedSquiggles
209        [color release]; // release the color UIColor
210        [super dealloc];
211    } // end method dealloc
212    @end
```

Fig. 9.9 | Methods motionEnded:withEvent:, alertView:clickedButtonAtIndex:, canBecomeFirstResponder and dealloc of class MainView. (Part 2 of 2.)

Declaring the MainViewController Interface

MainViewController.h (Fig. 9.10) defines the class MainViewController, a subclass of UIViewController. This class is the controller for the frontside of our app. Its main functions are to show the flipside when the info button is touched and to pass messages from the flipside to MainView. We declare the MainViewController class as a subclass of UIViewController (line 6). MainViewController also conforms to the FlipsideViewControllerDelegate protocol, which is defined in FlipsideViewController.h. The showInfo: method creates a new FlipsideViewController and displays it when the info button is touched (line 11).

```
1     // MainViewController.h
2     // Controller for the front side of the Painter app.
3     // Implementation in MainViewController.m
4     #import "FlipsideViewController.h"
5
6     @interface MainViewController : UIViewController
7         <FlipsideViewControllerDelegate>
8     {
9     } // end instance variable declaration
10
11    - (IBAction)showInfo; // flip the app to the flipside
12    @end // end interface MainViewController
```

Fig. 9.10 | MainViewController interface.

Implementing the MainViewController Class

MainViewController.m (Fig. 9.11) provides the definition of class MainViewController. The viewDidAppear: and viewDidDisappear: methods (lines 9–20) are inherited from UIViewController. They are called when MainView is going to be shown or hidden, respectivly. For MainView to receive notifications about motion events, it must be the first responder. These notifications are necessary for the "shake to erase" feature to work. We don't want MainView to be the first responder when it's hidden, so we make it the first responder when it appears by using the becomeFirstResponder method (line 12). We then remove the first-responder status when the MainView disappears by using the resignFirstResponder method (line 19).

```
1   // MainViewController.m
2   // Controller for the front side of the Painter app.
3   #import "MainViewController.h"
4   #import "MainView.h"
5
6   @implementation MainViewController
7
8   // make the main view the first responder
9   - (void)viewDidAppear:(BOOL)animated
10  {
11     [super viewDidAppear:animated]; // pass message to superclass
12     [self.view becomeFirstResponder]; // make main view the first responder
13  } // end method viewDidAppear
14
15  // resign the main view as the first responder
16  - (void)viewDidDisappear:(BOOL)animated
17  {
18     [super viewDidDisappear:animated]; // pass message to superclass
19     [self.view resignFirstResponder]; // resign view as first responder
20  } // end method viewDidDisappear:
21
22  // called when the Done button on the flipside is touched
23  - (void)flipsideViewControllerDidFinish:(FlipsideViewController *)c
24  {
25     // make the app flip back to the main view
26     [self dismissModalViewControllerAnimated:YES];
27  } // end method flipsideViewControllerDidFinish:
28
29  // called when the info button is touched
30  - (IBAction)showInfo
31  {
32     // load a new FlipsideViewController from FlipsideView.xib
33     FlipsideViewController *controller = [[FlipsideViewController alloc]
34        initWithNibName:@"FlipsideView" bundle:nil];
35
36     controller.delegate = self; // set the delegate of controller
37
38     // set the animation effect and show the flipside
39     controller.modalTransitionStyle = UIModalTransitionStyleFlipHorizontal;
40     [self presentModalViewController:controller animated:YES];
41
42     // set the sliders on the flipside to the current values in view
43     MainView *view = (MainView *)self.view;
44     [controller setColor:view.color lineWidth:view.lineWidth];
45     [controller release]; // we are done with controller so release it
46  } // end method showInfo
47
```

Fig. 9.11 | Controller for the front side of the **Painter** app. (Part 1 of 2.)

```
48  // set the color of the main view
49  - (void)setColor:(UIColor *)color
50  {
51     MainView *view = (MainView *)self.view; // get main view as a MainView
52     view.color = color; // update the color in the main view
53  } // end method setColor:
54
55  // set the line width of the main view
56  - (void)setLineWidth:(float)width
57  {
58     MainView *view = (MainView *)self.view; // get main view as a MainView
59     view.lineWidth = width; // update the line width in the main view
60  } // end method setLineWidth:
61
62  // clear the paintings in the main view
63  - (void)resetView
64  {
65     MainView *view = (MainView *)self.view; // get main view as a MainView
66     [view resetView]; // reset the main view
67  } // end method resetView
68  @end
```

Fig. 9.11 | Controller for the front side of the **Painter** app. (Part 2 of 2.)

The flipsideViewControllerDidFinish: method (lines 23–27) is called when the user touches the "**Done**" **Button** on the **FlipSideView**. The showInfo method (lines 30–46) switches to the **FlipsideView** when the info button is touched. Lines (33–34) create a new FlipsideViewcontroller, setting the view it controls to FlipsideView.xib. This is accessed via the controller pointer. We then set controller's delegate property to self—allowing the FlipsideViewController to access MainViewcontroller's methods and properties. Line 39 sets controller's modalTransitionStyle property (inherited from UIViewController) to UIModalTransitionStyleFlipHorizontal. This makes it flip horizontally between the **MainView** and the **FlipsideView**.

Line 43 gets a pointer to the **MainView**. Line 44 calls controller's setColor:line-Width: method, passing the **MainView**'s color and lineWidth properties as arguments. This initializes the **FlipsideView**'s GUI components to match the current painted line's color and width. Line 45 releases controller, because it's no longer needed by the Main-ViewController.

The setColor: method (lines 49–53) takes a UIColor—retrieving the **MainView** and setting its color property to the given UIColor. The setLineWidth method (lines 56–60) sets **MainView**'s lineWidth property in a similar manner. The resetView method (lines 63–67) simply calls the **MainView**'s resetView method.

Declaring the FlipsideViewController Interface

FlipsideViewController.h (Fig. 9.12) declares the FlipsideViewController class, which is a UIViewController subclass that controls the flipside of our app. Line 8 declares instance variable delegate (line 8), which is of type id and implements the FlipsideViewControllerDelegate protocol. This is the object that will receive a message when the user touches the "**Done**" **Button**. We next declare five outlets that will be connected to GUI components in Interface Builder. Four UISliders represent the **Sliders** used to set the color and width of the painted line (lines 9–13). The UIView shows a preview of the painting color. The clearScreen variable tracks whether the user has touched the "Clear Screen" Button.

```
 1    // FlipsideViewController.h
 2    // Controller for the flipside of the Painter app.
 3    // Implementation in FlipsideViewController.m
 4    @protocol FlipsideViewControllerDelegate; // declare a new protocol
 5
 6    @interface FlipsideViewController : UIViewController
 7    {
 8       id <FlipsideViewControllerDelegate> delegate; // this class's delegate
 9       IBOutlet UISlider *redSlider; // slider for changing amount of red
10       IBOutlet UISlider *greenSlider; // slider for changing amount of green
11       IBOutlet UISlider *blueSlider; // slider for changing amount of blue
12       IBOutlet UISlider *widthSlider; // slider for changing line width
13       IBOutlet UIView *colorView; // view that displays the current color
14       BOOL clearScreen; // was the Clear Screen button touched?
15    } // end instance variable declaration
16
17    // declare delegate and outlets as properties
18    @property(nonatomic, assign) id <FlipsideViewControllerDelegate> delegate;
19    @property(nonatomic, retain) IBOutlet UISlider *redSlider;
20    @property(nonatomic, retain) IBOutlet UISlider *greenSlider;
21    @property(nonatomic, retain) IBOutlet UISlider *blueSlider;
22    @property(nonatomic, retain) IBOutlet UISlider *widthSlider;
23    @property(nonatomic, retain) IBOutlet UIView *colorView;
24
25    - (IBAction)done; // called when the Done button is touched
26    - (IBAction)updateColor:sender; // called when a color slider is moved
27    - (IBAction)erase:sender; // called when the Erase button is touched
28    - (IBAction)clearScreen:sender; // called by Clear Screen button
29
30    // sets the color and line width
31    - (void)setColor:(UIColor *)c lineWidth:(float)width;
32    @end // end interface FlipsideViewController
33
34    // protocol that the delegate implements
35    @protocol FlipsideViewControllerDelegate
36    - (void)flipsideViewControllerDidFinish: // return to the MainView
37       (FlipsideViewController *)controller;
38    - (void)setColor:(UIColor *)color; // sets the current drawing color
39    - (void)setLineWidth:(float)width; // sets the current drawing line width
40    - (void)resetView; // erases the entire painting
41    @end // end protocol FlipsideViewControllerDelegate
```

Fig. 9.12 | FlipsideViewController interface.

The FlipsideViewcontroller class has five methods:

- done returns the user to the **MainView** when the "**Done**" **Button** is touched.

- updateColor updates the UIView previewing the chosen color when any of the color **Sliders**' thumbs are moved.

- erase sets the color of the painted line to white when the **"Eraser"** Button is touched. The **Sliders** move to the right to reflect the change.

- clearScreen:sender: is called when the **"Clear Screen"** Button is touched and causes the painting to be erased when the app returns to the **MainView**.

- setColor:lineWidth: sets the **Sliders'** thumb positions to match the current color and width of the painted line.

Implementing the FlipsideViewController Class

FlipsideViewController.m (Fig. 9.13) defines the FlipsideViewController class. The viewDidLoad method (lines 16–20) initializes FlipsideViewController's instance variables when its view loads. We set the view's backgroundColor property to the default UI-Color used for flipside views.

```
1    // Fig. 9.13: FlipsideViewController.m
2    // Controller for the flipside of the Painter app.
3    #import "FlipsideViewController.h"
4    #import "MainViewController.h"
5
6    @implementation FlipsideViewController
7
8    @synthesize delegate; // generate getter and setter for delegate
9    @synthesize redSlider; // generate getter and setter for redSlider
10   @synthesize greenSlider; // generate getter and setter for greenSlider
11   @synthesize blueSlider; // generate getter and setter for blueSlider
12   @synthesize widthSlider; // generate getter and setter for widthSlider
13   @synthesize colorView; // generate getter and setter for colorView
14
15   // called when view finishes loading
16   - (void)viewDidLoad
17   {
18      // initialize the background color to the default
19      self.view.backgroundColor = [UIColor viewFlipsideBackgroundColor];
20   } // end method viewDidLoad
21
22   // called when view is going to be displayed
23   - (void)viewWillAppear:(BOOL)animated
24   {
25      [super viewWillAppear:animated];
26      clearScreen = NO; // reset clearScreen
27   } // end method viewWillAppear:
28
29   // set the values for color and lineWidth
30   - (void)setColor:(UIColor *)c lineWidth:(float)width
31   {
32      // split the passed color into its RGB components
33      const float *colors = CGColorGetComponents(c.CGColor);
34
35      // update the sliders with the new value
36      redSlider.value = colors[0]; // set the red slider's value
```

Fig. 9.13 | FlipsideViewController class. (Part 1 of 3.)

```
37      greenSlider.value = colors[1]; // set the green slider's value
38      blueSlider.value = colors[2]; // set the blue slider's value
39
40      // update the color of colorView to reflect the sliders
41      colorView.backgroundColor = c;
42
43      // update the width slider
44      widthSlider.value = width;
45   } // end method setColor:lineWidth:
46
47   // called when any of the color sliders are changed
48   - (IBAction)updateColor:sender
49   {
50      // get the color from the sliders
51      UIColor *color = [UIColor colorWithRed:redSlider.value
52         green:greenSlider.value blue:blueSlider.value alpha:1.0];
53
54      // update colorView to reflect the new slider values
55      [colorView setBackgroundColor:color];
56   } // end method updateColor:
57
58   // called when the Eraser button is touched
59   - (IBAction)erase:sender
60   {
61      // do all the changes in an animation block so all the sliders finish
62      // moving at the same time
63      [UIView beginAnimations:nil context:nil]; // begin animation block
64      [UIView setAnimationDuration:0.5]; // set the animation length
65
66      // set all sliders to their max value so the color is white
67      [redSlider setValue:1.0]; // set the red slider's value to 1
68      [greenSlider setValue:1.0]; // set the green slider's value to 1
69      [blueSlider setValue:1.0]; // set the blue slider's value to 1
70
71      // update colorView to reflect the new slider values
72      [colorView setBackgroundColor:[UIColor whiteColor]];
73      [UIView commitAnimations]; // end animation block
74   } // end method erase:
75
76   // called when the Clear Screen button is touched
77   - (IBAction)clearScreen:sender
78   {
79      clearScreen = YES; // set clearScreen to YES
80   } // end method clearScreen:
81
82   // called when the Done button is touched
83   - (IBAction)done
84   {
85      // set the new values for color and line width
86      [self.delegate setColor:colorView.backgroundColor];
87      [self.delegate setLineWidth:widthSlider.value];
88
```

Fig. 9.13 | FlipsideViewController class. (Part 2 of 3.)

```
89      // if the user touched the Clear Screen button
90      if (clearScreen)
91          [self.delegate resetView]; // clear the canvas
92
93      // flip the view back to the front side
94      [self.delegate flipsideViewControllerDidFinish:self];
95  } // end method done
96
97  // free FlipsideViewController's memory
98  - (void)dealloc
99  {
100     [redSlider release]; // release the redSlider UISlider
101     [greenSlider release]; // release the greenSlider UISlider
102     [blueSlider release]; // release the blueSlider UISlider
103     [widthSlider release]; // release the widthSlider UISlider
104     [colorView release]; // release the colorView UIView
105     [super dealloc]; // call the superclass's dealloc method
106 } // end method dealloc
107 @end
```

Fig. 9.13 | FlipsideViewController class. (Part 3 of 3.)

The viewWillAppear method (lines 23–27) is called when the **FlipsideView** is about to be displayed. The method resets clearScreen to NO. We call the superclass's viewWill-Appear: method (line 25) to ensure that the UIView is ready to be displayed.

The setColor:lineWidth: method (lines 30–45) is used to update the GUI components on the flipside to match the current appearance of the painted line. Remember, a new FlipsideViewController is created every time the user touches the info button, but we want to save the settings through each one. The CGColorGetComponents function breaks down a CGColor into an array of its RGB values (line 33). Lines 36–38 update each **Slider**'s value property to the appropriate colors—moving the thumbs to their proper locations. The colorView UIView's backgroundColor is updated to display the current color of the painted line and widthSlider's value is updated to the current width (lines 41 and 44).

The updateColor method (lines 48–56) is called to update colorView each time a **Slider**'s thumbs is moved. We create a new UIColor object using the values of the **Slider**s (lines 51–52). We then update the background color of colorView to reflect the new color.

The erase method (lines 59–74) sets each color **Slider**'s value property to one—setting the color of the painted line to white. The **Slider**'s thumbs are moved to their new positions using animation. Line 63 begins a new Core Animation block by calling UIView's beginAnimations:context: method. The setAnimationDuration: method specifies that the animation will last half a second. Lines 67–69 set all of the Sliders' values to 1.0 using UISlider's setValue: method. The colorView UIView is then updated to display the color white. Line 73 calls UIView's commitAnimations method to end the animation block and start the animation.

The clearScreen: method (lines 77–80) sets clearScreen to YES when the "**Clear Screen**" **Button** is touched. This causes the painting to clear when the user switches back to the **MainView**.

The done method (lines 83–95) is called when the user touches the "**Done**" **Button**. We then call the delegate's setColor method—setting the color of the painted line equal to colorView's backgroundColor property (line 86). Line 87 sets the painted line width equal to the value of widthSlider using the delegate's setLineWidth method. If the "**Clear Screen**" **Button** was touched (line 90), we call the delegates's resetView method to erase the current painting. MainViewController's flipsideViewControllerDid-Finish: method returns the app to the **MainView**.

Building the Flipside View

The interface for the flipside view is contained in the file FlipsideView.xib. The flipside view contains components used to set the width and the color of the painted line. Begin by changing Title to Painter, then add a **Slider** for changing the line width and a **Label** to describe it. Select the **Slider** and open the **Inspector**. Change **Minimum** to 1.0, **Maximum** to 20.0 and **Current** to 5.0. Drag three more **Slider**s to set the RGB values of the painted line. In the **Inspector** check the checkbox **Continuous** for each one. This makes the **Slider** send events every time it's moved, rather than once only when it stops moving. Add a **Button** titled **Clear Screen** to allow the user to erase the canvas, and add a **Button** titled **Eraser** which will turn the painted line into an eraser. The finished interface is shown in Fig. 9.14.

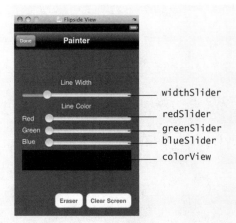

Fig. 9.14 | The finished flipside interface.

Next, connect the outlets and actions as we discussed in Section 4.6. In the **Flipside-View.xib** window, the FlipsideViewController object is represented by **File's Owner**. Select this object and connect its outlets as labeled in Fig. 9.14. Next, select the three color **Slider**s and connect their **Value Changed** event to the updateColor: method of **File's Owner**. Also connect the "**Eraser**" **Button**'s **Touch Up Inside** event to the erase: method and the "**Clear Screen**" **Button**'s event to the clearScreen: method.

9.4 Wrap-Up

In the **Painter** app, you learned more about how custom UIViews and UIViewControllers interact. We saw how to handle all three types of touch events, along with motion events generated when the user shakes the iPhone. We also saw how to store primitives and structures in collections using the NSValue class, and how to selectively redraw a UIView to optimize the app's performance.

In Chapter 10, we build the **Address Book** app. We introduce the **Table View** component to display a list of information. We show the different kinds of **Table View**s and how to populate them with information. We also introduce **Navigation Controllers**, which are used to manage a hierarchy of **View**s and are usually used in conjunction with **Table View**s. Both of these new classes are used in the context of the **Navigation-based Application** template.

Address Book App
Tables and UINavigationController

OBJECTIVES

In this chapter you'll learn:

- To use UITableViews to display contact information.

- To save memory by reusing UITableViewCells.

- To display different keyboard styles to match various input types using UIKeyboardStyles.

- To use the **Navigation-based Application** template to switch between **View**s using a **Navigation Controller**.

- To add **Button**s to a UINavigationItem so that one navigation bar can handle transitions between three **View**s.

- To extend UITableViewCell to create an editable cell.

Outline

10.1 Introduction

10.2 Test-Driving the **Address Book** App

10.3 Technologies Overview

10.4 Building the App

    10.4.1 Class `RootViewController`

    10.4.2 Class `AddViewController`

    10.4.3 Class `ContactViewController`

    10.4.4 Class `EditableCell`

10.5 Wrap-Up

10.1 Introduction

The **Address Book** app (Fig. 10.1) provides quick and easy access to stored contact information. On the main screen, the user can scroll through an alphabetical contact list, add contacts, delete contacts and view more information about individual contacts. Touching a contact's name displays a screen showing the contact's detailed information (Fig. 10.2). Touching the "**Back**" **Button** in the top-left corner of the details screen returns the user to the contacts list. You can add a new contact by touching the **Add Contact Button** (![+]) in the top-right corner of the app. This shows a screen containing editable **Text Fields** for entering the new contact's name, address, e-mail and phone number (Fig. 10.3). Touching the "**Done**" **Button** adds the new contact and returns the user to the main contact screen. Pressing the "**Edit**" **Button** in the top-left corner of the main screen displays the **Deletion Control Button**s (![-]) next to each contact (Fig. 10.4(a)). Touching one of these displays a

Touch to choose a contact to delete

Touch to add a new contact

Fig. 10.1 | List of contacts.

"**Delete**" **Button** next to the chosen contact's name (Fig. 10.4(b)). Pressing the "**Delete**" **Button** deletes the corresponding contact.

Touch to return to the
list of contacts

Fig. 10.2 | Viewing a single contact's details.

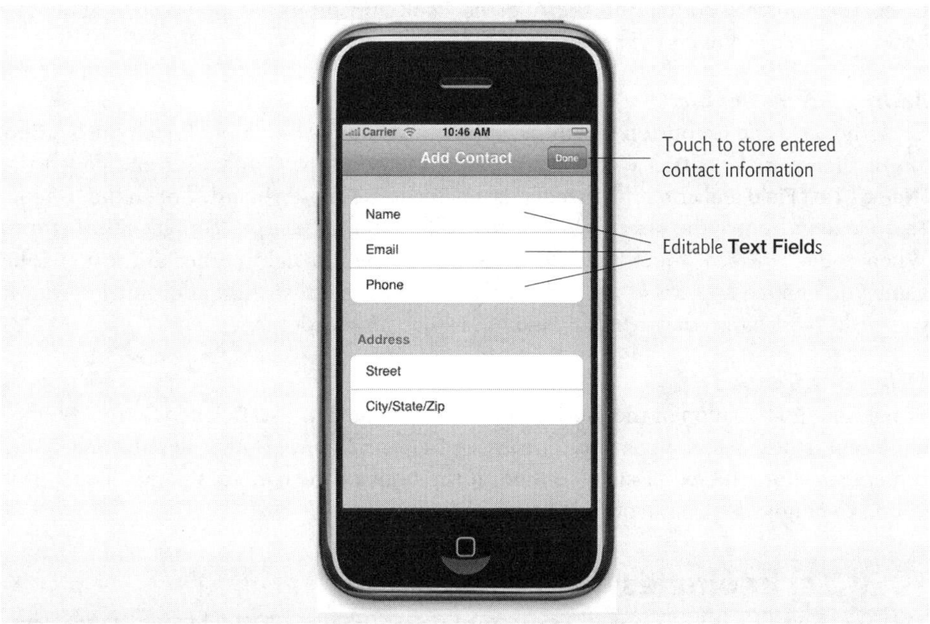

Touch to store entered
contact information

Editable **Text Field**s

Fig. 10.3 | **Add Contact** screen.

Fig. 10.4 | Deleting a contact.

10.2 Test-Driving the Address Book App

Opening the Completed Application
Open the directory containing the **Address Book** app project. Double click Address-Book.xcodeproj to open the project in Xcode.

Adding a New Contact
Click the **Build and Go** button to run the app in the iPhone Simulator. Touch the ➕ Button in the top-right corner of the app to view the **Add New Contact** screen. Touch the "**Name**" **Text Field** and enter the first and last name using the keyboard. Touch the "**Street**" **Text Field** and enter the street address, then fill in the remaining contact information. When you're finished, touch the "**Done**" **Button** in the top-right corner of the app. The name you entered appears as the only entry in the contact list. Add additional entries if you wish. Notice that they're maintained in alphabetical order.

Deleting a Contact
Touch the "**Edit**" **Button** in the top-left corner of the contacts list. **Deletion Control Buttons** (➖) appear next to each contact. Touch the **Deletion Control Button** next to one of the contacts to show the red "**Delete**" **Button** to the right of the contact's name. Touch this **Button** to remove the contact from the list.

10.3 Technologies Overview

This app displays a list of contacts in a *UITableView*—the standard table for iPhone apps. A UITableView allows the user to scroll through the contacts by dragging a finger up or down the screen. UITableViews contain UITableViewCells. We use both editable and non-editable cells in this app. To save memory and improve the app's performance, we reuse UITableViewCells in our UITableViews. For example, when the user is scrolling through a long list of contacts, only a limited number of contacts can appear on the screen at any time. Rather than creating new UITableViewCells for contacts as the appear on the screen, we can reuse the ones that are no longer visible by calling UITableView's de-queueReusableCellWithIdentifier: method. This saves memory and improves the app's performance. Similarly, we don't need new UITableViewCells for each new contact the user adds—we can simply reuse the cells in the UITableView for each new contact. For more information on programming with UITableViews, visit:

```
developer.apple.com/iphone/library/documentation/UserExperience/
    Conceptual/TableView_iPhone/
```

All UIViewControllers have a navigationController property of type UINaviga-tionController. We use this navigation bar to add **Button**s that the user can press to view, edit and add new contacts. UINavigationItems contain the **Button**s that are used to navigate through the app's screens. The RootViewController's view contains the contact-list UITableView. The RootViewController displays a new ContactViewController when the user touches an individual contact and creates an AddViewController when the user touches the ➕ **Button**. Various UIKeyboardTypes provide the user with the correct keyboard for the type of information being entered.

10.4 Building the App

Open Xcode and create a new project. Select the **Navigation-based Application** template and name the project AddressBook. The RootViewController class files are automatically generated.

10.4.1 Class RootViewController

The RootViewController class (Fig. 10.5) manages the **RootView**. This is the starting point of the **Address Book** app.

```
1   // RootViewController.h
2   // Controller for the main table of the Address Book app.
3   // Implementation in RootViewController.m
4   #import <UIKit/UIKit.h>
5   #import "AddViewController.h"
6   #import "ContactViewController.h"
7
8   // begin interface RootViewController
9   @interface RootViewController : UITableViewController
10      <AddViewControllerDelegate>
11  {
12      NSMutableArray *contacts; // contains all the added contacts
13      NSString *filePath; // the path of the save file
14  } // end instance variables declaration
```

Fig. 10.5 | Controller for the main table of the **Address Book** app. (Part 1 of 2.)

```
15
16   - (void)addContact; // present the view for adding a new contact
17   @end // end interface RootViewController
18
19   // begin NSDictionary's sorting category
20   @interface NSDictionary (sorting)
21      // compares this contact's name to the given contact's title
22      - (NSComparisonResult)compareContactNames:(NSDictionary *)contact;
23   @end // end category sorting of interface UIButton
```

Fig. 10.5 | Controller for the main table of the **Address Book** app. (Part 2 of 2.)

RootViewController is a subclass of *UITableViewController* (line 9)—which is a subclass of the UIViewController class we've used in previous apps. A UITableViewController manages UITableViews similar to the way UIViewController manages UIViews. Line 10 states that this class implements the AddViewControllerDelegate protocol—it defines the addViewControllerDidFinish: method.

RootViewController has two instance variables—contacts (line 12) and filePath (line 13). The contacts NSMutableArray contains NSDictionary objects—each represents the complete contact information for one person. The filePath contains the location of the file that stores the app's data. The addContact method (line 16) creates a new **AddContactView** so the user can add a new contact.

Lines 20–23 add the sorting category to NSDictionary. The sorting category has only one method—compareContactNames: (defined in Fig. 10.12). This compares the names of two contacts represented as NSDictionarys. We use this method to sort an NSMutableArray of contacts in alphabetical order.

Defining the RootViewController Class Implementation
The viewDidLoad method (Fig. 10.6, lines 9–48) initializes class RootViewController's instance variables after the view loads. Lines 12–13 use the NSSearchPathForDirectoriesInDomains function to get an NSArray with one item—the path name of the directory where this app can save data. The path name is stored in the directory NSString (line 16). Lines 19–20 concatenate the word contacts to the end of directory to specify the complete path of the file in which we'll save the contact information. Line 23 creates a new NSFileManager by calling NSFileManager's defaultManager static method. We use this object to determine whether the file already exists (line 26). If it does, we use NSMutableArray's static initWithContentsOfFile method to initialize contacts with the contents of that file (line 27). This method parses a plist file to create an NSMutableArray containing the file's contents. Otherwise, NSMutableArray contacts is initialized as a new, empty array (line 29). Lines 32–34 create an **Add Contact Button** (+) as a new *UIBarButtonItem* that, when touched, calls RootViewController's addContact method. A UIBarButtonItem functions similar to a UIButton, except that a UIBarButtonItem appears only inside a **Navigation Bar**. Lines 37–38 create another UIBarButtonItem titled Back. We then access RootViewController's navigationItem property (inherited from class UIViewController) to place the two UIBarButtonItems on the **Navigation Bar** at the top of the app (lines 41–42). The **Add Contact Button** is placed on the right side of the bar (line 41) and UIViewController's editButtonItem is placed on the left (line 42). Line 45 sets navigationItem's backBarButtonItem to backButton—causing the navigation controller to use

backButton as navigationItem's leftBarButtonItem when the user navigates away from the RootViewController's view.

```objc
 1  // RootViewController.m
 2  // Controller for the main table of the Address Book app.
 3  #import "RootViewController.h"
 4  #import "AddressBookAppDelegate.h"
 5
 6  @implementation RootViewController
 7
 8  // called when view finishes initializing
 9  - (void)viewDidLoad
10  {
11     // creates list of valid directories for saving a file
12     NSArray *paths = NSSearchPathForDirectoriesInDomains(
13        NSDocumentDirectory, NSUserDomainMask, YES);
14
15     // get the first directory because we only care about one
16     NSString *directory = [paths objectAtIndex:0];
17
18     // concatenate the file name "contacts" to the end of the path
19     filePath = [[NSString alloc] initWithString:
20        [directory stringByAppendingPathComponent:@"contacts"]];
21
22     // retrieve the default NSFileManager
23     NSFileManager *fileManager = [NSFileManager defaultManager];
24
25     // if the file exists, initialize contacts with its contents
26     if ([fileManager fileExistsAtPath:filePath])
27        contacts = [[NSMutableArray alloc] initWithContentsOfFile:filePath];
28     else // else initialize contacts as empty NSMutableArray
29        contacts = [[NSMutableArray alloc] init];
30
31     // create the button to add a new contact
32     UIBarButtonItem *plusButton = [[UIBarButtonItem alloc]
33        initWithBarButtonSystemItem:UIBarButtonSystemItemAdd target:self
34        action:@selector(addContact)];
35
36     // create the back UIBarButtonItem
37     UIBarButtonItem *backButton = [[UIBarButtonItem alloc]initWithTitle:
38        @"Back" style:UIBarButtonItemStylePlain target:nil action:nil];
39
40     // add the plus UIBarButtonItem to the top bar on the right
41     self.navigationItem.rightBarButtonItem = plusButton;
42     self.navigationItem.leftBarButtonItem = self.editButtonItem;
43
44     // set the back UIBarButtonItem to show if the user navigates away
45     self.navigationItem.backBarButtonItem = backButton;
46     [plusButton release]; // release the plusButton UIButton
47     [backButton release]; // release the backButton UIButton
48  } // end method viewDidLoad
49
```

Fig. 10.6 | Method viewDidLoad of class RootViewController.

Method addContact of Class RootViewController

The addContact method (Fig. 10.7) initializes a new AddViewController (lines 54–55). UIViewController's presentModalViewController:animated: method is called to display the controller's **View** (line 58).

```
50    // called when the user touches the plus button
51    - (void)addContact
52    {
53       // create new AddViewController
54       AddViewController *controller = [[AddViewController alloc] init];
55       controller.delegate = self; // set controller's delegate to self
56
57       // show the new controller
58       [self presentModalViewController:controller animated:YES];
59       [controller release]; // release the controller AddViewController
60    } // end method addContact
61
```

Fig. 10.7 | Method addContact of class RootViewController.

Method addViewControllerDidFinishAdding: of Class RootViewController

The addViewControllerDidFinishAdding: method (Fig. 10.8) adds a new contact then dismisses the AddViewController. Line 65 calls the AddViewController's values method (defined in Fig. 10.16), which returns an NSDictionary containing the data for the new contact. If the NSDictionary is not nil, we add the new contact using NSDictionary's addObject: method (line 70). Line 73 sorts contacts by their names using NSMutableArray's sortUsingSelector: method. We then hide AddViewController's view by calling UIViewController's dismissModalViewControllerAnimated: method (line 77). Line 80 saves the contents of the contacts dictionary to a file by calling NSMutableDictionary's writeToFile:atomically: method. Next, we reload the UITableView (line 82) to display the updated contact list data.

```
62    - (void)addViewControllerDidFinishAdding:(AddViewController *)controller
63    {
64       // get the values for the new person to be added
65       NSDictionary *person = [controller values];
66
67       // if there is a person
68       if (person != nil)
69       {
70          [contacts addObject:person]; // add person to contacts
71
72          // sort the contacts array in alphabetical name by order
73          [contacts sortUsingSelector:@selector(compareContactNames:)];
74       } // end if
75
```

Fig. 10.8 | Method addViewControllerDidFinishAdding: of class RootViewController. (Part 1 of 2.)

```
76      // make the AddViewControler stop showing
77      [self dismissModalViewControllerAnimated:YES];
78
79      // write contacts to file
80      [contacts writeToFile:filePath atomically:NO];
81
82      [self.tableView reloadData]; // refresh the table view
83   } // end method finishedAdding
84
```

Fig. 10.8 | Method addViewControllerDidFinishAdding: of class RootViewController.
(Part 2 of 2.)

Methods *tableView:NumberOfRowsInSection* and *tableView:cellForRowAt-IndexPath:* of Class *RootViewController*

Several methods inherited from UITableViewController control the table's formatting. These methods are defined in the *UITableViewDataSource* and *UITableViewDelegate* protocols, which UITableViewController implements. A UITableView gets its data from its specified *dataSource*. In this case, RootViewController is the dataSource. The number of rows in each section is specified by the UITableViewDataSource protocol's *tableView:numberOfRowsInSection: method* (Fig. 10.9, lines 86–90). We return the number of elements in the contacts array (line 89) in this case, since all of the saved contacts are shown in one section of the table.

```
85   // called by the table view to determine the number of rows in a section
86   - (NSInteger)tableView:(UITableView *)tableView numberOfRowsInSection:
87     (NSInteger)section
88   {
89      return contacts.count; //return the number of contacts
90   } // end method tableView:numberOfRowsInSection:
91
92   // returns tableView's cell at specified indexPath
93   - (UITableViewCell *)tableView:(UITableView *)tableView
94     cellForRowAtIndexPath:(NSIndexPath *)indexPath
95   {
96      // create cell identifier
97      static NSString *MyIdentifier = @"StandardCell";
98      UITableViewCell *cell = [tableView dequeueReusableCellWithIdentifier:
99         MyIdentifier]; // get a reusable cell
100
101     // if no reusable cells are available
102     if (cell == nil)
103     {
104        // create a new editable cell
105        cell = [[[UITableViewCell alloc] initWithStyle:
106           UITableViewCellStyleDefault reuseIdentifier:MyIdentifier]
107           autorelease];
108     } // end if
```

Fig. 10.9 | Methods and tableView:NumberOfRowsInSection: and
tableView:cellForRowAtIndexPath: of class RootViewController. (Part 1 of 2.)

```
109
110     // set up the cell
111     NSString *name = [[contacts objectAtIndex:indexPath.row] valueForKey:
112       @"Name"];
113     UILabel *label = [cell textLabel]; // get the label for the cell
114     label.text = name; // set the text of the label
115
116     // make the cell display an arrow on the right side
117     cell.accessoryType = UITableViewCellAccessoryDisclosureIndicator;
118     return cell; // return the updated cell
119   } // end method tableView:cellForRowAtIndexPath:
120
```

Fig. 10.9 | Methods and `tableView:NumberOfRowsInSection:` and `tableView:cellForRowAtIndexPath:` of class `RootViewController`. (Part 2 of 2.)

The *tableView:cellForRowAtIndexPath: method* returns a UITableViewCell for the given UITableView and *NSIndexPath*—an object that represents the index of a cell (i.e., contact) in the table. Line 97 creates an NSString which will be passed to UITableView's *dequeueReusableCellWithIdentifier:* method to get a UITableView-Cell from tableView (lines 98–99). The NSString specifies the type of cell we want to receive. This method attempts to reuse an existing UITableViewCell (with the specified identifier) which is not in use at the moment, possibly because it is not displayed on the screen. If tableView contains no editable UITableViewCells that can be reused (line 102), we create a new one using *UITableViewCell's initWithStyle:reuseIdentifier: method* (lines 105–107). UITableViewCell styles are new to iPhone OS 3.x, you can learn more about them by searching developer.apple.com for A Closer Look at Table-View Cells. Lines 111–112 get the name of the contact corresponding to the row we're retrieving. Lines 113–114 update cell's textLabel property to display the correct contact's name. We then return the configured cell to the UITableView (line 118).

Method tableView:didSelectRowAtIndexPath: of Class RootViewController
The UITableViewDelegate's *tableView:didSelectRowAtIndexPath: method* (Fig. 10.10) is called when the user touches a row of the UITableView. In this case, we display a **Contact-View** so the user can edit a contact. Lines 126–127 create a new ContactViewController. We then call ContactViewController's setPerson and updateTitle methods to initialize the **ContactView** with the data from the selected contact. Line 134 calls UINavigationController's *pushViewController:animated: method* to display the new **ContactView**.

```
121   // called when the user touches one of the rows in the table
122   - (void)tableView:(UITableView *)tableView didSelectRowAtIndexPath:
123     (NSIndexPath *)indexPath
124   {
```

Fig. 10.10 | Method `tableView:didSelectRowAtIndexPath:` of class `RootViewController`. (Part 1 of 2.)

```
125    // initialize a ContactViewController
126    ContactViewController *controller = [[ContactViewController alloc]
127       initWithNibName:@"ContactViewController" bundle:nil];
128
129    // give controller the data to display
130    [controller setPerson:[contacts objectAtIndex:[indexPath row]]];
131    [controller updateTitle]; // update the title with the new data
132
133    // show the ContactViewController
134    [self.navigationController pushViewController:controller animated:YES];
135    [controller release]; // release the controller ContactViewController
136 } // end method tableView:didSelectRowAtIndexPath:
137
```

Fig. 10.10 | Method `tableView:didSelectRowAtIndexPath:` of class RootViewController. (Part 2 of 2.)

Methods *tableView:commitEditingStyle:forRowAtIndexPath:*, *shouldAutorotateToInterfaceOrientation:* and *dealloc of Class* RootViewController

The UITableViewDataSource protocol's ***tableView:commitEditingStyle:forRowAtIndexPath: method*** (Fig. 10.11, lines 139–156) is called when the user edits the table, such as by deleting or inserting a row. Recall that the user can delete cells using when the app is in edit mode. If the given UITableViewCellEditingStyle is UITableViewCellEditingStyleDelete (line 144), the user touched the "**Delete**" **Button**, so line 147 calls contact's removeObjectAtIndex method to remove the element at indexPath.row. We call UITableView's ***deleteRowsAtIndexPaths:withRowAnimation: method*** to remove the deleted row from tableView (lines 150–151). We then write the updated contacts to the file (line 154).

```
138 // Override to support editing the table view.
139 - (void)tableView:(UITableView *)tableView commitEditingStyle:
140    (UITableViewCellEditingStyle)editingStyle forRowAtIndexPath:
141    (NSIndexPath *)indexPath
142 {
143    // "delete" editing style is committed
144    if (editingStyle == UITableViewCellEditingStyleDelete)
145    {
146       // remove contact at indexPath.row
147       [contacts removeObjectAtIndex:indexPath.row];
148
149       // delete the row from the data source
150       [tableView deleteRowsAtIndexPaths:[NSArray arrayWithObject:
151          indexPath] withRowAnimation:UITableViewRowAnimationFade];
152
```

Fig. 10.11 | Methods `tableView:commitEditingStyle:forRowAtIndexPath:`, `shouldAutorotateToInterfaceOrientation:` and `dealloc` of class RootViewController. (Part 1 of 2.)

```
153        // write contacts to file
154        [contacts writeToFile:filePath atomically:NO];
155     } // end if
156  } // end method tableView:commitEditingStyle:forRowAtIndexPath:
157
158  // called to determine what orientations our View allows
159  - (BOOL)shouldAutorotateToInterfaceOrientation:
160     (UIInterfaceOrientation)interfaceOrientation
161  {
162     // return YES for supported orientations
163     return (interfaceOrientation == UIInterfaceOrientationPortrait);
164  } // end method shouldAutorotateToInterfaceOrientation
165
166  // release MainViewController's memory
167  - (void)dealloc
168  {
169     [contacts release]; // release the contacts NSMutableArray
170     [super dealloc]; // call the superclass's dealloc method
171  } // end method dealloc
172  @end // end RootViewController implementation
173
```

Fig. 10.11 | Methods `tableView:commitEditingStyle:forRowAtIndexPath:`, `shouldAutorotateToInterfaceOrientation:` and `dealloc` of class `RootViewController`. (Part 2 of 2.)

The `shouldAutoRotateToInterfaceOrientation:` method (lines 159–164) is inherited from `UIViewController` and overridden by default in the **Navigation-based Application** template. This method is called by the iPhone OS to determine if this view should rotate when the iPhone's orientation changes. The `dealloc` method (lines 167–171) releases the `contacts` `NSMutableArray` and calls the superclass's `dealloc` method.

NSDictionary's sorting Category

Lines 175–182 implement method `compareContactNames:` of NSDictionary's sorting category (Fig. 10.12). Lines 179–180 use NSString's `caseInsensitiveCompare:` method to compare the value for key `Name` of the given NSDictionary to that of the NSDictionary receiving the `compareContactNames:` message.

```
174  // define NSDictionary's sorting category method
175  @implementation NSDictionary (sorting)
176  - (NSComparisonResult)compareContactNames:(NSDictionary *)contact
177  {
178     // compare this contact's title to that of the given contact
179     return [[self valueForKey:@"Name"]
180        caseInsensitiveCompare:[contact valueForKey:@"Name"]];
181  } // end method compareContactNames
182  @end // end NSDictionary's sorting category
```

Fig. 10.12 | NSDictionary's sorting category.

10.4.2 Class `AddViewController`

In Xcode, select **File > New File** and chose **UIViewController subclass**. Before pressing **Next**, ensure that the **With XIB for user interface** checkbox is checked so that Xcode automatically generates a nib file for the new class. Name the class **AddViewController** and save it in the default location provided. Open `AddViewController.xib` and drag a **Navigation Bar** to the top of the app window. Change the title of the **Navigation Item** to **Add Contact**. Next, drag a **Bar Button Item** from the Library to the right side of the **Navigation Bar**. Open the Inspector window to change the **Bar Button Item**'s **Title** to **Done**. Drag a **TableView** from the **Library** window and resize it to fill the remainder of the app window. Figure 10.13 shows the completed nib file.

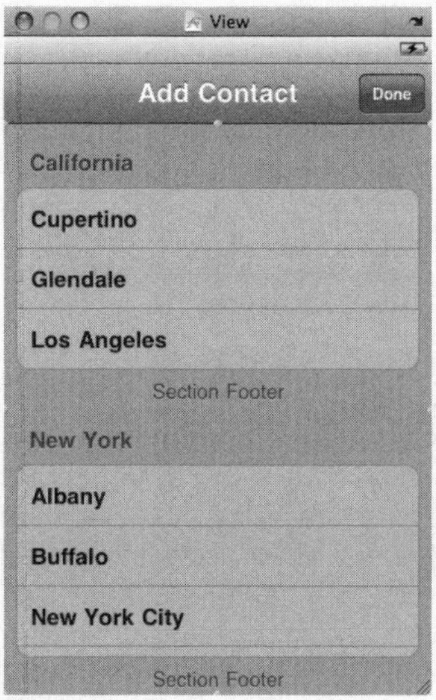

Fig. 10.13 | `AddViewController.xib` in Interface Builder after placing the default TableView.

AddViewController Interface Declaration

Class `AddViewController` (Fig. 10.14) is a subclass of `UIViewController` (line 10) and implements the `UITableViewDataSource` protocol. This means that `AddViewController` acts as a data source for a `UITableView`. It also implements the `EditableCellDelegate` protocol so that it can receive messages when a user begins editing a cell, stops editing a cell or touches the "**Done**" **Button**.

```
1   // AddViewController.h
2   // AddViewController's interface declaration.
3   // Implementation in AddViewController.m
4   #import <UIKit/UIKit.h>
5   #import "EditableCell.h"
```

Fig. 10.14 | `AddViewController`'s interface declaration. (Part 1 of 2.)

```
 6   static const int KEYBOARD_HEIGHT = 200; // the height of the keyboard
 7
 8   @protocol AddViewControllerDelegate; // AddViewControllerDelegate protocol
 9
10   @interface AddViewController : UIViewController <UITableViewDataSource,
11      EditableCellDelegate>
12   {
13      id <AddViewControllerDelegate> delegate; // this class's delegate
14      IBOutlet UITableView *table; // table that displays editable fields
15      NSArray *fields; // an array containing the field names
16      NSMutableDictionary *data; // dictionary containing contact data
17      BOOL keyboardShown; // is the keyboard visible?
18      EditableCell *currentCell; // the cell the user is currently editing
19   } // end instance variable declaration
20
21   // declare delegate and table as properties
22   @property (nonatomic, assign) id <AddViewControllerDelegate> delegate;
23   @property (nonatomic, retain) IBOutlet UITableView *table;
24   @property (readonly, copy, getter=values) NSDictionary *data;
25   - (IBAction)doneAdding:sender; // return to RootView
26   - (NSDictionary *)values; // return values NSDictionary
27   - (void)clearFields; // clear table cells
28   @end // end interface AddViewController
29
30   // notifies RootViewcontroller that Done Button was touched
31   @protocol AddViewControllerDelegate
32   - (void)addViewControllerDidFinishAdding:(AddViewController *)controller;
33   @end // end protocol AddViewControllerDelegate
```

Fig. 10.14 | AddViewController's interface declaration. (Part 2 of 2.)

Line 13 declares variable delegate of type id which implements the AddViewControllerDelegate protocol. This will be used to store the RootViewController. The UITableView table is declared as an outlet and will display the contact information for the chosen contact (line 14). In Interface Builder connect the new **Table View** to the table property of **File's Owner**. NSArray fields will store the field names for each of the fields in table (line 15). The NSMutableDictionary data contains the data for the new contact, once the user enters it (line 16). The BOOL variable keyboardShown indicates whether or not the keyboard is currently visible (line 17). Line 18 declares an EditableCell to store the UITableViewCell currently being edited by the user.

Lines 22–24 declare delegate, table and data as properties. The AddViewController class defines three methods:

- doneAdding:sender: returns the app to the **RootView** when the user touches the "Done" Button

- values returns an NSDictionary containing all the contact information stored in table.

- clearFields clears all of table's EditableCells.

Lines 31–33 declare the AddViewControllerDelegate protocol. Classes implementing this protocol define the addViewControllerDidFinishAdding: method. Root-

`ViewController` implements this protocol to hide the **AddView** when the "**Done**" **Button** is touched.

Method `initWithNibName:bundle:` of Class `AddViewController`

The `initWithNibName:bundle:` method (Fig. 10.15, lines 10–27) is called when the AddViewController loads. If the inherited superclass members initialize without error (line 14), lines 17–18 initialize the `fields` NSArray with names of the fields in the `table` UITableView using ***NSArray's `initWithObjects:` method***. This method takes a comma separated list of objects ending with `nil`. The last argument indicates the end of the list and is not included in the `NSArray`. Line 21 uses `NSMutableDictionary`'s `initWithCapacity:` method to create the `data` NSMutableDictionary with the same number of elements as `fields`.

```
 1   // AddViewController.m
 2   // Controls a view for adding a new contact.
 3   #import "AddViewController.h"
 4
 5   @implementation AddViewController
 6   @synthesize delegate;
 7   @synthesize table;
 8
 9   // initialize the AddViewController
10   - (id)initWithNibName:(NSString *)nibNameOrNil bundle:
11      (NSBundle *)nibBundleOrNil
12   {
13      // if the superclass initialized properly
14      if (self = [super initWithNibName:nibNameOrNil bundle:nibBundleOrNil])
15      {
16         // create the names of the fields
17         fields = [[NSArray alloc] initWithObjects:@"Name", @"Email",
18            @"Phone", @"Street", @"City/State/Zip", nil];
19
20         // initialize the data NSMutableDictionary
21         data = [[NSMutableDictionary alloc] initWithCapacity:fields.count];
22         keyboardShown = NO; // hide the keyboard
23         currentCell = nil; // there is no cell currently selected
24      } // end if
25
26      return self; // return this AddViewController
27   } // end method initWithNibName:bundle:
28
```

Fig. 10.15 | Methods `initWithNibName:bundle:` and `viewDidLoad` of class AddViewController.

Methods `doneAdding:` and `values` of Class `AddViewController`

The `doneAdding:` method (Fig. 10.16, lines 30–40) returns the app to the **RootView** when the user touches the "**Done**" **Button**. If there is a currently selected UITableViewCell (line 33), we call NSDictionary's `setValue:forKey:` method to update `data` with the selected UITableViewCell's text. Line 39 calls RootViewController's `addViewControllerDidFinishAdding:` method to switch views. If the user has not entered any contacts, the values method (lines 43–51) returns nil (line 47). Otherwise, it calls NSDictionary's dictionaryWithDictionary: method to create a new NSDictionary containing the same information as data (line 50).

```
29   // alert RootViewController that the "Done" Button was touched
30   - (IBAction)doneAdding:sender
31   {
32      // if there is a cell currently selected
33      if (currentCell != nil)
34         // update data with the text in the currently selected cell
35         [data setValue:currentCell.textField.text
36            forKey:currentCell.label.text];
37
38      // return to the RootView
39      [delegate addViewControllerDidFinishAdding:self];
40   } // end method doneAdding:
41
42   // returns a dictionary containing all the supplied contact information
43   - (NSDictionary *)values
44   {
45      // if the user did not supply a name
46      if ([data valueForKey:@"Name"] == nil)
47         return nil; // return nil
48
49      // returns a copy of the data NSDictionary
50      return [NSDictionary dictionaryWithDictionary:data];
51   } // end method values
52
```

Fig. 10.16 | Methods doneAdding: and values of class AddViewController.

Methods editableCellDidBeginEditing:, editableCellDidEndEditing: and editableCellDidEndOnExit: of Class AddViewController

The editableCellDidBeginEditing: method (Fig. 10.17, lines 54–78) is called when the user touches one of table's cells. If the keyboard is not currently displayed (line 57), we resize table to make room for the keyboard. We animate the resize to make it a visually smooth transition. Line 60 calls UIView's beginAnimations:context: method to begin a new animation block. We set the length of the animation to 0.25 seconds by calling UI-View's setAnimationDuration: method. We call UIView's setAnimationCurve method to specify that the animation starts slowly and accelerates until finishing. Lines 63–64 get table's frame and decrease frame's height by the height of the keyboard. We then apply the resized frame to table and call UIView's commitAnimations method to end the animation block and begin animating (lines 65–66). Next, we set keyboardShown equal to YES (line 69). Line 73 passes cell as an argument to UITableView's indexPathForCell: method to get an NSIndexPath representing cell's location in table. UITableView's scrollToRowAtIndexPath:atScrollPosition:animated: scrolls the table so that cell appears at the top of the screen (lines 76–77).

The editableCellDidEndEditing: method (lines 81–85) is called when the user finishes editing a cell—either by selecting another cell or hitting the "**Done**" **Button**. Line 84 stores the name of the cell and its content as a key/value pair in NSDictionary data.

```
53    // called when the user begins editing a cell
54    - (void)editableCellDidBeginEditing:(EditableCell *)cell
55    {
56        // if the keyboard is hidden
57        if (!keyboardShown)
58        {
59            // animate resizing the table to fit the keyboard
60            [UIView beginAnimations:nil context:NULL]; // begin animation block
61            [UIView setAnimationDuration:0.25]; // set the animation duration
62            [UIView setAnimationCurve:UIViewAnimationCurveEaseIn];
63            CGRect frame = table.frame; // get the frame of the table
64            frame.size.height -= KEYBOARD_HEIGHT; // subtract from the height
65            [table setFrame:frame]; // apply the new frame
66            [UIView commitAnimations]; // end animation block
67        } // end if
68
69        keyboardShown = YES; // the keyboard appears on the screen
70        currentCell = cell; // update the currently selected cell
71
72        // get the index path for the selected cell
73        NSIndexPath *path = [table indexPathForCell:cell];
74
75        // scroll the table so that the selected cell is at the top
76        [table scrollToRowAtIndexPath:path atScrollPosition:
77            UITableViewScrollPositionTop animated:YES];
78    } // end method cellBeganEditing:
79
80    // called when the user stops editing a cell or selects another cell
81    - (void)editableCellDidEndEditing:(EditableCell *)cell
82    {
83        // add the new entered data
84        [data setValue:cell.textField.text forKey:cell.label.text];
85    } // end method editableCellDidEndEditing:
86
87    // called when the user touches the Done button on the keyboard
88    - (void)editableCellDidEndOnExit:(EditableCell *)cell
89    {
90
91        // resize the table to fit the keyboard
92        CGRect frame = table.frame; // get the frame of the table
93        frame.size.height += KEYBOARD_HEIGHT; // subtract from the height
94        [table setFrame:frame]; // apply the new frame
95
96        keyboardShown = NO; // hide the keyboard
97        currentCell = nil; // there is no cell currently selected
98    } // end method editableCellDidEndOnExit:
99
```

Fig. 10.17 | Methods editableCellDidBeginEditing:, editableCellDidEndEditing:
and editableCellDidEndOnExit: of class AddViewController.

The editableCellDidEndOnExit: method (lines 88–98) removes the keyboard when
the user touches the "**Done**" **Button**. Lines 92–94 resize table's frame to fill the entire
screen and line 96 sets keyboardShown to NO.

Methods numberOfSectionsInTableView:, tableView:numberOfRowsInSection: and tableView:titleForHeaderInSection: of Class **AddViewController**
The numberOfSectionsInTableView: method (Fig. 10.18, lines 101–104) returns the number of sections in the table—two. The tableView:numberOfRowsInSection: method (lines 107–115) returns the number of rows for a given section. The first section contains three rows (name, e-mail, phone) and table's remaining rows are in the second section (lines 111–114). The *tableView:titleForHeaderInSection: method* (lines 118–126) returns the title of a section. The first section is titled Address (lines 122–125). All other sections have no title, so passing them to this method returns the value nil.

```
100  // returns the number of sections in table
101  - (NSInteger)numberOfSectionsInTableView:(UITableView *)tableView
102  {
103     return 2; // the number of sections in the table
104  } // end method numberOfSectionsInTableView:
105
106  // returns the number of rows in the given table section
107  - (NSInteger)tableView:(UITableView *)tableView numberOfRowsInSection:
108     (NSInteger)section
109  {
110     // if it's the first section
111     if (section == 0)
112        return 3; // there are three rows in the first section
113     else
114        return fields.count - 3; // all other rows are in the second section
115  } // end method tableView:numberOfRowsInSection:
116
117  // returns the title for the given section
118  - (NSString *)tableView:(UITableView *)tableView titleForHeaderInSection:
119     (NSInteger)section
120  {
121     // if it's the second section
122     if (section == 1) // return the title
123        return @"Address";
124     else // none of the other sections have titles
125        return nil; // return nil
126  } // end method tableView:titleForHeaderInSection:
127
```

Fig. 10.18 | Methods numberOfSectionsInTableView:, tableView:numberOf-RowsInSection: and tableView:titleForHeaderInSection: of class AddViewController.

Methods tableView:cellForRowAtIndexPath:, shouldAutorotateToInterfaceOrientation: and dealloc of Class **AddViewController**
Line 132 creates an NSString that will be passed to UITableView's dequeueReusable-CellWithIdentifier: method to get an UITableViewCell from tableView (lines 135–136). If tableView contains no reusable UITableViewCells (line 139), we create a new one (lines 142–143). Once we've created a new cell or obtained one for reuse, we customize the cell using the saved data. Lines 146–148 get the correct label for the cell. We then set the text in the text field to what the user entered (line 151). Next, we set the keyboard

type for the cell's text field (lines 154–164). Most of the cells use the default keyboard, but the cell for entering an e-mail address and the cell for entering a phone number require special keyboards. Finally, we set the editing mode, delegate and selection style for the cell (lines 165–169). Line 170 returns the cell.

```
128  // returns the cell at the given index path
129  - (UITableViewCell *)tableView:(UITableView *)tableView
130     cellForRowAtIndexPath:(NSIndexPath *)indexPath
131  {
132     static NSString *identifier = @"EditableCell";
133
134     // get a reusable cell
135     EditableCell *cell = (EditableCell *)[table
136        dequeueReusableCellWithIdentifier:identifier];
137
138     // if no reusable cell exists
139     if (cell == nil)
140     {
141        // create a new EditableCell
142        cell = [[EditableCell alloc] initWithStyle:
143           UITableViewCellStyleDefault reuseIdentifier:identifier];
144     } // end if
145     // get the key for the given index path
146     NSString *key =
147        [fields objectAtIndex:indexPath.row + indexPath.section * 3];
148     [cell setLabelText:key]; // update the cell text with the key
149
150     // update the text in the text field with the value
151     cell.textField.text = [data valueForKey:key];
152
153     // if cell is going to store an e-mail address (1st section 2nd row)
154     if (indexPath.section == 0 && indexPath.row == 1)
155     {
156        // set the cells keyboard to email address keyboard
157        cell.textField.keyboardType = UIKeyboardTypeEmailAddress;
158     } // end if
159     // if the cell is going to store a phone number (1st section 3rd row)
160     else if (indexPath.section == 0 && indexPath.row == 2)
161     {
162        // set the cell's keyboard to the phone pad keyboard
163        cell.textField.keyboardType = UIKeyboardTypePhonePad;
164     } // end else if
165     cell.editing = NO; // cell is not in editing mode
166     cell.delegate = self; // set this object as the cell's delegate
167
168     // make the cell do nothing when it is selected
169     cell.selectionStyle = UITableViewCellSelectionStyleNone;
170     return cell; // return the customized cell
171  } // end method tableView:cellForRowAtIndexPath:
172
```

Fig. 10.19 | Method tableView:cellForRowAtIndexPath: of class AddViewController. (Part 1 of 2.)

```
173  // called to determine what orientations our View allows
174  - (BOOL)shouldAutorotateToInterfaceOrientation:
175    (UIInterfaceOrientation)interfaceOrientation
176  {
177    // return YES for supported orientations
178    return (interfaceOrientation == UIInterfaceOrientationPortrait);
179  } // end method shouldAutorotateToInterfaceOrientation:
180
181  // free AddViewController's memory
182  - (void)dealloc
183  {
184    [fields release]; // release the fields NSArray
185    [data release]; // release the data NSMutableDictionary
186    [table release]; // release the table UITableView
187    [super dealloc]; // release the superclass
188  } // end method dealloc
189  @end // end AddViewController's implementation
```

Fig. 10.19 | Method `tableView:cellForRowAtIndexPath:` of class `AddViewController`. (Part 2 of 2.)

10.4.3 Class `ContactViewController`

In Xcode, select **File > New File** and chose **UIViewController** subclass. Before pressing **Next**, ensure that the **With XIB for user interface** checkbox is checked to auto-generate a nib file. Name the class **ContactViewController** and save it in the default location provided. Drag a **TableView** from the **Library** window and resize it to fill the entire app window.

ContactViewController Interface Declaration
Class `ContactViewController` (Fig. 10.20) controls the **View** that displays a single existing contact's information. `ContactViewController` is a subclass of `UIViewController` and implements the `UITableViewDataSource` protocol (lines 7–8). The class has one instance variable, `person` (line 10) which is declared as a property at line 14. The update-Title method updates the navigation bar's title to the selected contact's name.

```
1   // ContactViewController.h
2   // ContactViewController's interface declaration.
3   // Implementation in ContactViewController.m
4   #import <UIKit/UIKit.h>
5
6   // begin ContactViewController interface
7   @interface ContactViewController : UIViewController
8      <UITableViewDataSource>
9   {
10     NSDictionary *person; // the data for the entry being viewed
11  } // end instance variable declaration
12
```

Fig. 10.20 | ContactViewController's interface declaration. (Part 1 of 2.)

```
13    // declare person as a property
14    @property(nonatomic, retain) NSDictionary* person;
15    - (void)updateTitle; // updates the title in the navigation bar
16    @end // end interface ContactViewController
```

Fig. 10.20 | ContactViewController's interface declaration. (Part 2 of 2.)

ContactViewController Class Definition

ContactViewController's updateTitle method (Fig. 10.21, lines 11–15) sets navigationItem's title property to the selected contact's name. The tableView:numberOfRowsInSection: method (lines 18–22) returns the total number of pieces of information contained in the person NSDictionary (line 21). This corresponds to the number of rows in the UITableView's only section.


```
1     // ContactViewController.m
2     // ContactViewController class displays information for a contact.
3     #import "ContactViewController.h"
4     #import "EditableCell.h"
5
6     @implementation ContactViewController
7
8     @synthesize person; // generate get and set methods for person
9
10    // update the title in the navigation bar
11    - (void)updateTitle
12    {
13       // set the title to the name of the contact
14       [self.navigationItem setTitle:[person valueForKey:@"Name"]];
15    } // end method updateTitle
16
17    // determines how many rows are in a given section
18    - (NSInteger)tableView:(UITableView *)tableView numberOfRowsInSection:
19       (NSInteger)section
20    {
21       return person.count; // return the number of total rows
22    } // end method tableView:numberOfRowsInSection:
23
24    // retrieve tableView's cell at the given index path
25    - (UITableViewCell *)tableView:(UITableView *)tableView
26       cellForRowAtIndexPath:(NSIndexPath *)indexPath
27    {
28       // used to identify cell as a normal cell
29       static NSString *MyIdentifier = @"NormalCell";
30
31       // get a reusable cell
32       UITableViewCell *cell =
33          [tableView dequeueReusableCellWithIdentifier:MyIdentifier];
34
```

Fig. 10.21 | ContactViewController class displays information for a contact. (Part 1 of 2.)

```
35    // if there are no cells to be reused, create one
36    if (cell == nil)
37    {
38       // create a new cell
39       cell = [[UITableViewCell alloc] initWithStyle:
40          UITableViewCellStyleDefault reuseIdentifier:identifier];
41    } // end if
42
43    // get the key at the appropriate index in the dictionary
44    NSString *key = [[person allKeys] objectAtIndex:indexPath.row];
45    NSString *value = [person valueForKey:key]; // get the value
46    UILabel *label = [cell textLabel]; // get the label for the cell
47
48    // update the text of the label
49    label.text = [NSString stringWithFormat:@"%@: %@", key, value];
50    return cell; // return the customized cell
51 } // end method tableView:cellForRowAtIndexPath:
52
53 // determines the title for a given table header
54 - (NSString *)tableView:(UITableView *)tableView titleForHeaderInSection:
55    (NSInteger)section
56 {
57    return nil; // there are no section headers
58 } // end method tableView:titleForHeaderInSection:
59
60 // determines if a table row can be edited
61 - (BOOL)tableView:(UITableView *)tableView canEditRowAtIndexPath:
62    (NSIndexPath *)indexPath
63 {
64    return NO; // none of the rows are editable
65 } // end method tableView:canEditRowAtIndexPath:
66
67 // called to determine what orientations our View allows
68 - (BOOL)shouldAutorotateToInterfaceOrientation:
69    (UIInterfaceOrientation)interfaceOrientation
70 {
71    // allow only the portrait orientation
72    return (interfaceOrientation == UIInterfaceOrientationPortrait);
73 } // end method shouldAutorotateToInterfaceOrientation:
74
75 // free ContactViewController's memory
76 - (void)dealloc
77 {
78    [person release]; // release the person NSDictionary
79    [super dealloc]; // call the superclass's dealloc method
80 } // end method dealloc
81 @end // end implementation of ContactViewController
```

Fig. 10.21 | `ContactViewController` class displays information for a contact. (Part 2 of 2.)

The `tableView:cellForRowAtIndexPath:` method (lines 25–52) returns the cell at the location specified by the `NSIndexPath`. Line 29 creates an `NSString` which we'll use to indicate that we want to retrieve cells as standard `UITableViewCells` (not editable ones). Lines 32–33 use `UITableView`'s `dequeueReusableCellWithIdentifier:` method to get a

UITableViewCell from tableView. This method attempts to reuse an existing cell which is no longer displayed on the screen. If tableView contains no reusable cells (line 36), we must create a new UITableViewCell (lines 39–40). Lines 44–55 retrieve the key–value pair of the given UITableViewCell from the person NSDictionary and line 46 retrieves that UITableViewCell's **Label**. We then update the **Label** with the retrieved data from person and return the cell (lines 49–50).

10.4.4 Class EditableCell

Select **File > New File...** and choose **Objective-C class**. Choose **UITableViewCell** from the **Subclass Of** drop-down menu. This specifies that our new class will extend class UITableViewCell. Press **Next** then name the class **EditableCell**. Although we programatically create EditableCells, it's also possible to load custom UITableViewCells from nib files. For information on doing this, see the section "A Closer Look at Table-View Cells" in the *Table View Programming Guide for iPhone OS*, which can be found at:

> developer.apple.com/iphone/library/documentation/UserExperience/
> Conceptual/TableView_iPhone/TableView_iPhone.pdf

EditableCell Interface Declaration
The EditableCell class (Fig. 10.22) extends UITableViewCell and implements the *UITextFieldDelegate protocol* (line 9), which states that EditableCell can respond to messages sent by a **Text Field** as the user edits that **Text Field**. All of these messages are optional, but EditableCell defines the textFieldDidBeginEditing: and textFieldDid-EndEditing: methods. Lines 11–13 declare EditableCell's instance variables.

```
1   // EditableCell.h
2   // Interface for UITableViewCell that contains a label and a text field.
3   // Implementation in EditableCell.m
4
5   #import <UIKit/UIKit.h>
6
7   @protocol EditableCellDelegate; // declare EditableCellDelegate Protocol
8
9   @interface EditableCell : UITableViewCell <UITextFieldDelegate>
10  {
11     id <EditableCellDelegate> delegate; // this class's delegate
12     UITextField *textField; // text field the user edits
13     UILabel *label; // label on the left side of the cell
14  } // end instance variables declaration
15
16  // declare textField as a property
17  @property (nonatomic, retain) UITextField *textField;
18
19  // declare label as a property
20  @property (readonly, retain) UILabel *label;
21
```

Fig. 10.22 | Interface for a UITableViewCell that contains a **Label** and a **Text Field**. (Part 1 of 2.)

```
22   //declare delegate as a property
23   @property (nonatomic, assign) id <EditableCellDelegate> delegate;
24
25   - (void)setLabelText:(NSString *)text; // set the text of label
26   - (void)clearText; // clear all the text out of textField
27   @end // end interface EditableCell
28
29   @protocol EditableCellDelegate // protocol for the delegate
30
31   // called when the user begins editing a cell
32   - (void)editableCellDidBeginEditing:(EditableCell *)cell;
33
34   // called when the user stops editing a cell
35   - (void)editableCellDidEndEditing:(EditableCell *)cell;
36
37   // called when the user touches the Done button on the keyboard
38   - (void)editableCellDidEndOnExit:(EditableCell *)cell;
39   @end // end protocol EditableCellDelegate
```

Fig. 10.22 | Interface for a `UITableViewCell` that contains a **Label** and a **Text Field**. (Part 2 of 2.)

Lines 17–23 declare each of `EditableCell`'s instance variables as properties. The `readonly` keyword is used for `label` so that other classes will not be able to directly change its text. Lines 25–26 declare two methods. The `setLabelText:` method sets `label`'s `text` property. The `clearText` method removes all text from `textField`. Lines 29–39 declare the `EditableCellDelegate` protocol. Any class implementing this protocol should define three methods—`editableCellDidBeginEditing:`, `editableCellDidEndEditing:` and `editableCellDidEndOnExit:`, which are called when the user starts editing a cell, stops editing a cell or touches the keyboard's "**Done**" **Button**, respectively.

EditableCell Class Definition
Lines 6–8 of class `EditableCell` (Fig. 10.23) synthesize each of `EditableCell`'s properties. The `initWithStyle:reuseIdentifier:` method (lines 11–34) initializes an `EditableCell`. If the superclass's inherited members are initialized without error (line 15), we create a **Label** on the left side of the `EditableCell` (line 18). Lines 21–22 create a new **Text Field** to the right of the **Label**. We then set this `EditableCell` as `textField`'s `delegate` so this class will receive the `textFieldDidBeginEditing:` and `textFieldDidEndEditing:` messages. Lines 27–28 call `UITextField`'s `addTarget:action:forControlEvents:` method to specify that this `EditableCell` object receives the `textFieldDidEndOnExit:` message when the user touches the keyboard's "**Done**" **Button**. We then add `label` and `textField` to the `EditableCell`'s view (lines 29–30).

```
1   // EditableCell.m
2   // EditcableCell's class definition
3   #import "EditableCell.h"
4   @implementation EditableCell
```

Fig. 10.23 | `EditableCell`'s class definition. (Part 1 of 3.)

```objc
 5
 6   @synthesize textField; // synthesize get and set methods for textField
 7   @synthesize label; // synthesize get and set methods for label
 8   @synthesize delegate; // synthesize get and set methods for delegate
 9
10   // initialize the cell
11   - (id)initWithStyle:(UITableViewCellStyle)style
12       reuseIdentifier:(NSString *)reuseIdentifier
13   {
14      // call the superclass
15      if (self = [super initWithStyle:style reuseIdentifier:reuseIdentifier])
16      {
17         // create the label on the left side
18         label = [[UILabel alloc] initWithFrame:CGRectMake(20, 10, 0, 20)];
19
20         // create the text field to the right of the label
21         textField =
22            [[UITextField alloc] initWithFrame:CGRectMake(0, 10, 0, 20)];
23
24         [textField setDelegate:self]; // set the delegate to this object
25
26         // call textFieldDidEndOnExit when the Done key is touched
27         [textField addTarget:self action:@selector(textFieldDidEndOnExit)
28             forControlEvents:UIControlEventEditingDidEndOnExit];
29         [self.contentView addSubview:label]; // add label to the cell
30         [self.contentView addSubview:textField]; // add textField to cell
31      } // end if
32
33      return self; // return this Editable cell
34   } // end method initWithFrame:reuseIdentifier:
35
36   // method is called when the user touches the Done button on the keyboard
37   - (void)textFieldDidEndOnExit
38   {
39      [textField resignFirstResponder]; // make the keyboard go away
40      [delegate editableCellDidEndOnExit:self]; // call the delegate method
41   } // end method textFieldDidEndOnExit
42
43   // set the text of the label
44   - (void)setLabelText:(NSString *)text
45   {
46      label.text = text; // update the text
47
48      // get the size of the passed text with the current font
49      CGSize size = [text sizeWithFont:label.font];
50      CGRect labelFrame = label.frame; // get the frame of the label
51      labelFrame.size.width = size.width; // size the frame to fit the text
52      label.frame = labelFrame; // update the label with the new frame
53
54      CGRect textFieldFrame = textField.frame; // get the frame of textField
55
```

Fig. 10.23 | EditableCell's class definition. (Part 2 of 3.)

```
56      // move textField to 30 pts to the right of label
57      textFieldFrame.origin.x = size.width + 30;
58
59      // set the width to fill the remainder of the screen
60      textFieldFrame.size.width =
61        self.frame.size.width - textFieldFrame.origin.x;
62      textField.frame = textFieldFrame; // assign the new frame
63    } // end method setLabelText:
64
65    // clear the text in textField
66    - (void)clearText
67    {
68      textField.text = @""; // update textField with an empty string
69    } // end method clearText
70
71    // delegate method of UITextField, called when a text field begins editing
72    - (void)textFieldDidBeginEditing:(UITextField *)textField
73    {
74      [delegate editableCellDidBeginEditing:self]; // inform the delegate
75    } // end method textFieldDidBeginEditing:
76
77    // delegate method of UITextField, called when a text field ends editing
78    - (void)textFieldDidEndEditing:(UITextField *)textField
79    {
80      [delegate editableCellDidEndEditing:self]; // inform the delegate
81    } // end method textFieldDidEndEditing:
82
83    // free EditableCell's memory
84    - (void)dealloc
85    {
86      [textField release]; // release the textField UITextField
87      [label release]; // release the label UILabel
88      [super dealloc]; // call the superclass's dealloc method
89    } // end method dealloc
90    @end // end EditableCell class definition
```

Fig. 10.23 | EditableCell's class definition. (Part 3 of 3.)

The textFieldDidEndOnExit method (lines 37–41) is called when the user touches the keyboard's "**Done**" **Button**. Calling UITextField's resignFirstResponder method deselects textField, causing the keyboard to disappear. Line 40 calls delegate's editableCellDidEndOnExit: method to indicate that the user touched the "**Done**" **Button**.

The setLabelText: method (lines 44–63) updates the text displayed by label. Line 46 sets label's text property to the given NSString. NSString's sizeWithFont: method is used to get a CGSize object representing the size of text when it appears in label's font. Lines 50–52 adjust label's frame to fit the new CGSize. Lines 54–62 adjust textField's frame to fill the remainder of the EditableCell.

The clearText method (lines 66–69) sets textField's text property to an empty string. The textFieldDidBeginEditing: and textFieldDidEndEditing: methods call their corresponding methods of delegate.

10.5 Wrap-Up

The **Address Book** app used several `UITableViews` to display contact information stored in the app. We handled navigation between the app's three views with a `UINavigationController`. We added **Button**s to a `UINavigationItem`, allowing the user to switch between views while displaying a navigation bar throughout the whole app. Each of the views displayed contact information in a `UITableView`. To allow the user to enter information into a `UITableView` we created a custom `EditableCell` subclass of `UITableViewCell`. The `EditableCell` class allowed the user to enter information in a `UITableView` for a new contact.

In Chapter 11, we'll develop the **Route Tracker** app. This app will track the user's path showing a map and satellite image of where the user has traveled. We'll do this using the Map Kit framework, which interacts with Google Maps web services, and using the Core Location framework, which interacts with the iPhone's GPS and compass to provide locations and maps for the user's current location.

Route Tracker App

Map Kit and Core Location (GPS and Compass)

OBJECTIVES

In this chapter you'll learn:

■ To use the Map Kit framework and MKMapView class to display Google Maps™ generated by Google web services.

■ To use the Core Location framework and CLLocationManager class to receive information on the iPhone's position and compass heading.

■ To display the user's route using GPS location data received in the form of CLLocation objects.

■ To orient the map to the user's current compass heading using data in CLHeading objects—a new feature of the iPhone 3GS.

■ To use NSDate objects to calculate the speed at which the user moves along the route.

Outline

11.1 Introduction[1]
11.2 Test-Driving the **Route Tracker** App
11.3 Technologies Overview
    11.4.1 Class `TrackingMapView`
    11.4.2 Class `Controller`
11.4 Building the App
11.5 Wrap-Up

11.1 Introduction[1]

The **Route Tracker** app monitors the user's location and heading (i.e., direction)—visually displaying a route on a map. The app initially presents the user with a world map containing a blue dot that approximates the iPhone's location (Fig. 11.1). The user touches the "**Start Tracking**" **Button** to zoom the map in, centered on the iPhone's current location (Fig. 11.2). The map shifts as the user moves, keeping the user's location centered in the map. The route is a line colored from green (the starting location) to blue (the current location). Black arrows appear at intervals along the route, indicating the user's direction as shown in Fig. 11.3(a) and (b). The map is always oriented in the user's direction and that direction always points to the top of the device. The user changes the look of the map by touching **Map**, **Satellite** or **Hybrid** in the **Segmented Control** in the app's top-right corner. Touching **Map** changes the display to show a Google™ Maps street map—the app's default. Touching **Satellite** displays a satellite image of the area around the user (Fig. 11.4(a)) and touching **Hybrid** shows the map overlaid on the satellite image (Fig. 11.4(b)). The user touches the "**Stop Tracking**" **Button** to end the current route. This displays an alert containing the total distance travelled and the user's average speed (Fig. 11.5).

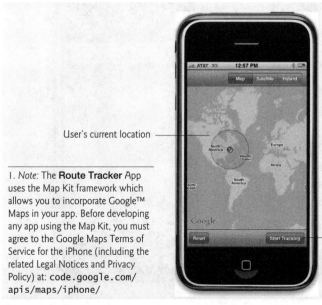

User's current location ⸺

1. *Note:* The **Route Tracker** App uses the Map Kit framework which allows you to incorporate Google™ Maps in your app. Before developing any app using the Map Kit, you must agree to the Google Maps Terms of Service for the iPhone (including the related Legal Notices and Privacy Policy) at: `code.google.com/apis/maps/iphone/`

Touch to begin tracking

Fig. 11.1 | Approximate user location on world map.

Fig. 11.2 | Map just after the user presses **Start Tracking**.

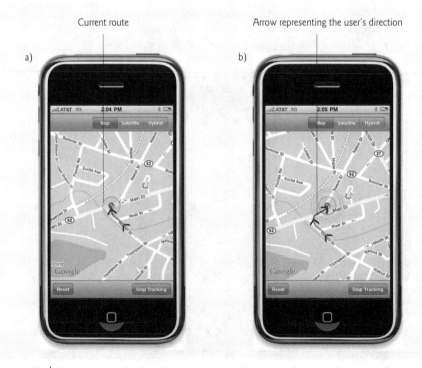

Fig. 11.3 | User's route displayed on the map with arrows showing the user's direction.

Fig. 11.4 | Satellite and hybrid map views.

Fig. 11.5 | Statistics for a completed route.

11.2 Test-Driving the Route Tracker App

Opening the Completed App
Open the directory containing the **Route Tracker** app project. Double click `RouteTracker.xcodeproj` to open the project in Xcode. The iPhone simulator does not have the ability to simulate the GPS capabilities of the iPhone 3GS. The app will run in the iPhone simulator, but it will show only the default location of Apple's headquarters in Cupertino, California. Please refer to the document **Program Portal User Guide** in the iPhone Developer Program Portal at

> `developer.apple.com/iphone/manage/overview/index.action`

for instructions on testing the app on your iPhone. The iPhone Developer Program Portal is available only to members of Apple's fee-based developer program. Also, although this app runs on any iPhone model with GPS support, iPhones prior to the iPhone 3GS cannot use the compass features.

Using the Route Tracker App
Once the **Route Tracker** App is running on your iPhone, touch the "**Start Tracking**" Button in the bottom-right corner of the app. Go outside and run, walk, jog or drive around the block. As you move, the blue dot representing the iPhone's location moves as well. Your route is marked with a line colored from green (the starting location) to blue (the current location). The iPhone 3GS compass ensures that the map is always oriented the way you're currently facing—this will not be the case on devices that do not have the compass feature. Touching **Map**, **Satellite** or **Hybrid** at the top of the app changes the map's display to a street map, a satellite image or an overlay of the two, respectively. When you've finished moving, touch the "**Stop Tracking**" Button in the bottom-right corner of the app. An alert displays your distance traveled and speed. Touch the "**Return**" Button to close the alert and return to the map. Touching the "**Reset**" Button in the lower-left corner of the app will erase your route from the map.

11.3 Technologies Overview

The **Route Tracker** app displays a map using the Map Kit framework's `MKMapView`. We'll use this class to rotate, zoom and draw to the map. The route is displayed by drawing directly to the `MKMapView`. The user's location and compass heading are provided by the Core Location framework. A `CLLocationManager` monitors the iPhone's location and compass heading and sends messages to our `Controller` class when either reading is updated. The user's location is represented by a `CLLocation` object, which provides the iPhone's latitude, longitude and altitude (in meters) at a specific time. Each time we receive a `CLLocation` from the `CLLocationManager`, we draw the route line to the new location. We also use the `CLLocation` class to calculate the distance between two `CLLocations`. This allows us to calculate the user's total distance traveled in a route.

The iPhone's heading is represented by a `CLHeading` object. Each time the `Controller` class receives a `CLHeading`, we rotate the map's orientation to the same direction as the user. Each time we start tracking a route, we initialize an `NSDate` object to the current time. When we stop tracking, we can ask this object how long it's been since tracking began and use that time to calculate the user's speed.

11.4 Building the App

Open Xcode and create a new project. Select the **Window-based Application** template and name the project RouteTracker. Open MainWindow.xib in Interface Builder. Drag **Toolbars** to the top and bottom of the app window and delete their default "Item" **Buttons**. Drag a **Map View** from the **Library** onto the app window between the **Toolbars** and size it to fill the remaining space. Drag **Flexible Space Bar Button Items** to the top and bottom of the window. A **_Flexible Space Bar Button Item_** is an invisible component that is used to add space between other **Bar Button Items**. Next, to the right side of the top **Flexible Space Bar Button Item** drag a **Segmented Control** and configure it to have three sections named Map, Satellite and Hybrid. Drag two **Round Rect Buttons** to the left and right of the bottom **Flexible Space Bar Button Item** and name them Reset and Start Tracking, respectively. Connect all of the appropriate IBOutlets and actions using the **Inspector** window. Fig. 11.6 shows the final nib file in Interface Builder.

Fig. 11.6 | **MainWindow.xib** in Interface Builder.

11.4.1 Class TrackingMapView

The TrackingMapView class (Fig. 11.7) is a subclass of UIView. We overlay an object of this class on the MKMapView. We could add the TrackingMapView as a subview of the MKMapView in Interface Builder; however, the TrackingMapView and MKMapView are the same size, so they would overlap in the nib file, making them difficult to work with. We chose to add the TrackingMapView programmatically to keep the nib file as simple as possible. TrackingMapView implements the *MKMapViewDelegate protocol* which declares several methods that respond to messages from MKMapView objects (line 9). The class *MKMapView* represents a map that can be displayed in our app and controlled programmatically. This class is part of the *Map Kit framework* that uses Google Maps web services. NSMutableArray points (line 11) stores CLLocations representing locations along the user's route. A *CLLocation* object represents the iPhone's geographical location at a specific time. Lines 14–15 declare two methods. The addPoint: method adds new CLLocations to NSMutableArray points. The reset method removes all the CLLocations from points. Both methods refresh the display after performing their tasks.

```
1   // TrackingMapView.h
2   // TrackingMapView interface declaration.
3   // Implementation in TrackingMapView.m
4   #import <UIKit/UIKit.h>
5   #import <MapKit/MapKit.h>
6   #import <CoreLocation/CoreLocation.h>
7
8   // begin TrackingMapView interface declaration
9   @interface TrackingMapView : UIView <MKMapViewDelegate>
10  {
11     NSMutableArray *points; // stores all points visited by the user
12  } // end instance variable declaration
13
14  - (void)addPoint:(CLLocation *)point; // add a new point to points
15  - (void)reset; // reset the MKMapView
16  @end // end interface TrackingMapView
```

Fig. 11.7 | TrackingMapView interface declaration.

Method *initWithFrame: of Class TrackingMapView*
TrackingMapView's initWithFrame: method (Fig. 11.8) is inherited from UIView and overridden. Line 13 calls the superclass's initWithFrame: method and checks that the superclass's inherited members were initialized without error. If so, line 15 sets this TrackingMapView's backgroundColor property to clear using UIColor's clearColor method and line 16 creates points as an empty NSMutableArray (line 16).

```
1   // TrackingMapView.m
2   // A view that displays lines connecting coordinates on a MKMapView.
3   #import "TrackingMapView.h"
4   #import <MapKit/MKMapView.h>
5   static const int ARROW_THRESHOLD = 50;
6
7   @implementation TrackingMapView
8
```

Fig. 11.8 | Method initWithFrame: of class TrackingMapView. (Part 1 of 2.)

```
 9    // initialize the view
10    - (id)initWithFrame:(CGRect)frame
11    {
12        // if the superclass initialized properly
13        if (self = [super initWithFrame:frame])
14        {
15            self.backgroundColor = [UIColor clearColor]; // set the background
16            points = [[NSMutableArray alloc] init]; // initialize points
17        } // end if
18
19        return self; // return this TrackingMapView
20    } // end method initWithFrame:
21
```

Fig. 11.8 | Method initWithFrame: of class TrackingMapView. (Part 2 of 2.)

Method drawRect: of Class TrackingMapView

The drawRect: method (Fig. 11.9) draws the route line and arrows representing the path traveled by the user. If there's only one CLLocation in points or the TrackingMapView's hidden property is YES, the method exits because no line needs to be drawn (lines 27–28). Line 31 gets the current graphics context using the UIGraphicsGetCurrentContext function. The CGContextSetLineWidth function sets the width of any line drawn in context to four pixels (line 32). This will be the width of the line representing the user's route on the map. Lines 33–34 declare the CGPoint point and float distance. Variable point is used to store the next point in the line during each iteration of the loop in lines 37–120. We initialize distance to zero. This variable helps us determine whether to place the next arrow on the line representing the route.

```
22    // called automatically when the view needs to be displayed
23    // this is where we do all of our drawing
24    - (void)drawRect:(CGRect)rect
25    {
26        // no drawing needed if there is only one point or the view is hidden
27        if (points.count == 1 || self.hidden)
28            return; // exit the method
29
30        // get the current graphics context
31        CGContextRef context = UIGraphicsGetCurrentContext();
32        CGContextSetLineWidth(context, 4.0); // set the line width
33        CGPoint point; // declare the point CGPoint
34        float distance = 0.0; // initialize distance to 0.0
35
36        // loop through all of the points
37        for (int i = 0; i < points.count; i++)
38        {
39            float f = (float)i; // cast i as a float and store in f
```

Fig. 11.9 | Method drawRect: of class TrackingMapView. (Part 1 of 3.)

```
40
41      // set the lines's color so that the whole line has a gradient
42      CGContextSetRGBStrokeColor(context, 0, 1 - f / (points.count - 1),
43         f / (points.count - 1), 0.8);
44
45      // get the next location
46      CLLocation *nextLocation = [points objectAtIndex:i];
47      CGPoint lastPoint = point; // store point in lastPoint
48
49      // get the view point for the given map coordinate
50      point = [(MKMapView *)self.superview convertCoordinate:
51         nextLocation.coordinate toPointToView:self];
52
53      // if this isn't the first point
54      if (i != 0)
55      {
56         // move to the last point
57         CGContextMoveToPoint(context, lastPoint.x, lastPoint.y);
58
59         // add a line
60         CGContextAddLineToPoint(context, point.x, point.y);
61
62         // add the length of the line drawn to distance
63         distance += sqrt(pow(point.x - lastPoint.x, 2) +
64            pow(point.y - lastPoint.y, 2));
65
66         // if distance is large enough
67         if (distance >= ARROW_THRESHOLD)
68         {
69            // load the arrow image
70            UIImage *image = [UIImage imageNamed:@"arrow.png"];
71            CGRect frame; // declare frame CGRect
72
73            // calculate the point in the middle of the line
74            CGPoint middle = CGPointMake((point.x + lastPoint.x) / 2,
75               (point.y + lastPoint.y) / 2);
76
77            // set frame's width to image's width
78            frame.size.width = image.size.width;
79
80            // set frame's height to image's height
81            frame.size.height = image.size.height;
82
83            // move frame's origin's x-coordinate halfway across the frame
84            frame.origin.x = middle.x - frame.size.width / 2;
85
86            // move frame's origin's y-coordinate halfway down the frame
87            frame.origin.y = middle.y - frame.size.height / 2;
88
89            // save the graphics state so we can restore it later
90            CGContextSaveGState(context);
91
```

Fig. 11.9 | Method drawRect: of class TrackingMapView. (Part 2 of 3.)

```
 92                // center the context where we want to draw the arrow
 93                CGContextTranslateCTM(context, frame.origin.x +
 94                   frame.size.width / 2, frame.origin.y + \
 95                   frame.size.height / 2);
 96
 97                // calculate the angle at which to draw the arrow image
 98                float angle = atan((point.y - lastPoint.y) / (point.x -
 99                   lastPoint.x));
100
101                // if this point is to the left of the last point
102                if (point.x < lastPoint.x)
103                   angle += 3.14159; // increase angle by pi
104
105                // rotate the context by the required angle
106                CGContextRotateCTM(context, angle);
107
108                // draw the image into the rotated context
109                CGContextDrawImage(context, CGRectMake(-frame.size.width / 2,
110                   -frame.size.height / 2, frame.size.width,
111                   frame.size.height), image.CGImage);
112
113                // restore context's original coordinate system
114                CGContextRestoreGState(context);
115                distance = 0.0; // reset distance
116             } // end if
117          } // end if
118
119          CGContextStrokePath(context); // draw the path
120       } // end for
121    } // end method drawRect:
122
```

Fig. 11.9 | Method drawRect: of class TrackingMapView. (Part 3 of 3.)

Lines 37–124 loop through each CLLocation in points. Line 39 stores the control variable in float variable f so that we can use the value in a floating-point division calculation. Lines 42–43 set the line color using the CGContextSetRGBStrokeColor function. The RGB values are calculated using f and points.count in such a way that the line will start green and become more blue with each additional location. Passing 0.8 as the last argument makes the line slightly transparent so the user can still see the underlying map. Line 46 gets the CLLocation at index i of points. Line 47 initializes the lastPoint CGPoint to point. This does nothing during the first iteration of the loop because point has not yet been initialized, but for each subsequent iteration this stores the previous CGPoint drawn into lastPoint. Lines 50–51 convert the nextLocation CLLocation to a CGPoint in TrackingMapView. We do this by first casting TrackingMapView's superview to an MKMapView (line 50)—as you'll see in Fig. 11.13, the controller sets TrackingMapView as a subview of MKMapView. We then call MKMapView's ***convertCoordinate:toPoint-ToView:*** method to receive a CGPoint in TrackingMapView representing nextLocation.

If this is not the first loop iteration (line 54), we call the CGContextMoveToPoint function to select the location in context of the last point drawn (line 57). The CGContext-AddLineToPoint function adds a line from the last point drawn to point's coordinates (line 60). Lines 63–64 use the formula for the distance between two points to calculate the length the last line segment and add that to distance. If this distance is greater than or equal to ARROW_THRESHOLD (line 67), we draw a new arrow onto the route. Line 70 declares a new UIImage using arrow.png and line 71 declares the frame CGRect. Lines 74–75 call the CGPointMake function to create a new CGPoint in the center of the last line segment. We then set frame's size to that of image (lines 78 and 81) and its origin to the coordinates in the line segment's center (lines 84–87).

The CGContextSaveGState function saves the coordinate system of the current graphics context (line 90) so we can revert back to it later. Lines 93–95 call the **CGContextTranslateCTM** *function* to translate context to the location at the center of the line segment where we wish to display the arrow. Lines 98–103 calculate the angle at which context needs to be rotated so that when we place the arrow on context it will be perpendicular to the second endpoint of the line. The CGContextRotateCTM function rotates the context by the calculated angle (line 106). Lines 109–111 call the CGContextDrawImage function to draw the image into the context. Line 114 uses the CGContextRestoreCGState function to restore context's original coordinate system. Line 119 draws the line representing the route by calling the function CGContextStrokePath. We do this after the arrow image is displayed so that the line appears on top of the arrow.

Methods addPoint: and reset of Class TrackingMapView

The addPoint: method (Fig. 11.10, lines 124–136) adds a new CLLocation to the points NSMutableArray. Before adding a new point, we ensure that it does not describe the same geographical coordinates as the last element in the NSMutableArray, which would indicate that the user has not moved from the prior position. Line 127 receives the last element in points using NSMutableArray's lastObject method. Lines 130–131 compare the latitude and longitude properties of CLLocations point and lastPoint. If either is different, we add the new CLLocaton to points (line 133). We then force TrackingMapView to redraw by calling UIView's setNeedsDisplay method (line 134). The reset method (lines 139–143) removes the visual representation of the user's route from the TrackingMapView by calling NSMutableArray's removeAllObjects method to empty points and calling setNeedsDisplay to force TrackingMapView to redraw (lines 141–142).

```
123  // add a new point to the list
124  - (void)addPoint:(CLLocation *)point
125  {
126     // store last element of point
127     CLLocation *lastPoint = [points lastObject];
128
129     // if new point is at a different location than lastPoint
130     if (point.coordinate.latitude != lastPoint.coordinate.latitude ||
131         point.coordinate.longitude != lastPoint.coordinate.longitude)
132     {
133        [points addObject:point]; // add the point
134        [self setNeedsDisplay]; // redraw the view
135     } // end if
136  } // end method addPoint:
```

Fig. 11.10 | Methods addPoint: and reset of class TrackingMapView. (Part 1 of 2.)

```
137
138   // remove all the points and update the display
139   - (void)reset
140   {
141      [points removeAllObjects]; // remove all the points
142      [self setNeedsDisplay]; // update the display
143   } // end method reset
144
```

Fig. 11.10 | Methods addPoint: and reset of class TrackingMapView. (Part 2 of 2.)

Methods *mapView:regionWillChangeAnimated:* and *mapView:regionDid-ChangeAnimated:* of Class *TrackingMapView.*

The *mapView:regionWillChangeAnimated: method* of the MKMapViewDelegate protocol (Fig. 11.11, lines 146–150) is called by the MKMapView when the area being displayed by the map is about to shift. Line 149 hides the TrackingMapView during this transition so that the line is not temporarily displayed out of place while the map shifts. When the map finishes shifting, the *mapView:regionDidChangeAnimated: method* of the MKMapViewDelegate protocol is called. Line 156 indicates that the TrackingMapView should display and line 157 calls UIView's setNeedsDisplay method so the TrackingMapView redraws.

```
145   // called by the MKMapView when the region is going to change
146   - (void)mapView:(MKMapView *)mapView regionWillChangeAnimated:
147      (BOOL)animated
148   {
149      self.hidden = YES; // hide the view during the transition
150   } // end method mapView:regionWillChangeAnimated:
151
152   // called by the MKMapView when the region has finished changing
153   - (void)mapView:(MKMapView *)mapView
154      regionDidChangeAnimated:(BOOL)animated
155   {
156      self.hidden = NO; // unhide the view
157      [self setNeedsDisplay]; // redraw the view
158   } // end method mapview:regionDidChangeAnimated:
159
160   // free TrackingMapView's memory
161   - (void)dealloc
162   {
163      [points release]; // release the points NSMutableArray
164      [super dealloc]; // call the superclass's dealloc method
165   } // end method dealloc
166   @end // end TrackingMapView class implementation
```

Fig. 11.11 | Methods mapView:regionWillChangeAnimated: and mapView:regionDidChangeAnimated: of class TrackingMapView.

11.4.2 Class Controller

Controller is a subclass of UIViewController and implements the MKMapViewDelegate protocol and the *CLLocationManagerDelegate protocol* (Fig. 11.12, lines 9–10), which indicates that this class can receive messages from a `CLLocationManager` object. Class *CLLocationManager* is a part of the Core Location framework and provides information on the iPhone's location and compass heading.

```
1   // Controller.h
2   // Controller class for the Route Tracker app interface declaration
3   // Implementation in Controller.m
4   #import <UIKit/UIKit.h>
5   #import <MapKit/MapKit.h>
6   #import <CoreLocation/CoreLocation.h>
7   #import "TrackingMapView.h"
8
9   @interface Controller : UIViewController <MKMapViewDelegate,
10     CLLocationManagerDelegate>
11  {
12     // touched to start or stop tracking
13     IBOutlet UIBarButtonItem *startButton;
14     TrackingMapView *trackingMapView; // View displaying the map and route
15     IBOutlet MKMapView *mapView; // represents the map
16     CLLocationManager *locationManager; // provides location information
17     BOOL tracking; // is the app tracking?
18     float distance; // the distance traveled by the user
19     NSDate *startDate; // stores the time when tracking began
20     CLHeading *heading; // the compass heading of the iPhone
21  } // end instance variable declaration
22
23     // declare our outlets as properties
24  @property (nonatomic,retain) IBOutlet UIBarButtonItem *startButton;
25  @property (nonatomic,retain) IBOutlet MKMapView *mapView;
26
27  - (IBAction)toggleTracking; // switch between tracking or not tracking
28  - (IBAction)resetMap; // resets the MKMapView
29  - (IBAction)selectMapMode:sender; // select type of map displayed
30  @end // end interface Controller
```

Fig. 11.12 | Controller class for the **Route Tracker** app interface declaration.

The `startButton` outlet (line 13) is connected to the **Button** pressed by the user to toggle whether or not the app is tracking the route. Line 14 declares a `TrackingMapView`. The `MKMapView` `mapView` represents the map displayed in the `TrackingMapView` (line 15). Line 16 declares a `CLLocationManager` that's used to get location and compass heading information needed to draw the user's route. `BOOL` variable `tracking` specifies whether the app is currently tracking the user's route and `distance` stores the total distance traveled in the current route. The *NSDate class* stores a date and time. Line 19 declares an `NSDate` object used to store the time when tracking starts. Line 20 declares a *CLHeading* representing the iPhone's compass heading.

Class `Controller` also declares three methods (lines 27–29):

- `toggleTracking`—tells the `CLLocationManager` to start tracking the iPhone's position if it isn't currently doing so. Otherwise, this method stops tracking and displays a `UIAlertView` containing the route's statistics.

- resetMap—clears the previous route from the map.
- selectMapMode:—switches between street map, satellite image and combination of the two.

Method viewDidLoad of Class Controller

Controller's viewDidLoad method (Fig. 11.13) begins by initializing the superclass's inherited members and setting tracking to NO. Lines 18–19 initializes trackingMapView to have the same size as mapView, because we're going to overlay the trackingMapView on the mapView. Line 22 calls UIView's addSubview: method to add trackingMapView as a subview of mapView. We then set mapView's delegate property to trackingMapView (line 26) so the mapView can deliver notifications to trackingMapView when the map moves. Lines 29 and 32 initialize locationManager and set its delegate to this Controller object. Setting locationManager's desiredAccuracy property to *kCLLocationAccuracy-Best* (line 35) specifies that the location and heading information provided by locationManager should be as accurate as the iPhone's hardware can provide.

```
1   // Controller.m
2   // Controller class for the Route Tracker app.
3   #import "Controller.h"
4
5   @implementation Controller
6
7   // generate get and set methods for our properties
8   @synthesize startButton;
9   @synthesize mapView;
10
11  // called when the main view finishes loading
12  - (void)viewDidLoad
13  {
14     [super viewDidLoad]; // initialize the superclass
15     tracking = NO; // set tracking to NO
16
17     // initialize the TrackingMapView
18     trackingMapView =
19        [[TrackingMapView alloc] initWithFrame:mapView.frame];
20
21     // add the trackingMapView subview to mapView
22     [mapView addSubview:trackingMapView];
23     [trackingMapView release]; // release the TrackingMapView
24
25     // set trackingMapView as mapView's delegate
26     mapView.delegate = trackingMapView;
27
28     // initialize location manager
29     locationManager= [[CLLocationManager alloc] init];
30
31     // set locationManager's delegate to self
32     locationManager.delegate = self;
33
```

Fig. 11.13 | Method viewDidLoad of class Controller. (Part 1 of 2.)

```
34        // set locationManager to provide the most accurate readings possible
35        locationManager.desiredAccuracy = kCLLocationAccuracyBest;
36     } // end method viewDidLoad
37
```

Fig. 11.13 | Method `viewDidLoad` of class `Controller`. (Part 2 of 2.)

Method `toggleTracking` of Class `Controller`

The `toggleTracking` method (Fig. 11.14) is called when the user touches the **Button** in the bottom-right corner of the app which alternates between **Start Tracking** and **Stop Tracking**, depending on the current tracking state. If the app is currently tracking the user's route (line 42) we set `tracking` to `NO` (line 44), then enable sleep mode for the iPhone by using UIApplication's ***setIdleTimerDisabled: method*** (line 47). We also set `startButton`'s `title` property to `Start Tracking` (line 48). We then send ***stopUpdatingLocation*** and ***stopUpdatingHeading*** messages to prevent the `locationManager` from monitoring the iPhone's position and orientation (lines 49–50). Lines 51–52 set ***mapView's scrollEnabled*** and ***zoomEnabled*** properties to YES, allowing the user to scroll through the map and zoom in and out.

```
38     // called when the user touches the "Start Tracking" button
39     - (IBAction)toggleTracking
40     {
41        // if the app is currently tracking
42        if (tracking)
43        {
44           tracking = NO; // stop tracking
45
46           // allow the iPhone to go to sleep
47           [[UIApplication sharedApplication] setIdleTimerDisabled:NO];
48           startButton.title = @"Start Tracking"; // update button title
49           [locationManager stopUpdatingLocation]; // stop tracking location
50           [locationManager stopUpdatingHeading]; // stop tracking heading
51           mapView.scrollEnabled = YES; // allow the user to scroll the map
52           mapView.zoomEnabled = YES; // allow the user to zoom the map
53
54           // get the time elapsed since the tracking started
55           float time = -[startDate timeIntervalSinceNow];
56
57           // format the ending message with various calculations
58           NSString *message = [NSString stringWithFormat:
59              @"Distance: %.02f km, %.02f mi\nSpeed: %.02f km/h, %.02f mph",
60              distance / 1000, distance * 0.00062, distance * 3.6 / time,
61              distance * 2.2369 / time];
62
63           // create an alert that shows the message
64           UIAlertView *alert = [[UIAlertView alloc]
65              initWithTitle:@"Statistics" message:message delegate:self
66              cancelButtonTitle:@"Return" otherButtonTitles:nil];
```

Fig. 11.14 | Method `toggleTracking` of class `Controller`. (Part 1 of 2.)

```
67          [alert show]; // show the alert
68          [alert release]; // release the alert UIAlertView
69      } // end if
70      else // start tracking
71      {
72          tracking = YES; // start tracking
73          mapView.scrollEnabled = NO; // prevent map scrolling by user
74          mapView.zoomEnabled = NO; // prevent map zooming by user
75
76          // keep the iPhone from going to sleep
77          [[UIApplication sharedApplication] setIdleTimerDisabled:YES];
78          startButton.title = @"Stop Tracking"; // update button title
79          distance = 0.0; // reset the distance
80          startDate = [[NSDate date] retain]; // store the start time
81          [locationManager startUpdatingLocation]; // start tracking location
82          [locationManager startUpdatingHeading]; // start tracking heading
83      } // end else
84  } // end method toggleTracking
85
```

Fig. 11.14 | Method `toggleTracking` of class `Controller`. (Part 2 of 2.)

Line 55 calls NSDate's ***timeIntervalSinceNow*** *method* to return a `float` containing the number seconds that have elapsed since `startDate` was created (i.e., when the app first started tracking). We then prepare an `NSString` containing the distance and speed the user traveled (lines 58–61), using both standard and metric measurement units. Lines 64–66 display that `NSString` in a `UIAlertView` containing a "**Return**" **Button**.

If the app had not previously been tracking (line 70), we set `tracking` to YES (line 72). Lines 73–74 set `mapView`'s `scrollEnabled` and `zoomEnabled` properties to `NO` so the user cannot scroll or zoom the map while the app is tracking. We then disable sleep mode for the iPhone by using `UIApplication`'s ***setIdleTimerDisabled:*** *method* (line 77). Lines 78–79 set `startButton`'s `title` property to `Stop Tracking` and reset `distance` to zero. We create a new `NSDate` object to monitor how much time passes during the user's route. We then send ***startUpdatingLocation*** and ***startUpdatingHeading*** messages to tell the `locationManager` to begin monitoring the iPhone's position and direction.

Methods *resetMap, selectMapMode:* and *mapView:viewForAnnotation:* of Class *Controller*

The `resetMap` method (Fig. 11.15, lines 87–90) calls `trackingMapView`'s `reset` method when the user touches the "**Reset**" **Button**. This will clear the previous route from the map. The `selectMapMode:` method (lines 93–109) updates the type of map displayed when the user touches the **Segmented Control** containing map options. Line 95 gets `UISegmentedControl`'s `selectedSegmentIndex` property which represents the index of the touched item. If `index` is zero, we set ***mapView's mapType*** *property* to ***MKMapTypeStandard***—causing `mapView` to display a standard street map (line 101). If `index` is 1, we set the `mapType` property to ***MKMapTypeSatellite*** (line 104) to display a satellite image. If `index` is 2, we set the `mapType` property to ***MKTypeHybrid*** to display a street map on a satellite image.

The `mapView:viewForAnnotation:` method (lines 112–116) returns `nil` because we do not use annotations in this app. The *MKAnnotationView class* represents annotations (such as push pins) that can be displayed on the map to mark locations.

```
 86    // called when the user touches the Reset button
 87    - (IBAction)resetMap
 88    {
 89        [trackingMapView reset]; // clear all the stored points
 90    } // end method resetMap
 91
 92    // called when the user touches a segment of the UISegmentedControl
 93    - (IBAction)selectMapMode:sender
 94    {
 95        int index = [sender selectedSegmentIndex]; // get the selected segment
 96
 97        // set the map type depending on the selected segment
 98        switch (index)
 99        {
100            // show the standard map
101            case 0: mapView.mapType = MKMapTypeStandard; break;
102
103            // show the satellite map
104            case 1: mapView.mapType = MKMapTypeSatellite; break;
105
106            // show the hybrid map
107            case 2: mapView.mapType = MKMapTypeHybrid; break;
108        } // end switch
109    } // end method selectMapMode:
110
111    // delegate method for the MKMapView
112    - (MKAnnotationView *)mapView:(MKMapView *)mapView viewForAnnotation:
113        (id <MKAnnotation>)annotation
114    {
115        return nil; // we don't want any annotations
116    } // end method mapView:viewForAnnotation:
117
```

Fig. 11.15 | Methods `resetMap`, `selectMapMode:` and `mapView:viewForAnnotation:` of class `Controller`.

Method locationManager:didUpdateToLocation:fromLocation: of Class Controller

The *locationManager:didUpdateToLocation:fromLocation:* method (Fig. 11.16) of the `CLLocationManagerDelegate` protocol is called each time our `CLLocationManager` updates the location of the iPhone. This method receives a `CLLocation` representing the iPhone's current position (`newLocation`) and a `CLLocation` representing the iPhone's previous position (lines 119–120). Line 123 passes the `newLocation` to `TrackingMapView`'s `addPoint` method. If this is not the first location added (line 126), we calculate the distance between the locations using `CLLocation`'s *getDistanceFrom: method* then add the result to distance. Line 133 uses `MapKit`'s *MKCoordinateSpanMake function* to create an

MKCoordinateSpan struct of size 0.005 degrees longitude and 0.005 degrees latitude. *MKCoordinateSpan* structs represent the size of the area covered in an MKCoordinate-Region. *MKCoordinateRegion structs* represent a portion of a total map to display. Lines 136–137 create a new MKCoordinateRegion the same size as span, centered around the newLocation. Line 140 passes this new region to UIMapView's setRegion method to center the user's location in mapView.

```
118   // called whenever the location manager updates the current location
119   - (void)locationManager:(CLLocationManager *)manager didUpdateToLocation:
120     (CLLocation *)newLocation fromLocation:(CLLocation *)oldLocation
121   {
122      // add the new location to the map
123      [trackingMapView addPoint:newLocation];
124
125      // if there was a previous location
126      if (oldLocation != nil)
127      {
128         // add distance from the old location to the total distance
129         distance += [newLocation getDistanceFrom:oldLocation];
130      }
131
132      // create a region centered around the new point
133      MKCoordinateSpan span = MKCoordinateSpanMake(0.005, 0.005);
134
135      // create a new MKCoordinateRegion centered around the new location
136      MKCoordinateRegion region = MKCoordinateRegionMake(
137         newLocation.coordinate, span);
138
139      // reposition the map to show the new point
140      [mapView setRegion:region animated:YES];
141   } // end method locationManager:didUpdateToLocation:fromLocation
142
```

Fig. 11.16 | Method locationManager:didUpdateToLocation:fromLocation: of class Controller.

Methods locationManager:didUpdateHeading: and locationManager:didFailWithError: of Class Controller

The *locationManager:didUpdateHeading:* *method* of the CLLocationManagerDelegate protocol (Fig. 11.17) is called each time our CLLocationManager updates the iPhone's compass heading. The newHeading's trueHeading property is converted to radians (from degrees) and stored in the float variable rotation (line 148). Line 151 resets *mapView's transform property* to *CGAffineTransformIdentity*. This returns mapView's coordinate system to its original settings. Lines 154–155 create a new CGAffineTransform and apply it to mapView, causing the map to rotate at the angle received from newHeading. The *locationManager:didFailWithError:* *method* (lines 159–167) checks the error code to determine whether the user denied the use of locaton services. If so, line 164 invokes CLLocationManager method stopUpdatingLocation to stop using the location services.

Line 166 writes to the log when the CLLocation manager fails. This can occur for several reasons, such as a hardware error or the user denying access to location services.

```
143  // called when the location manager updates the heading
144  - (void)locationManager:(CLLocationManager *)manager didUpdateHeading:
145    (CLHeading *)newHeading
146  {
147    // calculate the rotation in radians
148    float rotation = newHeading.trueHeading * M_PI / 180;
149
150    // reset the transform
151    mapView.transform = CGAffineTransformIdentity;
152
153    // create a new transform with the angle
154    CGAffineTransform transform = CGAffineTransformMakeRotation(-rotation);
155    mapView.transform = transform; // apply the new transform
156  } // end method locationManager:didUpdateHeading:
157
158  // Write an error to console if the CLLocationManager fails
159  - (void)locationManager:(CLLocationManager *)manager didFailWithError:
160  (NSError *)error
161  {
162    // stop using the location service if user disallowed access to it
163    if ([error code] == kCLErrorDenied)
164      [locationManager stopUpdatingLocation];
165
166    NSLog(@"location manager failed"); // log location manager error
167  } // end method locationManager:didFailWithError:
168
169  // free Controller's memory
170  - (void)dealloc
171  {
172    [startButton release]; // release the startButton UIBarButtonItem
173    [mapView release]; // release the mapView MKMapView
174    [locationManager release]; // release the CLLocationManager
175    [super dealloc]; // call the superclass's dealloc
176  } // end method dealloc
177  @end // end Controller implementation
```

Fig. 11.17 | Methods `locationManager:didUpdateHeading:` and `locationManager:didFailWithError:` of class `Controller`.

11.5 Wrap-Up

In the **Route Tracker** app, we displayed a map using the Map Kit framework, which relies on Google Maps web services to obtain map data. The MKMapView class allowed us to draw our route on top of the map and change the display mode between a street map, a satellite image and a combination of the two. The Core Location framework and CLLocationManager class allowed us to access the user's location and compass heading to draw the route and keep the map oriented in the same direction as the user. The NSDate class helped us determine the time it took the user to complete a route—allowing us to calculate the user's average speed along that route.

In Chapter 12, we build the **SlideShow** app, which allows the user to create and display slideshows using images and music. The app will allow the user to access the iPhone's music and photo libraries. The photo picker will be used to add new photos to the slide show, and the music picker will be used to choose a song to play during the slideshow.

12

Slideshow App
Photos and iPod Library Access

OBJECTIVES

In this chapter you'll learn:

- To use a `UIImagePickerController` to allow the user to add pictures from the iPhone's photo library to a slideshow.

- To use an `MPMediaPickerController` to allow the user to add music from the iPod library to a slideshow.

- To use a `UIActionSheet` to allow the user to choose how slideshow images transition from one to the next.

- To use an `MPMusicPlayerController` to play music from the iPod library during the slideshow.

- To allow the slideshow to be viewed in landscape mode by detecting orientation changes.

Outline

12.1 Introduction

12.2 Test-Driving the **Slideshow** App

12.3 Technologies Overview

12.4 Building the App

    12.4.1 Class RootViewController

    12.4.2 Class SlideshowViewController

    12.4.3 Class NameViewController

    12.4.4 Class SlideshowDataViewController

12.5 Wrap-Up

12.1 Introduction

The **Slideshow** app allows the user to create and manage slideshows using pictures and music from the iPhone photo album and iPod library. Each slideshow's title and first image are displayed in a table (Fig. 12.1). This app *does not save* slideshows when the app is closed—we add this capability in the next chapter's **Enhanced Slideshow** app. Touching the "**Play**" **Button** next to a slideshow plays that slideshow (Fig. 12.2(a)). Rotating the iPhone horizontally while the slideshow is playing displays its images in landscape orientation (Fig. 12.2(b)). Each of the images displays for five seconds, while a user-chosen song from the iPod library plays in the background. The images transition either by fading or by sliding to the left, as specified by the user when creating the slideshow. Touching the "**Edit**" **Button** in the top-left corner of the app displays **Deletion Control Buttons** (⊖) next

Fig. 12.1 | List of saved slideshows.

to each of the slideshows (Fig. 12.3 (a)). Touching one of these displays a "**Delete**" **Button** next to the selected slideshow (Fig. 12.3 (b)) that allows the user to remove that slideshow. The user touches the "**New**" **Button** to create a new slideshow.

Fig. 12.2 | Slideshow playing in portrait and landcape orientations.

Fig. 12.3 | Editing the list of slideshows.

Touching the "**New**" **Button** in the top-right corner of the app displays a **Text Field** requesting a name for the new slideshow (Fig. 12.4 (a)). The **Edit Slideshow** screen (Fig. 12.4 (b)) allows the user to add pictures, music and effects to the slideshow. Touching the "**Add Picture**" **Button** in the bottom-left corner of the app displays the iPhone's photo library (Fig. 12.5).

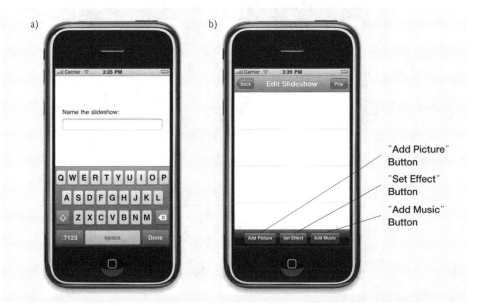

Fig. 12.4 | Creating a new slideshow.

Fig. 12.5 | Photo library.

Touching any of the albums displays the pictures in the album (Fig. 12.6 (a)). The user touches a picture to see a larger version of it. Touching the "**Choose**" **Button** adds that photo to the slideshow (Fig. 12.6 (b)).

a)

Return to photo library

Touch the "**Cancel**" **Button** to return to the **Edit Slideshow** screen

b)

Add current picture to slideshow

Fig. 12.6 | Picking a photo.

12.2 Test-Driving the Slideshow App

Opening the Completed App
Open the directory containing the **Slideshow** app project. Double click `Slideshow.xcodeproj` to open the project in Xcode.

Adding a New Slideshow
Touch the "**New**" **Button** at the top of the app to view the **Edit Slideshow** screen. Touch the "**Add Picture**" **Button** to view the iPhone's (or simulator's) photo library. If you're using the simulator, touch **Saved Photos**; otherwise, touch one of your personal photo folders. Touch any one of the photos to see a larger view of that photo and touch the "**Choose**" **Button** to add the picture to the slideshow and return to the **Edit Slideshow** screen. Touching the "**Cancel**" **Button** here returns you to the previous screen without adding the photo. Add two more images to this slideshow. Touch the reordering control (≡) next to the top picture and drag that picture to the bottom of the list so it's the last image displayed in this slideshow. Now touch the **Deletion Control Button** (⊖) next to the top picture then touch the "**Delete**" **Button** to remove that picture from this slideshow.

Touch the "**Add Effect**" **Button** and choose **Slide**. This will cause the slideshow to transition between images by sliding them to the left. If you're using an actual iPhone to test this app, touch the "**Add Music**" **Button** to view your iPod music library—this feature *is not* supported by the simulator. Select one or more of your songs to add them to the slideshow as background music. If your slideshow contains enough pictures, the slideshow will play the list of songs in the order you selected them; otherwise, the slideshow will likely end before the first song completes. Touch the "**Back**" **Button** in the top-left corner of the app to return to the list of slideshows.

Playing a Slideshow

Touch the "**Play**" **Button** next to your slideshow to play it. The images you added are displayed on the screen, sliding to the left when each new image transitions into view. Your chosen songs play in the background. Rotate the iPhone horizontally to view the slideshow in portrait mode. You can do this in the simulator by selecting **Hardware > Rotate Left** or **Hardware > Rotate Right** in the iPhone simulator.

Editing and Deleting a Slideshow

Touch the "**Modify**" **Button** next to your slideshow to return to the **Edit Slideshow** screen. Touch the "**Add Effect**" **Button** and choose **Fade**. You can add or delete photos as you did previously. If you choose different songs, the original song list is replaced. Return to the list of slideshows and play your slideshow again. The images now transition by fading from view instead of sliding off the screen.

Once the slideshow finishes, touch the "**Edit**" **Button** in the top-left corner of the app. Touch the **Deletion Control Button** (⊖) next to your slideshow then touch the "**Delete**" **Button** to erase your slideshow from the app.

12.3 Technologies Overview

The app's list of slideshows is displayed in a `UITableView` containing custom `UITableViewCells` in which we add "**Play**" and "**Modify**" **Button**s. The **Edit Slideshow** screen uses a `UITableView` with standard `UITableViewCells` to display the images in a selected slideshow. We'll use a `UINavigationController` with a `UIToolbar` to allow the user to navigate between the app's screens. `UIBarButtonItems` are used to switch between views and to delete images and slideshows.

The Photo API contains image pickers that provide a user interface for choosing photos from the iPhone's photo library. We create a `UIImagePickerController` to allow the user to add photos from the photo library to the slideshow. We use `MPMediaPickerController` to control a similar built-in interface that allows the user to choose the slideshow's background music from their iPod library. We store songs chosen from the iPod music library in an `MPMediaItemCollection`. An `MPMusicPlayerController` is used to play the selected song.

The user selects between different image transitions for a slideshow using a `UIActionSheet`. This displays a screen displaying several **Button**s describing different image transitions. Each of these buttons corresponds to a member of the `transitions` enum which is used to define the different transition styles our app supports.

12.4 Building the App

The `RootViewController` controls the view displaying the list of created slideshows. Users can play, modify and delete existing slideshows from this view. The `SlideshowViewController` controls the view used to play slideshows. New slideshows are named using the view controlled by the `NameViewController`, which provides a **Text Field** in which the user can specify the slideshow name. The user can add images, effects and music to a slideshow in the view controlled by the `SlideshowDataViewController`.

12.4.1 Class RootViewController

Class `RootViewController` (Fig. 12.7) is a subclass of `UITableViewController` and implements the `SlideshowCellDelegate` (Fig. 12.15) and `NameViewControllerDelegate` (Fig. 12.24) protocols (lines 10–11). The `NSMutableArray` variable `slideshows` (line 13) will store the user's slideshows. The `addSlideshow` method (line 16) displays the naming view, which allows the user to enter a title for a new slideshow. After being named, the slideshow is displayed in `RootViewController`'s list of slideshows.

```
1   // RootViewController.h
2   // RootViewController class controls the main list of slideshows.
3   // Implementation in RootViewController.m
4   #import <MediaPlayer/MediaPlayer.h>
5   #import "SlideshowDataViewController.h"
6   #import "SlideshowCell.h"
7   #import "NameViewController.h"
8
9   // RootViewController interface declaration
10  @interface RootViewController : UITableViewController
11      <SlideshowCellDelegate, NameViewControllerDelegate>
12  {
13      NSMutableArray *slideshows; // the created slideshows
14  } // end instance variable declaration
15
16  - (void)addSlideshow; // allows the user to add a new slideshow
17  @end // end interface RootViewController
```

Fig. 12.7 | `RootViewController` class controls the main list of slideshows.

Method viewDidLoad of Class RootViewController
The `viewDidLoad` method (Fig. 12.8) is called after the `RootViewController`'s view is initialized. Lines 10–11 call the superclass's `viewDidLoad` method and initialize the slideshows `NSMutableArray`. Line 12 calls `RootViewController`'s `navigationItem` property's `setTitle` method to display `Slideshows` at the top of the app.

```
1   // RootViewController.m
2   // This class controls the main list of slideshows.
3   #import "RootViewController.h"
4
5   @implementation RootViewController
6
7   // called after the view is initialized
8   - (void)viewDidLoad
9   {
10      [super viewDidLoad]; // initialize the superclass
11      slideshows = [[NSMutableArray alloc] init]; // initialize slideshows
```

Fig. 12.8 | Methods `viewDidLoad` of class `RootViewController`. (Part 1 of 2.)

```
12        [self.navigationItem setTitle:@"Slideshows"]; // set the bar title
13
14        // create the newSlideshowButton for adding a new slideshow
15        UIBarButtonItem *newSlideshowButton = [[UIBarButtonItem alloc]
16           initWithTitle:@"New" style:UIBarButtonItemStylePlain target:self
17           action:@selector(addSlideshow)];
18
19        // create the back button for when the user navigates away
20        UIBarButtonItem *backButton = [[UIBarButtonItem alloc]
21           initWithTitle:@"Back" style:UIBarButtonItemStylePlain target:nil
22           action:nil];
23
24        // add the newSlideshowButton to the right side of the navigation bar
25        [self.navigationItem setRightBarButtonItem:newSlideshowButton];
26        self.navigationItem.leftBarButtonItem = self.editButtonItem;
27
28        // set the back button to be displayed when the user navigates away
29        [self.navigationItem setBackBarButtonItem:backButton];
30        self.tableView.rowHeight = ROW_HEIGHT; // set the table's row height
31        [newSlideshowButton release]; // release the newSlideshowButton
32        [backButton release]; // release the backButton
33    } // end method viewDidLoad
34
```

Fig. 12.8 | Methods viewDidLoad of class RootViewController. (Part 2 of 2.)

Lines 15–17 create a new UIBarButtonItem titled New, which calls the addSlideshow method when touched. This allows the user to create a new slideshow. Lines 20–22 create a UIBarButtonItem titled Back, which is added to the navigation bar when the user leaves the RootViewController, so the user can return to this view. We then add the "**New**" **Button** to the right side of the navigation bar (line 25). Line 26 adds RootViewController's editButtonItem property to the left side of the navigation bar. This is the "**Edit**" **Button** used to delete slideshows. Line 29 passes backButton to UINavigationItem's setBackBarButtonItem: method to specify that backButton should appear when the user navigates to a different view.

Methods viewWillAppear: and addSlideshow of Class RootViewController
The viewWillAppear: method (Fig. 12.9, lines 36–43) is called each time the app displays the RootViewController's view. Line 38 calls the superclass's viewWillAppear: method. We then get RootViewController's UINavigationController and use its setNavigationBarHidden:animated: method to display the navigation bar (line 41). Line 42 calls UITableView's reloadData method to update RootViewController's table to any changes made in another view.

```
35    // called when the view is about to be displayed
36    - (void)viewWillAppear:(BOOL)animated
37    {
```

Fig. 12.9 | Method viewWillAppear: and addSlideshow of class RootViewController. (Part 1 of 2.)

```
38      [super viewWillAppear:animated]; // pass message to the superclass
39
40      // show the navigation bar
41      [self.navigationController setNavigationBarHidden:NO animated:YES];
42      [(UITableView *)self.view reloadData]; // update the table
43   } // end method viewWillAppear:
44
45   // called when the "New" button is touched
46   - (void)addSlideshow
47   {
48      // create a new NameViewController
49      NameViewController *controller = [[NameViewController alloc]
50         initWithNibName:@"NameViewController" bundle:nil];
51      controller.delegate = self; // set delegate to self
52
53      // display the NameViewController
54      [self presentModalViewController:controller animated:YES];
55   } // end method addSlideshow
56
```

Fig. 12.9 | Method `viewWillAppear:` and `addSlideshow` of class `RootViewController`. (Part 2 of 2.)

The `addSlideshow` method (lines 46–55) displays the `NameViewController` when the user touches the "**New**" **Button**. Lines 49–51 create a new `NameViewController` and set its delegate to `self`. We call `UIViewController`'s `presentModalViewController:animated:` method to display the **NameViewController** (line 54).

Methods nameViewController:didGetName: and tableView:numberOfRowsInSection: of Class RootViewController

The `nameViewController:didGetName:` method (Fig. 12.10, lines 58–73) is declared in the `NameViewDelegate` protocol (Fig. 12.24) and is called when the user finishes entering a name for a new slideshow. `UIViewController`'s `dismissModalViewControllerAnimated:` method hides the `NameViewController`'s view (line 62). Lines 65–67 create a new `SlideshowDataViewController` and add it to `slideshows` using `NSMutableArray`'s `addObject:` method. We then set the new `slideshow`'s `title` property to the given name. Line 71 calls `UINavigationController`'s `pushViewController:animated:` method to show the `SlideshowDataView` for the new slideshow. The `tableView:numberOfRowsInSection:` method (lines 76–80) specifies that `RootViewController`'s `UITableView`'s only section has as many rows as there are slideshows.

```
57   // gets slideshow name from the NameView then displays SlideshowDataView
58   - (void)nameViewController:(NameViewController *)controller
59      didGetName:(NSString *)name
60   {
61      // hide the NameView
62      [self dismissModalViewControllerAnimated:YES];
```

Fig. 12.10 | `RootViewController` methods `nameViewController:didGetName:`, and `tableView:numberOfRowsInSection:`. (Part 1 of 2.)

```
63
64    // create a new SlideshowDataViewController
65    SlideshowDataViewController *slideshow =
66       [[SlideshowDataViewController alloc] init];
67    [slideshows addObject:slideshow]; // add it to the list of slideshows
68    slideshow.title = name; // title the slideshow with the given name
69
70    // show the create slideshow view
71    [self.navigationController pushViewController:slideshow animated:YES];
72    [slideshow release]; // release the SlideshowDataViewController
73 } // end method nameViewController:didGetName:
74
75 // called by the table view to get the number of rows in a given section
76 - (NSInteger)tableView:(UITableView *)tableView numberOfRowsInSection:
77    (NSInteger)section
78 {
79    return slideshows.count; // return one row for each slideshow
80 } // end method tableView:numberOfRowsInSection:
81
```

Fig. 12.10 | RootViewController methods nameViewController:didGetName:, and tableView:numberOfRowsInSection:. (Part 2 of 2.)

Method tableView:cellForRowAtIndexPath: of Class RootViewController

The tableView:cellForRowAtIndexPath: method (Fig. 12.11) retrieves the UITable-ViewCell specified by the given NSIndexPath. Lines 87–100 attempt to reuse a UITableViewCell from the given tableView using UITableView's dequeReusableCell-WithIdentifier: method. We set the new SlideshowCell's delegate to this RootView-Controller (line 103). Line 105 sets the UITableViewCell's selectionStyle property to UITableViewCallSelectionStyleNone to indicated that no action is taken when the UITableViewCell is touched. Lines 108–109 get the SlideshowDataViewController corresponding to the touched UITableViewCell. Line 112 calls the SlideshowDataViewController's firstImage method to get a UIImage representing the first picture in the selected slideshow. Lines 113–114 set the SlideshowCell's thumbnail to that UIImage and title to the SlideshowDataViewController's title.

```
82 // called by the table view to get the cells it needs to populate itself
83 - (UITableViewCell *)tableView:(UITableView *)tableView
84    cellForRowAtIndexPath:(NSIndexPath *)indexPath
85 {
86    // create cell identifier
87    static NSString *CellIdentifier = @"SlideshowCell";
88
89    // get a reusable cell
90    SlideshowCell *cell = (SlideshowCell *)[tableView
91       dequeueReusableCellWithIdentifier:CellIdentifier];
92
```

Fig. 12.11 | Method tableView:cellForRowAtIndexPath: of class RootViewController. (Part 1 of 2.)

```
93      // if no reusable cells are available
94      if (cell == nil)
95      {
96         // create a new cell
97         cell = [[[SlideshowCell alloc] initWithStyle:
98            UITableViewCellStyleDefault reuseIdentifier:CellIdentifier]
99            autorelease];
100     } // end if
101
102     cell.delegate = self; // set this object as cell's delegate
103
104     // make the cell do nothing when selected
105     cell.selectionStyle = UITableViewCellSelectionStyleNone;
106
107     // get the SlideshowDataViewController for the given row
108     SlideshowDataViewController *controller =
109        [slideshows objectAtIndex:indexPath.row];
110
111     // get the first image in the slideshow at the correct index
112     UIImage *image = [controller firstImage];
113     cell.thumbnail.image = image; // set the cell's thumbnail image
114     cell.title.text = controller.title; // set the cell's text
115
116     return cell; // return the configured cell to the table view
117  } // end method tableView:cellForRowAtIndexPath:
118
```

Fig. 12.11 | Method `tableView:cellForRowAtIndexPath:` of class `RootViewController`. (Part 2 of 2.)

Methods `slideshowCellDidSelectEditButton:` and `slideshowCellDidSelectPlayButton:` of Class `RootViewController`
The `slideshowCellDidSelectEditButton:` method (Fig. 12.12, lines 120–126) is declared by the `SlideshowCellDelegate` protocol and displays the `SlideshowDataViewController`'s view for the touched slideshow. This allows the user to edit the selected slideshow.

```
119  // called when the user touches the modify button of a SlideshowCell
120  - (void)slideshowCellDidSelectEditButton:(SlideshowCell *)cell
121  {
122     // get the index path for the touched cell
123     NSIndexPath *indexPath = [self.tableView indexPathForCell:cell];
124     [self.navigationController pushViewController:
125        [slideshows objectAtIndex:indexPath.row] animated:YES];
126  } // end method slideshowCellDidSelectEditButton:
127
128  // called when the user touches the play button of a SlideshowCell
129  - (void)slideshowCellDidSelectPlayButton:(SlideshowCell *)cell
130  {
```

Fig. 12.12 | Methods `slideshowCellDidSelectEditButton:` and `slideshowCellDidSelectPlayButton:` of class `RootViewController`. (Part 1 of 2.)

```
131      // find the index path where the given cell is located
132      NSIndexPath *indexPath = [self.tableView indexPathForCell:cell];
133
134      // get the SlideshowDataViewController at the index path
135      SlideshowDataViewController *data =
136         [slideshows objectAtIndex:indexPath.row];
137
138      // create a new SlideshowViewController
139      SlideshowViewController *controller =
140         [[SlideshowViewController alloc] init];
141      controller.pictures = data.pictures; // set controller's pictures
142      controller.effect = data.effect; // set controller's effect
143      controller.music = data.music; // set controller's music
144
145      // hide the navigation bar
146      [self.navigationController setNavigationBarHidden:YES animated:YES];
147
148      // show the slideshow
149      [self.navigationController pushViewController:controller animated:YES];
150   } // end method slideshowCellDidSelectPlayButton:
151
```

Fig. 12.12 | Methods slideshowCellDidSelectEditButton: and slideshowCell-DidSelectPlayButton: of class RootViewController. (Part 2 of 2.)

The slideshowCellDidSelectPlayButton: method (lines 129–150) plays a slideshow when the user touches its "**Play**" **Button**. Lines 132–136 get the SlideshowData-ViewController at the UITableViewCell selected by the given NSIndexPath. We then create a new SlideshowViewController to play the selected slideshow (lines 139–140). Lines 141–143 set the SlideshowViewController's pictures, effect and music to those of the selected slideshow. We hide the navigation bar then call UINavigationController's pushViewController:animated: method to display the slideshow (lines 146–149).

Method tableView:commitEditingStyle:forRowAtIndexPath: of Class Root-ViewController
Method tableView:commitEditingStyle:forRowAtIndexPath: (Fig. 12.13) specifies that RootViewController's UITableViewCells support editing. This allows the user to delete slideshows.

```
152   // Override to support editing the table view.
153   - (void)tableView:(UITableView *)tableView commitEditingStyle:
154      (UITableViewCellEditingStyle)editingStyle forRowAtIndexPath:
155      (NSIndexPath *)indexPath
156   {
157      // "delete" editing style is committed
158      if (editingStyle == UITableViewCellEditingStyleDelete)
159      {
```

Fig. 12.13 | Method tableView:commitEditingStyle:forRowAtIndexPath: of class RootViewController. (Part 1 of 2.)

```
160        // remove contact at indexPath.row
161        [slideshows removeObjectAtIndex:indexPath.row];
162
163        // delete the row from the table view
164        [tableView deleteRowsAtIndexPaths:[NSArray arrayWithObject:
165           indexPath] withRowAnimation:UITableViewRowAnimationFade];
166     } // end if
167 } // end method tableView:commitEditingStyle:forRowAtIndexPath:
168
```

Fig. 12.13 | Method `tableView:commitEditingStyle:forRowAtIndexPath:` of class `RootViewController`. (Part 2 of 2.)

Methods `tableView:moveRowAtIndexPath:toIndexPath:` and `tableView:canMoveRowAtIndexPath:` of Class RootViewController

The `tableView:moveAtIndexPath:toIndexPath:` method (Fig. 12.14, lines 170–183) is called when the user moves a row in `RootViewController`'s `UITableView` by dragging a `UITableViewCell`'s reordering control (≡). Lines 174–178 get the `SlideshowDataViewController` for the row being dragged and remove it from slideshows using `NSMutableArray`'s `removeObjectAtIndex:` method. The `fromIndexPath` `NSIndexPath` specifies the `UITableViewCell` being dragged. Line 181 inserts the `SlideshowDataViewController` back in slideshows at the index to which the `UITableViewCell` was dragged. The `toIndexPath` `NSIndexPath` specifies the end location of the dragged `UITableViewCell`. Method `tableView:canMoveRowAtIndexPath:` (lines 186–190) always returns `YES` in this example to indicate that the user can move all of the `UITableViewCells`.

```
169 // called when the user moves a row in the table
170 - (void)tableView:(UITableView *)tableView moveRowAtIndexPath:
171    (NSIndexPath *)fromIndexPath toIndexPath:(NSIndexPath *)toIndexPath
172 {
173     // get the SlideshowDataViewController for the moved row
174     SlideshowDataViewController *data =
175        [[slideshows objectAtIndex:fromIndexPath.row] retain];
176
177     // remove the moved SlideshowDataViewController
178     [slideshows removeObjectAtIndex:fromIndexPath.row];
179
180     // insert the SlideshowDataViewController in the new position
181     [slideshows insertObject:data atIndex:toIndexPath.row];
182     [data release]; // release the data SlideshowDataViewController
183 } // end method tableView:moveRowAtIndexPath:toIndexPath:
184
185 // called by the table view to check if a given row can be moved
186 - (BOOL)tableView:(UITableView *)tableView canMoveRowAtIndexPath:
187 (NSIndexPath *)indexPath
188 {
189    return YES; // all the rows in this table can be moved
190 } // end method tableView:canMoveRowAtIndexPath:
```

Fig. 12.14 | Methods `tableView:moveRowAtIndexPath:toIndexPath:` and `tableView:canMoveRowAtIndexPath:` of class `RootViewController`.

SlideshowCell Interface Declaration

The SlideshowCell class (Fig. 12.15) extends UITableViewCell to display a slideshow title, and "**Play**" and "**Modify**" **Buttons**. Lines 11–13 declare this class's delegate and other instance variables. We declare each of SlideshowCell's instance variables as properties (lines 17–19). The editSlideshow method (line 21) informs the delegate that the SlideshowCell's "**Edit**" **Button** was touched. The playSlideshow method (line 22) informs the delegate that the SlideshowCell's "**Play**" **Button** was touched. The SlideshowCellDelegate protocol (lines 26–33) defines two methods used to inform the delegate that SlideshowCell's **Buttons** were touched.

```objc
1   // SlideshowCell.h
2   // UITableViewCell for previewing a slideshow.
3   // Implementation in SlideshowCell.m
4   #import <UIKit/UIKit.h>
5
6   @protocol SlideshowCellDelegate; // declare SlideshowCellDelegate protocol
7
8   // SlideshowCell interface declaration
9   @interface SlideshowCell : UITableViewCell
10  {
11      id <SlideshowCellDelegate> delegate; // this class's delegate
12      UIImageView *thumbnail; // the first slide in the slideshow
13      UILabel *title; // the slideshow's title
14  } // end instance variable declarations
15
16  // declare delegate, thumbnail and title as properties
17  @property (nonatomic, assign) id <SlideshowCellDelegate> delegate;
18  @property (nonatomic, readonly) UIImageView *thumbnail;
19  @property (nonatomic, readonly) UILabel *title;
20
21  - (void)editSlideshow; // called when the user touches the edit button
22  - (void)playSlideshow; // called when the user touches the play button
23  @end // end interface SlideshowCell
24
25  // SlideshowCell Delegate protocol
26  @protocol SlideshowCellDelegate
27
28  // informs delegate that the edit button was touched
29  - (void)slideshowCellDidSelectEditButton:(SlideshowCell *)cell;
30
31  // informs delegate that the play button was touched
32  - (void)slideshowCellDidSelectPlayButton:(SlideshowCell *)cell;
33  @end // end protocol SlideshowCellDelegate
```

Fig. 12.15 | UITableViewCell for previewing a slideshow.

Method initWithFrame:reuseIdentifier: of Class SlideshowCell

The initWithFrame:reuseIdentifier: method (Fig. 12.16) initializes the SlideshowCell. Lines 19–20 create a new UIImageView on the left side of the SlideshowCell. This is used to show a thumbnail of the first image of the slideshow. Line 23 expands the thumbnail to fit the height of the SlideshowCell. Lines 26–27 create a new **Label** which we user later to title the slideshow. Lines 30–55 create UIButtons editButton and play-

Button. Touching the editButton calls SlideshowCell's editSlideshow method. Touching the playButton calls the playSlideshow method. We then call UIView's addSubview method to add the thumbnail image, title and **Button**s to this SlideshowCell's contentView to display them on the UITableViewCell (lines 58–61).

```
1    // SlideshowCell.m
2    // SlideshowCell implementation
3    #import "SlideshowCell.h"
4
5    @implementation SlideshowCell
6
7    @synthesize delegate; // generate get and set methods for delegate
8    @synthesize thumbnail; // generate get and set methods for thumbnail
9    @synthesize title; // generate get and set methods for title
10
11   // initialize the SlideshowCell
12   - (id)initWithStyle:(UITableViewCellStyle)style
13       reuseIdentifier:(NSString *)reuseIdentifier
14   {
15      // if the superclass initialized properly
16      if (self = [super initWithStyle:style reuseIdentifier:reuseIdentifier])
17      {
18         // initialize thumbnail
19         thumbnail =
20            [[UIImageView alloc] initWithFrame:CGRectMake(20, 10, 120, 76)];
21
22         // make the image scale to fit the view
23         thumbnail.contentMode = UIViewContentModeScaleAspectFit;
24
25         // initialize title
26         title =
27            [[UILabel alloc] initWithFrame:CGRectMake(148, 20, 152, 21)];
28
29         // initialize editButton
30         UIButton *editButton =
31            [UIButton buttonWithType:UIButtonTypeRoundedRect];
32
33         // set editButton's frame
34         editButton.frame = CGRectMake(228, 49, 72, 37);
35
36         // set editButton's title
37         [editButton setTitle:@"Modify" forState:UIControlStateNormal];
38
39         // make editButton call the editSlideshow method when touched
40         [editButton addTarget:self action:@selector(editSlideshow)
41            forControlEvents:UIControlEventTouchUpInside];
42
43         // initialize playButton
44         UIButton *playButton =
45            [UIButton buttonWithType:UIButtonTypeRoundedRect];
46
```

Fig. 12.16 | SlideshowCell method initWithFrame:reuseIdentifier:. (Part 1 of 2.)

```
47        // set playButton's title
48        [playButton setTitle:@"Play" forState:UIControlStateNormal];
49
50        // set playButton's frame
51        playButton.frame = CGRectMake(148, 49, 72, 37);
52
53        // make playButton call the playSlideshow method when touched
54        [playButton addTarget:self action:@selector(playSlideshow)
55            forControlEvents:UIControlEventTouchUpInside];
56
57        // add the components to contentView
58        [self.contentView addSubview:thumbnail]; // add thumbnail to View
59        [self.contentView addSubview:title]; // add title to View
60        [self.contentView addSubview:editButton]; // add editButton to View
61        [self.contentView addSubview:playButton]; // add playButton to View
62    } // end if
63
64    return self; // return this object
65 } // end method initWithFrame:reuseIdentifier:
66
```

Fig. 12.16 | SlideshowCell method initWithFrame:reuseIdentifier:. (Part 2 of 2.)

Methods *editSlideshow* and *playSlideShow* of Class *SlideshowCell*

The editSlideshow method (Fig. 12.17, lines 68–72) calls the delegate's slideshow-CellDidSelectEditButton: method (line 71). This displays the selected slideshow's SlideshowDataViewController so the user can edit that slideshow. The playSlideshow method (Fig. 12.17, lines 75–79) calls the delegate's slideshowCellDidSelectPlayButton: method to play the selected slideshow.

```
67 // called when the edit button is touched
68 - (void)editSlideshow
69 {
70    // inform the delegate that the edit button was touched
71    [delegate slideshowCellDidSelectEditButton:self];
72 } // end method editSlideshow
73
74 // called when the play button is touched
75 - (void)playSlideshow
76 {
77    // inform the delegate that the play button was touched
78    [delegate slideshowCellDidSelectPlayButton:self];
79 } // end method playSlideshow
80
81 // release SlideshowCell's memory
82 - (void)dealloc
83 {
84    [thumbnail release]; // release the thumbnail UIImageView
85    [title release]; // release the title UILabel
```

Fig. 12.17 | Methods editSlideshow and playSlideShow of class SlideshowCell. (Part 1 of 2.)

```
86        [super dealloc]; // call the superclass's dealloc method
87     } // end method dealloc
88     @end
```

Fig. 12.17 | Methods editSlideshow and playSlideShow of class SlideshowCell. (Part 2 of 2.)

12.4.2 Class SlideshowViewController

The SlideshowViewController's **View** plays a slideshow in full screen mode. The slideshow re-orients as the user rotates the iPhone.

SlideshowViewController *Interface Declaration*

The SlideshowViewController class (Fig. 12.18) controls a view that displays a user-created slideshow. Lines 7–11 create an ***enum type*** containing a set of integer symbolic constants. Values in an enum start with 0 and increment by 1 by default, so the constant TransitionEffectFade has the value 0 and TransitionEffectSlide has the value 1. The identifiers in an enumeration must be unique, but the values may be duplicated. To provide a specific value for a constant, assign the value to the enum constant in the enum declaration. Line 16 declares a TransitionEffect variable effect. If the user chooses **Fade** as this slideshow's effect, the effect variable is set to TransitionEffectFade. Choosing the **Slide** effect sets the variable effect to TransitionEffectSlide.

```
 1    // SlideshowViewController.h
 2    // Controller for a View that shows a slideshow.
 3    // Implementation in SlideshowViewController.m
 4    #import <UIKit/UIKit.h>
 5    #import <MediaPlayer/MediaPlayer.h>
 6
 7    typedef enum _transitionEffects
 8    {
 9       TransitionEffectFade, // represents fade image transition effect
10       TransitionEffectSlide // represents slide image transition effect
11    } TransitionEffect;
12
13    @interface SlideshowViewController : UIViewController
14    {
15       NSMutableArray *pictures; // the pictures in this slideshow
16       TransitionEffect effect; // the transition effect for the slideshow
17       MPMediaItemCollection *music; // the music to play during the slideshow
18       MPMusicPlayerController *musicPlayer; // plays the music
19       NSTimer *timer; // generates event to move to the next slide
20       UIImageView *currentImageView; // the current image being displayed
21       int pictureIndex; // the index in pictures of the current slide
22    } // end instance variable declaration
23
24    // declare pictures, effect and music as properties
25    @property (nonatomic, assign) NSMutableArray *pictures;
26    @property (nonatomic, assign) TransitionEffect effect;
27    @property (nonatomic, assign) MPMediaItemCollection *music;
```

Fig. 12.18 | Controller for a **View** that shows a slideshow. (Part 1 of 2.)

```
28
29    - (UIImageView *)nextImageView; // returns the next image to display
30    - (void)exitShow; // returns the app to the previous screen
31    - (void)timerFired:(NSTimer *)timer; // progresses the slideshow
32    @end // end interface SlideshowViewController
33
34    // additional method for UIImageView
35    @interface UIImageView (Scaling)
36
37    // scales the image view to fill the given bounds
38    - (void)expandToFill:(CGRect)bounds;
39    @end // end category Scaling of interface UIImageView
```

Fig. 12.18 | Controller for a **View** that shows a slideshow. (Part 2 of 2.)

Line 17 declares an **MPMediaItemCollection** used to store the background music for this slideshow. We declare an **MPMusicPlayerController** to play music from the iPod library (line 18). Lines 19–21 declare SlideshowViewController's remaining instance variables.

Lines 25–27 declare the NSMutableArray, TransitionEffect and MPMediaItemCollection as properties. The SlideshowViewController class declares three methods (lines 29–31):

- nextImageView—returns the new UIImage displayed in the current slideshow

- exitShow—returns the app to the **RootView**

- timerFired:—changes the slideshow's image every five seconds; if there are no slides left, this method calls exitShow

Lines 35–39 add the Scaling category to class UIImageView. The category's expandToFill: method scales a UIImageView to fill the given CGRect.

Methods *loadView* and *nextImageView* of Class *SlideshowViewController*
The loadView method (Fig. 12.19, lines 12–18) initializes the **SlideshowView** (line 14). We set the UIView's frame property makes the slideshowView fill the entire screen (line 17).

```
 1    // SlideshowViewController.m
 2    // Controller for a view that shows a slideshow
 3    #import "SlideshowViewController.h"
 4
 5    @implementation SlideshowViewController
 6
 7    @synthesize pictures; // generate getter and setter for pictures
 8    @synthesize effect; // generate getter and setter for effect
 9    @synthesize music; // generate getter and setter for music
10
```

Fig. 12.19 | Methods loadView and nextImageView of class SlideshowViewController. (Part 1 of 2.)

```
11   // setup the view
12   - (void)loadView
13   {
14      self.view = [[UIView alloc] init]; // initialize the main view
15
16      // size the main view to fill the entire screen
17      self.view.frame = [UIScreen mainScreen].bounds;
18   } // end method loadView
19
20   // Returns a UIImageView that contains the next image to display
21   - (UIImageView *)nextImageView
22   {
23      // get the image at the next index
24      UIImage *image = [pictures objectAtIndex:pictureIndex];
25      ++pictureIndex; // increment the index
26
27      // create an image view for the image
28      UIImageView *imageView = [[UIImageView alloc] initWithImage:image];
29
30      CGRect screenBounds = self.view.bounds; // get the screen bounds
31
32      // resize the image to fill the screen without distorting
33      [imageView expandToFill:screenBounds];
34
35      // position the image to appear in the center of the view
36      imageView.center = self.view.center;
37
38      // Makes the image move proportionally in any direction if the
39      // bounds of the superview change when the iPhone is rotated.
40      imageView.autoresizingMask = (UIViewAutoresizingFlexibleLeftMargin |
41         UIViewAutoresizingFlexibleRightMargin |
42         UIViewAutoresizingFlexibleTopMargin |
43         UIViewAutoresizingFlexibleBottomMargin);
44
45      return imageView;
46   } // end method nextImageView
47
```

Fig. 12.19 | Methods `loadView` and `nextImageView` of class `SlideshowViewController`. (Part 2 of 2.)

Method `nextImageView` (lines 21–46) returns a `UIImageView` displaying the slideshow's next image. We retrieve the next `UIImage` from `pictures` (line 24), then increment `pictureIndex` (line 25). Line 28 creates a new `UIImageView` using the retrieved `UIImage`. We access `SlideshowViewController`'s `UIView`'s bounds property to get a `CGRect` representing the screen's bounds (line 30). We pass this `CGRect` to `imageView`'s `expandToFill:` method to resize our **Image View** to fill the entire screen. This method expands the image as much as possible without distorting it. Line 36 centers the `UIImageView` in the screen.

`SlideshowViewController`'s *autoresizingMask property* (inherited from `UIView`) defines how the `UIView` resizes its subviews when the `UIView`'s bounds change. This occurs in this app when the user rotates the iPhone while a slideshow is playing. The autoresizingMask property is an integer containing bit flags so we set it by combining all desired options using the bitwise OR operator (|). Lines 40–43 specify that SlideshowViewController's UIImageView remains centered as the iPhone rotates.

Methods exitShow and timerFired of Class SlideshowViewController

The exitShow method (Fig. 12.20, lines 49–58) stops the background music by calling AVAudioPlayer's stop method (line 51). We call UIApplication's sharedApplication method to get the singleton UIApplication for this app (line 54). *UIApplication's set-StatusBarHidden method* is called to redisplay the status bar, which we hid when the slideshow began playing. The *status bar* normally appears at the top of the app and displays the iPhone's remaining battery life, service provider (e.g. AT&T) and current time among other things. Line 57 calls UINavigationController's popViewControllerAnimated: method to return to the previous view.

The timerFired: method (lines 61–119) displays the next slideshow image every five seconds. If there are no more images in the slideshow (line 64), we call the exitShow method to end the current slideshow (line 66). Otherwise, we call the nextImageView method to get a UIImageView representing the next picture in this slideshow (line 71). UIView's addSubview: method is used to display the image (line 72).

```
48    // called from timerFired: if there are no more images to be displayed
49    - (void)exitShow
50    {
51        [musicPlayer stop]; // stop the music
52
53        // display the status bar
54        [[UIApplication sharedApplication] setStatusBarHidden:NO];
55
56        // remove the slideshow view to return to the previous View
57        [self.navigationController popViewControllerAnimated:YES];
58    } // end method exitShow
59
60    // called every five seconds when the timer fires
61    - (void)timerFired:(NSTimer *)timer
62    {
63        // check if there's another image to display
64        if (pictureIndex >= pictures.count)
65        {
66            [self exitShow]; // if there's no image, exit the slideshow
67        } // end if
68        else
69        {
70            // get the next image to display
71            UIImageView *nextImageView = [self nextImageView];
72            [self.view addSubview:nextImageView]; // add the image to the view
73            CGRect frame;
74
75            // set the next image to its beginning state for the effect
76            switch (effect)
77            {
```

Fig. 12.20 | Methods exitShow and timerFired of class SlideshowViewController. (Part 1 of 2.)

```
78              case TransitionEffectFade: // the user chose the fade effect
79                  nextImageView.alpha = 0.0; // make the next image transparent
80                  break;
81              case TransitionEffectSlide: // the user chose the slide effect
82
83                  // position the next image to the right of the screen
84                  frame = nextImageView.frame; // get the next image's frame
85                  frame.origin.x += frame.size.width; // move frame off screen
86                  nextImageView.frame = frame; // apply the repositioned frame
87                  break;
88          } // end switch
89
90          // begin animation block
91          [UIView beginAnimations:nil context:nextImageView];
92          [UIView setAnimationDuration:2.0]; // set the animation length
93          [UIView setAnimationDelegate:self]; // set the animation delegate
94
95          // call the given method when the animation ends
96          [UIView setAnimationDidStopSelector:
97              @selector(transitionFinished:finished:context:)];
98
99          // make the next image appear with the chosen effect
100         switch (effect)
101         {
102             case TransitionEffectFade: // the user chose the fade effect
103                 [nextImageView setAlpha:1.0]; // fade in the next image
104                 [currentImageView setAlpha:0.0]; // fade out the old image
105                 break;
106             case TransitionEffectSlide: // the user chose the slide effect
107                 frame.origin.x -= frame.size.width; // slide new image left
108                 nextImageView.frame = frame; // apply the repositioned frame
109                 CGRect currentImageFrame = currentImageView.frame;
110
111                 // slide the old image to the left
112                 currentImageFrame.origin.x -= currentImageFrame.size.width;
113                 currentImageView.frame = currentImageFrame; // apply frame
114                 break;
115         } // end switch
116
117         [UIView commitAnimations]; // end animation block
118     } // end else
119 } // end method timerFired:
120
```

Fig. 12.20 | Methods exitShow and timerFired of class SlideshowViewController. (Part 2 of 2.)

The image is added to the screen using Core Animation according to the user's chosen effect. If the effect is TransitionEffectFade, the UIImageView's alpha property to set to 0.0, making the image transparent (lines 78–79). This allows us to fade in the image as the old image is faded out. If the effect is TransitionEffectSlide, we position the UIImageView to the right of the screen (lines 81–86). This allows us to slide the image in from the right edge of the screen. Lines 91–93 begin a Core Animation block defining an animation lasting two seconds. Lines 96–97 specify that the transitionFinished:finished:context: method is called when the animation ends.

We then set the final state of the image according to the chosen effect. If the effect is TransitionEffectFade the new UIImageView will have full opacity and the old UIImageView will be transparent (lines 101–102). If the effect is TransitionEffectSlide, we place the new UIImageView in the center of the screen (lines 106–109) and move the old UIImageView off the left side of the screen (lines 112–113). Line 117 calls UIView's commitAnimations method to animate the UIImageView's to their final state.

Methods *transitionFinished:finished:context:*, *viewWillAppear* and *viewDidDisappear* of Class *SlideshowViewController*

The transitionFinished:finished:context: method (Fig. 12.21, lines 122–128) is called when the image transition animation completes. Line 125 calls UIImageView's removeFromSuperview method to remove the old image. We release the previous UIImageView's memory and set currentImageView to the new image (lines 126–127).

```
121   // called when the image transition animation finishes
122   - (void)transitionFinished:(NSString *)animationId finished:(BOOL)finished
123       context:(void *)context
124   {
125       [currentImageView removeFromSuperview]; // remove the old image
126       [currentImageView release]; // release the memory for the old image
127       currentImageView = context; // assign the new image
128   } // end method transitionFinished:finished:context:
129
130   // called when the View appears
131   - (void)viewWillAppear:(BOOL)animated
132   {
133       [super viewWillAppear:animated]; // pass the message to the superclass
134       pictureIndex = 0; // reset the index
135
136       currentImageView = [self nextImageView]; // load the first image
137       [self.view addSubview:currentImageView]; // add the image to the view
138
139       // hide the status bar so the slideshow can appear fullscreen
140       [[UIApplication sharedApplication] setStatusBarHidden:YES];
141
142       // initialize the timer to fire every 5 seconds
143       timer = [NSTimer scheduledTimerWithTimeInterval:5.0 target:self
144           selector:@selector(timerFired:) userInfo:nil repeats:YES];
145
146       // if the user has selected music to play
147       if (music != nil)
148       {
149           // get the application music player
150           musicPlayer = [MPMusicPlayerController applicationMusicPlayer];
151           musicPlayer.shuffleMode = MPMusicShuffleModeOff; // turn off shuffle
152           musicPlayer.repeatMode = MPMusicRepeatModeNone; // turn off repeat
```

Fig. 12.21 | Methods transitionFinished:finished:context:, viewWillAppear and viewDidDisappear of class SlideshowViewController. (Part 1 of 2.)

```
153
154        // add the music the user selected to the queue
155        [musicPlayer setQueueWithItemCollection:music];
156        [musicPlayer play]; // play the music
157     } // end if
158 } // end method viewWillAppear:
159
160 // called when the View disappears
161 - (void)viewDidDisappear:(BOOL)animated
162 {
163     [super viewDidDisappear:animated];
164
165     // Stop the timer
166     [timer invalidate];
167     timer = nil; // set timer to nil
168     [currentImageView removeFromSuperview]; // remove the current image
169 } // end method viewDidDisappear:
170
```

Fig. 12.21 | Methods `transitionFinished:finished:context:`, `viewWillAppear` and `viewDidDisappear` of class `SlideshowViewController`. (Part 2 of 2.)

The `viewWillAppear` method (lines 131–158) is called when the app transitions to the `SlideshowViewController`'s view. Lines 136–137 use `UIView`'s `addSubview:` method to display the first image in the slideshow. `UIApplication`'s `setStatusBarHidden:` method is used to hide the iPhone status bar so the slideshow fills the entire screen. Lines 143–144 initialize our `NSTimer` to call the `timerFired:` method every five seconds.

If the user selected background music for this slideshow (line 147), we use an ***MPMusicPlayerController*** to play those files. Line 150 calls ***MPMusicPlayerController's applicationMusicPlayer method*** to get the app's singleton `MPMusicPlayerController` object. We prevent the `MPMusicPlayerController` from shuffling the selected songs by setting its `shuffleMode` property to ***MPMusicShuffleModeOff*** (line 151). We prevent the `MPMusicPlayerController` from repeating songs by setting its `repeatMode` property to ***MPMusicShuffleModeNone*** (line 152). Line 155 passes `music` to `MPMusicPlayer`'s `setQueueWithItemCollection:` method so the `MPMusicPlayer` plays each song in `music` when the `MPMusicPlayer`'s `play` method is called in line 156.

Method `viewDidDisappear:` (lines 161–169) is called when the app transitions from the `SlideshowViewController`'s view back to that of the `RootViewController` or the `SlideshowDataViewController`—this depends on where the user began playing the slideshow. We call the superclass's `viewDidDisappear` method (line 163) then use `NSTimer`'s `invalidate` method to stop `timer` and release it (line 166). Line 168 calls `UIImageView`'s `removeFromSuperView` method to remove the current image; otherwise, the next time the user plays a slideshow, the previous slideshow's last image will still be displayed.

Methods shouldAutorotateToInterfaceOrientation: and willRotateToInterfaceOrientation: of Class SlideshowViewController

The `shouldAutorotateToInterfaceOrientation:` method (Fig. 12.22, lines 172–176) returns YES indicating that the `SlideshowViewController`'s view can rotate to all possible iPhone orientations. Method `willRotateToInterfaceOrientation:duration:` (lines

179–189) is called when the user rotates the iPhone. Lines 184–185 create a new CGRect the same size as the screen. Line 188 calls imageView's expandToFill: method to resize the slideshow image according to the screen's new height and width.

```
171  // determines whether the view rotates when the iPhone orientation changes
172  - (BOOL)shouldAutorotateToInterfaceOrientation:
173      (UIInterfaceOrientation)interfaceOrientation
174  {
175     return YES; // allow rotation to all interface orientations
176  } // end method shouldAutorotateToInterfaceOrientation
177
178  // called when the iPhone orientation changes
179  - (void)willRotateToInterfaceOrientation:
180      (UIInterfaceOrientation)interfaceOrientation duration:
181      (NSTimeInterval)duration
182  {
183     // create a CGRect with the view's height and width flipped
184     CGRect bounds = CGRectMake(0, 0, self.view.bounds.size.height,
185        self.view.bounds.size.width);
186
187     // make the current image resize to fill the flipped bounds
188     [currentImageView expandToFill:bounds];
189  } // end method willRotateToInterfaceOrientation:
190
191  // free SlideshowViewController's memory
192  - (void)dealloc
193  {
194     [currentImageView release]; // release the currentImageView UIImageView
195     [super dealloc]; // call the superclass's dealloc method
196  } // end method dealloc
197  @end // end implementation SlideshowviewController
198
```

Fig. 12.22 | Methods shouldAutorotateToInterfaceOrientation: and willRotate-ToInterfaceOrientation: of class SlideshowViewController.

Scaling *Category of* UIImageView

Method expandToFill: (Fig. 12.23, lines 202–237) expands a UIImageView to fill the given CGRect. Lines 204–205 get this UIImageView's UIImage and frame. First, we check if the UIImage is bound by its height (lines 208–209). If it is, we expand its frame's height to match the given CGRect's height (line 212). We then calculate a new width to ensure the image is not distorted (lines 215–216). Lines 219–220 adjust the image's origin so it remains centered. If the UIImage is bound by its width (line 222), we expand its frame's height to match the given CGRect's width (line 225). We then calculate a new height so the image is not distorted (lines 228–229). Lines 232–233 adjust the image's origin so it remains centered.

```
199  @implementation UIImageView (Scaling) // extensions to UIImageView
200
```

Fig. 12.23 | Scaling category of UIImageView. (Part 1 of 2.)

```
201  // scale the view to fill the given bounds without distorting
202  - (void)expandToFill:(CGRect)bounds
203  {
204     UIImage *image = self.image; // get the image of this view
205     CGRect frame = self.frame; // get the frame of this view
206
207     // check if the image is bound by its height
208     if (image.size.height / image.size.width >
209        bounds.size.height / bounds.size.width)
210     {
211        // expand the new height to fill the entire view
212        frame.size.height = bounds.size.height;
213
214        // calculate the new width so the image isn't distorted
215        frame.size.width = image.size.width * bounds.size.height /
216           image.size.height;
217
218        // add to the x and y coordinates so the view remains centered
219        frame.origin.y += (self.frame.size.height - frame.size.height) / 2;
220        frame.origin.x += (self.frame.size.width - frame.size.width) / 2;
221     } // end if
222     else // the image is bound by its width
223     {
224        // expand the new width to fill the entire view
225        frame.size.width = bounds.size.width;
226
227        // calculate the new height so the image isn't distorted
228        frame.size.height = image.size.height * bounds.size.width /
229           image.size.width;
230
231        // add to the x and y coordinates so the view remains centered
232        frame.origin.y += (self.frame.size.height - frame.size.height) / 2;
233        frame.origin.x += (self.frame.size.width - frame.size.width) / 2;
234     } // end else
235
236     self.frame = frame; // assign the new frame
237  } // end method expandToFill:
238  @end // end implementation UIImageView (Scaling)
```

Fig. 12.23 | Scaling category of UIImageView. (Part 2 of 2.)

12.4.3 Class NameViewController

The NameViewController's view is displayed when the user touches the "**New**" Button above the slideshow list. The user enters the name of the new slideshow into a **Text Field**.

NameViewController Interface Declaration

The NameViewController class (Fig. 12.24) extends UIViewController. Line 11 declares this class's delegate and line 12 declares an outlet that responds to events from the **Text Field** used to name the slideshow. Lines 16–17 declare delegate and textField as properties. Method finishedNaming: is called when the user finishes naming a new slideshow. The NameViewControllerDelegate protocol declares the nameViewController:didGet-Name: method (lines 26–27), which passes the slideshow's name to the delegate.

```
 1   // NameViewController.h
 2   // Controls a View for naming a slideshow.
 3   #import <UIKit/UIKit.h>
 4
 5   // declare NameViewControllerDelegate protocol
 6   @protocol NameViewControllerDelegate;
 7
 8   // begin NameRecordingViewController interface
 9   @interface NameViewController : UIViewController
10   {
11      id <NameViewControllerDelegate> delegate; // declare class's delegate
12      IBOutlet UITextField *textField; // text field for entering name
13   } // end instance variable declaration
14
15   // declare delegate and textField as properties
16   @property (nonatomic, assign) id <NameViewControllerDelegate> delegate;
17   @property (nonatomic, retain) UITextField *textField;
18
19   - (IBAction)finishedNaming:sender; // the user finished entering the name
20   @end // end interface NameViewController
21
22   // begin NameDelegate protocol
23   @protocol NameViewControllerDelegate
24
25   // informs the delegate that the user chose a name
26   - (void)nameViewController:(NameViewController *)
27     controller didGetName:(NSString *)fileName;
28   @end // end protocol NameDelegate
```

Fig. 12.24 | Controls a **View** for naming a slideshow.

NameViewController Class Implementation

Method viewDidLoad (Fig. 12.25, lines 11–17) calls the superclass's viewDidLoad method (line 13) then selects the **Text Field** by calling UITextField's becomeFirstResponder method to display the keyboard. The finishedNaming: method (lines 20–24) passes the textField's text property to the delegate's nameViewController:didGetName: method. This gives the RootViewController the user-entered name for the new slideshow.

```
 1   // NameViewController.m
 2   // Implementation of NameViewController.
 3   #import "NameViewController.h"
 4
 5   @implementation NameViewController
 6
 7   @synthesize delegate; // synthesize get and set methods for delegate
 8   @synthesize textField; // synthesize get and set methods for textField
 9
10   // called when the View finishes loading
11   - (void)viewDidLoad
12   {
```

Fig. 12.25 | Implementation of NameViewController. (Part 1 of 2.)

```
13      [super viewDidLoad]; // calls the superclass's viewDidLoad method
14
15      // select the text field to make the keyboard appear
16      [textField becomeFirstResponder];
17  } // end method viewDidLoad
18
19  // call when the user touches the Done button on the keyboard
20  - (IBAction)finishedNaming:sender
21  {
22      // inform the delegate that the user chose a name
23      [delegate nameViewController:self didGetName:textField.text];
24  } // end method finishedNaming:
25  @end // NameRecoringViewController implementation
```

Fig. 12.25 | Implementation of NameViewController. (Part 2 of 2.)

12.4.4 Class SlideshowDataViewController

The class SlideshowDataViewController controls the view where the user edits a slide-show. The view contains buttons for adding pictures, music and effects, and displays controls for deleting and reordering slides.

SlideshowDataViewController Interface Declaration

Create a new UIViewController subclass named SlideshowDataViewController. Its class declaration is shown in SlideshowDataViewController.h (Fig. 12.26).

```
1   // SlideshowDataViewController.h
2   // Manages the pictures, sounds and effects of a slideshow.
3   // Implementation in SlideshowDataViewController.m
4   #import <MediaPlayer/MediaPlayer.h>
5   #import "SlideshowViewController.h"
6
7   const static float ROW_HEIGHT = 100; // the height of the rows
8
9   // SlideshowDataViewController interface declaration
10  @interface SlideshowDataViewController : UITableViewController
11      <UIImagePickerControllerDelegate, UINavigationControllerDelegate,
12      MPMediaPickerControllerDelegate, UIActionSheetDelegate>
13  {
14      UIImagePickerController *imagePicker; // controller for picking images
15      MPMediaPickerController *musicPicker; // controller for picking music
16      MPMediaItemCollection *music; // the chosen music for the slideshow
17
18      // View used to play the slideshow
19      SlideshowViewController *slideshowViewController;
20      UIActionSheet *effectSheet; // a sheet for choosing an effect
21      UIToolbar *toolbar; // the toolbar at the bottom
22      NSMutableArray *pictures; // the chosen pictures
23      TransitionEffect effect; // the transition effect
24      NSString *title; // this slideshow's title
25      BOOL firstLoad; // is this the first load of this object?
```

Fig. 12.26 | Manages the pictures, sounds and effects of a slideshow. (Part 1 of 2.)

```
26      BOOL returnFromImagePicker; // are we returning from the image picker?
27   } // end instance variable declaration
28
29   // declare pictures, effect, music and title as properties
30   @property (nonatomic, readonly) NSMutableArray *pictures;
31   @property (nonatomic, readonly) TransitionEffect effect;
32   @property (nonatomic, readonly) MPMediaItemCollection *music;
33   @property (nonatomic, retain) NSString *title;
34
35   - (void)addPhoto; // adds a new photo to the slideshow
36   - (void)addMusic; // adds music to the slideshow
37   - (void)addEffect; // adds the effect for the slideshow
38   - (void)startSlideshow; // begins the slideshow
39   - (UIImage *)firstImage; // return the first image in the slideshow
40   @end // end interface SlideshowDataViewController
```

Fig. 12.26 | Manages the pictures, sounds and effects of a slideshow. (Part 2 of 2.)

Lines 10–12 declare the protocols that SlideshowDataViewController implements. We then declare a *UIImagePickerController* (line 14), which controls a view that prompts the user to choose a picture from the photo library. We also declare a *MPMedia-PickerController* (line 15), which controls a view that prompts the user to pick music from the iPod music library. The music *MPMediaItemCollection* represents the songs the user chose using the MPMediaPickerController.

The SlideshowViewController (line 19) controls the view that displays the slideshow. Line 20 declares a *UIActionSheet*—a GUI component that prompts the user to choose between multiple options. We declare a UIToolbar (line 21), an NSMutableArray to hold the chosen pictures (line 22), a TransitionEffect to store the transition effect (line 23) and an NSString to store the slideshow's title (line 24). We also declare two BOOLs (lines 25–26) that store whether this is the first time the view is appearing and whether the app is returning from picking an image. The SlideshowDataViewController interface declares five methods:

- addPhoto—prompts the user to add a new photo to the slideshow
- addMusic—prompts the user to choose music to play during the slideshow
- addEffect—displays the choices for the slideshow's transition effect
- startSlideshow—begins playing the slideshow
- firstImage—returns the first image in the slideshow

Method viewDidLoad of Class SlideshowDataViewController
SlideshowDataViewController's class implementation can be found in SlideshowData-ViewController.m (Fig. 12.27). Lines 7–10 synthesize the properties. We override the viewDidLoad method (lines 13–80) to set up our view. First, we set the navigationItem's title (line 16) and initialize pictures (line 18). Then we create the four UIBarButtonItems for adding pictures, music, effects and playing the slideshow (lines 22–52). We add the UIBarButtonItem for playing the slideshow to the UINavigationItem (line 27) and add the other UIBarButtonItems to the bottom toolbar (lines 55–56). We also add a **Flexible Space Bar Button Item** (created at lines 50–52) to the bottom toolbar to center the other

components. Lines 65–69 position the toolbar at the bottom of the main view. We then put the **Table View** in editing mode (line 73) and set the **Table View**'s row height (line 76).

```objc
1   // SlideshowDataViewController.m
2   // Manages the pictures, sounds and effects of a slideshow.
3   #import "SlideshowDataViewController.h"
4
5   @implementation SlideshowDataViewController
6
7   @synthesize pictures; // generate get method for pictures
8   @synthesize effect; // generate get method for effect
9   @synthesize music; // generate get method for music
10  @synthesize title; // generate get and set methods for title
11
12  // method is called when view finishes initializing
13  - (void)viewDidLoad
14  {
15      [super viewDidLoad]; // initialize the superclass
16      [self.navigationItem setTitle:@"Edit Slideshow"]; // set the bar title
17
18      pictures = [[NSMutableArray alloc] init]; // initialize pictures
19
20      // create the "Play" button
21      // the "black translucent" style makes the button blue
22      UIBarButtonItem *playButton = [[UIBarButtonItem alloc]
23          initWithTitle:@"Play" style:UIBarStyleBlackTranslucent
24          target:self action:@selector(startSlideshow)];
25
26      // add the "Play" button to the top navigation bar on the right side
27      [self.navigationItem setRightBarButtonItem:playButton];
28      [playButton release]; // release the playButton UIBarButtonItem
29
30      // create the toolbar at the bottom
31      toolbar = [[UIToolbar alloc] init];
32      [toolbar setBarStyle:UIBarStyleBlack]; // make toolbar black
33
34      // create a "Add Picture" button for adding new photos
35      UIBarButtonItem *pictureButton = [[UIBarButtonItem alloc]
36          initWithTitle:@"Add Picture" style:UIBarStyleBlack target:self
37          action:@selector(addPhoto)];
38
39      // create the "Add Music" button
40      UIBarButtonItem *musicButton = [[UIBarButtonItem alloc]
41          initWithTitle:@"Add Music" style:UIBarStyleBlack target:self
42          action:@selector(addMusic)];
43
44      // create the "Add Effect" button
45      UIBarButtonItem *effectButton = [[UIBarButtonItem alloc]
46          initWithTitle:@"Set Effect" style:UIBarStyleBlack target:self
47          action:@selector(addEffect)];
48
```

Fig. 12.27 | Method `viewDidLoad` of class `SlideshowDataViewController`. (Part 1 of 2.)

```
49      // create a flexible space bar button item
50      UIBarButtonItem *space = [[UIBarButtonItem alloc]
51          initWithBarButtonSystemItem:UIBarButtonSystemItemFlexibleSpace
52          target:nil action:NULL];
53
54      // add the buttons to toolbar in the given order
55      [toolbar setItems:[NSArray arrayWithObjects:space, pictureButton,
56          effectButton, musicButton, space, nil]];
57
58      [pictureButton release]; // release the pictureButton UIBarButtonItem
59      [musicButton release]; // release the musicButton UIBarButtonItem
60      [effectButton release]; // release the effectButton UIBarButtonItem
61
62      // add the toolbar to the superview
63      [[self.navigationController view] addSubview:toolbar];
64
65      [toolbar sizeToFit]; // expand the toolbar to include all the buttons
66      CGRect frame = toolbar.frame; // get the frame of toolbar
67      frame.origin.y = self.navigationController.view.bounds.size.height -
68          toolbar.bounds.size.height; // move toolbar to the bottom edge
69      [toolbar setFrame:frame]; // apply the new frame
70
71      // put the table's cells in editing mode so they display reorder and
72      // delete controls
73      [(UITableView *)self.view setEditing:YES];
74
75      // set the height of each row
76      [(UITableView *)self.view setRowHeight:ROW_HEIGHT];
77
78      firstLoad = YES; // this is the first load of this view
79      returnFromImagePicker = NO; // we're not returning from image picker
80  } // end method viewDidLoad
81
```

Fig. 12.27 | Method viewDidLoad of class SlideshowDataViewController. (Part 2 of 2.)

Method viewDidAppear: and viewDidDisappear: of Class SlideshowData-ViewController

Methods viewDidAppear: and viewDidDisappear: (Fig. 12.28) adjust the GUI component's sizes as necessary for hiding and showing the view. In viewDidAppear: (lines 83–114) we first check if this is the first time the view is appearing (line 88). If so, we adjust the size of the **Table View** to fit the toolbar (lines 92–96) otherwise, an animation displays the toolbar (lines 101–109). In viewWillDisappear: we hide the toolbar by moving it below the screen (lines 122–126).

```
82      // called when view appears
83      - (void)viewDidAppear:(BOOL)animated
84      {
85          [super viewDidAppear:animated]; // pass the message to the superclass
```

Fig. 12.28 | Method viewDidAppear: and viewDidDisappear: of class SlideshowDataViewController. (Part 1 of 2.)

```
 86
 87      // if this is the first time the view is appearing
 88      if (firstLoad)
 89      {
 90         // resize the table to fit the toolbar at the bottom
 91         firstLoad = NO; // the View has loaded once already
 92         CGRect frame = [self.view frame]; // fetch the frame of view
 93
 94         // decrease the height of the table
 95         frame.size.height -= [toolbar bounds].size.height;
 96         [self.view setFrame:frame]; // apply the new frame
 97      } // end if
 98      else
 99      {
100         // unhide the toolbar and navigation bar
101         CGRect frame = toolbar.frame; // fetch the toolbar's frame
102
103         // set the frame to be just below the bottom of the screen
104         frame.origin.y = self.navigationController.view.bounds.size.height;
105         [toolbar setFrame:frame]; // apply the new frame
106         [UIView beginAnimations:nil context:toolbar]; // begin animation
107         frame.origin.y -= frame.size.height; // move the toolbar up
108         [toolbar setFrame:frame]; // apply the new frame
109         [UIView commitAnimations]; // end animation block
110
111         // show the navigation bar at the top
112         [self.navigationController setNavigationBarHidden:NO animated:YES];
113      } // end else
114   } // end method viewDidAppear:
115
116   // called when the view is going to disappear
117   - (void)viewWillDisappear:(BOOL)animated
118   {
119      [super viewWillDisappear:animated]; // pass message to the superclass
120
121      // hide the toolbar
122      [UIView beginAnimations:nil context:toolbar]; // begin animation block
123      CGRect frame = [toolbar frame]; // fetch the frame of toolbar
124      frame.origin.y += frame.size.height; // move the toolbar down
125      [toolbar setFrame:frame]; // apply the new frame
126      [UIView commitAnimations]; // end animation block
127   } // end method viewWillDisappear:
128
```

Fig. 12.28 | Method viewDidAppear: and viewDidDisappear: of class
SlideshowDataViewController. (Part 2 of 2.)

Methods *addPhoto and imagePickerController:didFinishPickingImage:* of Class *SlideshowDataViewController*

The next two methods (Fig. 12.29) allow the user to choose an image from the photo library and add it to the slideshow. The addPhoto method (lines 130–148) is called when the user touches the "**Add Picture**" UIBarButtonItem. First, we initialize the *UIImagePickerController* if it hasn't been initialized yet (lines 132–142). We set the *allowsImage-*

Editing property to YES (line 136) to allow the user to edit the image before it is added to the slideshow. We also set the *sourceType* to UIImagePickerControllerSourceTypePhotoLibrary to specify that the image is to be picked from the user's photo library. We then show the image picker (line 147).

```
129  // add a new photo to the slideshow
130  - (void)addPhoto
131  {
132     if (imagePicker == nil) // create the image picker
133     {
134        // initialize imagePicker
135        imagePicker = [[UIImagePickerController alloc] init];
136        imagePicker.allowsImageEditing = YES; // allow image editing
137
138        // set the image source as the photo library
139        imagePicker.sourceType =
140           UIImagePickerControllerSourceTypePhotoLibrary;
141        imagePicker.delegate = self; // set imagePicker's delegate
142     } // end if
143
144     returnFromImagePicker = YES; // we're returning from image picker
145
146     // show the image picker
147     [self presentModalViewController:imagePicker animated:YES];
148  } // end method addPhoto
149
150  // add the chosen image to the slideshow
151  - (void)imagePickerController:(UIImagePickerController *)picker
152     didFinishPickingImage:(UIImage *)img editingInfo:
153     (NSDictionary *)editInfo
154  {
155     [pictures addObject:img]; // add the picked image to the image list
156     UITableView *table = (UITableView *)self.view;
157
158     // insert a new row in the table for the new picture
159     [table insertRowsAtIndexPaths:[NSArray arrayWithObject:[NSIndexPath
160        indexPathForRow:pictures.count - 1 inSection:0]] withRowAnimation:
161        UITableViewRowAnimationRight];
162
163     // make the image picker go away
164     [self dismissModalViewControllerAnimated:YES];
165  } // end method imagePickerController:didFinishPickingImage:
166
```

Fig. 12.29 | Methods addPhoto and imagePickerController:didFinishPickingImage: of class SlideshowDataViewController.

The imagePickerController:didFinishPickingImage:editingInfo: method is called when the user finishes picking an image using a UIImagePickerController. The chosen image is passed as the img property. First, we add the chosen image to pictures (line 155). We then insert a new row in the table for the image (lines 159–161) and dismiss the UIImagePickerController (line 164).

Methods addMusic and mediaPicker:didPickMediaItems: of Class Slideshow-DataViewController

The addMusic and mediaPicker:didPickMediaItems: methods (Fig. 12.30) allow the user to choose music from the iPod similarly to how they chose images from the photo library. In the addMusic method (lines 168–179) we create a new *MPMediaPickerController* (lines 171–172). We specify MPMediaTypeMusic to only allow the media picker to pick music. We set the *allowsPickingMultipleItems property* to YES to allow the user to pick multiple songs. We then show the MPMediaPickerController (line 177).

The MPMediaPickerController calls method mediaPicker:didPickMediaItems: when the user finishes picking songs. We store the chosen music (line 185) and dismiss the MPMediaPickerContorller (line 188).

```
167  // called when the user touches the Add Music button
168  - (void)addMusic
169  {
170      // create a new media picker configured for picking music
171      musicPicker = [[MPMediaPickerController alloc] initWithMediaTypes:
172          MPMediaTypeMusic];
173      musicPicker.allowsPickingMultipleItems = YES;
174      musicPicker.delegate = self;
175
176      // show the music picker
177      [self presentModalViewController:musicPicker animated:YES];
178      [musicPicker release];
179  } // end method addMusic
180
181  // called when the user touches the done button in the media picker
182  - (void)mediaPicker: (MPMediaPickerController *)mediaPicker
183    didPickMediaItems:(MPMediaItemCollection *)mediaItemCollection
184  {
185      music = [mediaItemCollection retain]; // get the returned songs
186
187      // make the media picker go away
188      [self dismissModalViewControllerAnimated:YES];
189  } // end method mediaPicker:didPickMediaItems:
190
```

Fig. 12.30 | Methods addMusic and mediaPicker:didPickMediaItems: of class SlideshowDataViewController.

Methods addEffect, actionSheet:clickedButtonAtIndex:, startSlideshow and firstImage of Class SlideshowDataViewController

Figure 12.31 defines the addEffect, actionSheet:clickedButtonAtIndex: and start-Slideshow methods. The addEffect method (lines 192–203) creates the UIActionSheet (from which the user chooses an effect) if it hasn't been initialized yet (lines 194–200). We then show the UIActionSheet (line 202).

The actionSheet:clickedButtonAtIndex: method is called when the user touches one of the choices on the UIActionSheet. We update effect with the selected choice.

The startSlideshow method begins the slideshow. First, we create slideshowView-Controller if it hasn't been created yet (lines 216–217). We then update slideshowView-

Controller's properties (lines 220–222) with the correct pictures, transition effect and music. We hide the navigation bar (line 225) and show the slideshowViewController (lines 228–229). The firstImage method (lines 233–240) returns the first UIImage in the pictures array, if one exists.

```objc
191  // called when the user touches the Add Effect button
192  - (void)addEffect
193  {
194     if (effectSheet == nil) // first time the user touches the button
195     {
196        // create a new sheet with the given title and button titles
197        effectSheet = [[UIActionSheet alloc] initWithTitle:@"Choose Effect"
198           delegate:self cancelButtonTitle:nil destructiveButtonTitle:nil
199           otherButtonTitles:@"Fade", @"Slide In", nil];
200     } // end if
201
202     [effectSheet showInView:self.view]; // show the sheet
203  } // end method addEffect
204
205  // called when the user touches one of the options in the effect sheet
206  - (void)actionSheet:(UIActionSheet *)actionSheet clickedButtonAtIndex:
207     (NSInteger)buttonIndex
208  {
209     effect = buttonIndex; // keep track of which effect is selected
210  } // end method actionSheet:clickedButtonAtIndex:
211
212  // called when the user touches the Start Slideshow button
213  - (void)startSlideshow
214  {
215     // first time button was touched
216     if (slideshowViewController == nil)
217        slideshowViewController = [[SlideshowViewController alloc] init];
218
219     // set the pictures to appear in the slideshow
220     slideshowViewController.pictures = pictures;
221     slideshowViewController.effect = effect; // set the slideshow effect
222     slideshowViewController.music = music; // set the slideshow music
223
224     // hide the navigation bar so the screen is clear for the slideshow
225     [self.navigationController setNavigationBarHidden:YES animated:YES];
226
227     // show the view that plays the slideshow
228     [self.navigationController pushViewController:slideshowViewController
229        animated:YES];
230  } // end method startSlideshow
231
232  // called by RootViewController to get thumbnails for the table
233  - (UIImage *)firstImage
234  {
```

Fig. 12.31 | Methods addEffect and startSlideshow of class SlideshowDataViewController. (Part 1 of 2.)

```
235    // if no pictures are in the slideshow
236    if (pictures.count == 0)
237       return nil; // return nil
238
239    return [pictures objectAtIndex:0]; // return the first picture
240 } // end method firstImage
241
```

Fig. 12.31 | Methods addEffect and startSlideshow of class SlideshowDataViewController. (Part 2 of 2.)

UITableViewDataSource methods of Class SlideshowDataViewController

The next methods in SlideshowDataViewController are declared in the UITableView-DataSource protocol. Method tableView:numberOfRowsInSection: (Fig. 12.32, lines 243–247) returns the number of pictures in the slideshow to indicate the number of rows.

```
242 // called by the table view to get the number of rows in a given section
243 - (NSInteger)tableView:(UITableView *)tableView numberOfRowsInSection:
244    (NSInteger)section
245 {
246    return pictures.count;
247 } // end method tableView:numberOfRowsInSection:
248
249 // called by the table view to get the cells it needs to populate itself
250 - (UITableViewCell *)tableView:(UITableView *)tableView
251    cellForRowAtIndexPath:(NSIndexPath *)indexPath
252 {
253    static NSString *CellIdentifier = @"Cell";
254
255    // get a reused cell
256    UITableViewCell *cell =
257       [tableView dequeueReusableCellWithIdentifier:CellIdentifier];
258
259    // if no reusable cells were available
260    if (cell == nil)
261    {
262       // create a new cell
263       cell = [[[UITableViewCell alloc] initWithStyle:
264          UITableViewCellStyleDefault reuseIdentifier:CellIdentifier]
265          autorelease];
266    } // end if
267
268    // remove any views that exist in a reused cell
269    for (UIView *view in cell.contentView.subviews)
270       [view removeFromSuperview];
271
272    // get the image for the given row
273    UIImage *image = [pictures objectAtIndex:indexPath.row];
274
```

Fig. 12.32 | Method tableView:cellForRowAtIndexPath: of class SlideshowDataViewController. (Part 1 of 2.)

```
275     // create an image view for the image
276     UIImageView *view = [[UIImageView alloc] initWithImage:image];
277
278     // resize the image without distorting it
279     float newWidth = image.size.width * ROW_HEIGHT / image.size.height;
280     CGRect frame;
281
282     // create the image shifted to the left of the center by 50 pts
283     frame.origin.x = cell.center.x - newWidth / 2 - 50;
284     frame.origin.y = 0; // the image will fill the height of the cell
285     frame.size.width = newWidth; // the width so there is no distortion
286     frame.size.height = ROW_HEIGHT; // the image will fill the whole height
287     view.frame = frame; // assign the new frame
288     [cell.contentView addSubview:view]; // add the image to the cell
289
290     return cell; // return the configured cell
291  } // end method tableView:cellForRowAtIndexPath:
292
```

Fig. 12.32 | Method `tableView:cellForRowAtIndexPath:` of class `SlideshowDataViewController`. (Part 2 of 2.)

The `tableView:cellForRowAtIndexPath:` method (lines 250–290) first creates or reuses a `UITableViewCell` (lines 253–266). We then remove any views that may have been previously added to the cell (lines 269–270). Lines 273–276 create the `UIImageView` for this cell, which we then resize (lines 279–287). We add the configured `UIImageView` to the cell (line 288) and return the cell (line 290).

Additional UITableViewDataSource methods of Class SlideshowDataViewController

In `tableView:commitEditingStyle:forRowAtIndexPath:` (Fig. 12.33, lines 294–308) we handle the event generated when the user deletes a row. If the user deleted the row (line 299), we remove that entry from `pictures` (line 301) and remove the row from the table (lines 305–306). In the `tableView:moveRowAtIndexPath:toIndexPath:` method (lines 310–319) we move the object in `pictures` from the `UItableviewcell` specified by `fromIndexPath` to the `UItableviewcell` specified by `toIndexPath`. In `tableView:canMoveRowAtIndexPath:` we return `YES` because all the rows are reorderable.

```
293  // called by the table when the user touches the delete button
294  - (void)tableView:(UITableView *)tableView commitEditingStyle:
295     (UITableViewCellEditingStyle)editingStyle forRowAtIndexPath:
296     (NSIndexPath *)indexPath
297  {
298     // if the user touched a delete button
299     if (editingStyle == UITableViewCellEditingStyleDelete)
300     {
```

Fig. 12.33 | Methods `tableView:commitEditingStyle:forRowAtIndexPath:`, `tableView:moveRowAtIndexPath:toIndexPath:` and `tableView:canMoveRowAtIndexPath:` of class `SlideshowDataViewController`. (Part 1 of 2.)

```
301        // remove the object at the deleted row
302        [pictures removeObjectAtIndex:indexPath.row];
303
304        // remove the row from the table
305        [tableView deleteRowsAtIndexPaths:[NSArray arrayWithObject:
306            indexPath] withRowAnimation:UITableViewRowAnimationLeft];
307     } // end if
308 } // end method tableView:commitEditingStyle:forRowAtIndexPath:
309
310 - (void)tableView:(UITableView *)tableView moveRowAtIndexPath:
311     (NSIndexPath *)fromIndexPath toIndexPath:(NSIndexPath *)toIndexPath
312 {
313     // get the image at the moved row
314     UIImage *image = [pictures objectAtIndex:fromIndexPath.row];
315     [pictures removeObject:image]; // remove the image from the list
316
317     // insert the image into the list at the specified index
318     [pictures insertObject:image atIndex:toIndexPath.row];
319 } // end method tableView:moveRowAtIndexPath:toIndexPath:
320
321 // called by the table view to check if a given row can be moved
322 - (BOOL)tableView:(UITableView *)tableView canMoveRowAtIndexPath:
323     (NSIndexPath *)indexPath
324 {
325     return YES; // all the rows in this table can be moved
326 } // end method tableView:canMoveRowAtIndexPath:
327
328 // release this object's memory
329 - (void)dealloc
330 {
331     [imagePicker release]; // release imagePicker UIImagePickerController
332     [slideshowViewController release]; // release slideshowViewController
333     [pictures release]; // release the pictures NSMutableArray
334     [toolbar release]; // release the toolbar UIToolbar
335     [music release]; // release the music MPMediaItemCollection
336     [super dealloc]; // call the superclass's dealloc method
337 } // end method dealloc
338 @end // end SlideshowDataViewController class
```

Fig. 12.33 | Methods `tableView:commitEditingStyle:forRowAtIndexPath:`, `tableView:moveRowAtIndexPath:toIndexPath:` and `tableView:canMoveRowAtIndexPath:` of class `SlideshowDataViewController`. (Part 2 of 2.)

12.5 Wrap-Up

The **Slideshow** app enables users to create slideshows using pictures and music stored on their iPhones. You saw how to use class `UIImagePickerController` to display a standard interface for choosing images, and class `MPMediaPickerController` for picking music from the iPod library. We used class `MPMusicPlayerController` to play the selected music. We also used the `UIActionSheet` component to present the user with a list of transition effect choices. Lastly, you learned how to enable an app to operate in portrait and landscape orientations by responding to orientation change events.

In Chapter 13, we'll build the **Enhanced Slideshow** app, which enhances the **Slideshow** app with support for video and saving slideshows. You'll see how to use the `NSCoding` protocol and the `NSKeyedArchiver` class to serialize an object to a file. You'll also see how to use the `UIImagePickerController` class to allow the user to select videos, and how to use the `MPMoviePlayerController` class to play them.

Enhanced Slideshow App

Serialization Data with NSCoder and Playing Video

OBJECTIVES

In this chapter you'll learn:

- To use an MPMoviePlayerController to play videos from the iPhone's photo library.

- To use a UIImagePickerController to allow the user to chose images and videos from the iPhone's photo library.

- To add new image transitions using Core Animation.

- To use an NSCoder to serialize and deserialize objects.

- To use an NSKeyedArchiver to serialize all saved slideshows to memory so the app can reload the slideshows the next time it executes.

- To use the app's delegate class to save data when the app closes.

Outline

13.1 Introduction
13.2 Test-Driving the **Enhanced Slideshow** App
13.3 Overview of the Technologies
13.4 Building the App
  13.4.1 Class `MediaItem`
  13.4.2 Class `Slideshow`
  13.4.3 Class `RootViewController`
  13.4.4 Class `SlideshowDataViewController`
  13.4.5 Class `EnhancedSlideshowAppDelegate`
  13.4.6 Class `SlideshowViewController`
13.5 Suggested Enhancements
13.6 Wrap-Up

13.1 Introduction

The **Enhanced Slideshow** app adds video capabilities to Chapter 12's **SlideShow** app. When modifying a slideshow, the user touches the "**Add Picture/Video**" **Button** to view the iPhone's photo library, which now includes videos (Fig. 13.1). Selecting a video's thumbnail displays a close-up of that thumbnail (Fig. 13.2). The user touches the play **Button** to play the video without adding it to the slideshow. Touching the "**Choose**" **Button** adds the selected video to the slideshow. A new effect is displayed when the user touches the "**Set Effect**" **Button** (Fig. 13.3). The **Flip** effect rotates the previous image horizontally to reveal the next image on its reverse (Fig. 13.4). All user-created slideshows are saved and available each time the app is run.

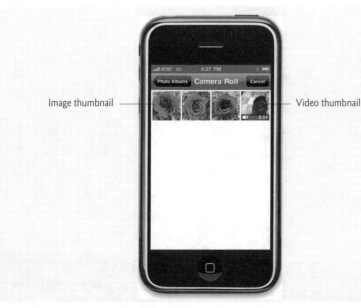

Image thumbnail — | — Video thumbnail

Fig. 13.1 | iPhone photo library.

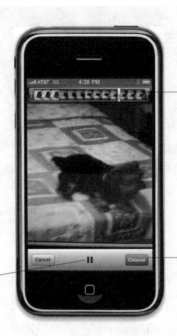

Position in the video playback
Touch to add this video to the slideshow
Touch to play/ pause the video
Cancel
Choose

Fig. 13.2 | Viewing a video.

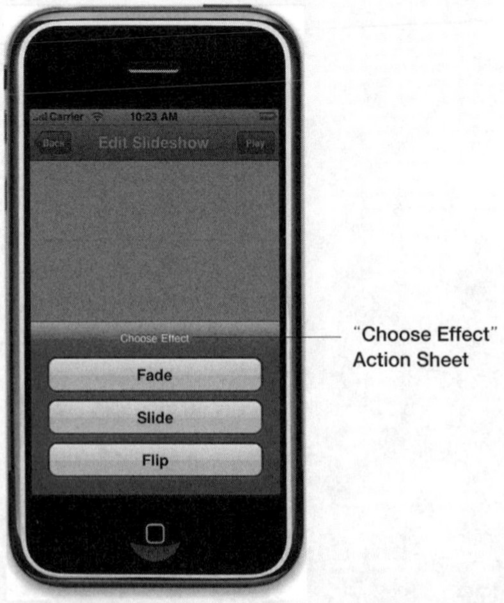
10:23 AM
Edit Slideshow
Choose Effect
Fade
Slide
Flip
"Choose Effect" Action Sheet

Fig. 13.3 | Setting the image transition effect.

Fig. 13.4 | **Flip** effect—rotates slide horizontally revealing the next slide underneath.

13.2 Test-Driving the Enhanced Slideshow App

Opening the completed application
Open the **Enhanced Slideshow** app project's directory and double click EnhancedSlide-show.xcodeproj to open it in Xcode. Apps running in the iPhone simulator cannot access the iPod music library, so if you're using the simulator you cannot add slideshow background music. Also, you cannot add video to the photo libraries of iPhones older than the 3GS (nor to the simulator's photo library), so slideshows running on those devices are limited to images. This test-drive assumes you're running the app on an iPhone 3GS.

Creating a New Slideshow
Touch the "**New**" **Button** in the top-right corner of the app and enter My Slideshow1 in the "**Name this slideshow**" **Text Field.** Touch the "**Add Picture/Video**" **Button** to view the iPhone's photo library. This library stores pictures and videos taken by the iPhone's camera. Touch a video's thumbnail to see a close-up of that thumbnail. Press the play **Button** to watch the video. Add the video to the slideshow by touching the "**Choose**" **Button.** Enter My Video1 in the "**Add a title for the video**" **Text Field.** Your video is displayed in the "**Edit Slideshow**" screen, represented by a thumbnail and the title you specified. Add two more pictures or videos, then select background music for this slideshow. Touch the "**Set Effect**" **Button** and choose **Flip.** Touch the "**Back**" **Button** to return to the list of slideshows.

Playing a Slideshow
Touch the "**Play**" **Button** next to your slideshow. Your videos and images are displayed. Images remain on the screen for five seconds while the background music plays. Videos

remain on the screen for their entire duration. Each video silences the background music in favor of the video's audio. Exit the app and touch its icon to run the **Enhanced Slideshow** again. Unlike the original **Slideshow** app, notice that the slideshows are persistent.

13.3 Overview of the Technologies

The **Enhanced Slideshow** app plays videos from the iPhone's photo library using an MPMoviePlayerController. The user chooses videos for the slideshow using a UIImagePickerController. We specify that all available media types in the photo library (images and videos) are available to the user by setting the UIImagePickerController's mediaTypes property.

We added another Core Animation image transition to this version of the app. The UIViewAnimationTransitionFlipFromRight animation transition flips a slideshow image horizontally to reveal the next image.

In the **Enhanced Slideshow** app, slideshows are stored on the iPhone for viewing later. We've saved textual data previously, but saving objects (such as those representing images and videos) requires a technique called *object serialization*. A so-called serialized object is an object represented as a sequence of bytes that includes the object's data as well as information about the object's type and the types of data stored in the object. We serialize an object (also referred to as *encoding* in Objective-C) using a subclass of the NSCoder abstract class. This class acts as an interface for storing Objective-C objects on disk (referred to as archiving). Class NSKeyedArchiver is a concrete subclass of NSCoder used to save the entire slideshow list's object graph to a file. An *object graph* is a representation of an object, all of the objects that it references, all of the objects that those objects reference, and so on. The NSKeyedArchiver handles creation of the object graph and serializing it.

After a serialized object has been written to a file, it can be read from the file and *deserialized*—that is, the type information and bytes that represent the object and its data can be used to recreate the object graph in memory. This is also referred to as *decoding* or *unarchiving* and is accomplished with a subclass of NSCoder.

13.4 Building the App

Only classes and methods that have changed from Chapter 12's **Slideshow** app are shown here. The complete source code is located in the project's directory. For any class or method that was previously discussed in Chapter 12 and that is shown in this chapter, we highlight the new or changed lines. For new classes and methods, we highlight new and important lines, as per our usual convention.

13.4.1 Class MediaItem

The new class MediaItem (Fig. 13.5) represents an image or video in a slideshow. Lines 6–10 declare the _mediaType enum. The typedef allows us to refer to this enum as MediaType. The MediaTypeImage enum constant indicates that a MediaItem represents a picture and the MediaTypeVideo constant indicates that a MediaItem represent a video.

MediaItem implements the ***NSCoding protocol*** (line 12), which declares two methods to encode and decode objects of the implementing class. This allows us to store MediaItems on the iPhone. The ***initWithCoder: method*** creates a MediaItem using an NSCoder object. The ***encodeWithCoder: method*** encodes a MediaItem, also using an NSCoder.

```
 1   // MediaItem.h
 2   // MediaItem class represents an image or a video.
 3   #import <Foundation/Foundation.h>
 4
 5   // the type of media this MediaItem represents
 6   typedef enum _mediaType
 7   {
 8      MediaTypeImage, // MediaItem represents an image
 9      MediaTypeVideo // MediaItem represents a video
10   } MediaType;
11
12   @interface MediaItem : NSObject <NSCoding>
13   {
14      MediaType type; // the type of the MediaItem
15      NSString *description; // a description of the MediaItem
16      id data; // the media, either an image or a video
17   } // end instance variable declaration
18
19   // declare type, description and data as properties
20   @property MediaType type;
21   @property (nonatomic, retain) NSString *description;
22   @property (nonatomic, retain) id data;
23
24   // creates a new MediaItem with the given type, description and data
25   - (id)initWithType:(MediaType)theType description:
26      (NSString *)theDescription data:(id)theData;
27   @end // end interface MediaItem
```

Fig. 13.5 | MediaItem class represents an image or a video.

Class MediaItem declares three instance variables (lines 14–16). The MediaType variable (line 14) type indicates if this MediaItem represents an image or a video. The NSString description (line 15) stores a brief title of this MediaItem if it's a video. Images do not store anything in description. The variable data of type id (line 16) represents the file path of this MediaItem's image or video. Lines 20–22 declare each of MediaItem's instance variables as properties. The initWithType:description:data: method (lines 25–26) receives arguments corresponding to each of MediaItem's instance variables and creates a new MediaItem.

MediaItem Class Definition
The initWithType:description:data: method (Fig. 13.6, lines 12–24) creates a new MediaType. Lines 18–20 set each of MediaItem's instance variables to their respective arguments.

```
 1   // MediaItem.m
 2   // MediaItem class implementation.
 3   #import "MediaItem.h"
 4
 5   @implementation MediaItem
```

Fig. 13.6 | MediaItem class implementation. (Part 1 of 2.)

```
6
7  @synthesize type; // generate get and set methods for type
8  @synthesize description; // generate get and set methods for description
9  @synthesize data; // generate get and set methods for data
10
11 // initalize the Media type with the given type, description and data
12 - (id)initWithType:(MediaType)theType description:
13   (NSString *)theDescription data:(id)theData
14 {
15    // if the superclass initializes properly
16    if (self = [super init])
17    {
18       self.type = theType; // update type with the given type
19       self.description = theDescription; // update description
20       self.data = theData; // update data with the given data
21    } // end if
22
23    return self; // return this object
24 } // end method initWithType:description:data:
25
26 // initialize the MediaItem with the given NSCoder
27 - (id)initWithCoder:(NSCoder *)decoder
28 {
29    // if the superclass initializes properly
30    if (self = [super init])
31    {
32       // get the type from the NSCoder
33       self.type = [decoder decodeIntForKey:@"type"];
34
35       // get the description from the NSCoder
36       self.description = [decoder decodeObjectForKey:@"description"];
37
38       // get the data from the NSCoder
39       self.data = [decoder decodeObjectForKey:@"data"];
40    } // end if
41
42    return self; // return this object
43 } // end method initWithCoder:
44
45 // encode this object into the given NSCoder
46 - (void)encodeWithCoder:(NSCoder *)coder
47 {
48    [coder encodeInt:type forKey:@"type"]; // encode type
49
50    // encode description
51    [coder encodeObject:description forKey:@"description"];
52    [coder encodeObject:data forKey:@"data"]; // encode data
53 } // end method encodeWithCoder:
54 @end // end class MediaItem
```

Fig. 13.6 | MediaItem class implementation. (Part 2 of 2.)

The initWithCoder: method (lines 27–43) decodes each of MediaItem's instance variables from the given NSCoder. This method is called to deserialize a MediaItem. Line

33 decodes a value for the MediaType using NSCoder's *decodeIntForKey: method.* We supply "type" as the key for this decoding since we use this same key when encoding this instance variable. Lines 36 and 39 decode values for MediaItem's remaining instance variables using NSCoder's *decodeObjectForKey: method.*

The encodeWithCoder: method (lines 46–53) serializes the MediaItem by encoding each of MediaItem's instance variables using the given NSCoder. Line 48 passes the key "type" to NSCoder's *encodeIntForKey: method.* The key identifies the encoding and is required for decoding. Lines 51–52 encode MediaItem's remaining instance variables using NSCoder's *encodeObjectForKey: method.*

MediaItemCreator Interface Declaration

The new class MediaItemCreator (Fig. 13.7) controls a view that allows the user to title a selected video. Lines 10–11 declare MediaItemCreator's delegate and the **Text Field** used to enter a video name. The NSURL variable media stores the location of the video that is being titled. Lines 16–17 declare delegate and media as properties. Method finished-Naming: (line 20) passes the video's name to the delegate when the user touches the "**Done**" **Button** on the keyboard. Lines 27–28 declare the NameChooserDelegate. Method mediaItemCreator:didCreateMediaItem: is called to pass the new video MediaItem to the delegate.

```
1   // MediaItemCreator.h
2   // Presents the user with an interface for creating a MediaItem.
3   #import <UIKit/UIKit.h>
4   #import "MediaItem.h"
5
6   @protocol NameChooserDelegate;
7
8   @interface MediaItemCreator : UIViewController
9   {
10     id <NameChooserDelegate> delegate; // this class's delegate
11     IBOutlet UITextField *textField; // text field where user enters a name
12     NSURL *media; // the video
13   } // end instance variable declaration
14
15   // declare delegate and media as properties
16   @property (nonatomic, assign) id <NameChooserDelegate> delegate;
17   @property (nonatomic, retain) NSURL *media;
18
19   // called when the user is finished naming the media
20   - (IBAction)finishedNaming:sender;
21   @end // end interface NameChooser
22
23   // NameChooserDelegate
24   @protocol NameChooserDelegate
25
26   // informs the delegate that this object has finished creating a MediaItem
27   - (void)mediaItemCreator:(MediaItemCreator *)creator didCreateMediaItem:
28     (MediaItem *)item;
29   @end // end protocol NameChooserDelegate
```

Fig. 13.7 | Presents the user with an interface for creating a MediaItem.

To build this view's GUI, open `MediaItemCreator.xib` in Interface builder then add a **Label** and set its text to `Add a label for the video`. Add a **Text Field** below the **Label** then open the Inspector window and connect the `finishedNaming:` method to the **Text Field**'s **Did End On Exit** event in the Inspector window.

MeidaItemCreator Class Definition

Lines 7–8 of class `MediaItemCreator` (Fig. 13.8) synthesize properties `delegate` and `media`. This `viewDidLoad` method (lines 11–15) sets up `MediaItemCreator`'s view. We call the superclass's `viewDidLoad` method (line 13) then call `UITextField`'s `becomeFirstResponder` method to select the "**Add a label for the video**" **Text Field** (line 14). This displays the keyboard. The `finishedNaming:` method (lines 18–26) creates a new `MediaItem` that is labeled using the `textField`'s `text` property (lines 21–22) and passes the `MediaItem` to the `delegate`'s `mediaItemCreator:didCreateMediaItem:` method (line 25). This passes to the `SlideshowDataViewController` a `MediaItem` representing the selected video with the user-entered title.

```
1   // MediaItemCreator.m
2   // MediaItemCreator class implementation.
3   #import "MediaItemCreator.h"
4
5   @implementation MediaItemCreator
6
7   @synthesize delegate; // generate get and set methods for delegate
8   @synthesize media; // generate get and set method for media
9
10  // set up the main view
11  - (void)viewDidLoad
12  {
13     [super viewDidLoad]; // call the superclass's viewDidLoad method
14     [textField becomeFirstResponder]; // make the keyboard appear
15  } // end method viewDidLoad
16
17  // called when the user touches the Done button on the keyboard
18  - (IBAction)finishedNaming:sender
19  {
20     // create a new MediaItem with the text the user entered
21     MediaItem *item = [[MediaItem alloc] initWithType:MediaTypeVideo
22        description:textField.text data:media];
23
24     // pass the MediaItem to the delegate
25     [delegate mediaItemCreator:self didCreateMediaItem:item];
26  } // end method finishedNaming:
27  @end // end MediaItemCreator class
```

Fig. 13.8 | `MediaItemCreator` class implementation.

13.4.2 Class Slideshow

The `Slideshow` class (Fig. 13.9) represents a user-created slideshow. In the original **Slideshow** app, we did not create a separate class to represent slideshows. The increased complexity of slideshows in the **Enhanced Slideshow** app and the requirements for archiving slideshows make it important to follow the Model-View-Controller design pattern. So we create a new class representing a slideshow. The **Enhanced Slideshow** app adds an enumeration constant to the TransitionEffect enum (lines 8–13). TransitionEffectFlip (line 12) represents an image transition which flips the previous image horizontally to reveal the next image on its the backside.

```
1   // Slideshow.h
2   // Interface for class which represents a slideshow.
3   #import <Foundation/Foundation.h>
4   #import <MediaPlayer/MediaPlayer.h>
5   #import "MediaItem.h"
6
7   // the transition effect in the slideshow
8   typedef enum _transitionEffects
9   {
10      TransitionEffectFade = 0, // fade from one slide to the next
11      TransitionEffectSlide = 1, // move next slide in from the right
12      TransitionEffectFlip = 2, // flip from one slide to the next
13   } TransitionEffect;
14
15   // Slideshow interface
16   @interface Slideshow : NSObject <NSCoding>
17   {
18      NSMutableArray *media; // the slides in the slideshow
19      MPMediaItemCollection *music; // the music for the slideshow
20      TransitionEffect effect; // the effect to transition between slides
21      NSString *title; // the slideshow's title
22   } // end instance variable declaration
23
24   // declare music, effect, media and title as properties
25   @property (nonatomic, retain) MPMediaItemCollection *music;
26   @property TransitionEffect effect;
27   @property (nonatomic, retain) NSMutableArray *media;
28   @property (nonatomic, retain) NSString *title;
29
30   - (UIImage *)firstImage; // returns the first image in the slideshow
31   @end // end interface Slideshow
32
33   // NSCoding category
34   @interface UIImage (NSCoding) // add NSCoding protocol methods to UIImage
35   - (id)initWithCoder:(NSCoder *)decoder; // create slideshow from archive
36   - (void)encodeWithCoder:(NSCoder *)encoder; // archive slideshow
37   @end // end Slideshow class
```

Fig. 13.9 | Interface for class Slideshow which represents a slideshow.

The NSMutableArray variable media stores the images and videos in this Slideshow (line 18). Line 19 declares an MPMediaItemCollection that stores the background music for a Slideshow. We use a TransitionEffect (line 20) to represent the type of animated transition between this Slideshow's slides. An NSString stores this Slideshow's title. Lines 25–28 declare Slideshow's instance variables as properties. Slideshow's firstImage method (lines 30) returns the Slideshow's first image, which will not be the first slide if the Slideshow starts with a video.

Lines 34–37 declare a category named NSCoding which adds the two NSCoding protocol methods to UIImage (lines 35–36). The initWithCoder: method uses an NSCoder to deserialize a UIImage and the encodeWithCoder: method uses an NSCoder to serialize a UIImage.

Methods init and initWithCoder: of Class Slideshow

The init method (Fig. 13.10, lines 12–20) calls the superclass's init method (line 16) then initializes the media NSMutableArray (line 17). The initWithCoder: method (lines 23–42) receives an NSCoder that is used to deserialize a Slideshow. Lines 29–38 use NSCoder's decodeObjectForKey method to deserialize each Slideshow instance variable.

```objc
1   // Slideshow.m
2   // Represents a slideshow.
3   #import "Slideshow.h"
4
5   @implementation Slideshow
6
7   @synthesize media; // generate get and set methods for media
8   @synthesize music; // generate get and set methods for music
9   @synthesize effect; // generate get and set methods for effect
10  @synthesize title; // generate get and set methods for title
11
12  // initialize this object
13  - (id)init
14  {
15     // if the superclass initializes properly
16     if (self = [super init])
17        media = [[NSMutableArray alloc] init]; // initialize media
18
19     return self; // return this object
20  } // end method init
21
22  // initialize this object from the given NSCoder
23  - (id)initWithCoder:(NSCoder *)decoder
24  {
25     // if the superclass initializes properly
26     if (self = [super init])
27     {
28        // decode media from the NSCoder
29        self.media = [decoder decodeObjectForKey:@"media"];
30
31        // decode effect from the NSCoder
32        self.effect = [decoder decodeIntForKey:@"effect"];
33
34        // decode music from the NSCoder
35        self.music = [decoder decodeObjectForKey:@"music"];
36
37        // decode title from the NSCoder
38        self.title = [decoder decodeObjectForKey:@"title"];
39     } // end if
40
```

Fig. 13.10 | Methods init and initWithCoder: of class Slideshow. (Part 1 of 2.)

```
41      return self; // return this object
42  } // initWithCoder:
43
```

Fig. 13.10 | Methods init and initWithCoder: of class Slideshow. (Part 2 of 2.)

Methods encodeWithCoder: and firstImage of Class Slideshow

The encodeWithCoder: method (Fig. 13.11, lines 45–51) uses NSCoder's encodeObject:forKey: method to serialize Slideshow's media, music and title instance variables. We can encode the media because we made MediaItem implement the NSCoding protocol earlier in the chapter. We use NSCoder's encodeInt:forKey: method to serialize the TransitionEffect enum value because an enum is equivalent to an int.

The firstImage method (lines 54–73) returns the first image slide in this Slideshow. Lines 60–70 loop through each MediaItem and check if its type property is MediaTypeImage (line 65). If it is, this MediaItem represents a picture and is assigned to firstImage (line 67). Line 68 sets found to YES indicating that the first image has been found.

```
44  // encode this object into the given NSCoder
45  - (void)encodeWithCoder:(NSCoder *)coder
46  {
47      [coder encodeObject:media forKey:@"media"]; // encode media
48      [coder encodeInt:effect forKey:@"effect"]; // encode effect
49      [coder encodeObject:music forKey:@"music"]; // encode music
50      [coder encodeObject:title forKey:@"title"]; // encode title
51  } // end method encodeWithCoder:
52
53  // returns the first image in this slideshow
54  - (UIImage *)firstImage
55  {
56      UIImage *firstImage = nil; // set first image to nil until we find one
57      BOOL found = NO; // we've not found the first image yet
58
59      // loop through each slide
60      for (int i = 0; i < media.count && !found; i++)
61      {
62          MediaItem *item = [media objectAtIndex:i]; // get slide at index i
63
64          // if the slide is an image
65          if (item.type == MediaTypeImage)
66          {
67              firstImage = item.data; // assign item to firstImage
68              found = YES; // we found the first image
69          } // end if
70      } // end for
71
72      return firstImage; // return the first image
73  } // end method firstImage
74
```

Fig. 13.11 | Methods encodeWithCoder: and firstImage of class Slideshow. (Part 1 of 2.)

```
75   // release this object's memory
76   - (void)dealloc
77   {
78      [media release]; // release the media NSMutableArray
79      [music release]; // release the music MPMediaItemCollection
80      [title release]; // release the title NSString
81      [super dealloc]; // call the superclass's dealloc method
82   } // end method dealloc
83   @end // end Slideshow class
84
```

Fig. 13.11 | Methods encodeWithCoder: and firstImage of class Slideshow. (Part 2 of 2.)

NSCoding category For UIImage

Class UIImage does not implement the NSCoding protocol, so we use the category feature of Objective-C to add the required serialization methods to UIImage. Method initWith-Coder: (Fig. 13.12, lines 89–100) initializes a UIImage using an NSCoder. NSCoder's decodeObjectForKey: method returns an NSData object representing the UIImage (line 94). We pass this to UIImage's initWithData: method to initialize the UIImage from the saved data (line 95).

```
85    // NSCoding category for UIImage
86    @implementation UIImage (NSCoding)
87
88    // initialize the UIImage with the given NSCoder
89    - (id)initWithCoder:(NSCoder *)decoder
90    {
91       // if the superclass initializes properly
92       if (self = [super init])
93       {
94          // decode the NSData from the NSCoder
95          NSData *data = [decoder decodeObjectForKey:@"UIImage"];
96          self = [self initWithData:data]; // initialize the UIImage with data
97       } // end if
98
99       return self; // return this object
100   } // end method initWithCoder:
101
102   // encode the UIImage into the given NSCoder
103   - (void)encodeWithCoder:(NSCoder *)encoder
104   {
105      // get the PNG representation of the UIImage
106      NSData *data = UIImagePNGRepresentation(self);
107
108      // encode the data using the NSCoder
109      [encoder encodeObject:data forKey:@"UIImage"];
110   } // end method encodeWithCoder:
111   @end // end NSCoding category
```

Fig. 13.12 | NSCoding category For UIImage.

The encodeWithCoder: method (lines 103 –110) gets an NSData object representing this UIImage using the ***UIImagePNGRepresentation*** *function* (line 105). We then serialize this object by passing the NSData object to NSCoder's encodeObject:forKey: method (line 108).

13.4.3 Class RootViewController

This section shows only the updated portions of the RootViewController class from Section 12.4.1.

Method *viewDidLoad* of class *RootViewController*

RootViewController's viewDidLoad method (Fig. 13.13) loads the list of slideshows from the app's data directory on the iPhone each time RootViewController's view is loaded. Lines 15–16 call the NSSearchPathForDirectoriesInDomains function to get an NSArray containing one element—the path for this app's documents directory. We retrieve this directory path (line 19), then append the name of the slideshow data file (data.slideshow) to the app's data directory.

```
 9   // set up the main view
10   - (void)viewDidLoad
11   {
12      [super viewDidLoad]; // call the superclass's viewDidLoad method
13
14      // find this app's documents directory
15      NSArray *paths = NSSearchPathForDirectoriesInDomains(
16         NSDocumentDirectory, NSUserDomainMask, YES);
17
18      // get the first directory
19      NSString *directory = [paths objectAtIndex:0];
20
21      // concatenate the file name "data.slideshows" to the end of the path
22      NSString *filePath = [[NSString alloc] initWithString:
23         [directory stringByAppendingPathComponent:@"data.slideshows"]];
24
25      // unarchive slideshows from the file data.slideshows
26      slideshows =
27         [[NSKeyedUnarchiver unarchiveObjectWithFile:filePath] mutableCopy];
28      [filePath release]; // release the filePath NSString
29
30      // if no data was unarchived from data.slideshows
31      if (slideshows == nil)
32         slideshows = [[NSMutableArray alloc] init]; // create slideshows
33
34      [self.navigationItem setTitle:@"Slideshows"]; // set the bar title
35
36      // create the New Slideshow button for adding a new slideshow
37      UIBarButtonItem *newSlideshowButton = [[UIBarButtonItem alloc]
38         initWithTitle:@"New" style:UIBarButtonItemStylePlain target:self
39         action:@selector(addSlideshow)];
40
```

Fig. 13.13 | Method viewDidLoad of class RootViewController. (Part 1 of 2.)

```
41      // create the back button for when the user navigates away
42      UIBarButtonItem *backButton = [[UIBarButtonItem alloc]
43         initWithTitle:@"Back" style:UIBarButtonItemStylePlain target:nil
44         action:nil];
45
46      // add the "New" Button to the right side of the navigation bar
47      self.navigationItem.rightBarButtonItem = newSlideshowButton;
48
49      // add the "Edit" Button to the left side of the navigation bar
50      self.navigationItem.leftBarButtonItem = self.editButtonItem;
51
52      // set the back button to be displayed when the user navigates away
53      [self.navigationItem setBackBarButtonItem:backButton];
54      [newSlideshowButton release]; // release the newSlideshowButton
55      [backButton release]; // release the backButton
56   } // end method viewDidLoad
```

Fig. 13.13 | Method `viewDidLoad` of class `RootViewController`. (Part 2 of 2.)

Lines 26–27 get an `NSMutableArray` containing all of the slideshows by deserializing the `data.slideshows` file. `NSKeyedUnarchiver`'s **unarchiveObjectWithFile:** *method* returns an *object graph* of type `id`, representing the `NSArray` of saved slideshows. **NSKeyed-Unarchiver** is a concrete subclass of `NSCoder` that deserializes an object. `NSObject`'s muta-bleCopy method converts the `NSArray` to an `NSMutableArray`. If there are no saved slideshows, we initialize `slideshows` as a new `NSMutableArray` (lines 31–32). Lines 34–55 set up the app's navigation bar the same way as in the original **Slideshow** app.

Method nameViewController:didGetName: of class RootViewController
The `nameViewController:didGetName:` method (Fig. 13.14) is called when the user finishes entering a name for a new slideshow. `UIViewController`'s `dismissModalViewControllerAnimated:` method hides the `NameViewController`'s view (line 85). Lines 88–89 create a new `Slideshow` and set its `title` property to the given `NSString`. We then create a new `SlideshowDataViewController` using the `initWithSlideshow:` method (lines 92–93). We call `NSMutableArray`'s `addObject:` method to add the new `Slideshow` to the list of `Slideshow`s.

```
80   // called when the user picks a name using the NameViewController
81   - (void)nameViewController:(NameViewController *)controller
82      didGetName:(NSString *)name
83   {
84      // hide the NameViewContorller
85      [self dismissModalViewControllerAnimated:YES];
86
87      // create a new Slideshow
88      Slideshow *slideshow = [[Slideshow alloc] init];
89      slideshow.title = name; // update slideshow's name
90
```

Fig. 13.14 | Method `nameViewController:didGetName:` of class `RootViewController`. (Part 1 of 2.)

```
91        // create a new SlideshowDataViewController with the Slideshow
92        SlideshowDataViewController *dataController =
93           [[SlideshowDataViewController alloc] initWithSlideshow:slideshow];
94        [slideshows addObject:slideshow]; // add to the list of slideshows
95
96        // show the slideshow creator
97        [self.navigationController pushViewController:dataController
98           animated:YES];
99        [slideshow release]; // release the Slideshow
100       [dataController release]; // release the SlideshowDataViewController
101    } // end method nameViewController:didGetName:
```

Fig. 13.14 | Method `nameViewController:didGetName:` of class `RootViewController`.
(Part 2 of 2.)

Method *slideshowCellDidSelectEditButton:* of class *RootViewController*

Method `slideshowCellDidSelectEditButton:` (Fig. 13.15) displays the view for editing
the selected Slideshow. Line 107 calls method UITableView's `indexPathForCell:` to get
an NSIndexPath representing the index of the touched UITableViewCell. We create a new
SlideshowDataViewController using its `initWithSlideshow` method (lines 110–112).
Line 112 gets the selected Slideshow by passing the NSIndexPath's row property to NS-
MutableArray method `objectAtIndex:`. Lines 115–116 call UINavigationController's
`pushViewController:animated:` method to display the Slideshow-editing view.

```
103    // called when the user touched the edit button of a SlideshowCell
104    - (void)slideshowCellDidSelectEditButton:(SlideshowCell *)cell
105    {
106       // find the index path where the given cell is located
107       NSIndexPath *indexPath = [self.tableView indexPathForCell:cell];
108
109       // create a new SlideshowDataViewController
110       SlideshowDataViewController *controller =
111          [[SlideshowDataViewController alloc] initWithSlideshow:
112          [slideshows objectAtIndex:indexPath.row]];
113
114       // show the SlideshowDataViewController
115       [self.navigationController pushViewController:controller
116          animated:YES];
117    } // end method slideshowCellDidSelectPlayButton:
```

Fig. 13.15 | Method `slideshowCellDidSelectEditButton:` of class
`RootViewController`.

Method *tableView:cellForRowAtIndexPath:* of Class *RootViewController*

Method `tableView:cellForRowAtIndexPath:` (Fig. 13.16) retrieves the UITableView-
Cell specified by the given NSIndexPath. Lines 153–165 attempt to reuse a cell from the
given tableView using UITableView's `dequeReusableCellWithIdentifier:` method. We
set the new SlideshowCell's delegate to this RootViewController (line 167). Line 170
sets the UITableViewCell's selectionStyle property to UITableViewCellSelection-
StyleNone so that no action is taken when the UITableViewCell is touched. Line 173 gets

the `SlideShow` corresponding to the touched `UITableViewCell`. Line 176 calls the `Slide-show`'s `firstImage` method to get a `UIImage` representing the first picture in the selected `Slideshow`. Lines 177–178 set the `SlideshowCell`'s thumbnail to that `UIImage` and title to the `Slideshow`'s title.

```
149   // called by the table view to get the cells it needs to populate itself
150   - (UITableViewCell *)tableView:(UITableView *)tableView
151           cellForRowAtIndexPath:(NSIndexPath *)indexPath
152   {
153       static NSString *CellIdentifier = @"SlideshowCell";
154
155       // get a reusable cell
156       SlideshowCell *cell = (SlideshowCell *)[tableView
157           dequeueReusableCellWithIdentifier:CellIdentifier];
158
159       // if no reusable cells are available, create one
160       if (cell == nil)
161       {
162           cell = [[[SlideshowCell alloc] initWithStyle:
163               UITableViewCellStyleDefault reuseIdentifier:CellIdentifier]
164               autorelease];
165       } // end if
166
167       cell.delegate = self; // set cell's delegate to this controller
168
169       // make the cell do nothing when selected
170       cell.selectionStyle = UITableViewCellSelectionStyleNone;
171
172       // get the Slideshow for the given row
173       Slideshow *slideshow = [slideshows objectAtIndex:indexPath.row];
174
175       // get the first image in the Slideshow at the correct index
176       UIImage *image = [slideshow firstImage];
177       cell.thumbnail.image = image; // set the cell's thumbnail image
178       cell.title.text = slideshow.title; // set the cell's title
179
180       return cell; // return the configured cell to the table view
181   } // end method tableView:cellForRowAtIndexPath:
```

Fig. 13.16 | Method `tableView:cellForRowAtIndexPath:` of class `RootViewController`.

13.4.4 Class `SlideshowDataViewController`

This section shows only the updated portions of the `SlideshowDataViewController` class from Section 12.4.4.

Method `initWithSlideshow:` of Class `SlideshowDataViewController`
The **Enhanced Slideshow** app's `SlideshowDataViewController` class (Fig. 13.17) has one additional instance variable not in the original **Slideshow** app. The slideshow currently being edited is stored as a pointer to an object of the new `Slideshow` class. Line 13 sets this `slideshow` instance variable to the given `Slideshow` and calls its `retain` method—increasing its retain count by one and ensuring that the `Slideshow`'s memory is not freed until the `SlideshowViewController` no longer needs it.

```
 8    // initialize with the given slideshow
 9    - (id)initWithSlideshow:(Slideshow *)show
10    {
11       // if the superclass initializes properly
12       if (self = [super init])
13          slideshow = [show retain]; // take ownership of the Slideshow
14
15       return self; // return this object
16    } // end method initWithSlideshow
```

Fig. 13.17 | Method initWithSlideshow: of class SlideshowDataViewController.

Method addPhoto of Class SlideshowDataViewController

The addPhoto method (Fig. 13.18) allows the user to choose an image or video from the photo library and add it to the slideshow when the user touches the "**Add Picture/Video**" **Bar Button Item**. First, we initialize the UIImagePickerController if it hasn't been initialized yet (lines 137–140). We set the allowsImageEditing property to YES (line 141) to allow the user to edit the image or video before it's added to the slideshow. For example, the user can zoom into a particular part of an image with a pinch gesture, or the user can trim a video by dragging the handles at the left or right side of the video's thumbnail strip at the top of the screen. We set the sourceType to UIImagePickerControllerSource-TypePhotoLibrary to specify that the image or video is to be picked from the user's photo library. Lines 148–150 call UIImagePickerController's availableMediaTypesFor-SourceType method, passing as an argument the source type representing the iPhone's photo library (UIImagePickerControllerSourceTypePhotoLibrary). We assign the result to imagePicker's mediaTypes property to specify that we want the imagePicker to display both images and videos. We then show the imagePicker (line 157).

```
133    // prompts the user to add a new photo or video to the slideshow
134    - (void)addPhoto
135    {
136       // if imagePicker hasn't been initialized yet
137       if (imagePicker == nil)
138       {
139          // create the image picker
140          imagePicker = [[UIImagePickerController alloc] init];
141          imagePicker.allowsEditing = YES; // allow user to edit images
142
143          // pick images from the photo library
144          imagePicker.sourceType =
145             UIImagePickerControllerSourceTypePhotoLibrary;
146
147          // allow all media types available in the photo library
148          imagePicker.mediaTypes =
149             [UIImagePickerController availableMediaTypesForSourceType:
150             UIImagePickerControllerSourceTypePhotoLibrary];
151          imagePicker.delegate = self; // set delegate to this object
152       } // end if
```

Fig. 13.18 | Method addPhoto of class SlideshowDataViewController. (Part 1 of 2.)

```
153
154    returnFromImagePicker = YES; // we're going to the image picker
155
156    // show the image picker
157    [self presentModalViewController:imagePicker animated:YES];
158  } // end method addPhoto
```

Fig. 13.18 | Method addPhoto of class SlideshowDataViewController. (Part 2 of 2.)

Method imagePickerController:didFinishPickingMediaWithInfo: of Class SlideshowDataViewController

The imagePickerController:didFinishPickingMediaWithInfo: method (Fig. 13.19) is called when the user adds an image or video from the image picker to the slideshow. Line 165 hides the image picker by calling UIViewController's dismissModalViewController-Animated: method. The info NSDictionary contains information on the chosen image or video. We use NSDictionary's valueForKey: method to get info's value for key UIImage-PickerControllerMediaType (line 168). If this value equals kuTypeImage, we know the user touched an image. Lines 172–173 get info's UIImage for key UIImagePickerCon-trollerEditedImage. This is the user's chosen picture. We then create a new MediaItem using the UIImage and add the MediaItem to the Slideshow (lines 176–180). Line 183 gets SlideshowDataViewController's UITableView. We then insert the new MediaItem into the UITableView of slides (lines 186–188).

```
160  // called when the user finishes picking a photo or video
161  - (void)imagePickerController:(UIImagePickerController *)picker
162      didFinishPickingMediaWithInfo:(NSDictionary *)info
163  {
164    // make the image picker go away
165    [self dismissModalViewControllerAnimated:NO];
166
167    // if the user chose an image
168    if ([[info valueForKey:@"UIImagePickerControllerMediaType"]
169        isEqualToString:kUTTypeImage])
170    {
171      // get the image the user chose
172      UIImage *image =
173        [info objectForKey:UIImagePickerControllerEditedImage];
174
175      // create a MediaItem with the image
176      MediaItem *item = [[MediaItem alloc] initWithType:MediaTypeImage
177        description:nil data:image];
178
179      // add the MediaItem to the slideshow
180      [slideshow.media addObject:item];
181
182      // insert the new image into the table
183      UITableView *table = (UITableView *)self.view;
```

Fig. 13.19 | Method imagePickerController:didFinishPickingMediaWithInfo: of class SlideshowDataViewController. (Part 1 of 2.)

```
184
185          // insert a new row in the table for the new picture
186          [table insertRowsAtIndexPaths:[NSArray arrayWithObject:[NSIndexPath
187              indexPathForRow:slideshow.media.count - 1 inSection:0]]
188              withRowAnimation:UITableViewRowAnimationRight];
189      } // end if
190      else // if the user chose a video
191      {
192          // get the URL for the selected video
193          NSURL *url = [info objectForKey:UIImagePickerControllerMediaURL];
194
195          // get the name of the video
196          NSString *name = [[url absoluteString] lastPathComponent];
197
198          // find the location of this app's documents directory
199          NSArray *paths = NSSearchPathForDirectoriesInDomains(
200              NSDocumentDirectory, NSUserDomainMask, YES);
201
202          // get the first directory
203          NSString *directory = [paths objectAtIndex:0];
204
205          // create a path in the documents directory for the video
206          NSString *newPath = [directory stringByAppendingPathComponent:name];
207
208          // get the default file manager
209          NSFileManager *manager = [NSFileManager defaultManager];
210
211          // move video from the temporary directory to documents directory
212          [manager copyItemAtPath:[url path] toPath:newPath error:nil];
213
214          // create a new MediaItemCreator
215          MediaItemCreator *creator = [[MediaItemCreator alloc]
216              initWithNibName:@"MediaItemCreator" bundle:nil];
217          creator.delegate = self; // set delegate to this object
218
219          // set the media to the chosen video
220          creator.media = [NSURL fileURLWithPath:newPath];
221
222          // show the MediaItemCreator
223          [self presentModalViewController:creator animated:YES];
224          [creator release]; // release the creator MediaItemCreator
225      } // end else
226  } // end method imagePickerController:didFinishPickingMediaWithInfo:
227
```

Fig. 13.19 | Method imagePickerController:didFinishPickingMediaWithInfo: of class SlideshowDataViewController. (Part 2 of 2.)

If the user did not touch an image they must have touched a video. Line 193 gets info's NSURL for the key UIImagePickerControllerMediaURL. This represents the chosen video's location on the iPhone. We use NSURL's absoluteString method to get a NSString representing the URL then call NSString's lastPathComponent to extract the video's name from the end of its file path. The NSSearchPathForDirectoriesInDomains function returns an NSString representing the directory path for this app's documents directory (lines 199–200). The video file was automatically saved in a temporary directory. We need to move the video out of this directory, so that it's not deleted when the app closes. NSString's stringByAppendingPathComponent: method is used to append the video's name to the end of the documents directory path to get the video's current file path (line 202). Line 209 gets the default NSFileManager. NSFileManager's copyItemAtPath:new-Path:error: method is used to move the video file from the temporary directory to the app's data directory. We get the path for the video file in the temporary directory is saved using NSURL's path method (line 212).

Lines 215–217 create a new MediaItemCreator and set its delegate to self. We use NSURL's fileURLWithPath: method to convert the video file path in the app's data directory to an NSURL (line 220). Line 226 calls UIViewController's presentModalViewController:animated: method to display MediaItemCreator's view.

Method mediaItemCreator:didCreateMediaItem: of Class SlideshowDataViewController

The mediaItemCreator:didCreateMediaItem: method (Fig. 13.20) is called when the user finishes naming a video MediaItem using MediaItemCreator's view. Line 232 adds the MediaItem to the current Slideshow. Lines 238–243 add a new row displaying the new MediaItem to SlideshowDataViewController's UITableView and hides MediaItem-Creator's view.

```
228  // called when the user finishes naming the media
229  - (void)mediaItemCreator:(MediaItemCreator *)creator didCreateMediaItem:
230     (MediaItem *)item;
231  {
232     [slideshow.media addObject:item]; // add the media to the slideshow
233
234     // add a new row in the table for the media
235     UITableView *table = (UITableView *)self.view;
236
237     // insert a new row in the table for the new picture
238     [table insertRowsAtIndexPaths:[NSArray arrayWithObject:[NSIndexPath
239        indexPathForRow:slideshow.media.count - 1 inSection:0]]
240        withRowAnimation:UITableViewRowAnimationRight];
241
242     // dismiss the MediaItemCreator
243     [self dismissModalViewControllerAnimated:YES];
244  } // end method mediaItemCreator:didCreateMediaItem:
```

Fig. 13.20 | Method mediaItemCreator:didCreateMediaItem: of class SlideshowDataViewController.

Methods mediaPicker:didPickMediaItems: and addEffect of Class SlideshowDataViewController

The mediaPicker:addPickMediaItems: method (Fig. 13.21, lines 263–271) is called when the user touches the "**Done**" **Button** after selecting songs from the iPod music library. Line 267 assigns the MPMediaItemCollection containing the selected songs to the Slideshow's music property. UIViewController's dismissModalViewControllerAnimated:

removes the media picker from view (line 270). The addEffect method (lines 274–286) displays a UIActionSheet when the user touches the "**Add Effect**" Button. Lines 280–282 create the UIActionSheet that displays the transition options. We add the Flip effect as a third argument to otherButtonTitles:.

```
262  // called when the user touches the done button in the media picker
263  - (void)mediaPicker: (MPMediaPickerController *)mediaPicker
264    didPickMediaItems:(MPMediaItemCollection *)mediaItemCollection
265  {
266     // update the music of the slideshow
267     slideshow.music = mediaItemCollection;
268
269     // make the media picker go away
270     [self dismissModalViewControllerAnimated:YES];
271  } // end method mediaPicker:didPickMediaItems:
272
273  // called when the user touches the "Add Effect" Button
274  - (void)addEffect
275  {
276     // if effectSheet hasn't been created yet
277     if (effectSheet == nil)
278     {
279        // create a new sheet with the given title and button titles
280        effectSheet = [[UIActionSheet alloc] initWithTitle:@"Choose Effect"
281           delegate:self cancelButtonTitle:nil destructiveButtonTitle:nil
282           otherButtonTitles:@"Fade", @"Slide", @"Flip", nil];
283     } // end if
284
285     [effectSheet showInView:self.view]; // show the sheet
286  } // end method addEffect
287
```

Fig. 13.21 | Methods mediaPicker:didPickMediaItems: and addEffect of class SlideshowDataViewController.

Methods *startSlideshow* and *actionSheet:clickedButtonAtIndex:* of Class *SlideshowDataViewController*

Method startSlideshow (Fig. 13.22, lines 289–303) begins the slideshow. First, we create the SlideshowViewController (lines 291–292) then set its slideshow property to the current Slideshow (line 295). We hide the navigation bar (line 298) then show the SlideshowViewController using UINavigationController's pushViewController:animated: method (line 301). Method actionSheet:clickedButtonAtIndex: (lines 306–310) sets this Slideshow's effect property to the given NSInteger representing the effect the user selected. This saves the user's choice of image transition effect.

```
288  // called when the user touches the Start Slideshow button
289  - (void)startSlideshow
290  {
```

Fig. 13.22 | Methods startSlideshow and actionSheet:clickedButtonAtIndex: of class SlideshowDataViewController. (Part I of 2.)

```
291    SlideshowViewController *controller =
292        [[SlideshowViewController alloc] init];
293
294    // set the pictures to appear in the slideshow
295    controller.slideshow = slideshow;
296
297    // hide the navigation bar so the screen is clear for the slideshow
298    [self.navigationController setNavigationBarHidden:YES animated:YES];
299
300    // show the view that shows the slideshow
301    [self.navigationController pushViewController:controller animated:YES];
302    [controller release]; // release the controller SlideshowViewController
303 } // end method startSlideshow
304
305 // called when the user touches one of the options in the effect sheet
306 - (void)actionSheet:(UIActionSheet *)actionSheet clickedButtonAtIndex:
307    (NSInteger)buttonIndex
308 {
309    slideshow.effect = buttonIndex; // update the selected effect
310 } // end method actionSheet:clickedButtonAtIndex:
```

Fig. 13.22 | Methods startSlideshow and actionSheet:clickedButtonAtIndex: of class SlideshowDataViewController. (Part 2 of 2.)

Method tableView:cellForRowAtIndexPath: of Class SlideshowDataViewController

Method tableView:cellForRowAtIndexPath: (Fig. 13.23) retrieves the UITableViewCell at the given NSIndexPath. Lines 328–339 attempt to reuse a cell from the tableView. We empty any subviews from the UITableViewCell using UIView's removeFromSuperView method (lines 342–343). Line 346 gets the MediaItem corresponding to the touched UITableViewCell. If this MediaItem's type is MediaTypeImage, the MediaItem represents an image so we access its data property to receive a UIImage (349–352). Line 355 creates a new UIImageView using the retrieved UIImage, then resizes it to fit the cell (lines 358–367). We then add the configured UIImageView to the cell (line 368). If the MediaItem represents a video, we need to title the UITableCell with the video's title. Lines 376–378 create a new UILabel and set its text to "Video:" followed by the MediaItem's description. Lines 379–383 size and position the **Label** then add it to the UITableViewCell.

```
324 // called by the table view to get the cells it needs to populate itself
325 - (UITableViewCell *)tableView:(UITableView *)tableView
326    cellForRowAtIndexPath:(NSIndexPath *)indexPath
327 {
328    static NSString *CellIdentifier = @"Cell";
329
330    // get a reused cell
331    UITableViewCell *cell =
332        [tableView dequeueReusableCellWithIdentifier:CellIdentifier];
```

Fig. 13.23 | Method tableView:cellForRowAtIndexPath: of class SlideshowDataViewController. (Part 1 of 3.)

```
333
334    // if there were no cells that could be reused
335    if (cell == nil)
336        // create a new cell
337        cell = [[[UITableViewCell alloc] initWithStyle:
338            UITableViewCellStyleDefault reuseIdentifier:CellIdentifier]
339            autorelease];
340
341    // loop through all the existing subviews in the cell
342    for (UIView *view in cell.contentView.subviews)
343        [view removeFromSuperview]; // remove the view from the cell
344
345    // get the MediaItem at the appropriate row for this cell
346    MediaItem *item = [slideshow.media objectAtIndex:indexPath.row];
347
348    // if the MediaItem represents an image
349    if (item.type == MediaTypeImage)
350    {
351        // get the image for the given row
352        UIImage *image = item.data;
353
354        // create an image view for the image
355        UIImageView *view = [[UIImageView alloc] initWithImage:image];
356
357        // resize the image without distorting it
358        float newWidth = image.size.width * rowHeight / image.size.height;
359        CGRect frame;
360
361        // create the image shifted to the right of the center by 50 points
362        frame.origin.x = (cell.frame.size.width / 2) - (newWidth / 2) - 50;
363        frame.origin.y = 0; // the image will fill the height of the cell
364        frame.size.width = newWidth; // the width so there's no distortion
365        frame.size.height = rowHeight; // the image fills the entire height
366        view.center = CGPointMake(cell.center.x - 50, cell.center.y);
367        view.frame = frame; // assign the new frame
368        [cell.contentView addSubview:view]; // add the image to the cell
369        [view release]; // release the view UIImageView
370    } // end if
371    else  // if the MediaItem represents a video
372    {
373        UILabel *label = [[UILabel alloc] init]; // create a new label
374
375        // set the label's text using the user's description of the video
376        label.text = [NSString stringWithFormat:@"Video: %@",
377            item.description];
378        CGRect frame = label.frame; // get the label's frame
379        frame.origin.x = 20; // update the x-coordinate
380        frame.size.height = rowHeight; // update the height
381        frame.size.width = cell.contentView.frame.size.width; // set width
382        label.frame = frame; // apply the new frame
383        [cell.contentView addSubview:label]; // add the label to the cell
```

Fig. 13.23 | Method `tableView:cellForRowAtIndexPath:` of class `SlideshowDataViewController`. (Part 2 of 3.)

```
384        [label release]; // release the label UILabel
385    } // end else
386
387    return cell; // return the configured cell
388 } // end method tableView:cellForRowAtIndexPath:
```

Fig. 13.23 | Method `tableView:cellForRowAtIndexPath:` of class `SlideshowDataViewController`. (Part 3 of 3.)

Method `tableView:moveRowAtIndexPath:toIndexPath:` of Class `Slideshow-DataViewController`

When the user reorders slideshow items, method `tableView:moveRowAtIndexPath:toIndexPath:` (Fig. 13.24) moves a `MediaItem` from the `UITableViewCell` specified by `fromIndexPath` to the `UITableViewCell` specified by `toIndexPath`. We use `NSMutableArray`'s `objectAtIndex:` and `insertObject:atIndex:` methods to reorder the `Slideshow`'s media array according to the `NSIndexPaths`.

```
 1  // used to reorder UITableViewCells
 2  - (void)tableView:(UITableView *)tableView moveRowAtIndexPath:
 3      (NSIndexPath *)fromIndexPath toIndexPath:(NSIndexPath *)toIndexPath
 4  {
 5      // get the image at the moved row
 6      MediaItem *item =
 7          [[slideshow.media objectAtIndex:fromIndexPath.row] retain];
 8
 9      // remove the MediaItem
10      [slideshow.media removeObjectAtIndex:fromIndexPath.row];
11
12      // insert the image into the list at the specified index
13      [slideshow.media insertObject:item atIndex:toIndexPath.row];
14      [item release]; // release the item MediaItem
15  } // end method tableView:moveRowAtIndexPath:toIndexPath:
```

Fig. 13.24 | Method `tableView:moveRowAtIndexPath:toIndexPath:` of class `SlideshowDataViewController`.

13.4.5 Class EnhancedSlideshowAppDelegate

An *app delegate* (subclass of *UIApplicationDelegate*) responds to messages from the app's singleton `UIApplication` object after the app loads and just before it terminates. Xcode generates app delegate classes for each project which can be overwritten to add behavior at load or launch.

Method `applicationWillTerminate:` of Class `EnhancedSlideshowAppDelegate`

The `EnhancedSlideshowAppDelegate` class was automatically created by Xcode when we created the **Enhanced Slideshow** app project. We ignored this file in the previous **Slideshow** app; however, to save the slideshows when the user exits the app, we must add code to the app delegate's `applicationWillTerminate:` method (Fig. 13.25). Lines 34–38 get this app's data directory. We add `data.slideshows` to the end of this directory path. Lines 45–46 access the `UINavigationController`'s `viewController` property to get the app's

RootViewController. We pass the RootViewController's NSMutableArray of Slide-shows to NSKeyedArchiver's **archiveRootObject:toFile: method**. This serializes the slideshow list's object graph (i.e., the slideshows and their contents) so it can be loaded the next time the app executes.

```
30  // called when the application is going to close
31  - (void)applicationWillTerminate:(UIApplication *)application
32  {
33      // creates list of valid directories for saving a file
34      NSArray *paths = NSSearchPathForDirectoriesInDomains(
35          NSDocumentDirectory, NSUserDomainMask, YES);
36
37      // get the first directory because we care about only one
38      NSString *directory = [paths objectAtIndex:0];
39
40      // concatenate the file name "data.slideshows" to the end of the path
41      NSString *filePath = [[NSString alloc] initWithString:
42          [directory stringByAppendingPathComponent:@"data.slideshows"]];
43
44      // get the root view controller
45      RootViewController *controller =
46          [navigationController.viewControllers objectAtIndex:0];
47
48      // get all the slideshows from controller
49      NSArray *slideshows = controller.slideshows;
50
51      // archive the slideshows to the file data.slideshows
52      [NSKeyedArchiver archiveRootObject:slideshows toFile:filePath];
53  } // end method applicationWillTerminate:
```

Fig. 13.25 | Method applicationWillTerminate: of class EnhancedSlideshowAppDelegate.

13.4.6 Class SlideshowViewController

The SlideshowViewController class (Fig. 13.26) controls a view that plays the Slide-show stored in the slideshow instance variable (line 10). An MPMoviePlayerController is used to play full screen movies (lines 12). Video on the iPhone plays only in landscape orientation, so the video will not rotate in response to reorienting the iPhone. Line 18 declares Slideshow as a property.

```
1  // SlideshowViewController.h
2  // Controller for a view that shows a slideshow.
3  // Implementation in SlideshowViewController.m
4  #import <UIKit/UIKit.h>
5  #import <MediaPlayer/MediaPlayer.h>
6  #import "Slideshow.h"
7
8  @interface SlideshowViewController : UIViewController
9  {
```

Fig. 13.26 | Controller for a view that shows a slideshow. (Part I of 2.)

```
10      Slideshow *slideshow; // the Slideshow that's being played
11      MPMusicPlayerController *musicPlayer; // plays the slideshow's music
12      MPMoviePlayerController *moviePlayer; // plays the slideshow's video
13      UIImageView *currentImageView; // the current image being displayed
14      int pictureIndex; // the index of the current place in Slideshow
15   } // end instance variable declaration
16
17   // declare slideshow as a property
18   @property (nonatomic, retain) Slideshow *slideshow;
19
20   // returns an image view for the given MediaItem
21   - (UIImageView *)nextImageViewWithMedia:(MediaItem *)item;
22
23   // transitions the slideshow to a new image
24   - (void)displayNewImage:(MediaItem *)item;
25
26   // transitions the slideshow to a new video
27   - (void)displayNewVideo:(MediaItem *)item;
28   - (void)videoFinished:(NSNotification *)n; // called when video finishes
29   - (void)exitShow; // ends the slideshow and returns to the previous view
30   - (void)changeSlide; // moves to the next slide in the slideshow
31
32   // called when the transition between two slides finishes
33   - (void)transitionFinished:(NSString *)animationId finished:(BOOL)finished
34      context:(void *)context;
35   @end // end SlideshowViewController interface
36
37   // additional method for UIImageView
38   @interface UIImageView (Scaling)
39
40   // scales the image view to fill the given bounds
41   - (void)expandToFill:(CGRect)bounds;
42   @end // end category Scaling of interface UIImageView
```

Fig. 13.26 | Controller for a view that shows a slideshow. (Part 2 of 2.)

SlideshowViewController declares seven methods (lines 21–34):

- nextImageViewWithMedia:—returns a UIImage representing a given MediaItem's image. This method is called only for MediaItem's representing images.

- displayNewImage:—displays a MediaItem representing the next image in the slideshow

- displayNewVideo:—displays a MediaItem representing the next video in the slideshow

- videoFinished:—moves to the next slide in the slideshow when a video finishes playing

- exitShow:—stops the music and returns to the previous view.

- changeSlide:—moves to the next slide in the slideshow or calls the exitShow method if there are no more slides

- transitionFinished:finished:context:—called when an image transition animation completes

Method `nextImageViewWithMedia:` of Class `SlideshowViewController`

Method `nextImageViewWithMedia` (Fig. 13.27) returns a `UIImageView` representing the given `MediaItem`. We retrieve the `UIImage` by accessing the `MediaItem`'s data property (line 22). Line 25 creates a new `UIImageView` using the retrieved `UIImage`. Line 27 accesses `SlideshowViewController`'s `UIView`'s bounds property to get a `CGRect` representing the screen's bounds. We pass this `CGRect` to `imageView`'s `expandToFill:` method to resize our `UIImageView` to fill the entire screen (line 30). This expands the image as much as possible in the current orientation without distorting it. Lines 31–36 get the expanded `UIImageView`'s frame and center the `UIImageView` in the screen. Lines 40–43 specify that `SlideshowViewController`'s `UIImageView` remains centered as the iPhone rotates. We set the `UIImageView`'s `autoresizingMask` property by combining all desired options using the bitwise OR operator (|).

```
18   // returns a UIImageView that contains the next image to display
19   - (UIImageView *)nextImageViewWithMedia:(MediaItem *)item
20   {
21       // get the image at the next index
22       UIImage *image = item.data;
23
24       // create an image view for the image
25       UIImageView *imageView = [[UIImageView alloc] initWithImage:image];
26
27       CGRect screenBounds = self.view.bounds; // get the screen bounds
28
29       // resize the image to fill the screen without distorting
30       [imageView expandToFill:screenBounds];
31       CGRect frame = imageView.frame; // get the frame of the image
32
33       // position the image to appear in the center of the view
34       frame.origin.x = (screenBounds.size.width - frame.size.width) / 2;
35       frame.origin.y = (screenBounds.size.height - frame.size.height) / 2;
36       imageView.frame = frame; // assign the new frame
37
38       // Makes the image move proportionally in any direction if the
39       // bounds of the superview change. Used during orientation changes.
40       imageView.autoresizingMask = (UIViewAutoresizingFlexibleLeftMargin |
41           UIViewAutoresizingFlexibleRightMargin |
42           UIViewAutoresizingFlexibleTopMargin |
43           UIViewAutoresizingFlexibleBottomMargin);
44
45       return imageView; // return the configured image view
46   } // end method nextImageViewWithMedia:
```

Fig. 13.27 | Method `nextImageViewWithMedia:` of class `SlideshowViewController`.

Method `changeSlide` of Class `SlideshowViewController`

Method `changeSlide` method (Fig. 13.28) advances the `Slideshow` by displaying its next image or video. If `pictureIndex` equals the number of slides in this `Slideshow` (slideshow.media.count), we call the `exitShow` method to end the `Slideshow` (lines 64–65). Otherwise, we get this `Slideshow`'s next `MediaItem` (line 69). If the `MediaItem`'s type property is `MediaTypeImage`, we pass the `MediaType` to the `displayNewImage:` method to display that picture as the next slide (lines 72–73). Otherwise, the MediaItem represents a video so we pass it to the displayNewVideo: method (lines 74–75).

```
60   // changes to the next slide in the slideshow
61   - (void)changeSlide
62   {
63       // check if there's another slide to display
64       if (pictureIndex >= slideshow.media.count)
65           [self exitShow]; // if there's no image, exit the slideshow
66       else
67       {
68           // get the next MediaItem
69           MediaItem *item = [slideshow.media objectAtIndex:pictureIndex];
70
71           // if the MediaItem represents an image
72           if (item.type == MediaTypeImage)
73               [self displayNewImage:item]; // display the image
74           else // the MediaItem represents a video
75               [self displayNewVideo:item]; // display the video
76
77           ++pictureIndex; // increment the index
78       } // end else
79   } // end method changeSlide
```

Fig. 13.28 | Method changeSlide of class SlideshowViewController.

Method displayNewImage: of Class SlideshowViewController
Method displayNewImage: (Fig. 13.29) displays an image (represented by the given MediaItem) as the next slide in this Slideshow. Lines 89–137 implement the **Fade** and **Slide** transitions the same way as in the original **Slideshow** app.

If this Slideshow uses the **Flip** image transition (line 138), we start a new Core Animation block describing an animation with a duration of two seconds which calls the transitionFinished:finished:context: method upon completion (lines 146–147). We call UIView's setAnimationTransition:forView:cache: method, supplying UIViewAnimationTransitionFlipFromRight as the animation transition (lines 150–152). Lines 154–156 remove the previous UIImageView, add the new UIImageView and begin the animation. Lines 161–162 use the performSelector:withObject:afterDelay: method to call the changeSlide method after a five-second delay.

```
81   // displays a new image in the slideshow
82   - (void)displayNewImage:(MediaItem *)item
83   {
84       // get the next image to display
85       UIImageView *nextImageView = [self nextImageViewWithMedia:item];
86       CGRect frame; // declare a new CGRect
87
88       // transition to the image based on the transition effect
89       switch (slideshow.effect)
90       {
```

Fig. 13.29 | Method displayNewImage: of class SlideshowViewController. (Part 1 of 3.)

```
 91        // if the transition effect is fade
 92        case TransitionEffectFade:
 93           [self.view addSubview:nextImageView]; // add the image to view
 94           nextImageView.alpha = 0.0; // make the next image transparent
 95
 96           // begin animation block
 97           [UIView beginAnimations:nil context:nextImageView];
 98           [UIView setAnimationDuration:2.0]; // set the animation length
 99           [UIView setAnimationDelegate:self]; // set the animation delegate
100
101           // call the given method when the animation ends
102           [UIView setAnimationDidStopSelector:
103              @selector(transitionFinished:finished:context:)];
104
105           [nextImageView setAlpha:1.0]; // fade in the next image
106           [currentImageView setAlpha:0.0]; // fade out the old image
107
108           [UIView commitAnimations]; // end animation block
109           break;
110
111        // if the transition effect is slide
112        case TransitionEffectSlide:
113           // position the next image to the right of the screen
114           [self.view addSubview:nextImageView]; // add the image to view
115           frame = nextImageView.frame;
116           frame.origin.x += frame.size.width;
117           nextImageView.frame = frame;
118
119           // begin animation block
120           [UIView beginAnimations:nil context:nextImageView];
121           [UIView setAnimationDuration:2.0]; // set the animation length
122           [UIView setAnimationDelegate:self]; // set the animation delegate
123
124           // call the given method when the animation ends
125           [UIView setAnimationDidStopSelector:
126              @selector(transitionFinished:finished:context:)];
127
128           frame.origin.x -= frame.size.width; // slide new image left
129           nextImageView.frame = frame; // apply the new frame
130           CGRect currentImageFrame = currentImageView.frame;
131
132           // slide the old image to the left
133           currentImageFrame.origin.x -= currentImageFrame.size.width;
134           currentImageView.frame = currentImageFrame;
135
136           [UIView commitAnimations]; // end animation block
137           break;
138        case TransitionEffectFlip: // if the transition effect is flip
139
140           // begin the animation block
141           [UIView beginAnimations:@"flip" context:nextImageView];
142           [UIView setAnimationDuration:2.0]; // set the animation duration
```

Fig. 13.29 | Method displayNewImage: of class SlideshowViewController. (Part 2 of 3.)

```
143              [UIView setAnimationDelegate:self]; // set delegate to self
144
145              // call the given method when the animation finishes
146              [UIView setAnimationDidStopSelector:
147                 @selector(transitionFinished:finished:context:)];
148
149              // set the transition to flip from the right side
150              [UIView setAnimationTransition:
151                 UIViewAnimationTransitionFlipFromRight forView:
152                 self.view cache:NO];
153
154              [currentImageView removeFromSuperview]; // remove the last image
155              [self.view addSubview:nextImageView]; // add the new image
156              [UIView commitAnimations]; // start the animation
157              break;
158        } // end switch
159
160        // change the slide after 5 seconds
161        [self performSelector:@selector(changeSlide) withObject:nil
162            afterDelay:5.0];
163   } // end method displayNewImage
164
```

Fig. 13.29 | Method displayNewImage: of class SlideshowViewController. (Part 3 of 3.)

Methods displayNewVideo: and videoFinished of Class SlideshowViewController

Method displayNewVideo: (lines 166–178) displays a video as the next slide in the slideshow. First, we add self as an observer of the MPMoviePlayerPlaybackDidFinish-Notification (lines 169–171). Class **NSNotificationCenter** manages notifications and observers. Notifications are objects that represent an event—in this example the event occurs when a movie's playback finishes. An observer is an object that should be notified when the event occurs. We access the **defaultCenter** singleton object, which is where system notifications are posted. Lines 169–171 indicate that the videoFinished method should be called when a MPMoviePlayer finishes playback. We then initialize moviePlayer with the URL of the movie to be played (lines 175–176) and play the movie (line 177).

```
165   // displays a new video in the slideshow
166   - (void)displayNewVideo:(MediaItem *)item
167   {
168        // receive notifications when a movie player finishes playback
169        [[NSNotificationCenter defaultCenter] addObserver:self
170            selector:@selector(videoFinished:)
171            name:MPMoviePlayerPlaybackDidFinishNotification object:nil];
172        [moviePlayer release]; // release the old movie player
173
174        // create a new movie player with the video URL
175        moviePlayer =
176            [[MPMoviePlayerController alloc] initWithContentURL:item.data];
```

Fig. 13.30 | Method displayNewVideo: of class SlideshowViewController. (Part 1 of 2.)

```
177    [moviePlayer play]; // play the video
178  } // end method displayNewVideo
179
180  // called when the video finishes playing
181  - (void)videoFinished:(NSNotification *)n
182  {
183      // stop receiving notifications when videos finish
184      [[NSNotificationCenter defaultCenter] removeObserver:self];
185
186      // hide the status bar
187      [[UIApplication sharedApplication] setStatusBarHidden:YES];
188      [self changeSlide]; // change to the next slide
189  } // end method videoFinished
```

Fig. 13.30 | Method displayNewVideo: of class SlideshowViewController. (Part 2 of 2.)

The videoFinished method is called when the movie stops playing. We remove self as an observer from the NSNotificationCenter using the ***removeObserver: method***. This stops the object from receiving notifications about movies ending. We then hide the status bar (line 187) and change to the next slide (line 188).

13.5 Suggested Enhancements

The **Enhanced Slideshow** app provides numerous capabilities not found in its predecessor but there are still features which can improve the app. Currently, each image displays for five seconds before moving to the next slide. Providing a means for the user to adjust this time would allow the slideshow to be more customized. Additionally, the app could enable the user to navigate through the slideshow while it's playing—left swipe could advance to the next slide and a right swipe could return to the previous slide.

13.6 Wrap-Up

The **Enhanced Slideshow** app played videos from the iPhone's photo library using an MP-MoviePlayerController. We used a UIImagePickerController to create a graphical interface for the user to chose images and videos. We added a new image transition using Core Animation. The UIViewAnimationTransitionFlipFromRight animation transition enabled images to transition by flipping horizontally. We saved slideshows so they would be accessible between multiple executions of the app using object serialization. We encoded objects using a subclass of NSCoder. An NSKeyedArchiver was used to save the entire slideshow list's object graph to a file.

In Chapter 14, we build the **Voice Recorder** app. We use the AVFoundation framework and an AVAudioRecorder object to record the user's speech through the iPhone's microphone. We'll change the app's AVAudioSession to switch between settings for recording and audio playback. We'll also use an MFMailComposeViewController to allow the user to send a voice recording as an e-mail attachment directly from the app.

14

Voice Recorder App

Audio Recording and Playback

OBJECTIVES

In this chapter you'll learn:

- To record audio files using an AVAudioRecorder and the AV Foundation framework.

- To set the AVAudioSession to accommodate playback and recording.

- To verify text input using an NSPredicate object and a regular expression.

- To use metering to create a visual representation of the user's audio input.

- To create an NSData object representing an audio file and use an MFMailComposeViewController to send an e-mail with the recording attached.

14.1 Introduction
14.2 Test-Driving the **Voice Recorder** App
14.3 Overview of the Technologies
14.4 Building the App
    14.4.1 Class `VoiceRecorderViewController`
    14.4.2 Class `NameRecordingViewController`
    14.4.3 Class `Visualizer`
    14.4.4 Class `PlaybackViewController`
14.5 Speech Synthesis and Recognition
14.6 Wrap-Up

14.1 Introduction

The **Voice Recorder** app allows the user to record sounds using the iPhone's microphone and save the audio files for playback later. The app has a red record **Button** which the user presses to begin recording audio (Fig. 14.1). At this point, the screen becomes a visualizer, displaying bars in reaction to the strength of the user's voice (Fig. 14.2). During recording, the record **Button** changes to a stop **Button**, which the user can touch to end the recording and display a **Text Field** used to enter the file name for the saved recording (Fig. 14.3).

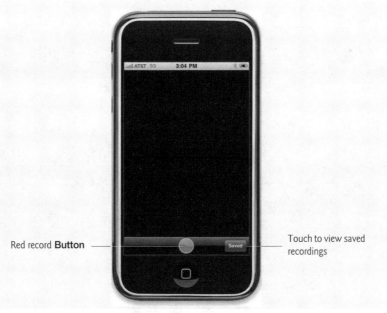

Fig. 14.1 | **Voice Recorder** app ready to record.

Saved recordings can be viewed by touching the "**Saved**" **Button** in the app's lower-right corner. They're displayed in a table. Touching a recording's name (Fig. 14.4) plays that recording. You can drag the **Slider** above the table of names to move forward or backward in the audio file—just like in the iPod app. The **Slider** at the bottom of the app con-

Fig. 14.2 | Visualizer during a recording.

Fig. 14.3 | Naming a recording.

trols the playback's volume. Touching the e-mail **Button** next to a recording's name opens an e-mail dialog with the audio file attached (Fig. 14.5). The user can send an e-mail containing the audio file without leaving the **Voice Recorder** app. Touching the "**Record**"

Button returns the user to the app's original screen. This app introduces the iPhone's speech-based capabilities, but this powerful tool is not fully explored here. Please see Section 14.5 for more information on speech synthesis and recognition.

Recording name

Send this recording as an e-mail attachment

Return to the audio recording screen

Fig. 14.4 | Playing a saved recording.

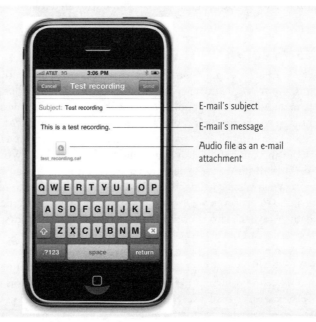

E-mail's subject

E-mail's message

Audio file as an e-mail attachment

Fig. 14.5 | E-mailing a recording.

14.2 Test-Driving the Voice Recorder App

Opening the Completed App

Open the directory containing the **Voice Recorder** app project. Double click VoiceRe-corder.xcodeproj to open the project in Xcode. This project will compile and run in the iPhone Simulator, but you will not be able to make recordings.

Recording a New Audio File

Touch the red record **Button** at the bottom of the app to begin recording sound. Speak into the iPhone and notice that the app's visualizer reacts to the intensity of your voice. When you're done recording, hit the white stop **Button** then enter Test Recording into the "**Name your recording**" **Text Field.**

Playing a Recording

Touch the "**Saved**" **Button** in the lower-right corner of the app to see a table containing the names of any audio files recorded with this app. Touch **Test Recording** and your recording will play through the iPhone's speaker. Slide the thumb of the **Slider** at the bottom of the app to adjust the volume and do the same for the top **Slider** to adjust the playback's position in the audio file. Touch the "**Record**" **Button** in the bottom-right corner of the app to return to the recording screen.

E-mailing a Recording

Touch the "**Saved**" **Button** to return to the app's flipside and touch the e-mail **Button** next to any of the saved audio file's names. An e-mail dialog appears with the audio file as an attachment. Enter a destination e-mail address and hit **Send** to e-mail the audio file. (This assumes that you've configured your iPhone with an e-mail account that can send e-mail.)

14.3 Overview of the Technologies

The **Voice Recorder** app uses the AV Foundation framework to record and play back sounds. An AVAudioRecorder records sounds using the iPhone's microphone and saves them to audio files in the app. We access the AVAudioSession singleton object belonging to this app to change the iPhone's audio session. The *singleton design pattern* guarantees that a system instantiates a maximum of one object of a given class. This is useful here because the app can handle only one audio session at a time. When the app is recording we use the AVAudioSessionCategoryRecord session to silence any audio that might be playing. An AVAudioSessionCategoryPlayback session is used to play back recordings and to force audio to play even when the Ring/Silent switch is set to silent. The AVAudioSession-CategoryPlayback also continues playback while the iPhone is locked. The flipside of the app contains a UITableView displaying the name of each saved audio recording. An AVAudioPlayer plays a files when the user touches the name of a prior recording.

We use the NSPredicate class and a regular expression to verify that the user entered a valid file name, which can't include special characters such as slashes or ampersands. We allow the user to e-mail a saved audio recording by converting the saved file to an NSData object, then pass that as an attachment to an MFMailComposeViewController. This class opens an e-mail dialog in the app.

14.4 Building the App

In the next several subsections, we define the app's views and controllers. We begin with the app's VoiceRecorderViewController.

14.4.1 Class VoiceRecorderViewController

Create a new project in Xcode using the **View-based Application** template and name it VoiceRecorder. The files VoiceRecorderViewController.h, VoiceRecorderViewController.m and VoiceRecorderViewController.xib are created for you.

VoiceRecorderViewController *Interface Declaration*
The VoiceRecorderViewController class (Fig. 14.6) extends UIViewController and implements the PlaybackViewControllerDelegate and NameRecordingDelegate protocols (lines 10–11)—defined by this app's two other UIViewControllers (Figs. 14.20 and 14.13, respectively).

```
 1   // Fig. 14.6: VoiceRecorderViewController.h
 2   // VoiceRecorderViewController interface declaration.
 3   #import <AVFoundation/AVFoundation.h>
 4   #import <CoreAudio/CoreAudioTypes.h>
 5   #import "Visualizer.h"
 6   #import "PlaybackViewController.h"
 7   #import "NameRecordingViewController.h"
 8
 9   // begin VoiceRecorderVewController interface declaration
10   @interface VoiceRecorderViewController : UIViewController
11      <PlaybackViewControllerDelegate, NameRecordingDelegate>
12   {
13      IBOutlet Visualizer *visualizer; // store Visualizer
14      IBOutlet UIButton *recordButton; // touched to start and stop recording
15      AVAudioRecorder *recorder; // records user sound input
16      NSTimer *timer; // updates the visualizer every .05 seconds
17   } // end instance variable declaration
18
19   // declare visualizer and recordButton as properties
20   @property (nonatomic, retain) Visualizer *visualizer;
21   @property (nonatomic, retain) UIButton *recordButton;
22
23   - (IBAction)record:sender; // toggle recording
24   - (IBAction)flip:sender; // moves to the flipside
25   @end // end interface VoiceRecorderViewController
```

Fig. 14.6 | VoiceRecorderViewController interface declaration.

Line 13 declares an outlet for a new Visualizer. This is a subclass of UIView (defined in 14.16) that displays a visualizer that reacts to the intensity of the user's voice. The UIButton recordButton (line 14) is touched by the user to start and stop recording. Line 15 declares an instance variable of type *AVAudioRecorder*. Objects of this class can record audio through the iPhone's microphone. The NSTimer (line 16) generates events which redraw the Visualizer 20 times per second for smooth animation of the visualizer's bars.

VoiceRecorderViewController's interface declares two methods (lines 23–24). Method record: starts recording audio when the user touches the red record **Button**. When the user touches the white stop **Button**, this method ends the recording and displays a NameRecordingView, which allows users to name their recordings. The flip: method transitions the app to the **PlaybackView** when the "Saved" **Button** is touched.

Defining the VoiceRecorderViewController's View
Open the file VoiceRecorderViewController.xib in Interface Builder. Double-click **View** to edit its contents. Drag a **Toolbar** from the **Library** window to the bottom of **View**. Set its **Style** to **Black Opaque**. Drag a **Fixed Space Bar Button Item** onto the **Toolbar**, followed by a **Bar Button Item**. Change the **Bar Button Item**'s **Identifier** to **Custom** and change its **Image** to record.png. Resize the **Fixed Space Bar Button Item** so that the record **Button** is centered in the **Toolbar**. Next, drag a **Flexible Space Bar Button Item** onto the **Toolbar**, followed by another **Bar Button Item** and set the **Button**'s text to Saved. Finally, drag a **View** above the **Toolbar** and position it to fill the remaining space in the app. Change its **Class** to Visualizer. Figure 14.7 shows the final layout.

Fig. 14.7 | VoiceRecorderViewController's finished view.

Next, connect the recordButton outlet of **File's Owner** to the middle **Button** in the **Toolbar**, and connect the visualizer outlet to the **View** above the **Toolbar**. Connect the **Touch Up Inside** event from the record **Button** to the record: action of **File's Owner**, and connect the **Touch Up Inside** event from the "Saved" **Button** to the flip: action.

Method viewDidLoad of Class VoiceRecorderViewController
The viewDidLoad method sets up the VoiceRecorderViewController's **View**. After passing the viewDidLoad message to the superclass (line 12), we activate the AVAudioSession (line 15). AVAudioSession's *sharedInstance method* returns the singleton AVAudioSession object for this app. This object can be used to set audio preferences, such as how to react to incoming calls or whether to continue audio when the screen locks. The AVAudioSession's behavior is determined by its *category property*—there are different categories for recording and playing back audio.

```
1   // Fig. 14.8: VoiceRecorderViewController.m
2   // VoiceRecorderViewController class implementation.
3   #import "VoiceRecorderViewController.h"
4
5   @implementation VoiceRecorderViewController
6   @synthesize visualizer; // generate get and set methods for visualizer
7   @synthesize recordButton; // generate get and set methods for recordButton
8
9   // setup the View
10  - (void)viewDidLoad
11  {
12      [super viewDidLoad]; // call the superclass's viewDidLoad method
13
14      // activate the current audio session
15      [[AVAudioSession sharedInstance] setActive:YES error:nil];
16  } // end method viewDidLoad
17
```

Fig. 14.8 | Methods initWithNibName:bundle: and viewDidLoad of class VoiceRecorderViewController.

Method record: of Class VoiceRecorderViewController

The record: method (Fig. 14.9) toggles whether or not the app is recording. If the app was recording when the method was called (line 22), we invalidate timer so it stops generating events and redrawing the Visualizer. Line 26 tells the recorder AVAudioRecorder to stop recording. Lines 29–30 pass AVAudioSessionCategorySoloAmbient to AVAudioSession's *setCategory: method.* This sets the iPhone back to its default audio session. In this case, it indicates that the app is no longer in recording mode. We create a new UIImage variable recordImage using record.png and use UIButton's setImage:forState: method to display this image for recordButton (line 36). Lines 39–41 create a new NameRecordingViewController and set its delegate to self. Line 44 presents the view for naming recordings using method UIViewController's presentModalViewController:animated:. This view allows the user to enter a name for the audio recording.

```
18  // called when the user touches the record/stop recording button
19  - (IBAction)record:sender
20  {
21      // if we're currently recording
22      if (recorder.recording)
23      {
24          [timer invalidate]; // stop the timer from generating events
25          timer = nil; // set time to nil
26          [recorder stop]; // stop recording
27
28          // set the category of the current audio session
29          [[AVAudioSession sharedInstance] setCategory:
30              AVAudioSessionCategorySoloAmbient error:nil];
31
```

Fig. 14.9 | Method record: of class VoiceRecorderViewController. (Part 1 of 3.)

```
32            // load the record image
33            UIImage *recordImage = [UIImage imageNamed:@"record.png"];
34
35            // set the image on the record button
36            [recordButton setImage:recordImage forState:UIControlStateNormal];
37
38            // create a new NameRecordingViewController
39            NameRecordingViewController *controller =
40               [[NameRecordingViewController alloc] init];
41            controller.delegate = self; // set controller's delegate to self
42
43            // show the NameRecordingViewController
44            [self presentModalViewController:controller animated:YES];
45         } // end if
46         else
47         {
48            // set the audio session's category to record
49            [[AVAudioSession sharedInstance] setCategory:
50               AVAudioSessionCategoryRecord error:nil];
51
52            // find the location of the document directory
53            NSArray *paths = NSSearchPathForDirectoriesInDomains(
54               NSDocumentDirectory, NSUserDomainMask, YES);
55
56            // get the first directory
57            NSString *dir = [paths objectAtIndex:0];
58
59            // create a name for the file using the current system time
60            NSString *filename = [NSString stringWithFormat:@"%f.caf",
61               [[NSDate date] timeIntervalSince1970]];
62
63            // create the path using the directory and file name
64            NSString *path = [dir stringByAppendingPathComponent:filename];
65
66            // create a new NSMutableDictionary for the record settings
67            NSMutableDictionary *settings = [[NSMutableDictionary alloc] init];
68
69            // record using the Apple lossless format
70            [settings setValue: [NSNumber
71               numberWithInt:kAudioFormatAppleLossless] forKey:AVFormatIDKey];
72
73            // set the sample rate to 44100 Hz
74            [settings setValue:[NSNumber
75               numberWithFloat:44100.0] forKey:AVSampleRateKey];
76
77            // set the number of channels for recording
78            [settings setValue:[NSNumber numberWithInt:1]
79               forKey:AVNumberOfChannelsKey];
80
81            // set the bit depth
82            [settings setValue:[NSNumber numberWithInt:16]
83               forKey:AVLinearPCMBitDepthKey];
```

Fig. 14.9 | Method record: of class VoiceRecorderViewController. (Part 2 of 3.)

```
 84
 85        // set whether the format is big endian
 86        [settings setValue:[NSNumber numberWithBool:NO]
 87           forKey:AVLinearPCMIsBigEndianKey];
 88
 89        // set whether the audio format is floating point
 90        [settings setValue:[NSNumber numberWithBool:NO]
 91           forKey:AVLinearPCMIsFloatKey];
 92        [visualizer clear]; // clear the visualizer
 93
 94        [recorder release]; // release the recorder AVAudioRecorder
 95
 96        // initialize recorder with the URL and settings
 97        recorder =
 98           [[AVAudioRecorder alloc] initWithURL:[NSURL fileURLWithPath:path]
 99           settings:settings error:nil];
100        [recorder prepareToRecord]; // prepare the recorder to record
101        recorder.meteringEnabled = YES; // enable metering for the recorder
102        [recorder record]; // start the recording
103
104        // start a timer
105        timer = [NSTimer scheduledTimerWithTimeInterval:0.05 target:self
106           selector:@selector(timerFired:) userInfo:nil repeats:YES];
107
108        // create the stop recording image
109        UIImage *stopImage = [UIImage imageNamed:@"stop.png"];
110
111        // change the image on recordButton to the stop image
112        [recordButton setImage:stopImage forState:UIControlStateNormal];
113     } // end else
114  } // end method record:
115
```

Fig. 14.9 | Method record: of class VoiceRecorderViewController. (Part 3 of 3.)

If the app wasn't recording (line 46), we pass AVAudioSessionCategoryRecord to AVAudioSession's setCategory: method. This silences any playback audio so we can properly record the user's voice. The NSSearchPathForDirectoriesInDomains function is used to get an NSArray containing only this app's documents directory (lines 53–54). Line 57 stores that directory name in NSString variable dir. The NameRecordingView-Controller later allows the user to enter a recording name, but for now we need to save the clip to a temporary location. Lines 60–61 create a file name using the current system time (to ensure unique names) and the .caf extension, which stands for Core Audio File—a type of container used by the Core Audio framework that supports many types of audio files, such as WAV and AIFF. Lines 67–91 initialize the settings NSMutableDictionary with the standard settings for iPhone audio recording. For more information on iPhone these settings visit

developer.apple.com/iphone/library/documentation/AVFoundation/
Reference/AVAudioRecorder_ClassReference/Reference/Reference.html

and scroll to the section **Constants**.

Lines 92 and 94 clear the visualizer and release the previous recorder. Lines 97–102 assign recorder a new AVAudioRecorder that writes to the temporary location we chose, and that uses the settings specified in the settings NSMutableDictionary. We then call recorder's **prepareToRecord method** (line 100). This is required to set recorder's **allowMetering property** to YES (line 101), which allows us to sample the recording's intensity level so we can animate the visualizer. Line 102 starts the recording by calling AVAudioRecorder's **record method**. We then create a new NSTimer which generates an event calling the timerFired: method 20 times per second. Lines 109–112 use UIButton's setImage:forState: method to change the record **Button** to a stop **Button**.

Method nameRecordingViewController:didGetName: of Class Voice-RecorderViewController

The nameRecordingViewController:didGetName: method (Fig. 14.10) receives from the NameRecordingViewController an NSString chosen by the user to name an audio recording. Line 121 appends the caf file extension to the end of the given fileName using NSString's stringByAppendingPathExtension: method. Accessing recorder's url property and calling its **path method** (line 124) returns an NSString representing the file path of the last recorded audio file. Line 127 uses NSString's stringByDeletingLastPathComponent method to remove the last part of the path in the string (i.e., the file name of that recording) and store only the directory. We append the given fileName and the .caf extension to the end of this directory.

```
116   // called when the user finishes picking a name for the recording
117   - (void)nameRecordingViewController:(NameRecordingViewController *)
118   controller didGetName:(NSString *)fileName
119   {
120       // append the extension to the chosen name
121       fileName = [fileName stringByAppendingPathExtension:@"caf"];
122
123       // get the path for the last recorded file
124       NSString *path = [recorder.url path];
125
126       // get the directory the last file was saved in
127       NSString *dir = [path stringByDeletingLastPathComponent];
128
129       // append the new file name to the path
130       NSString *newPath = [dir stringByAppendingPathComponent:fileName];
131
132       // get the default file manager
133       NSFileManager *fileManager = [NSFileManager defaultManager];
134
135       // rename the old file to the new name the user picked
136       [fileManager moveItemAtPath:path toPath:newPath error:nil];
137
138       // make the NameRecordingViewController go away
139       [self dismissModalViewControllerAnimated:YES];
140   } // end method nameRecordingViewController:didGetName:
141
```

Fig. 14.10 | Method nameRecordingViewController:didGetName: of class VoiceRecorderViewController.

Line 133 gets the default NSFileManager using NSFileManager's static defaultMan-ager method. NSFileManager's ***moveItemAtPath:toPath: method*** is used to change the default file name of the recording to the user's chosen file name (line 136).[1] Line 139 hides the **NameRecordingView** using UIViewController's dismissModalViewController-Animated: method.

Method flip: of Class VoiceRecorderViewController
The flip: method (Fig. 14.11) transitions the app to the playback **View** when the user touches the "**Saved**" **Button**. Lines 146–147 initialize a new PlaybackViewController. We set playback's modalTransitionStyle property to UIModalTransitionStyleCross-Dissolve so the recording **View** will fade into the playback **View** (line 150). We then set playback's delegate to this VoiceRecorderViewController. Line 154 calls UIViewCon-troller's presentModalViewController:animated: method to transition to the Play-backRecordingViewController's view.

```
142  // transition the app to the PlaybackView
143  - (IBAction)flip:sender
144  {
145     // create a new PlaybackViewController
146     PlaybackViewController *playback =
147        [[PlaybackViewController alloc] init];
148
149     // set the transition style to fade
150     playback.modalTransitionStyle = UIModalTransitionStyleCrossDissolve;
151     playback.delegate = self; // set playback's delegate to self
152
153     // show the PlaybackViewController
154     [self presentModalViewController:playback animated:YES];
155     [playback release]; // release the playback PlaybackViewController
156  } // end method flip:
157
```

Fig. 14.11 | Method flip: of class VoiceRecorderViewController.

Methods playbackViewControllerDidFinish: and timerFired: of Class VoiceRecorderViewController
Method playbackViewControllerDidFinish: (Fig. 14.12, lines 159–164) is called when the user touches the "**Record**" **Button** in the playback **View**. Line 163 calls UIView-Controller's dismissModalViewControllerAnimated: method to transition the app back to the recorder **View**.

Method timerFired: (lines 167–174) is called 20 times a second to update visual-izer. We use the AVAudioRecorder **updateMeters method** to cause the recorder to refresh its meters based on the recording's power levels (i.e., intensities). Line 172 calls our visualizer's setPower: method, passing the result of recorder's ***averagePowerForChannel: method***. We use the first channel (0) because the iPhone's microphone has only one channel. Line 173 calls UIView's setNeedsDisplay method to redraw the visualizer.

---

1. In this app, we assume that the file name specified by the user *does not* already exist. If it does, the move operation will fail.

```
158    // delegate method for the PlaybackViewController
159    - (void)playbackViewControllerDidFinish:
160        (PlaybackViewController *)controller
161    {
162        // return to the VoiceRecorderView
163        [self dismissModalViewControllerAnimated:YES];
164    } // end method playbackViewControllerDidFinish:
165
166    // called every .05 seconds when the timer generates an event
167    - (void)timerFired:(NSTimer *)timer
168    {
169        [recorder updateMeters]; // sample the recording to get new data
170
171        // set the visualizer's average power level
172        [visualizer setPower:[recorder averagePowerForChannel:0]];
173        [visualizer setNeedsDisplay]; // redraw the visualizer
174    } // end method timerFired:
175
176    // release this object's memory
177    - (void)dealloc
178    {
179        [visualizer release]; // release the Visualizer
180        [recordButton release]; // release the recordButton UIButton
181        [recorder release]; // release the recorder AVAudioRecorder
182        [super dealloc]; // call the superclass's dealloc method
183    } // end method dealloc
184    @end // VoiceRecorderViewController class
```

Fig. 14.12 | Methods playbackViewControllerDidFinish: and timerFired: of class VoiceRecorderViewController.

14.4.2 Class NameRecordingViewController

Create a new UIViewController subclass named NameRecordingViewController and check the **With XIB for user interface** checkbox to generate the header, source and nib files.

NameRecordingViewController Interface Declaration

The NameRecordingViewController class (Fig. 14.13) is a sublcass of UIViewController whichs implements the UITextFieldDelegate protocol, indicating that it can respond to events generated by a **Text Field**. Lines 11–12 declare this class's delegate and a UITextField outlet which responds to events from the "**Name your recording**" **Text Field**. Line 16 declares delegate as a property. The finishedNaming: method (line 19) verifies that the input audio file's name is valid and passes it on to the delegate. Lines 23–28 declare the NameRecordingDelegate protocol which contains one method declaration. The nameRecordingViewController:didGetName: method (lines 26–27) is used by the delegate to receive an audio file name when the user touches the keyboard's "**Done**" **Button**.

```
1    // Fig. 14.13: NameRecordingViewController.h
2    // Controls a View for naming a recording.
3    #import <UIKit/UIKit.h>
```

Fig. 14.13 | Controls a **View** for naming a recording. (Part 1 of 2.)

```
 4
 5    @protocol NameRecordingDelegate; // declare NameRecordingDelegate protocol
 6
 7    // begin NameRecordingViewController interface
 8    @interface NameRecordingViewController : UIViewController
 9       <UITextFieldDelegate>
10    {
11       id <NameRecordingDelegate> delegate; // declare the class's delegate
12       IBOutlet UITextField *textField; // text field for entering the name
13    } // end instance variable declaration
14
15    // declare delegate and textField as a properties
16    @property (nonatomic, assign) id <NameRecordingDelegate> delegate;
17    @property (nonatomic, retain) UITextField *textField;
18
19    - (IBAction)finishedNaming:sender; // the user finished entering the name
20    @end // end interface NameRecordingViewController
21
22    // begin NameRecordingDelegate protocol
23    @protocol NameRecordingDelegate
24
25    // informs the delegate that the user chose a name
26    - (void)nameRecordingViewController:(NameRecordingViewController *)
27       controller didGetName:(NSString *)fileName;
28    @end // end protocol NameRecordingDelegate
```

Fig. 14.13 | Controls a **View** for naming a recording. (Part 2 of 2.)

Defining the NameRecordingViewController's View

Open the file NameRecordingViewController.xib in Interface Builder. Open **View** and drag a **Text Field** and a **Label** onto it. Position and name the components as seen in Fig. 14.14. Connect the textField outlet of **File's Owner** to the **Text Field** and connect the **Did End On Exit** event of the **Text Field** to the finishedNaming: method of **File's Owner**.

Fig. 14.14 | Finished layout of NameRecordingViewController's view.

NameRecordingViewController *Class Definition*

The viewDidLoad method (Fig. 14.15, lines 11–15) is called when the **NameRecord-ingView** loads. Line 13 calls the superclass's viewDidLoad method and line 14 uses UIText-Field's becomeFirstResponder method to select textField and display the keyboard.

The finishedNaming: method (lines 18–22) is called when the user touches the keyboard's "**Done**" Button after entering a save name for the audio recording. Line 21 passes the name to delegate's nameRecordingViewController:didGetName: method to inform the VoiceRecorderViewController of the chosen name.

```
1   // Fig. 14.15: NameRecordingViewController.m
2   // Implementation of NameRecordingViewController
3   #import "NameRecordingViewController.h"
4
5   @implementation NameRecordingViewController
6
7   @synthesize delegate; // synthesize get and set methods for the delegate
8   @synthesize textField; // synthesize get and set methods for textField
9
10  // called when the View finishes loading
11  - (void)viewDidLoad
12  {
13     [super viewDidLoad]; // calls the superclass's viewDidLoad method
14     [textField becomeFirstResponder]; // show the keyboard
15  } // end method viewDidLoad
16
17  // call when the user touches the "Done" button on the keyboard
18  - (IBAction)finishedNaming:sender
19  {
20     // inform the delegate that the user chose a name
21     [delegate nameRecordingViewController:self didGetName:textField.text];
22  } // end method finishedNaming:
23
24  // called every time the user edits text in the text field
25  - (BOOL)textField:(UITextField *)field shouldChangeCharactersInRange:
26     (NSRange)range replacementString:(NSString *)string
27  {
28     // string that will exist once this method returns YES
29     NSString *newString = [field.text stringByReplacingCharactersInRange:
30        range withString:string];
31
32     // create a new predicate that matches characters valid for file names
33     NSPredicate *regex = [NSPredicate predicateWithFormat:
34        @"SELF MATCHES '.*[^-_.a-zA-Z0-9].*'"];
35     BOOL matches = [regex evaluateWithObject:newString]; // check for match
36
37     // if the new string is an invalid file name
38     if (matches)
39        field.textColor = [UIColor redColor]; // change the text to red
40     else // if the string is a valid file name
41        field.textColor = [UIColor blackColor]; // change the text to black
```

Fig. 14.15 | Implementation of NameRecordingViewController. (Part 1 of 2.)

```
42
43      return YES; // allow the edit
44    } // end method textField:shouldChangeCharactersInRange:replacementString:
45
46    // called when the user touches the "Done" button on the keyboard
47    - (BOOL)textFieldShouldReturn:(UITextField *)field
48    {
49        // create a new predicate that matches characters valid for file names
50        NSPredicate *regex = [NSPredicate predicateWithFormat:
51            @"SELF MATCHES '.*[^-_.a-zA-Z0-9].*'"];
52        return (![regex evaluateWithObject:field.text]); // check for a match
53    } // end method textFieldShouldReturn:
54    @end // NameRecoringViewController implementation
```

Fig. 14.15 | Implementation of `NameRecordingViewController`. (Part 2 of 2.)

The ***textField:shouldChangeCharactersInRange:replacementString:*** *method* is a method of the `UITextFieldDelegate` protocol which a `UITextField` calls each time the user enters a new character in that `UITextField`. If this method returns YES, the character is appended to the end of the **Text Field**'s `text` property; otherwise, it's not appended. The `NSString` parameter `string` represents the user's edit to the **Text Field**. We first apply the user's change so we can work with the new value (lines 29–30). Lines 33–34 create a new ***NSPredicate*** object using `NSPredicate`'s static ***predicateWithFormat:*** *method*. This is used to define a regular expression which matches only invalid file name strings. For more information on regular expressions, visit `www.deitel.com/regularexpressions/`.

Line 35 uses `NSPredicate`'s ***evaluateWithObject:*** *method* to compare the string to the regular expression. This returns YES for valid strings and NO for invalid ones. We then set the color of the text in the **Text Field**—black if the string is valid, red if it isn't. We return YES to allow all edits, even if they are invalid.

The `textFieldShouldReturn:` method is called when the user touches the **Return** button on the keyboard. If this method returns YES, the user's file name is valid and the **Text Field** will call our `finishedNaming:` method. To determine whether the name is valid, we create an `NSPredicate` object with an appropriate regular expression (lines 50–51), then use the regular expression to validate the name (line 52).

14.4.3 Class `Visualizer`

Create a new `UIView` subclass named `Visualizer` to generate the files `Visualizer.h` and `Visualizer.m`. This class renders a graphic of the user's voice intensity during recording.

Visualizer Interface Declaration
Class `Visualizer` (Fig. 14.16) is a subclass of `UIView` (line 6). Variable `powers` (line 8) represents the power levels received from the `VoiceRecorderViewController`. The lowest recorded power level for the current recording is stored in `minPower` (line 9). Lines 12–13 declare two methods. The `setPower:` method (line 12) adds a new power level to the `powers` `NSMutableArray` and updates `minPower` when necessary. The `clear` method (line 13) removes all elements from the `powers` `NSMutableArray`, thus clearing the `Visualizer`.

```
 1    // Fig. 14.16: Visualizer.h
 2    // View that displays a visualization of a recording in progress.
 3    #import <UIKit/UIKit.h>
 4
 5    // begin Visualizer interface definition
 6    @interface Visualizer : UIView
 7    {
 8       NSMutableArray *powers; // past power levels in the recording
 9       float minPower; // the lowest recorded power level
10    } // end instance variable declaration
11
12    - (void)setPower:(float)p; // set the powerLevel
13    - (void)clear; // clear all the past power levels
14    @end // end interface Visualizer
```

Fig. 14.16 | **View** that displays a visualization of a recording in progress.

Method initWithCoder: of Class Visualizer

The initWithCoder: method (Fig. 14.17) initializes the Visualizer. Line 11 checks if the superclass initialized correctly. If so, we initialize the powers array with a capacity of half the screen's width using NSMutableArray's initWithCapacity: method (lines 14–15). This initializes the NSMutableArray to contain the same number of elements as half the number of pixels in the screen's width. We'll display a power-level line for every other pixel in the width of the screen.

```
 1    // Fig. 14.17: Visualizer.m
 2    // VoiceRecorder
 3    #import "Visualizer.h"
 4
 5    @implementation Visualizer
 6
 7    // initialize the Visualizer
 8    - (id)initWithCoder:(NSCoder *)aDecoder
 9    {
10       // if the superclass initializes properly
11       if (self = [super initWithCoder:aDecoder])
12       {
13          // initialize powers with an entry for every other pixel of width
14          powers = [[NSMutableArray alloc]
15             initWithCapacity:self.frame.size.width / 2];
16       } // end if
17
18       return self; // return this BarVisualizer
19    } // end method initWithCoder:
20
```

Fig. 14.17 | Method initWithCoder: of class Visualizer.

Methods setPower: and clear of Class Visualizer

The setPower: method (Fig. 14.18, lines 22–33) adds the recording's current power to the Visualizer. Line 24 wraps the given float in an NSNumber object and adds it to the powers array. Recall that primitives such as floats can't be directly inserted in collections like NSMutableArrays. Line 27 checks whether there are enough power levels to fill the entire screen. If so, we use NSMutableArray's removeObjectAtIndex: method to remove the oldest entries in powers (line 28). Line 31 checks if the given power level is lower than any level previously recorded. If there are too many, we update minPower to the given value (line 32). The clear method (lines 36–39) calls NSMutableArray's removeAllObjects method to remove all elements from powers. This clears the Visualizer's display.

```
21    // sets the current power in the recording
22    - (void)setPower:(float)p
23    {
24        [powers addObject:[NSNumber numberWithFloat:p]]; // add value to powers
25
26        // while there are enough entries to fill the entire screen
27        while (powers.count * 2 > self.frame.size.width)
28            [powers removeObjectAtIndex:0]; // remove the oldest entry
29
30        // if the new power is less than the smallest power recorded
31        if (p < minPower)
32            minPower = p; // update minPower with the new power
33    } // end method setPower:
34
35    // clears all the points from the visualizer
36    - (void)clear
37    {
38        [powers removeAllObjects]; // remove all objects from powers
39    } // end method clear
40
```

Fig. 14.18 | Methods setPower: and clear of class Visualizer.

Method drawRect: of Class Visualizer
The drawRect: method (Fig. 14.19) draws each power level in the Visualizer. Line 45 retrieves the current graphics context using the UIGraphicsGetCurrentContext function. We then access Visualizer's frame property's size to get a CGSize representing the size of the Visualizer (line 46).

```
41    // draws the visualizer
42    - (void)drawRect:(CGRect)rect
43    {
44        // get the current graphics context
45        CGContextRef context = UIGraphicsGetCurrentContext();
46        CGSize size = self.frame.size;
47
48        // draw a line for each point in powers
49        for (int i = 0; i < powers.count; i++)
50        {
51            // get next power level
52            float newPower = [[powers objectAtIndex:i] floatValue];
```

Fig. 14.19 | Method drawRect: of class Visualizer. (Part 1 of 2.)

```
53
54        // calculate the height for this power level
55        float height = (1 - newPower / minPower) * (size.height / 2);
56
57        // move to a point above the middle of the screen
58        CGContextMoveToPoint(context, i * 2, size.height / 2 - height);
59
60        // add a line to a point below the middle of the screen
61        CGContextAddLineToPoint(context, i * 2, size.height / 2 + height);
62
63        // set the color for this line segment based on f
64        CGContextSetRGBStrokeColor(context, 0, 1, 0, 1);
65        CGContextStrokePath(context); // draw the line
66     } // end for
67  } // end method drawRect:
68
69  // free Visualizer's memory
70  - (void)dealloc
71  {
72     [powers release]; // release the powers NSMutableArray
73     [super dealloc]; // call the superclass's dealloc method
74  } // end method dealloc
75  @end // end visualizer implementation
```

Fig. 14.19 | Method drawRect: of class Visualizer. (Part 2 of 2.)

Lines 49–66 loop through each power level in powers and draw a line representing that level. Line 52 gets a float value representing the power level at index i. NSMutableArray's objectAtIndex: method is used to retrieve the NSNumber at the current index and NSNumber's floatValue method converts that to a float. Line 55 uses this value to calculate the height for this power level's line, scaled by the minPower. The line is drawn so that it is bisected by the vertical center of the screen. Line 58 uses the CGContextMoveToPoint function to select the point in context that is half of the line's height above the vertical center of the screen. This will be the line's top endpoint. Line 61 draws the line to the point in context half of the line's height below the vertical center of the screen. Line 64 sets the stroke color to green using the CGContextSetRGBStrokeColor function. The CGContextStrokePath function draws the line to context (line 65).

14.4.4 Class PlaybackViewController

Create a new UIViewController subclass named PlayBackViewController and check the **With XIB for user interface** checkbox to generate the class's header, source and nib files.

PlaybackViewController Interface Declaration

The PlaybackViewController class (Fig. 14.20) is a subclass of UIViewController that implements the UITableViewDataSource and UITableViewDelegate protocols (lines 9–10) indicating that this class is a data model for a UITableView and receives messages when the user interacts with that UITableView. Line 13 declares a PlaybackViewControllerDelegate for this class. Lines 14–19 declare outlets used to connect to the interactive GUI components in this view. The AVAudioPlayer variable player is used to play back saved recordings and the NSMutableArray variable files stores the list of the recordings' file paths (lines 20–21). Line 22 declares an NSTimer which will generate events to update the progress and volume Sliders to correspond to the current position and volume of the playback. Lines 26–32 declare delegate and the outlets as a properties.

```objc
 1   // Fig. 14.20: PlaybackViewController.h
 2   // Controls the View where the user plays existing sound files.
 3   #import <UIKit/UIKit.h>
 4   #import <MessageUI/MessageUI.h>
 5
 6   @protocol PlaybackViewControllerDelegate;
 7
 8   // begin interface PlaybackViewController's declaration
 9   @interface PlaybackViewController : UIViewController
10      <UITableViewDataSource, UITableViewDelegate,
11      MFMailComposeViewControllerDelegate>
12   {
13      id <PlaybackViewControllerDelegate> delegate; // this class's delegate
14      IBOutlet UITableView *table; // displays a list of recordings
15      IBOutlet UIToolbar *toolbar; // top toolbar
16      IBOutlet UISlider *progressSlider; // controls the playback progress
17      IBOutlet UISlider *volumeSlider; // controls the playback volume
18      IBOutlet UIBarButtonItem *timeLabel; // shows the playback time
19      IBOutlet UIBarButtonItem *playButton; // button to play/pause playback
20      AVAudioPlayer *player; // plays the recordings
21      NSMutableArray *files; // a list of the recordings
22      NSTimer *timer; // fires to update the progress slider and time label
23   } // end instance variable declaration
24
25   // declare delegate and the outlets as properties
26   @property(nonatomic, assign) id <PlaybackViewControllerDelegate> delegate;
27   @property (nonatomic, retain) UITableView *table;
28   @property (nonatomic, retain) UIToolbar *toolbar;
29   @property (nonatomic, retain) UISlider *progressSlider;
30   @property (nonatomic, retain) UISlider *volumeSlider;
31   @property (nonatomic, retain) UIBarButtonItem *timeLabel;
32   @property (nonatomic, retain) UIBarButtonItem *playButton;
33
34   - (IBAction)sliderMoved:sender; // called when progressSlider is moved
35   - (IBAction)togglePlay:sender; // called when playButton is touched
36   - (IBAction)updateVolume:sender; // called when volumeSlider is moved
37   - (IBAction)record:sender; // called when the "record" button is touched
38   - (void)timerFired:(NSTimer *)t; // called when the timer fires
39   - (void)playSound; // plays the current sound
40   - (void)stopSound; // stops playback
41   @end // end interface PlaybackViewController
42
43   @protocol PlaybackViewControllerDelegate
44
45   // informs the delegate that the user finished playback
46   - (void)playbackViewControllerDidFinish:
47      (PlaybackViewController *)controller;
48   @end // end protocol PlaybackControllerDelegate
```

Fig. 14.20 | Controls the **View** where the user plays existing sound files.

This class declares seven methods (lines 34–40):

- `sliderMoved:`—adjusts the position in the audio playback when the user moves the progress **Slider**'s thumb

- `togglePlay:`—starts the audio playback if no recording is currently playing; otherwise, it stops the currently playing audio recording

- `updateVolume:`—adjusts the audio playback's volume when the user moves the volume **Slider**'s thumb

- `record:`—returns the app to the recorder **View** when the user touches **Record**

- `timerFired:`—adjusts the progress and volume **Slider**s to match the state of the audio playback 10 times per second

- `playSound`—plays an `AVAudioPlayer` representing the selected audio

- `stopSound`—stops the currently playing `AVAudioRecorder`

Lines 43–48 declare the `PlaybackViewControllerDelegate`. The `playbackViewControllerDidFinish:` method is called to inform the `RootViewController` that the user has finished playing back saved audio recordings and touched the red record **Button**.

Building the PlaybackViewController's View

Open the file `PlaybackViewController.xib` in Interface Builder. Open the **View** object to edit its contents. Drag two **Toolbar**s from the **Library** window onto **View** and position one at the top and one at the bottom. Change the **Style** of both **Toolbar**s to **Black Opaque**. Drag a **Bar Button Item** onto the top toolbar, change its **Identifier** to `Play` and uncheck **Enabled**. Drag a **Slider** and a **Label** onto the top toolbar. Set the label's text to `0:00`, uncheck the **Enabled** checkbox in the **Inspector**, expand the **Slider** to fill the extra space and check the **Slider**'s **Continuous** checkbox. Drag another **Slider** onto the bottom **Toolbar**. Set the **Slider**'s **Min Image** to `low_volume.png` and **High Image** to `high_volume.png`. Drag a **Bar Button Item** onto the bottom **Toolbar** and name it `Record`. Expand the bottom **Slider** to fill any empty space. Finally, drag a **Table View** onto **View** and expand it to fill all the space between the top and bottom **Toolbar**s. Figure 14.21 shows the finished GUI.

Fig. 14.21 | Completed `PlaybackViewController` GUI.

Connect the playButton outlet of **File's Owner** to the **Button** on the left side of the top **Toolbar**. Connect progressSlider to the top **Slider** and timeLabel to the **Label** on the right side. Connect toolbar to the top **Toolbar** and table to the **Table View** in the middle. Connect volumeSlider to the bottom **Slider**.

Next, connect the selector action of the left **Bar Button Item** in the top **Toolbar** to the togglePlay: method of **File's Owner**. Connect the **Value Changed** event of the top **Slider** to the sliderMoved: method and the **Value Changed** event of the bottom **Slider** to the updateVolume: method. Finally, connect the **selector** action of the red record **Bar Button Item** to the record: method.

Method *viewDidLoad* of Class *PlaybackViewController*

PlaybackViewController's viewDidLoad method (Fig. 14.22) begins by initializing the files NSMutableArray. Lines 22–23 use the NSSearchPathForDirectoriesInDomains function to get an array of one element, which is the directory path for this app's data. Line 24 stores that directory in the dir NSString variable.

```
 1   // Fig. 14.22: PlaybackViewController.m
 2   // Implementation for PlaybackViewController.
 3   #import <AVFoundation/AVFoundation.h>
 4   #import "PlaybackViewController.h"
 5
 6   @implementation PlaybackViewController
 7
 8   @synthesize delegate; // generate get and set methods for the delegate
 9   @synthesize table; // generate get and set methods for table
10   @synthesize toolbar; // generate get and set methods for toolbar
11   @synthesize progressSlider; // generate get and set methods for the slider
12   @synthesize volumeSlider; // generate get and set methods for the slider
13   @synthesize timeLabel; // generate get and set methods for timeLabel
14   @synthesize playButton; // generate get and set methods for playButton
15
16   // setup the view
17   - (void)viewDidLoad
18   {
19       files = [[NSMutableArray alloc] init]; // initialize files
20
21       // find the directory that the recordings are saved in
22       NSArray *paths = NSSearchPathForDirectoriesInDomains(
23           NSDocumentDirectory, NSUserDomainMask, YES);
24       NSString *dir = [paths objectAtIndex:0];
25
26       // get the default file manager
27       NSFileManager *filemanager = [NSFileManager defaultManager];
28
29       // get a list of all the files in the directory
30       NSArray *filelist = [filemanager directoryContentsAtPath:dir];
31
32       // iterate through each file in the directory
33       for (NSString *file in filelist)
34       {
```

Fig. 14.22 | Implementation for PlaybackViewController. (Part 1 of 2.)

```
35        // if the file's extension is "caf"
36        if ([[file pathExtension] isEqualToString:@"caf"])
37            // add the path to files
38            [files addObject:[dir stringByAppendingPathComponent:file]];
39    } // end for
40
41    [table reloadData]; // refresh the table
42    } // end method viewDidLoad
43
```

Fig. 14.22 | Implementation for `PlaybackViewController`. (Part 2 of 2.)

NSFileManager's static `defaultManager` method returns an instance of the default NSFileManager (line 27). Line 30 stores a list of all files in the app's data directory by calling the new fileManager's ***directoryContentsAtPath: method***. Lines 33–39 loop though each file, using NSString's ***pathExtension method*** to get each file's extension then check if the extension matches caf (line 36). Line 38 uses NSString's stringByAppendingPathComponent: method to append each file name to the app's data directory, then adds the .caf file's complete path to the files array. Line 41 calls table's reloadData method to refresh the UITableView and display the newly added file names.

Methods *sliderMoved:*, *togglePlay:* and *updateVolume:* of Class *PlaybackViewController*

The sliderMoved: method (Fig. 14.23, lines 45–51) changes the current playback location when the user adjusts the **Slider** at the top of the app. If the player is currently playing a recording (line 48), we set player's currentTime property to progressSlider's value.

The togglePlay: method (lines 54–61) is called when the user touches the **Button** next to the progress **Slider** that alternates between play and pause. If the player is already playing (line 57), line 58 calls the stopSound method to end the playback. Otherwise, if player exists (line 59), line 60 calls the playSound method to play the recording.

Method updateVolume: (lines 64–67) sets player's volume property to volumeSlider's value, which allows the user to adjust the playback's volume by moving the **Slider**'s thumb.

```
44    // called when the user moves the playback slider
45    - (IBAction)sliderMoved:sender
46    {
47        // if the player is currently playing a recording
48        if (player != nil)
49            // update the player's playback time
50            player.currentTime = progressSlider.value;
51    } // end method sliderMoved:
52
53    // called when the user touches the play/pause button
54    - (IBAction)togglePlay:sender
55    {
```

Fig. 14.23 | Methods sliderMoved:, togglePlay and updateVolume: of class PlaybackViewController. (Part 1 of 2.)

```
56      // if the player is playing a recording
57      if (player.playing)
58         [self stopSound]; // stop playback
59      else if (player != nil) // if the player has been created
60         [self playSound]; // play the player's sound
61   } // end method togglePlay:
62
63   // called when the user moved the volume slider
64   - (IBAction)updateVolume:sender
65   {
66      player.volume = volumeSlider.value; // update player's volume
67   } // end method updateVolume:
68
```

Fig. 14.23 | Methods sliderMoved:, togglePlay and updateVolume: of class PlaybackViewController. (Part 2 of 2.)

Methods timerFired: and record: of Class PlaybackViewController

The timerFired: method (Fig. 14.24, lines 70–89) is called 10 times per second to update the progressSlider and timeLabel according to the current playback position. If the AVAudioPlayer is currently playing (line 73), we get the current playback's time by accessing player's *currentTime property*. Line 78 calls progressSlider's setValue:animated: method to move the **Slider**'s thumb to match player's currentTime. Lines 81–82 use NSString's stringWithFormat: method to update timeLabel to display the current time elapsed in the audio playback. If the player isn't playing (line 84), the playback must have reached its end. We call our stopSound method to perform any necessary cleanup, and we reset progressSlider to the beginning (line 87).

The record: method (lines 92–96) is called when the user touches the "**Record**" **Button** to the bottom-right corner of the app. Line 95 calls delegate's playbackViewControllerDidFinish: method to return the app to the recorder **View**.

```
69   // update progressSlider and timeLabel when the timer fires
70   - (void)timerFired:(NSTimer *)t
71   {
72      // if the player is playing
73      if (player.playing)
74      {
75         double time = player.currentTime; // get the current playback time
76
77         // update progressSlider with the time
78         [progressSlider setValue:time animated:NO];
79
80         // update timeLabel with the time in minutes:seconds
81         timeLabel.title = [NSString stringWithFormat:@"%i:%.02i",
82            (int)time / 60, (int)time % 60];
83      } // end if
84      else // if the player isn't playing
85      {
```

Fig. 14.24 | PlaybackViewController methods timerFired: and record:. (Part 1 of 2.)

```
86          [self stopSound]; // stop the playback
87          [progressSlider setValue:0 animated:YES]; // move slider to start
88       } // end else
89  } // end method timerFired:
90
91  // called when the user touches the "Record" Button
92  - (IBAction)record:sender
93  {
94      // inform the delegate that the user is done playing recordings
95      [delegate playbackViewControllerDidFinish:self];
96  } // end method record:
97
```

Fig. 14.24 | PlaybackViewController methods timerFired: and record:. (Part 2 of 2.)

Method playSound of Class PlaybackViewController

PlaybackViewController's playSound method (Fig. 14.25) plays a saved audio recording. Lines 102–103 set the audio session to AVAudioSessionCategoryPlayback using AVAudioSession's setCategory: method. We then play the AVAudioPlayer (line 104). Lines 107–108 initialize the timer to generate an event every .1 second which calls the timerFired: method. Lines 111–113 create a new UIBarButtonItem that calls the togglePlay: method when touched. This **Button** pauses the playback.

```
 98  // plays the current recording
 99  - (void)playSound
100  {
101      // set the audio session's category to playback
102      [[AVAudioSession sharedInstance] setCategory:
103          AVAudioSessionCategoryPlayback error:nil];
104      [player play]; // play the audio player
105
106      // initialize the timer
107      timer = [NSTimer scheduledTimerWithTimeInterval:0.1 target:self
108          selector:@selector(timerFired:) userInfo:nil repeats:YES];
109
110      // create a pause button
111      UIBarButtonItem *pauseButton = [[UIBarButtonItem alloc]
112          initWithBarButtonSystemItem:UIBarButtonSystemItemPause target:self
113          action:@selector(togglePlay:)];
114
115      // get the items in the toolbar
116      NSMutableArray *items = [toolbar.items mutableCopy];
117
118      // replace the play button with the pause button
119      [items removeObjectAtIndex:0]; // remove the play button
120      [items insertObject:pauseButton atIndex:0]; // add the pause button
121      [pauseButton release]; // release the pauseButton UIBarButtonItem
122      [toolbar setItems:items animated:NO]; // update toolbar's items
123  } // end method playSound
124
```

Fig. 14.25 | Method playSound of class PlaybackViewController.

We must alter toolbar's items property to add the pauseButton to the **Toolbar**. We can't alter items directly, so we use the mutableCopy method to store an NSMutableArray copy of items (line 116). Line 119 calls NSMutableArray's removeObjectAtIndex: method to remove the playButton from the copy of items. We then insert the pause-Button at the same index using NSMutableArray's insertObject:atIndex: method (line 120). We then call UIToolbar's setItems:animated: method to replace items with our altered copy which includes the pauseButton.

Methods stopSound, numberOfSectionsInTableView: and tableView:number-OfRowsInSection: of Class PlaybackViewController

The stopSound method (Fig. 14.26, lines 126–143) ends the playback of the current audio recording. Lines 128–129 stop the timer and set it to nil. Line 130 stops player from playing the recording by calling AVAudioPlayer's pause method. Lines 133–134 return the app's audio session to the default AVAudioSessionCategorySoloAmbient. We then store a copy of the items in toolbar using NSMutableArrays's mutableCopy method. Lines 140–141 remove the pauseButton from the copy of items and replace it with the play-Button. We then set toolbar's items property to the altered copy. Method tableView:numberOfRowsInSection: (lines 152–156) returns the value of files.count because our UITableView has one row for each saved audio recording file.

```
125  // stops the playback of current recording
126  - (void)stopSound
127  {
128      [timer invalidate]; // stop and release the timer
129      timer = nil; // assign the timer to nil
130      [player pause]; // pause the audio player
131
132      // set the audio session's category to ambient
133      [[AVAudioSession sharedInstance] setCategory:
134         AVAudioSessionCategorySoloAmbient error:nil];
135
136      // get the items in the toolbar
137      NSMutableArray *items = [toolbar.items mutableCopy];
138
139      // replace the pause button with the play button
140      [items removeObjectAtIndex:0]; // remove the pause button
141      [items insertObject:playButton atIndex:0]; // add the play button
142      [toolbar setItems:items animated:NO]; // update the toolbar's items
143  } // end method stopSound
144
145  // called by the table view to determine its number of sections
146  - (NSInteger)numberOfSectionsInTableView:(UITableView *)tableView
147  {
148      return 1; // this table has only one section
149  } // end method numberOfSectionsInTableView:
150
```

Fig. 14.26 | Methods stopSound, numberOfSectionsInTableView: and tableView:numberOfRowsInSection: of class PlaybackViewController. (Part 1 of 2.)

```
151  // called by the table view to determine the number of rows in a section
152  - (NSInteger)tableView:(UITableView *)tableView numberOfRowsInSection:
153  (NSInteger)section
154  {
155      return files.count; // return the number of files
156  } // end method tableView:numberOfRowsInSection:
157
```

Fig. 14.26 | Methods stopSound, numberOfSectionsInTableView: and tableView:numberOfRowsInSection: of class PlaybackViewController. (Part 2 of 2.)

Method tableView:cellForRowAtIndexPath: of Class PlaybackViewController

Method tableView:cellForRowAtIndexPath: (Fig. 14.27) returns a cell in a UITableView specified by an NSIndexPath. Line 162 creates a new NSString that identifies the type of UITableViewCell in our table. Lines 160–161 call UITableViewCell's dequeueReusableCellWithIdentifier: to request a currently unused cell of that type. If there are no unused cells available (line 169), lines 171–172 create a new UITableViewCell.

```
158  // called by the table view to get a cell for the given index path
159  - (UITableViewCell *)tableView:(UITableView *)tableView
160      cellForRowAtIndexPath:(NSIndexPath *)indexPath
161  {
162      static NSString *ID = @"Cell"; // create a cell identifier
163
164      // get a reused cell using the identifier
165      UITableViewCell *cell =
166          [tableView dequeueReusableCellWithIdentifier:ID];
167
168      // if there were no cells available for reuse
169      if (cell == nil)
170          // create a new cell
171          cell = [[[UITableViewCell alloc] initWithStyle:
172              UITableViewCellStyleDefault reuseIdentifier:ID] autorelease];
173
174      // get the file name for this cell
175      NSString *text =
176          [[files objectAtIndex:indexPath.row] lastPathComponent];
177
178      // delete the .caf from the path
179      cell.textLabel.text = [text stringByDeletingPathExtension];
180
181      // load the e-mail icon
182      UIImage *mailImage = [UIImage imageNamed:@"envelope.png"];
183
184      // create a new button
185      UIButton *mailButton =
186          [[UIButton alloc] initWithFrame:CGRectMake(0, 0, 32, 32)];
187
```

Fig. 14.27 | Method tableView:cellForRowAtIndexPath: of class PlaybackViewController. (Part 1 of 2.)

```
188    // use the email icon for the button
189    [mailButton setImage:mailImage forState:UIControlStateNormal];
190    mailButton.tag = indexPath.row; // tag the button with the current row
191
192    // make the button call the mailButtonTouched: method when touched
193    [mailButton addTarget:self action:@selector(mailButtonTouched:)
194        forControlEvents:UIControlEventTouchUpInside];
195
196    // make the button the accessory view of the cell
197    cell.accessoryView = mailButton;
198    return cell; // return the configured cell
199 } // end method tableView:cellForRowAtIndexPath:
200
```

Fig. 14.27 | Method `tableView:cellForRowAtIndexPath:` of class `PlaybackViewController`. (Part 2 of 2.)

Lines 175–176 get the file name of the recording specified by the `indexPath` using `NSMutableArray`'s `objectAtIndex:` method. `NString`'s `lastPathComponent` method is used to remove the file name from the full path that is returned. Line 179 removes the `.caf` extension from the file name using `NSString`'s `stringByDeletingPathExtension` method. We then create a new **Button** with the e-mail icon (lines 185–186) and make it this cell's *accessoryView* (line 197)—a view that's displayed at the right side of the cell's contents. We use the **tag** *property* of `UIView` to store the row in which the **Button** is being added (line 190). This property helps identify the view. We retrieve this value in the `mail-ButtonTouched:` method to identify the row in which the touched **Button** resides, so we know which audio recording to add to the e-mail.

Method `tableView:commitEditingStyle:forRowAtIndexPath:` of Class PlaybackViewController

The `tableView:commitEditingStyle:forRowAtIndexPath:` method (Fig. 14.28) of the `UITableViewDataSource` protocol is called when the user edits a cell in our `UITableView`. Line 207 checks whether the user deleted a cell, which is the only type of editing our `UITableView` is configured to allow. Line 210 gets the default `NSFileManager` and line 213 gets the file name from `files` specified by the given `indexPath`.

```
201  // called when the user edits the table view
202  - (void)tableView:(UITableView *)tableView commitEditingStyle:
203      (UITableViewCellEditingStyle)editingStyle forRowAtIndexPath:
204      (NSIndexPath *)indexPath
205  {
206      // if the user deleted the element
207      if (editingStyle == UITableViewCellEditingStyleDelete)
208      {
209          // get the default file manager
210          NSFileManager *fileManager = [NSFileManager defaultManager];
```

Fig. 14.28 | Method `tableView:commitEditingStyle:forRowAtIndexPath:` of class `PlaybackViewController`. (Part 1 of 2.)

```
211
212        // get the path for the deleted recording
213        NSString *path = [files objectAtIndex:indexPath.row];
214
215        // if the recording being deleted is also being played
216        if ([[player.url path] isEqualToString:path])
217        {
218            [self stopSound]; // stop the playback
219            [player release]; // release the player AVAudioPlayer
220            player = nil; // set player to nil
221        } // end if
222
223        [fileManager removeItemAtPath:path error:nil]; // delete recording
224
225        // remove the entry from files
226        [files removeObjectAtIndex:indexPath.row];
227
228        // remove the row from the table
229        [tableView deleteRowsAtIndexPaths:[NSArray arrayWithObject:
230            indexPath] withRowAnimation:UITableViewRowAnimationRight];
231    } // end if
232 } // end method tableView:commitEditingStyle:forRowAtIndexPath:
233
```

Fig. 14.28 | Method `tableView:commitEditingStyle:forRowAtIndexPath:` of class `PlaybackViewController`. (Part 2 of 2.)

Before deleting the file, we first check if the file is currently playing (line 216). If it is, we stop the playback and release `player` so that the sound file can be deleted. `NSFileManager`'s `removeItemAtPath` method deletes the audio recording from the app. Line 226 removes the corresponding file name from the `files` `NSMutableArray`. We then call `UITableView`'s `deleteRowsAtIndexPaths:withRowAnimation:` to remove the deleted entry from `tableView`. Passing `UITableViewRowAnimationRight` specifies that the deleted row will slide out to the right before being removed from the screen.

Method `tableView:didSelectRowAtIndexPath:` of Class `PlaybackViewController`
Method `tableView:didSelectRowAtIndexPath:` (Fig. 14.29) of the `UITableViewDelegate` protocol is called when the user touches any of the `tableView`'s rows. Line 239 retrieves the file path at the given `indexPath`. We then use `NSURL`'s static `URLWithString:` method to create a new `NSURL` using the file path.

```
234 // called when the user touches a row of the table view
235 - (void)tableView:(UITableView *)tableView didSelectRowAtIndexPath:
236     (NSIndexPath *)indexPath
237 {
```

Fig. 14.29 | Method `tableView:didSelectRowAtIndexPath:` of class `PlaybackViewController`. (Part 1 of 2.)

```
238      // get the file name for the touches row
239      NSString *file = [files objectAtIndex:indexPath.row];
240
241      // create a URL with the file's path
242      NSURL *url = [NSURL URLWithString:file];
243      [player release]; // release the player AVAudioPlayer
244
245      // create a new AVAudioPlayer with the URL
246      player = [[AVAudioPlayer alloc] initWithContentsOfURL:url error:nil];
247      player.volume = volumeSlider.value; // set player's volume
248
249      // set the maximum value of the slider to reflect the recording length
250      progressSlider.maximumValue = player.duration;
251      [self playSound]; // play the selected recording
252      playButton.enabled = YES; // enable the play/pause button
253  } // end method tableView:didSelectRowAtIndexPath:
254
```

Fig. 14.29 | Method `tableView:didSelectRowAtIndexPath:` of class `PlaybackViewController`. (Part 2 of 2.)

Line 243 releases the old `player` and line 246 reinitializes `player` as a new AVAudio-Player using the selected file path. We set `player`'s `volume` property equal to the position of the volume **Slider**'s thumb (line 247). Line 250 sets `progressSlider`'s `maximumValue` to `player`'s `duration`, so that the position of the **Slider**'s thumb always corresponds to the current location in the playback. Lines 251–252 call our `playSound` method to play the newly created recording and enable the `playButton`, respectively.

Methods `mailButtonTouched:` and `mailComposeController:didFinishWith-Result:error:` of Class `PlaybackViewController`
Method `mailButtonTouched` (Fig. 14.30, lines 256–277) displays an e-mail dialog when the user touches the **Button** next to a file's name. Line 259 retrieves the file path that corresponds to the touched **Button**. When we added the **Button** to the `UITableViewCell`, we set its `tag` property to be its row in the table, so here we can retrieve the **Button**'s tag and use it to identify the row. We then create an `NSData` object containing the contents of the selected audio file using `NSData`'s static ***dataWithContentsOfFile: method. NSData*** objects represent stored data (byte buffers).

```
255  // called when the user touches the mail button on a cell
256  - (void)mailButtonTouched:sender
257  {
258      // get the file for the touched row
259      NSString *file = [files objectAtIndex:[sender tag]];
260
261      // create an NSData object with the selected recording
262      NSData *data = [NSData dataWithContentsOfFile:file];
```

Fig. 14.30 | Methods `tableView:accessoryButtonTappedForRowWithIndexPath:` and `mailComposeController:didFinishWithResult:error:` of class `PlaybackViewController`. (Part 1 of 2.)

```
263
264     // create an MFMailComposeViewController for sending an e-mail
265     MFMailComposeViewController *controller =
266        [[MFMailComposeViewController alloc] init];
267
268     // add the recording as an attachment
269     [controller addAttachmentData:data mimeType:@"audio/mp4" fileName:
270        [file lastPathComponent]];
271
272     // set controller's delegate to this object
273     controller.mailComposeDelegate = self;
274
275     // show the MFMailComposeViewController
276     [self presentModalViewController:controller animated:YES];
277  } // end method tableView:accessoryButtonTappedForRowWithIndexPath:
278
279  // called when the user finishes sending an e-mail
280  - (void)mailComposeController:(MFMailComposeViewController*)controller
281     didFinishWithResult:(MFMailComposeResult)result error:(NSError*)error
282  {
283     // make the MFMailComposeViewController disappear
284     [self dismissModalViewControllerAnimated:YES];
285  } // end method mailComposeController:didFinishWithResult:error:
286
287  // release this object's memory
288  - (void)dealloc
289  {
290     [player release]; // release the player AVAudioPlayer
291     [files release]; // release the files NSMutableArray
292     [super dealloc]; // call the superclass's dealloc method
293  } // end method dealloc
294  @end // end implementation of PlaybackViewController
```

Fig. 14.30 | Methods `tableView:accessoryButtonTappedForRowWithIndexPath:` and `mailComposeController:didFinishWithResult:error:` of class `PlaybackViewController`. (Part 2 of 2.)

Lines 265–266 create a new *MFMailComposeViewController* which controls an e-mail dialog **View**, allowing the user to send e-mail without leaving the app. MFMail-ComposeViewController's *addAttachmentData:mimeType:fileName:* method adds the selected audio file (the NSData object created in line 262) as an e-mail attachment. We get the file's name using NSString's lastPathComponent method and pass that as the file-Name argument. Line 273 sets controller's *mailComposeDelegate* to self so that this PlaybackViewController will receive a *mailComposeController:didFinishWithResult:error:* message (from the protocol *MFMailComposeViewControllerDelegate* protocol) when the user finishes with the e-mail dialog. Line 276 calls UIViewController's presentModalViewController:animated: method to display the e-mail dialog.

The mailComposeController:didFinishWithResult:error: method is called when the user finishes with the e-mail dialog box, either by sending an e-mail or by touching **Cancel**. Line 284 hides the MFMailComposeViewController by calling UIViewController's dismissModalViewControllerAnimated: method.

14.5 Speech Synthesis and Recognition

The iPhone 3.x APIs are divided into two sections—public and private. Public APIs are documented on Apple's website and are free for any developer to use. Private APIs are not documented, and Apple will not approve any app that uses them. The iPhone currently supports both speech recognition and speech synthesis, but the APIs used to access them are private. There are currently no public APIs for speech recognition, and speech synthesis is available only through the UI Accessibility framework. This framework allows visually impaired users to hear descriptions of screen components, but does not allow you to access the iPhone speech synthesis capabilities programmatically. Apple may make these APIs public in the future.

14.6 Wrap-Up

The **Voice Recorder** app used the AV Foundation framework and an AVAudioRecorder to record sounds using the iPhone's microphone, then save them for playback later. The AVAudioSessionCategoryRecord audio session silenced any playback while we were recording. When playing back recordings we used the AVAudioSessionCategoryPlayback audio session to set the iPhone's ringer to silent and to continue playback while the iPhone is locked. The flipside of the app contained a UITableView displaying the name of each saved audio recording. AVAudioPlayers were used to play the files.

The NSPredicate class and a regular expression were used to verify that the user entered a valid file name for each saved recording—disallowing invalid characters such as spaces and punctuation. We also converted saved audio files to NSData objects that could be attached to e-mails. We used the MFMailComposeViewController to open an e-mail dialog allowing the user to send e-mail from the app.

15

Enhanced Address Book App
Managing and Transferring Persistent Data

OBJECTIVES

In this chapter you'll learn:

- To use the Core Data framework to separate our data model from the rest of the app according to the Model-View-Controller design pattern.

- To visually design our data model using the data model editor.

- To use an NSManagedObject to programmatically interact with the Core Data model.

- To use an NSFetchedResultsController to coordinate between the app's data and its UITableViews.

- To use the Game Kit framework and the GKSession class to transfer data between two devices using Bluetooth.

- To allow the user to choose from nearby peers using a GKPeerPickerController.

Outline

15.1 Introduction

15.2 Test-Driving the Enhanced Address Book App

15.3 Technologies Overview

15.4 Building the App

    15.4.1 Building the Core Data Model

    15.4.2 Class `ContactViewController`

    15.4.3 Class `RootViewController`

15.5 Wrap-Up

15.1 Introduction

The **Enhanced Address Book** app is an enhanced version of the **Address Book** app created in Chapter 10. This version allows the user to transfer contacts between iPhones using Bluetooth technology. [*Note:* The Bluetooth capabilities do not work in the iPhone Simulator.] When viewing a single contact (Fig. 15.1), touching the **Button** in the top-right corner of the app searches for nearby iPhones and iPod Touches that are running the **Enhanced Address Book** app (Fig. 15.2 (a)). The app shows a list of all nearby devices (Fig. 15.2 (b)). The user touches the device's name to send the contact, then the receiving device receives a **Connection Request** alert (Fig. 15.3). Touching **Accept** transfers the contact and adds it to that device's **Enhanced Address Book**.

Transfer contact's information to another iPhone

Fig. 15.1 | Viewing a contact.

Fig. 15.2 | Requesting a connection.

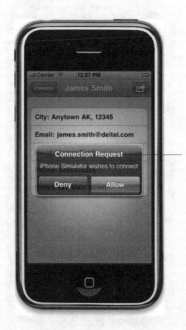

Fig. 15.3 | Getting a Bluetooth **Connection Request**.

15.2 Test-Driving the Enhanced Address Book App

Opening the Completed App

Open the directory containing the **Enhanced Address Book** app project and double click
EnhancedAddressBook.xcodeproj to open the project in Xcode. To test the Bluetooth ca-
pabilities of this app you'll need to run the app simultaneously on at least two iPhones (or
Bluetooth-enabled iPod Touches). The iPhone Simulator does not support Bluetooth.

Sending a Contact

Run the **Enhanced Address Book** app on two iPhones in close proximity. Create a new
contact on one of the iPhones then touch the new contact's name to view it in more detail.
Touch the ⬀ **Button** in the top-right corner of the app to search for nearby iPhones.
When the list of nearby devices appears, touch the name of the other iPhone and wait for
a **Connection Request** alert to appear on the receiving iPhone. Touch **Accept** on the receiving iPhone and the transferred contact appears in both iPhone's list of contacts.

15.3 Technologies Overview

The *Core Data framework* allows us to graphically define our app's data model in a manner similar to building GUIs in Interface Builder. The framework allows apps to follow
the Model-View-Controller design pattern by completely separating the data model from
the controller. A Core Data data model is known as a *managed object model* and is created
visually. The managed object model defines model objects (also known as *entities*) and
their relationships. The **Enhanced Address Book** has a simple managed object model con-
sisting of only the Person entity for storing a contact's information. Each entity typically
has several *attributes*. For example, our Person entity contains name, address and phone
number attributes. The interface between the managed object model and our code is the
Managed Object Context, which is represented by class *NSManagedObjectContext*. We use
an object of this class to add, retrieve and update information in the data model.

Entities are represented by class *NSEntityDescription*. To create a new object representing a data object you must use class *NSManagedObject*. In this app, an individual contact's data is represented by an NSManagedObject received from the NSEntityDescription
representing the Person entity. You manipulate this object in Objective-C code then
insert it back into the data model.

Information is retrieved using *fetch requests* (represented by class *NSFetchRequest*).
This works similarly to querying databases, in that you specify the exact kind of data that's
returned. For example, in the **Enhanced Address Book** app we could construct a fetch
request asking for all people from the state of Alaska, or all people whose first name begins
with the letter M. We use a *FetchedRequestController* to update both the Core Data
stored information and our UITableView displaying the contact information. We use one
instance of class *NSFetchRequest* which is shared in the RootViewController.

The *Game Kit framework* allows multiple iPhones to interact via Bluetooth. [*Note:*
App users might need to enable Bluetooth on their devices.] We use the *GKPeerPickerCon-
troller* class to create a view displaying nearby iPhones running the **Enhanced Address
Book** app. We specify whether or not the iPhone is receiving or transmitting data using a
GKSession. An NSKeyedArchiver is used to serialize the NSMutableArray representing a
contact's information to an NSData object that we can transmit between iPhones using
GKSession's sendDataToAllPeers:withDataMode: method.

15.4 Building the App

Create a new project named `EnhancedAddressBook.xcodeproj` using the **Navigation-based Application** template. Make sure the **Use Core Data for storage** checkbox is checked when you choose the template so that you can use Core Data functionality in the app.

15.4.1 Building the Core Data Model

The Core Data data model is stored in `EnhancedAddressBook.xcdatamodel`, under the **Resources** group in Xcode's **Groups and Files** window. Double-click this file to open it in the *data model editor* (Fig. 15.4). Click the `Event` entity class. In the top-right corner of the screen, rename the entity `Person`. Select the `timeStamp` attribute, rename it to `Name` in the top-right corner of the screen and change its type to `String`. Click the plus button in the center of the screen to add a new attribute. Name the new attribute `Email`. Add three more attributes named `City`, `Phone` and `Street` then close the data model editor. Figure 15.4 shows the completed data model.

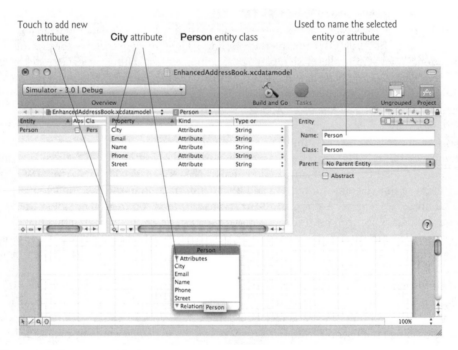

Touch to add new attribute   **City** attribute   **Person** entity class   Used to name the selected entity or attribute

Fig. 15.4 | Data model editor.

15.4.2 Class `ContactViewController`

Class `ContactViewController` (Fig. 15.5) is a subclass of `UIViewController` which implements the `UITableViewDataSource` protocol (lines 7–8). `ContactViewController` also implements the *GKSessionDelegate protocol* (line 8) so that it can receive messages when a visible peer device changes its state. This class also implements the *GKPeerPickerControllerDelegate protocol* (line 8) so that it can respond to messages from a *GKPeerPickerController*, which provides a standard user interface for connecting to other iPhones.

```
 1   // ContactViewController.h
 2   // Controller that displays the contact information for a created contact.
 3   // Implementation in ContactViewController.m
 4   #import <UIKit/UIKit.h>
 5   #import <GameKit/GameKit.h>
 6
 7   @interface ContactViewController : UIViewController
 8   <UITableViewDataSource, GKSessionDelegate, GKPeerPickerControllerDelegate>
 9   {
10      NSManagedObject *person; // the person we're loading information from
11   } // end instance variable declaration
12
13   @property(retain) NSManagedObject* person; // declare person as a property
14
15   - (void)updateTitle; // updates the navigation item's title from person
16   @end // end interface ContactViewController
```

Fig. 15.5 | Controller that displays the contact information for a created contact.

ContactViewController has an ***NSManagedObject*** instance variable representing the Core Data object for the selected contact (line 10). Line 13 declares the NSManagedObject as a property. The updateTitle method (line 15) updates the navigation bar's title to display the contact's name.

Methods *viewDidLoad* and *send of Class* ContactViewController
The viewDidLoad method (Fig. 15.6, lines 10–17) sets up ContactViewController's view. Lines 13–15 create a new UIBarButtonItem that, when touched, calls the send method to allow the user to send a contact to another iPhone. We pass UIBarButtonSystemItemAction enum constant as the BarButtonSystemItem parameter to get a system item action **Button** ( ). Line 16 calls UINavigationItem's setRightBarButtonItem: method to add the **Button** to the right side of the navigation bar.

The send method (lines 20–28) is called when the user touches the UIBarButtonItem in the top-right corner of the app. Lines 23–24 create a new GKPeerPickerController to display all nearby iPhones. We set peerPicker's delegate to self (line 25) so this ContactViewController will receive a message when the user chooses a peer. Line 26 sets peerPicker's ***connectionTypesMask*** *property* to ***GKPeerPickerConnectionTypeNearby***, which indicates that we'd like to see a list of the devices that are reachable via a Bluetooth connection. Line 27 calls peerPicker's ***show*** *method* to displays the peerPicker's view.

```
 1   // ContactViewController.m
 2   // Implementation of ContactViewController.
 3   #import "ContactViewController.h"
 4
 5   @implementation ContactViewController
 6
 7   @synthesize person; // generate get and set methods for person
 8
```

Fig. 15.6 | Methods viewDidLoad and send of class ContactViewController. (Part 1 of 2.)

```
 9    // setup the view once it's loaded
10    - (void)viewDidLoad
11    {
12       // create the button for sending a contact
13       UIBarButtonItem *sendButton = [[UIBarButtonItem alloc]
14          initWithBarButtonSystemItem:UIBarButtonSystemItemAction target:self
15          action:@selector(send)];
16       [self.navigationItem setRightBarButtonItem:sendButton];
17    } // end method viewDidLoad
18
19    // displays a list of other iPhones to send this contact to
20    - (void)send
21    {
22       // create a new GKPeerPickerController for connecting to a peer
23       GKPeerPickerController *peerPicker =
24          [[GKPeerPickerController alloc] init];
25       peerPicker.delegate = self; // set the delegate to this object
26       peerPicker.connectionTypesMask = GKPeerPickerConnectionTypeNearby;
27       [peerPicker show]; // show the peer picker
28    } // end method send
29
```

Fig. 15.6 | Methods viewDidLoad and send of class ContactViewController. (Part 2 of 2.)

Method *peerPickerController:didConnectPeer:toSession:* of Class ContactViewController

The ***peerPickerController:didConnectPeer:toSession:*** *method* (Fig. 15.7) of the GK-PeerPickerControllerDelegate protocol is called when the user chooses a peer device to which contact information should be sent. Line 35 retrieves an NSDictionary containing the selected contact's information. NSManagedObject's ***entity*** *method* gets an NSEntity-Description representing the Person entity. NSEntityDescription's ***propertiesByName*** *method* returns an NSDictionary containing the names of the entity's properties as keys and NSAttributeDescriptions as the values. We initialize a new NSMutableDictionary to store the information that will be sent to the peer device. Next, we iterate through the keys in personDictionary and use those keys to retrieve the corresponding values from the person object. We add these keys and values to the NSMutableDictionary. Line 47 serializes the dictionary to an NSData object using NSKeyedArchiver's archivedDataWith-RootObject: method. We then call the given GKSession's ***sendDataToAllPeers:with-DataMode:*** *method* to send the serialized contact information to the connected devices. The GKSendReliable argument specifies that the data will be continuously sent until it all arrives successfully or the connection times out.

```
30    // called when the user chooses a peer to send this contact to
31    - (void)peerPickerController:(GKPeerPickerController *)picker
32       didConnectPeer:(NSString *)peerID toSession:(GKSession *)session
33    {
```

Fig. 15.7 | Method peerPickerController:didConnectPeer:toSession: of class ContactViewController. (Part 1 of 2.)

```
34       // get the property names from person
35       NSDictionary *personDictionary = [[person entity] propertiesByName];
36
37       // create a new NSMutableDictionary to store the data
38       NSMutableDictionary *dictionary = [[NSMutableDictionary alloc] init];
39
40       // iterate through each property name in person
41       for (NSString *key in [personDictionary allKeys])
42
43          // add the property and its value in person to the dictionary
44          [dictionary setValue:[person valueForKey:key] forKey:key];
45
46       // archive dictionary
47       NSData *data = [NSKeyedArchiver archivedDataWithRootObject:dictionary];
48
49       // send the data to all connected peers
50       [session sendDataToAllPeers:data withDataMode:GKSendDataReliable
51          error:nil];
52       [picker dismiss]; // dismiss the peer picker
53       [picker release]; // release the picker GKPeerPickerController
54    } // end method peerPickerController:didConnectPeer:toSession:
55
```

Fig. 15.7 | Method peerPickerController:didConnectPeer:toSession: of class ContactViewController. (Part 2 of 2.)

Methods peerPickerControllerDidCancel:, updateTitle and tableView:numberOfRowsInSection: of Class ContactViewController

The *peerPickerControllerDidCancel: method* (Fig. 15.8, lines 57–61) of the GKPeer-PickerControllerDelegate protocol calls the GKPeerPickerController's dismiss method to hide its view when the user touches the "**Cancel**" **Button**. The updateTitle method (lines 64–68) sets the navigation bar's title to the contact's name using UINavigationItem's setTitle: method.

```
56    // called when the user touches the cancel button of the peer picker
57    - (void)peerPickerControllerDidCancel:(GKPeerPickerController *)picker
58    {
59       [picker dismiss]; // dismiss the peer picker
60       [picker release]; // release the picker GKPeerPickerController
61    } // end method peerPickerControllerDidCancel:
62
63    // set the navigation item's title depending on person
64    - (void)updateTitle
65    {
66       // set the title to the contact's name
67       [self.navigationItem setTitle:[person valueForKey:@"Name"]];
68    } // end method updateTitle
69
```

Fig. 15.8 | Methods peerPickerControllerDidCancel:, updateTitle and tableView:numberOfRowsInSection: of class ContactViewController. (Part 1 of 2.)

```
70   // called by the table view to find the number of rows in a given section
71   - (NSInteger)tableView:(UITableView *)tableView numberOfRowsInSection:
72     (NSInteger)section
73   {
74     return [[person entity] properties].count; // return number of fields
75   } // end method tableView:numberOfRowsInSection:
76
```

Fig. 15.8 | Methods peerPickerControllerDidCancel:, updateTitle and tableView:numberOfRowsInSection: of class ContactViewController. (Part 2 of 2.)

Method tableView:numberOfRowsInSection: (lines 71–75) returns the number of rows in ContactViewController's UITableView. We get an NSEntityDescription on which we call the ***properties** method* to obtain an NSArray containing all of the fields in the person data model (line 74). We then use the NSArray's count property to determine the number of rows in the UITableView.

Method tableView:cellForRowAtIndexPath: of Class ContactViewController

Method tableView:cellForRowAtIndexPath: (Fig. 15.9, lines 78–101) returns the UI-TableViewCell at the given NSIndexPath in the UITableView. Lines 81–90 attempt to re-use an existing cell from the UITableView. We retrieve person's NSEntityDescription then call its propertiesByName method to get an NSDictionary representing person's properties (line 93). Lines 93–94 use NSDictionary's allKeys method to obtain an NSArray of the dictionary's keys, then use the NSIndexPath's row property to get the selected key from the array. Line 95 gets the value for the selected key from the person object. Line 96 gets the UILabel of the selected UITableViewCell using its textLabel method. Lines 99–100 update the UITableViewCell's UILabel with the contact information then return the configured cell.

```
77   // called by the table view to get a cell for the given index path
78   - (UITableViewCell *)tableView:(UITableView *)tableView
79     cellForRowAtIndexPath:(NSIndexPath *)indexPath
80   {
81     static NSString *identifier = @"NormalCell";
82
83     // get a reused cell
84     UITableViewCell *cell =
85       [tableView dequeueReusableCellWithIdentifier:identifier];
86
87     // if there are no cells to be reused, create one
88     if (cell == nil)
89       cell = [[[UITableViewCell alloc] initWithFrame:CGRectZero
90         reuseIdentifier:identifier] autorelease];
91
92     // get the key at the appropriate index in the dictionary
93     NSString *key = [[[[person entity] propertiesByName] allKeys]
94       objectAtIndex:indexPath.row];
```

Fig. 15.9 | Method tableView:cellForRowAtIndexPath: of class ContactViewController. (Part 1 of 2.)

```
95      NSString *value = [person valueForKey:key]; // get the value
96      UILabel *label = [cell textLabel]; // get the label for the cell
97
98      // update the text of the label
99      label.text = [NSString stringWithFormat:@"%@: %@", key, value];
100     return cell; // return the configured cell
101 } // end method tableView:cellForRowAtIndexPath:
102
103 // determines what orientations the view supports
104 - (BOOL)shouldAutorotateToInterfaceOrientation:
105     (UIInterfaceOrientation)interfaceOrientation
106 {
107     // we only support the portrait orientation
108     return (interfaceOrientation == UIInterfaceOrientationPortrait);
109 } // end method shouldAutorotateToInterfaceOrientation:
110
111 // release this object's memory
112 - (void)dealloc
113 {
114     [person release]; // release the person NSManagedObject
115     [super dealloc]; // call the superclass's dealloc method
116 } // end method dealloc
117 @end // end implementation ContactViewController
```

Fig. 15.9 | Method `tableView:cellForRowAtIndexPath:` of class `ContactViewController`. (Part 2 of 2.)

15.4.3 Class RootViewController

Class `RootViewController` (Fig. 15.10) implements the ***NSFetchedResultsController-Delegate*** protocol (line 8) so that it can respond to messages from an ***NSFetchedResults-Controller***, which updates a `UITableView` with information fetched from Core Data objects. The class also implements the `GKSessionDelegate` protocol (line 8) so that it can receive messages when a visible peer device changes its state.

```
1  // RootViewController.h
2  // Controls the main View of the Enhanced Address Book app.
3  #import <GameKit/GameKit.h>
4  #import "AddViewController.h"
5
6  // begin RoorViewController interface
7  @interface RootViewController : UITableViewController
8      <NSFetchedResultsControllerDelegate, AddViewControllerDelegate,
9      GKSessionDelegate>
10 {
11     GKSession *serverSession; // session other devices can connect to
12     NSString *connectingPeerID; // the ID of the connecting peer
13
14     // provides the data for the UITableView
15     NSFetchedResultsController *fetchedResultsController;
16
```

Fig. 15.10 | Controls the main view of the **Enhanced Address Book** app. (Part 1 of 2.)

```
17      // the managed object context fetchedResultsController was created from
18      NSManagedObjectContext *managedObjectContext;
19  } // end instance variable declaration
20
21  // declare fetchedResultsController and managedObjectContext as properties
22  @property (nonatomic, retain) NSFetchedResultsController
23      *fetchedResultsController;
24  @property (nonatomic, retain) NSManagedObjectContext
25      *managedObjectContext;
26  @end // end interface RootViewController
```

Fig. 15.10 | Controls the main view of the **Enhanced Address Book** app. (Part 2 of 2.)

We declare a GKSession (line 11) to connect to other iPhones (peers) via Bluetooth. Line 12 declares an NSString used to identify the iPhone which is trying to send a contact. We use an NSFetchedResultsController (line 15) to populate RootViewController's UITableView with information from our Core Data model. Line 18 declares an **NSManaged-ObjectContext**, which enables the app to interact with the Core Data services. Lines 22–25 declare our NSFetchedResultsController and NSManagedObjectContext as properties.

Method viewDidLoad of Class RootViewController

The viewDidLoad method (Fig. 15.11) sets up RootViewController's view when it loads. Line 16 adds the "**Edit**" Button to the left-side of the navigation bar using UINavigation-Item's leftBarButtonItem property. We then create the ➕ **Button** and add it to the right-side of the navigation bar (lines 19–24). Line 28 creates an **NSError** pointer to an object representing error information. We pass this to our **NSFetchedResultsController's performFetch: method** (line 31). If this method fails to retrieve data from our Core Data model (line 31), we write to console detailing the error using the NSLog function (line 32). Lines 35–36 initialize a new GKSession, passing **GKSessionModeServer** as the sessionMode parameter. This type of GKSession informs nearby devices of this iPhone's peer ID and that it's ready to receive information. We set the GKSession's delegate to self then call its **setDataReceiveHandler:withContext: method** to specify that this RootViewController gets any data received during the GKSession (lines 37–40). Line 41 sets the GKSession's **available property** to YES to begin accepting connections.

```
1   // RootViewController.m
2   // RootViewController class implementation
3   #import "RootViewController.h"
4   #import "ContactViewController.h"
5
6   @implementation RootViewController
7
8   @synthesize fetchedResultsController, managedObjectContext;
9
10  // set up the View once it initializes
11  - (void)viewDidLoad
12  {
```

Fig. 15.11 | Method viewDidLoad of class RootViewController. (Part 1 of 2.)

```
13        [super viewDidLoad]; // call the superclass's viewDidLoad method
14
15        // set up the edit and add buttons
16        self.navigationItem.leftBarButtonItem = self.editButtonItem;
17
18        // create the plus button
19        UIBarButtonItem *addButton = [[UIBarButtonItem alloc]
20           initWithBarButtonSystemItem:UIBarButtonSystemItemAdd target:self
21           action:@selector(insertNewObject)];
22
23        // add the plus button to the navigation bar's right side
24        self.navigationItem.rightBarButtonItem = addButton;
25        [addButton release]; // release the addButton UIBarButtonItem
26
27
28        NSError *error; // create a new NSError
29
30        // if fetchedResultsController failed to retrieve data
31        if (![[self fetchedResultsController] performFetch:&error])
32           NSLog(@"Could not load data: %@", [error description]);
33
34        // initialize serverSession as a server
35        serverSession = [[GKSession alloc] initWithSessionID:nil
36           displayName:nil sessionMode:GKSessionModeServer];
37        serverSession.delegate = self; // set the delegate to this object
38
39        // this object will receive data from serverSession
40        [serverSession setDataReceiveHandler:self withContext:NULL];
41        serverSession.available = YES; // begin accepting connections
42     } // end method viewDidLoad
43
```

Fig. 15.11 | Method viewDidLoad of class RootViewController. (Part 2 of 2.)

Method session:didReceiveConnectionRequestFromPeer: of Class *RootViewController*

The ***session:didReceiveConnectionRequestFromPeer: method*** (Fig. 15.12) of the GK-SessionDelegate protocol is called when this app's GKSession receives a connection request from another device. Line 48 saves the NSString representing the connecting iPhone's peer ID. We get that iPhone's display name (as set by its owner) using GKSession's ***displayNameForPeer: method***. Lines 54–61 create a new UIAlertView informing the user which iPhone is requesting to connect and providing "**Allow**" and "**Deny**" **Buttons**.

```
44     // called when the GKSession receives a connection request
45     - (void)session:(GKSession *)session didReceiveConnectionRequestFromPeer:
46        (NSString *)peerID
47     {
48        connectingPeerID = peerID; // save peerID
49
```

Fig. 15.12 | Method session:didReceiveConnectionRequestFromPeer: of class RootViewController. (Part 1 of 2.)

```
50      // get the display name for the connecting peer
51      NSString *name = [session displayNameForPeer:connectingPeerID];
52
53      // display an alert prompting the user if the peer can connect
54      NSString *message =
55         [NSString stringWithFormat:@"%@ wishes to connect", name];
56
57      // create the UIAlertView
58      UIAlertView *connectionAlert = [[UIAlertView alloc] initWithTitle:
59         @"Connection Request" message:message delegate:self
60         cancelButtonTitle:@"Deny" otherButtonTitles:@"Allow", nil];
61      [connectionAlert show]; // show the alert
62   } // end method session:didRecieveConnectionRequestFromPeer:
63
```

Fig. 15.12 | Method session:didReceiveConnectionRequestFromPeer: of class RootViewController. (Part 2 of 2.)

Methods *alertView:clickedButtonAtIndex:* and *alertViewCancel:* of Class *RootViewController*

The alertView:clickedButtonAtIndex: method (Fig. 15.13, lines 65–70) is called when the user touches the "**Accept**" **Button** on the **Connection Request** UIAlertView. Line 69 calls GKSession's ***acceptConnectionFromPeer:error:*** *method* to accept the connection and receive contact information from the sending iPhone. The alertViewCancel: method (lines 73–77) calls GKSession's ***denyConnectionFromPeer:*** *method* to not connect to the requesting device (line 76).

```
64   // called when the user touches a button of the alert view
65   - (void)alertView:(UIAlertView *)alertView clickedButtonAtIndex:
66      (NSInteger)buttonIndex
67   {
68      // accept the connection request
69      [serverSession acceptConnectionFromPeer:connectingPeerID error:nil];
70   } // end method alertView:clickedButtonAtIndex:
71
72   // called when the user touches the cancel button of the alert view
73   - (void)alertViewCancel:(UIAlertView *)alertView
74   {
75      // deny the connection request
76      [serverSession denyConnectionFromPeer:connectingPeerID];
77   } // end method alertViewCancel:
78
```

Fig. 15.13 | Methods alertView:clickedButtonAtIndex: and alertViewCancel: of class RootViewController.

Method *receiveData:fromPeer:inSession:context:* of Class *RootViewController*

The ***receiveData:fromPeer:inSession:context:*** *method* (Fig. 15.14) is called by the GKSession when the app receives data from a connected device. Lines 84–85 deserialize the given NSData object into an NSMutableDictionary containing contact information. We know the NSData object represents an NSMutableDictionary because that's the only type of object we transfer in this app.

Lines 88–89 use NSFetchedResultsController's managedObjectContext method to get the app's NSManagedObjectContext. Lines 92–93 get the NSEntityDescription from the NSFetchedResultsController. We then create a new NSManagedObject to represent the received contact's information (lines 96–98). Lines 101–104 loop through the key–value pairs in the NSDictionary and add them to the NSManagedObject using its **set-Value:forKey: method**. Lines 106–112 call NSManagedObject's **save method** to add this data to the Core Data model, and if an error occurs, write a message to the console with function NSLog. Otherwise, we call UITableView's insertRowsAtIndexPaths: method to insert a new empty row into RootViewController's UITableView (lines 114–119). Line 120 calls UITableView's reloadData method to load in a new contact into the empty row.

```objc
79    // called when we receive data from a connected peer
80    - (void)receiveData:(NSData *)data fromPeer:(NSString *)peer inSession:
81      (GKSession *)session context:(void *)context
82    {
83       // extract the NSDictionary from the received data
84       NSDictionary *dictionary =
85          [NSKeyedUnarchiver unarchiveObjectWithData:data];
86
87       // get the managed object context from the fetched results controller
88       NSManagedObjectContext *objectContext =
89          [fetchedResultsController managedObjectContext];
90
91       // get the entity description from the fetched results controller
92       NSEntityDescription *entity =
93          [[fetchedResultsController fetchRequest] entity];
94
95       // insert a new object into objectContext with the given name
96       NSManagedObject *newManagedObject =
97          [NSEntityDescription insertNewObjectForEntityForName:entity.name
98          inManagedObjectContext:objectContext];
99
100      // loop through all the keys in the received dictionary
101      for (NSString *key in [dictionary allKeys])
102
103         // update the values in the new managed object we're inserting
104         [newManagedObject setValue:[dictionary valueForKey:key] forKey:key];
105
106      NSError *error; // declare an NSError for the save operation
107
108      // if the context doesn't save properly
109      if (![objectContext save:&error])
110      {
111         // log the error
112         NSLog(@"Error saving context: %@", [error description]);
113      } // end if
```

Fig. 15.14 | Method receiveData:fromPeer:inSession:context: of class RootViewController. (Part 1 of 2.)

```
114     else
115     {
116        // insert a new row in the table view for the new object
117        [self.tableView insertRowsAtIndexPaths:[NSArray arrayWithObject:
118           [NSIndexPath indexPathForRow:0 inSection:0]] withRowAnimation:
119           UITableViewRowAnimationLeft];
120        [self.tableView reloadData]; // refresh the table view
121     } // end else
122  } // end method receiveData:fromPeer:inSession:context:
123
```

Fig. 15.14 | Method receiveData:fromPeer:inSession:context: of class RootViewController. (Part 2 of 2.)

Methods insertNewObject and addViewControllerDidFinishAdding: of Class RootViewController

The insertNewObject method (Fig. 15.15, lines 125–133) allows the user to enter a new contact when they touch the ➕ **Button** in the top-right corner of the app. We create a new AddViewController and set its delegate to self (lines 128–129). We call UIView-Controller's presentModalViewController:animated: method to show AddViewController's view (line 132).

```
124  // called when the user touches the plus button
125  - (void)insertNewObject
126  {
127     // create new AddViewController
128     AddViewController *controller = [[AddViewController alloc] init];
129     controller.delegate = self; // set controller's delegate to self
130
131     // show the new controller
132     [self presentModalViewController:controller animated:YES];
133  } // end method insertNewObject
134
135  // called when the user touches the Done button in the AddViewController
136  - (void)addViewControllerDidFinishAdding:(AddViewController *)controller
137  {
138     // get the managed object context from the fetched results controller
139     NSManagedObjectContext *objectContext =
140        [fetchedResultsController managedObjectContext];
141
142     // get the entity description from the fetched results controller
143     NSEntityDescription *entity =
144        [[fetchedResultsController fetchRequest] entity];
145
146     // insert a new object into objectContext with the given name
147     NSManagedObject *newManagedObject =
148        [NSEntityDescription insertNewObjectForEntityForName:entity.name
149        inManagedObjectContext:objectContext];
```

Fig. 15.15 | Methods insertNewObject and addViewControllerDidFinishAdding: of class RootViewController. (Part 1 of 2.)

```
150
151    NSDictionary *values = [controller values]; // get the entered data
152
153    // loop through the field names in the entered data
154    for (NSString *key in values)
155
156       // add the contact's information to the object under the key
157       [newManagedObject setValue:[values valueForKey:key] forKey:key];
158
159    NSError *error; // declare an NSError for the save operation
160
161    // if the context doesn't save properly
162    if (![objectContext save:&error])
163       NSLog(@"Error saving context: %@", [error description]);
164
165    // dismiss the AddViewController
166    [self dismissModalViewControllerAnimated:YES];
167    [self.tableView reloadData]; // refresh the table view's data
168 } // end method addViewControllerDidFinishAdding
169
```

Fig. 15.15 | Methods insertNewObject and addViewControllerDidFinishAdding: of class RootViewController. (Part 2 of 2.)

Method addViewControllerDidFinishAdding: (lines 136–168) from our AddView-ControllerDelegate protocol (Fig. 10.14) is called when the user has finished adding a new contact and touches the "**Done**" **Button** in AddViewController's view. Lines 139–149 get the app's NSManagedObjectContext, NSEntityDescription and NSManagedObject. We then get the NSDictionary representing the new contact information from the Root-ViewController (line 151). Lines 154–157 loop through the key–value pairs and add them to the NSManagedObject using its setValue:forKey: method. Lines 159–163 call NSManagedObject's save method to save the data, writing to NSLog if the save fails. We then hide the AddViewController and refresh the UITableView (lines 166–167).

Methods *numberOfSectionsInTableView:* and *tableView:numberOfRowsIn-Section:* of Class *RootViewController*
The numberOfSectionsInTableView: method (Fig. 15.16, lines 171–181) returns the number of sections in the given UITableView. Line 174 calls NSFretchedResultsCon-troller's **sections method** to get an NSArray representing the UITableView's sections. We call NSArray's count method to get the number of sections. If count is 0, we set it to 1 (lines 177–178). We do this to fix an incompatability between the NSFetchResultsCon-troller and UITableView class in iPhone OS 3.x. For more information, visit

developer.apple.com/iPhone/library/documentation/CoreData/Reference/
NSFetchedResultsController_Class/Reference/Reference.html

Method tableView:numberOfRowsInSection: (lines 184–203) returns the number of rows in the given UITableView's section specified by the supplied NSInteger. We start by getting an NSArray representing the UITableView's sections by calling NSFetched-ResultsController's sections method (line 188). If this array contains at least one section (line 192), we get the object at the given NNSInteger (lines 195–196). This object implements the ***NSFetchedResultsSectionInfo** protocol* (line 195) and we call its ***numberOfObjects** method* to get the number of rows in the selected UITableView section.

```
170    // called by the table view to find the number of secitons it has
171    - (NSInteger)numberOfSectionsInTableView:(UITableView *)tableView
172    {
173       // get the number of sections from the fetched results controller
174       NSUInteger count = [[fetchedResultsController sections] count];
175
176       // if the fetched results controller reports 0 sections
177       if (count == 0)
178          count = 1; // change count to 1
179
180       return count; // return the number of sections
181    } // end method numberOfSectionsInTableView:
182
183    // called by the table view to find the number of rows in a given section
184    - (NSInteger)tableView:(UITableView *)tableView
185       numberOfRowsInSection:(NSInteger)section
186    {
187       // get all the sections in the fetched results controller
188       NSArray *sections = [fetchedResultsController sections];
189       NSUInteger count = 0; // initialize count to 0
190
191       // if sections contains at least one object
192       if ([sections count])
193       {
194          // get the object at the given index
195          id <NSFetchedResultsSectionInfo> sectionInfo =
196             [sections objectAtIndex:section];
197
198          // get the number of rows in the section
199          count = [sectionInfo numberOfObjects];
200       } // end if
201
202       return count; // return the number of rows in the section
203    } // end method tableView:numberOfRowsInSection:
204
```

Fig. 15.16 | Methods numberOfSectionsInTableView: and tableView:numberOfRowsInSection: of class RootViewController.

Methods tableView:cellForRowAtIndexPath: *and* tableView:didSelectRowAtIndexPath: *of Class* RootViewController

Method tableView:cellForRowAtIndexPath: (Fig. 15.17, lines 206–234) attempts to reuse an existing UITableViewCell using the dequeueReusableCellWithIdentifier: method (lines 209–221). Lines 224–225 call the ***NSFetchedResultsController's** objectAtIndexPath: method* to get the NSManagedObject at the specified NSIndexPath.

The tableView:didSelectRowAtIndexPath: method (lines 237–255) is called when the user touches one of the UITableView's rows. Lines 241–242 create a new Contact-

ViewController. We use NSFetchedResultsController's objectAtIndexPath: method to get the NSManagedObject specified by the given NSIndexPath. Lines 249–250 set the ContactViewController's person property to the NSManagedObject then call its update-Title method. We call UINavigationController's pushViewController:animated: method to display the ContactViewController's view. Line 232 sets cell's accessory-Type property to UITableViewCellAccessoryDisclosureIndicator to indicate that more details will be displayed when the UITableViewCell is touched.

```
205   // called by the UITableView to get a cell for the given index path
206   - (UITableViewCell *)tableView:(UITableView *)tableView
207       cellForRowAtIndexPath:(NSIndexPath *)indexPath
208   {
209       static NSString *CellIdentifier = @"Cell"; // normal cell identifier
210
211       // get a reused cell
212       UITableViewCell *cell =
213           [tableView dequeueReusableCellWithIdentifier:CellIdentifier];
214
215       // if no reusable cells are available
216       if (cell == nil)
217
218           // create a new cell
219           cell = [[[UITableViewCell alloc]
220               initWithStyle:UITableViewCellStyleDefault
221               reuseIdentifier:CellIdentifier] autorelease];
222
223       // get the managed object for the given index path
224       NSManagedObject *managedObject =
225           [fetchedResultsController objectAtIndexPath:indexPath];
226
227       // update the text in the cell with the contact's name
228       cell.textLabel.text =
229           [[managedObject valueForKey:@"Name"] description];
230
231       // make the cell display an arrow on the right side
232       cell.accessoryType = UITableViewCellAccessoryDisclosureIndicator;
233       return cell; // return the configured cell
234   } // end method tableView:cellForRowAtIndexPath:
235
236   // called when the user touches one of the rows in the table view
237   - (void)tableView:(UITableView *)tableView
238       didSelectRowAtIndexPath:(NSIndexPath *)indexPath
239   {
240       // create a new ContactViewController
241       ContactViewController *controller = [[ContactViewController alloc]
242           initWithNibName:@"ContactViewController" bundle:nil];
243
244       // get the managed object at the given index path
245       NSManagedObject *selectedObject =
246           [[self fetchedResultsController] objectAtIndexPath:indexPath];
```

Fig. 15.17 | Methods tableView:cellForRowAtIndexPath: and tableView:didSelectRowAtIndexPath: of class RootViewController. (Part 1 of 2.)

```
247
248     // set the ContactViewController's person to be the managed object
249     controller.person = selectedObject;
250     [controller updateTitle]; // update the title in controller
251
252     // show the ContactViewController
253     [self.navigationController pushViewController:controller animated:YES];
254     [controller release]; // release the controller ContactViewContorller
255  } // end method tableView:didSelectRowAtIndexPath:
256
```

Fig. 15.17 | Methods tableView:cellForRowAtIndexPath: and
tableView:didSelectRowAtIndexPath: of class RootViewController. (Part 2 of 2.)

Methods *tableView:commitEditingStyle:forRowAtIndexPath: and tableView:canMoveRowAtIndexPath: of Class RootViewController*

The tableView:commitEditingStyle:forRowAtIndexPath: method (Fig. 15.18, lines
258–283) is called when the user deletes a row from RootViewController's UITableView.
Line 263 checks if the given UITableViewCellEditingStyle is UITableViewCellEditingStyleDelete. If so, we call NSFetchedResultsController's managedObjectContext
method to get the app's NSManagedObjectContext (lines 266–267). Lines 270–271 delete
the contact from our data using NSManagedObjectContext's *deleteObject: method.* We
then save this change using NSManageObjectContext's save: method and write an error
message with NSLog if save fails (lines 273–277). Lines 280–281 call UITableView's del-
eteRowsAtIndexPaths:withRowAnimation: method to remove the deleted cell. Method
tableView:canMoveRowAtIndexPath: (lines 286–290) returns NO to indicate that the
UITableViewCells cannot be reordered.

```
257  // called when the user edits a cell in the table view
258  - (void)tableView:(UITableView *)tableView
259     commitEditingStyle:(UITableViewCellEditingStyle)editingStyle
260     forRowAtIndexPath:(NSIndexPath *)indexPath
261  {
262     // if the user deleted a cell
263     if (editingStyle == UITableViewCellEditingStyleDelete)
264     {
265        // get the managed object context
266        NSManagedObjectContext *context =
267           [fetchedResultsController managedObjectContext];
268
269        // delete the managed object in the context at the given index path
270        [context deleteObject:
271           [fetchedResultsController objectAtIndexPath:indexPath]];
272
273        NSError *error; // declare an NSError for the save operation
274
```

Fig. 15.18 | Methods tableView:commitEditingStyle:forRowAtIndexPath: and
tableView:canMoveRowAtIndexPath: of class RootViewController. (Part 1 of 2.)

```
275        // if the context fails to save
276        if (![context save:&error])
277            NSLog(@"Error saving context: %@", [error description]);
278
279        // delete the row from the table view
280        [tableView deleteRowsAtIndexPaths:[NSArray arrayWithObject:
281            indexPath] withRowAnimation:UITableViewRowAnimationFade];
282     } // end if
283 } // end method tableView:commitEditingStyle:forRowAtIndexPath:
284
285 // called by the table view to determine if a given row is re-orderable
286 - (BOOL)tableView:(UITableView *)tableView
287     canMoveRowAtIndexPath:(NSIndexPath *)indexPath
288 {
289     return NO; // none of the cells in this table can be moved
290 } // end method tableView:canMoveRowAtIndexPath:
291
```

Fig. 15.18 | Methods tableView:commitEditingStyle:forRowAtIndexPath: and tableView:canMoveRowAtIndexPath: of class RootViewController. (Part 2 of 2.)

Method fetchedResultsController of Class RootViewController
Method fetchedResultsController (Fig. 15.19) is auto-generated by Xcode to initialize the NSFetchedResultsController used throughout the app. We customize this method to our data model as highlighted in the source code.

```
292 // returns the fetched results controller that controls this table
293 - (NSFetchedResultsController *)fetchedResultsController
294 {
295     // if a fetched results controller has already been initialized
296     if (fetchedResultsController != nil)
297         return fetchedResultsController; // return the controller
298
299     // create the fetch request for the entity
300     NSFetchRequest *fetchRequest = [[NSFetchRequest alloc] init];
301
302     // edit the entity name as appropriate.
303     NSEntityDescription *entity = [NSEntityDescription entityForName:
304         @"Person" inManagedObjectContext:managedObjectContext];
305     [fetchRequest setEntity:entity];
306
307     // edit the sort key as appropriate.
308     NSSortDescriptor *sortDescriptor =
309         [[NSSortDescriptor alloc] initWithKey:@"Name" ascending:YES];
310     NSArray *sortDescriptors =
311         [[NSArray alloc] initWithObjects:sortDescriptor, nil];
312
313     [fetchRequest setSortDescriptors:sortDescriptors];
314
```

Fig. 15.19 | Method fetchedResultsController of class RootViewController. (Part 1 of 2.)

```
315    // edit the section name key path and cache name if appropriate
316    // nil for section name key path means "no sections"
317    NSFetchedResultsController *aFetchedResultsController =
318        [[NSFetchedResultsController alloc] initWithFetchRequest:
319        fetchRequest managedObjectContext:managedObjectContext
320        sectionNameKeyPath:nil cacheName:@"Root"];
321
322    aFetchedResultsController.delegate = self;
323    self.fetchedResultsController = aFetchedResultsController;
324
325    [aFetchedResultsController release]; // release temporary controller
326    [fetchRequest release]; // release fetchRequest NSFetcheRequest
327    [sortDescriptor release]; // release sortDescriptor NSSortDescriptor
328    [sortDescriptors release]; // release sortDescriptor NSArray
329
330    return fetchedResultsController;
331 } // end method fetchedResultsController
332
333 // releases this object's memory
334 - (void)dealloc
335 {
336    [fetchedResultsController release]; // release fetchedResultsController
337    [managedObjectContext release]; // release managedObjectContext
338    [super dealloc]; // call the superclass's dealloc method
339 } // end method dealloc
340 @end // end class RootViewController
```

Fig. 15.19 | Method fetchedResultsController of class RootViewController. (Part 2 of 2.)

Line 296 checks whether fetchedResultsController is already initialized. If so, this method has already been called and we return the existing NSFetchedResultsController. Otherwise, line 300 creates a new NSFetchRequest. Lines 303–304 declare the NSEntity-Description representing the entity to be stored in the table. The Person entity was created by us to store contact information, so we pass Person as the entityForName argument. NSFetchedRequest's setEntity method sets the Person entity as the one that the NSFetchedRequest is currently manipulating.

Lines 308–309 create a new **NSSortDescriptor**, which is used to sort the Person entities by their Name attributes. Lines 310–311 add the NSSortDescriptor to a new NSArray and pass this to **NSFetchRequest's setSortDescriptors:** *method* to specify the sorting order of the fetches.

Lines 317–322 initialize an NSFetchedResultsController and set its delegate to this RootViewController. We then assign the new NSFetchedResultsController to RootViewController's fetchedResultsController property.

15.5 Wrap-Up

In the **Enhanced Address Book** app, we used the Core Data framework to separate our data model from the rest of the app according to the Model-View-Controller design pattern. We visually designed a Person entity, which contained attributes representing a contact's name, e-mail and address. We programmatically interacted with the data model via an NS-

`ManagedObject`. Xcode generated an `NSFetchedResultsController` which allowed us to make fetch requests to update our `UITableView`. We used the Game Kit framework to transfer contact information among multiple iPhones using Bluetooth technology. The `GKPeerPickerController` class displayed a view that enabled the user to choose a nearby iPhone to which a contact would be transferred. We then used a `GKSession` to transmit an `NSData` object representing the contact information.

In Chapter 16, we'll build the **Twitter® Discount Airfares** app which uses Twitter web services to display current discounted jetBlue® flights. We'll use an `NSURLConnection` to receive an Atom feed (similar to an RSS Feed) from Twitter then parse the feed using an `NSXMLParser`. We'll also use a **Web View** to allow the user to view the jetBlue web page where discounted flights can be purchased.

Twitter® Discount Airfares App

Internet Enabled Applications

OBJECTIVES

In this chapter you'll learn:

- To use Twitter web services to search for tweets that match a given criterion.

- To use the NSURLConnection class to connect to Twitter and retrieve data.

- To use the NSXMLParser class to read the XML data provided by Twitter.

- To use the UIWebView class to display a web page in your app.

- To create a custom UITableViewCell that includes labels and an image.

Outline

16.1 Introduction
16.2 Test-Driving the **Twitter Discount Airfares** App
16.3 Technologies Overview
16.4 Building the App
16.5 Wrap-Up

16.1 Introduction

The **Twitter®** **Discount Airfares** app (Fig. 16.1) uses Twitter web services to discover discount airfares from jetBlue®. Typically, these discounts expire at the end of the business day on which the tweet occurred. The app's main screen displays a list of the discounted flights retrieved from Twitter. Each entry contains four pieces of data—the origin airport, the destination airport, the flight cost and the full tweet that describes the deal. The origin and destination airports are given by their three-letter codes, which can be found at

    www.world-airport-codes.com

The airport codes appear in blue at the top of each table, with an icon of an airplane flying from the origin to the destination airport. The trip cost appears to the right in green, and the tweet that provides the airfare information appears under the other items in black.

Fig. 16.1 | **Twitter Discount Airfares** app showing several discount airfares.

A refresh **Button** (🔄) appears in the upper-left corner. When the user presses it, the app refreshes the list of tweets to display any new jetBlue tweets since the last update. While the tweets are refreshing, the refresh button turns into an **Activity Indicator** (☀)—a small component that spins to indicate a task is in progress. When the user touches an entry in the table, a **Web View** appears—if the deal's still active, the **Web View** allows the user to buy tickets for that flight.

16.2 Test-Driving the Twitter Discount Airfares App

Opening the Completed Application
Open the directory containing the **Twitter Discount Airfares** app project. Double click the file TwitterDiscountAirfares.xcodeproj to open the project in Xcode.

Viewing the Discounted Flights List
Click the **Build and Go** button to run the app in the iPhone Simulator. When the app loads, it automatically refreshes the list of jetBlue discount-airfare tweets. You should see the **Activity Indicator** (🌀) spinning in the app's top-left corner. The **Activity Indicator** stops spinning when the list is populated with flights, at which point the **Activity Indicator** is replaced with a refresh **Button** (🔁).

Booking a Flight
If a flight looks interesting to you, touch its entry in the table. Another view will appear and load a website for buying tickets. Touch the "**Discount Airfares**" **Button** to return to the list of flights.

16.3 Technologies Overview

The **Twitter Discount Airfares** app connects to Twitter using class NSURLConnection. We construct a Twitter URL and pass it to the NSURLConnection, which handles the networking issues. NSURLConnection informs its delegate object when events occur, such as receiving a response from the server, an authentication request or when the connection ends. We receive responses from Twitter in Atom format—an XML vocabulary that's a popular RSS alternative. We then parse the XML using the class NSXMLParser. We store the parsed data in an NSMutableArray and display it in a UITableView with custom UITableViewCells. When the user touches a cell, we display a web page where the user can view the discounted airfare deal and purchase tickets if the deal has not expired. We display the page using a UIWebView, which takes any URL and displays the web site.

16.4 Building the App

Open Xcode and create a new project. Select the **Navigation-based Application** template and name the project TwitterDiscountAirfares.

Declaring the Airfare Interface
We begin by creating the Airfare class to store information about a single airfare (Fig. 16.2). The class consists of four properties—the flights's cost, the origin airport, the destination airport and the tweet that contains the deal.

```
1   // Fig. 16.2: Airfare.h
2   // Class that represents an airfare.
3   // Implementation in Airfare.m
4   #import <Foundation/Foundation.h>
5
```

Fig. 16.2 | Class that represents an airfare. (Part 1 of 2.)

```
 6  @interface Airfare : NSObject
 7  {
 8     NSString *tweet; // the tweet that this airfare came from
 9     NSString *cost; // the flight's cost
10     NSString *origin; // the flight's origin airport
11     NSString *destination; // the flight's destination
12  } // end instance variable declaration
13
14  // declare all the instance variables as properties
15  @property (nonatomic, retain) NSString *tweet;
16  @property (nonatomic, retain) NSString *cost;
17  @property (nonatomic, retain) NSString *origin;
18  @property (nonatomic, retain) NSString *destination;
19  @end
```

Fig. 16.2 | Class that represents an airfare. (Part 2 of 2.)

Airfare *Class Implementation*

The Airfare class's implementation (Fig. 16.3) consists of four @synthesize directives (lines 7–10) that generate *get* and *set* methods for the properties.

```
 1  // Fig. 16.3: Airfare.m
 2  // Implementation of class Airfare.
 3  #import "Airfare.h"
 4
 5  @implementation Airfare
 6
 7  @synthesize tweet; // generate get and set methods for tweet
 8  @synthesize cost; // generate get and set methods for cost
 9  @synthesize origin; // generate get and set methods for origin
10  @synthesize destination; // generate get and set methods for destination
11  @end
```

Fig. 16.3 | Implementation of class Airfare.

Declaring the RootViewController *interface*

The files RootViewController.h and RootViewController.m are automatically created by the **Navigation-based Application** template. The RootViewController class (Fig. 16.4) manages the table of discounted flights. This is the app's main view.

```
 1  // Fig. 16.4: RootViewController.h
 2  // Controller for the root view of the Twitter Discount Airfares app.
 3  // Implementation in RootViewController.m
 4  #import "TwitterConnection.h"
 5  #import "AirfareFinder.h"
 6  #import "AirfareCell.h"
 7
 8  // begin RootViewController interface declaration
 9  @interface RootViewController : UITableViewController
```

Fig. 16.4 | Controller for the root **View** of the **Twitter Discount Airfares** app. (Part 1 of 2.)

```
10   <AirfareFinderDelegate>
11   {
12      AirfareFinder *airfareFinder; // finds and parses the tweets
13      NSArray *airfares; // the Airfare objects returned from airfareFinder
14      UIActivityIndicatorView *activityView; // indicates the app is working
15   } // end instance variable declarations
16
17   // declare airfares as a property
18   @property (nonatomic, retain) NSArray *airfares;
19
20   - (void)refreshFares; // refreshes the list of fares
21   @end // end interface RootViewController
```

Fig. 16.4 | Controller for the root **View** of the **Twitter Discount Airfares** app. (Part 2 of 2.)

Class `RootViewController` is a subclass of `UITableViewController` (line 9). It contains three instance variables—an `AirfareFinder` (line 12) for finding new airfares, an `NSArray` for storing the airfares (line 13) and a `UIActivityIndicatorView` for telling the user that the app is refreshing the data (line 14). A *UIActivityIndicatorView* is a component that displays a spinning animation to indicate that the app is performing a task. `RootViewController.h` declares the `refreshFares` method (line 20), which refreshes the list by searching Twitter.

RootViewController Class Implementation

Our `RootViewController` implementation (Fig. 16.5) begins by declaring the constant `rowHeight` (line 6), which specifies the height of each row in the table. You'll see where we got this number when we discuss the `AirfareCell` class (Figs. 16.18–16.19).

```
1    // Fig. 16.5: RootViewController.m
2    // RootViewController class implementation.
3    #import "RootViewController.h"
4    #import "WebViewController.h"
5
6    static const int rowHeight = 117; // the height of each row in the table
7
8    @implementation RootViewController
9
10   @synthesize airfares; // generate get and set methods for airfares
11
12   // called when the main view finishes loading
13   - (void)viewDidLoad
14   {
15      [super viewDidLoad]; // call the superclass's viewDidLoad method
16      self.tableView.rowHeight = rowHeight; // set the table's row height
17
18      // create activityView
19      activityView = [[UIActivityIndicatorView alloc] initWithFrame:
20         CGRectMake(0, 0, 20, 20)];
21
```

Fig. 16.5 | `RootViewController` class implementation. (Part 1 of 2.)

```
22      airfareFinder = [[AirfareFinder alloc] init]; // create airfareFinder
23      airfareFinder.delegate = self; // set airfareFinder's delegate
24      [self refreshFares]; // refresh the list of fares
25   } // end method viewDidLoad
26
27   - (void)refreshFares
28   {
29      // create a button to display the activity indicator
30      UIBarButtonItem *activityButton =
31         [[UIBarButtonItem alloc] initWithCustomView:activityView];
32
33      // place the button on the left side of the bar
34      self.navigationItem.leftBarButtonItem = activityButton;
35      [activityButton release]; // release the activitybutton UIBarButtonItem
36      [activityView startAnimating]; // start the activity view spinning
37      [airfareFinder getAirfares]; // get the new list of airfares
38   } // end method refreshFares
39
40   // delegate method of AirfareFinder, called when it finds airfares
41   - (void)airfareFinder:(AirfareFinder *)finder
42      didFindAirfares:(NSArray *)fares
43   {
44      self.airfares = fares; // update airfares with the new items
45      [activityView stopAnimating]; // stop the activity view spinning
46
47      // create a new button to replace the activity view
48      UIBarButtonItem *refreshButton = [[UIBarButtonItem alloc]
49         initWithBarButtonSystemItem:UIBarButtonSystemItemRefresh target:self
50         action:@selector(refreshFares)];
51
52      // place the new button in place of the activity view
53      self.navigationItem.leftBarButtonItem = refreshButton;
54      [refreshButton release]; // release the refreshButton UIBarButtonItem
55      [self.tableView reloadData]; // refresh table to display new entries
56   } // end method airfareFinder:didFindAirfares:
57
```

Fig. 16.5 | RootViewController class implementation. (Part 2 of 2.)

The viewDidLoad method (lines 13–25) sets up the interface. Line 16 sets the rowHeight of tableView and lines 19–20 initialize activityView. We then initialize airfareFinder (an object of class AirFareFinder which is declared in Figs. 16.11–16.17) and set this RootViewController as its delegate (lines 22–23). Then we call method refreshFares to get data from Twitter and update the rows in tableView.

The refreshFares method (lines 27–38) first creates a UIBarButtonItem to contain the activityView using UIBarButtonItem's initWithCustomView: method. We add this item to the navigation bar's left side (line 34) and start activityView's spinning animation (line 36). Then we call the getAirfares method of AirfareFinder to start searching Twitter for new airfares.

When the AirfareFinder finishes finding airfares, it calls the airfareFinder:did-FindAirfares: method (lines 41–56). We assign the found flights to the airfares NSArray (line 44), then stop the activityView's spinning animation (line 45). Lines 48–

50 create a new `UIBarButtonItem` (a refresh **Button**) to replace the `activityView` (the **Activity Indicator**). We replace the navigation bar's left `UIBarButtonItem` with the new `UIBarButtonItem` (line 53), then refresh the table to display the new airfares (line 55).

*UITableView **Delegate and Data Source Methods of Class** RootViewController*
The next three methods of `RootViewController` are the delegate and data source methods of `UITableView` (Fig. 16.6). In `tableView:numberOfRowsInSection:` (lines 59–63) we re-turn the size of the `airfares` array because we want the table to have one row for each airfare.

```
58   // called by the table view to find how many rows are in a given section
59   - (NSInteger)tableView:(UITableView *)tableView
60       numberOfRowsInSection:(NSInteger)section
61   {
62       return airfares.count; // return the number of total airfares
63   } // end method tableView:numberOfRowsInSection:
64
65   // called by the table view to get a cell for the given index path
66   - (UITableViewCell *)tableView:(UITableView *)tableView
67       cellForRowAtIndexPath:(NSIndexPath *)indexPath
68   {
69       static NSString *CellIdentifier = @"AirfareCell";
70
71       // get an AirfareCell by reusing an old one
72       AirfareCell *cell = (AirfareCell *)
73           [tableView dequeueReusableCellWithIdentifier:CellIdentifier];
74
75       // if there weren't any cells available for reuse
76       if (cell == nil)
77
78           // create a new AirfareCell
79           cell = [[[AirfareCell alloc] initWithStyle:
80               UITableViewCellStyleDefault reuseIdentifier:CellIdentifier]
81               autorelease];
82
83       // get the Airfare object for the cell at the given index
84       Airfare *fare = [airfares objectAtIndex:indexPath.row];
85
86       // set all the labels on the cell to correspond with the Airfare
87       cell.originLabel.text = fare.origin; // set the origin label
88       cell.destinationLabel.text = fare.destination; // set destination label
89       cell.priceLabel.text = fare.cost; // set the price label
90       cell.tweetLabel.text = fare.tweet; // set the tweet label
91       return cell; // return the configured cell
92   } // end method tableView:cellForRowAtIndexPath:
93
94   // called when the user touches a cell
95   - (void)tableView:(UITableView *)tableView didSelectRowAtIndexPath:
96       (NSIndexPath *)indexPath
97   {
```

Fig. 16.6 | `UITableView` delegate and data source methods of class `RootViewController`. (Part 1 of 2.)

```
 98      // create a new WebViewController
 99      WebViewController *controller = [[WebViewController alloc]
100         initWithNibName:@"WebViewController" bundle:nil];
101
102      // show the controller
103      [self.navigationController pushViewController:controller animated:YES];
104      [controller release]; // release the controller WebViewController
105   } // end method tableView:didSelectRowAtIndexPath:
106
107   // release the RootViewController's memory
108   - (void)dealloc
109   {
110      [airfareFinder release]; // release airfareFinder
111      [airfares release]; // release the airfares NSMutableArray
112      [activityView release]; // release activityView
113      [super dealloc]; // call the superclass's dealloc method
114   } // end method dealloc
115   @end
```

Fig. 16.6 | UITableView delegate and data source methods of class RootViewController. (Part 2 of 2.)

The tableView:cellForRowAtIndexPath: method (lines 66–92) returns a customized UITableViewCell for a given table row. This table uses objects of class AirfareCell (Figs. 16.18–16.19). First, we create a new AirfareCell or reuse an existing one (lines 72–81). Line 84 gets the Airfare at the correct index and updates the cell's labels to correspond to the Airfare's properties (lines 87–90). Line 91 returns the customized cell.

The tableView:didSelectRowAtIndexPath: method (lines 95–105) is called when the user touches one of the UITableView's rows. Lines 99–100 create a WebViewController, a subclass of UIViewController that displays a web page. Line 103 displays the WebViewController.

Declaring the WebViewController Class

In Xcode, create a new UIViewController subclass. Ensure that **With XIB for user interface** is checked to automatically generate the nib file. The finished WebViewController.h is shown in Fig. 16.7. We add as outlets a UIWebView (line 8) and a UIActivityIndicatorView. *UIWebView* is a subclass of UIView that displays a webpage. Once you've updated WebViewController.h, open the file WebViewController.xib in Interface Builder. Double-click **View** to open it in a separate window. Drag a **Web View** from the **Library** window onto **View** and resize it to fill the entire window. Also drag an **Activity Indicator** and position it in the middle of the **Web View**. Connect the webView outlet of **File's Owner** to the new **Web View** and the activity outlet to the **Activity Indicator**. Also, connect the delegate outlet of the **Web View** to **File's Owner**.

```
1   // Fig. 16.7: WebViewController.h
2   // View that displays the website for purchasing flight tickets.
3   #import <UIKit/UIKit.h>
```

Fig. 16.7 | **View** that displays the website for purchasing flight tickets. (Part 1 of 2.)

```
 4
 5    // begin interface WebViewConroller declaration
 6    @interface WebViewController : UIViewController
 7    {
 8       IBOutlet UIWebView *webView; // view for displaying web page
 9       IBOutlet UIActivityIndicatorView *activity; // shows page is loading
10    } // end instance variable declaration
11
12    // declare webView as a property
13    @property (nonatomic,retain) IBOutlet UIWebView *webView;
14    @property (nonatomic,retain) IBOutlet UIActivityIndicatorView *activity;
15    @end // end interface WebViewController
```

Fig. 16.7 | **View** that displays the website for purchasing flight tickets. (Part 2 of 2.)

WebViewController *Class Implementation*

In WebViewController.m (Fig. 16.8), we override the viewDidLoad method (lines 11–21). Line 16 creates an NSURL for the website where users can buy tickets. We then create an **NSURLRequest** from the NSURL (line 19) and call the UIWebView's ***loadRequest:*** method (line 20), which receives the NSURLRequest and displays the URL's contents. Line 21 animates the UIActivityIndicator to indicate that the UIWebView is loading a page.

```
 1    // Fig. 16.8: WebViewController.m
 2    // View that displays a website for purchasing flight tickets.
 3    #import "WebViewController.h"
 4
 5    @implementation WebViewController
 6
 7    // generate get and set methods for our property
 8    @synthesize webView;
 9
10    // load the website in the web view
11    - (void)viewDidLoad
12    {
13       [super viewDidLoad]; // call the superclass's viewDidLoad method
14
15       // create an NSURL from the url string
16       NSURL *url = [NSURL URLWithString:@"http://bit.ly/mobilecheeps"];
17
18       // create an NSURLRequest from the NSURL
19       NSURLRequest *urlRequest = [NSURLRequest requestWithURL:url];
20       [webView loadRequest:urlRequest]; // show the website in webView
21       [activity startAnimating]; // animate the activity indicator
22    } // end method viewDidLoad
23
24    // called when webView finishes loading the page
25    - (void)webViewDidFinishLoad:(UIWebView *)webView
26    {
27       [activity stopAnimating]; // stop the activity indicator's animation
28       activity.hidden = YES; // hide the activity indicator
29    } // end method webViewDidFinishLoad:
```

Fig. 16.8 | **View** that displays a website for purchasing flight tickets. (Part 1 of 2.)

```
30
31   // release this object's memory
32   - (void)dealloc
33   {
34      [webView release]; // release the webView UIWebView
35      [activity release]; // release the activity UIActivityIndicatorView
36      [super dealloc]; // call the superclass's dealloc method
37   } // end method dealloc
38   @end
```

Fig. 16.8 | **View** that displays a website for purchasing flight tickets. (Part 2 of 2.)

The UIWebView delegate method webViewDidFinishLoad: (lines 25–29) is called when the UIWebView finishes loading the web page. We use this method to stop and hide the UIActivityIndicator when the web page finishes loading.

Declaring the TwitterConnection Class

The TwitterConnection class is declared in TwitterConnection.h (Fig. 16.9). TwitterConnection connects to Twitter and returns any received data to its delegate. The delegate is declared as an object of type id that conforms to the TwitterConnectionDelegate protocol (line 11). Instance variable receivedData stores the data received from Twitter. Its type is *NSMutableData*—the mutable counterpart of NSData. The performSearch: method (line 17) begins a Twitter search using its NSString argument. When the object finishes receiving data from Twitter, it calls the twitterConnection:didReceiveData: method (lines 23–24) of the TwitterConnectionDelegate.

```
1    // Fig. 16.9: TwitterConnection.h
2    // Class that connects with Twitter web services and returns data.
3    // Implementation in TwitterConnection.m
4    #import <Foundation/Foundation.h>
5
6    @protocol TwitterConnectionDelegate;
7
8    // begin TwitterConnection interface declaration
9    @interface TwitterConnection : NSObject
10   {
11      id <TwitterConnectionDelegate> delegate; // this class's delegate
12      NSMutableData *receivedData; // the data received from Twitter
13   } // end instance variable declarations
14
15   // declare delegate as a property
16   @property (nonatomic, assign) id <TwitterConnectionDelegate> delegate;
17   - (void)performSearch:(NSString *)search; // performs a Twitter search
18   @end // end interface TwitterConnection
19
20   @protocol TwitterConnectionDelegate
21
```

Fig. 16.9 | Class that connects with Twitter web services and returns data. (Part 1 of 2.)

```
22  // called when the TwitterConnection finishes receiving data
23  - (void)twitterConnection:(TwitterConnection *)connection
24     didReceiveData:(NSData *)data;
25  @end // end protocol TwitterConnectionDelegate
```

Fig. 16.9 | Class that connects with Twitter web services and returns data. (Part 2 of 2.)

TwitterConnection *Class Implementation*

In TwitterConnection.m (Fig. 16.10), the performSearch: method (lines 9–39) performs a Twitter web service call with the given NSString. First, lines 12–13 URL encode the string for security purposes by escaping any special characters in the string. We then create an NSURL object by concatenating the search query to the Twitter search URL. The URLs can be found in the Twitter API documentation at:

apiwiki.twitter.com/Twitter-API-Documentation

Line 20 creates an NSURLRequest using the NSURL and lines 23–24 create an NSURL-Connection using the NSURLRequest. An *NSURLConnection* loads a URL then informs the delegate of any responses from the server. If the NSURLConnection was created successfully (line 28), we initialize receivedData (line 31). We also display the standard activity indicator in the status bar by setting UIApplication's *networkActivityIndicatorVisible* property to YES (lines 34–35). This icon indicates that the iPhone is performing network activity. If the NSURLConnection was not created successfully (line 37), we log an error message.

```
1   // Fig. 16.10: TwitterConnection.m
2   // Implementation of class TwitterConnection.
3   #import "TwitterConnection.h"
4
5   @implementation TwitterConnection
6
7   @synthesize delegate; // generate get and set methods for delegate
8
9   - (void)performSearch:(NSString *)search
10  {
11     // encode the search string with percent escapes
12     search = [search stringByAddingPercentEscapesUsingEncoding:
13        NSUTF8StringEncoding];
14
15     // create the NSURL for performing the specified search
16     NSURL *searchURL = [NSURL URLWithString:[NSString stringWithFormat:
17        @"http://search.twitter.com/search.atom?q=%@", search]];
18
19     // create an NSURLRequest from the created NSURL
20     NSURLRequest *request = [[NSURLRequest alloc] initWithURL:searchURL];
21
22     // create an NSURLConnection object with the created NSURLRequest
23     NSURLConnection *connection =
24        [[NSURLConnection alloc] initWithRequest:request delegate:self];
```

Fig. 16.10 | Implementation of TwitterConnection. (Part 1 of 2.)

```
25      [request release]; // release the request NSURLRequest
26
27      // if the NSURLConnection was successfully created
28      if (connection)
29      {
30         // create received data
31         receivedData = [[NSMutableData data] retain];
32
33         // display the standard network activity indicator in the status bar
34         [UIApplication sharedApplication].networkActivityIndicatorVisible =
35            YES;
36      } // end if
37      else
38         NSLog(@"search \"%@\" could not be performed", search);
39   } // end method performSearch:
40
41   // called when the NSURLConnection receives a response to the connection
42   - (void)connection:(NSURLConnection *)connection
43      didReceiveResponse:(NSURLResponse *)response
44   {
45      receivedData.length = 0; // reset the data
46   } // end method connection:didReceiveResponse:
47
48   // called when the NSURLConnection receives data
49   - (void)connection:(NSURLConnection *)connection
50      didReceiveData:(NSData *)data
51   {
52      [receivedData appendData:data]; // append the data to receivedData
53   } // end method connection:didRecieveData:
54
55   // called when the NSURLConnection fails
56   - (void)connection:(NSURLConnection *)connection
57      didFailWithError:(NSError *)error
58   {
59      [receivedData release]; // release the receivedData NSMutableData
60      [connection release]; // release the connection NSURLConnection
61   } // end method connection:didFailWithError:
62
63   // called when the NSURLConnection finishes
64   - (void)connectionDidFinishLoading:(NSURLConnection *)connection
65   {
66      // hide the network activity indicator in the status bar
67      [UIApplication sharedApplication].networkActivityIndicatorVisible = NO;
68
69      // pass the received data to the delegate
70      [delegate twitterConnection:self didReceiveData:receivedData];
71      [receivedData release]; // release the receivedData NSMutableData
72      [connection release]; // release the connection NSURLConnection
73   } // end method connectionDidFinishLoading:
74   @end
```

Fig. 16.10 | Implementation of `TwitterConnection`. (Part 2 of 2.)

The last four methods of class `TwitterConnection` are the delegate methods called by
`NSURLConnection`. Method `connection:didReceiveResponse:` (lines 42–46) is called
when the `NSURLConnection` receives a response from the server. We reset `receivedData`
(line 45) to discard any data we might have received before this response. The connection:`didReceiveData:` method (lines 49–50) is called when the `NSURLConnection`
receives data from Twitter. This method can be called multiple times before the connection closes, so we accumulate all the received data by appending the new data to `received-
Data` (line 52). The `connection:didFailWithError:` message (lines 56–57) is called when
the connection fails—we simply release the objects we allocated. The `connectionDidFin-
ishLoading:` method is called when the connection finishes loading successfully. This
means our Twitter search request has completed, so we stop the activity indicator, pass the
received data to our delegate (line 70) and release the instance variables we allocated (lines
71–72).

Declaring the `AirfareFinder` Interface
`AirfareFinder.h` declares the `AirfareFinder` class (Fig. 16.11). This class gets tweets
from Twitter using the `TwitterConnection` class, then parses each tweet for the flight cost,
origin and destination. The `AirfareFinder` compiles a list of `Airfare` objects and passes
the list to its delegate after parsing all the tweets.

```
 1   // Fig. 16.11: AirfareFinder.h
 2   // Class that gets tweets and parses them for information.
 3   // Implementation in AirfareFinder.m
 4   #import <Foundation/Foundation.h>
 5   #import "TwitterConnection.h"
 6   #import "Airfare.h"
 7
 8   @protocol AirfareFinderDelegate;
 9
10   // begin AirfareFinder interface declaration
11   @interface AirfareFinder : NSObject <TwitterConnectionDelegate>
12   {
13      id <AirfareFinderDelegate> delegate; // this class's delegate
14      NSMutableArray *airfares; // all the Airfares constructed so far
15      Airfare *currentAirfare; // the Airfare currently in progress
16      NSMutableString *currentString; // the string currently in progress
17      BOOL isAirfare; // is the current entry an airfare?
18   } // end instance variable declarations
19
20   // declare delegate as a property
21   @property (nonatomic, assign) id <AirfareFinderDelegate> delegate;
22
23   - (void)getAirfares; // begins the process of finding the airfares
24   @end // end interface AirfareFinder
25
26   @protocol AirfareFinderDelegate // begin AirfareFinderDelegate declaration
27
```

Fig. 16.11 | Class that gets tweets and parses them for information. (Part 1 of 2.)

```
28    // called when the AirfareFinder finishes finding airfares
29    - (void)airfareFinder:(AirfareFinder *)finder
30      didFindAirfares:(NSArray *)fares;
31    @end // end protocol AirfareFinderDelegate
32
33    @interface NSString (parsing) // begin parsing category declaration
34    - (NSString *)parseCost; // parses the flight cost from the tweet
35    - (NSArray *)parseLocations; // parses the origin and destination
36    - (NSString *)removeLink; // removes the link from the tweet's end
37    @end // end parsing category declaration
```

Fig. 16.11 | Class that gets tweets and parses them for information. (Part 2 of 2.)

AirfareFinder's delegate adheres to the AirfareFinderDelegate protocol (line 13). It also contains an NSMutableArray (line 14), which stores the Airfares objects as they're created. The remaining instance variables (lines 15–17) store data as we parse the XML returned by the Twitter web service. The currentAirfare variable stores the Airfare currently being processed, currentString stores the string we'll use to display the data and isAirfare stores whether or not the current tweet has information about an airfare.

The getAirfares method (lines 23) begins the process of connecting to Twitter and parsing the returned XML. The airfareFinder:didFindAirfares: delegate method is called when the AirfareFinder finishes parsing all the XML. AirfareFinder.h also declares some new methods for NSString (lines 33–37). The parseCost method looks for a price in the current string and returns it. The parseLocations method searches for airport names in the string and returns them, and the removeLink method looks for a link and returns a string without it.

Defining the AirfareFinder Class Implementation
The getAirfares method (Fig. 16.12, lines 10–20) begins the process of getting new airfares from Twitter. We initialize the instance variables (lines 12–13), then create a new TwitterConnection (line 16). Line 18 performs a search that will yield tweets about discounted airfares from the Twitter account jetbluecheeps.

```
1    // Fig. 16.12: AirfareFinder.m
2    // AirfareFinder class implementation.
3    #import "AirfareFinder.h"
4
5    @implementation AirfareFinder
6
7    @synthesize delegate; // generate get and set methods for delegate
8
9    // creates a new connection to Twitter and performs the search
10   - (void)getAirfares
11   {
12      airfares = [[NSMutableArray alloc] init]; // initialize airfares
13      isAirfare = YES; // initialize isAirfare to YES
14
```

Fig. 16.12 | AirfareFinder class implementation. (Part 1 of 2.)

```
15      // create a new TwitterConnection
16      TwitterConnection *connection = [[TwitterConnection alloc] init];
17      connection.delegate = self; // set the TwitterConnection's delegate
18      [connection performSearch:@"from:jetbluecheeps"]; // search for tweets
19      [connection release]; // release the connection TwitterConnection
20   } // end method getAirfares
21
22   // called when the TwitterConnection receives all the data from Twitter
23   - (void)twitterConnection:(TwitterConnection *)connection
24      didReceiveData:(NSData *)data
25   {
26      // create a new NSXMLParser with the given data
27      NSXMLParser *parser = [[NSXMLParser alloc] initWithData:data];
28      parser.delegate = self; // set the parser's delegate to this object
29      [parser parse]; // begin parsing the data
30      [parser release]; // release the parser NSXMLParser
31   } // end method twitterConnection:didReceiveData:
32
```

Fig. 16.12 | AirfareFinder class implementation. (Part 2 of 2.)

The twitterConnection:didReceiveData: method is called after the Twitter-Connection receives data from Twitter. We requested that Twitter return the data in Atom format (Fig. 16.10, lines 12–13). To view a sample of the returned data, open a web browser, enter search.twitter.com/search.atom?q=*searchTerms* and view the page's source. The XML data contains an entry element for each returned tweet. Figure 16.13 shows the structure of an entry element containing data about a tweet.

```
1    <entry>
2        <id>id of tweet</id>
3        <published>date the tweet was published</published>
4        <link type="text/html" href=link to tweet rel="alternate"/>
5        <title>title of tweet</title>
6        <content type="html">text of tweet</content>
7        <updated>date the tweet was updated</updated>
8        <link type=format of image href=link to profile image rel="image"/>
9        <twitter:source>applicatoin that posted the tweet</twitter:source>
10       <twitter:lang>the language of the tweet</twitter:lang>
11       <author>
12           <name>name of the twitter account</name>
13           <uri>link for the twitter account</uri>
14       </author>
15   </entry>
```

Fig. 16.13 | XML containing information about a single tweet.

To retrieve the data from the XML, we use the class *NSXMLParser*—an event-driven XML parser included in Cocoa. NSXMLParser sends messages to its delegate as it parses XML data, informing the delegate of each start tag, the text within a tag and and each end tag. We initialize parser (Fig. 16.12, line 27), set its delegate to this object (line 28) and begin parsing by calling the parse method (line 29).

Implementing NSXMLParser *Delegate Methods*
The next three methods of AirfareFinder (Fig. 16.14) are the delegate methods called by
the NSXMLParser. Method parser:didStartElement:namespaceURI:qualifiedName:at-
tributes: (lines 34–51) is called for an element's start tag. Method parser:didEndEle-
ment:namespaceURI:qualifiedName: (lines 54–96) is called for an element's end tag.
Method parser:foundCharacters: (lines 101–108) is called for the text between an element's start and end tags. It simply appends the tweet's text to currentString.

```
33   // called when the NSXMLParser begins a new XML element
34   - (void)parser:(NSXMLParser *)parser didStartElement:
35     (NSString *)elementName namespaceURI:(NSString *)namespaceURI
36     qualifiedName:(NSString *)qualifiedName attributes:
37     (NSDictionary *)attributeDict
38   {
39     // if the parser found a <entry> tag
40     if ([elementName isEqualToString:@"entry"])
41     {
42       currentAirfare = [[Airfare alloc] init]; // initialize new Airfare
43       isAirfare = YES; // initialize isAirfare to YES
44     } // end if
45
46     // if the parser found a <content> tag
47     else if ([elementName isEqualToString:@"content"])
48
49       // initialize currentString with a capacity of 50
50       currentString = [[NSMutableString alloc] initWithCapacity:50];
51   } // end parser:didStartElement:namespaceURI:qualifiedName:attributes:
52
53   // called when the NSXMLParser ends an XML tag
54   - (void)parser:(NSXMLParser *)parser didEndElement:(NSString *)elementName
55     namespaceURI:(NSString *)namespaceURI qualifiedName:(NSString *)qName
56   {
57     // if the parser found a </entry> tag
58     if ([elementName isEqualToString:@"entry"])
59     {
60       // if the current entry is an airfare
61       if (isAirfare)
62         [airfares addObject:currentAirfare]; // add object to airfares
63       [currentAirfare release]; // release the currentAirfare Airfare
64       currentAirfare = nil; // assign currentAirfare a value of nil
65     } // end if
66
67     // if the parser found a </content> tag
68     else if ([elementName isEqualToString:@"content"])
69     {
70       // find the entire tweet minus the link at the end
71       currentAirfare.tweet = [currentString removeLink];
72
73       // find how much the flight costs from the tweet
74       currentAirfare.cost = [currentString parseCost];
75
```

Fig. 16.14 | NSXMLParser delegate methods. (Part 1 of 2.)

```
76      // if the tweet didn't include a price
77      if (currentAirfare.cost == nil)
78          isAirfare = NO; // this tweet is not an airfare
79
80      // get the origin and destination from the tweet
81      NSArray *locations = [currentString parseLocations];
82
83      // assign the origin and destination to the Airfare
84      currentAirfare.origin = [locations objectAtIndex:0];
85      currentAirfare.destination = [locations objectAtIndex:1];
86   } // end else
87
88   // if the parser found a </feed> tag
89   else if ([elementName isEqualToString:@"feed"])
90      // pass the found airfares to the delegate
91      [delegate airfareFinder:self didFindAirfares:
92          [airfares autorelease]];
93
94   [currentString release]; // release the currentString NSMutableString
95   currentString = nil; // assign currentString a value of nil
96   } // end method parser:didEndElement:namespaceURI:qualifiedName:
97
98   // called when the NSXMLParser finds characters inside an element
99   - (void)parser:(NSXMLParser *)parser foundCharacters:(NSString *)string
100  {
101     // if currentString has been initialized
102     if (currentString != nil)
103
104        // append the found characters to currentString
105        [currentString appendString:string];
106  } // end method parser:foundCharacters:
107  @end
108
```

Fig. 16.14 | NSXMLParser delegate methods. (Part 2 of 2.)

In method parser:didStartElement:namespaceURI:qualifiedName:attributes:, we begin by checking if the element is an entry element (40–44). If so, we initialize a new Airfare (line 42) to hold the entry. If it was a content tag, we initialize currentString to hold the text of the tweet (line 50).

In parser:didEndElement:namespaceURI:qualifiedName:, we first check if the end tag terminates an entry element (line 58). If so, and if isAirfare is YES, we add the created Airfare object to airfares (line 62). (Some tweets are not discount airfares.) If it was a content tag (line 68), we update the current working Airfare with currentString (lines 71–85). First we get the full tweet minus the hyperlink by calling the removeLink method (line 71). Then we get the flight cost using the parseCost method (line 74) of our parsing category. If the parser couldn't find a cost, we set isAirfare to NO (line 78)— meaning that the tweet was not about a discount airfare. We then get the origin and destination airports in an array using the parseLocations method (line 81) of our parsing category, then update currentAirfare with them (lines 84–85). Line 89 checks for the end of a feed tag, which indicates the end of the XML document. In this case, line 92 calls the delegate method with the found Airfares. We autorelease airfares so the delegate is not responsible for releasing the object.

Implementing the parsing Category's parseCost Method

Method parseCost (Fig. 16.15) finds the price in the tweet. First, we get the index of a $ sign in the tweet (line 115) using the *rangeOfString: method*. Then, we find the index of the next non-digit character (lines 120–129) and create a substring using the *substringWithRange: method* (line 136), which we pass index as the starting position and the difference between index and i as the length. Line 138 returns the substring.

```
109  @implementation NSString (parsing) // begin category parsing of NSString
110
111  // returns the cost of the airfare, if one is found
112  - (NSString *)parseCost
113  {
114     // get the index of the $ sign
115     int index = [self rangeOfString:@"$"].location;
116     int i = index + 1; // initalize i
117     BOOL found = NO; // initalize found to NO
118
119     // while a character other than a digit hasn't been found
120     while (!found && i < self.length)
121     {
122        char c = [self characterAtIndex:i]; // get the character at index i
123
124        // if the character is not a digit
125        if (c <= '0' || c >= '9')
126           found = YES; // a non-digit has been found
127
128        ++i; // increment i
129     } // end while
130
131     NSString *cost = nil; // initialize cost to nil
132
133     // if a dollar sign was found
134     if (index < self.length)
135        // get the $ plus the digits
136        cost = [self substringWithRange:NSMakeRange(index, i - index)];
137
138     return cost; // return the result
139  } // end method parseCost
140
```

Fig. 16.15 | Method parseCost of category parsing of class NSString.

Implementing the parsing Category's parseLocations Method

The parseLocations method (Fig. 16.16) of the parsing category returns an NSArray in which the first element is the origin airport and the second is the destination. Because the tweets give three-letter airport codes, we find the airports by searching for sequences of three capital letters. First, we initialize origin, destination and capitalCount (lines 145–146). Then lines 149–174 iterate through each character in the tweet. If the character is in uppercase (line 154), we increment capitalCount. If we've found three capital letters in a row (line 160), we assign those characters to origin (line 165) or destination (line 170) depending on whether each has been assigned a value—the origin will always be assigned a value before the destination. We then construct an NSArray with origin as the first value and destination as the second (line 181) and return it (line 183).

```
141   // return the origin and destination of the airfare
142   - (NSArray *)parseLocations
143   {
144      // initialize origin and destination to nil
145      NSString *origin = nil, *destination = nil;
146      int capitalCount = 0; // found zero capital letters so far
147
148      // iterate through each character in the string
149      for (int i = 0; i < self.length; i++)
150      {
151         char c = [self characterAtIndex:i]; // get the character at index i
152
153         // if the character is a capital letter
154         if (c >= 'A' && c <= 'Z')
155            ++capitalCount; // increment capitalCount
156         else
157            capitalCount = 0; // reset capitalCount
158
159         // if three sequential capital letters have been found
160         if (capitalCount == 3)
161         {
162            // if a origin hasn't been found yet
163            if (origin == nil)
164               // assign the three capital letters to origin
165               origin = [self substringWithRange:NSMakeRange(i - 2, 3)];
166
167            // if a destination hasn't been found yet
168            else if (destination == nil)
169               // assign the three capital letters to destination
170               destination = [self substringWithRange:NSMakeRange(i - 2, 3)];
171
172            capitalCount = 0; // reset capitalCount
173         } // end if
174      } // end for
175
176      NSArray *locations = nil; // initialize locations to nil
177
178      // if both a origin and a destination were found
179      if (origin != nil && destination != nil)
180         // create locations with the origin and destination
181         locations = [NSArray arrayWithObjects:origin, destination, nil];
182
183      return locations; // return the found locations
184   } // end method parseLocations
185
```

Fig. 16.16 | Method parseLocation of category parsing of class NSString.

Implementing the parsing Category's removeLink Method

Method removeLink (Fig. 16.17) searches for a link in the tweet and returns the portion of the tweet's text that appears before the link. Line 190 gets the location where the link begins. Line 196 gets the portion of the string that comes before the link and line 198 returns it. We subtract 3 from index to remove the word Go before the link.

```
186    // removes the part of the tweet containing a link
187    - (NSString *)removeLink
188    {
189        // find the location of the link
190        int index = [self rangeOfString:@"<a href="].location;
191        NSString *substring = nil; // initialize substring to nil
192
193        // if a link was found
194        if (index < self.length)
195            // create substring that doesn't include the link
196            substring = [self substringWithRange:NSMakeRange(0, index - 3)];
197
198        return substring; // return the substring
199    } // end method removeLink
200    @end // end category parsing of class NSString
```

Fig. 16.17 | Method removeLink of category parsing of class NSString.

Declaring the AirfareCell Interface

Class AirfareCell (Fig. 16.18) is a subclass of UITableView that displays information about a single airfare. It consists of four UILabels and a UIImageView. The priceLabel UILabel (line 8) displays the flight's cost, originLabel (line 9) displays the origin airport, destinationLabel (line 10) displays the destination airport and tweetLabel (line 11) displays the tweet's text. The planeView UIImageView (line 12) displays a directional image of an airplane flying from the origin airport to the destination airport. All four UILabels are declared as readonly properties (lines 16–19). This allows other objects to change the text in the UILabels, but not the UILabels themselves.

```
1    // Fig. 16.18: AirfareCell.h
2    // UITableViewCell that displays information about an airfare.
3    // Implementation in AirfareCell.m
4    #import <UIKit/UIKit.h>
5
6    @interface AirfareCell : UITableViewCell
7    {
8        UILabel *priceLabel; // label that shows the airfare price
9        UILabel *originLabel; // label that shows the origin airport
10       UILabel *destinationLabel; // label that shows the destination
11       UILabel *tweetLabel; // shows the tweet the airfare came from
12       UIImageView *planeView; // shows a directional image of a plane
13    } // end instance variable declarations
14
```

Fig. 16.18 | UITableViewCell that displays information about an airfare. (Part 1 of 2.)

```
15  // declare all the UILabel instance variables as properties
16  @property (nonatomic, readonly) UILabel *priceLabel;
17  @property (nonatomic, readonly) UILabel *originLabel;
18  @property (nonatomic, readonly) UILabel *destinationLabel;
19  @property (nonatomic, readonly) UILabel *tweetLabel;
20  @end // end interface AirfareCell
```

Fig. 16.18 │ UITableViewCell that displays information about an airfare. (Part 2 of 2.)

Class AirfareCell Implementation

Lines 7–10 of AirfareCell.m (Fig. 16.19) synthesize the four properties we declared in the header file. Method initWithStyle:reuseIdentifier: (lines 13–72) initializes an AirfareCell. We initialize originLabel and destinationLabel first (lines 21–24). To get the configuration information for the frames of the GUI components in AirfareCell, we created a temporary nib file with a UITableViewCell in it. We laid out all the cell's components in Interface Builder, then used the **Inspector** window to view each component's location, width and height. Next, we used those values programmatically in Xcode (lines 21–24). You can also load UITableViewCells directly from a nib file. Apple provides a guide for this under the heading **Loading Custom Table-View Cells From Nib Files** at:

> developer.apple.com/iphone/library/documentation/UserExperience/
> Conceptual/TableView_iPhone/TableViewCells/TableViewCells.html

```
 1  // Fig. 16.19: AirfareCell.m
 2  // AirfareCell class implementation.
 3  #import "AirfareCell.h"
 4
 5  @implementation AirfareCell
 6
 7  @synthesize priceLabel; // generate get and set methods for priceLabel
 8  @synthesize originLabel; // generate get and set methods for originLabel
 9  @synthesize destinationLabel; // get and set methods for destinationLabel
10  @synthesize tweetLabel; // generate get and set methods for tweetLabel
11
12  // initializes the AirfareCell
13  - (id)initWithStyle:(UITableViewCellStyle)style
14      reuseIdentifier:(NSString *)reuseIdentifier
15  {
16      // if the superclass initializes properly
17      if ( self =
18          [super initWithStyle:style reuseIdentifier:reuseIdentifier])
19      {
20          // create the origin and destination labels
21          originLabel =
22              [[UILabel alloc] initWithFrame:CGRectMake(20, 5, 70, 64)];
23          destinationLabel =
24              [[UILabel alloc] initWithFrame:CGRectMake(171, 5, 70, 64)];
25
```

Fig. 16.19 │ AirfareCell class implementation. (Part 1 of 3.)

```
26        // create the font for the origin and destination labels
27        UIFont *locationFont =
28           [UIFont fontWithName:@"CourierNewPS-BoldMT" size:33];
29        originLabel.font = locationFont; // apply font to originLabel
30        destinationLabel.font = locationFont; // apply font to destination
31
32        // set the text color of originLabel to dark blue
33        originLabel.textColor =
34           [UIColor colorWithRed:0 green:0 blue:0.8 alpha:1];
35
36        // set the text color of destinationLabel to dark blue
37        destinationLabel.textColor =
38           [UIColor colorWithRed:0 green:0 blue:0.8 alpha:1];
39
40        // create the price label
41        priceLabel =
42           [[UILabel alloc] initWithFrame:CGRectMake(250, 2, 83, 64)];
43
44        priceLabel.font = [UIFont systemFontOfSize:30]; // set label's font
45
46        // set priceLabel's text color
47        priceLabel.textColor =
48           [UIColor colorWithRed:0 green:0.95 blue:0 alpha:1];
49
50        // create tweetLabel
51        tweetLabel =
52           [[UILabel alloc] initWithFrame:CGRectMake(20, 55, 280, 61)];
53        tweetLabel.font = [UIFont systemFontOfSize:14]; // set label's font
54        tweetLabel.numberOfLines = 3; // set the number of lines in label
55
56        // create the plane image
57        UIImage *plane = [UIImage imageNamed:@"plane.png"];
58
59        // create an image view for the image
60        planeView = [[UIImageView alloc] initWithImage:plane];
61        planeView.frame = CGRectMake(102, 20, 51, 34); // set the frame
62
63        // add the views to the contentView
64        [self.contentView addSubview:originLabel];
65        [self.contentView addSubview:destinationLabel];
66        [self.contentView addSubview:priceLabel];
67        [self.contentView addSubview:tweetLabel];
68        [self.contentView addSubview:planeView];
69     } // end if
70
71     return self; // return this object
72  } // end method initWithStyle:reuseIdentifer:
73
74  // release the AirfareCell's memory
75  - (void)dealloc
76  {
77     [originLabel release]; // release the originLabel UILabel
```

Fig. 16.19 | AirfareCell class implementation. (Part 2 of 3.)

```
78     [destinationLabel release]; // release the destinationLabel UILabel
79     [priceLabel release]; // release the priceLabel UILabel
80     [tweetLabel release]; // release the tweetLabel UILabel
81     [super dealloc]; // call the superclass's dealloc method
82  } // end method dealloc
83  @end
```

Fig. 16.19 | AirfareCell class implementation. (Part 3 of 3.)

We next create the font to use with originLabel and destinationLabel (lines 27–28). We apply it to the UILabels (lines 29–30), then set the text color (lines 33–38). We initialize priceLabel (lines 41–42) and set its font (line 44) and text color (lines 47–48). Next, we initialize tweetLabel (lines 51–52) and set its font (line 53). We also set its numberOfLines property (line 54) so the label has three lines of text. We initialize plane-View with a plane image stored in our app's **Resources** group (lines 57–61), then add all the initialized components to the cell's contentView (lines 64–68).

16.5 Wrap-Up

In the **Twitter Discount Airfares** app, we interacted with Twitter web services using the NSURLRequest and NSURLConnection classes. We used NSURLConnection's delegate methods to retrieve data and determine when the connection closed. We then parsed the retrieved XML data with an NSXMLParser. We searched the parsed data for useful information, such as the origin airport, destination airport and cost of the flight, then displayed the data in a **Table View**. We used custom UITableViewCells to present the data in a user-friendly format. We also used the UIWebView class to display a the web page linked to each discount airfare tweet.

We hope you enjoyed *iPhone for Programmers* as much as we enjoyed writing it. We'd appreciate your feedback. Please send your comments, suggestions or corrections to deitel@deitel.com. Check out our growing list of iPhone-related Resource Centers at www.deitel.com/ResourceCenters.html. To stay up-to-date with the latest news about Deitel publications and corporate training, sign up for the free weekly *Deitel® Buzz Online* e-mail newsletter at www.deitel.com/newsletter/subscribe.html, and follow us on Facebook (www.deitel.com/deitelfan) and Twitter (@deitel). To learn more about Deitel & Associates' worldwide on-site programming training for your company or organization, visit www.deitel.com/training or e-mail deitel@deitel.com.

Index

Symbols

!= operator 80
?: operator **182**
(CSR) Certificate Signing Request **26**
@"*string*" NSString literal **80**
@encode compiler directive **177**
@selector **98**
@synthesize directive 176
* operator 81
/ operator 81
& (address of) operator **177**
# preprocessor operator 72
#import macro **72**
% operator 81
- operator 81
+ operator 81
< operator 81
<= operator 81
== operator 80
> operator 81
>= operator 81

Numerics

148Apps app review site 46

A

absoluteString method of class NSURL 297
Abstract Factory design pattern 10
abstract factory design pattern **91**
accelerometer 6
acceptConnection-FromPeer:error: method of class GKSession **354**
access a property with dot (.) notation 79
accessibility 7, 32

Accessibility Programming Guide for iPhone OS 35
accessories 13, 14
accessoryView property of class UITableViewCell **337**
action **73**
actionSheet:clickedButtonAtIndex: of protocol UIActionSheetDelegate 272
Ad 25
Ad Hoc distribution 25, **29**, 32
addAttachmentData:mimeType:fileName: method of class MFMailComposeViewController **340**
addition 81
addObject: method of class NSMutableArray 248, 292
Address Book 12
Address Book app xxx, 15
Address Book UI 11
address of (&) operator **177**
addSubView: method of class UIView 233
addTarget:action:forControlEvents: method of a GUI component **98**, **100**
addTarget:action:forControlEvents: of class UIControl 216
AdMob 37, 47
advertising revenue 37
AdWhirl 37, 47
alertView:clickedButtonAtIndex: of protocol UIAlertViewDelegate 183
allKeys method of class NSDictionary 350
allObjects of class NSSet **182**
allowMetering property of class AVAudioRecorder **320**

allowsImageEditing property of class UIImagePickerController 270, 295
allowsPickingMultipleItems property of class MPMediaPickerController **272**
alpha property of class UIImageView 260
alpha transparency 20
alphabetical order 84
altitude 224
Amazon Mobile app 37
Android 49
Anecdotes 48
animation 132
  manually perform with timer events 156
API 11
apiwiki.twitter.com/ 49
app xxxv
app approval process 24
app delegate **302**
app development xxxv
app distribution 29
App ID 25, **27**
app review sites
  148Apps 46
  AppCraver 46
  Apple iPhone School 46
  Appletell 46
  Apptism 46
  AppVee 46
  Ars Technica 46
  Fresh Apps 46
  Gizmodo 46
  iPhone App reviews 45
  iPhone Toolbox 46
  iusethis 46
  Macworld 46

app review sites (cont.)
   The App Podcast 46
   What's on iPhone 45
App Store xxxi, xxxv, 3, 7, 24,
   25, 37, 41, 45
   Books category 7
   Business category 7
   Education category 7
   Entertainment category 7
   Finance category 7
   Games category 7
   Healthcare and Fitness cate-
      gory 7
   Lifestyle category 7
   Medical category 7
   Music category 7
   Navigation category 7
   News category 8
   Photography category 8
   Productivity category 8
   Reference category 8
   Social Networking category
      8
   Sports category 8
   Travel category 8
   Utilities category 8
   Weather category 8
App Store 5
App Store distribution 25, 29,
   32
AppCraver app review site 46
app-driven approach xxx, **2**
Apple developer account xxxv
Apple Inc. 9
Apple iPhone School app review
   site 46
Apple Macintosh 9
Apple online documentation 2
Apple Push Notification **13**, 32
Appletell app review site 46
applicationMusicPlayer
   method of class MPMusic-
   PlayerController **262**
apps
   Amazon Mobile 37
   Bank of America 37
   Comcast Mobile 37
   ESPN ScoreCenter 37
   Nationwide Mobile 37
Apptism app review site 46

AppVee app review site 46
archivedDataWithRootOb-
   ject: method of class NS-
   KeyedArchiver 348
archiveRootObject:toFile:
   method of class NSKeyed-
   Archiver **303**
archiving **282**
arithmetic operators 81
Ars Technica app review site 46
arstechnica.com/apple/
   iphone/apps/ 46
assign keyword **124**
association **17**
Atom format 366
attribute **16**
attribute of an entity (Core Data) **345**
audio xxxi
audio book **14**
audio messages 9
Audio Toolbox 12
Audio Unit 12
audiobooks 9
autofocus camera 6
autorelease message 122
autorelease method of class
   NSObject **122**
autorelease pool **122**
autoresizingMask property of
   class UIView **258**
AV Foundation 12
AV Foundation framework 314
available property of class GK-
   Session **352**
availableMediaTypesFor-
   SourceType method of class
   UIImagePickerController
   295
AVAudioPlayer class 132, 133,
   158, 314, 334
   currentTime property **333**
   pause method 335
   volume property 332
AVAudioRecorder class **315**
   allowMetering property
      320
   averagePowerForChannel:
      method **321**

AVAudioRecorder class (cont.)
   prepareToRecord method
      320
   record method **320**
   updateMeters method **321**
AVAudioSession class 314, 334
   category property 316
   setCategory: method **317**,
      319
   sharedInstance method
      316
AVaudioSession class
   setCategory: method 334
AVAudioSessionCategory-
   Playback 334
AVAudioSessionCategory-
   Playback class 314
AVAudioSessionCategory-
   Record 319
AVAudioSessionCategory-
   Record class 314
AVAudioSessionCategory-
   SoloAmbient 317, 335
averagePowerForChannel:
   method of class
   AVAudioRecorder **321**
AVFoundation framework 132
awakeFromNib message **79**
awakeFromNib method **78**

B

backBarButtonItem property of
   class UINavigationItem 198
backgroundColor of class
   UIView 190
backgroundColor property of
   class UIView 191, 226
Bank of America app 37
Bar Button Item 86
becomeFirstResponder method of a GUI component **79**
becomeFirstResponder method of class UITextField 286,
   324
becomeFirstResponder method of class UIViewCon-
   troller 185
Before You Begin xxxv

beginAnimations:context:
method of class UIView **138**, 190, 208

behavior **16**

binary 40

Bing 49

bitwise OR operator 259, 305

BlackBerry 49

blog.wundrbar.com/ 48

Blogger 44

blogging 44

Bluetooth 7, 13, 14

brand awareness 37

Build and Debug button (Xcode) 18, 55

Build and Go button (Xcode) **18**, 55, 61

Build and Run button (Xcode) 18, 55

Bundle Indentifier **27**

Bundle Programming Guide 34, 50

Bundle Seed ID **27**

Button 18, **86**

C

C# xxx

C++ xxx

CALayer class 132, 141, 145
presentationLayer method **141**
removeAllAnimations method 146

Calculator 5

CalDAV 9

Calendar 9

Calendar 5

call a function after a specified delay 132

Camera 5

camera 4, 6

camera, autofocus 6

canBecomeFirstResponder of class UIResponder **183**

Cannon Game app xxx, xxxi, 12, 15

category **91**, 101, 121, 198, 204, 257, 288
enhance an existing class **91**

category (cont.)
methods added to a class at runtime 91

category property of class AVAudioSession 316

Certificate Signing Request (CSR) **26**

Certificates 26, 27, 29

CFNetwork 13

CGAffineTransformIdentity **237**

CGColorGetComponents function **190**

CGContext class 168

CGContextAddLineToPoint function of CGContext Reference 229

CGContextDrawImage function of CGContext Reference 169

CGContextMoveToPoint function of CGContext Reference 169, 229, 328

CGContextRestoreCGState function of the CoreGraphics framework 230

CGContextRotateCTM function of the CoreGraphics framework 230

CGContextSaveGState function of the CoreGraphics framework 230

CGContextScaleCTM function **168**

CGContextSelectFont function of CGContext Reference **169**

CGContextSetLineWidth function of the CoreGraphics framework 227

CGContextSetRGBFillColor function of CGContextReference **169**

CGContextSetRGBStrokeColor function of CGContextReference 328

CGContextSetRGBStrokeColor function of the CoreGraphics framework 229

CGContextShowTextAtPoint function of CGContextReference 169

CGContextStrokePath function 180

CGContextStrokePath function of CGContext Reference 169, 328

CGContextStrokePath function of the CoreGraphics framework 230

CGContextTranslateCTM function 168

CGContextTranslateCTM function of the CoreGraphics framework **230**

CGImage class 169

CGImage property of class UIView 169

CGMakeRect function of CGGeometry Reference 169

CGPoint **96**, 176

CGPoint class 227, 229

CGPointMake function of CGGeometry Reference 230

CGRect class **96**, 169, 257, 263

CGRectMake function of CGGeometry Reference 169

CGSize class 96, **99**, 327

CGSizeMake **99**

Chain-of-Responsibility design pattern 10, **141**

characteristics of great apps 35

chat 14

choosing photos from the iPhone's photo library 245

Chrome 49

class **16**
interface 72

Class Actions 91

class cluster **91**

class declaration 65

class implementation 65

class library **10**

Class Outlets 91

Classes
AVAudioPlayer 132, 133, 158, 314, 334
AVAudioRecorder **315**
AVAudioSession 314, 334

Classes (cont.)

AVAudioSessionCategory-Playback 314

AVAudioSessionCategoryRecord 314

CALayer 132, 141, 145

CGContext 168

CGImage 169

CGPoint 227, 229

CGRect **96**, 169, 257, 263

CGSize 96, **99**, 327

CLHeading 224, **232**

CLLocation 224, **226**, 229, 230

CLLocationManager 224, **232**, 236, 237

FetchedRequestController **345**

FlipsideViewController 188

GKPeerPickerController **345**, **346**, 347

GKSession 345, 348, 352, 354

MFMailComposeViewController 314, **340**

MKAnnotationView **236**

MKMapView 224, **226**

MPMediaItemCollection 245, **257**, **267**, 287

MPMediaPickerController 245, **267**, **272**

MPMoviePlayerController 282

MPMusicPlayer 262

MPMusicPlayerController 245, **257**, **262**

NSArray **91**, 207

NSAutoreleasePool 122

NSBundle **112**

NSCoder 282, 284, 288

NSData **339**, 348, 355

NSDate 224, **232**

NSDictionary **90**, 98, 200, 296, 348, 350, 355

NSEntityDescription **345**, 348, 350, 355

NSError 352

Classes (cont.)

NSFetchedResultsController **351**, **352**, 355, 358

NSFetchRequest **345**

NSFileManager **94**, 198, 298, 332

NSIndexPath **202**, 214, 249, 251, 293, 300, 350, 358

NSKeyedArchiver 282, 303, 348

NSKeyedUnarchiver **292**

NSLocale 80

NSManagedObject **345**, **347**, 348, 358

NSManagedObjectContext **345**, **352**

NSMutableArray **86**, **91**, 133, 178, 198, 226, 246, 252, 288, 292, 326, 327

NSMutableData **373**

NSMutableDictionary **86**, **90**, 178, 200, 348, 355

NSNotificationCenter **308**

NSNumber **111**, 137, 326, 328

NSNumberFormatter 80

NSObject 112

NSPredicate 314, 325

NSSet **140**

NSSortDescriptor **362**

NSString **73**, 297, 332

NSTimer **156**, **158**, 161, 262, 315

NSURL **100**, 297, 298, 372

NSURLConnection 366, **374**

NSURLRequest **372**

NSUserDefault **137**

NSValue **177**

NSXMLParser 366, **378**

UIActionSheet 245, **267**, 299

UIActivityIndicatorView **368**

UIAlertView 118, 353

UIApplication 259, 262, 302

UIBarButtonItem **198**, 245, 247, 267, 334, 347, 369

UIButton 97, 253, 315

Classes (cont.)

UIColor 174, 188, 226

UIImage 132, 169, 249, 258, 288, 294, 296, 305

UIImagePickerController 245, **267**, **270**, 282, 295

UIImageView **53**, 59, 132, 257, 259, 262, 305

UILabel **53**, 350

UINavigationController 245, 247, 248, 251, 259, 293, 359

UINavigationItem 247, 349, 352

UIScrollView 88

UISlider 190

UITableView **196**, 201, 202, 214, 247, 248, 249, 293, 296, 332, 350, 351, 355, 366

UITableViewCell 197, 210, 249, 293, 300, 350, 358, 366

UITableViewCellEditingStyle 203

UITableViewController 198, 246

UITextField 216, 286, 322, 324

UIToolbar 245, 267

UITouch 132, **140**, 182

UIView 178, 187, 190, 198, 225, 233, 257, 258, 262, 325

UIViewController **111**, 198, 200, 264, 292, 296, 315, 322, 346

UIWebView 366, **371**

Classes group 55, 71, 89

classified listings 17

clearColor method of class UIColor 226

CLHeading class 224, **232**

  trueHeading property **237**

ClickPress 46

client of a class **16**

CLLocation class 224, **226**, 229, 230

  getDistanceFrom: method 236

CLLocation class (cont.)
  latitude property 230
  longitude property 230
CLLocationManager class 224, **232**, 236, 237
  startUpdatingHeading method **235**
  startUpdatingLocation method **235**
  stopUpdatingHeading method **234**
  stopUpdatingLocation method **234**, 237
CLLocationManagerDelegate protocol **231**, 236, 237
  locationManager:did-FailWithError: **237**
  locationManager:didUp-dateHeading: **237**
  locationManager:didUp-dateToLocation:from-Location: 236
Cocoa xxix, xxx, xxxi, 2, **10**, 11, 16
  frameworks **10**, 11
Cocoa frameworks 55, **56**
  Address Book 12
  Address Book UI 11
  Audio Toolbox 12
  Audio Unit 12
  AV Foundation 12
  CFNetwork 13
  Cocoa Touch Layer 11
  Core Audio 12
  Core Data 12
  Core Foundation 12
  Core Graphics 12
  Core Location 12
  Core OS Layer 13
  Core Services Layer 12
  External Accessory 13
  Foundation 12
  Map Kit 11
  Media Layer 12
  Media Player 12
  Message UI 11

Cocoa frameworks (cont.)
  Mobile Core Services 12
  OpenGL ES 12
  Quartz Core 12
  Security 13
  Store Kit 13
  System 13
  System Configuration 13
  UIKit 11
Cocoa Touch 10
Cocoa Touch Class 71
Cocoa Touch Layer 11
code examples xxxv
code highlighting 2
code license xxix
code walkthrough 2
code.google.com 49
code.google.com/chromium/ 49
Comcast Mobile app 37
Command design pattern 10, **100**
commitAnimations method of class UIView **138**, 190, 208
Compass 5
compass 6
compass heading 224
component **15**
Components
  Flexible Space Bar Button Item **225**
Composite design pattern 10
connection:didFailWithEr-ror: of protocol NSURLCon-nectionDelegate 376
connection:didReceiveData: of protocol NSURLConnec-tionDelegate 376
connection:didReceiveRe-sponse: of protocol NSURL-ConnectionDelegate 376
connectionDidFinishLoad-ing: of protocol NSURLCon-nectionDelegate 376
connectionTypesMask property class GKPeerPickerCon-troller **347**
const qualifier **110**
constant **89**, **158**
consumables 42

Contacts 4, 5
contentView property of class UIView 254
continue audio when the screen locks 316
contract information 34
Contracts, Tax & Banking In-formation 43
controller (in MVC) **71**
Controls
  Button 18
  Label 18
  Slider 18
  View 18
convertCoordinate:toPoint-ToView: method of class MK-MapView **229**
copy and paste 8
copy text 8
copyItemAtPath:newPath:er-ror: method of class NSFile-Manager 298
copyright xxix
Core Animation 260, 282, 309
Core Animation block **138**, 190, 306
Core Animation framework 132, 156
Core Animation Layer 132
Core Audio 12
Core Audio File 319
Core Data 12, 351
Core Data data model 345
Core Data framework xxxi, **345**
Core Data object 347
Core Foundation 12
Core Graphics 12
Core Graphics framework 157
Core Location 12
Core Location framework xxxi, 224, **232**
Core OS Layer 13
Core Services Layer 12
count property 335
count property of class NSMut-ableArray 335
CPU usage xxxi
CraigsList (www.craigs-list.org) 17
create derivative apps xxix

cStringUsingEncoding method of class NSString **169**
current system time 319
currentTime property of class AVAudioPlayer 332, **333**
cut and paste 8
cut text 8

D

dailymobile.se/2009/02/11/iphone-humor-cell-phone-reunion/ 49
data model editor **346**
dataSource of class UITableView **201**
dataWithContentsOfFile: method of class NSData **339**
Decktrade 48
decodeIntForKey: method of class NSCoder **285**
decodeObjectForKey method of class NSCoder **285**, 288
decoding **282**
Decorator design pattern 10, **121**
Default Apps 4
  App Store 5
  Calculator 5
  Calendar 5
  Camera 5
  Compass 5
  Contacts 5
  iPod 5
  iTunes 5
  Mail 5
  Maps 5
  Messages (SMS/MMS) 5
  Notes 5
  Phone 5
  Photos 5
  Safari 5
  Settings 5
  Stocks 5
  Voice Memos 5
  Weather 5
  YouTube 5
default install location for the SDK xxxvi
defaultCenter of class NSNotificationCenter **308**

defaultManager method of class NSFileManager 198, 332
Deitel® Buzz Online Newsletter (www.deitel.com/newsletter/subscribe.html) xxxiii, xxxvi, 17, 386
Deitel® Training (deitel.com/training) 386
delay before calling a function 132
delegate 121
delegate protocol 121
deleteObject: method of class NSManagedObjectContext **360**
deleteRowsAtIndexPaths:withRowAnimation: method of class UITableView **203**, 338
Delicious (www.delicious.com) 17, 44
denyConnectionFromPeer: method of class GKSession **354**
dequeReusableCellWithIdentifier: method of class UITableView 249, 293
dequeueReusableCellWithIdentifier: method of class UITableView 197, **202**, 210, 214, 358
deserialized **282**
Design patterns xxxi, 10, 71
  Abstract Factory 10, **91**
  Chain of Responsibility 10
  Command 10, **100**
  Composite 10
  Decorator 10, **121**
  Facade 10
  Memento 11
  Model View Controller 10
  Singleton 11, **94**
  Template Method 11, **79**
Detail Disclosure Button 86
detect performance problems 169
developer.apple.com/ 14, 53
developer.apple.com/cocoa/ 11, 56

developer.apple.com/documentation/Cocoa/Conceptual/CocoaFundamentals/CocoaFundamentals.pdf 3
developer.apple.com/documentation/Cocoa/Conceptual/CodingGuidelines/CodingGuidelines.pdf 3
developer.apple.com/documentation/Cocoa/Conceptual/ObjCRuntimeGuide/ObjCRuntimeGuide.pdf 3
developer.apple.com/documentation/Cocoa/Conceptual/ObjectiveC/ObjC.pdf 3
developer.apple.com/documentation/DeveloperTools/Conceptual/Xcode_Overview/Contents/Resources/en.lproj/Xcode_Overview.pdf 3
developer.apple.com/documentation/DeveloperTools/Conceptual/XcodeDebugging/Xcode_Debugging.pdf 3
developer.apple.com/documentation/UserExperience/Conceptual/AppleHIGuidelines/XHIGIntro/XHIGIntro.html 3
developer.apple.com/iphone/ xxxii, 2, 25, 43
developer.apple.com/iphone/index.action# downloads xxxv
developer.apple.com/iphone/library/documentation/Cocoa/Conceptual/Strings/introStrings.html 80

developer.apple.com/
    iphone/library/
    documentation/
    CoreFoundation/
    Conceptual/CFBundles/
    Introduction/
    Introduction.html 50

developer.apple.com/
    iphone/library/
    documentation/iPhone/
    Conceptual/
    iPhoneOSProgrammingGuide
    /Introduction/
    Introduction.html 50

developer.apple.com/
    iphone/library/
    documentation/
    userexperience/
    conceptual/mobilehig/
    Introduction/
    Introduction.html 3, 50,
    30

developer.apple.com/
    iphone/library/
    documentation/Xcode/
    Conceptual/
    iphone_development/000-
    Introduction/
    introduction.html) 50

developer.apple.com/
    iPhone/library/
    navigation/Frameworks/
    index.html 11

developer.apple.com/
    iphone/library/
    navigation/index.html 50

developer.apple.com/
    iphone/program/start/
    register/ xxxv

developer.apple.com/tools/
    xcode/xcodeprojects.html
    3

developer.myspace.com/
    community/ 50

developer.palm.com/ 49

developer.symbian.org/ 49

developer.yahoo.com 49

developers.facebook.com/ 49

Development Certificate 26

Development Provisioning Pro-
    file **27**
development tool xxxvi
device name **27**
dictionaryWithDictionary:
    of class NSDictionary 208
Digg 44
directoryContentsAtPath:
    method of class NSFileMan-
    ager **332**
dismissModalViewControlle-
    rAnimated: method of class
    UIViewController **120**, 200,
    248, 292, 296
display the keyboard 265
display the numeric keyboard 79
displayNameForPeer: method
    of class GKSession **353**
distribution certificate 29
Distribution Provisioning Pro-
    file **29**, 30
division 81
Dock Connector 4, 13, 14
dot (.) notation 79
    cannot be used to invoke
    methods 79
double tap 4, 15
drag 4, 15
drawRect: of class UIView 227
drive sales 37
dynamic binding 100
dynamically typed **73**

E

earnings 37
ease of use 30
EditableCellDelegate proto-
    col 205
editButtonItem property of
    class UIViewController 247
encapsulation **16**
encodeInt:forKey: method of
    class NSCoder **285**, 289
encodeObject:forKey: meth-
    od of class NSCoder **285**, 289
encodeWithCoder: method of
    protocol NSCoder **282**
encoding **282**
@end keyword **73**

Enhanced Address Book app xxx,
    9, 11, 12, 14
Enhanced Slideshow app xxx
entity in a managed object mod-
    el **345**
entity method of class NSMan-
    agedObject **348**
enum 282
enum constant 282
enum keyword 287
enum type **256**
enumeration constant 287
equality 80
ESPN ScoreCenter app 37
evaluateWithObject: method
    of class NSPredicate **325**
event **75**
Events
    Editing Changed **75**
    Value Changed **75**
events **10**
Examples xxxvi
Examples.zip xxxvi
External Accessory 13

F

Facade design pattern 10
FaceBook 17
Facebook xxxiii, **44**, 49
    fan 45
    fan page 44
    friend 45
    www.deitel.com/deitel-
    fan 386
factory settings **6**
fan in Facebook 45
fan page in Facebook 44
Favorite Twitter Searches app xxx,
    10, 11, 12
fee-based app 8
fetch request **345**
FetchedRequestController
    class **345**
fetchedResultsController
    method 361
fileExistsAtPath
    94
fileURLWithPath: method of
    class NSURL 298
Financial Reports 43

financial transaction 41
Find My iPhone **6**
Finder xxxvi
Finder window **18**
Flag Quiz Game app xxx, xxxi, 10
Flexible Space Bar Button Item
component **225**, 267
flick 4, 15
Flickr 17, 44
flipside view 106, 191
used for settings 106
FlipsideViewController class
188
FlipsideViewControllerDel-
egate protocol **109**, 123
float 227, 327
floatValue method of class
NSNumber 328
for...in operator 95
format specifier **80**, 100
formatting string objects 80
Foundation 12
frame property 96
frame property of class UIView
257
Frameworks
AV Foundation 314
AVFoundation 132
Core Animation 132, 156
Core Data **345**
Core Graphics 157
Core Location 224
Game Kit **345**
Map Kit 224, **226**
Store Kit 41
UIKit 56
free app 8, 36, 41
Free Applications contract **34**
Fresh Apps app review site 46
friend 45
friend in Facebook 45
frontside view 106
function 16

G

Game Kit 32
Game Kit framework xxxi, **14**,
345
games 14, 35
generic pointer **80**

gesture **4**
Gestures
double tap 4
drag 4
flick 4
pinch 4
swipe 4
tap 4
touch and hold 4
getDistanceFrom: method of
class CLLocation 236
getValue: method of class NS-
Value **180**
Gizmodo app review site 46
gizmodo.com/5300060/find-
my-iphone-saved-my-
phone-from-a-thief 49
gizmodo.com/tag/iphone-
apps-directory/ 46
GKPeerPickerConnection-
TypeNearby constant **347**
GKPeerPickerController class
345, **346**, 347
connectionTypesMask
property **347**
show method **347**
GKPeerPickerControllerDelegate protocol **346**, 348, 349
peerPickerCon-
troller:didConnect-
Peer:toSession:
method **348**
peerPickerController-
DidCancel: method **349**
GKSendReliable constant **348**
GKSession class **345**, 348, 352,
354
acceptConnection-
FromPeer:error: meth-
od **354**
available property **352**
denyConnectionFromPeer:
method **354**
displayNameForPeer:
method **353**
initialize 352
sendDataToAllPeers:
withDataMode: method
345, **348**

GKSession class (cont.)
setDataReceiveHan-
dler:withContext:
method **352**
GKSessionDelegate protocol
346, 351, 353
session:didReceiveCon-
nectionRequest-
FromPeer: method **353**
GKSessionModeServer **352**
global variables **109**
Google 49
Google Maps xxxi, **13**
Google Maps web services 226
Google Mobile Maps Service 14
GPS 224
Graphical User Interface (GUI)
9
graphics xxxi
graphics context **168**, 178, 227
greater than 81
greater than or equal to 81
Groups and Files window 55, 71,
108, 109, 122
guesture 15
GUI (Grahical User Interface) **9**
GUI Components
Bar Button Item 86
Button 86
Detail Disclosure Button 86
Image View 53, **86**, 107
Info Button 106, **108**, **125**
Label 53, 67, **86**, 107, 133
Rounded Rect Button 86, 87
Scroll View 86, 88
Segmented Control 106, 110,
127
Slider 65, 68, **86**, 190
Switch 123
Tab Bar 86
Tab Bar Item 86
Text Field 66, 87, 285
Toolbar 86
View 86
GUI design 35

H

hashtag **45**
header file **71**, 108
heading, compass 224

headset jack 4
hearing impaired **7**
Home button 4
Humor 49

I
i-Newswire 47
IBAction **73**
IBOutlet **72**
icon 32, **33**
icon design firms
    icondesign 33
    IconDrawer 33
    Razorianfly Graphic Design
        33
    The Iconfactory 33
id <*ProtocolName*> 124
id generic pointer type **80**
id type **73**
    implicit 97
IDE (integrated development
    environment) xxxi, 14
if...else keyword 80
image picker 245, 296
image property of class
    UIImageView 132, 141
image transition 245
Image View **53**, 59, 61, 86
Image View GUI component 107
imagePickerController:did-
    FinishPickingImage:edit-
    ingInfo method of protocol
    UIImagePickerCon-
    trollerDelegate 271
images xxxi
implementation file **78**
@implementation keyword **78**
in-app advertising 36, **37**
In App Purchase **13**, 32, 41, 42
in-game voice communication
    14
indexPathForCell: method of
    class UITableView 293
indexPathForCell: of class
    UITableView 208
inequality 80
info button 18, 31
Info Button GUI Component
    106, **108**, **125**
information hiding **16**

inheritance **16**, 65, 72, **111**
inherits **72**
init method **92**
init of class NSMutableDic-
    tionary **94**
initialize an NSFetched-
    ResultsController 361
initWithCapacity: method of
    class NSMutableArray **111**,
    326
initWithCapacity: of class NS-
    MutableDictionary 207
initWithCoder: method of
    class NSObject **159**
initWithCoder: method of
    class UIView 177
initWithCoder: method of
    protocol NSCoder **282**
initWithCoder: method of
    protocol NSCoding 288
initWithContentsOfFile
    94
initWithContentsOfFile:
    method of class NSMutable-
    Array 198
initWithCustomView: of class
    UIBarButtonItem 369
initWithNibName:bundle: of
    class UIViewController 207
initWithObjects: method of
    class NSArray 207
initWithString: method of
    class NSString **94**
initWithStyle:reuseIdenti-
    fier: method of class
    UITableViewCell **202**, 384
initWithTitle:dele-
    gate:cancelButtonTi-
    tle:destructiveButtonTit
    le:otherButtonTitles:
    method of class UIAction-
    Sheet 299
insertRowsAtIndexPaths
    method of class
    UITableView 355
Inspector window **61**, 66, **73**,
    87, 91, 122
instance **16**
instance method **73**

instance variable **16**, 71, 73,
    133, 198
instantiated 16
Instruments tool xxxi, 53, 169
    Activity Monitor template
        169
    checking for memory leaks
        118
integrated development envi-
    ronment (IDE) xxxi, 14
Intel-based Mac xxxv
interface 16, 78
Interface Builder 9, 10, **14**, 53
interface of a class 72
international App Stores 32
Internet Public Relations
    ClickPress 46
    i-Newswire 47
    InternetNewsBureau.com
        47
    Marketwire 46
    openPR 47
    PR Leap 46
    Press Release Writing 47
    PRLog 47
    PRWeb 46
    PRX Builder 47
Internet telephony 17
Internet tethering **7**
InternetNewsBureau.com 47
invalidate method of class
    NSTimer **166**
iPhone 3G xxix, 3
iPhone 3GS xxix, 3
iPhone App Reviews 45
*iPhone Application Programming
    Guide* 34, 50
iPhone Developer Center 43
iPhone Developer Program 2,
    24, 25
iPhone Developer Program Por-
    tal 25, 26, 27, 28, 29
iPhone Developer University
    Program **3**
iPhone Development Certificate
    26
iPhone Development Guide 32,
    50
iPhone Development Team **25**

iPhone Distribution Certificate 29

iPhone for Programmers website www.deitel.com/books/iPhoneFP/ xxix

iPhone Human Interface Guidelines 24, **30**, 33, 34, 50

iPhone OS 3 Readiness Checklist 32

iPhone OS 3.0 8

iPhone OS 3.x 41

iPhone OS 3.x compatible 32

iPhone Reference Library 50

iPhone sales 3

iPhone SDK xxxv, xxxvi, 14

iPhone SDK 3.x xxix, xxxi, 13

iPhone simulator 14, 52

  rotate left 245

  rotate right 245

iPhone Toolbox app review site 46

iphone.iusethis.com/ 46

iPhoneSDK.mpkg xxxvi

iphonetoolbox.com/category/application/ 46

iPod 3, 9

iPod 4, 5

iPod library access xxxi, 14, 32

iPod music library 267, 281, 298

iPod Touch 2, 8

iterate through the items in a collection 95

iTunes 4, 7, 9, 39, 42

iTunes 5

iTunes Connect 24, 41, **42**

iTunes Connect Developer Guide 32, 33, 34, 42

iTunes Connect Modules 43

iTunes Store 9

itunesconnect.apple.com 38, 42

iusethis app review site 46

J

Java xxx

Jobs, Steve 9

K

kCLLocationAccuracyBest constant **233**

keyboard 4

  how to display 79

  how to set the type 210

  layout 9

Keychain Access 26, 27, 29

Keywords 32, 33

  for...in 95

  id **73**

  if...else 80

  nil **93**

  self **92**

  struct **158**

  super **92**

kUTypeImage class 296

L

Label GUI Component 18, **53**, 61, 67, 86, 107, 133, 191

landscape keyboard **6**, 8

language support 9

lastObject method of class NSMutableArray 230

lastPathComponent method of class NSString **112**, 297

latitude 224

latitude property of class CLLocation 230

launch image 32, **34**, 34

layer property of class UIView 141, 145

leftBarButtonItem property of class UINavigationItem 352

less than 81

less than or equal to 81

Library window 59, 67, 87, 91, 122

LinkedIn 44, 50

literal

  NSString 80

loadView method of class UIView 257

local variable

  declared static 79

localization 40

locate your iPhone 6

location (GPS) 224

location-based app 14

locationInView: method of class UIView **141**

locationManager:didFailWithError: of protocol CLLocationManagerDelegate **237**

locationManager:didUpdateHeading: of protocol CLLocationManagerDelegate **237**

locationManager:didUpdateToLocation:fromLocation: of protocol CLLocationManagerDelegate 236

lock the iPhone 4

longitude 224

longitude property of class CLLocation 230

M

Mac xxx

Mac OS X xxx, xxxv, 8, 9

Macintosh 9

Macworld app review site 46

Mail 4, 5

mailComposeController:didFinishWithResult:error: method of protocol MFMailComposeViewControllerDelegate **340**

mailComposeDelegate property of class MFMailComposeViewController **340**

mainBundle method of class NSBundle **112**

Manage Users 43

Manage Your Applications 43

Managed Object Context **345**

managed object model **345**

managedObjectContext method of class NSFetchedResultsController 355

map 14

Map Kit 11

Map Kit framework **xxxi**, **14**, 224, **226**

Maps 5

mapType property of class MKMapView **235**

mapView:regionDidChangeAn-
imated: of protocol MK-
MapViewDelegate **231**

mapView:regionWillChange-
Animated: of protocol MK-
MapViewDelegate **231**

marketing xxxi

Marketwire 46

mashup **13**

Media Layer 12

Media Player 12

Media Player framework xxxi,
14

Medialets 47

mediaPicker:didPickMedia-
Items: of protocol MPMedia-
PickerControllerDelegate
272

mediaTypes property of class
UIImagePickerController
282, 295

Memento design pattern 11

memory leak xxxi

memory limitation 30

memory management 106, 107
developer.apple.com/
iPhone/library/
documentation/Cocoa/
Conceptual/
MemoryMgmt/
MemoryMgmt.html 107

menu name xxxv

Menus
Build 54
Subclass of 71

message **75**, **79**

Message UI 11

Messages (SMS/MMS) 5

method implementations that
enhance an existing class 91

method of a class **16**, 71

MFMailComposeViewCon-
troller class 314, **340**
addAttachmentData:mime-
Type:fileName: method
340
mailComposeDelegate
property **340**

MFMailComposeViewCon-
trollerDelegate protocol
340
mailComposeController:
didFinishWithResult:
error: method **340**

micro blogging 44, 45

microphone 4, **8**

Microsoft Exchange ActiveSync
9

MKAnnotationView class **236**

MKCoordinateRegion struct
237

MKCoordinateSpan struct
237

MKCoordinateSpanMake function of MapKit 236

MKMapTypeSatellite map type
constant **235**

MKMapTypeStandard map type
constant **235**

MKMapView class 224, **226**
transform property **237**
convertCoordi-
nate:toPointToView:
method **229**
mapType property **235**
scrollEnabledproperty 234
zoomEnabledproperty 234

MKMapViewDelegate protocol
226
mapView:regionDid-
ChangeAnimated: **231**
mapView:regionWill-
ChangeAnimated: **231**

MKTypeHybrid map type constant **235**

MMS (Multimedia Messaging
Service) 9

mobile advertising network 37,
47
AdMob 37, 47
AdWhirl 37, 47
Decktrade 48
Medialets 47
Pinch Media 38
PinchMedia 48
Quattro Wireless 47
Tapjoy 37, 48

Mobile Core Services 12

MobileMe **6**, 49

modalTransitionStyle property of class UIViewController
121, 186

model (in MVC) **71**

Model-View-Controller (MVC)
design pattern xxxi, 10, **71**,
286, 345

modulus operator 116

monetization 47

monetize apps 37

monetizing apps 24

motionEnded:withEvent: of
class UIResponder **183**

mount xxxvi

mounted image xxxvi

moveItemAtPath:toPath:
method of class NSFileManager 321

movies 9

MPMediaItemCollection class
245, **257**, **267**, 287

MPMediaPickerController
class 245, **267**, **272**
allowsPickingMulti-
pleItems property **272**

MPMediaPickerController-
Delegate protocol
mediaPicker:didPick-
MediaItems: 272

MPMoviePlayerController
class 282

MPMusicPlayer class 262
play method 262
setQueueWithItemCollec-
tion: method 262

MPMusicPlayerController
class 245, **257**, **262**

MPMusicShuffleModeNone **262**

MPMusicShuffleModeOff **262**

msdn.microsoft.com/en-us/
windowsmobile/
default.aspx 49

MSMutableArray class
removeAllObjects method
327

multi-touch events 132

Multi-Touch screen 4, 11

multimedia xxxi

Multimedia Messaging Service (MMS) 9
multiplayer game 14
multiplication 81
music **14**
music library 9
mutableCopy method of class NSMutableArray 335
mutableCopy method of class NSObject **112**
mutually exclusive options 106
MVC (Model-view-controller) xxxi
MySpace 17, 44, 50

N

na.blackberry.com/eng/services/appworld/? 49
Nationwide Mobile app 37
navigate between an app's screens 245
navigation bar 198, 347, 349, 352
Navigation-based Application template 197, 204, 366
navigationController property of class UIViewController 197
navigationItem property of class UIViewController 198, 246
network activity xxxi
networkActivityIndicatorVisible of classl UIApplication **374**
New App ID button 27
New Project dialog **53**
NeXT 9, 56
NeXT Interface Builder 14
NeXTSTEP operating system 9
NeXTSTEP programming environment 56
nib file 14, 56, 92
Nike + iPod Sensor 14
nil keyword **93**
nonatomic keyword **109**
non-consumables 42
Notes 5, 9
nouns in a system specification 17

NSArray class **91**, 207
initWithObjects: method 207
NSAutoreleasePool class 122
NSBundle class **112**
mainBundle method **112**
pathForResource:ofType: method **112**, 134
NSCoder class 282, 284, 288
decodeInt:forKey: method **285**
decodeObject:forKey method **285**, 288
encodeInt:forKey: method **285**, 289
encodeObject:forKey: method **285**, 289
encodeWithCoder: method **282**
initWithCoder: method **282**
NSCoding protocol **282**, 288
initWithCoder: method 288
NSData class **339**, 355
dataWithContentsOfFile: method **339**
NSDataclass 348
NSDate class 224, **232**
timeIntervalSinceNow method **235**
NSDictionary class **90**, 98, **198**, 200, 296, 348, 350, 355
allKeys method 350
dictionaryWithDictionary: 208
valueForKey: method 296
writeToFile:atomically: method **98**
NSEntityDescription class **345**, 348, 350, 355
properties method **350**
propertiesByName method 348, 350
NSError class 352
NSFetchedResultsController class **351**, **352**, 355, 358
initialize 361
managedObjectContext method 355

NSFetchedResultsController class (cont.)
objectAtIndexPath: method 358
performFetch: method **352**
sections method 357
NSFetchedResultsControllerDelegate protocol **351**
NSFetchedResultsSectionInfo protocol **358**
numberOfObjects method **358**
NSFetchRequest class **345**
setSortDescriptors: method **362**
NSFileManager class **94**, 198, 298, 332
copyItemAtPath:newPath:error: method 298
defaultManager method 198, 332
directoryContentsAtPath: method **332**
moveItemAtPath:toPath: method 321
NSIndexPath class **202**, 214, 249, 251, 293, 300, 350, 358
row property 293, 350
NSKeyedArchiver class 282, 303, 348
archivedDataWithRootObject: method 348
archiveRootObject:toFile: method **303**
NSKeyedUnarchiver class **292**
unarchiveObjectWithFile: method **292**
NSLocale class 80
NSLog function of the Foundation framework 352, 355
NSManagedObject class **345**, **347**, 348, 358
entity method **348**
save method **355**, 357
setValue:forKey: method **355**
NSManagedObjectContext class **345**, **352**
deleteObject: method **360**

NSMutableArray **198**

NSMutableArray class **86, 91,** 133, 178, 198, 226, 246, 252, 288, 292, 326, 327, 335

  addObject: method 248, 292

  initWithCapacity: method **111**, 326

  initWithContentsOfFile: method 198

  lastObject method 230

  mutableCopy method 335

  objectAtIndex: method 328

  removeAllObjects method 230

  removeObjectAtIndex: method 252, 327

  sortUsingSelector: method 99

NSMutableData class **373**

NSMutableDictionary class **86, 90,** 178, 200, 348, 355

  init **94**

  initWithCapacity: 207

  removeAllObjects method 178

  setValue:forKey: **97**

  writeToFile:atomically: 200

NSNotificationCenter class **308**

  defaultCenter **308**

  removeObserver: **309**

NSNumber class **111,** 137, 326, 328

  floatValue method 328

  numberWithBool: method **111**

NSNumberFormatter class 80

NSObject class 112

  autorelease **122**

  initWithCoder: method **159**

  mutableCopy method **112**

  release method **107, 112**

  retain method **107, 112**

NSObject class performSelector:withObject:AfterDelay: method **116,** 137

NSPredicate class 314, 325

  evaluateWithObject: method **325**

  predicateWithFormat: method **325**

NSSearchPathForDirectoriesInDomains function 319, 331

NSSearchPathForDirectoriesInDomains funtion of the Foundation framework 198, 291

NSSet class **140**

  allObjects **182**

NSSortDescriptor class **362**

NSString class **73,** 297, 332

  @"*string*" literal **80**

  cStringUsingEncoding method **169**

  initWithString: method **94**

  lastPathComponent method **112,** 297

  pathExtension method **332**

  rangeOfString: method **381**

  sizeWithFont: 218

  stringByAddingPercentEscapesUsingEncoding: method 374

  stringByAppendingPathComponent: method **94,** 298, 332

  stringByDeletingLastPathComponent method 320

  stringWithFormat: method 333

  substringWithRange: method **381**

NSString literal 80

NSTemporaryDirectory function 297

NSTimer class **156, 158,** 161, 262, 315

  invalidate method **166**

NSURL class **100,** 297, 298, 372

  absoluteString method 297

NSURL class (cont.)

  fileURLWithPath: method 298

  path method **320**

  URLWithString: method 338

NSURLConnection class 366, **374**

NSURLConnectionDelegate protocol

  connection:didFailWithError: 376

  connection:didReceiveData: 376

  connection:didReceiveResponse: 376

  connectionDidFinishLoading: 376

NSURLRequest class **372**

NSUserDefault class **137**

  setValue:forKey: method **146**

  valueForKey: method **137**

NSValue class **177**

  getValue: method **180**

  valueWithBytes:objCType: **177**

  valueWithPointer: **182**

NSXMLParser class 366, **378**

NSXMLParserDelegate protocol

  parser:didEndElement:namespaceURI:qualifiedName: 379

  parser:didStartElement:namespaceURI:qualifiedName:attributes: 379

  parser:foundCharacters: 379

numberOfObjects method of protocol NSFetchedResultsSectionInfo **358**

numberOfSectionsInTableView: method of class UITableViewController 210, 248

numberWithBool: method of class NSNumber **111**

numeric keyboard, display 79

O

Object 91
object **15**, 16
object (or instance) 16
object graph **282**, **292**, 303
object messaging 100
object-oriented design (OOD) **16**
object-oriented language **16**
object-oriented programming (OOP) **9**, **16**
object serialization **282**, 309
object technology **15**
objectAtIndex: method of class NSMutableArray **94**, 328
objectAtIndexPath: method of class NSFetchedResults-Controller 358
Objective-C xxix, xxx, 2, **9**
Objective-C code xxxv
Objective-C command xxxv
on-screen component xxxv
OOD (object-oriented design) **16**
OOP (object-oriented programming) **9**, **16**
Open GL ES 2.0 12, 32
openPR 47
OpenStep 11
openURL method of class UIApplication **101**
operating system 8
operating system requirements xxxv
Operators
  - 81
  != 80
  ?: **182**
  * 81
  / 81
  % 81
  + 81
  < 81
  <= 81
  == 80
  > 81
  >= 81
Orkut 44
OS X 9

P

paid app 41
Paid Applications contract **34**
Painter app xxx, **17**
Parental Controls 9, 32, 39
parser:didEndElement:namespaceURI:qualifiedName: of protocol NSXMLParserDelegate 379
parser:didStartElement:namespaceURI:qualifiedName:attributes: of protocol NSXMLParserDelegate 379
parser:foundCharacters: of protocol NSXMLParserDelegate 379
paste text 8
path method of class NSURL **320**
pathExtension method of class NSString **332**
pathsForResourcesOfType: method of class NSBundle **112**, 134
pause method of class AVAudioPlayer 335
payment 42
peer ID 353
peerPickerController:didConnectPeer:toSession: method of protocol GKPeerPickerControllerDelegate **348**
peerPickerControllerDidCancel: method of protocol GKPeerPickerControllerDelegate **349**
peer-to-peer connectivity **14**
peer-to-peer games 9
Performance and Threading (developer.apple.com/documentation/Cocoa/Conceptual/ObjectiveC/Articles/ocProperties.html#//apple_ref/doc/uid/TP30001163-CH17-SW12) 109

outlet **72**, **109**, **124**, 186, 232, 264, 315, 328

performance problems, detect 169
performFetch: method of class NSFetchedResultsController **352**
performSelector:withObject:AfterDelay: method of NSObject **116**, 137
Phone 4, 5
Photo API 245
photo sharing 17, 44
Photos 5
photos 4
pinch 4, 15
Pinch Media 38, 48
play method of class MPMusicPlayer 262
.plist extension 98
plist file 198
plist format 98
podcast **14**
pointer
  generic **80**
pointer to the sender component 80
popViewControllerAnimated: method of class UINavigationController 259
power the iPhone 4
PR Leap 46
predicateWithFormat: method of class NSPredicate **325**
prepareToRecord method of class AVAudioRecorder **320**
preprocessor **72**
presentationLayer method of class CALayer **141**
presentModalViewController:animated: method of class UIViewController 200, 248, 317
Press Release Writing 47
price 8, 36
price tier 40
Pricing Matrix 40
primary screenshot 34
privacy **6**
PRLog 47
Programatically update user interface 96

programmatically select a component 79

programming languages
Objective-C 10

project **53**

Project Structure group **55**

properties method of class NSEntityDescription **350**

propertiesByName method of class NSEntityDescription 348, 350

property **109**, 257, 264, 322
access with dot (.) notation 79
readonly 175

property-list format 98

property of an object **16**

protocol **109**
delegate 121
similar to an interface in other programming languages 109

Protocols
CLLocationManagerDelegate 236, 237
EditableCellDelegate 205
GKPeerPickerControllerDelegate 348, 349
GKSessionDelegatel 353
MFMailComposeViewControllerDelegate **340**
NSFetchedResultsSectionInfo **358**
UITableViewDataSource **201**, 205, 212, 328
UITableViewDelegate **201**, 328
UITextFieldDelegate **215**, 322, 325

Provisioning 28

Provisioning Profile 25, **27**

PRWeb 46

PRX Builder 47

public relations 46

purchase 41

purchasing interface 42

Push Notification 2, **13**

pushViewController:animated: method of class UINavigationController **202**, 248, 251, 293, 359

Q

Quartz Core 12

Quattro Wireless 47

R

radio button 106

random number generator **111**

rangeOfString: method of class NSString **381**

rating apps 39

react to incoming calls 316

readonly 383

readonly property 175

receive data from a connected device **354**

receiveData:fromPeer:
inSession:context: method **354**

receiver 79

record method of class AVAudioRecorder **320**

Registered iPhone Developer 2

regular expression **325**

relational operators 80

release date 40

release method of class NSObject **107**, 112

reloadData method of class UITableView 247, 332, 355

remainder operator, % 81

Remote Wipe **6**

removeAllAnimations method of class CALayer 146

removeAllObjects method of class NSMutableArray **95**, 230, 327

removeAllObjects method of class NSMutableDictionary 178

removeAllObjects of class NSMutableDictionary 178

removeFromSuperView method of class UIView **95**, 112, 145, 261, 262

removeObjectAtIndex: method of class NSMutableArray 252, 327

removeObserver: of class NSNotificationCenter **309**

Request Promotional Codes 43

resignFirstResponder method of class UIViewController 185

resignFirstResponder method of class UIResponder 218

Resource Centers
(www.deitel.com/
ResourceCenters.html) 17

Resources group 55, 58

responder chain 141

REST xxxi

retain count **106**, **112**

retain counting 106

retain keyword **109**

retain method of class NSObject **107**, **112**

reuse **17**

reuse UITableViewCells 197

RGB values **87**, 191, 229

Rhapsody 11

Ring/Silent switch 4

rotate left (iPhone simulator) 245

rotate right (iPhone simulator) 245

Rounded Rect Button **86**, 87

Route Tracker app xxx, 2, 6, 11, 12, 14, 15

row property of class NSIndexPath 293, 350

run loop **122**

S

Safari 4, 5, 9

Sales/Trend Reports 43

Salesforce 17

save data on the iPhone 84

save method of class NSManagedObject **355**, 357

scheduledTimerWithTimeInterval:target:select:userInfo:repeats: method of class NSTimer **161**

screen size 30

screenshot 32

scroll 4

Scroll View 86, 88

`scrollEnabled` property of class `MKMapView` 234

`scrollToRowAtIndex-Path:atScrollPosi-tion:animated:` of class `UITableView` 208

SDK (Software Development Kit) xxxv

SDK beta xxxv

SDK documentation xxxv

search 9

Second Life 17

`sections` method of class `NS-FetchedResultsController` 357

Security 13

seed (random number generation) 111

Segmented Control GUI Component 106, 110, 122, 127
dynamically created 115

select a component programmatically 79

`selectedSegmentIndex` property of class `UISegmentedControl` 235

`selectionStyle` property of class `UITableViewCell` 249, 293

`self` keyword **92**

`sendDataToAllPeers:with-DataMode:` method of class `GKSession` 345, **348**

sender of an event **80**

serialized object 282

`session`
didReceiveConnectionRequestFromPeer: method of protocol `GKSessionDelegate` **353**

set the keyboard type 210

`setAnimationCurve:` method of class `UIView` **139**, 208

`setAnimationDidStopSelector:` method of class `UIView` **139**, **144**

`setAnimationDuration:` method of class `UIView` **139**, 190, 208

`setBackBarButtonItem:` method of class `UINavigation-Item` 247

`setCategory:` method of class `AVAudioSession` **317**, 319, 334

`setContentSize:` method of class `UIScrollView` **99**

`setDataReceiveHan-dler:withContext:` method of class `GKSession` **352**

`setIdleTimerDisabled:` of class `UIApplication` 234, 235

`setNavigationBarHidden:an-imated:` method of class `UI-NavigationController` 247

`setNeedsDisplay` method of class `UIView` 165, 178, 230

`setNeedsDisplayInRect:` method of class `UIView` 182

`setQueueWithItemCollec-tion:` method of class `MPMu-sicPlayer` 262

`setRegion:` method of class `UIMapView` **237**

`setRightBarButtonItem:` method of class `UINaviga-tionItem` 347

`setSortDescriptors:` method of class `NSFetchRequest` **362**

`setStatusBarHidden:` method of class `UIApplication` **259**

`setStatusBarHidden:` method of class `UIApplication` 262

Settings 5

`setTitle:` method of class `UI-NavigationItem` 246, 349

`setValue:` method of class `UIS-lider` 190

`setValue:animated:` method of class `UISlider` 333

`setValue:forKey:` method of class `NSManagedObject` **355**

`setValue:forKey:` method of class `NSUserDefault` **146**

`setValue:forKey:` of class `NS-MutableDictionary` **97**

Shake to Shuffle 9

`sharedApplication` method of class `UIApplication` **101**, 259

`sharedInstance` method of class `AVAudioSession` 316

sheet **57**

shine effect 33

`shouldAutorotateToInter-faceOrientation:` method of class `UIViewController` **204**, 262

`show` method of class `GKPeer-PickerController` **347**

SIM card tray 4

simulator 32

singleton 262, 302, 314, 316

Singleton design pattern 11, 94, **101, 314**

`sizeWithFont:` of class `NS-String` 218

Skype 17

Sleep/Awake button 4

Slider 18, 65, 68, 86, 191

Slider GUI component 190

Slideshow app xxx, 6, 12, **14**

social bookmarking 17, 44

social media 44

social media sites
Blogger 44
Delicious 44
Digg 44
Flickr 44
LinkedIn 44
Squidoo 44
StumbleUpon 44
Tip'd 44
Wordpress 44
YouTube 44

social networking 17, 44

social news 44

Software Development Kit (SDK) xxxv

sort an `NSMutableArray` 91

`sortUsingSelector:` method of class `NSMutableArray` 99

sound 132

source code 2

source-code listing 2

sourceType property of class UIImagePickerController **271**, 295

speaker 4

speech recognition xxxi

speech synthesis xxxi

Spotlight 9

Spot-On Game app xxx, 10, 12, 20

Squidoo 44

srandom library method **111**

stackoverflow.com/questions/740127/how-was-your-iphone-developer-experience 48

standardUserDefaults method **137**

startUpdatingHeading method of class CLLocationManager **235**

startUpdatingLocation method of class CLLocationManager **235**

static global variable **110**

static keyword
    local variable 79

Static method **73**

staticly typed object **73**

status bar **259**

StepStone 9

Stocks 5

stopUpdatingHeading method of class CLLocationManager **234**

stopUpdatingLocation method of class CLLocationManager **234**, 237

Store Kit 2, 13, 32

Store Kit framework **13**, 41, 42

Store Kit Framework Reference 42

Store Kit Programming Guide 42

string format specifier 169

string formatting 80

string literal that begins with @ 80

stringByAddingPercentEscapesUsingEncoding: method of class NSString 374

stringByAppendingPathComponent: method of class NSString **94**, 298, 332

stringByDeletingLastPathComponent method of class NSString 320

stringWithFormat: method of class NSString 333

struct keywords **158**

structure **96**, 157, **158**

structure members **158**

structure tag **158**

stucture type 158

StumbleUpon 44

subscription 42

substringWithRange: method of class NSString **381**

subtraction 81

subview **95**

subviews property **95**

super keyword **92**

superview **95**

swipe 4, 15

Switch GUI Component **123**

Symbian 49

sync 7, 9

syntax shading 2

synthesize a property 111

@synthesize directive 177, 367

@synthesize keyword **111**

System 13

System Configuration 13

T

Tab Bar 86

Tab Bar Item 86

tableView:canMoveRowAtIndexPath: method of class UITableViewController 252

tableView:cellForRowAtIndexPath: method of class UITableView 249, 293, 300

tableView:cellForRowAtIndexPath: method of protocol UITableViewDataSource **202**, 214, 275, 350, 371

tableView:commitEditingStyle:forRowAtIndexPath: method of class UITableViewController 251

tableView:commitEditingStyle:forRowAtIndexPath: method of protocol UITableViewDataSource **203**, 275, 337

tableView:didSelectRowAtIndexPath: method of protocol UITableViewDelegate **202**, 338, 371

tableView:moveAtIndexPath:toIndexPath: method of class UITableViewController 252

tableView:moveRowAtIndexPath:toIndexPath: of protocol UITableViewDataSource 275, 302

tableView:numberOfRowsInSection: method of class UITableView 213

tableView:numberOfRowsInSection: method of class UITableViewController 248

tableView:numberOfRowsInSection: method of protocol UITableViewDataSource **201**, 274, 350, 370

tableView:numberOfRowsInSection: of class UITableViewDataSource 210

tableView:titleForHeaderInSection: method of protocol UITableViewDataSource **210**

tag property of class UIView **337**

tap 4, 15

tapCount property of class UITouch **171**

Tapjoy 37, 48

Team Admin 25, 26, 34

Team Agent **25**, 29

Team Member 25, 26

template **54**

Template Method design pattern 11, **79**

testing xxxv

Text Field 66, 87, 285

textField:should-
ChangeCharactersIn-
Range:replacementString:
method of protocol UIText-
FieldDelegate 325

textFieldDidBeginEditing:
of protocol UITextFieldDelegate 215

textFieldDidEndEditing: of
protocol UITextFieldDele-
gate 215

textLabel method of class
UITableViewCell 350

The App Podcast app review site
46

theapppodcast.com/ 46

time library function **111**

timeIntervalSinceNow method of class NSDate **235**

Tip Calculator app xxx, 10, 11, 15

Tip'd 44

tipd.com/ 44

title property of class UIButton 234

Toolbar 86

touch and hold 4, 15

touch handling 132

Touch Up Inside event **92**

touchesBegan method of class
UIView 132

touchesBegan:withEvent:
method of class UIResponder
139

touchesBegan:withEvent: of
class UIResponder 182

touchesEnded:withEvent: of
class UIResponder 183

transform property of class MK-
MapView **237**

trueHeading property of class
CLHeading **237**

TV shows 9

tweet **45**

Twitter xxxi, xxxiii, 17, **45**, 49,
100

@deitel 386

hashtag **45**

tweet **45**

Twitter app xxx

Twitter Discount Airfares app 13

Twitter search 84

operators 84

typedef keyword 282

typedef specifier **158**

U

UDID (Unique Device Identifier) **27**

UIActionSheet class 245, **267**,
299

initWithTitle:dele-
gate:cancelButtonTi-
tle:destructiveButton
Title:otherButtonTi-
tles: method 299

UIActionSheetDelegate protocol

actionSheet:clickedBut-
tonAtIndex: 272

UIActivityIndicatorView
class **368**

UIAlertView class 118, 353

UIAlertViewDelegate protocol

alertView:clickedBut-
tonAtIndex: 183

UIApplication class **100**, 259,
262, 302

networkActivityIndica-
torVisible **374**

openURL method **101**

setIdleTimerDisabled:
234, 235

setStatusBarHidden:
method **259**

setStatusBarHidden:
method 262

sharedApplication meth-
od 259

UIApplicationDelegate
protocol **302**

UIBarButtonItem class **198**,
245, 247, 267, 334, 347, 369

initWithCustomView: 369

UIBarButtonSystemItemAc-
tion 347

UIButton class 97, 253, 315

title property 234

UIColor class 174, 188, 226

clearColor method 226

UIControl class

addTarget:action:for-
ControlEvents: 216

UIControlTouchUpInside **98**

UIGraphicsGetCurrentCon-
text function **168**

UIGraphicsGetCurrentCon-
text function of CGContext
Reference 327

UIGraphicsGetCurrentCon-
text function of the UIKit
framework 227

UIImage class 132, 169, 249,
258, 288, 294, 296, 305

UIImagePickerController
class 245, **267**, **270**, 282, 295

allowsImageEditing 270

allowsImageEditing prop-
erty 295

availableMediaTypesFor-
SourceType method 295

mediaTypes property 282,
295

sourceType **271**

sourceType property 295

UIImagePickerCon-
trollerDelegate protocol

imagePickerCon-
troller:didFinish-
PickingImage:editingI
nfo: 271

UIImagePickerControllerEd-
itedImage 296

UIImagePickerControllerMediaURL 297

UIImagePickerController-
SourceTypePhotoLibrary
295

UIImagePNGRepresentation
function **291**

UIImageView class **53**, 59, 132,
257, 259, 262, 305

alpha property 260

image property 132, 141

UIImageView class (cont.)
  removeFromSuperView
    method 261, 262
UIKeyboardType 197
UIKit 11
UIKit framework 56
UIKit header file **72**
UILabel class **53**, 350
UIMapView class
  setRegion: method **237**
UIModalTransitionStyle-
  CrossDissolve 321
UIModalTransitionStyle-
  FlipHorizontalUIModal-
  TransitionStyle **121**
UINavigationController class
  245, 247, 248, 251, 259, 293,
  359
  pushViewController:
    animated: method **202**,
    248, 251, 259, 293, 359
  setNavigationBarHidden:
    animated: method 247
  viewController property
    302
UINavigationItem class 247,
  349, 352
  backBarButtonItem proper-
    ty 198
  leftBarButtonItem proper-
    ty 352
  setBackBarButtonItem:
    method 247
  setRightBarButtonItem:
    method 347
  setTitle: method 246, 349
UIResponder class
  canBecomeFirstResponder
    183
  motionEnded:withEvent:
    183
  resignFirstResponder 218
  touchesBegan:withEvent:
    182
  touchesEnded:withEvent:
    139, 183
UIScrollView 88
UISegmentedControl class
  selectedSegmentIndex
    property 235

UISlider class 190
  setValue: method 190
  setValue:animated: meth-
    od 333
  value property 190
UITable ViewCell class
  customized 371
UITableView class **196**, 197,
  201, 202, 247, 248, 249, 293,
  296, 332, 350, 351, 355, 366
  dataSource **201**
  deleteRowsAtIndex-
    Paths:withRowAnima-
    tion: method **203**, 338
  dequeueReusableCell-
    WithIdentifier:
    method **202**, 210, 214,
    249, 293, 358
  indexPathForCell: meth-
    od 208, 293
  insertRowsAtIndexPaths
    method 355
  reloadData method 247,
    355
  scrollToRowAtIndex-
    Path:atScrollPosi-
    tion:animated: 208
  tableView:cellForRowAt-
    IndexPath: method 249,
    293, 300
  tableView:numberOfRow-
    sInSection: method 213
UITableViewCallSelection-
  StyleNone 249, 293
UITableViewCell class 197,
  202, 210, 214, 249, 252, 293,
  300, 350, 358, 366
  accessoryView property **337**
  initWithStyle:reuse-
    Identifier: method
    202, 384
  selectionStyle property
    249, 293
  textLabel method 350
UITableViewCellEditing-
  Style class 203
UITableViewController class
  198, 246
  numberOfSectionsIn-
    TableView: method 248

UITableViewController class
  (cont.)
  tableView:canMoveRowAt-
    IndexPath: method 252
  tableView:commitEdit-
    ingStyle:forRowAtIn-
    dexPath: method 251
  tableView:moveAtIndex-
    Path:toIndexPath:
    method 252
  tableView:numberOfRow-
    sInSection: method 248
UITableViewDataSource protocol **201**, 205, 212, 328, 346
  numberOfSectionsIn-
    TableView: 210
  tableView:cellForRowAt-
    IndexPath: method **202**,
    214, 275, 350, 371
  tableView:commitEdit-
    ingStyle:forRowAtIn-
    dexPath: method **203**,
    275, 337
  tableView:moveRowAtIn-
    dexPath:toIndexPath:
    275, 302
  tableView:numberOfRows-
    InSection: method **201**,
    210, 274, 350, 370
  tableView:titleForHea-
    derInSection: **210**
UITableViewDelegate class
  tableView:didSelectRow-
    AtIndexPath: **202**, 371
UITableViewDelegate protocol **201**, 328
  tableView:didSelectRo-
    wAtIndexPath: method
    338
UITextField class 216, 286,
  322, 324
  becomeFirstResponder
    method 286, 324
UITextFieldDelegate class
  textFieldDidBeginEdit-
    ing: 215
  textFieldDidEndEditing:
    215
UITextFieldDelegate protocol **215**, 322, 325

`UITextFieldDelegate` protocol (cont.)
  `textField:should-`
    `ChangeCharactersIn-`
    `Range:replacementStri`
    `ng:` method **325**
`UIToolbar` class 245, 267
`UITouch` class 132, **140**, 182
  `tapCount` property **171**
`UIView` class 178, 187, 190, 198, 225, 233, 257, 258, 262, 325
  `addSubView:` method 233
  `autoresizingMask` property **258**
  `backgroundColor` 190
  `backgroundColor` property 191, 226
  `beginAnimation:withContext:` method **138**
  `beginAnimations:context:` 208
  `beginAnimations:context:` method 190
  `CGImage` property 169
  `commitAnimations` 208
  `commitAnimations` method **138**, 190
  `contentView` property 254
  `drawRect:` 227
  `frame` property 257
  `initWithCoder:` method 177
  `layer` property 141, 145
  `loadView` method 257
  `locationInView:` method **141**
  `removeFromSuperView` method **112**, 145
  `setAnimationCurve:` method **139**, 208
  `setAnimationDidStopSelector:` method **139**, **144**
  `setAnimationDuration:` method **139**, 190, 208
  `setNeedsDisplay` method 165, 178, 230
  `setNeedsDisplayInRect:` 182

`UIView` class (cont.)
  `tag` property **337**
  `touchesBegan` method 132
  `viewDidAppear` method 190
  `viewDidLoad` method 134
`UIViewController` class **111**, 198, 200, 264, 292, 296, 315, 322, 346
  `becomeFirstResponder` method 185
  `dismissModalViewControllerAnimated:` method **120**, 200, 248, 292, 296
  `editButtonItem` property 247
  `initWithNibName:bundle:` method 207
  `modalTransitionStyle` property **121**, 186
  `navigationController` property 197
  `navigationItem` property 198, 246
  `presentModalViewController:animated:` method 200, 248, 317
  `resignFirstResponder` method 185
  `shouldAutorotateToInterfaceOrientation:` method **204**, 262
  `viewDidAppear:` method 184, 269
  `viewDidDisappear:` method 184
  `viewDidLoad` method **198**, 286, 291, 324, 347
  `viewWillAppear:` method 247
  `viewWillDisappear:` method 269
`UIWebView` class 366, **371**
`UIWebViewDelegate` protocol
  `webViewDidFinishLoad:` 373
`unarchiveObjectWithFile:` method of class `NSKeyedUnarchiver` **292**
unarchiving **282**

Unique Device Identifier (UDID) **27**
unlock the iPhone 4
`updateMeters` method of class `AVAudioRecorder` **321**
upload finished apps xxxv
URL encode a string 374
`URLWithString:` method of class `NSURL` 338
utilities 35
Utility Application template 107, **109**, 120, 123, 175

V
`value` property of class `UISlider` 190
`valueForKey` **97**
`valueForKey:` method of class `NSDictionary` 296
`valueForKey:` method of class `NSUserDefault` **137**
`valueWithBytes:objCType:` of class `NSValue` **177**
`valueWithPointer:` of class `NSValue` **182**
video xxxi, 4, 6
video sharing 17, 44
View 18, **86**
view (in MVC) **71**
view controller 106
`viewController` property of class `UINavigationController` 302
`viewDidAppear` method of class `UIView` 190
`viewDidAppear:` of class `UIViewController` 184, 269
`viewDidDisappear:` of class `UIViewController` 184
`viewDidLoad` method of class `UIView` 134
`viewDidLoad` method of class `UIViewController` **198**, 286, 291, 324, 347, 352
`viewWillAppear:` method of class `UIViewController` 247
`viewWillDisappear:` of class `UIViewController` 269
viral marketing 44
virtual goods 41, 47

virtual world 17

visible peer 346, 351

vision impaired **7**

Viximo 41

voice controls 9

Voice Memos 9

Voice Memos 5

Voice Recorder app xxx

VoiceOver **7**

Volume buttons 4

volume property of class AVAudioPlayer 332

W

Weather 5

Web 2.0 **17**

web services xxxi, **13**, **226**

webOS 49

`webViewDidFinishLoad:` of protocol `UIWebViewDelegate` 373

Welcome app xxx, 11, 14, 15

Welcome to Xcode window **53**

What's on iPhone app review site 45

Wi-Fi 9

Wikipedia 17

Window-based Application template 54, **56**, 66, 86, 225

Windows xxxv

Windows Mobile 49

word-of-mouth marketing 44

Wordpress 44

Wozniak, Steve 9

`writeToFile:atomically:` method of class `NSDictionary` **98**

`writeToFile:atomically:` method of class `NSMutableDictionary` 200

WWDR intermediate certificate **27**, 29

www.148apps.com/ 46

www.admob.com/ 37

www.adwhirl.com/ 47

www.appcraver.com/ 46

www.apple.com/downloads/ macosx/ development_tools/ iphonesdk.html xxxv

www.apple.com/iphone/apps-for-iphone/ 8

www.apple.com/iphone/ iphone-3gs/ accessibility.html 7

www.apple.com/iphone/ softwareupdate/ 8

www.appleiphoneschool.com/ 46

www.appletell.com/apple/ tag/iphone+app+reviews/ 46

www.apptism.com/ 46

www.appvee.com/ 46

www.bing.com/developers 49

www.bis.doc.gov/licensing/ exportingbasics.htm 38

www.blogger.com 44

www.clickpress.com 46

www.craigslist.org 13

www.deitel.com xxxvi, 22

www.deitel.com/books/ iPhoneFP/ (*iPhone for Programmers* website) xxix,

www.deitel.com/books/ iPhonefp/ (*iPhone for Programmers* website) xxxii, xxxiii

www.deitel.com/Cocoa/ (Cocoa Resource Center) xxxii

www.deitel.com/deitelfan/ (Deitel Facebook Page) xxxiii

www.deitel.com/internetpr/ 46

www.deitel.com/iPhone/ (iPhone Resource Center) xxxii, xxxv, xxxvi, 2

www.deitel.com/newsletter/ subscribe.htm (*Deitel Buzz Online* newsletter) xxxiii, xxxvi

www.deitel.com/ObjectiveC/ (Objective-C Resource Center) xxxii

www.deitel.com/ ResourceCenters.html (Deitel Resource Centers) xxxii

www.deitel.com/training 386

www.delicious.com 44

www.digg.com 44

www.facebook.com 44

www.flickr.com 44

www.freshapps.com/ 46

www.google.com/mobile/ #p=android 49

www.housingmaps.com 13

www.i-newswire.com/ 47

www.internetnewsbureau.com / 47

www.iphoneappreviews.net/ 45

www.iphonebuzz.com/ category/apple-iphone-humor 49

www.khronos.org/opengles 54

www.linkedin.com 44

www.linkedin.com/ static?key=developers_wi dgets&trk=hb_ft_widgets 50

www.macworld.com/appguide/ index.html 46

www.marketwire.com 46

www.myspace.com 44

www.openpr.com 47

www.orkut.com 44

www.press-release-writing.com/ 47

www.prleap.com/ 46

www.prlog.org/pub/ 47

www.prweb.com 46

www.prxbuilder.com/x2/ 47

www.squidoo.com 44

www.stumbleupon.com 44

www.techcrunch.com/2009/02/ 15/experiences-of-a-newbie-iphone-developer/ 48

www.touchtip.com/iphone-and-ipod-touch/worlds-youngest-iphone-developer/ 48

www.twitter.com 44

www.whatsoniphone.com/ 45

www.wired.com/gadgets/ wireless/magazine/16-02/ ff_iphone?currentPage=al 1 48

www.wordpress.com 44
www.youtube.com 44

X

Xcode xxix, xxxv, 2, 10, 14, **18**, 34
  Build and Debug button 18
  Build and Run button 18
Xcode Groups
  Classes 55, 71
  Project Structure **55**
  Resources 55, 58

Xcode toolbar 54
Xcode toolset xxxv
Xcode Windows
  Groups and Files 71, 108, 109, 122
  Groups and Files window 55
  Inspector **61**, **73**, 87, 91, 122
  Library 59, 67, 87, 91, 122
  Welcome to Xcode **53**
Xerox PARC (Palo Alto Research Center) 9
.xib 56

Y

Yahoo 49
Yellow Box API 11
YouTube 6, 9, 17, 44
YouTube app 5

Z

zoom 4
zoomEnabled property of class MKMapView 234